Lecture Notes in Computer Science   10831

Commenced Publication in 1973
Founding and Former Series Editors:
Gerhard Goos, Juris Hartmanis, and Jan van Leeuwen

Editorial Board

David Hutchison
  Lancaster University, Lancaster, UK
Takeo Kanade
  Carnegie Mellon University, Pittsburgh, PA, USA
Josef Kittler
  University of Surrey, Guildford, UK
Jon M. Kleinberg
  Cornell University, Ithaca, NY, USA
Friedemann Mattern
  ETH Zurich, Zurich, Switzerland
John C. Mitchell
  Stanford University, Stanford, CA, USA
Moni Naor
  Weizmann Institute of Science, Rehovot, Israel
C. Pandu Rangan
  Indian Institute of Technology Madras, Chennai, India
Bernhard Steffen
  TU Dortmund University, Dortmund, Germany
Demetri Terzopoulos
  University of California, Los Angeles, CA, USA
Doug Tygar
  University of California, Berkeley, CA, USA
Gerhard Weikum
  Max Planck Institute for Informatics, Saarbrücken, Germany

More information about this series at http://www.springer.com/series/7410

Antoine Joux · Abderrahmane Nitaj
Tajjeeddine Rachidi (Eds.)

Progress in Cryptology – AFRICACRYPT 2018

10th International Conference on Cryptology in Africa
Marrakesh, Morocco, May 7–9, 2018
Proceedings

 Springer

Editors
Antoine Joux
Fondation Partenariale de Sorbonne
  Université
Paris
France

Tajjeeddine Rachidi
Al Akhawayn University
Ifrane
Morocco

Abderrahmane Nitaj
Université de Caen
Caen
France

ISSN 0302-9743   ISSN 1611-3349 (electronic)
Lecture Notes in Computer Science
ISBN 978-3-319-89338-9   ISBN 978-3-319-89339-6 (eBook)
https://doi.org/10.1007/978-3-319-89339-6

Library of Congress Control Number: 2018937402

LNCS Sublibrary: SL4 – Security and Cryptology

Printed on acid-free paper

This Springer imprint is published by the registered company Springer International Publishing AG
part of Springer Nature
The registered company address is: Gewerbestrasse 11, 6330 Cham, Switzerland

Preface

AFRICACRYPT 2018, the 10th International Conference on the Theory and Application of Cryptographic Techniques in Africa, took place in Marrakesh, Morocco, May 7–9, 2018. The conference was organized by Al Akhawayn University in Ifrane in cooperation with the International Association for Cryptologic Research (IACR).

The conference received a total of 54 submissions. Each submission was anonymized for the reviewing process and was assigned to three reviewers out of the 41 Program Committee members.

The Program Committee, aided by reports from 37 external reviewers, produced a total of 156 reviews. After highly interactive discussions and careful deliberation, the Program Committee selected 19 papers for presentation. The authors of accepted papers were given a week to prepare final versions of their papers for these proceedings. The revised versions of these papers are included in these proceedings and classified into two topics: symmetric cryptography and asymmetric cryptography.

The program was completed with two invited talks by Joan Daemen from Radboud University in Nijmegen, The Netherlands, and STMicroelectronics; and by Léo Ducas from CWI, Amsterdam, The Netherlands. We are very grateful to them for accepting our invitation.

We would like to thank all authors who submitted papers. The submissions came from: Australia, Austria, Belgium, Brazil, Canada, China, France, Germany, India, Iran, Japan, Morocco, Norway, Portugal, Romania, Senegal, Singapore, Sweden, Switzerland, Taiwan, The Netherlands, UAE, UK, and USA. We regret that the Program Committee rejected some very good papers. We know that this can be very disappointing. We sincerely hope that these works, eventually, get the attention they deserve elsewhere.

We are deeply grateful to the Program Committee and to the external reviewers for their hard work, enthusiasm, and conscientious efforts to ensure that each paper received a thorough and fair review.

We would also like to thank Springer for agreeing to an accelerated schedule for printing these proceedings, the EasyChair team for allowing us to use their platform, and Al Akhawayn University in Ifrane for supporting the conference.

We also thank the local Organizing Committee for their commitment and hard work to make the conference an enjoyable experience. We also thank Driss Ouaouicha and Kevin Smith, respectively, President and Dean of the School of Science and Engineering at Al Akhawayn University, for their financial and unconditional moral support. We extend our gratitude to the conference sponsors S2M Morocco for financially supporting the conference.

Last but not least, we thank everyone else, speakers, session chairs, and rump session chairs for their contribution to the program of Africacrypt 2018.

Finally, we wish to thank the participants and presenters. They all made Africacrypt 2018 a highly recognized forum for researchers to interact and share their works and knowledge with their peers, for the overall growth and development of cryptology research in the world and in Africa in particular.

May 2018

Antoine Joux
Abderrahmane Nitaj
Tajjeeddine Rachidi

Organization

Africacrypt 2018 was organized by Al Akhawayn University in Ifrane, Morocco.

General Chair

Tajjeeddine Rachidi   Al Akhawayn University in Ifrane, Morocco

Program Chairs

Antoine Joux   Fondation Partenariale de Sorbonne Université, IMJ-PRG, Paris, France
Abderrahmane Nitaj   University of Caen Normandie, France
Tajjeeddine Rachidi   Al Akhawayn University in Ifrane, Morocco

Organizing Committee

Latifa El Mortaji (Chair)   Al Akhawayn University, Ifrane, Morocco
Bouchra Saad   Al Akhawayn University, Ifrane, Morocco

Program Committee

Elena Andreeva   Katholieke Universiteit Leuven, Belgium
Hatem M. Bahig   Ain Shams University, Cairo, Egypt
Magali Bardet   University of Rouen, France
Hussain Benazza   University of Meknes, Morocco
Colin Boyd   Norwegian University of Science and Technology, Norway
Dario Catalano   Università di Catania, Italy
Xing Chaoping   Nanyang Technological University, Singapore
Sherman S. M. Chow   The Chinese University of Hong Kong, SAR China
Nicolas Courtois   University College London, UK
Luca De Feo   University de Versaille – Saint-Quentin-en-Yvelines, France
Milena Djukanovic   University of Montenegro
Nadia El Mrabet   SAS - CGCP - EMSE, France
Pierre-Alain Fouque   University of Rennes, France
Aline Gouget   Gemalto, France
Gottfried Herold   ENS Lyon, France
Javier Herranz   Universitat Politècnica de Catalunya, Spain
Hieuphan Duong   University of Limoges, France
Sorina Ionica   Université de Picardie, France

Tetsu Iwata	Nagoya University, Japan
Antoine Joux	Fondation Partenariale de Sorbonne Université, IMJ-PRG, Paris, France
Juliane Kramer	TU Darmstadt, Germany
Fabien Laguillaumie	University of Lyon I/LIP, France
Tancrède Lepoint	SRI International, USA
Abderrahmane Nitaj	University of Caen Normandie, France
Ayoub Otmani	University of Rouen Normandie, France
Elizabeth A. Quaglia	Royal Holloway, University of London, UK
Tajjeeddine Rachidi	Al Akhawayn University in Ifrane, Morocco
Adeline Roux-Langlois	CNRS-IRISA, France
Magdy Saeb	Arab Academy for Science, Technology Institute Maritime Transport, Alexandria, Egypt
Rei Safavi-Naini	University of Calgary, Canada
Palash Sarkar	Indian Statistical Institute, India
Alessandra Scafuro	North Carolina State University, Raleigh, USA
Peter Schwabe	Radboud University Nijmegen, The Netherlands
Djiby Sow	University of Dakar, Senegal
Pontelimon Stanica	Naval Postgraduate School, Monterey, USA
Noah Stephens-Davidowitz	New York University, USA
Willy Susilo	University of Wollongong, Australia
Joseph Tonien	University of Wollongong, Australia
Damien Vergnaud	Sorbonne Université, Paris, France
Vanessa Vitse	University of Grenoble, France
Amr M. Youssef	Concordia University, Canada

Additional Reviewers

Luca Nizzardo	Sumit Pandey	Subhadip Singha
Michael Walter	Nicolas Gama	Olivier Sanders
Ashley Fraser	Mohamed Elsheikh	Khoa Nguyen
Karim Bigou	Marine Minier	Fabrice Mouhartem
Guilherme Perin	Antoine Loiseau	Pierre Karpman
Sepideh Avizheh	Viet Cuong Trinh	Matteo Scarlata
Hisham Galal	Peter Spacek	Thomas De Cnudde
Mamun Akand	Julien Eynard	Paul Germouty
Sebati Ghosh	Kerem Varici	Brice Minaud
Yongjun Zhao	Valentin Suder	Sabyasachi Karati
Mohamed Tolba	Begül Bilgin	
Pauline Bert	Joan Daemen	

Invited Speakers

| Joan Daemen | Radboud University in Nijmegen, The Netherlands, and STMicroelectronics |
| Léo Ducas | CWI, Amsterdam, The Netherlands |

Sponsoring Institutions

Al Akhawayn University in Ifrane, Morocco
Société Maghrébine de Monétique (S2M), Morocco, http://www.s2m.ma

Contents

Symmetric Cryptography

A Complete Characterization
of Plateaued Boolean Functions in Terms
# of Their Cayley Graphs

Constanza Riera[1], Patrick Solé[2], and Pantelimon Stănică[3](✉)

[1] Department of Computing, Mathematics, and Physics,
Western Norway University of Applied Sciences, 5020 Bergen, Norway
csr@hvl.no
[2] CNRS/LAGA, University of Paris 8, 2 rue de la Liberté, 93 526 Saint-Denis, France
patrick.sole@telecom-paristech.fr
[3] Department of Applied Mathematics, Naval Postgraduate School, Monterey, CA
93943, USA
pstanica@nps.edu

Abstract. In this paper we find a complete characterization of plateaued Boolean functions in terms of the associated Cayley graphs. Precisely, we show that a Boolean function f is s-plateaued (of weight $= 2^{(n+s-2)/2}$) if and only if the associated Cayley graph is a complete bipartite graph between the support of f and its complement (hence the graph is strongly regular of parameters $e = 0, d = 2^{(n+s-2)/2}$). Moreover, a Boolean function f is s-plateaued (of weight $\neq 2^{(n+s-2)/2}$) if and only if the associated Cayley graph is strongly 3-walk-regular (and also strongly ℓ-walk-regular, for all odd $\ell \geq 3$) with some explicitly given parameters.

Keywords: Plateaued Boolean functions · Cayley graphs
Strongly regular · Walk regular

1 Introduction

Boolean functions are very important objects in cryptography, coding theory, and communications, and have connections with many areas of discrete mathematics [4,5]. In particular bent functions, which offer optimal resistance to linear cryptanalysis, when used in symmetric cryptosystems, have been extensively studied [12,14]. They were shown in [1,2] to be connected to strongly regular graphs. This connection occurs through the Cayley graph with generator set the support of the Boolean function (denoted by Ω_f below). Namely, having two nonzero components in the Walsh-Hadamard spectrum translates at the Cayley graph level as having three eigenvalues. This link is often referred to as the *Bernasconi-Codenotti correspondence*.

In this paper, we extend this connection by relating semibent and, in general, plateaued functions with a special class of walk-regular graphs. Plateaued

© Springer International Publishing AG, part of Springer Nature 2018
A. Joux et al. (Eds.): AFRICACRYPT 2018, LNCS 10831, pp. 3–10, 2018.
https://doi.org/10.1007/978-3-319-89339-6_1

Boolean functions are characterized as having three values in their Walsh-Hadamard spectrum [11]. Their corresponding Cayley graphs belong to a special class of regular graphs with either three or four eigenvalues in their spectrum. The three eigenvalue case is dealt with by the strong regularity and the four eigenvalues case corresponds to the strongly t-walk-regular graphs introduced by Fiol and Garriga [8]. The special case of four eigenvalues of these graphs was studied in particular in [7].

The material is organized as follows. The next section compiles the necessary notions and definitions on Boolean functions and graph spectra. Section 3 derives the main characterization result of the paper.

2   Preliminaries

2.1   Boolean Functions

Let $\mathbb{F}_2$ be the finite field with two elements and $\mathbb{Z}$ be the ring of integers. For any $n \in \mathbb{Z}^+$, the set of positive integers, let $[n] = \{1, \ldots, n\}$. The Cartesian product of n copies of $\mathbb{F}_2$ is $\mathbb{F}_2^n = \{\mathbf{x} = (x_1, \ldots, x_n) : x_i \in \mathbb{F}_2, i \in [n]\}$ which is an n-dimensional vector space over $\mathbb{F}_2$, which we will denote by $\mathbb{V}_n$. We will denote by $\oplus$, respectively, $+$, the operations on $\mathbb{F}_2^n$, respectively, $\mathbb{Z}$. For any $n \in \mathbb{Z}^+$, a function $F : \mathbb{V}_n \to \mathbb{F}_2$ is said to be a *Boolean function* in n variables. The set of all Boolean functions will be denoted by $\mathcal{B}_n$. A Boolean function can be regarded as a multivariate polynomial over $\mathbb{F}_2$, called the *algebraic normal form* (ANF)

$$f(x_1, \ldots, x_n) = a_0 \oplus \sum_{1 \leq i \leq n} a_i x_i \oplus \sum_{1 \leq i < j \leq n} a_{ij} x_i x_j \oplus \cdots \oplus a_{12\ldots n} x_1 x_2 \ldots x_n,$$

where the coefficients $a_0, a_i, a_{ij}, \ldots, a_{12\ldots n} \in \mathbb{F}_2$. The maximum number of variables in a monomial is called the *(algebraic) degree*.

For a Boolean function $f \in \mathcal{B}_n$, we define its sign function $\hat{f}$ by $\hat{f}(\mathbf{x}) = (-1)^{f(\mathbf{x})}$. For $\mathbf{u} = (u_1, \ldots, u_n)$, $\mathbf{x} = (x_1, \ldots, x_n)$, we let $\mathbf{u} \cdot \mathbf{x} = \sum_{i=1}^n u_i x_i$ be the regular scalar (inner) product on $\mathbb{V}_n$. For a binary string $\mathbf{s}$, we let $\bar{\mathbf{s}}$ denote the binary complement of $\mathbf{s}$. The (Hamming) *weight* of a binary string $\mathbf{s}$, denoted by $wt(\mathbf{s})$, is the number of nonzero bits in $\mathbf{s}$.

We order $\mathbb{F}_2^n$ lexicographically, and denote $\mathbf{v}_0 = (0, \ldots, 0, 0)$, $\mathbf{v}_1 = (0, \ldots, 0, 1)$, $\mathbf{v}_{2^n-1} = (1, \ldots, 1, 1)$. The *truth table* of a Boolean function $f \in \mathcal{B}_n$ is the binary string of length 2^n, $[f(\mathbf{v}_0), f(\mathbf{v}_1), \ldots, f(\mathbf{v}_{2^n-1})]$ (we will often omit the commas). The (Hamming) *weight* of a function f is the cardinality of the support $\Omega_f = \{\mathbf{x} : f(\mathbf{x}) = 1\}$, that is, is the weight of its truth table. We define the *Fourier transform* of f by

$$\mathcal{W}_f(\mathbf{u}) = \sum_{\mathbf{x} \in \mathbb{V}_n} f(\mathbf{x})(-1)^{\mathbf{u} \cdot \mathbf{x}},$$

and the *Walsh-Hadamard transform* of f by

$$\mathcal{W}_{\hat{f}}(\mathbf{u}) = \sum_{\mathbf{x} \in \mathbb{V}_n} (-1)^{f(\mathbf{x})}(-1)^{\mathbf{u} \cdot \mathbf{x}}.$$

A function f for which $|\mathcal{W}_{\hat{f}}(\mathbf{u})| = 2^{n/2}$ for all $\mathbf{u} \in \mathbb{V}_n$ is called a *bent* function [13]. Further recall that $f \in \mathcal{B}_n$ is called *plateaued* if $|\mathcal{W}_{\hat{f}}(\mathbf{u})| \in \{0, 2^{(n+s)/2}\}$ for all $\mathbf{u} \in \mathbb{V}_n$ for a fixed integer s depending on f (we also call f then *s-plateaued*). If $s = 1$ (n must then be odd), or $s = 2$ (n must then be even), we call f *semibent*. For more on Boolean functions (bent, semibent, plateaued, etc.), the reader can consult [3–5,12] and the references therein.

2.2 A Short Primer on Strong Regularity and Walk Regularity

A graph is *regular of degree r* (or *r-regular*) if every vertex has degree r, where the degree of a vertex is defined as the number of edges incident to it. We say that an r-regular graph G with v vertices is a *strongly regular graph* (srg) with parameters (v, r, e, d) if there exist nonnegative integers e, d such that for all vertices $\mathbf{u}, \mathbf{v}$ the number of vertices adjacent to both $\mathbf{u}, \mathbf{v}$ is e, (resp. d), if $\mathbf{u}, \mathbf{v}$ are adjacent, (resp. nonadjacent). See [6] for further properties of these graphs.

For a Boolean function f on $\mathbb{V}_n$, we define the *Cayley graph* of f to be the graph $G_f = (\mathbb{V}_n, E_f)$ whose vertex set is $\mathbb{V}_n$, and whose set of edges is defined by

$$E_f = \{(\mathbf{w}, \mathbf{u}) \in \mathbb{V}_n \times \mathbb{V}_n : f(\mathbf{w} \oplus \mathbf{u}) = 1\}.$$

The adjacency matrix A_f is the matrix whose entries are $A_{i,j} = f(\mathbf{i} \oplus \mathbf{j})$ (where $\mathbf{i}$ is the binary representation as an n-bit vector of the index i). It is simple to prove that A_f has the dyadic property: $A_{i,j} = A_{i+2^{k-1}, j+2^{k-1}}$. One can derive from its definition that G_f is a *regular graph of degree* $wt(f) = |\Omega_f|$ (see [6, Chap. 3] for further definitions and properties of these graphs).

Given a graph, G_f, and its adjacency matrix, A, the *spectrum* $Spec(G_f)$ is the set of eigenvalues of A (called also the eigenvalues of G_f). We assume throughout that G_f is connected (in fact, one can show that all connected components of G_f are isomorphic) [1,6].

It is known (see [6, pp. 194–195]) that a connected r-regular graph is strongly regular if and only if it has exactly three distinct eigenvalues $\lambda_0 = r, \lambda_1, \lambda_2$ (so $e = r + \lambda_1\lambda_2 + \lambda_1 + \lambda_2, d = r + \lambda_1\lambda_2$). Bent functions exactly correspond to those strongly regular graphs with $e = d$ (Bernasconi-Codenotti correspondence).

The following result is known [6, Theorem 3.32, p. 103] (the second part follows from a counting argument and is also well known).

Proposition 1. *If A is the adjacency matrix of a strongly r-regular graph of parameters e, d and $|V| = v$, then*

$$A^2 = (e - d)A + (r - d)I + dJ,$$

where J is the all 1 matrix. Further, $r(r - e - 1) = d(v - r - 1)$.

The distance in the graph $\Gamma = (V, E)$ between two vertices $x, y \in V$, denoted by $d(x, y)$, is given by the length of the shortest path between x and y. The diameter of a graph is $D = \max_{x,y \in V} d(x, y)$. A connected graph is called *distance-regular* of parameters (c_i, a_i, b_i) (called intersection numbers), if, for all $0 \leq i \leq D$, and for all vertices x, y with $d(x, y) = i$, among the neighbors of y, there are c_i that are at distance $i - 1$ from x, a_i at distance i, and b_i at distance $i + 1$ (thus Γ is regular of degree $r = b_0$).

Fiol and Garriga [8] introduced t-walk-regular graphs as a generalization of both distance-regular and walk-regular graphs. We call a graph $\Gamma = (V, E)$ a t-*walk-regular* (assuming Γ has its diameter at least t) if the number of walks of every given length ℓ between two vertices $x, y \in V$ depends only on the distance between x, y, provided it is $\leq t$. In [7], van Dam and Omidi generalized this concept and called Γ a *strongly ℓ-walk-regular* with parameters $(\sigma_\ell, \mu_\ell, \nu_\ell)$ if there are $\sigma_\ell, \mu_\ell, \nu_\ell$ walks of length ℓ between every two adjacent, every two non-adjacent, and every two identical vertices, respectively. Certainly, every strongly regular graph of parameters (v, r, e, d) is a strongly 2-walk-regular graph with parameters (e, d, r).

Similarly to Proposition 1, the adjacency matrix A of a strongly ℓ-walk-regular graph will satisfy the following property.

Proposition 2 ([7]). *Let $\ell > 1$, and A be the adjacency matrix of a graph Γ. Then Γ is a strongly ℓ-walk-regular with parameters $(\sigma_\ell, \mu_\ell, \nu_\ell)$ if and only if*

$$A^\ell + (\mu_\ell - \sigma_\ell)A + (\mu_\ell - \nu_\ell)I = \mu_\ell J.$$

3 Plateaued Boolean Functions

In general, the spectrum of the Cayley graph of an s-plateaued Boolean function $f : \mathbb{F}_2^n \to \mathbb{F}_2$ will be 4-valued, and therefore the graph will not be strongly regular (see [5, Theorem 9.7]). This can be easily deduced from the fact that, if the Walsh-Hadamard transform of a Boolean function takes values in $\{0, \pm k\}$ (for s-plateaued functions, $k = 2^{(n+s)/2}$), then the Fourier transform of f takes values in $\{wt(f), 0, \pm\frac{k}{2}\}$ (recall that the Fourier transform of f gives the graph spectrum of the corresponding Cayley graph), as the following argument shows.

By [5, Eq. (2.15)],

$$\mathcal{W}_f(\mathbf{w}) = 2^{n-1}\delta(\mathbf{w}) - \frac{1}{2}\mathcal{W}_{\hat{f}}(\mathbf{w}),$$

where δ is the Kronecker delta. Note that, for $\mathbf{w} = \mathbf{0}, \mathcal{W}_f(\mathbf{0}) = wt(f)$. By Parseval's identity (see [5]), $2^{2n} = \sum_{\mathbf{w} \in \mathbb{F}_2^n} |\mathcal{W}_{\hat{f}}(\mathbf{w})|^2$, the multiplicity of $\pm k$ is $\frac{2^{2n}}{k^2}$.

Hence, the multiplicity of these eigenvalues will be (assuming $wt(f) \neq \frac{k}{2}$; the other case follows easily):

(i) If f is balanced, then $\mathcal{W}_{\hat{f}}(\mathbf{0}) = 0$, while $\mathcal{W}_f(\mathbf{0}) = wt(f)$. Then, the multiplicity of $\lambda_1 = wt(f)$ is 1, the multiplicity of $\lambda_3 = 0$ is $2^n - \frac{2^{2n}}{k^2} - 1$, while the multiplicities of $\lambda_2, \lambda_4 = \pm\frac{k}{2}$ will sum to $\frac{2^{2n}}{k^2}$.

(ii) If f is not balanced, then $\mathcal{W}_{\hat{f}}(\mathbf{0}) = \pm k$, while $\mathcal{W}_f(\mathbf{0}) = wt(f)$. Then, the multiplicity of $\lambda_1 = wt(f)$ is 1, the multiplicity of 0 is $2^n - \frac{2^{2n}}{k^2}$, while the multiplicities of $\pm\frac{k}{2}$ will sum to $\frac{2^{2n}}{k^2} - 1$.

Example: $n = 3$, $f = x_1x_2 \oplus x_1x_3 \oplus x_2x_3$, which is semibent, since $\mathcal{W}_{\hat{f}}(\mathbf{w}) = (0\ 4\ 4\ 0\ 4\ 0\ 0\ -4))^T$. We compute that $\mathcal{W}_f(\mathbf{w}) = (4\ -2\ -2\ 0\ -2\ 0\ 0\ 2)^T$, which is 4-valued.

Certainly, if f is semibent, the multiplicities are more precisely known (see [11], for example). For instance, if n is odd (without loss of generality, we assume that $f(\mathbf{0}) = 0$), the multiplicities of the spectra coefficients of $\hat{f}$ are

value	multiplicity
0	2^{n-1}
$2^{(n+1)/2}$	$2^{n-2} + 2^{(n-3)/2}$
$-2^{(n+1)/2}$	$2^{n-2} - 2^{(n-3)/2}$.

We show in Fig. 1 the Cayley graph of a semibent function.

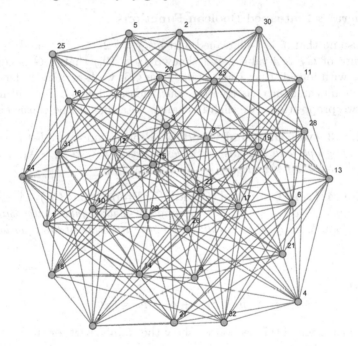

Fig. 1. Cayley graph associated to the semibent $f(\mathbf{x}) = x_1x_2 \oplus x_3x_4 \oplus x_1x_4x_5 \oplus x_2x_3x_5 \oplus x_3x_4x_5$

3.1 s-Plateaued Boolean Functions f with $wt(f) = 2^{(n+s-2)/2}$

Theorem 1. *If $f : \mathbb{F}_2^n \to \mathbb{F}_2$ is s-plateaued and $wt(f) = 2^{(n+s-2)/2}$, then G_f (if connected) is the complete bipartite graph between the vectors in Ω_f and vectors in $\mathbb{F}_2^n \setminus \Omega_f$ (if disconnected, it is a union of complete bipartite graphs). Moreover, G_f is a strongly regular graph with $(e, d) = \left(0, 2^{(n+s-2)/2}\right)$.*

Proof. We know that the Walsh-Hadamard spectra of $\hat{f}$ in this case is $\{0, \pm 2^{(n+s)/2}\}$ and therefore, the spectra of f is also 3-valued, that is, $\{wt(f), 0, \pm 2^{(n+s-2)/2}\} = \{0, \pm 2^{(n+s-2)/2}\}$, and thus, the Cayley graph of f in this case is strongly regular. Now, from [6], we know that if G_f has three distinct eigenvalues $\lambda_0 = wt(f) > \lambda_1 = 0 > \lambda_2 = -\lambda_0$, then G_f is the complete bipartite graph between the nodes in Ω_f and nodes in $\mathbb{F}_2^n \setminus \Omega_f$.

Since the eigenvalues of the strongly regular graph G_f of f can be expressed in terms of the parameters e, d, namely

$$\lambda_0 = wt(f), \ \lambda_{1,2} = \frac{1}{2}\left(e - d \pm \sqrt{(e-d)^2 - 4(d - wt(f))}\right),$$

or equivalently, $e = r + \lambda_1\lambda_2 + \lambda_1 + \lambda_2, d = r + \lambda_1\lambda_2$, and given the Walsh-Hadamard spectra of f, the last claim follows. □

3.2   General s-Plateaued Boolean Functions

We now assume that f is s-plateaued and $wt(f) \neq 2^{(n+s-2)/2}$, and, therefore, the spectrum of G_f is 4-valued. It is known (see [10]) that if G is connected and regular with four distinct eigenvalues, then G is walk-regular. In fact, in our case a result much stronger is true (see our theorem below). We will need the following two propositions (we slightly change notations, to be consistent).

Proposition 3 (van Dam and Omidi [7, Proposition 4.1]**).** *Let Γ be a connected regular graph with four distinct eigenvalues $r > \lambda_2 > \lambda_3 > \lambda_4$. Then Γ is strongly 3-walk-regular if and only if $\lambda_2 + \lambda_3 + \lambda_4 = 0$.*

Proposition 4 (van Dam and Omidi [7, Proposition 3.1]**).** *A connected r-regular graph Γ on v vertices is strongly ℓ-walk-regular with parameters $(\sigma_\ell, \mu_\ell, \nu_\ell)$ if and only if all eigenvalues except r are roots of the equation*

$$x^\ell + (\mu_\ell - \sigma_\ell)x + \mu_\ell - \nu_\ell = 0,$$

and r satisfies

$$r^\ell + (\mu_\ell - \sigma_\ell)r + \mu_\ell - \nu_\ell = \mu_\ell v.$$

In our main theorem of this section we show the counterpart for the Bernasconi-Codenotti equivalence in the case of plateaued functions.

Theorem 2. *Let $f : \mathbb{F}_2^n \to \mathbb{F}_2$ be a Boolean function, and assume that G_f is connected, and that $r := wt(f) \neq 2^{(n+s-2)/2}$. Then, f is s-plateaued (with 4-valued spectra for f) if and only if G_f is strongly 3-walk-regular of parameters $(\sigma, \mu, \nu) = (2^{-n}r^3 + 2^{n+s-2} - 2^{s-2}r, 2^{-n}r^3 - 2^{s-2}r, 2^{-n}r^3 - 2^{s-2}r)$ (hence $\mu = \nu$).*

Proof. We first assume that f is s-plateaued and so, its spectra is $\{0, \pm 2^{(n+s)/2}\}$. Consequently, the spectra of G_f is 4-valued (since $r := wt(f) \neq 2^{(n+s-2)/2}$), namely $\{r = wt(f), \lambda_2 = 2^{(n+s-2)/2}, \lambda_3 := 0, \lambda_4 := -2^{(n+s-2)/2}\}$. The fact that G_f is strongly 3-walk-regular follows from Proposition 3, since $\lambda_2 + \lambda_3 + \lambda_4 = 0$, which certainly happens for our graphs. Moreover, the parameters (σ, μ, ν) (we removed, for convenience, the subscripts $\ell = 3$) can be found using Proposition 4 as solutions to the diophantine system (recall that in our case $v = 2^n$ and $r = wt(f)$)

$$0 = 2^{3(n+s-2)/2} + (\mu - \sigma)2^{(n+s-2)/2} + \mu - \nu,$$
$$0 = -2^{3(n+s-2)/2} - (\mu - \sigma)2^{(n+s-2)/2} + \mu - \nu,$$
$$\mu\, 2^n = r^3 + (\mu - \sigma)r + \mu - \nu,$$

namely, $(\sigma, \mu, \nu) = (2^{-n}r^3 + 2^{n+s-2} - 2^{s-2}r, 2^{-n}r^3 - 2^{s-2}r, 2^{-n}r^3 - 2^{s-2}r)$.

Conversely, assuming G_f is a 3-walk-regular graph with the above parameters, then the eigenvalues $\lambda_2 > \lambda_3 > \lambda_4$ will satisfy the equation

$$x^3 + (\mu - \sigma)x + \mu - \nu = 0,$$

which will render the roots, $\lambda_2 = 2^{(n+s-2)/2}, \lambda_3 = 0, \lambda_4 = -2^{(n+s-2)/2}$. The claim is shown. □

Remark 1. Using a result of Godsil [9] one can easily show (under mild conditions – thus removing strongly regular ones, for example) that the graphs corresponding to plateaued functions are not distance-regular.

In fact, from [7] we know that the graph with four distinct eigenvalues is ℓ-walk-regular for any odd $\ell \geq 3$, but in our case we can show a lot more, by finding the involved parameters precisely.

Theorem 3. *If A is the adjacency matrix of the Cayley graph corresponding to an s-plateaued with 4-valued spectra (of f), then C_f is strongly ℓ-walk-regular for any odd ℓ of parameters $(\sigma_\ell, \mu_\ell, \nu_\ell)$, where $\ell = 2t + 1$, $\sigma_\ell = \mu \frac{2^{(n+s-2)t} - r^{2t}}{2^{n+s-2} - r^2} + 2^{(n+s-2)t}$, $\mu_\ell = \nu_\ell = \mu \frac{2^{(n+s-2)t} - r^{2t}}{2^{n+s-2} - r^2}$. Further, the following identity holds, for all $t \geq 1$,*

$$A^{2t+1} = 2^{(n+s-2)t}A + \mu \frac{2^{(n+s-2)t} - r^{2t}}{2^{n+s-2} - r^2}\, J,$$

where $(\sigma, \mu, \nu) = (2^{-n}r^3 + 2^{n+s-2} - 2^{s-2}r, 2^{-n}r^3 - 2^{s-2}r, 2^{-n}r^3 - 2^{s-2}r)$.

Proof. From our Theorem 2, we know that

$$A^3 = (\sigma - \mu)A + \mu J,$$

since we know that $\mu = \nu$. We will show our result by induction, and so, for simplicity we label $x_1 := \sigma - \mu = 2^{n+s-2}, y_1 := \mu = 2^{-n}r^3 - 2^{s-2}r$. Assume now that

$$A^{2t+1} = x_t A + y_t J. \tag{1}$$

First, observe that, since our graph is regular of degree r, then $AJ = rJ$, and more general, $A^k J = r^k J$. Multiplying (1) by A^2, we get

$$A^{2t+3} = x_t A^3 + y_t A^2 J$$
$$= x_t(x_1 A + y_1 J) + y_t r^2 J$$
$$= x_t x_1 A + (x_t y_1 + y_t r^2)J,$$

and consequently, we get the recurrences

$$x_{t+1} = x_t x_1$$
$$y_{t+1} = x_t y_1 + y_t r^2.$$

Solving the system, we get $x_{t+1} = x_1^{t+1} = (\sigma - \mu)^{t+1} = 2^{(n+s-2)(t+1)}$ and $y_{t+1} = y_1 \dfrac{x_1^{t+1} - r^{2(t+1)}}{x_1 - r^2} = \mu \dfrac{2^{(n+s-2)(t+1)} - r^{2(t+1)}}{2^{n+s-2} - r^2}$, and our claim is shown. $\square$

References

1. Bernasconi, A., Codenotti, B.: Spectral analysis of Boolean functions as a graph eigenvalue problem. IEEE Trans. Comput. **48**(3), 345–351 (1999)
2. Bernasconi, A., Codenotti, B., VanderKam, J.M.: A characterization of bent functions in terms of strongly regular graphs. IEEE Trans. Comput. **50**(9), 984–985 (2001)
3. Budaghyan, L.: Construction and Analysis of Cryptographic Functions. Springer, Heidelberg (2014). https://doi.org/10.1007/978-3-319-12991-4
4. Carlet, C.: Boolean models and methods in mathematics, computer science, and engineering. In: Hammer, P., Crama, Y. (eds.) Boolean Functions for Cryptography and Error Correcting Codes, pp. 257–397. Cambridge University Press, Cambridge (2010)
5. Cusick, T.W., Stănică, P.: Cryptographic Boolean Functions and Applications, 2nd edn. Academic Press, San Diego (2017). 1st edn. (2009)
6. Cvetkovic, D.M., Doob, M., Sachs, H.: Spectra of Graphs. Academic Press, New York (1979)
7. van Dam, E.R., Omidi, G.R.: Strongly walk-regular graphs. J. Comb. Theory Ser. A **120**, 803–810 (2013)
8. Fiol, M.A., Garriga, E.: Spectral and geometric properties of k-walk-regular graphs. Electron. Notes Discrete Math. **29**, 333–337 (2007)
9. Godsil, C.D.: Bounding the diameter of distance-regular graphs. Combinatorica **8**(4), 333–343 (1988)
10. Huang, X., Huang, Q.: On regular graphs with four distinct eigenvalues. Linear Algebra Appl. **512**, 219–233 (2017)
11. Mesnager, S.: On semi-bent functions and related plateaued functions over the Galois field $\mathbb{F}_{2^n}$. In: Koç, Ç.K. (ed.) Open Problems in Mathematics and Computational Science, pp. 243–273. Springer, Cham (2014). https://doi.org/10.1007/978-3-319-10683-0_11
12. Mesnager, S.: Bent Functions: Fundamentals and Results. Springer, New York (2016). https://doi.org/10.1007/978-3-319-32595-8
13. Rothaus, O.S.: On bent functions. J. Comb. Theory Ser. A **20**, 300–305 (1976)
14. Tokareva, N.: Bent Functions, Results and Applications to Cryptography. Academic Press, San Diego (2015)

Chameleon-Hashes with Dual Long-Term Trapdoors and Their Applications

Stephan Krenn[1]([✉]), Henrich C. Pöhls[2], Kai Samelin[3], and Daniel Slamanig[1]

[1] AIT Austrian Institute of Technology GmbH, Vienna, Austria
{stephan.krenn,daniel.slamanig}@ait.ac.at
[2] ISL & Chair of IT-Security, University of Passau, Passau, Germany
hp@sec.uni-passau.de
[3] TU Darmstadt, Darmstadt, Germany
ks@sec.uni-passau.de

Abstract. A chameleon-hash behaves likes a standard collision-resistant hash function for outsiders. If, however, a trapdoor is known, arbitrary collisions can be found. Chameleon-hashes with ephemeral trapdoors (CHET; Camenisch et al., PKC 17) allow prohibiting that the holder of the long-term trapdoor can find collisions by introducing a second, ephemeral, trapdoor. However, this ephemeral trapdoor is required to be chosen freshly for *each* hash.

We extend these ideas and introduce the notion of chameleon-hashes with *dual long-term* trapdoors (CHDLTT). Here, the second trapdoor is not chosen freshly for each new hash; Rather, the hashing party can decide if it wants to generate a fresh second trapdoor or use an existing one. This primitive generalizes CHETs, extends their applicability and enables some appealing new use-cases, including *three-party* sanitizable signatures, group-level selectively revocable signatures and break-the-glass signatures. We present two provably secure constructions and an implementation which demonstrates that this extended primitive is efficient enough for use in practice.

1 Introduction

Standard chameleon-hashes have proven to be useful in very different areas such as on/offline signatures [28,33,56], (tightly) secure signatures [14,43,50], but also sanitizable signature [2,17,22,40] and identity-based encryption [58]. They are also useful in context of trapdoor-commitments, direct anonymous attestation, Σ-protocols and distributed hashing [1,10,16]. Recently, they have been extended to have ephemeral trapdoors, which allow one to find collisions if, and

The project leading to this work has received funding from the European Union's Horizon 2020 research and innovation programme under grant agreement No 644962 PRISMACLOUD and No 321310 PERCY.

K. Samelin—This work was done while the third author was also at IBM Research – Zurich.

A. Joux et al. (Eds.): AFRICACRYPT 2018, LNCS 10831, pp. 11–32, 2018.
https://doi.org/10.1007/978-3-319-89339-6_2

only if, two trapdoors at the same time are known [22]. One of those trapdoors is long-term, while the second one is chosen freshly for each new hash.

The first application of these so called CHETs were invisible sanitizable signatures [7,22]. In this primitive, a semi-trusted third party, named the sanitizer having its own key pair, can modify signer-chosen admissible parts of a signed message to arbitrary bit-strings [2,17]. The derived signatures still verify, while an outsider cannot decide which parts are actually modifiable. However, the current formalization of those chameleon-hashes inherently requires that the ephemeral trapdoor is chosen freshly for *each* new hash. Thus, for each generated hash, the hashing party can decide if, and when, the holder of the long-term trapdoor can find collisions. This requirement, however, is quite restricting and once it is lifted, several new interesting use-cases are possible.

Motivation and Contribution. We introduce chameleon-hashes with dual long-term trapdoors (CHDLTT). In this primitive, the second trapdoor no longer needs to be freshly generated on every hash computation, but can be re-used in several hash computations. This has several advantages over CHETs as defined by Camenisch et al. [22]. For example, our definitions allow that the trapdoors can be generated in advance (and thus can, e.g., be registered at a PKI before usage), re-used multiple times (which adds flexibility and saves computational costs) and are inherently independent of any other hashing keys created. In other words, releasing the second trapdoor allows the holder of the long-term secret to find collisions for *all* hashes created using the corresponding second public hashing key that corresponds to the trapdoor. Thus, our new primitive strictly generalizes CHETs: using a fresh trapdoor for each generated hash within our extended definition of CHDLTT resembles the behavior of a CHET.

We introduce a suitable framework, along with corresponding security definitions and two provably secure constructions. The first construction is based on standard collision-resistant chameleon-hashes, while the second one is based on the one-more RSA-Assumption. To demonstrate the usefulness of our new primitive, we show how one can construct *three*-party sanitizable signatures. In this new primitive, a *signer*-designated third party can decide if, and when, the sanitizer is able to sanitize the admissible parts of messages. This new primitive enables several new use-cases for sanitizable signatures scheme. For example, consider the following scenario, where "standard" sanitizable signatures [2] are not sufficient. Assume a supply chain, where the delivery person needs to claim that it delivered the goods as instructed by the sender, while also the recipient needs to vouch for the correct delivery at time of successful reception. In standard sanitizable signature schemes, either a fresh signature is generated at delivery, which is approved by the recipient, or vice versa. However, in this case, the sender has no control what is actually signed. Our extended primitives allows to tackle this problem: the sender can sign what has been commissioned, while the delivery person can approve that it has successfully delivered the goods, if, and only if, the recipient allows the delivery man to do this, i.e., by releasing an additional trapdoor. To some extend, this resembles "four-eyes"-signatures [12], but in a more sophisticated manner, as in our case also damaged goods can be reported *within the same report*, e.g., using special blocks of the message.

Additional application scenarios include group-level selectively revocable signatures and break-the-glass signatures. Revocable signatures have already been mentioned by Camenisch et al. [22] as a potential additional application scenario, while break-the-glass signatures are a new concept. Moreover, our evaluation shows that the primitive is practically efficient. Summarized, our work leads to some new interesting applications of chameleon-hashes, which may give rise to new use-cases which have not been considered yet.

Related Work and State-of-the-Art. Chameleon-hashes were introduced by Krawczyk and Rabin [46], based on the work done by Brassard et al. [16]. Later, they have been ported to the identity-based setting, i.e., ID-based chameleon-hash functions, where the holder of some master secret key can extract new secret keys for new identities [4,6,55,57]. However, most of the schemes presented suffer from the key-exposure problem [5,27,46]. Key-exposure means that seeing a single collision in the hash allows to find further collisions by extracting the corresponding trapdoor, i.e., the secret key.[1] This problem was addressed by the introduction of "key-exposure free" chameleon-hashes [5,26,27,38,39,55], which prohibit extracting the secret key if a collision was seen. This also includes combinations of both techniques [29]. Such schemes allow for re-using secret key-material. However, the definition of collision-resistance is defined w.r.t. some additional label L.[2] This label L is used to define a "collision-domain", i.e., such hashes do *not* prohibit that once a collision is made public for a label L, an adversary cannot produce additional collisions w.r.t. that label L. We stress that our framework does not require such a label, i.e., it is collision-resistant in the "usual" sense. Brzuska et al. also proposed a formal framework for tag-based chameleon-hashes secure under random-tagging attacks, i.e., they add an additional *random* tag to the input of the hashing algorithm [17]. We stress that all of the mentioned approaches are orthogonal to our primitive, as in our case two keys at *the same time* are required. Camenisch et al. presented a new type of chameleon-hash, where the hashing party can prohibit that the holder of the long-term secret can find collisions by adding a second, i.e., ephemeral, trapdoor [22], which is chosen freshly for each new hash. Their work can be seen as the starting point for our work. Additional related work is discussed when presenting the applications of our new primitive.

2   Preliminaries

Let us give our notation and assumptions first. Additional standard formal security definitions are given in the full version of this paper.

---

[1] In the case of identity-based chameleon-hashes w.r.t. to some identity.

[2] Also referred to as nonce or tag.

Notation. $\lambda \in \mathbb{N}$ denotes our security parameter. All algorithms implicitly take 1^λ as an additional input. We write $a \leftarrow A(x)$ if a is assigned to the output of algorithm A with input x. An algorithm is efficient if it runs in probabilistic polynomial time (ppt) in the length of its input. All algorithms are ppt, if not explicitly mentioned otherwise. Most algorithms may return a special error symbol $\perp \notin \{0,1\}^*$, denoting an exception. Returning output ends an algorithm. If S is a set, we write $a \leftarrow S$ to denote that a is chosen uniformly at random from S. For a list we require that there is an injective, and efficiently reversible, encoding, mapping the list to $\{0,1\}^*$. In the definitions, we speak of a general message space $\mathcal{M}$ to be as generic as possible. For our instantiations, however, we let the message space $\mathcal{M}$ be $\{0,1\}^*$ to reduce unhelpful boilerplate notation. A function $\nu : \mathbb{N} \to \mathbb{R}_{\geq 0}$ is negligible, if it vanishes faster than every inverse polynomial, i.e., $\forall k \in \mathbb{N}, \exists n_0 \in \mathbb{N}$ such that $\nu(n) \leq n^{-k}, \forall n > n_0$. Moreover, we require that one can derive a public key from the private key. This is not explicitly checked. This can be achieved by appending the randomness used to generate the key pair to the secret key.

The One-More-RSA-Assumption [9]. Let $(n, e, d, p, q) \leftarrow \mathsf{RSA}(1^\lambda)$ be an RSA-key generator returning an RSA modulus $n = pq$, where p and q are random distinct primes, $e > 1$ an integer co-prime to $\varphi(n)$, and $d \equiv e^{-1} \bmod \varphi(n)$. The one-more-RSA-assumption associated to RSA is provided an inversion oracle $\mathcal{I}$, which inverts any element $x \in \mathbb{Z}_n^*$ w.r.t. e, and a challenge oracle $\mathcal{C}$, which at each call returns a random element $y_i \in \mathbb{Z}_n^*$. An adversary wins if, given n and e, it is able to invert more elements received by $\mathcal{C}$ than is makes calls to $\mathcal{I}$. The corresponding assumption states that for every ppt adversary $\mathcal{A}$ there exists a negligible function ν such that:

$$\Pr[(n, p, q, e, d) \leftarrow \mathsf{RSA}(1^\lambda), X \leftarrow \mathcal{A}(n, e)^{\mathcal{C}(n), \mathcal{I}(d, n, \cdot)} :$$
$$\text{more values returned by } \mathcal{C} \text{ are inverted than queries to } \mathcal{I}] \leq \nu(\lambda)$$

Here, X is the set of inverted challenges.

We require that e is larger than any possible n w.r.t. λ and that it is prime. Re-stating the assumption with this condition is straightforward. In this case, it is also required that e is drawn independently from p, q, or n (and d is then calculated from e, and not vice versa). This can, e.g., be achieved by demanding that e is drawn uniformly from $[n' + 1, \ldots, 2n'] \cap \{p \mid p \text{ is prime}\}$, where n' is the largest RSA modulus possible w.r.t. to λ. The details are left to the concrete instantiation of RSA.

Chameleon-Hashes. The given framework is the one by Camenisch et al. [22].

Definition 1. *A chameleon-hash* CH *consists of five algorithms* (PGen, KGen, Hash, Ver, Adap), *such that:*

PGen. *It outputs the public parameters of the scheme:*

$$\mathsf{pp}_{ch} \leftarrow \mathsf{PGen}(1^\lambda)$$

We assume that pp_{ch} *is an implicit input to all other algorithms.*
KGen. *On input* pp_{ch}, *it outputs the private and public key of the scheme:*

$$(\mathsf{sk}_{ch}, \mathsf{pk}_{ch}) \leftarrow \mathsf{KGen}(\mathsf{pp}_{ch})$$

Hash. *It gets as input a public key* pk_{ch} *and a message* m *to hash. It outputs a hash* h *and some randomness* r: $(h, r) \leftarrow \mathsf{Hash}(\mathsf{pk}_{ch}, m)$.[3]
Ver. *This deterministic algorithm gets as input the public key* pk_{ch}, *a message* m, *randomness* r *and a hash* h. *It outputs a decision* $d \in \{0, 1\}$ *indicating whether* $(d = 1)$ *or not* $(d = 0)$ *the hash* h *is valid:*

$$d \leftarrow \mathsf{Ver}(\mathsf{pk}_{ch}, m, r, h)$$

Adap. *On input of secret key* sk_{ch}, *the message* m, *the randomness* r, *hash* h *and a new message* m', *it outputs new randomness* r':

$$r' \leftarrow \mathsf{Adap}(\mathsf{sk}_{ch}, m, m', r, h)$$

The standard correctness definition is given in the full version of this paper.

Indistinguishability. Indistinguishability requires that r does not reveal if it was obtained through Hash or Adap. The messages are chosen by the adversary.

Definition 2 (Indistinguishability). *A chameleon-hash* CH *is indistinguishable, if for any ppt adversary* $\mathcal{A}$ *there exists a negligible function* ν *such that* $\left| \Pr[\mathsf{Ind}_{\mathcal{A}}^{\mathsf{CH}}(\lambda) = 1] - \frac{1}{2} \right| \leq \nu(\lambda)$. *The corresponding experiment is depicted in Fig. 1.*

Collision Resistance. Collision resistance says, that even if an adversary has access to an adapt oracle, it cannot find any collisions for messages other than the ones queried to the adapt oracle. Note, this is a stronger definition than key-exposure freeness [5,27], as key-exposure freeness does *not* guarantee that for a given collision no additional ones can be found [26].

Definition 3 (Collision-Resistance). *A chameleon-hash* CH *is collision-resistant, if for any ppt adversary* $\mathcal{A}$ *there exists a negligible function* ν *such that* $\Pr[\mathsf{CollRes}_{\mathcal{A}}^{\mathsf{CH}}(1^\lambda) = 1] \leq \nu(\lambda)$. *The corresponding experiment is depicted in Fig. 2.*

Uniqueness. Uniqueness requires that it is hard to come up with two different randomnesses for the same message m^* such that the hashes are equal, for the same adversarially chosen pk^*.

---

[3] The randomness r is also sometimes called "check value" [3].

Experiment $\mathsf{Ind}_{\mathcal{A}}^{\mathsf{CH}}(\lambda)$

   $\mathsf{pp}_{\mathsf{ch}} \leftarrow \mathsf{PGen}(1^{\lambda})$
   $(\mathsf{sk}_{\mathsf{ch}}, \mathsf{pk}_{\mathsf{ch}}) \leftarrow \mathsf{KGen}(\mathsf{pp}_{\mathsf{ch}})$
   $b \leftarrow \{0, 1\}$
   $a \leftarrow \mathcal{A}^{\mathsf{HashOrAdapt}(\mathsf{sk}_{\mathsf{ch}},\cdot,\cdot,\cdot,b),\mathsf{Adap}(\mathsf{sk}_{\mathsf{ch}},\cdot,\cdot,\cdot,\cdot)}(\mathsf{pk}_{\mathsf{ch}})$
     where HashOrAdapt on input $\mathsf{sk}_{\mathsf{ch}}, m, m', b$:
       $(h, r) \leftarrow \mathsf{Hash}(\mathsf{pk}_{\mathsf{ch}}, m')$
       $(h', r') \leftarrow \mathsf{Hash}(\mathsf{pk}_{\mathsf{ch}}, m)$
       $r'' \leftarrow \mathsf{Adap}(\mathsf{sk}_{\mathsf{ch}}, m, m', r', h')$
       If $r = \bot \lor r'' = \bot$, return $\bot$
       if $b = 0$, return (h, r)
       if $b = 1$, return (h', r'')
   return 1, if $a = b$
   return 0

Fig. 1. Indistinguishability

Experiment $\mathsf{CollRes}_{\mathcal{A}}^{\mathsf{CH}}(\lambda)$

   $\mathsf{pp}_{\mathsf{ch}} \leftarrow \mathsf{PGen}(1^{\lambda})$
   $(\mathsf{sk}_{\mathsf{ch}}, \mathsf{pk}_{\mathsf{ch}}) \leftarrow \mathsf{KGen}(\mathsf{pp}_{\mathsf{ch}})$
   $\mathcal{Q} \leftarrow \emptyset$
   $(m^*, r^*, m'^*, r'^*, h^*) \leftarrow \mathcal{A}^{\mathsf{Adap}'(\mathsf{sk}_{\mathsf{ch}},\cdot,\cdot,\cdot,\cdot)}(\mathsf{pk}_{\mathsf{ch}})$
     where Adap' on input $\mathsf{sk}_{\mathsf{ch}}, m, m', r, h$:
       return $\bot$, if $\mathsf{Ver}(\mathsf{pk}_{\mathsf{ch}}, m, r, h) \neq 1$
       $r' \leftarrow \mathsf{Adap}(\mathsf{sk}_{\mathsf{ch}}, m, m', r, h)$
       return $\bot$, if $r' = \bot$
       $\mathcal{Q} \leftarrow \mathcal{Q} \cup \{m, m'\}$
       return r'
   return 1, if $\mathsf{Ver}(\mathsf{pk}_{\mathsf{ch}}, m^*, r^*, h^*) = 1 \land$
      $\mathsf{Ver}(\mathsf{pk}_{\mathsf{ch}}, m'^*, r'^*, h^*) = 1 \land$
      $m'^* \notin \mathcal{Q} \land m^* \neq m'^*$
   return 0

Fig. 2. Collision resistance

Experiment $\mathsf{Uniqueness}_{\mathcal{A}}^{\mathsf{CH}}(\lambda)$

   $\mathsf{pp}_{\mathsf{ch}} \leftarrow \mathsf{PGen}(1^{\lambda})$
   $(\mathsf{pk}^*, m^*, r^*, r'^*, h^*) \leftarrow \mathcal{A}(\mathsf{pp}_{\mathsf{ch}})$
   return 1, if $\mathsf{Ver}(\mathsf{pk}^*, m^*, r^*, h^*) = \mathsf{Ver}(\mathsf{pk}^*, m^*, r'^*, h^*) = 1 \land r^* \neq r'^*$
   return 0

Fig. 3. Uniqueness

Definition 4 (Uniqueness). *A chameleon-hash* CH *is unique, if for any ppt adversary* $\mathcal{A}$ *there exists a negligible function* ν *such that* $\Pr[\mathsf{Uniqueness}_{\mathcal{A}}^{\mathsf{CH}}(1^{\lambda}) = 1] \leq \nu(\lambda)$. *The corresponding experiment is depicted in Fig. 3.*

Definition 5 (Secure Chameleon-Hashes). *A chameleon-hash* CH *is secure, if it is correct, indistinguishable, and collision-resistant.*

It depends on the concrete use-case, if CH needs to be unique.

3   CHs with Dual Long-Term Trapdoors

As already mentioned, a chameleon-hash with dual long-term trapdoors (CHDLTT) allows to prevent the holder of some long-term trapdoor $\mathsf{sk}_{\mathsf{chret}}$ from finding collisions, as long as no additional second trapdoor std is known. This additional trapdoor can can be re-used for multiple hash generation, but may also be chosen freshly. This, e.g., allows to generate trapdoors in advance and to make one of the trapdoors public beforehand. Clearly, providing or withholding the second trapdoor information corresponding to the public part ptd of the second trapdoor thus allows to decide if finding a collision is possible for the holder of the long-term trapdoor. Due to this new possibility, we need to introduce a new framework, given subsequently, which is also accompanied by suitable security definitions. This framework is inspired by, and compatible to, the one given by Camenisch et al. [22] and it can be seen as a generalization of their ideas.

Definition 6 (CHDLTT). *A chameleon-hash with dual long-term trapdoors* CHDLLT *is a tuple* (PGen, KGen, TDGen, Hash, Ver, Adap), *such that:*

PGen. *It outputs the public parameters:*

$$pp_{chret} \leftarrow PGen(1^\lambda)$$

   which are input to all other algorithms, which we sometimes may not make explicit for notational convenience.

KGen. *On input* pp_{chret}, *it outputs the long-term private and public key of the scheme:*

$$(sk_{chret}, pk_{chret}) \leftarrow KGen(pp_{chret})$$

TDGen. *It outputs a private and public trapdoor pair:*

$$(std, ptd) \leftarrow TDGen(pp_{chret})$$

Hash. *It gets as input a public key* pk_{chret}, ptd *and a message* m *to hash. It outputs a hash* h *and randomness* r:

$$(h, r) \leftarrow Hash(pk_{chret}, ptd, m)$$

Ver. *It gets as input the public key* pk_{chret}, ptd, *a message* m, *a hash* h *and randomness* r. *It outputs a decision bit* $d \in \{0,1\}$, *indicating whether the given hash is correct:*

$$d \leftarrow Ver(pk_{chret}, ptd, m, r, h)$$

Adap. *It gets as input* sk_{chret}, *the old message* m, *the old randomness* r, *the new message* m', *the hash* h *and the trapdoor information* std. *It outputs new randomness:*

$$r' \leftarrow Adap(sk_{chret}, m, m', r, h, std)$$

Correctness is straightforward and is defined in the full version of this paper. We also require some security guarantees, which we introduce next.

Indistinguishability. Indistinguishability requires that the randomnesses r does not reveal if it was obtained through Hash or Adap. In other words, an outsider cannot decide whether a message is the original one or not. Note, however, that both secrets are generated honestly, i.e., for adversarially generated keys no security guarantees are given. Moreover, only one trapdoor pair is generated; security for multiple trapdoor information pairs can be shown for any indistinguishable CHDLTT using a simple hybrid argument.

Definition 7 (Indistinguishability). *A* CHDLTT *is indistinguishable, if for every ppt adversary* $\mathcal{A}$ *there exists a negligible function* ν *such that* $\left| \Pr[Ind_{\mathcal{A}}^{CHDLTT}(\lambda) = 1] - \frac{1}{2} \right| \leq \nu(\lambda)$. *The corresponding experiment is depicted in Fig. 4.*

Experiment $\mathsf{Ind}_{\mathcal{A}}^{\mathsf{CHDLTT}}(\lambda)$

$\mathsf{pp}_{\mathsf{chret}} \leftarrow \mathsf{PGen}(1^\lambda)$
$(\mathsf{sk}_{\mathsf{chret}}, \mathsf{pk}_{\mathsf{chret}}) \leftarrow \mathsf{KGen}(\mathsf{pp}_{\mathsf{chret}})$
$(\mathsf{std}, \mathsf{ptd}) \leftarrow \mathsf{TDGen}(\mathsf{pp}_{\mathsf{chret}})$
$b \leftarrow \{0, 1\}$
$a \leftarrow \mathcal{A}_{\mathsf{Adap}(\mathsf{sk}_{\mathsf{chret}}, \cdot, \cdot, \cdot, \cdot, \cdot)}^{\mathsf{HashOrAdapt}(\mathsf{sk}_{\mathsf{chret}}, \mathsf{std}, \cdot, \cdot, b)}(\mathsf{pk}_{\mathsf{chret}}, \mathsf{ptd})$
  where HashOrAdapt on input $\mathsf{sk}_{\mathsf{chret}}, \mathsf{std}, m, m', b$:
    let $(h, r) \leftarrow \mathsf{Hash}(\mathsf{pk}_{\mathsf{chret}}, \mathsf{ptd}, m')$
    let $(h', r') \leftarrow \mathsf{Hash}(\mathsf{pk}_{\mathsf{chret}}, \mathsf{ptd}, m)$
    let $r'' \leftarrow \mathsf{Adap}(\mathsf{sk}_{\mathsf{chret}}, m, m', r', h', \mathsf{std})$
    if $r'' = \bot \vee r' = \bot$, return $\bot$
    if $b = 0$, return (h, r)
    if $b = 1$, return (h', r'')
return 1, if $a = b$
return 0

Experiment $\mathsf{Uniqueness}_{\mathcal{A}}^{\mathsf{CHDLTT}}(\lambda)$

$\mathsf{pp}_{\mathsf{chret}} \leftarrow \mathsf{PGen}(1^\lambda)$
$(\mathsf{pk}^*, m^*, r^*, r'^*, \mathsf{ptd}^*, h^*) \leftarrow \mathcal{A}(\mathsf{pp}_{\mathsf{ch}})$
return 1, if $\mathsf{Ver}(\mathsf{pk}_{\mathsf{chret}}, \mathsf{ptd}^*, m^*, r^*, h^*) =$
  $\mathsf{Ver}(\mathsf{pk}_{\mathsf{chret}}, \mathsf{ptd}^*, m^*, r'^*, h^*) = 1 \wedge r^* \neq r'^*$
return 0

Fig. 4. Indistinguishability   **Fig. 5.** Uniquessness

Public Collision Resistance. Public collision resistance requires that, even if an adversary has access to an Adap oracle, it cannot find any collisions by itself, even if it can chose ptd. Clearly, the collision must be fresh, i.e., must not be produced using the Adap oracle.

Definition 8 (Public Collision-Resistance). *A* CHDLTT *is publicly collision-resistant, if for any ppt adversary $\mathcal{A}$ there exists a negligible function ν such that* $\Pr[\mathsf{PublicCollRes}_{\mathcal{A}}^{\mathsf{CHDLTT}}(1^\lambda) = 1] \leq \nu(\lambda)$. *The corresponding experiment is depicted in Fig. 6.*

Private Collision-Resistance. Private collision-resistance requires that even the holder of the secret key $\mathsf{sk}_{\mathsf{chret}}$ cannot find collisions as long as std is unknown, even if it can request collisions for different pks. This catches the idea that the hashes for a given ptd may be equivocated for different $\mathsf{pk}_{\mathsf{chret}}$s. This is formalized by a honest adaption oracle which returns collisions for other key pairs. Hence, $\mathcal{A}$'s goal is to return an actual collision for a public key pk^*, for an honestly generated ptd, for which it did not see a collision generated by the oracle, but for an arbitrary $\mathsf{sk}_{\mathsf{chret}}$.

Definition 9 (Private Collision-Resistance). *A* CHDLTT *is privately collision-resistant, if for any ppt adversary $\mathcal{A}$ there exists a negligible function ν such that* $\Pr[\mathsf{PrivateCollRes}_{\mathcal{A}}^{\mathsf{CHDLTT}}(1^\lambda) = 1] \leq \nu(\lambda)$. *The corresponding experiment is depicted in Fig. 7.*

Uniqueness. Uniquess requires that even if the adversary can generate the public key and the corresponding public trapdoor, it cannot find two different randomnesses for the same hash and message such that both are valid.

Definition 10 (Uniqueness). *A* CHDLTT *is unique, if for any ppt adversary $\mathcal{A}$ there exists a negligible function ν such that* $\Pr[\mathsf{Uniqueness}_{\mathcal{A}}^{\mathsf{CHDLTT}}(1^\lambda) = 1] \leq \nu(\lambda)$. *The corresponding experiment is depicted in Fig. 5.*

Experiment PublicCollRes$_\mathcal{A}^{\mathsf{CHDLTT}}(\lambda)$

  $\mathsf{pp}_{\mathsf{chret}} \leftarrow \mathsf{PGen}(1^\lambda)$
  $(\mathsf{sk}_{\mathsf{chret}}, \mathsf{pk}_{\mathsf{chret}}) \leftarrow \mathsf{KGen}(\mathsf{pp}_{\mathsf{chret}})$
  $\mathcal{Q} \leftarrow \emptyset$
  $(m^*, r^*, m'^*, r'^*, \mathsf{ptd}^*, h^*) \leftarrow \mathcal{A}^{\mathsf{Adap}'(\mathsf{sk}_{\mathsf{chret}}, \cdots)}(\mathsf{pk}_{\mathsf{chret}})$
    where Adap$'$ on input $\mathsf{sk}_{\mathsf{chret}}, m, m', r, \mathsf{std}, \mathsf{ptd}, h$:
      return $\bot$, if $\mathsf{Ver}(\mathsf{pk}_{\mathsf{chret}}, \mathsf{ptd}, m, r, h) = 0$
      $r' \leftarrow \mathsf{Adap}(\mathsf{sk}_{\mathsf{chret}}, m, m', r, h, \mathsf{std})$
      If $r' = \bot$, return $\bot$
      $\mathcal{Q} \leftarrow \mathcal{Q} \cup \{(\mathsf{ptd}, m), (\mathsf{ptd}, m')\}$
      return r'
  return 1, if $\mathsf{Ver}(\mathsf{pk}_{\mathsf{chret}}, \mathsf{ptd}^*, m^*, r^*, h^*) = 1 \wedge$
    $\mathsf{Ver}(\mathsf{pk}_{\mathsf{chret}}, \mathsf{ptd}^*, m'^*, r'^*, h^*) = 1 \wedge$
    $(\mathsf{ptd}^*, m'^*) \notin \mathcal{Q} \wedge m^* \neq m'^*$
  return 0

Fig. 6. Public collision-resistance

Experiment PrivateCollRes$_\mathcal{A}^{\mathsf{CHDLTT}}(\lambda)$

  $\mathsf{pp}_{\mathsf{chret}} \leftarrow \mathsf{PGen}(1^\lambda)$
  $(\mathsf{std}, \mathsf{ptd}) \leftarrow \mathsf{TDGen}(\mathsf{pp}_{\mathsf{chret}})$
  $\mathcal{Q} \leftarrow \emptyset$
  $(\mathsf{pk}^*, m^*, r^*, m'^*, r'^*, h^*) \leftarrow \mathcal{A}^{\mathsf{Adap}'(\mathsf{std}, \cdots, \cdots)}(\mathsf{ptd})$
    where Adap$'$ on input $\mathsf{std}, \mathsf{sk}_{\mathsf{chret}}$,
    $\mathsf{pk}_{\mathsf{chret}}, m, m', r, h$:
      return $\bot$, if $\mathsf{Ver}(\mathsf{pk}_{\mathsf{chret}}, \mathsf{ptd}, m, r, h) = 0$
      $r' \leftarrow \mathsf{Adap}(\mathsf{sk}_{\mathsf{chret}}, m, m', r, h, \mathsf{std})$
      return $\bot$, if $r' = \bot$
      $\mathcal{Q} \leftarrow \mathcal{Q} \cup \{(\mathsf{pk}_{\mathsf{chret}}, m), (\mathsf{pk}_{\mathsf{chret}}, m')\}$
      return r'
  return 1, if $\mathsf{Ver}(\mathsf{pk}^*, \mathsf{ptd}, m^*, r^*, h^*) = 1 \wedge$
    $\mathsf{Ver}(\mathsf{pk}^*, \mathsf{ptd}, m'^*, r'^*, h^*) = 1 \wedge$
    $(\mathsf{pk}^*, m'^*) \notin \mathcal{Q} \wedge m^* \neq m'^*$
  return 0

Fig. 7. Private collision-resistance

Definition 11 (Secure CHDLTT). *We call a* CHDLTT *secure, if it is correct, indistinguishable, publicly collision-resistant and privately collision-resistant.*

As for CHs, it depends on the concrete use-case, if uniqueness is required.

4 Constructions

We first show how to bootstrap a CHDLTT scheme in a black-box fashion from any given existing secure chameleon-hash CH, inspired by the ideas given by Camenisch et al. [22] who also proposed a suitable chameleon-hash CH based on the ideas by Brzuska et al. [17]. We then present a direct construction in the hidden order group setting based on the one-more RSA-Assumption.

Black-Box Construction. We now present a black-box construction from any existing chameleon-hash CH. Namely, we show how one can achieve our goals by combining two instances of a secure chameleon-hash CH. However, instead of hashing the messages alone, one also requires to hash the public keys $\mathsf{pk}_{\mathsf{chret}}$ and ptd in question to achieve our strengthened definitions. This is described in detail in Construction 1.

Theorem 1. *If* CH *is secure (and unique), then Construction 1 is a secure (and unique)* CHDLTT.

We sketch the proof below. The detailed proof of Theorem 1 is given in the full version of this paper.

Proof (Sketch). Indistinguishability follows from the indistinguishability of the underlying chameleon-hashes. If an adversary can find a collision (either for public and private collision-resistance), than either h_1 or h_2 must be a fresh

---

PGen(1^λ). Return $pp_{chret} \leftarrow$ CH.PGen(1^λ).
KGen(pp_{chret}). Return $(sk_{chret}, pk_{chret}) \leftarrow$ CH.KGen(pp_{chret}).
TDGen(pp_{chret}). Return $(std, ptd) \leftarrow$ CH.KGen(pp_{chret}).

Hash(pk_{chret}, ptd, m). Let $(h_1, r_1) \leftarrow$ CH.Hash($pk_{chret}, (pk_{chret}, ptd, m)$) and $(h_2, r_2) \leftarrow$ CH.Hash($ptd, (pk_{chret}, ptd, m)$). Return $((h_1, h_2), (r_1, r_2))$.
Ver(pk_{chret}, ptd, m, r, h). Let $b_1 \leftarrow$ CH.Ver($pk_{chret}, (pk_{chret}, ptd, m), r_1, h_1$) and $b_2 \leftarrow$ CH.Ver($ptd, (pk_{chret}, ptd, m), r_2, h_2$). If $b_1 = 0 \lor b_2 = 0$, return 0. Return 1.
Adap($sk_{chret}, m, m', r, h, std$). If $0 =$ Ver(pk_{ch}, m, r, h), return $\perp$. Compute $r_1' \leftarrow$ CH.Adap($sk_{chret}, (pk_{chret}, ptd, m), (pk_{chret}, ptd, m'), r_1, h_1$), and $r_2' \leftarrow$ CH.Adap($std, (pk_{chret}, ptd, m), (pk_{chret}, ptd, m'), r_2, h_2$). Return (r_1', r_2').

Construction 1: Black-box construction of CHDLTT

collision, which can easily be extracted. The need to also hash the public keys comes from the fact that the adversary is, in our model, allowed to choose the trapdoor. For uniqueness, the adversary must find two randomness values for the same hash and message. Thus, the randomness for either h_1 or h_2 must be non-unique.

It remains to show if we can also directly construct a CHDLTT, which we answer to the affirmative subsequently.

A Direct Construction. We now present a direct construction, based on the one-more RSA-Assumption. It is inspired by ideas due to Brzuska et al. [17], Pöhls et al. [52] and Camenisch et al. [22], enriched with the trick to also hash the public keys, as introduced in our first construction.

In our construction (illustrated in Construction 2), the public trapdoor ptd is an additional RSA-modulus n'. Thus, only if the factorization of $n' = p'q'$, contained in std, and $n = pq$, which is the secret key sk_{ch}, is known, a collision can be produced. We assume that the bit-length of n and n' is the same, which is implicitly given by the security parameter λ. Furthermore, we assume that an algorithm aborts if a modulus is too large for the given security parameter. We note that the condition on the size of e also implies $\gcd(\varphi(nn'), e) = 1$, which makes the construction a bit more efficient than the solution by Camenisch et al. [22] which require $e > n^3$. Let $\mathcal{H}_n : \{0, 1\}^* \to \mathbb{Z}_n^*$, where $n \in \mathbb{N}$, denote a random oracle.

Theorem 2. *If the one-more RSA-Assumption holds, then Construction 2 is a secure CHDLTT in the random-oracle model.*

We sketch the proof below; the full proof is given in the full version of this paper.

Proof (Sketch). Indistinguishability follows from the fact that a random oracle behaves as a function, while RSA defines a permutation with the restrictions given and the values are distributed uniformly in $\mathbb{Z}_{nn'}^*$. If an adversary can find a collision (either for public or private collision-resistance), than a reduction can extract an eth root of one of the moduli, while uniqueness follows from the same fact used for indistinguishability.

$\mathsf{PGen}(1^\lambda)$. Call RSA with the restriction that e is larger than any possible n w.r.t λ and e prime. Return e.

$\mathsf{KGen}(\mathsf{pp}_{\mathsf{chret}})$. Generate two primes p and q using $\mathsf{RSA}(1^\lambda)$. Set $\mathsf{sk}_{\mathsf{ch}} \leftarrow (p,q)$. Let $n \leftarrow pq$. Set $\mathsf{pk}_{\mathsf{ch}} \leftarrow n$. Return $(\mathsf{sk}_{\mathsf{chret}}, \mathsf{pk}_{\mathsf{chret}})$.

$\mathsf{TDGen}(\mathsf{pp}_{\mathsf{chret}})$. Generate two primes p' and q' using $\mathsf{RSA}(1^\lambda)$. Set $\mathsf{std} \leftarrow (p',q')$, $n' \leftarrow p'q'$, and $\mathsf{ptd} \leftarrow n'$. If $\gcd(n,n') \neq 1$, start over. Return $(\mathsf{std}, \mathsf{ptd})$.

$\mathsf{Hash}(\mathsf{pk}_{\mathsf{chret}}, \mathsf{ptd}, m)$. Draw $r \leftarrow \mathbb{Z}^*_{nn'}$. Let $g \leftarrow \mathcal{H}_{nn'}(m,n,n')$ and $h \leftarrow gr^e \bmod nn'$. Return (h,r).

$\mathsf{Ver}(\mathsf{pk}_{\mathsf{chret}}, \mathsf{ptd}, m, r, h)$. Return $\bot$, if $r \notin \mathbb{Z}^*_{nn'}$. Let $g \leftarrow \mathcal{H}_{nn'}(m,n,n')$ and $h' \leftarrow gr^e \bmod nn'$. Return 1, if $h = h'$. Return 0.

$\mathsf{Adap}(\mathsf{sk}_{\mathsf{chret}}, m, m', r, h, \mathsf{std})$. Check that $n' = p'q'$, where p' and q' are taken from std. If this is not the case, return $\bot$. If $\mathsf{Ver}(\mathsf{pk}_{\mathsf{ch}}, m, r, h) = 0$, return $\bot$. Let d s.t. $de \equiv 1 \bmod \varphi(nn')$, $g \leftarrow \mathcal{H}_{nn'}(m,n,n')$, $h \leftarrow gr^e \bmod nn'$, $g' \leftarrow \mathcal{H}_{nn'}(m',n,n')$ and $r' \leftarrow (h(g'^{-1}))^d \bmod nn'$. Return r'.

Construction 2: CHDLTT from the one-more RSA-Assumption

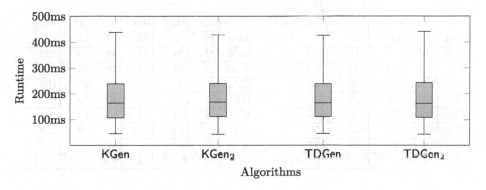

Fig. 8. Key generation algorithm runtime in ms

5   Evaluation

To demonstrate the practicality of our schemes, we have implemented them in Java. We implemented both CHDLTT construction, whereas for the first we use the standard RSA-based chameleon-hash as the underlying primitive. All RSA-moduli have a fixed bit-length of $2,048$ Bit (with balanced primes). Likewise, e has $2,050$ Bit. The random oracles were implemented using SHA-512 in standard counter-mode [11,23,37].

The measurements were performed on a Lenovo W530 with an Intel i7-3470QM@2.70 GHz, and 16 GiB of RAM. No performance optimization such as CRT were implemented and the computation is performed by a single thread. The reason for this choice is to obtain a lower bound of the runtime and any additional optimization will only speed up the calculation. The overall results are depicted in Figs. 8, 9, Tables 1 and 2. In the figure and tables the algorithms of Construction 1 have no subscript, while the algorithms of Construction 2 are

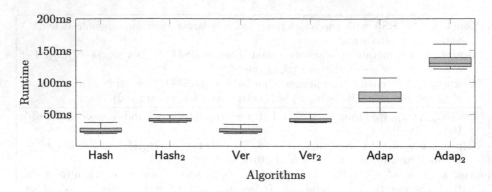

Fig. 9. Other algorithms' runtime in ms

Table 1. Percentiles for key generation in ms

	KGen	KGen₂	TDGen	TDGen₂
Min.	45	43	45	43
25%	107	112	111	109
Med.	164	168	164	163
75%	239	240	238	243
90%	331	319	320	329
95%	383	374	368	390
Max.	525	505	533	553
Avg.	186	186	184	187
SD	99.34	96.00	95.50	101.30

Table 2. Percentiles for the other algorithms in ms

	Hash	Hash₂	Ver	Ver₂	Adap	Adap₂
Min.	20	37	20	37	53	121
25%	22	39	22	38	70	125
Med.	23	40	23	39	75	130
75%	28	43	27	43	85	139
90%	35	49	33	49	106	154
95%	45	54	43	54	138	164
Max.	137	107	153	91	399	258
Avg.	27	42	27	42	85	135
SD	12.75	6.73	12.36	6.21	35.32	14.93

sub-scripted with "2". $1,000$ runs were taken. Parameter generation is omitted, as this is a one-time setup, i.e., drawing a random prime.

As demonstrated by the runtime measurements, both primitives can be considered practical. The lion's share is finding suitable primes during key generation. All exponentiations within the algorithms only have a negligible overhead, as seen by the runtime. However, as key generation only needs to be done once, this seems to be acceptable, even with realistic security parameters and rather expensive RSA-based primitives.

6   Application: Three-Party Sanitizable Signatures 3SSS

We now present applications of our CHDLTTs. The first are *three-party* sanitizable signatures. Sanitizable signatures (SSS) allow a signer to determine which blocks $m[i]$ of a message $m = (m[1], m[2], \ldots, m[i], \ldots, m[\ell])$ are admissible. Any such admissible block can be changed to an arbitrary bitstring $m[i]' \in \{0,1\}^*$, where $i \in \{1, 2, \ldots, \ell\}$, by a semi-trusted party named the sanitizer, if it had received an additional secret. In a nutshell, sanitization of a message m results in an altered message $m' = (m[1]', m[2]', \ldots, m[i]', \ldots, m[\ell]')$, where $m[i] = m[i]'$

for every non-admissible block, and also a signature σ', which verifies for m' under the original public key. Sanitizable signatures enforce that either a block cannot be altered at all, or only by a semi-trusted third party. In a 3SSS, the signer additionally appoints a third party which needs to provide its secret key before the sanitizer can alter certain blocks.

Related Work and State-of-the-Art for SSS. Sanitizable signatures have been introduced by Ateniese et al. [2]. Most of the current security properties were formalized by Brzuska et al. [17]. Later on, extensions such as (strong) unlinkability [19,21,36] and non-interactive public accountability [20,21] were introduced. Additional extensions such as limiting the sanitizer to certain values [24,32,45,54], multi-sanitizer and multi-signer environments [18,21,25], as well as sanitization of signed encrypted data [30,34] have been considered. They have also been used as a tool to make other primitives accountable [53] and to construct other primitives, such as redactable signatures [12,49]. We stress that all previous work, in contrast to our three-party setting (where two parties are required for sanitizing *at the same time*), only the two-party setting is considered and we refer for more detailed overviews to [13,31].

The Framework for Three-Party Sanitizable Signature Schemes. Subsequently, we introduce the used framework for 3SSSs. The definitions are inspired by the ones given by Camenisch et al. [22], which are itself based on existing work [2,17,20,21,40,47]. However, due to our goals, we need to re-define the framework. Like Camenisch et al , we do not consider "non-interactive public accountability" [20,21,44], which allows some external party to decide which party is accountable, as transparency is mutually exclusive to this property. But if needed this is very easy to achieve, e.g., by signing the signature again [20].

For brevity, we now set some additional notation. This notation is similar to existing definitions, to make reading more comfortable [17,22]. For a message $m = (m[1], m[2], \ldots, m[\ell])$, we call $m[i]$ a block, while $\ell \in \mathbb{N}$ denotes the number of blocks in a message m. The variable ADM is a tuple containing the set of indices of the admissible blocks and the number ℓ of blocks in a message m. We write $\mathrm{ADM}(m) = 1$, if ADM is valid w.r.t. m, i.e., ADM contains the correct ℓ and all indices are in m. For example, let $\mathrm{ADM} = (\{1, 2, 4\}, 4)$. Then, m must contain four blocks, while all but the third will be admissible. If we write $m_i \in \mathrm{ADM}$, we mean that m_i is admissible. MOD is a set containing pairs $(i, m[i]')$ for those blocks that shall be modified, meaning that $m[i]$ is replaced with $m[i]'$. We write $\mathrm{MOD}(\mathrm{ADM}) = 1$, if MOD is valid w.r.t. ADM, meaning that the indices to be modified are contained in ADM. To allow a compact presentation of our construction, we write $[X]_{n,m}$, with $n \leq m$, for the vector $(X_n, X_{n+1}, X_{n+2}, \ldots, X_{m-1}, X_m)$.

Definition 12 (Three-Party Sanitizable Signature). *A three-party sanitizable signature scheme* 3SSS *consists of nine ppt algorithms* (PGen, KGen$_{\mathsf{sig}}$, KGen$_{\mathsf{san}}$, TGen, Sign, Sanit, Verify, Proof, Judge) *such that:*

PGen. *On input security parameter* λ, *it generates the public parameters:* $\mathsf{pp_{3SSS}} \leftarrow \mathsf{PGen}(1^\lambda)$. *We assume that* $\mathsf{pp_{3SSS}}$ *is implicitly input to all other algorithms.*

KGen$_{\mathsf{sig}}$. *It takes the public parameters* $\mathsf{pp_{3SSS}}$ *and returns the signer's private key and the corresponding public key:* $(\mathsf{sk_{sig}}, \mathsf{pk_{sig}}) \leftarrow \mathsf{KGen_{sig}}(\mathsf{pp_{3SSS}})$.

KGen$_{\mathsf{san}}$. *It takes the public parameters* $\mathsf{pp_{3SSS}}$ *and returns the sanitizer's private key and the corresponding public key:* $(\mathsf{sk_{san}}, \mathsf{pk_{san}}) \leftarrow \mathsf{KGen_{san}}(\mathsf{pp_{3SSS}})$.

TGen. *It takes the public parameters* $\mathsf{pp_{3SSS}}$, *and returns the private and public trapdoor pair:* $(\mathsf{tdpriv}, \mathsf{tdpub}) \leftarrow \mathsf{TGen}(\mathsf{pp_{3SSS}})$.

Sign. *It takes as input a message* m, $\mathsf{sk_{sig}}$, $\mathsf{pk_{san}}$, tdpub, *as well as a description* ADM *of the admissible blocks. If* $\mathrm{ADM}(m) = 0$, *it returns* $\perp$. *It outputs a signature:* $\sigma \leftarrow \mathsf{Sign}(m, \mathsf{sk_{sig}}, \mathsf{pk_{san}}, \mathsf{tdpub}, \mathrm{ADM})$.

Sanit. *It takes a message* m, *modification instruction* MOD, *a signature* σ, $\mathsf{pk_{sig}}$, $\mathsf{sk_{san}}$ *and* tdpriv. *It outputs* m' *together with* σ': $(m', \sigma') \leftarrow \mathsf{Sanit}(m, \mathrm{MOD}, \sigma, \mathsf{pk_{sig}}, \mathsf{sk_{san}}, \mathsf{tdpriv})$ *where* $m' \leftarrow \mathrm{MOD}(m)$ *is message* m *modified according to the modification instruction* MOD. *If* $\mathrm{ADM}(m') = 0$, *this algorithm returns* $\perp$.

Verify. *It takes as input the signature* σ *for a message* m *w.r.t. the public keys* $\mathsf{pk_{sig}}$, $\mathsf{pk_{san}}$, *and* tdpub. *It outputs a decision* $d \in \{1, 0\}$: $d \leftarrow \mathsf{Verify}(m, \sigma, \mathsf{pk_{sig}}, \mathsf{pk_{san}}, \mathsf{tdpub})$. *This algorithm is deterministic.*

Proof. *It takes as input* $\mathsf{sk_{sig}}$, *a message* m, *a signature* σ, *a set of polynomially many additional message/signature pairs* $\{(m_i, \sigma_i)\}$, $\mathsf{pk_{san}}$ *and* tdpub. *It outputs a string* $\pi \in \{0, 1\}^*$ *which can be used by the* Judge *to decide which party is accountable given a message/signature pair* (m, σ): $\pi \leftarrow \mathsf{Proof}(\mathsf{sk_{sig}}, m, \sigma, \{(m_i, \sigma_i) \mid i \in \mathbb{N}\}, \mathsf{pk_{san}}, \mathsf{tdpub})$.

Judge. *It takes as input a message* m, *a signature* σ, $\mathsf{pk_{sig}}$, $\mathsf{pk_{san}}$, tdpub, *as well as a proof* π. *Note, this means that once a proof* π *is generated, the accountable party can be derived by anyone for that message/signature pair* (m, σ). *It outputs a decision* $d \in \{\mathsf{Sig}, \mathsf{San}, \perp\}$, *indicating whether the message/signature pair has been created by the signer, or the sanitizer:* $d \leftarrow \mathsf{Judge}(m, \sigma, \mathsf{pk_{sig}}, \mathsf{pk_{san}}, \mathsf{tdpub}, \pi)$.

Defining correctness of 3SSS is straightforward and therefore omitted.

Security of 3SSSs. Next, we introduce the security model. It is based on the work done for sanitizable signatures by Brzuska et al. [17]. However, due to our goals, we need to modify it significantly. In the security framework (for the unforgeability definitions), the public trapdoor tdpub is always generated by the adversary, as the holder of tdpriv should never be able to generate forgeries. This simplifies our framework significantly, as an adversary generating tdpub has more power than an adversary only receiving an honestly generated tdpub.

Due to space limitations, we can only sketch the security requirements here. The formal game-based definitions are given in the full version of this paper.

Unforgeability. This definition requires that an adversary $\mathcal{A}$ not having any secret keys is not able to produce a valid signature σ^* on a *new* message m^*. As $\mathcal{A}$ has full oracle access *new* means that $\mathcal{A}$ has not seen the message genuinely being signed before.

Immutability. A sanitizer must only be able to sanitize the admissible blocks defined by ADM. This also prohibits deleting or appending blocks from a given message m. The adversary is given full oracle access, while it is also allowed to generate the sanitizer key pair itself.

Immutability2. Even if the signer, and the sanitizer, work together, they must be not able to generate a valid sanitization, if std is not known. However, as the signer can clearly sign whatever it wants (including any ADM), we define this immutability property such that the adversary cannot generate a proof π^* that it sanitized the message, as it should not be able to do so. The adversary also receives full adaptive oracle access, also for other pks, modeling the case where for different pks sanitizations where generated.

Privacy. The notion of privacy is related to the indistinguishability of ciphertexts. The adversary is allowed to input two messages with the same ADM which are sanitized to the exact same message. The adversary then has to decide which of the input messages was used to generate the sanitized one. The adversary receives full adaptive oracle access.

Transparency. Transparency guarantees that the accountable party of a message m remains anonymous. This is important if discrimination may follow from learning that sanitizations have taken place [2,17]. In a nutshell, the adversary to transparency has to decide whether it sees a freshly computed signature, or a sanitized one. The adversary has full (but proof-restricted) oracle access.

Signer-Accountability. For signer-accountability, a signer must not be able to blame a sanitizer if the sanitizer is actually not responsible for a given message. Hence, the adversary $\mathcal{A}$ has to generate a proof π^* which makes Judge to decide that the sanitizer is accountable, if it is not for a message m^* output by $\mathcal{A}$. Here, the adversary gains access to all oracles related to sanitizing.

Sanitizer-Accountability. Sanitizer-accountability requires that the sanitizer cannot blame the signer for a message/signature pair not created by the signer. In particular, the adversary has to make Proof generate a proof π which makes Judge decide that for a given (m^*, σ^*) generated by $\mathcal{A}$ the signer is accountable, while it is not. Thus, the adversary $\mathcal{A}$ gains access to all signer-related oracles, while ptd can always be derived from std by assumption.

Unlinkability. In line with Camenisch et al. [22], we do not consider unlinkability [19,21,36,48] in our construction, as it seems to be very hard to achieve with the underlying construction paradigm.

Definition 13 (Secure 3SSS). *An 3SSS secure, if it is correct, private, transparent, unforgeable, immutable, immutable 2, sanitizer-accountable and signer-accountable.*

Additional Building Blocks. For the construction, we require PRGs, PRFs and digital signatures (Σs). The formal definitions are given in the full version of this paper.

Construction. Subsequently, we present the construction of 3SSS. The underlying construction paradigm is an augmented version of the one by Brzuska et al. [17]. In a nutshell, each admissible block is hashed using a CHDLTT. Then, the hashes (along with the non-admissible blocks) are signed to achieve accountability. Note, however, that the used CHDLTT is not required to be unique.

$\mathsf{PGen}(1^\lambda)$: Let $\mathsf{pp}_{\mathsf{chret}} \leftarrow \mathsf{PGen}(1^\lambda)$. Return $\mathsf{pp}_{\mathsf{3SSS}} = \mathsf{pp}_{\mathsf{chret}}$.

$\mathsf{KGen}_{\mathsf{sig}}(\mathsf{pp}_{\mathsf{3SSS}})$: Let $(\mathsf{sk}_\Sigma, \mathsf{pk}_\Sigma) \leftarrow \mathsf{KGen}_\Sigma(1^\lambda)$. Pick a key for a PRF, i.e., $\kappa \leftarrow \mathsf{KGen}_{\mathsf{prf}}(1^\lambda)$. Return $((\kappa, \mathsf{sk}_\Sigma), \mathsf{pk}_\Sigma)$.

$\mathsf{KGen}_{\mathsf{san}}(\mathsf{pp}_{\mathsf{3SSS}})$: Let $(\mathsf{sk}_{\mathsf{chret}}, \mathsf{pk}_{\mathsf{chret}}) \leftarrow \mathsf{KGen}(\mathsf{pp}_{\mathsf{chret}})$. Return $(\mathsf{sk}_{\mathsf{chret}}, \mathsf{pk}_{\mathsf{chret}})$.

$\mathsf{TGen}(\mathsf{pp}_{\mathsf{3SSS}})$: Let $(\mathsf{std}, \mathsf{ptd}) \leftarrow \mathsf{TDGen}(\mathsf{pp}_{\mathsf{chret}})$. Return $(\mathsf{std}, \mathsf{ptd})$.

$\mathsf{Sign}(m, \mathsf{sk}_{\mathsf{sig}}, \mathsf{pk}_{\mathsf{san}}, \mathsf{tdpub}, \mathsf{ADM})$: If $\mathsf{ADM}(m) = 0$, return $\bot$. Draw $x \leftarrow \{0,1\}^\lambda$. Let $x' \leftarrow \mathsf{Eval}_{\mathsf{prf}}(\kappa, x)$. Let $\tau \leftarrow \mathsf{Eval}_{\mathsf{prg}}(x')$. For each block $i \in \mathsf{ADM}$, do $(h_i, r_i) \leftarrow \mathsf{Hash}(\mathsf{pk}_{\mathsf{chret}}, \mathsf{tdpub}, (i, m[i], \mathsf{pk}_{\mathsf{sig}}, \mathsf{tdpub}))$. For each block $i \notin \mathsf{ADM}$, let $h_i \leftarrow m[i]$, and $r \leftarrow \emptyset$. Let $(h_0, r_0) \leftarrow \mathsf{Hash}(\mathsf{pk}_{\mathsf{chret}}, (0, m, x, \ell, \tau, [h]_{1,\ell}, \mathsf{pk}_{\mathsf{sig}}, \mathsf{tdpub}))$. Sign $\sigma \leftarrow \mathsf{Sign}_\Sigma(\mathsf{sk}_\Sigma, ([h]_{0,\ell}, \ell, \mathsf{pk}_{\mathsf{sig}}, \mathsf{pk}_{\mathsf{san}}, \mathsf{ADM}, x, \mathsf{tdpub}))$. Return $(\sigma', ([h]_{0,\ell}, \mathsf{ADM}, \ell, x, \tau, [r]_{0,\ell}))$.

$\mathsf{Verify}(m, \sigma, \mathsf{pk}_{\mathsf{sig}}, \mathsf{pk}_{\mathsf{san}}, \mathsf{tdpub})$: For each block $i \in \mathsf{ADM}$, let $b_i \leftarrow \mathsf{Ver}(\mathsf{pk}_{\mathsf{chret}}, \mathsf{tdpub}, (i, m[i], \mathsf{pk}_{\mathsf{sig}}, \mathsf{tdpub}), r_i, h_i)$. Let $b_0 \leftarrow \mathsf{Ver}(\mathsf{pk}_{\mathsf{chret}}, \mathsf{tdpub}, (0, m, x, \ell, \tau, [h]_{1,\ell}, \mathsf{pk}_{\mathsf{sig}}, \mathsf{tdpub}), r_i, h_i)$. If any $b_i = 0$, return 0. Return $\mathsf{Verify}_\Sigma(\mathsf{pk}_\Sigma, ([h]_{0,\ell}, , \ell, \mathsf{pk}_{\mathsf{sig}}, \mathsf{pk}_{\mathsf{san}}, \mathsf{ADM}, x, \mathsf{tdpub}), \sigma')$.

$\mathsf{Sanit}(m, \mathsf{MOD}, \sigma, \mathsf{pk}_{\mathsf{sig}}, \mathsf{sk}_{\mathsf{san}}, \mathsf{tdpriv})$: Run $b \leftarrow \mathsf{Verify}(m, \sigma, \mathsf{pk}_{\mathsf{sig}}, \mathsf{pk}_{\mathsf{san}}, \mathsf{tdpub})$. If $b = 0$, return $\bot$. If $\mathsf{MOD}(\mathsf{ADM}) = 0$, return $\bot$. For each $(i, m[i]) \in \mathsf{MOD}$, let $r'_i \leftarrow \mathsf{Adap}(\mathsf{sk}_{\mathsf{chret}}, (i, m[i], \mathsf{pk}_{\mathsf{sig}}, \mathsf{tdpub}), (i, m'[i], \mathsf{pk}_{\mathsf{sig}}, \mathsf{tdpub}), r_i, h_i, \mathsf{std})$. Otherwise, let $r'_i \leftarrow r_i$. Draw $\tau' \leftarrow \{0,1\}^{2\lambda}$. Let $r'_0 \leftarrow \mathsf{Adap}(\mathsf{sk}_{\mathsf{chret}}, (0, m, x, \ell, \tau, [h]_{1,\ell}, \mathsf{pk}_{\mathsf{sig}}, \mathsf{tdpub}), (0, m', x, \ell, \tau', [h]_{1,\ell}, \mathsf{pk}_{\mathsf{sig}}, \mathsf{std}), r_0, h_0, \mathsf{std})$. Return $(\sigma', ([h]_{0,\ell}, \mathsf{ADM}, \ell, x, \tau', [r']_{0,\ell}))$.

$\mathsf{Proof}(\mathsf{sk}_{\mathsf{sig}}, m, \sigma, \{(m_i, \sigma_i) \mid i \in \mathbb{N}\}, \mathsf{pk}_{\mathsf{san}}, \mathsf{tdpub})$: Return $\bot$, if $0 = \mathsf{Verify}(m, \sigma, \mathsf{pk}_{\mathsf{sig}}, \mathsf{pk}_{\mathsf{san}}, \mathsf{tdpub})$. Verify each signature in the list, i.e., run $d_i \leftarrow \mathsf{Verify}(m_i, \sigma_i, \mathsf{pk}_{\mathsf{sig}}, \mathsf{pk}_{\mathsf{san}}, \mathsf{tdpub})$. If for any $d_i = 0$, return $\bot$. Go through the list of (m_i, σ_i), and find a (non-trivial) colliding tuple of the chameleon-hash with (m, σ), i.e., $h_0 = h'_0$, where also $1 = \mathsf{Ver}(\mathsf{pk}_{\mathsf{san}}, (0, m, x, \ell, \tau, [h]_{1,\ell}, \mathsf{pk}_{\mathsf{sig}}, \mathsf{tdpub}), r_0, h_0)$, and $1 = \mathsf{Ver}(\mathsf{pk}_{\mathsf{san}}, (0, m', x, \ell, \tau', [h]_{1,\ell}, \mathsf{pk}_{\mathsf{sig}}, \mathsf{tdpub}), r'_0, h'_0)$ for some different tag τ' or message m'. Let this signature/message pair be $(\sigma', m') \in \{(m_i, \sigma_i) \mid i \in \mathbb{N}\}$. Return $\pi = ((\sigma', m'), \mathsf{PRF}(\kappa, x))$, where x is contained in (σ, m).

$\mathsf{Judge}(m, \sigma, \mathsf{pk}_{\mathsf{sig}}, \mathsf{pk}_{\mathsf{san}}, \pi, \mathsf{tdpub})$: Check if π is of the form $((\sigma', m'), v)$ with $v \in \{0,1\}^\lambda$. If not, return Sig. Return $\bot$, if $0 = \mathsf{Verify}(m', \sigma', \mathsf{pk}_{\mathsf{sig}}, \mathsf{pk}_{\mathsf{san}}, \mathsf{tdpub})$, or $0 = \mathsf{Verify}(m, \sigma, \mathsf{pk}_{\mathsf{sig}}, \mathsf{pk}_{\mathsf{san}}, \mathsf{tdpub})$. Let $\tau'' \leftarrow \mathsf{PRG.Eval}_{\mathsf{prg}}(v)$. If $\tau' \neq \tau''$, return Sig, where τ' is taken from (σ', m'). If we have $h_0 = h'_0$, with a non-trivial colliding tuple $1 = \mathsf{Ver}(\mathsf{pk}_{\mathsf{san}}, (0, m, x, \ell, \tau, [h]_{0,\ell}, \mathsf{pk}_{\mathsf{sig}}, \mathsf{tdpub}), r_0, h_0) = \mathsf{Ver}(\mathsf{pk}_{\mathsf{san}}, (0, m', x, \ell, \tau', [h]_{0,\ell}, \mathsf{pk}_{\mathsf{sig}}, \mathsf{tdpub}), r'_0, h'_0)$, return San. Return Sig.

Construction 3: Secure 3SSS

Theorem 3. *If Σ and CHDLTT are secure, while PRF and PRG are both pseudorandom, then Construction 3 is secure.*

We sketch the proof below. The detailed proof of Theorem 3 is given in the full version of this paper.

Proof (Sketch). Unforgeability follows from the unforgeability of the underlying signature scheme and the public collision-resistance of the CHDLTT, as the adversary either needs to find a new signature or a collision in the hash. Immutability also follows from the unforgeability of the signature scheme, as each fixed block is signed. Immutability2, however, follows from private collision-resistance, as an adversary must find a collision for an honestly generated second trapdoor. Privacy and Transparency follow from the indistinguishability of the CHDLTT and pseudo-randomness of the PRF and PRG. Signer-accountability follows from the collision-resistance of the CHDLTT, as the proof must contain a collision which has never been published. Sanitizer-Accountability, follows from the unforgeability of the signature and the pseudo-randomness of PRF (and PRG).

Extensions. Subsequently, we present extensions to our basic scheme. We do not provide full-fledged formal security frameworks, as they are straightforward extensions to the one provided. However, these alterations increase the flexibility to delegate actions and may lead to new application scenarios for this primitive, and thus deserve to be mentioned.

Always Sanitizable Blocks. In the construction, the sanitizer can only sanitize, if it knows tdpriv. It may, however, be desirable that the sanitizer can always sanitize certain blocks, while others need tdpriv. This can easily be achieved by using a standard chameleon-hash instead of CHDLTT for those blocks. A formalization is straightforward and thus omitted.

Mixing Admissible Blocks. It may also be desirable that some blocks become sanitizable if tdpriv is released, and others if other tdprivs are released, i.e., there is more than one tdpriv for different blocks. Clearly, this can easily be achieved by using new tdpubs for each new block, perhaps even the same tdpubs for several blocks. Again, a formalization is straightforward and thus omitted. We did not implement and measure this scheme, but the additional overhead is essentially one more single signature and some PRG and PRF evaluations.

7 Additional Applications

This section is devoted to sketch some additional application scenarios of our new primitive. These use-cases include the already mentioned notion of group-level selectively revocable signatures and break-glass signatures.

Group-Level Selectively Revocable Signatures. Revoking (single) signatures is a long-standing open problem [8,15,42]. Using CHDLTT, however, we get one step closer to a satisfying solution. In particular, one can extend chameleon signatures [46] as follows: Instead of signing the hashed message m using the public key (of a standard chameleon-hash) of the recipient, one also uses ptd as an identifier for some group, e.g., an employee's name, or for a specific task. Then, to revoke signatures bound to this group, one simply releases std, i.e., makes it public, just as in a standard PKI where revoked public keys are made public. The corresponding ptd can be generated in advance by some entity, e.g., a server. All revoked signatures must then be considered invalid by a verifier, as all recipients could "fake" (i.e., adapt) arbitrary messages after revocation for that specific ptd. This is, essentially, the same argumentation as for standard chameleon signatures. Namely, as now any message can be "signed" by anyone[4] including the recipients, the signature loses all cryptographic value as an authentication of origin.

Break-The-Glass Emergency Signatures. Assume that some employees are not allowed to sign certain messages under "normal" conditions. Further assume the messages in question are an order form, or an approval, which requires explicit interaction with the department's head. If, however, the department's head is not reachable, e.g., due to sickness, but the signature must be generated, a designated employee may get access to some additional secret which allows to generate exactly this signature. If, however, this secret is revealed, it must be traceable that the secret was released, which can be enforced using standard policies. Our new primitive allows to technically map this workflow as follows: The employee able to sign a message in emergency generates a key pair for a standard signature scheme, but hashes an empty message to the corresponding ptd. The corresponding std can, e.g., be generated at some server within the same company. The employee can then gain access to std, and can thus sign any message it wants using Adap. This resembles a more sophisticated version of blank signatures [41]. This also resembles the emergency modes of access control, known as 'Break-Glass' or 'Break-The-Glass' (BTG), but for signature generation, e.g., those found in hospital information systems [35], and the server can log the distributed std to generate an audit trail of this emergency event.

References

1. Alsouri, S., Dagdelen, Ö., Katzenbeisser, S.: Group-based attestation: enhancing privacy and management in remote attestation. In: Acquisti, A., Smith, S.W., Sadeghi, A.-R. (eds.) Trust 2010. LNCS, vol. 6101, pp. 63–77. Springer, Heidelberg (2010). https://doi.org/10.1007/978-3-642-13869-0_5
2. Ateniese, G., Chou, D.H., de Medeiros, B., Tsudik, G.: Sanitizable signatures. In: di Vimercati, S.C., Syverson, P., Gollmann, D. (eds.) ESORICS 2005. LNCS, vol. 3679, pp. 159–177. Springer, Heidelberg (2005). https://doi.org/10.1007/11555827_10
3. Ateniese, G., Magri, B., Venturi, D., Andrade, E.R.: Redactable blockchain - or - rewriting history in bitcoin and friends. In: EuroS&P, pp. 111–126 (2017)
4. Ateniese, G., de Medeiros, B.: Identity-based Chameleon hash and applications. In: Juels, A. (ed.) FC 2004. LNCS, vol. 3110, pp. 164–180. Springer, Heidelberg (2004). https://doi.org/10.1007/978-3-540-27809-2_19
5. Ateniese, G., de Medeiros, B.: On the key exposure problem in Chameleon hashes. In: Blundo, C., Cimato, S. (eds.) SCN 2004. LNCS, vol. 3352, pp. 165–179. Springer, Heidelberg (2005). https://doi.org/10.1007/978-3-540-30598-9_12

---

[4] Note, there might be corner cases for authorizing everyone as described by Pöhls [51].

6. Bao, F., Deng, R.H., Ding, X., Lai, J., Zhao, Y.: Hierarchical identity-based Chameleon hash and its applications. In: Lopez, J., Tsudik, G. (eds.) ACNS 2011. LNCS, vol. 6715, pp. 201–219. Springer, Heidelberg (2011). https://doi.org/10.1007/978-3-642-21554-4_12

7. Beck, M.T., Camenisch, J., Derler, D., Krenn, S., Pöhls, H.C., Samelin, K., Slamanig, D.: Practical strongly invisible and strongly accountable sanitizable signatures. In: Pieprzyk, J., Suriadi, S. (eds.) ACISP 2017. LNCS, vol. 10342, pp. 437–452. Springer, Cham (2017). https://doi.org/10.1007/978-3-319-60055-0_23

8. Beck, M.T., Krenn, S., Preiss, F.-S., Samelin, K.: Practical signing-right revocation. In: Franz, M., Papadimitratos, P. (eds.) Trust 2016. LNCS, vol. 9824, pp. 21–39. Springer, Cham (2016). https://doi.org/10.1007/978-3-319-45572-3_2

9. Bellare, M., Namprempre, C., Pointcheval, D., Semanko, M.: The one-more-RSA-inversion problems and the security of Chaum's blind signature scheme. J. Cryptol. **16**(3), 185–215 (2003)

10. Bellare, M., Ristov, T.: A characterization of Chameleon hash functions and new, efficient designs. J. Cryptol. **27**(4), 799–823 (2014)

11. Bellare, M., Rogaway, P.: Random oracles are practical: a paradigm for designing efficient protocols. In: CCS, pp. 62–73, New York, NY, USA (1993)

12. Bilzhause, A., Huber, M., Pöhls, H.C., Samelin, K.: Cryptographically enforced four-eyes principle. In: ARES, pp. 760–767 (2016)

13. Bilzhause, A., Pöhls, H.C., Samelin, K.: Position paper: The past, present, and future of sanitizable and redactable signatures. In: ARES, pp. 87:1–87:9 (2017)

14. Blazy, O., Kakvi, S.A., Kiltz, E., Pan, J.: Tightly-secure signatures from chameleon hash functions. In: Katz, J. (ed.) PKC 2015. LNCS, vol. 9020, pp. 256–279. Springer, Heidelberg (2015). https://doi.org/10.1007/978-3-662-46447-2_12

15. Boneh, D., Ding, X., Tsudik, G., Wong, C.: A method for fast revocation of public key certificates and security capabilities. In: USENIX (2001)

16. Brassard, G., Chaum, D., Crépeau, C.: Minimum disclosure proofs of knowledge. J. Comput. Syst. Sci. **37**(2), 156–189 (1988)

17. Brzuska, C., Fischlin, M., Freudenreich, T., Lehmann, A., Page, M., Schelbert, J., Schröder, D., Volk, F.: Security of sanitizable signatures revisited. In: Jarecki, S., Tsudik, G. (eds.) PKC 2009. LNCS, vol. 5443, pp. 317–336. Springer, Heidelberg (2009). https://doi.org/10.1007/978-3-642-00468-1_18

18. Brzuska, C., Fischlin, M., Lehmann, A., Schröder, D.: Sanitizable signatures: how to partially delegate control for authenticated data. In: BIOSIG, pp. 117–128 (2009)

19. Brzuska, C., Fischlin, M., Lehmann, A., Schröder, D.: Unlinkability of sanitizable signatures. In: Nguyen, P.Q., Pointcheval, D. (eds.) PKC 2010. LNCS, vol. 6056, pp. 444–461. Springer, Heidelberg (2010). https://doi.org/10.1007/978-3-642-13013-7_26

20. Brzuska, C., Pöhls, H.C., Samelin, K.: Non-interactive public accountability for sanitizable signatures. In: De Capitani di Vimercati, S., Mitchell, C. (eds.) EuroPKI 2012. LNCS, vol. 7868, pp. 178–193. Springer, Heidelberg (2013). https://doi.org/10.1007/978-3-642-40012-4_12

21. Brzuska, C., Pöhls, H.C., Samelin, K.: Efficient and perfectly unlinkable sanitizable signatures without group signatures. In: Katsikas, S., Agudo, I. (eds.) EuroPKI 2013. LNCS, vol. 8341, pp. 12–30. Springer, Heidelberg (2014). https://doi.org/10.1007/978-3-642-53997-8_2

22. Camenisch, J., Derler, D., Krenn, S., Pöhls, H.C., Samelin, K., Slamanig, D.: Chameleon-hashes with ephemeral trapdoors. In: Fehr, S. (ed.) PKC 2017. LNCS, vol. 10175, pp. 152–182. Springer, Heidelberg (2017). https://doi.org/10.1007/978-3-662-54388-7_6

23. Camenisch, J., Lehmann, A., Neven, G., Samelin, K.: Virtual smart cards: how to sign with a password and a server. In: Zikas, V., De Prisco, R. (eds.) SCN 2016. LNCS, vol. 9841, pp. 353–371. Springer, Cham (2016). https://doi.org/10.1007/978-3-319-44618-9_19

24. Canard, S., Jambert, A.: On extended sanitizable signature schemes. In: Pieprzyk, J. (ed.) CT-RSA 2010. LNCS, vol. 5985, pp. 179–194. Springer, Heidelberg (2010). https://doi.org/10.1007/978-3-642-11925-5_13

25. Canard, S., Jambert, A., Lescuyer, R.: Sanitizable signatures with several signers and sanitizers. In: Mitrokotsa, A., Vaudenay, S. (eds.) AFRICACRYPT 2012. LNCS, vol. 7374, pp. 35–52. Springer, Heidelberg (2012). https://doi.org/10.1007/978-3-642-31410-0_3

26. Chen, X., Tian, H., Zhang, F., Ding, Y.: Comments and improvements on key-exposure free chameleon hashing based on factoring. In: Lai, X., Yung, M., Lin, D. (eds.) Inscrypt 2010. LNCS, vol. 6584, pp. 415–426. Springer, Heidelberg (2011). https://doi.org/10.1007/978-3-642-21518-6_29

27. Chen, X., Zhang, F., Kim, K.: Chameleon hashing without key exposure. In: Zhang, K., Zheng, Y. (eds.) ISC 2004. LNCS, vol. 3225, pp. 87–98. Springer, Heidelberg (2004). https://doi.org/10.1007/978-3-540-30144-8_8

28. Chen, X., Zhang, F., Susilo, W., Mu, Y.: Efficient generic on-line/off-line signatures without key exposure. In: Katz, J., Yung, M. (eds.) ACNS 2007. LNCS, vol. 4521, pp. 18–30. Springer, Heidelberg (2007). https://doi.org/10.1007/978-3-540-72738-5_2

29. Chen, X., Zhang, F., Susilo, W., Tian, H., Li, J., Kim, K.: Identity-based Chameleon hash scheme without key exposure. In: Steinfeld, R., Hawkes, P. (eds.) ACISP 2010. LNCS, vol. 6168, pp. 200–215. Springer, Heidelberg (2010). https://doi.org/10.1007/978-3-642-14081-5_13

30. Damgård, I., Haagh, H., Orlandi, C.: Access control encryption: enforcing information flow with cryptography. In: Hirt, M., Smith, A. (eds.) TCC 2016. LNCS, vol. 9986, pp. 547–576. Springer, Heidelberg (2016). https://doi.org/10.1007/978-3-662-53644-5_21

31. Demirel, D., Derler, D., Hanser, C., Pöhls, H.C., Slamanig, D., Traverso, G.: PRISMACLOUD D4.4: overview of functional and malleable signature schemes. Technical report, H2020 Prismacloud (2015). www.prismacloud.eu

32. Derler, D., Slamanig, D.: Rethinking privacy for extended sanitizable signatures and a black-box construction of strongly private schemes. In: Au, M.-H., Miyaji, A. (eds.) ProvSec 2015. LNCS, vol. 9451, pp. 455–474. Springer, Cham (2015). https://doi.org/10.1007/978-3-319-26059-4_25

33. Even, S., Goldreich, O., Micali, S.: On-line/off-line digital signatures. J. Cryptol. 9(1), 35–67 (1996)

34. Fehr, V., Fischlin, M.: Sanitizable signcryption: sanitization over encrypted data (full version). IACR Cryptology ePrint Archive, Report 2015/765 (2015)

35. Ferreira, A., Cruz-Correia, R., Antunes, L., Farinha, P., Oliveira-Palhares, E., Chadwick, D.W., Costa-Pereira, A.: How to break access control in a controlled manner. In: 19th IEEE Symposium on Computer-Based Medical Systems (CBMS 2006), pp. 847–854 (2006)

36. Fleischhacker, N., Krupp, J., Malavolta, G., Schneider, J., Schröder, D., Simkin, M.: Efficient unlinkable sanitizable signatures from signatures with re-randomizable keys. In: Cheng, C.-M., Chung, K.-M., Persiano, G., Yang, B.-Y. (eds.) PKC 2016. LNCS, vol. 9614, pp. 301–330. Springer, Heidelberg (2016). https://doi.org/10.1007/978-3-662-49384-7_12

37. Frädrich, C., Pöhls, H.C., Popp, W., Rakotondravony, N., Samelin, K.: Integrity and authenticity protection with selective disclosure control in the cloud & IoT. In: Lam, K.Y., Chi, C.H., Qing, S. (eds.) ICICS. LNCS, pp. 197–213. Springer, Cham (2016). https://doi.org/10.1007/978-3-319-50011-9_16

38. Gao, W., Li, F., Wang, X.: Chameleon hash without key exposure based on Schnorr signature. Comput. Stand. Interfaces **31**(2), 282–285 (2009)

39. Gao, W., Wang, X., Xie, D.: Chameleon hashes without key exposure based on factoring. J. Comput. Sci. Technol. **22**(1), 109–113 (2007)

40. Gong, J., Qian, H., Zhou, Y.: Fully-secure and practical sanitizable signatures. In: Lai, X., Yung, M., Lin, D. (eds.) Inscrypt 2010. LNCS, vol. 6584, pp. 300–317. Springer, Heidelberg (2011). https://doi.org/10.1007/978-3-642-21518-6_21

41. Hanser, C., Slamanig, D.: Blank digital signatures. In: ASIACCS (2013)

42. Hanzlik, L., Kutyłowski, M., Yung, M.: Hard invalidation of electronic signatures. In: Lopez, J., Wu, Y. (eds.) ISPEC 2015. LNCS, vol. 9065, pp. 421–436. Springer, Cham (2015). https://doi.org/10.1007/978-3-319-17533-1_29

43. Hohenberger, S., Waters, B.: Short and stateless signatures from the RSA assumption. In: Halevi, S. (ed.) CRYPTO 2009. LNCS, vol. 5677, pp. 654–670. Springer, Heidelberg (2009). https://doi.org/10.1007/978-3-642-03356-8_38

44. Höhne, F., Pöhls, H.C., Samelin, K.: Rechtsfolgen editierbarer signaturen. Datenschutz Datensicherheit **36**(7), 485–491 (2012)

45. Klonowski, M., Lauks, A.: Extended sanitizable signatures. In: Rhee, M.S., Lee, B. (eds.) ICISC 2006. LNCS, vol. 4296, pp. 343–355. Springer, Heidelberg (2006). https://doi.org/10.1007/11927587_28

46. Krawczyk, H., Rabin, T.: Chameleon hashing and signatures. In: NDSS (2000)

47. Krenn, S., Samelin, K., Sommer, D.: Stronger security for sanitizable signatures. In: Garcia-Alfaro, J., Navarro-Arribas, G., Aldini, A., Martinelli, F., Suri, N. (eds.) DPM/QASA -2015. LNCS, vol. 9481, pp. 100–117. Springer, Cham (2016). https://doi.org/10.1007/978-3-319-29883-2_7

48. Lai, R.W.F., Zhang, T., Chow, S.S.M., Schröder, D.: Efficient sanitizable signatures without random oracles. In: Askoxylakis, I., Ioannidis, S., Katsikas, S., Meadows, C. (eds.) ESORICS 2016. LNCS, vol. 9878, pp. 363–380. Springer, Cham (2016). https://doi.org/10.1007/978-3-319-45744-4_18

49. de Meer, H., Pöhls, H.C., Posegga, J., Samelin, K.: On the relation between redactable and sanitizable signature schemes. In: Jürjens, J., Piessens, F., Bielova, N. (eds.) ESSoS 2014. LNCS, vol. 8364, pp. 113–130. Springer, Cham (2014). https://doi.org/10.1007/978-3-319-04897-0_8

50. Mohassel, P.: One-time signatures and Chameleon hash functions. In: Biryukov, A., Gong, G., Stinson, D.R. (eds.) SAC 2010. LNCS, vol. 6544, pp. 302–319. Springer, Heidelberg (2011). https://doi.org/10.1007/978-3-642-19574-7_21

51. Pöhls, H.C.: Contingency revisited: secure construction and legal implications of verifiably weak integrity. In: Fernández-Gago, C., Martinelli, F., Pearson, S., Agudo, I. (eds.) IFIPTM 2013. IAICT, vol. 401, pp. 136–150. Springer, Heidelberg (2013). https://doi.org/10.1007/978-3-642-38323-6_10

52. Pöhls, H.C., Peters, S., Samelin, K., Posegga, J., de Meer, H.: Malleable signatures for resource constrained platforms. In: Cavallaro, L., Gollmann, D. (eds.) WISTP 2013. LNCS, vol. 7886, pp. 18–33. Springer, Heidelberg (2013). https://doi.org/10.1007/978-3-642-38530-8_2

53. Pöhls, H.C., Samelin, K.: Accountable redactable signatures. In: ARES (2015)

54. Pöhls, H.C., Samelin, K., Posegga, J.: Sanitizable signatures in XML signature — performance, mixing properties, and revisiting the property of transparency. In: Lopez, J., Tsudik, G. (eds.) ACNS 2011. LNCS, vol. 6715, pp. 166–182. Springer, Heidelberg (2011). https://doi.org/10.1007/978-3-642-21554-4_10

55. Ren, Q., Mu, Y., Susilo, W.: Mitigating Phishing by a new ID-based Chameleon hash without key exposure. In: AusCERT, pp. 1–13 (2007)

56. Shamir, A., Tauman, Y.: Improved online/offline signature schemes. In: Kilian, J. (ed.) CRYPTO 2001. LNCS, vol. 2139, pp. 355–367. Springer, Heidelberg (2001). https://doi.org/10.1007/3-540-44647-8_21

57. Zhang, F., Safavi-naini, R., Susilo, W.: Id-based chameleon hashes from bilinear pairings. IACR Cryptol. ePrint Archive **2003**, 208 (2003)

58. Zhang, R.: Tweaking TBE/IBE to PKE transforms with Chameleon hash functions. In: Katz, J., Yung, M. (eds.) ACNS 2007. LNCS, vol. 4521, pp. 323–339. Springer, Heidelberg (2007). https://doi.org/10.1007/978-3-540-72738-5_21

Ubiquitous Weak-Key Classes
of BRW-Polynomial Function

Kaiyan Zheng[1,2,3], Peng Wang[1,2,3](✉), and Dingfeng Ye[1,2,3]

[1] State Key Laboratory of Information Security,
Institute of Information Engineering, Chinese Academy of Sciences,
Beijing 100093, China
zhengkaiyan@iie.ac.cn, {wp,ydf}@is.ac.cn
[2] Data Assurance and Communication Security Research Center,
Chinese Academy of Sciences, Beijing 100093, China
[3] School of Cyber Security, University of Chinese Academic Science,
Beijing 100049, China

Abstract. BRW-polynomial function is suggested as a preferred alternative of polynomial function, owing to its high efficiency and seemingly non-existent weak keys. In this paper we investigate the weak-key issue of BRW-polynomial function as well as BRW-instantiated cryptographic schemes. Though, in BRW-polynomial evaluation, the relationship between coefficients and input blocks is indistinct, we give out a recursive algorithm to compute another $(2^{v+1} - 1)$-block message, for any given $(2^{v+1} - 1)$-block message, such that their output-differential through BRW-polynomial evaluation, equals any given s-degree polynomial, where $v \geq \lfloor \log_2(s+1) \rfloor$. With such algorithm, we illustrate that any non-empty key subset is a weak-key class in BRW-polynomial function. Moreover any key subset of BRW-polynomial function, consisting of at least 2 keys, is a weak-key class in BRW-instantiated cryptographic schemes like the Wegman-Carter scheme, the UHF-then-PRF scheme, DCT, etc. Especially in the AE scheme DCT, its confidentiality, as well as its integrity, collapses totally, when using weak keys of BRW-polynomial function, which are ubiquitous.

Keywords: Weak key · Polynomial evaluation hash
BRW-polynomial · DCT · Message authentication code
Authenticated encryption

1   Introduction

Universal Hash Function. Universal hash functions (short as UHFs) were firstly introduced by Carter and Wegman [8,37], and have become common components in numerous cryptographic constructions, like message authentication code (short as MAC) schemes [7,11,13,13], tweakable enciphering schemes [10,19,35] and authenticated encryption (short as AE) schemes [3,21],

© Springer International Publishing AG, part of Springer Nature 2018
A. Joux et al. (Eds.): AFRICACRYPT 2018, LNCS 10831, pp. 33–50, 2018.
https://doi.org/10.1007/978-3-319-89339-6_3

etc. A UHF is a keyed function. Compared with other primitives like pseudo-random permutations (short as PRPs) and pseudorandom functions (short as PRFs), UHFs have no strength of pseudorandomness. The only requirement is some simple combinatorial properties, which makes UHFs high-performance but brittle and vulnerable to weak-key analyses [1,14,25,27,39] and related-key attacks [34,36].

Weak-Key Analysis. Handschuh and Preneel [14] initiated the study of the weak-key issue of UHFs, as they pointed out that "in symmetric cryptology, a class of keys is called a weak-key class if for the members of that class the algorithm *behaves in an unexpected way* and if it is easy to *detect* whether a particular unknown key belongs to this class. Moreover, if a weak-key class is of size C, one requires that identifying that a key belongs to this class requires testing fewer than C keys by exhaustive search and fewer than C verification queries." Following such definition, they investigated several weak-key classes of UHFs in MACs. Later on the weak-key analyses of UHFs mainly focused on a specific UHF, i.e. polynomial function.

Polynomial Function. Polynomial function, which evaluates a polynomial in the key with the data blocks as coefficients, is one of the most widely used UHFs [4,5,10,15,17,20,35]. However the weak-key issue of polynomial function in cryptographic schemes such as MACs was extensively studied and was found unavoidable, especially in the example of GCM/GMAC which uses polynomial function in its authentication component. Saarrinen [27] found that the keys of polynomial function satisfying $K^t = K$ formed a weak-key class in GCM. Procter and Cid [25] found that any subset $\mathcal{W}$ is a weak-key class in GCM and GMAC, if $|\mathcal{W}| \geq 3$ or $|\mathcal{W}| \geq 2$ and $0 \in \mathcal{W}$, exploiting the so-called forgery polynomial $q(K) = \Sigma_{H \in \mathcal{W}}(K - H)$. Zhu et al. [39] pointed out that any subset $\mathcal{W}$ consisting of at least 2 keys is a weak-key class. Sun et al. [34] applied the above results to tweakable enciphering schemes based on polynomial function. Abdelraheem et al. [1] further proposed twisted polynomials from Ore rings to construct sparse forgery polynomials, which greatly facilitate key recovery attacks.

The weak-key issue casts shadow on the further application of polynomial function. For example, during the CAESAR competition, due to the weak-key issue of polynomial function in the AE scheme POET [2], the designers [3] decided to abandon the polynomial-function-based POET and retain the four-round-AES-based version.

BRW-Polynomial Function. Bernstein [6] proposed a variant of polynomial function, after the work of Rabin and Winograd [26], which is named as BRW (short for Bernstein-Rabin-Winograd) in [28]. BRW-polynomial function performs more highly-efficient than polynomial function, as it decreases nearly a half of multiplications in polynomial evaluation. BRW-polynomial function is widely-used in lots of cryptographic schemes, including authentication schemes [6,30], tweakable enciphering schemes [9,28,29], authenticated encryption schemes [12], etc.

Furthermore, unlike the case of polynomial function, the weak-key issue of BRW-polynomial function seems avoidable. By now, no weak-key problem of BRW-polynomial function has been found [12,14], which makes BRW-polynomial function an ideal UHF candidate in cryptographic schemes to alleviate the threat of weak keys. For example, the designers of DCT, a deterministic authenticated encryption scheme [12], suggested using BRW-polynomial function to instantiate its UHF to avoid the weak-key issue.

Our Contributions. This work investigates the weak-key problem of BRW-polynomial function and BRW-instantiated schemes. Unlike polynomial function, in BRW-polynomial evaluation, the relationship between coefficients and input blocks is indistinct owing to its recursive definition. Nevertheless we give out a recursive algorithm -$SumBRWpoly$- which, for any given $(2^{v+1} - 1)$-block message M and any given s-degree polynomial $q(K) = Q_0 K^s + Q_1 K^{s-1} + \cdots + Q_s$ that $v \geq \lfloor \log_2(s+1) \rfloor$, computes another $(2^{v+1} - 1)$-block message M' such that $BRW_K(M') = BRW_K(M) + q(K)$.

With $SumBRWpoly$, we illustrate that any s-key subset $\mathcal{W} = \{H_0, \cdots, H_{s-1}\}$ is a weak-key class of BRW-polynomial function. Moreover similar to the case of polynomial function, any $\mathcal{W}$, as long as $s \geq 2$, is also a weak-key class in BRW-instantiated schemes, even when padding rules are taken into consideration, which negates the suggestion of substituting BRW-polynomial function for polynomial function to mitigate the weak-key threat.

For example, when instantiating with BRW-polynomial, both the Wegman-Carter scheme and the UHF-then-PRF scheme suffer the forgery attack if the UHF key falls into $\mathcal{W}$, and it is easy to detect if the unknown UHF key belongs to $\mathcal{W}$. Furthermore, the BRW-instantiated DCT, a deterministic AE scheme, suffers both the distinguishing attack and the forgery attack once its UHF key is in $\mathcal{W}$, implying that the confidentiality, as well as the integrity, of DCT totally collapses when using weak keys of BRW-polynomial, which are ubiquitous.

The remaining of the paper is structured as following: after reviewing the weak-key problem of polynomial-based MACs in Sect. 2, $SumBRWpoly$ is illustrated in Sect. 3, together with ubiquitous weak keys of BRW-polynomial and BRW-instantiated MACs. Section 4 discuss weak-key classes of DCT, and Sect. 5 makes a simple conclusion of this work.

2   Preliminaries

2.1   Notations

For a finite set $\mathcal{S}$, let $x \xleftarrow{\$} \mathcal{S}$ denote selecting an element x uniformly at random from the set $\mathcal{S}$ and $\#\mathcal{S}$ denote the number of members in $\mathcal{S}$. Let $|s|$ represent the bit length of s. For $b \in \{0,1\}$, b^m denotes m bits of b. Let $\|$ denote the concatenation of two bit-strings, and $\Longleftrightarrow$ means if and only if. For a function $H : \mathcal{K} \times \mathcal{D} \to \mathcal{R}$ where $\mathcal{K}$ is a key space, we often write $H(K, M)$ as $H_K(M)$, where $(K, M) \in \mathcal{K} \times \mathcal{D}$. Without loss of generality, most of operations, such as additions, multiplications, in the remaining are defined over the finite filed

$\mathbb{GF}(2^n)$. $M = M_0 \cdots M_{m-1}$ is a m-block message where $M_i \in \mathbb{GF}(2^n)$ for $i = 0, \cdots, m - 1$.

2.2 Universal Hash Functions

Two commonly-used UHFs are almost-universal (AU) hash function and almost-XOR-universal (AXU) hash function. Both UHFs satisfy some simple combinatorial properties for *any* two different inputs.

For AU hash function, the output-collision probability of any two different inputs is negligible.

Definition 1 (AU [32]). $H : \mathcal{K} \times \mathcal{D} \to \mathcal{R}$ *is an ϵ-almost-universal (ϵ-AU) hash function, if for any $M, M' \in \mathcal{D}$, $M \neq M'$,*

$$\Pr[K \xleftarrow{\$} \mathcal{K} : H_K(M) = H_K(M')] = \frac{\#\{K \in \mathcal{K} : H_K(M) = H_K(M')\}}{\#\mathcal{K}} \leq \epsilon.$$

When ϵ is negligible we say that H is AU. Generally, $\epsilon = \max\limits_{M \neq M'} \Pr[K \xleftarrow{\$} \mathcal{K} : H_K(M) = H_K(M')]$.

For AXU hash function, the output-differential distribution of any two different inputs is almost uniform.

Definition 2 (AXU [33]). *Let $(\mathcal{R}, +)$ be an abelian group where the addition is exclusive-OR (XOR). $H : \mathcal{K} \times \mathcal{D} \to \mathcal{R}$ is an ϵ-almost-xor-universal (ϵ-AXU), if for any $M, M' \in \mathcal{D}$, $M \neq M'$, and any $C \in \mathcal{R}$,*

$$\Pr[K \xleftarrow{\$} \mathcal{K} : H_K(M) + H_K(M') = C] = \frac{\#\{K \in \mathcal{K} : H_K(M) + H_K(M') = C\}}{\#\mathcal{K}} \leq \epsilon.$$

When ϵ is negligible we say that H is AXU. Generally, $\epsilon = \max\limits_{M \neq M', C} \Pr[K \xleftarrow{\$} \mathcal{K} : H_K(M) + H_K(M') = C]$.

Clearly, if H is ϵ-AXU, it is also ϵ-AU, for ϵ-AU is a special case of ϵ-AXU when $C = 0$.

2.3 UHF-Based MACs

One popular design of UHF-based MACs is to firstly compress the variable-length input message into a fixed-length digest by a UHF and secondly encrypt it into a tag. For example, the Wegman-Carter scheme [18,31,37] masks the digest with the keystream of a block-cipher, while the UHF-then-PRF scheme [31] maps the digest into a tag by a PRF.

More specifically, let $H : \mathcal{K} \times \mathcal{D} \to \mathcal{R}$ be a UHF and $E : \mathcal{K}' \times \mathcal{R} \to \mathcal{R}$ be a secure block-cipher. Two common UHF-based MACs are as following:

- The Wegman-Carter scheme WC : $(\mathcal{K} \times \mathcal{K}') \times \mathcal{N} \times \mathcal{D} \to \mathcal{R}$, for $M \in \mathcal{D}, N \in \mathcal{N}$ and $K \xleftarrow{\$} \mathcal{K}, K' \xleftarrow{\$} \mathcal{K}'$,

$$\mathrm{WC}_{K,K'}(N, M) = E_{K'}(N) + H_K(M).$$

- The UHF-Then-PRF scheme UTP : $(\mathcal{K} \times \mathcal{K}') \times \mathcal{D} \to \mathcal{R}$, for $M \in \mathcal{D}$ and $K \xleftarrow{\$} \mathcal{K}, K' \xleftarrow{\$} \mathcal{K}'$,

$$\mathrm{UTP}_{K,K'}(M) = E_{K'}(H_K(M)).$$

In the Wegman-Carter scheme, N denotes a non-repeated Nonce which is required fresh in each computation.

The Security of MACs. Without loss of generality, assuming that the key is uniform-randomly chosen, i.e. $K \xleftarrow{\$} \mathcal{K}, K' \xleftarrow{\$} \mathcal{K}'$, the MAC scheme $\mathcal{O}$ often consists of two algorithms: (let $\mathcal{O} \in \{\mathrm{WC}, \mathrm{UTP}\}$)

- Tag-generation $\mathcal{T}^{\mathcal{O}}$: When $\mathcal{O} = \mathrm{WC}$, on the input (N, M) where N is non-repeated nonce, calculate $T = \mathrm{WC}_{K,K'}(N, M)$; otherwise on the input M, calculate $T = \mathrm{UTP}_{K,K'}(M)$. Return T.
- Verification $\mathcal{V}^{\mathcal{O}}$: When $\mathcal{O} = \mathrm{WC}$, on the input (N, M, T), compute $T' = \mathrm{WC}_{K,K'}(N, M)$; otherwise on the input (M, T) compute $T' = \mathrm{UTP}_{K,K'}(M)$. If $T' = T$, return 1; else return 0.

During the communication between two parties who have shared a secret key (K, K'), the sender generates tags of his messages by the tag-generation algorithm $\mathcal{T}^{\mathcal{O}}$ and transmits the message-tag pairs, while the receiver validates the received message-tag pairs when the verification algorithm $\mathcal{V}^{\mathcal{O}}$ returns 1.

The security goal of MACs is to resist the forgery attack. More specifically, any adversary who has access to both the tag-generation oracle $\mathcal{T}^{\mathcal{O}}$ and the verification oracle $\mathcal{V}^{\mathcal{O}}$, is said to have made a successful forgery, once it outputs a new message-tag pair, i.e. a triple (N, M, T) when $\mathcal{O} = \mathrm{WC}$ or a duplet (M, T) when $\mathcal{O} = \mathrm{UTP}$, which is not produced by $\mathcal{T}^{\mathcal{O}}$ but is validated by $\mathcal{V}^{\mathcal{O}}$.

It has been proved that the Wegman-Carter scheme is secure if H is an AXU and E is a PRP [18], and that the UHF-then-PRF scheme is secure if H is an AU and E is a PRP [31].

2.4 Weak Keys of Polynomial Function and Polynomial-Based MACs

Polynomial Function. Polynomial function is defined as

$$Poly_K(M) = M_0 K^{m-1} + M_1 K^{m-2} + \cdots + M_{m-1}$$

where $K \in \mathrm{GF}(2^n)$, $M = M_0 M_1 \cdots M_{m-1}$, $M_i \in \mathrm{GF}(2^n)$ for $i = 0, 1, \cdots, m-1$. Obviously $Poly_K(M)$ determines a polynomial in $\mathrm{GF}(2^n)[K]$.

It is easy to deduce that $Poly_K(\cdot)$ is a $(m-1)/2^n$-AU, and that $K \cdot Poly_K(\cdot)$ is a $m/2^n$-AXU. Because for any distinct M, M' and any $C \in \mathrm{GF}(2^n)$, the equation $Poly_K(M') = Poly_K(M)$ has at most $(m-1)$ roots in $\mathbb{GF}(2^n)$, while the equation $K \cdot Poly_K(M) + K \cdot Poly_K(M') = C$ has at most m roots.

Weak-Key Classes of *Poly* and *Poly*-Based MACs. Unfortunately, the weak-key issue of polynomial function is unavoidable. As shown in [25,34,39], any subset $\mathcal{W}$, as long as $|\mathcal{W}| \geq 2$, is a weak-key class of polynomial function in GCM and GMAC, both *Poly*-based schemes. We just give it a brief explanation in the following, and more details refer to [14,25,34,39].

For any key subset $\mathcal{W} = \{H_0, H_1, \cdots, H_{s-1}\}$ that $s \geq 2$, define

$$q(K) = (K - H_0)(K - H_1)\cdots(K - H_{s-1}) = Q_0 K^s + Q_1 K^{s-1} + \cdots + Q_s,$$

where $Q_0 = 1$. It is obvious that

$$K \in \mathcal{W} \iff q(K) = 0. \tag{1}$$

In polynomial function, each coefficient corresponds exactly each input block, and it is easy to find message pairs whose output-differential after polynomial evaluating equals $q(K)$. Specifically, for arbitrary m-block M that $m > s$, compute

$$Poly_K(M) + q(K) = M'_0 K^{m-1} + M'_1 K^{m-2} + \cdots + M'_{m-1},$$
$$K \cdot Poly_K(M) + q(K) = K \cdot \left(M''_0 K^{m-1} + M''_1 K^{m-2} + \cdots + M''_{m-1}\right) + Q_s.$$

Let $M' = M'_0 M'_1 \cdots M'_{m-1}$ and $M'' = M''_0 M''_1 \cdots M''_{m-1}$, and by (1),

$$K \in \mathcal{W} \iff Poly_K(M) = Poly_K(M'), \tag{2}$$
$$K \in \mathcal{W} \iff K \cdot Poly_K(M) = K \cdot Poly_K(M'') + Q_s. \tag{3}$$

By (2) (3), it is trivial that $\Pr\left[K \xleftarrow{\$} \mathcal{W} : Poly_K(M) = Poly_K(M')\right] = 1$ and $\Pr\left[K \xleftarrow{\$} \mathcal{W} : K \cdot Poly_K(M) = K \cdot Poly_K(M'') + Q_s\right] = 1$, which implies that the AU property of $Poly_K(\cdot)$, as well as the AXU property of $K \cdot Poly_K(\cdot)$, totally disappears in the key subset $\mathcal{W}$.

Furthermore, once the key of *Poly* falls into $\mathcal{W}$, the security of *Poly*-based schemes also collapses, and it is easy to detect whether the unknown key of *Poly* belongs to $\mathcal{W}$. Thus $\mathcal{W}$ ($|\mathcal{W}| \geq 2$) is a weak-key class of *Poly* in *Poly*-based schemes. Take two common *Poly*-based MACs, i.e. UTP and WC, as examples, that is, $\text{UTP}_{K,K'}(M) = E_{K'}(Poly_K(M))$, and $\text{WC}_{K,K'}(N, M) = E_{K'}(N) + K \cdot Poly_K(M)$. Since $E_{K'}$ is a PRP, according to (2) (3), it is easy to deduce that

$$K \in \mathcal{W} \iff \text{UTP}_{K,K'}(M) = \text{UTP}_{K,K'}(M'), \tag{4}$$
$$K \in \mathcal{W} \iff \text{WC}_{K,K'}(N, M) = \text{WC}_{K,K'}(N, M'') + Q_s, \tag{5}$$

which means that (1) when $K \in \mathcal{W}$, neither UTP nor WC can resist the forgery attack, and (2) by verifying if the UTP tags between M and M' or the WC tags between (N, M) and (N, M'') are equal, it is able to detect if K belongs to $\mathcal{W}$.

From above, it is crucial that, for arbitrary key subset $\mathcal{W}$, it is easy to find message pairs whose output-differential after polynomial evaluating equals $q(K)$, the so-called forgery polynomial defined by $\mathcal{W}$. To deal with variable-length inputs in real applications, inputs to polynomial function are padded firstly. However even when padding rules are taken into consideration, such message pairs are easy to find, and examples include GCM and GMAC [1,25,27,39].

3 Weak Keys of BRW-Polynomial Function and BRW-Instantiated MACs

3.1 The Description of BRW-Polynomial Function

BRW-polynomial function [6,23] is defined recursively, just as follows:

- $BRW_K(\varepsilon) = 0^n$;
- $BRW_K(M_0) = M_0$;
- $BRW_K(M_0 M_1) = M_0 K + M_1$;
- $BRW_K(M_0 M_1 M_2) = (M_0 + K)(M_1 + K^2) + M_2$;
- $BRW_K(M_0 \cdots M_{m-1}) = BRW_K(M_0 \cdots M_{t-2})(K^t + M_{t-1}) + BRW_K(M_t \cdots M_{m-1})$
  for $t \in \{4, 8, 16, 32, \cdots\}$ and $t \le m < 2t$ (i.e. $t = 2^{\lfloor \log_2 m \rfloor}$);

where ε is an empty string, $K \in \mathbb{GF}(2^n), M_i \in \mathbb{GF}(2^n)$ for $i = 0, \cdots, m - 1$. When $m \ge 3$, let $t = 2^{\lfloor \log_2 m \rfloor}$, $BRW_K(\cdot)$ is a monic polynomial with the degree of $(2t - 1)$. And it is easy to conclude that $BRW_K(\cdot)$ is $(2t - 1)/2^n$-AU and $K \cdot BRW_K(\cdot)$ is $2t/2^n$-AXU [28].

Unlike the case of polynomial function, in BRW-polynomial evaluation, each input block may affect multiple coefficients in the meantime, and its difficult to track the coefficients after modifying input blocks. However, even though the relationship between input blocks and coefficients is not so obvious as that in polynomial function, there are efficient methods to find message pairs whose output-differential after BRW-polynomial evaluating equals some given polynomial, and BRW-polynomial function suffers the same weak-key issue as polynomial function.

In the following, we firstly give out a recursive algorithm, $SumBRWpoly$ in Algorithm 1, which finds another new $(2^{v+1} - 1)$-block message for any given $(2^{v+1} - 1)$-block message such that their output-differential after BRW-polynomial evaluating equals any given s-degree polynomial, where $v \ge \lfloor \log_2(s+1) \rfloor$. Secondly, we study the weak-key problem of BRW-polynomial function and BRW-instantiated MACs, i.e. BRW-based UTP and WC, with the recursive algorithm.

3.2 The Description of $SumBRWpoly$

Given any s-degree polynomial $q(K) = Q_0 K^s + Q_1 K^{s-1} + \cdots + Q_s$ and any m-block message M that $m = 2^{v+1} - 1$ and $v \ge \lfloor \log_2(s + 1) \rfloor$, $SumBRWpoly$, exploiting the observations about the BRW-polynomial evaluation of the specific

$(2^{v+1} - 1)$-block inputs, computes another new m-block message M' such that $BRW_K(M')$ is exactly the sum of $BRW_K(M)$ and $q(K)$.

In this section, we first introduce the observations about the BRW-polynomial evaluation of $(2^{v+1} - 1)$-block inputs, and then explain how $SumBRWpoly$ works, where $v \geq 2$.

BRW-Polynomial Evaluation of $(2^{v+1}-1)$-Block Inputs. When $v \geq 2$, let $m = 2^{v+1} - 1$ and $t = 2^{\lfloor \log_2(m) \rfloor} = 2^v$. To an m-block message M,

$$BRW_K(M_0 \cdots M_{t-2}M_{t-1}M_t \cdots M_{2t-2}) =$$
$$BRW_K(M_0 \cdots M_{t-2}) \cdot K^t + M_{t-1} \cdot BRW_K(M_0 \cdots M_{t-2}) + BRW_K(M_t \cdots M_{2t-2}),$$

and the observations exploited in $SumBRWpoly$ are as following:

(1) $BRW_K(M)$ is a monic polynomial with the degree of $(2t - 1)$, i.e. m or $2^{v+1} - 1$;
(2) Both $BRW_K(M_0 \cdots M_{t-2})$ and $BRW_K(M_t \cdots M_{2t-2})$ are monic polynomials with the degree of $(t - 1)$, i.e. $(2^v - 1)$, and thus the coefficient of K^{t-1} is $(M_{t-1} + 1)$;
(3) The last $(t - 1)$ blocks of M, i.e. $M_t \cdots M_{2t-2}$, only affect the terms with a degree lower than $(t - 1)$;
(4) Only the first $(t - 1)$ blocks of M, i.e. $M_0 \cdots M_{t-2}$, affect the terms with a degree greater than t.
(5) The last block of M, i.e. M_{2t-2}, only affects the constant term, and the constant term in $BRW_K(M_0 \cdots M_{t-2})$ (if any) turns out to be the coefficient of K^t.

Note that when $v = 0, 1$ and $m = 1, 3$ respectively, the evaluation of $BRW_K(M)$ is simple.

How $SumBRWpoly$ Works. The description of $SumBRWpoly$ is shown in Algorithm 1. It is required that $m > s$. Otherwise there is no such m-block message pair M, M' satisfying $BRW_K(M') = BRW_K(M) + q(K)$ since both $BRW_K(M')$ and $BRW_K(M)$ are monic polynomials with the degree of m. By $2^{v+1} - 1 > s$, let $v \geq \lfloor \log_2(s + 1) \rfloor$ for simplicity. Besides, m is often expected to be as small as possible to make the attacks efficient. For any s, the shortest messages dealt by $SumBRWpoly$ is $m_{\min} = 2^{\lfloor \log_2(s+1) \rfloor + 1} - 1$, i.e. $s < m_{\min} \leq (2s + 1)$.

When $s = 0$. Note that when $s = 0$, $\mathcal{W} = \emptyset$, which is actually insignificant, and this case is given to complete the recursive algorithm. And $v = 0$ is included in this case. Let $q(K) = Q_0$ that $Q_0 \in \mathbb{GF}(2^n)$. To be simple, let $M'_{m-1} = M_{m-1} + Q_0$, as the last block of the $(2^{v+1} - 1)$-block message only affect the constant term in BRW-polynomial evaluation for $v \geq 0$.

When $v = 1$ and $s = 1, 2$. In this case, the specific message that $SumBRWpoly$ processes is of 3 blocks, i.e $m = 3$. According to

$$\begin{cases} BRW_K(M'_0 M'_1 M'_2) = K^3 + M'_0 K^2 + M'_1 K + M'_0 M'_1 + M'_2 \\ BRW_K(M_0 M_1 M_2) = K^3 + M_0 K^2 + M_1 K + M_0 M_1 + M_2 \end{cases},$$

Algorithm 1. The description of $SumBRWpoly$

Input: $q(K) = Q_0 K^s + Q_1 K^{s-1} + \cdots + Q_s$, $M = M_0 \cdots M_{m-1}$, where
$\quad m = 2^{v+1} - 1$ and $v \geq \lfloor \log_2(s+1) \rfloor$.
Output: $M' = M'_0 \cdots M'_{m-1}$.
if $s = 0$ **then**
$\quad\mid M'_0 \cdots M'_{m-2} = M_0 \cdots M_{m-2}$;
$\quad\mid M'_{m-1} = M_{m-1} + Q_s$;
else
$\quad\mid v = \lfloor \log_2 m \rfloor$;
$\quad\mid t = 2^v$;
$\quad\mid$ **if** $v = 1$ **then**
$\quad\quad\mid$ **if** $s = 1$ **then**
$\quad\quad\quad\mid M'_0 = M_0$;
$\quad\quad\quad\mid M'_1 = M_1 + Q_0$;
$\quad\quad\quad\mid M'_2 = M_2 + Q_1 + M_0 Q_0$;
$\quad\quad\mid$ **if** $s = 2$ **then**
$\quad\quad\quad\mid M'_0 = M_0 + Q_0$;
$\quad\quad\quad\mid M'_1 = M_1 + Q_1$;
$\quad\quad\quad\mid M'_2 = M_2 + Q_2 + M_0 Q_1 + M_1 Q_0 + Q_0 Q_1$;
$\quad\mid$ **else**
$\quad\quad\mid$ **if** $s < t - 1$ **then**
$\quad\quad\quad\mid M'_0 \cdots M'_{t-1} = M_0 \cdots M_{t-1}$;
$\quad\quad\quad\mid M'_t \cdots M'_{2t-2} = SumBRWpoly(q(K), M_t \cdots M_{2t-2})$;
$\quad\quad\mid$ **if** $s \geq t - 1$ **then**
$\quad\quad\quad\mid$ **if** $s \geq t$ **then**
$\quad\quad\quad\quad\mid q_1(K) = \sum_{i=0}^{s-t} Q_{s-t-i} K^i$;
$\quad\quad\quad\quad\mid M'_0 \cdots M'_{t-2} = SumBRWpoly(q_1(K), M_0 \cdots M_{t-2})$;
$\quad\quad\quad\mid$ **else**
$\quad\quad\quad\quad\mid q_1(K) = \varepsilon$;
$\quad\quad\quad\quad\mid M'_0 \cdots M'_{t-2} = M_0 \cdots M_{t-2}$;
$\quad\quad\quad\mid M'_{t-1} = M_{t-1} + Q_{s-t+1}$;
$\quad\quad\quad\mid q_2(K) = \sum_{i=0}^{t-2} Q_{s-i} K^i + Q_{s-t+1} \cdot \left(BRW_K(M_0 \cdots M_{t-2}) + K^{t-1} \right) +$
$\quad\quad\quad\quad (M_{t-1} + Q_{s-t+1}) \cdot q_1(K)$;
$\quad\quad\quad\mid M'_t \cdots M'_{2t-2} = SumBRWpoly(q_2(K), M_t \cdots M_{2t-2})$;

return M'

---

it is easy to define M' satisfying $BRW_K(M') = BRW_K(M) + q(K)$ for $s = 1, 2$. One simple way to define M' is given in Algorithm 1.

When $v \geq 2$. In this case, $SumBRWpoly$ runs in a recursive way by exploiting the observations about the BRW-polynomial evaluation of $(2^{v+1} - 1)$-block inputs. Let $t = 2^v$ (see Algorithm 1).

If $s < t - 1$, because the last $(t - 1)$ input blocks only affect the terms with the degree lower than $(t - 1)$ in BRW-polynomial evaluation, to be simple, $SumBRWpoly(q(K), M)$ keeps the first t blocks of M' the same as that of M, and computes the remaining $(t-1)$ blocks of M' by making a recursive call of $SumBRWpoly(q(K), M_t \cdots M_{2t-2})$. That is,

$$SumBRWpoly\,(q(K), M) = M_0 \cdots M_{t-1} \| SumBRWpoly\,(q(K), M_t \cdots M_{2t-2}).$$

Note that in this specific case $s < t-1$ and $v \geq \lfloor \log_2(s+1) \rfloor$, thus $v-1 \geq \lfloor \log_2(s+1) \rfloor$ which means that the recursive call of $SumBRWpoly(q(K), M_t \cdots M_{2t-2})$ is reasonable.

However when $s \geq t-1$, the problem is a bit complex. Rewrite the terms of $q(K)$ into three parts as following:

$$q(K) = \left(Q_0 K^s + \cdots + Q_{s-t} K^t\right) + Q_{s-t+1} K^{t-1} + \left(Q_{s-t+2} K^{t-2} + \cdots + Q_s\right)$$
$$= q_1(K) \cdot K^t + Q_{s-t+1} K^{t-1} + \left(Q_{s-t+2} K^{t-2} + \cdots + Q_s\right), \tag{6}$$

where when $s \geq t$, $q_1(K) = Q_0 K^{s-t} + Q_1 K^{s-t-1} + \cdots + Q_{s-t}$, and when $s = t-1$, $q_1(K) = \varepsilon$.

When $s \geq t$, because only the first $(t-1)$ input blocks affect the terms whose degree is greater than t in BRW-polynomial evaluation, $SumBRWpoly(q(K), M)$ first calls $SumBRWpoly(q_1(K), M_0 \cdots M_{t-2})$ to computes $M'_0 \cdots M'_{t-2}$. The recursive call is reasonable, since $M_0 \cdots M_{t-2}$ is a $(2^{(v-1)+1} - 1)$-block input and the relationship between $(v-1)$ and the degree of $q_1(K)$, i.e. $(s-t)$, satisfies the requirement of $SumBRWpoly$. Due to the property of floor number, $(s+1) \leq 2^{2\lfloor \log_2(s+1) \rfloor - 1} + 2^{\lfloor \log_2(s+1) \rfloor - 1}$ for $s \geq 1$, and

$$s - t + 1 = s - 2^v + 1 \leq s + 1 - 2^{\lfloor \log_2(s+1) \rfloor} \leq 2^{\lfloor \log_2(s+1) \rfloor - 1}.$$

Since $v-1 \geq \lfloor \log_2(s+1) \rfloor - 1$, it is easy to deduce that $v-1 \geq \lfloor \log_2(s-t+1) \rfloor$. Otherwise when $s = t-1$, since $q_1(K) = \varepsilon$, let $M'_0 \cdots M'_{t-2} = M_0 \cdots M_{t-2}$.

After that $SumBRWpoly$ figures out how $q_1(K)$ affects the remaining lower-degree terms. Moreover let $M'_{t-1} = M_{t-1} + Q_{s-t+1}$, and then

$$BRW_K(M'_0 \cdots M'_{t-2}) \cdot \left(K^t + M'_{t-1}\right) \tag{7}$$
$$= (BRW_K(M_0 \cdots M_{t-2}) + q_1(K)) \cdot \left(K^t + M_{t-1} + Q_{s-t+1}\right)$$
$$= BRW_K(M_0 \cdots M_{t-2}) \cdot \left(K^t + M_{t-1}\right) + q_1(K) \cdot K^t$$
$$\quad + (M_{t-1} + Q_{s-t+1}) \cdot q_1(K) + Q_{s-t+1} \cdot BRW_K(M_0 \cdots M_{t-2})$$
$$= BRW_K(M_0 \cdots M_{t-2}) \cdot \left(K^t + M_{t-1}\right) + q_1(K) \cdot K^t + Q_{s-t+1} K^{t-1}$$
$$\quad + (M_{t-1} + Q_{s-t+1}) \cdot q_1(K) + Q_{s-t+1} \cdot \left(BRW_K(M_0 \cdots M_{t-2}) + K^{t-1}\right).$$

To deal with the lower-degree terms, by (6) (7), let

$$q_2(K) = Q_{s-t+2} K^{t-2} + \cdots + Q_s$$
$$\quad + (M_{t-1} + Q_{s-t+1}) \cdot q_1(K) + Q_{s-t+1} \cdot \left(BRW_K(M_0 \cdots M_{t-2}) + K^{t-1}\right),$$

and the degree of $q_2(K)$ is either smaller than $(t-1)$ or equal to that of $q_1(K)$, and thus satisfies the requirement to call $SumBRWpoly(q_2(K), M_t \cdots M_{2t-2})$.

That is, the remaining blocks $M'_t \cdots M'_{2t-2}$ can be computed by making another recursive call of $SumBRWpoly(q_2(K), M_t \cdots M_{2t-2})$, and then

$$BRW_K(M'_t \cdots M'_{2t-2}) = BRW_K(M_t \cdots M_{2t-2}) + q_2(K). \tag{8}$$

Therefore when $s \geq t - 1$, by (7) (8),

$$
\begin{aligned}
& BRW_K(M'_0 \cdots M'_{t-2} M'_{t-1} M'_t \cdots M'_{2t-2}) \\
&= BRW_K(M'_0 \cdots M'_{t-2}) \cdot (K^t + M'_{t-1}) + BRW_K(M'_t \cdots M'_{2t-2}) \\
&= BRW_K(M_0 \cdots M^{t-2}) \cdot (K^t + M_{t-1}) + BRW_K(M_t \cdots M_{2t-2}) \\
&\quad + q_1(K) \cdot K^t + Q_{s-t+1} K^{t-1} + q_2(K) \\
&\quad\quad + (M_{t-1} + Q_{s-t+1}) \cdot q_1(K) + Q_{s-t+1} \cdot (BRW_K(M_0 \cdots M_{t-2}) + K^{t-1}) \\
&= BRW_K(M_0 \cdots M_{t-2} M_{t-1} M_t \cdots M_{2t-2}) + q(K).
\end{aligned}
$$

3.3 Weak Keys of BRW-Polynomial in MACs

Weak keys in BRW-polynomial function are found ubiquitous, which also threats BRW-based schemes. In this section, we explain how a key subset of BRW-polynomial function turns out to be a weak-key class, and then briefly discuss the weak-key issue of BRW-instantiated MACs.

For any key subset $\mathcal{W} = \{H_0, H_1, \cdots, H_{s-1}\}$ that $s \geq 1$, define

$$q(K) = (K - H_0)(K - H_1) \cdots (K - H_{s-1}) = Q_0 K^s + Q_1 K^{s-1} + \cdots + Q_s$$

where $Q_0 = 1$, similarly. Moreover let $\overline{q}(K) = Q_0 K^{s-1} + Q_1 K^{s-2} + \cdots + Q_{s-1}$ and then $q(K) = K \cdot \overline{q}(K) + Q_s$.

Choose arbitrary m-block message M where $m = 2^{v+1} - 1$ and $v = \lfloor \log_2(s + 1) \rfloor$, i.e. $s < m \leq (2s + 1)$. Compute M' and M'' by calling $SumBRWpoly$, that is $M' = SumBRWpoly(q(K), M)$ and $M'' = SumBRWpoly(\overline{q}(K), M)$. By

$$BRW_K(M') = BRW_K(M) + q(K),$$
$$K \cdot BRW_K(M'') = K \cdot BRW_K(M) + K \cdot \overline{q}(K),$$

it is obvious that

$$K \in \mathcal{W} \iff BRW_K(M') = BRW_K(M), \tag{9}$$
$$K \in \mathcal{W} \iff K \cdot BRW_K(M'') = K \cdot BRW_K(M) + Q_s. \tag{10}$$

Thus the AU property of $BRW_K(\cdot)$, as well as the AXU property of $K \cdot BRW_K(\cdot)$, totally disappears in $\mathcal{W}$, as $\Pr\left[K \xleftarrow{\$} \mathcal{W} : BRW_K(M) = BRW_K(M') \right] = 1$ and $\Pr\left[K \xleftarrow{\$} \mathcal{W} : K \cdot BRW_K(M) = K \cdot BRW_K(M'') + Q_s \right] = 1$.

Besides, once the key of BRW falls into $\mathcal{W}$, the security of the BRW-based scheme also collapses, and it is easy to detect whether the unknown key of BRW belongs to $\mathcal{W}$. So $\mathcal{W}$ is a weak-key class of BRW in the BRW-based schemes.

Take two BRW-instantiated MACs, i.e. UTP and WC, as examples, any $\mathcal{W}$ is a weak-key class, as long as $|\mathcal{W}| \geq 2$, because that:

- $\text{UTP}_{K,K'}(M) = E_{K'}(BRW_K(M))$
  (1) Forgery attack. Make a single tag-generation query of M and get its tag T. Once $K \in \mathcal{W}$, (M', T) is a successful forgery, since $E_{K'}$ is a PRP and then $T = E_{K'}(BRW_K(M)) = E_{K'}(BRW_K(M'))$ according to (9).
  (2) Detection. Simply make a tag-generation query of M to get its tag T, and one more verification query of (M', T). If 1 is returned, $BRW_K(M) = BRW_K(M')$ since $E_{K'}$ is a PRP, and thus $K \in \mathcal{W}$ according to (9), otherwise $K \notin \mathcal{W}$.
- $\text{WC}_{K,K'}(N, M) = E_{K'}(N) + K \cdot BRW_K(M)$
  (1) Forgery attack. Make a single tag-generation query of (N, M) and get its tag T. Once $K \in \mathcal{W}$, $(N, M'', T + Q_s)$ is a successful forgery, since $T + Q_s = E_{K'}(N) + K \cdot BRW_K(M) + Q_s = E_{K'}(N) + K \cdot BRW_K(M'')$ according to (10).
  (2) Detection. Make a single tag-generation query of (N, M) to get its T, and one more verification query of $(N, M'', T + Q_s)$. If 1 is returned, $K \in \mathcal{W}$ according to (10), otherwise $K \notin \mathcal{W}$.

Both forgery attack and detection given above require at least 1 tag-generation query and 1 verification query, and to avoid non-sense weak-key classes, it is required that $|\mathcal{W}| \geq 2$. In real applications, inputs are often padded firstly to deal with variable-length inputs. However even when padding rules are taken into consideration, *SumBRWpoly* still works by some tricks, such as the one used in the weak-key discussion of DCT (Sect. 4.2), and more refer to [1, 25, 27, 39].

4   Weak Keys of BRW-Polynomial in DCT

DCT [12], short for Deterministic Counter in Tweak, is a Beyond-Birthday-Bound-secure AE scheme, which is constructed from an efficient UHF, a CCA-secure PRP and a Beyond-Birthday-Bound-secure encryption scheme. Forler et al., the designers of DCT, suggest instantiating the underlying UHF with BRW-polynomial function, rather than polynomial function, to avoid the weak-key issue. However BRW-polynomial function suffers the same weak-key problem, which can be extended to DCT when instantiating with BRW-polynomial function.

4.1   A Brief Introduction to DCT

The encryption of DCT takes the input (A, P), where A is the associated data and P is the plaintext, and outputs the ciphertext C. The decryption of DCT takes the input (A, C), and outputs the plaintext P if the verification is passed.

The encryption and decryption of DCT are illustrated in Table 1. The block length is n-bit. $Encode_\tau(P)$ puts 0^τ on the left of P and then partitions the data into two part $P_L \| P_R$ where $|P_L| = n$. E is a block cipher. $\mathcal{E}$ is an encryption scheme and $\mathcal{D}$ is its inverse. If the left τ bits of P_L are zeroes, $Decode_\tau(P_L, P_R)$

Table 1. The encryption and decryption of DCT.

$DCT.enc_{K_1,K_2,K_3}(A,P)$	$DCT.dec_{K_1,K_2,K_3}(A,C)$
$P_L\|P_R = Encode_\tau(P)$	$C_L\|C_R = C$
$X = H_{K_1}(A, P_R)$	$P_R = \mathcal{D}_{K_3}(C_L, C_R)$
$Y = P_L + X$	$X = H_{K_1}(A, P_R)$
$C_L = E_{K_2}(Y)$	$Y = E_{K_2}^{-1}(C_L)$
$C_R = \mathcal{E}_{K_3}(C_L, P_R)$	$P_L = Y - X$
return $C_L\|C_R$	**return** $Decode_\tau(P_L, P_R)$

deletes the zeroes and returns the rest bits of $P_L\|P_R$, otherwise $Decode_\tau$ returns $\perp$ indicating the verification is failed.

In DCT, $\mathcal{E}$ is instantiated by the stream-cipher mode CTRT [24]. For simplicity, let $CTRT.Gen_{K_3}(C_L, l)$ be the function that outputs l-bit keystream in the key K_3, and once C_L is new, the l-bit keystream looks random at all. And then

$$\begin{cases} \mathcal{E}_{K_3}(C_L, P_R) = P_R + CTRT.Gen_{K_3}(C_L, |P_R|) \\ \mathcal{D}_{K_3}(C_L, C_R) = C_R + CTRT.Gen_{K_3}(C_L, |C_R|) \end{cases}.$$

The underlying UHF is defined as

$$H_{K_1}(A, P_R) = K_1 \cdot BRW_{K_1}(pad(A)\|pad(P_R)\|L)$$

where the function $pad(X)$ pads X with the minimal number of trailing zeroes such that its length after padding are multiples of n, $L = len(A)\|len(P_R)$ that $len(X)$ is an $(n/2)$-bit variable representing the bit length of X. Note that the UHF description here is a bit different from the original design in [12], but it doesn't affect the weak-key discussion in the following.

4.2   Weak Keys of BRW-Polynomial Function in DCT

When instantiating with BRW-polynomial function, which is suggested by its designers, DCT suffers the unavoidable weak-key problem, owing to ubiquitous weak keys of its BRW-polynomial UHF component, and the details are given out in the following.

AE schemes are designed to provide both the confidentiality of plaintexts and the integrity of plaintexts and associated data. However when weak keys are used, at least one of the security goal is broken. For example, GCM, one of the standardized AE schemes, fails to provide the integrity when using weak keys of its polynomial-function UHF, which is proved by the forgery attacks given in [1,14,25,27,39]. Another example is the robust AE scheme AEZ [16], which, when using weak keys given in [22], fails to offer the confidentiality, as its ciphertexts can be distinguished from random bits efficiently. As for BRW-instantiated DCT, both its confidentiality and integrity collapse, when using weak keys of BRW-polynomial. Besides it is easy to detect if the unknown key of BRW-polynomial belongs to some weak-key class.

Inherited from BRW-polynomial function, any subset $\mathcal{W} = \{H_0, \cdots, H_{s-1}\}$ is a weak-key class of DCT, as long as $s \geq 2$. That is, once $K_1 \in \mathcal{W}$, the confidentiality, as well as the integrity, of DCT collapses totally, and it is easy to detect whether $K_1 \in \mathcal{W}$.

Construct Message Pairs. The crux is how to construct distinct message pairs, say $(A, P), (A', P')$, for any $\mathcal{W}$, satisfying that

$$K_1 \in \mathcal{W} \iff H_{K_1}(A', P'_R) = H_{K_1}(A, P_R).$$

In the following, we explain how to find such pairs with $SumBRWpoly$ and a little trick to deal with the padding rule.

For any s-key subset $\mathcal{W}$, let $m = 2^{v+1} - 1$ and $v = \lfloor \log_2(s+1) \rfloor$, i.e. $s < m \leq (2s+1)$. Let A be arbitrary m-block message, i.e. $A = M_0 \cdots M_{m-1}$ where $M_i \in \{0,1\}^n$ for $i = 0, \cdots, m-1$. Let $q(K_1) = (K_1 - H_0) \cdots (K_1 - H_{s-1})$ and $A' = M'_0 \cdots M'_{m-1} = SumBRWpoly(q(K_1), M_0 \cdots M_{m-1})$, thus

$$BRW_{K_1}(M'_0 \cdots M'_{m-1}) = BRW_{K_1}(M_0 \cdots M_{m-1}) + q(K_1). \tag{11}$$

Besides, let $P_R = P'_R = 0^n \| U$ where $U \in \bigcup_{l=0}^{(m-2)n} \{0,1\}^l$, and

$$\begin{cases} pad(A) \| pad(P_R) \| L & = & M_0 \cdots M_{m-1} & \| & 0^n \| pad(U) \| L \\ pad(A') \| pad(P'_R) \| L' & = & M'_0 \cdots M'_{m-1} & \| & 0^n \| pad(U) \| L' \end{cases} \tag{12}$$

where $L = len(A) \| len(P_R)$, $L' = len(A') \| len(P'_R)$ and $L = L'$. Obviously, $(m+2)n \leq | pad(A) \| pad(P_R) \| L | \leq 2mn$, i.e. at most $2(2s+2)$ blocks, and $| pad(A) \| pad(P_R) \| L | = | pad(A') \| pad(P'_R) \| L |$.

Therefore, by (11) (12),

$$
\begin{aligned}
& BRW_{K_1}(pad(A') \| pad(P'_R) \| L') \\
= {} & BRW_{K_1}(pad(A') \| pad(P'_R) \| L) \\
= {} & BRW_{K_1}(M'_0 \cdots M'_{m-1}) \cdot (K_1^{m+1} + 0^n) + BRW_{K_1}(pad(U) \| L) \\
= {} & (BRW_{K_1}(M_0 \cdots M_{m-1}) + q(K_1)) \cdot (K_1^{m+1} + 0^n) + BRW_{K_1}(pad(U) \| L) \\
= {} & BRW_{K_1}(M_0 \cdots M_{m-1}) \cdot (K_1^{m+1} + 0^n) + BRW_{K_1}(pad(U) \| L) + q(K_1) \cdot K_1^{m+1} \\
= {} & BRW_{K_1}(pad(A) \| pad(P_R) \| L) + q(K_1) \cdot K_1^{m+1},
\end{aligned}
$$

and thus

$$K_1 \in \mathcal{W} \bigcup \{0\} \iff H_{K_1}(A', P'_R) = H_{K_1}(A, P_R). \tag{13}$$

Moreover, with $H_{K_1}(A', P'_R) = H_{K_1}(A, P_R)$, let $P = V \| P_R, P' = V \| P'_R$ where $V \in \{0,1\}^{n-\tau}$, and thus

$$C'_L = C_L, \tag{14}$$

where $C'_L \| C'_R = DCT.enc_{K_1, K_2, K_3}(A', P')$, $C_L \| C_R = DCT.enc_{K_1, K_2, K_3}(A, P)$.

Weak-Key Classes in DCT. For any key subset $\mathcal{W}$ of BRW-polynomial function, with the message pair $(A, P), (A', P')$ that satisfy (13) (14) found, both confidentiality and integrity of DCT collapse when $K_1 \in \mathcal{W}$. More specifically, when $K_1 \in \mathcal{W}$, the following attacks are successful:

- **Distinguishing attack.** Make two encryption queries of $(A, P), (A', P')$, and denote the ciphertexts as $C_L \| C_R, C'_L \| C'_R$ respectively. According to (14), $C_L = C'_L$ is always true in DCT, while happens with the small probability of 2^{-n} in the random case.
- **Forgery attack.** Make a single encryption query of (A, P) to get its ciphertext $C_L \| C_R$, and forge the ciphertext of (A', P') as $C_L \| (P'_R + P_R + C_R)$, where $P_R + C_R$ is the keystream which is produced by the CTRT encryption component $\mathcal{E}$, i.e. $P_R + C_R = CTRT.Gen_{K_3}(C_L, |P_R|)$.
  More specifically, let $C'_L \| C'_R = DCT.enc_{K_1,K_2,K_3}(A', P')$. By (14), $C'_L = C_L$, and then $CTRT.Gen_{K_3}(C'_L, |P'_R|) = CTRT.Gen_{K_3}(C_L, |P_R|)$ since $|P_R| = |P'_R|$. Thus $C'_R = P'_R + CTRT.Gen_{K_3}(C_L, |P'_R|) = P'_R + P_R + C_R$.

Moreover it is easy to detect whether $K_1 \in \mathcal{W} \bigcup \{0\}$. Simply make two encryption queries of $(A, P), (A', P')$ and denote the ciphertexts as $C_L \| C_R$, $C'_L \| C'_R$ respectively. Once $C'_L = C_L$, $H_{K_1}(A', P'_R) = H_{K_1}(A, P_R)$ as the block-cipher E is a PRP, and by (13), $K_1 \in \mathcal{W}$.

Besides, if $K_1 = 0$, the UHF outputs 0 for arbitrary input, and thus when $0 \notin \mathcal{W}$, by 1 more encryption query, it is able to detect either $K_1 = 0$ or $K_1 \in \mathcal{W}$. That is, make a encryption query of some input (A'', P'') for any A'' and $P'' = V \| P''_R$, and observe if its first n-bit ciphertext equals C_L.

Thus, any key subset $\mathcal{W}$ of BRW-polynomial function that $|\mathcal{W}| \geq 2$ is a weak-key class in BRW-instantiated DCT. Again, $|\mathcal{W}| \geq 2$ is required to avoid non-sense weak-key classes.

5   Conclusions

This work studies the weak-key problem of BRW-polynomial function and BRW-instantiated schemes. It is found that weak keys in BRW-polynomial function are ubiquitous, and that any key subset of BRW-polynomial which consists of at least 2 keys is a weak-key class in BRW-based cryptographic schemes like the Wegman-Carter scheme, the UHF-then-PRF scheme, DCT, etc. Similar weak-key classes also exist in more BRW-instantiated schemes [6,9,28–30]. Although the weak-key attack seems impossible to break the provable security of these schemes, the ubiquity of weak keys is a potential security risk.

Acknowledgements. The authors would like to thank the anonymous reviewers for their helpful comments and suggestions. The work of this paper is supported by the National Key Basic Research Program of China (2014CB340603) and the National Natural Science Foundation of China (Grants 61472415, 61732021, 61772519).

References

1. Abdelraheem, M.A., Beelen, P., Bogdanov, A., Tischhauser, E.: Twisted polynomials and forgery attacks on GCM. In: Oswald, E., Fischlin, M. (eds.) EUROCRYPT 2015. LNCS, vol. 9056, pp. 762–786. Springer, Heidelberg (2015). https://doi.org/10.1007/978-3-662-46800-5_29
2. Abdelraheem, M.A., Bogdanov, A., Tischhauser, E.: Weak-key analysis of poet. Cryptology ePrint Archive, Report 2014/226 (2014). http://eprint.iacr.org/2014/226
3. Abed, F., Fluhrer, S., Foley, J., Forler, C., List, E., Lucks, S., McGrew, D., Wenzel, J.: The POET family of on-line authenticated encryption schemes (2014). http://competitions.cr.yp.to/caesar-submissions.html
4. Andreeva, E., Bogdanov, A., Lauridsen, M.M., Luykx, A., Mennink, B., Tischhauser, E., Yasuda, K.: AES-COBRA (2014). http://competitions.cr.yp.to/caesar-submissions.html
5. Bernstein, D.J.: The Poly1305-AES message-authentication code. In: Gilbert, H., Handschuh, H. (eds.) FSE 2005. LNCS, vol. 3557, pp. 32–49. Springer, Heidelberg (2005). https://doi.org/10.1007/11502760_3
6. Bernstein, D.J.: Polynomial Evaluation and Message Authentication (2011). http://cr.yp.to/papers.html#pema
7. Black, J., Halevi, S., Krawczyk, H., Krovetz, T., Rogaway, P.: UMAC: fast and secure message authentication. In: Wiener [38], pp. 216–233 (1999). https://doi.org/10.1007/3-540-48405-1_14
8. Carter, L., Wegman, M.N.: Universal classes of hash functions. J. Comput. Syst. Sci. 18(2), 143–154 (1979)
9. Chakraborty, D., Mancillas-López, C.: Double ciphertext mode: a proposal for secure backup. IJACT 2(3), 271–287 (2012). https://doi.org/10.1504/IJACT.2012.045588
10. Chakraborty, D., Sarkar, P.: HCH: a new tweakable enciphering scheme using the hash-encrypt-hash approach. In: Barua, R., Lange, T. (eds.) INDOCRYPT 2006. LNCS, vol. 4329, pp. 287–302. Springer, Heidelberg (2006). https://doi.org/10.1007/11941378_21
11. Etzel, M., Patel, S., Ramzan, Z.: SQUARE hash: fast message authenication via optimized universal hash functions. In: Wiener [38], pp. 234–251 (1999). https://doi.org/10.1007/3-540-48405-1_15
12. Forler, C., List, E., Lucks, S., Wenzel, J.: Efficient beyond-birthday-bound-secure deterministic authenticated encryption with minimal stretch. In: Liu, J.K., Steinfeld, R. (eds.) ACISP 2016. LNCS, vol. 9723, pp. 317–332. Springer, Cham (2016). https://doi.org/10.1007/978-3-319-40367-0_20
13. Halevi, S., Krawczyk, H.: MMH: software message authentication in the Gbit/second rates. In: Biham, E. (ed.) FSE 1997. LNCS, vol. 1267, pp. 172–189. Springer, Heidelberg (1997). https://doi.org/10.1007/BFb0052345
14. Handschuh, H., Preneel, B.: Key-recovery attacks on universal hash function based MAC algorithms. In: Wagner, D. (ed.) CRYPTO 2008. LNCS, vol. 5157, pp. 144–161. Springer, Heidelberg (2008). https://doi.org/10.1007/978-3-540-85174-5_9
15. Harris, S.: The Enchilada authenticated ciphers (2014). http://competitions.cr.yp.to/caesar-submissions.html
16. Hoang, V.T., Krovetz, T., Rogaway, P.: Robust authenticated-encryption AEZ and the problem that it solves. In: Oswald, E., Fischlin, M. (eds.) EUROCRYPT 2015. LNCS, vol. 9056, pp. 15–44. Springer, Heidelberg (2015). https://doi.org/10.1007/978-3-662-46800-5_2

17. IEEE Std 1619.2-2010: IEEE standard for wide-block encryption for shared storage media (2011)
18. Krawczyk, H.: LFSR-based hashing and authentication. In: Desmedt, Y.G. (ed.) CRYPTO 1994. LNCS, vol. 839, pp. 129–139. Springer, Heidelberg (1994). https://doi.org/10.1007/3-540-48658-5_15
19. McGrew, D.A., Fluhrer, S.R.: The extended codebook (XCB) mode of operation. IACR Cryptology ePrint Archive 2004, 278 (2004). http://eprint.iacr.org/2004/278
20. McGrew, D.A., Viega, J.: The Galois/Counter mode of operation (GCM) (2004). http://csrc.nist.gov/groups/ST/toolkit/BCM/
21. McGrew, D.A., Viega, J.: The security and performance of the Galois/Counter mode of operation (full version). IACR Cryptology ePrint Archive 2004, 193 (2004). http://eprint.iacr.org/2004/193
22. Mennink, B.: Weak keys for AEZ, and the external key padding attack. In: Handschuh, H. (ed.) CT-RSA 2017. LNCS, vol. 10159, pp. 223–237. Springer, Cham (2017). https://doi.org/10.1007/978-3-319-52153-4_13
23. Morales-Luna, G.: On formal expressions of BRW-polynomials. IACR Cryptology ePrint Archive 2013, 3 (2013). http://eprint.iacr.org/2013/003
24. Peyrin, T., Seurin, Y.: Counter-in-tweak: authenticated encryption modes for tweakable block ciphers. In: Robshaw, M., Katz, J. (eds.) CRYPTO 2016. LNCS, vol. 9814, pp. 33–63. Springer, Heidelberg (2016). https://doi.org/10.1007/978-3-662-53018-4_2
25. Procter, G., Cid, C.: On weak keys and forgery attacks against polynomial-based MAC schemes. In: Moriai, S. (ed.) FSE 2013. LNCS, vol. 8424, pp. 287–304. Springer, Heidelberg (2014). https://doi.org/10.1007/978-3-662-43933-3_15
26. Rabin, M.O., Winograd, S.: Fast evaluation of polynomials by rational preparation. Commun. Pure Appl. Math. 25(4), 433–458 (1972)
27. Saarınen, M.-J.O.: Cycling attacks on GCM, GHASH and other polynomial MACs and hashes. In: Canteaut, A. (ed.) FSE 2012. LNCS, vol. 7549, pp. 216–225. Springer, Heidelberg (2012). https://doi.org/10.1007/978-3-642-34047-5_13
28. Sarkar, P.: Efficient tweakable enciphering schemes from (block-wise) universal hash functions. IEEE Trans. Inf. Theory 55(10), 4749–4760 (2009). https://doi.org/10.1109/TIT.2009.2027487
29. Sarkar, P.: Tweakable enciphering schemes using only the encryption function of a block cipher. Inf. Process. Lett. 111(19), 945–955 (2011). https://doi.org/10.1016/j.ipl.2011.06.014
30. Sarkar, P.: Modes of operations for encryption and authentication using stream ciphers supporting an initialisation vector. Crypt. Commun. 6(3), 189–231 (2014). https://doi.org/10.1007/s12095-013-0097-7
31. Shoup, V.: Sequences of games: a tool for taming complexity in security proofs. IACR Cryptology ePrint Archive 2004, 332 (2004). http://eprint.iacr.org/2004/332
32. Stinson, D.R.: Universal hashing and authentication codes. In: Feigenbaum, J. (ed.) CRYPTO 1991. LNCS, vol. 576, pp. 74–85. Springer, Heidelberg (1992). https://doi.org/10.1007/3-540-46766-1_5
33. Stinson, D.R.: On the connections between universal hashing, combinatorial designs and error-correcting codes. In: Electronic Colloquium on Computational Complexity (ECCC), vol. 2, no. 52 (1995). http://eccc.hpi-web.de/eccc-reports/1995/TR95-052/index.html

34. Sun, Z., Wang, P., Zhang, L.: Weak-key and related-key analysis of hash-counter-hash tweakable enciphering schemes. In: Foo, E., Stebila, D. (eds.) ACISP 2015. LNCS, vol. 9144, pp. 3–19. Springer, Cham (2015). https://doi.org/10.1007/978-3-319-19962-7_1
35. Wang, P., Feng, D., Wu, W.: HCTR: a variable-input-length enciphering mode. In: Feng, D., Lin, D., Yung, M. (eds.) CISC 2005. LNCS, vol. 3822, pp. 175–188. Springer, Heidelberg (2005). https://doi.org/10.1007/11599548_15
36. Wang, P., Li, Y., Zhang, L., Zheng, K.: Related-key almost universal hash functions: definitions, constructions and applications. In: Peyrin, T. (ed.) FSE 2016. LNCS, vol. 9783, pp. 514–532. Springer, Heidelberg (2016). https://doi.org/10.1007/978-3-662-52993-5_26
37. Wegman, M.N., Carter, L.: New hash functions and their use in authentication and set equality. J. Comput. Syst. Sci. 22(3), 265–279 (1981)
38. Wiener, M. (ed.): CRYPTO 1999. LNCS, vol. 1666. Springer, Heidelberg (1999). https://doi.org/10.1007/3-540-48405-1
39. Zhu, B., Tan, Y., Gong, G.: Revisiting MAC forgeries, weak keys and provable security of galois/counter mode of operation. In: Abdalla, M., Nita-Rotaru, C., Dahab, R. (eds.) CANS 2013. LNCS, vol. 8257, pp. 20–38. Springer, Cham (2013). https://doi.org/10.1007/978-3-319-02937-5_2

Lightweight MDS Serial-Type Matrices with Minimal Fixed XOR Count

Dylan Toh[1], Jacob Teo[1], Khoongming Khoo[2], and Siang Meng Sim[2,3]([⊠])

[1] NUS High School of Math and Science, Singapore, Singapore
[2] DSO National Laboratories, Singapore, Singapore
kkhoongm@dso.org.sg, ssim011@e.ntu.edu.sg
[3] Nanyang Technological University, Singapore, Singapore

Abstract. Many block ciphers and hash functions require the diffusion property of Maximum Distance Separable (MDS) matrices. Serial matrices with the MDS property obtain a trade-off between area requirement and clock cycle performance to meet the needs of lightweight cryptography. In this paper, we propose a new class of serial-type matrices called Diagonal-Serial Invertible (DSI) matrices with the sparse property. These matrices have a fixed XOR count (contributed by the connecting XORs) which is half that of existing matrices. We prove that for matrices of order 4, our construction gives the matrix with the lowest possible fixed XOR cost. We also introduce the Reversible Implementation (RI) property, which allows the inverse matrix to be implemented using the similar hardware resource as the forward matrix, even when the two matrices have different finite field entries. This allows us to search for serial-type matrices which are lightweight in both directions by just focusing on the forward direction. We obtain MDS matrices which outperform existing lightweight (involutory) matrices.

Keywords: MDS matrix · Serial matrix · Lightweight cryptography
XOR count

1 Introduction

Diffusion [1] is a key property of a secure cipher which refers to the propagation of changes in the input to the entire output. In many ciphers, the diffusion property is brought about by a linear diffusion matrix as part of a round function component. Effectively, a modification of even a single bit in the input results in drastic changes in the output, providing stronger defence against differential and linear cryptanalysis attacks. Hence, matrices known as Maximum Distance Separable (MDS) matrices are commonly used in ciphers [2–5] to maximise the diffusion ability of the diffusion layer. They have the property that the diffusion provided is optimal.

S. M. Sim—Supported by the Singapore National Research Foundation Fellowship 2012 (NRF-NRFF2012-06).

© Springer International Publishing AG, part of Springer Nature 2018
A. Joux et al. (Eds.): AFRICACRYPT 2018, LNCS 10831, pp. 51–71, 2018.
https://doi.org/10.1007/978-3-319-89339-6_4

However, the guarantee of strong diffusion power often results in a high hardware computation cost. Thus, it is necessary to find lightweight MDS matrices that can be incorporated into ciphers while minimising hardware requirements and maximising efficiency. However, due to the size of the search space it is impossible to perform a naive exhaustive search. Thus, various constructions [6–9] have been studied in order to narrow the search space to obtain lightweight MDS matrices. Other methods have also been proposed to increase overall efficiency.

One example is so-called *serial matrices* [5], which utilise a trade-off to reduce hardware requirement while incurring additional time cost. These matrices have the property that their k-th power is MDS (k-MDS), thus by applying the matrix k times in a series of k clock cycles, diffusion ability can still be maximised. [7] proposed the idea of cyclic matrices (generalisation of circulant matrices) in a serial-based implementation to simulate serial matrix implementation and to achieve low hardware cost. In both cases, the trade-off area (XOR count) with throughput (number of clock cycles) is kind of balance and proportional, reducing the XOR count by a factor of k while increasing the clock cycle by a factor of k.

Very often, the search for lightweight diffusion matrix focused on the forward direction and paid little attention to the implementation cost of the inverse matrix (backward direction). Although there are scenarios like OFB, CFB and counter mode which only requires the block cipher encryption to be lightweight, in other cases where both encryption and decryption are required, such matrices tends to pay more for its inverse matrix. There are other works which attempt to overcome this problem by considering involution (self-inverse) matrices like in [6,7,9]. In this case, both the forward and backward direction will cost the same. However, it often comes with a higher cost because of the involution restriction.

In this work, we aim to search for new serial-type matrices which outperform existing lightweight matrices and also have efficient implementation in both forward and backward direction. This will be useful for constrained devices where lightweight implementation is required but high throughput is not necessary.

Contributions. We propose a new class of serial-type matrices known as *Diagonal-Serial Invertible* (DSI) matrices. This matrix is potentially k-MDS while maintaining a low original weight, which can increase the probability of finding lightweight matrices possessing the targeted properties. By introducing the *sparse* condition for DSI matrices, we actually made a favourable trade-off between the area and clock cycle; we reduced the XOR count by almost a factor of $2k$ at a cost of k clock cycles.

We introduce the concept of Reversible Implementation (RI) property which allows us to better understand the implementation of serial-type matrices. We show that its implementation cost for the backward direction can be as low as the forward direction, giving us the advantage of having efficient implementation for both forward and backward directions. Because of this RI property, we can focus our search on lightweight matrices in the forward direction without worrying its inverse cost or to limit our search to involution matrices.

Our construction led us to finding new lightweight serial-type matrices, which are lighter than existing diffusion matrices in serialised implementation.

Lastly, we prove for diffusion matrices of order 4 that our sparse DSI matrices achieve the lowest possible fixed cost implementation. Meaning that there does not exist other serial-type matrix construction that would be lighter than our sparse DSI construction.

Organisation. We give the preliminaries in Sect. 2, introduce our new serial-type matrix construction and its properties in Sect. 3. Next, we introduce the concept of the RI property and describe how the implementation cost of a diffusion matrix is evaluated in Sect. 4, and present our search results in Sect. 5. Finally, we prove optimality for our sparse DSI matrix in Sect. 6 and end with our conclusion and some thoughts about future work in Sect. 7.

2   Preliminaries

In this section, we give a preliminary overview of concepts and definitions used in the rest of the paper.

2.1   Finite Fields and MDS Matrices

We denote by $GF(2^n)$ the finite field with 2^n elements. It is isomorphic to polynomials in $GF(2)[X]$ modulo an irreducible polynomial $p(X)$ of degree n. The elements of $GF(2^n)$ may be written in two ways: in polynomial representation, $\sum b_i X^i$ or in bitwise representation, $b_{n-1}b_{n-2}...b_2b_1b_0$, where $b_i \in GF(2)$. For example, in $GF(2^8)$, the 8-bit string 11100001 corresponds to the polynomial $X^7 + X^6 + X^5 + 1$, written 0xe1 in hexadecimal.

The addition operation on $GF(2^n)$ is simply the bitwise XOR on the coefficients of the polynomial representation of the elements. The multiplication of two elements is the modulo $p(X)$ reduction of the product of the polynomial representations of the two elements. For simplicity, we append the irreducible polynomial in hexadecimal form to the finite field. For instance, suppose $p(X) = X^4 + X^1 + 1$ is the modulo reduction of the product of field elements in $GF(2^4)$, we denote the finite field as $GF(2^4)/0x13$.

Definition 1 [7]. *The **branch number** of a matrix M of order k over finite field $GF(2^n)$ is the minimum number of nonzero components of the input vector v and output vector $u = M \cdot v$ as we range over all nonzero $v \in [GF(2^n)]^k$.*

Using matrices with high branch number for the diffusion layer of block ciphers protect them against differential and linear cryptanalysis (protecting against the latter requires the transpose of the diffusion matrix instead to have a high branch number).

Definition 2 [10]. *A **maximum distance separable (MDS)** matrix of order k is a matrix that attains the optimal branch number $k + 1$.*

Fixing the input vector to have only 1 nonzero element, the output vector will have at best, all its k entries nonzero; therefore the branch number is bounded above by $k + 1$.

Definition 3. *A matrix of order k is **q-MDS** if it is MDS when raised to the q-th power.*

Such matrix is also known as **recursive MDS** matrix, but since we will be discussing cases where $q \neq k$ (see Sect. 6), we chose the notation q-MDS for clearer indication of the number of iterations.

The following proposition is used to check if a matrix satisfies the MDS property:

Proposition 1 [11]. *A matrix is MDS if and only if its square submatrices are all nonsingular.*

Proposition 2 [7]. *For any permutation matrices P and Q, the branch numbers of these two matrices M and PMQ are the same.*

This provides some symmetry in terms of general construction in the later parts of the paper.

2.2   XOR Count

The way to perceive and estimate the implementation cost of the diffusion layer has evolved over time. It was a common belief that finite field elements with low Hamming weight has lower hardware implementation cost. In 2014, the authors of [12] proposed estimating the implementation cost by counting the number of XOR gates (denoted as d-XOR [13]) needed to implement the field element from its multiplication matrix. They also showed that, unlike the common belief, higher Hamming weight elements may also have low implementation cost. Several work [6,7,9,14] adopted this metric to estimate the implementation cost of diffusion matrix. An improved metric s-XOR [13], proposed by authors of [13] was introduced to better gauge the implementation cost in practice. In this paper, we adopt this new metric to calculate the implementation cost of the diffusion layer.

Definition 4 [13]. *The **s-XOR count** of an element α in $GF(2^n)/p(X)$ (where $p(X)$ is the generator polynomial), is the minimum number of XOR operations for implementing the field element multiplication, where the minimum is taken over all implementation sequences.*

Example 1 [13]. Given the finite field $GF(2^3)/\text{0xb}$, the multiplication of $\alpha = 7$ seen as $(1, 1, 1) \in [GF(2)]^3$ can be computed by:

$$(1, 1, 1)(b_2, b_1, b_0) = (b_2 \oplus b_0, b_2 \oplus b_1, b_1) \oplus (b_1, b_2 \oplus b_0, b_2) \oplus (b_2, b_1, b_0)$$
$$= (b_1 \oplus b_0, b_0, b_2 \oplus b_1 \oplus b_0),$$

where (b_2, b_1, b_0) is an arbitrary element of $GF(2^3) \cong (GF(2))^3$. Expressing the same computation as a matrix multiplication, it rewrites as

$$\begin{bmatrix} 0 & 1 & 1 \\ 0 & 0 & 1 \\ 1 & 1 & 1 \end{bmatrix} \begin{bmatrix} b_2 \\ b_1 \\ b_0 \end{bmatrix} = \begin{bmatrix} b_1 \oplus b_0 \\ b_0 \\ b_2 \oplus b_1 \oplus b_0 \end{bmatrix}.$$

From the multiplication matrix, we can see that d-XOR$(\alpha) = 3$ XOR count. In practice, one can upward-rotate the input vector components, XOR the second component to the first, followed by XORing the first component to the third to obtain the same desired output. Therefore, we get s-XOR$(\alpha) = 2 <$ d-XOR(α).

In [13], the authors denoted it as s-XOR(α) to distinguish it from the metric proposed in [12] which was denoted as d-XOR(α). Since we are adopting this new metric (s-XOR), we simply use XOR(α) to be concise in this paper. In this paper, we focus on the finite fields $GF(2^4)/0x13$ and $GF(2^8)/0x1c3$, where most of the lightweight diffusion matrices are found.

3   Diagonal-Serial Invertible Matrices

First, let us recall the matrix structure of serial matrices. To distinguish it from the other serial-type matrices that we studied in this paper, we shall call this matrix a Linear Feedback Serial (LFS) matrix.

The LFS matrix $L = LFS(z_0, z_1, ..., z_{k-1})$ from [5] is of specific interest in this study. Because $LFS(z_0, z_1, ..., z_{k-1})$ corresponds to a Linear Feedback Shift Register (LFSR) where the feedback taps are given by the last row of the matrix, hence the name. Properties of the LFS matrices have been investigated in [15], among which is the lightweight expression of the inverse, L^{-1}. In particular, the expression of LFS matrix and its inverse are shown below:

$$L_{ij} = \begin{cases} z_j, & i = k-1 \\ 1, & i+1 = j \\ 0, & \text{otherwise.} \end{cases} \qquad L_{ij}^{-1} = \begin{cases} \frac{z_{j+1}}{z_0}, & i = 0, z_k = 1 \\ 1, & i = j+1 \\ 0, & \text{otherwise.} \end{cases}$$

From this expression, the authors of [15] concluded that if $z_0 = 1$, then both a LFS matrix and its inverse has the same finite field entries $z_1, z_2, \ldots, z_{k-1}$ which will lead to both matrices requiring the same hardware resource to implement. We show later in this paper a new technique that allows us to implement LFS matrix and its inverse with the same hardware resources even when $z_0 \neq 1$.

3.1   Diagonal-Serial Invertible (DSI) Matrix

Definition 5. *A **Diagonal-Serial Invertible (DSI)** matrix $D = (D_{ij})_{1 \leq i,j \leq k} \in [GF(2^n)]^{k \times k}$, is determined by 2 vectors, $\mathbf{a} = (a_i)_{1 \leq i \leq k} \in [GF(2^n)\backslash\{0\}]^k$ and $\mathbf{b} = (b_i)_{1 \leq i \leq k-1} \in [GF(2^n)]^{k-1}$, as follows[1]:*

---

[1] The indices starts from 1 for the convenience of latter discussions.

$$D_{ij} = \begin{cases} a_1, & i = 1, j = k \\ a_i, & i = j + 1 \\ b_i, & i = j \le k - 1 \\ 0, & \text{otherwise.} \end{cases}$$

The design is motivated by the $LFS(z_0, z_1, ..., z_{k-1})$ matrix construction. Keeping to the structure of a permutation matrix, the underlying intuition is that pairwise linear combinations of rows will provide a higher diffusion power. We will first prove some elementary properties of the DSI matrix:

Theorem 1. *Every DSI matrix $D = DSI(\mathbf{a}, \mathbf{b})$ is invertible.*

Proof. We have $det(D) = D_{1k} \cdot det(M_{1k}) = a_1 \cdot det(M_{1k})$ by cofactor expansion along the rightmost column (where M_{1k} is the matrix formed by removing the topmost row and rightmost column); M_{1k} is upper triangular thus its determinant is simply the product of its diagonal entries, $det(M_{1k}) = a_2 a_3 a_4 \ldots a_k$. Therefore $det(D) = a_1 a_2 a_3 \ldots a_k \ne 0$ ($\forall i, a_i \ne 0$) and D is invertible.

To express the q-th power of the general DSI matrix $D = DSI(\mathbf{a}, \mathbf{b})$, we view it as a weighted adjacency matrix to a directed graph with vertices labeled 1 to k (D_{ij} is the weight of the directed edge from vertex i to vertex j). Then for any $q \in \mathbb{N}$, we have:

$$(D^q)_{ij} = \sum_{\text{length } q \text{ paths from } i \text{ to } j} (\text{product of all weights along the path})$$

with the sum taken over all all paths of length q from vertex i to vertex j. In the above expression, we note that an edge with weight 0 will never contribute to the sum; therefore edges with weight 0 may be added or removed without consequence.

For the ease of notation, we denote $b_k = 0$, and

$$P_i(\{s_1, s_2, \ldots, s_{|S|}\}) = \sum_{p_1 + p_2 + \cdots + p_{|S|} = i; \, p_j \ge 0} s_1^{p_1} s_2^{p_2} \ldots s_{|S|}^{p_{|S|}}; \text{ then we have, for a}$$

general DSI matrix D:

$$(D^k)_{ij} = \begin{cases} P_{i-j}(\{b_t | t \in \{j, \ldots, i\}\}) \cdot \prod_{u \in \{j-1, \ldots, i\}} a_u, & i > j \\ b_i^k + \prod_{u=1}^{k} a_u, & i = j \\ P_{j-i}(\{b_t | t \in \{1, \ldots, i\} \cup \{j, \ldots, k\}\}) \cdot \prod_{u \in \{1, \ldots, i\} \cup \{j+1, \ldots, k\}} a_u, & i < j \end{cases}$$

$$(1)$$

The expressions above are obtained by drawing the associated graph, with vertices 1 to k arranged anticlockwise in a circle; the edge weighted a_i points clockwise from vertex i to vertex $i - 1$ (mod k), while the edge weighted b_i points from vertex i to itself. For $i \ne j$, a path of length k from vertex i to vertex j must take the path through the $j - i$ (mod k) clockwise edges $i \to i - 1 \to \cdots \to j$, while passing through any $i - j$ (mod k) self-pointing edges along the way. A path of length k from vertex i to itself, on the other hand, may be the one passing through all clockwise edges $i \rightarrow i - 1 \rightarrow \cdots \rightarrow i$, or the path obtained by traversing the self-pointing edge $i \rightarrow i$ for k times.

The graph also illustrates the symmetry of the matrix; the vertices may be relabeled 1 through k still in an anticlockwise fashion but starting at an arbitrary vertex, which will shift the $b_k = D_{kk} = 0$ element to another element along the main diagonal of the matrix. Note the similarity with Proposition 2, taking $Q^{-1} = P =$ (the permutation matrix corresponding to the permutation of vertices as described).

Example 2. The DSI matrix $D = DSI(\mathbf{a}, \mathbf{b})$ of order 4 is expressed below together with its associated graph, shown in Fig. 1, of which it is the weighted adjacency matrix:

$$D = \begin{pmatrix} b_1 & 0 & 0 & a_1 \\ a_2 & b_2 & 0 & 0 \\ 0 & a_3 & b_3 & 0 \\ 0 & 0 & a_4 & 0 \end{pmatrix}$$

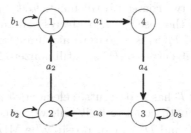

Fig. 1. Weighted adjacency graph associated with DSI matrix of order 4

Note that there is no self-pointing edge on vertex 4 because $b_4 = 0$. The fourth power can thus be expressed as shown below:

$$D^4 = \begin{pmatrix} b_1^4 + a_1 a_4 a_3 a_2 & P_1(\{b_1, b_3, b_2\}) a_1 a_4 a_3 & P_2(\{b_1, b_3\}) a_1 a_4 & P_3(\{b_1\}) a_1 \\ P_3(\{b_2, b_1\}) u_2 & b_2^4 + a_2 a_1 a_4 a_3 & P_1(\{b_2, b_1, b_3\}) a_2 a_1 a_4 & P_2(\{b_2, b_1\}) a_2 a_1 \\ P_2(\{b_3, b_2, b_1\}) a_3 a_2 & P_3(\{b_3, b_2\}) a_3 & b_3^4 + a_3 a_2 a_1 a_4 & P_1(\{b_3, b_2, b_1\}) a_3 a_2 a_1 \\ P_1(\{b_3, b_2, b_1\}) a_4 a_3 a_2 & P_2(\{b_3, b_2\}) a_4 a_3 & P_3(\{b_3\}) a_4 & a_4 a_3 a_2 a_1 \end{pmatrix}.$$

We also reach the following result:

Theorem 2. *Given DSI matrix D of order k, k is the minimum power of D for all entries to have a nonzero algebraic expression (and thus possibly MDS).*

Proof. The shortest path from vertex k to itself is the clockwise path passing through all vertices, $k \rightarrow k - 1 \rightarrow k - 2 \rightarrow \cdots \rightarrow 1 \rightarrow k$, of length k, therefore $(D^i)_{kk} = 0$ for all $i < k$. The algebraic expression of all coefficients of D^k have been evaluated above in (1).

3.2 Sparse DSI Matrix

However, for the DSI construction, pairwise linear combination of rows would generate maximum diffusion power with inherent redundancy! We can possibly further reduce the number of nonzero entries and consequently lower the fixed cost, as proposed in the following subclass of DSI matrices:

Definition 6. *A DSI matrix* $D = DSI(\mathbf{a}, \mathbf{b})$ *of order* k *is* **sparse** *if* $\mathbf{b}$ *satisfies:*
$$\begin{cases} b_2 = b_4 = b_6 = \cdots = b_{k-2} = 0, & \text{if } k \text{ is even} \\ b_2 = b_4 = b_6 = \cdots = b_{k-3} = 0, & \text{if } k \text{ is odd} \end{cases}$$

Although sparse DSI matrices do have lesser nonzero entries, a natural question to ask is whether sparse DSI matrices of order k can potentially be k-MDS. Extending the result from Theorem 2, we have the following corollary.

Corollary 1. *Sparse DSI matrices can potentially be k-MDS.*

Proof. By Definition 5, all the a_i's are nonzero. For each appearance of $P_i(S)$ in (1), we want to ensure that there exists nonzero term in the set S. For the case $i > j$, S contains at least two consecutive elements b_j, b_{j+1}, of which at least one term is not set to 0. For the case $i < j$, S always contains b_1 which is nonzero. Thus each appearance of $P_i(S)$ is a nonzero algebraic expression; therefore the algebraic expressions of all entries of D^k are still nonzero for a sparse DSI matrix D.

In fact, if DSI matrix D has 2 consecutive elements b_j, b_{j+1} (with consecutive indices modulo k) with both equal to 0, it follows from (1) that $(D^k)_{(j+1)j} = P_{k-1}(\{b_{j+1}, b_j\})a_{j+1} = 0$ and D^k cannot possibly be MDS; therefore the sparse restriction to the general DSI matrix sets the most number of entries in $\mathbf{b}$ to 0 while still allowing the possibility of D^k being MDS.

In [16], the authors proposed a new serial-type construction based on Type-II Generalized Feistel Structure (GFS). Although this matrix type is similar to our sparse DSI matrix, it is fundamentally different from ours, detailed in Sect. 6.

4 RI Property and Serial-Type Matrices

In this section, we introduce a property called the *Reversible Implementation* (RI) which allows us to understand more about the implementation of serial-type matrices and their inverse. Next, we describe how the implementation cost of the serial-type matrices and their inverse are computed.

4.1 Reversible Implementation (RI) Property

Definition 7. *Given some set of objects* S, *a function* $f : S^n \to S^n$ *has the* **Reversible Implementation (RI) property** *if there exists a sequence of transformations whereby each transformation is either a permutation of the n-tuple components, involution (self-inverse), or the transformation itself has the RI property. Such sequence of transformations is also called the RI sequence.*

Proposition 3. *If a function f has a RI sequence, then there exists an implementation of the inverse function f^{-1} that has the same implementation cost as the RI sequence.*

Proof. Given a RI sequence, we construct a sequence of transformations to implement the inverse function with the same implementation cost as the RI sequence. First, we reverse the entire sequence of transformations, that is starting from the last transformation of the RI sequence. If a transformation is some permutation of the n-tuple components, we implement the inverse permutation on the components. Since permutation is simply rewiring of the circuit in hardware, it is basically free. If a transformation is involution, we apply the exact same transformation with the same implementation cost. If a transformation has the RI property, it has some RI sequence of its own and we can recursively implement its inverse with the same implementation cost.

Example 3. The field multiplication of $7 \in \mathrm{GF}(2^3)/\mathrm{0xb}$ has the RI property as we can see from Example 1, the sequence of transformation: upward-rotate the input vector components, XOR the second component to the first component, and XOR the first component to the third component. This is an RI sequence since it consists of permutation and XOR instructions that are involutions. The inverse of this field multiplication can be implemented as follows: XOR the first component to the third component, XOR the second component to the first component, and downward-rotate the input vector components, which has the same implementation cost of 2 XORs as element 7.

In fact, under the s-XOR metric introduced in [13], we can conveniently conclude that *any nonzero finite field element has the RI property and its inverse has the same XOR count as itself* [2].

It is to note that this RI property is different from a function being involution. While being involution means the same circuit could be reused for forward and backward implementation at a cost of some multiplexers, more multiplexers might be needed to reuse the RI sequence circuit in the reverse order. Instead of reusing of circuit, our RI property is useful for identifying the implementation of the inverse requires the similar hardware resources.

4.2   RI Property in Serial-Type Matrices

The sparse matrix structure of serial-type matrices allows us to analyse the sequence of transformations easily. We illustrate the implementation sequence of the two serial-type matrices of order 4 in Fig. 2, which can also be generalised to any order k. One can observe that both LFS and DSI matrices have the RI property.

Previous, it was believed that LFS matrix has the same implementation cost for both forward and backward implementation only when $z_0 = 1$ [15]. However, under the s-XOR metric, field element multiplications have the RI property, the

---

[2] This observation has also been pointed out in [8].

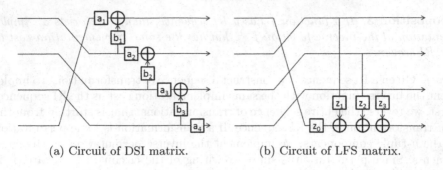

(a) Circuit of DSI matrix.   (b) Circuit of LFS matrix.

Fig. 2. Circuit of LFS and DSI matrices of order 4.

implementation cost of z_0 is actually the same as its inverse z_0^{-1}. Therefore, *LFS matrix has the same implementation cost for both forward and backward direction for any nonzero z_0.*

Similar argument holds for DSI matrix. One can implement the inverse of DSI matrix by first updating the last component with field multiplication a_k^{-1}, which as the same implementation cost as a_k. Next, multiply the last component with b_{k-1} and XOR it to the second last component. Repeat these process until the first component. Update the first component with a_1^{-1} and finally upward-rotate the components to obtain the final output vector. The entire process has the same implementation cost as the forward DSI matrix implementation.

4.3   Evaluating the Implementation Cost of Serial-Type Matrices

For round-based MDS matrices, a direct consequence of Proposition 1 is that all entries have to be nonzero. Thus, the conventional way of estimating the implementation cost of an MDS matrix over $GF(2^n)$ is to take the sum of the implementation cost of all nonzero field multiplications (so-called the *variable cost*), and add $(k-1)$ many n-bit XOR count for each row to generate the output components (so-called the *fixed cost*).

Things are a bit different for serial-type q-MDS matrices, there can be zero entries in the matrix, thus the fixed cost for each row is 1 less than the number of nonzero entries many n-bit XOR count. For the variable cost, we can apply a small technique to save some implementation cost of the field multiplication for some special cases.

Take DSI matrix of order 4 as an example, notice that if $b_1 = a_2$, we can rearrange the order of the field multiplication and the XOR operation so that we only need to compute one field multiplication and not both b_1 and a_2 separately, as shown in Fig. 3a. Thus, we only count the implementation cost of b_i when it is not equal to a_{i+1}.

Similar strategy can be applied to LFS matrices, when there are multiple z_i's of the same field element, we can first XOR these branches together before applying a single field multiplication, then XOR to the last component, Fig. 3b illustrates an example of LFS matrix of order 4. Therefore, we only need to count the implementation cost of the distinct z_i's in the last row.

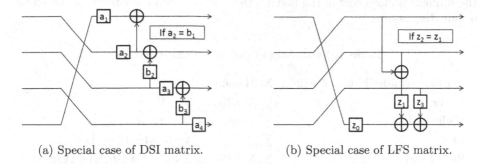

(a) Special case of DSI matrix.   (b) Special case of LFS matrix.

Fig. 3. Saving implementation cost for serial-type matrices.

While such trick can be applied to these two serial-type matrices, it is non-trivial to apply it to other types of matrices like Hadamard or circulant matrices. Thus, it remains an open question if similar trick can be applied to other matrices too.

5   Main Results

In this section, we present new serial-type k-MDS matrices which have lower XOR count than previously known MDS/k-MDS matrices. To obtain lightweight matrices, we searched through $k \times k$ sparse DSI and LFS matrices over the finite field $GF(2^8)$ defined by the irreducible polynomial 0x1c3 for $4 \leq k \leq 8$. To check if a matrix is k-MDS, we raise the matrix to power of k and recursively check that each submatrix is non-singular. Once a submatrix is singular, we exit prematurely and move on to the next candidate. Else, this candidate would be a k-MDS matrix. Besides searching directly in GF(2^8), we also use the subfield construction [12, Sect. 7.2] where we search over GF(2^4) defined by the irreducible polynomial 0x13, and interleave two copies to obtain a diffusion matrix with the same branch number over GF(2^8). The search can be completed relatively fast on a personal laptop from a few minutes when $k = 4$ to a few hours when $k = 7$. The lightweight sparse DSI and LFS k-MDS matrices are denoted by $D_{k,n}$ and $L_{k,n}$ respectively.

We reiterate that we are considering scenario where lightweight implementation is required but high throughput is not necessary. That is, we do a tradeoff for lower area at the cost of higher clock cycles. For serial-type matrices, such tradeoff is natural and the implementation cost is the XOR count of the entire matrix. For cyclic matrices, for instance circulant/left-circulant matrices, it can be implemented in a serialized manner by implementing one row of the matrix and reusing the same row [7]. Although it is non-trivial to implement Hadamard matrices in a serialized manner, we give the benefit of the doubt and assume that it can be done too. Therefore, we compare these round-based matrices by the XOR count for one of its row, see Table 1. Note that we are considering only the implementation cost of the matrix, the cost of multiplexer is out of the scope of our discussion.

Table 1. XOR count of various serialized matrices

Matrices of order k (over $GF(2^n)$)	XOR count
Cyclic	$\sum XOR(c_i) + (k-1) \cdot n$
Hadamard	$\sum XOR(h_i) + (k-1) \cdot n$
LFS	$\sum_{z_i \mid \forall j < i, z_i \neq z_j} XOR(z_i) + (k-1) \cdot n$
Sparse DSI	$\sum XOR(a_i) + \sum_{b_i \neq a_{i+1}} XOR(b_i) + \lceil k/2 \rceil \cdot n$

Where c_i's (resp. h_i's) are the entries in a row of cyclic (resp. Hadamard) matrix.

For fair comparison, we recalculated the implementation cost of the existing matrices under the same metric (s-XOR) as ours when possible. In Table 2 (resp. Table 3), we compare serialized MDS matrices and k-MDS serial-type matrices of order $4 \leq k \leq 8$ over GF(2^4) (resp. GF(2^8)) in both the forward and backward direction. In particular, we compare the DSI and LFS matrices that we found with circulant [9], left-circulant [7,8], Hadamard [6] and LFS [5,12,17] matrices. One may also consider unrolling DSI/LFS matrices to simulate round-based matrices for comparison with cyclic/Hadamard matrices in a round-based implementation scenario. That is to implement k copies of DSI/LFS matrices in series to achieve the MDS property in one clock cycle. The XOR count of all the matrices would simply be k times of what the tables have shown.

For the entries of the diffusion matrix, some literature considered invertible binary matrices rather than the finite field elements, for those cases, we indicate the entry type as GL(n, GF(2)).

5.1   Comparing Matrices Where $n = 4$

We ran our search on both sparse DSI and LFS k-MDS matrices of order $4 \leq k \leq 8$ over GF(2^4)/0x13. The results are summarised in Table 2.

In [17], the authors considered 8-MDS matrix of order 4 to extend their search for lighter diffusion matrices. Although they obtained LFS matrix with lower XOR count than other 4-MDS LFS matrices, in serial-based implementation, the number of clock cycle needed is doubled.

Although we could not find sparse DSI k-MDS matrices of order higher than 4, we would like to point out that this is quite common even for other matrix types due to the small field size. As we can see in Table 2 that there are lesser matrices that we can compare as the matrix size increases.

For circulant matrices from [9] and serial-type matrices from [16], the entries of the matrix are non-singular binary matrices of order n. In [8], the irreducible

Table 2. Comparison of MDS/k-MDS matrices for $n = 4$

k	Matrix type	Field/Ring	Forward	Backward	Reference
4	Hadamard	$GF(2^4)/\text{0x13}$	17	19	[6]
4	Involutory Hadamard	$GF(2^4)/\text{0x13}$	17	17	[6]
4	Involutory circulant	$GL(4, GF(2))$	17	17	[9]
4	Left-circulant	$GF(2^4)$	15	–	[8]
4	Circulant	$GL(4, GF(2))$	15	–	[9]
4	Left-circulant	$GF(2^4)/\text{0x13}$	15	29	[7]
4	**LFS**	$GL(4, GF(2))$	15	-	[16]
4	**LFS**	$GF(2^4)/\text{0x13}$	15	15	[12]
4	8-MDS **LFS**	$GF(2^4)/\text{0x13}$	13	13	[17]
4	**GFS**	$GL(4, GF(2))$	10	-	[16]
4	**Sparse DSI** $D_{4,4}$	$GF(2^4)/\text{0x13}$	10	10	This paper
5	IMDS left-circulant	$GF(2^4)/\text{0x13}$	27	27	[7]
5	Left-circulant	$GF(2^4)$	24	–	[8]
5	Left-circulant	$GF(2^4)/\text{0x13}$	20	26	[7]
5	**LFS**	$GL(4, GF(2))$	19	-	[16]
5	**LFS** A_{100}	$GF(2^4)/\text{0x13}$	18	18	[5]
5	**LFS** $L_{5,4}$	$GF(2^4)/\text{0x13}$	18	18	This paper, A_{100}
6	Left-circulant	$GF(2^4)/\text{0x13}$	30	40	[7]
6	**LFS** A_{144}	$GF(2^4)/\text{0x13}$	28	28	[5]
6	**LFS**	$GL(4, GF(2))$	25	-	[16]
6	**LFS** $L_{6,4}$	$GF(2^4)/\text{0x13}$	25	25	This paper
7	**LFS** A_{196}	$GF(2^4)/\text{0x13}$	31	31	[5]
7	**LFS**	$GL(4, GF(2))$	30	-	[16]
7	**LFS** $L_{7,4}$	$GF(2^4)/\text{0x13}$	30	30	This paper
8	Involutory Hadamard	$GF(2^4)/\text{0x13}$	53	53	[6]
8	Hadamard	$GF(2^4)/\text{0x13}$	48	56	[6]
8	**LFS** A_{256}	$GF(2^4)/\text{0x13}$	47	47	[5]
8	**LFS**	$GF(2^4)/\text{0x13}$	41	41	[12]
8	**LFS**	$GL(4, GF(2))$	37	-	[16]
8	**LFS** $L_{8,4}$	$GF(2^4)/\text{0x13}$	36	36	This paper

polynomial is not defined. Therefore, it is unclear how we can obtain the inverse of those matrices.

Besides obtaining the same LFS matrix as [5] for $k = 5$, we found new lightweight serial-type k-MDS matrices that outperform or match the existing lightweight matrices. For matrices over $GF(2^4)$, the room for improvement is small due to the small field size, one can see larger improvements for matrices over $GF(2^8)$ in the next section.

Table 3. Comparison of MDS/k-MDS matrices for $n = 8$

k	Matrix type	Field/Ring	Forward	Backward	Reference
4	Hadamard	$[GF(2^4)/0x13]^2$	2×17	2×19	[6]
4	Involutory Hadamard	$[GF(2^4)/0x13]^2$	2×17	2×17	[6]
4	Involutory circulant	$GL(8, GF(2))$	33	33	[9]
4	**LFS**	$GF(2^8)/0x11d$	33	33	[12]
4	Left-circulant	$GF(2^8)/0x1c3$	31	75	[7]
4	Left-circulant	$GF(2^8)$	30	-	[8]
4	8-MDS **LFS**	$GF(2^8)/0x1c3$	27	27	[17]
4	Circulant	$GL(8, GF(2))$	27	-	[9]
4	**LFS**	$GL(8, GF(2))$	27	-	[16]
4	**Sparse DSI** $D_{4,8}$	$GF(2^8)/0x1c3$	22	22	This paper
4	**Sparse DSI** $[D_{4,4}]^2$	$[GF(2^4)/0x13]^2$	2×10	2×10	This paper
4	**GFS**	$GL(8, GF(2))$	18	-	[16]
5	IMDS left-circulant	$GF(2^8)/0x165$	65	65	[7]
5	Left-circulant	$GF(2^8)/0x1c3$	42	90	[7]
5	Left-circulant	$GF(2^8)$	40	-	[8]
5	**LFS**	$GL(8, GF(2))$	35	-	[16]
5	**Sparse DSI** $D_{5,8}$	$GF(2^8)/0x1c3$	31	31	This paper
6	IMDS left-circulant	$GF(2^8)/0x165$	77	77	[7]
6	**LFS** A_{288}	$GF(2^8)/0x11b$	57	57	[5]
6	Left-circulant	$GF(2^8)/0x1c3$	55	115	[7]
6	Left-circulant	$GF(2^8)$	54	-	[8]
6	**LFS**	$GL(8, GF(2))$	45	-	[16]
6	**GFS**	$GF(2^8)$	≥ 42	-	[16]
6	**Sparse DSI** $D_{6,8}$	$GF(2^8)/0x1c3$	31	31	This paper
7	IMDS left-circulant	$GF(2^8)/0x139$	107	107	[7]
7	Left-circulant	$GF(2^8)/0x1c3$	66	120	[7]
7	Left-circulant	$GF(2^8)$	64	-	[8]
7	**LFS**	$GL(8, GF(2))$	54	-	[16]
7	**Sparse DSI** $D_{7,8}$	$GF(2^8)/0x1c3$	54	54	This paper
8	Involutory Hadamard	$GF(2^8)/0x1c3$	96	96	[6]
8	Hadamard	$GF(2^8)/0x1c3$	88	179	[6]
8	Left-circulant	$GF(2^8)$	82	-	[8]
8	Left-circulant	$GF(2^8)/0x1c3$	80	160	[7]
8	**LFS** $[L_{8,4}]^2$	$[GF(2^4)/0x13]^2$	2×36	2×36	This paper
8	**LFS**	$GL(8, GF(2))$	65	-	[16]

5.2   Comparing Matrices Where $n = 8$

In addition to running our search on both sparse DSI and LFS k-MDS matrices of order $4 \leq k \leq 8$ over $GF(2^8)/0x1c3$, we also considered the subfield construction [12, Sect. 7.2] where we use 2 copies of the serial-type matrices over $GF(2^4)/0x13$, denoted by $[\cdot]^2$, hence doubling the XOR count[3]. The results are summarised in Table 3.

Similar to the case $n = 4$, it is unclear how the inverse of the matrices from [8,9,16] are obtained. In [17], the authors considered 8-MDS matrix of order 4 to have lower XOR count. However, in serial-based implementation, this results in more clock cycles and higher latency compared to other serial-type matrices.

For $5 \leq k \leq 7$, we found sparse DSI matrices that outperform existing lightweight matrices in both forward and backward direction. For $k = 6$, the authors of [16] pointed out that there exists 6-MDS GFS matrix over finite field without giving an actual example, assuming that it can be constructed with some field element with the lowest possible XOR count of 3, we obtain, at best, an estimation of XOR count 42.

When $k = 8$, the search space for sparse DSI and LFS matrices are too large to cover and we have not found a k-MDS matrix yet. Similar problem was faced by the authors of [12] when they search for LFS matrices. Nevertheless, we can construct a competitive candidate matrix from $L_{8,4}$ using subfield construction.

Although we did not outperform the matrices from [16] for the case $k = 4, 8$, it is to note that the choice of matrix entry is different. While it is possible to search for lightweight DSI matrices over invertible binary matrices, it requires very different search strategy and it is beyond the scope of our work.

Notice that for non-involution round-based matrices, its inverse could be significantly larger. However for serial-type matrices, we do not have such problem thanks to the RI property. Thus, when the implementation of the backward direction is required, our matrices are more favourable.

The lightweight sparse DSI and LFS k-MDS matrices, denoted by $D_{k,n}$ and $L_{k,n}$ respectively, found are listed in Table 4.

6   Advantages of Sparse DSI Matrices

In this section, we look at the reasons behind why sparse DSI matrices tend to yield better results than other matrix types like Hadamard, cyclic and LFS matrices. In addition, we prove that sparse DSI matrix of order 4 has the lowest possible fixed XOR count. Since diffusion matrix of order 4 is probably the most commonly used matrix size for the diffusion layer, sparse DSI matrix is a great candidate for designing lightweight ciphers.

---

[3] We can multiply the XOR counts of all matrices in Table 2 by 2 to get matrices over $GF(2^8)$ but we do not include most of them in Table 3 to prevent congestion. But we can easily see that the best (sparse DSI) matrices we get directly from $GF(2^8)/0x1c3$ do outperform 2 copies of the best matrices over $GF(2^4)$ for $5 \leq k \leq 7$.

Table 4. Sparse DSI and LFS matrix examples. If the matrix has double digit hexadecimal entries, it belongs to $GF(2^8)/\texttt{0x1c3}$. If it has single digit hexadecimal entries, it belongs to $GF(2^4)/\texttt{0x13}$.

Order	Sparse DSI	LFS
4	$D_{4,4} = \begin{pmatrix} 1 & 0 & 0 & 1 \\ 1 & 0 & 0 & 0 \\ 0 & 1 & 0x9 & 0 \\ 0 & 0 & 0x2 & 0 \end{pmatrix}, D_{4,8} = \begin{pmatrix} 1 & 0 & 0 & 1 \\ 1 & 0 & 0 & 0 \\ 0 & 1 & 0xe1 & 0 \\ 0 & 0 & 0x02 & 0 \end{pmatrix}$	-
5	$D_{5,8} = \begin{pmatrix} 1 & 0 & 0 & 0 & 1 \\ 1 & 0 & 0 & 0 & 0 \\ 0 & 1 & 0x04 & 0 & 0 \\ 0 & 0 & 1 & 0x02 & 0 \\ 0 & 0 & 0 & 0x02 & 0 \end{pmatrix}$	$L_{5,4} = \begin{pmatrix} 0 & 1 & 0 & 0 & 0 \\ 0 & 0 & 1 & 0 & 0 \\ 0 & 0 & 0 & 1 & 0 \\ 0 & 0 & 0 & 0 & 1 \\ 0x1 & 0x2 & 0x9 & 0x9 & 0x2 \end{pmatrix}$
6	$D_{6,8} = \begin{pmatrix} 1 & 0 & 0 & 0 & 0 & 1 \\ 1 & 0 & 0 & 0 & 0 & 0 \\ 0 & 1 & 0x91 & 0 & 0 & 0 \\ 0 & 0 & 1 & 0 & 0 & 0 \\ 0 & 0 & 0 & 1 & 0x02 & 0 \\ 0 & 0 & 0 & 0 & 0x02 & 0 \end{pmatrix}$	$L_{6,4} = \begin{pmatrix} 0 & 1 & 0 & 0 & 0 & 0 \\ 0 & 0 & 1 & 0 & 0 & 0 \\ 0 & 0 & 0 & 1 & 0 & 0 \\ 0 & 0 & 0 & 0 & 1 & 0 \\ 0 & 0 & 0 & 0 & 0 & 1 \\ 0x1 & 0xd & 0x9 & 0x4 & 0x9 & 0xd \end{pmatrix}$
7	$D_{7,8} = \begin{pmatrix} 0x1c & 0 & 0 & 0 & 0 & 0 & 1 \\ 1 & 0 & 0 & 0 & 0 & 0 & 0 \\ 0 & 1 & 0x02 & 0 & 0 & 0 & 0 \\ 0 & 0 & 0x02 & 0 & 0 & 0 & 0 \\ 0 & 0 & 0 & 1 & 0xb5 & 0 & 0 \\ 0 & 0 & 0 & 0 & 1 & 0xe1 & 0 \\ 0 & 0 & 0 & 0 & 0 & 0xe1 & 0 \end{pmatrix}$	$L_{7,4} = \begin{pmatrix} 0 & 1 & 0 & 0 & 0 & 0 & 0 \\ 0 & 0 & 1 & 0 & 0 & 0 & 0 \\ 0 & 0 & 0 & 1 & 0 & 0 & 0 \\ 0 & 0 & 0 & 0 & 1 & 0 & 0 \\ 0 & 0 & 0 & 0 & 0 & 1 & 0 \\ 0 & 0 & 0 & 0 & 0 & 0 & 1 \\ 0x1 & 0x2 & 0x7 & 0x1 & 0x1 & 0x7 & 0x2 \end{pmatrix}$
8	-	$L_{8,4} = \begin{pmatrix} 0 & 1 & 0 & 0 & 0 & 0 & 0 & 0 \\ 0 & 0 & 1 & 0 & 0 & 0 & 0 & 0 \\ 0 & 0 & 0 & 1 & 0 & 0 & 0 & 0 \\ 0 & 0 & 0 & 0 & 1 & 0 & 0 & 0 \\ 0 & 0 & 0 & 0 & 0 & 1 & 0 & 0 \\ 0 & 0 & 0 & 0 & 0 & 0 & 1 & 0 \\ 0 & 0 & 0 & 0 & 0 & 0 & 0 & 1 \\ 0x1 & 0xe & 0x2 & 0xd & 0x9 & 0xd & 0x2 & 0xe \end{pmatrix}$

6.1   Reducing the Fixed XOR Count

The biggest limitation to MDS matrix was the fixed XOR cost. For matrices like Hadamard or cyclic matrices, a necessary condition for a matrix to be MDS is not to have any zero entries. This means that for each row of the matrix, there are up to k finite field multiplications as variable cost (some may be element 1 which is free), and these k components have to be summed together, incurring a fixed cost of $(k-1) \cdot n$ XOR count.

While most of the existing work focused on reducing the variable cost by considering various type of matrix structure, LFS matrix was introduced as a trade-off between hardware implementation cost and clock cycle. However, the fixed cost in the last row of the LFS matrix remains the same as we can see from the following:

Theorem 3. *If a LFS matrix is k-MDS, then $z_i \neq 0$ for all i.*

Due to space constraint, we leave the proof to the full version[4].

This means that the fixed cost of a LFS k-MDS matrix is necessarily $(k-1)\cdot n$, similar to the fixed cost of a row of MDS Hadamard or cyclic matrix. However, we managed to overcome this limitation by using sparse DSI matrix. The fundamental reason is that sparse DSI matrix can have lesser connecting XORs than other existing matrix structures while still be potentially k-MDS.

As we can see from Table 1, the fixed XOR count of a sparse DSI matrix (contributed by the connecting XORs independent of the choice of matrix entries) is approximately half that of cyclic, Hadamard and LFS matrices. Although there are more a_i and b_i entries in a DSI matrix than in a row of the other matrices, the overall XOR count is greatly compensated by the fact that the fixed XOR count is halved. This is especially so if we can keep the XOR count of a_i and b_i down by choosing them to be 1 or other very lightweight elements. As an example, the lightest sparse DSI k-MDS matrix we found for $n = 8$ and $k = 6$ has a total XOR count of 31, this is already less than the fixed XOR count of cyclic, Hadamard and LFS matrices which is $(6-1)\cdot 8 = 40$. Therefore when we search for lightweight sparse DSI or LFS k-MDS matrices, if we find sparse DSI k-MDS matrix that has XOR count lesser than the fixed cost of LFS matrices, we do not have to run our search on LFS matrices in hope for finding lighter matrices.

In Comparison with GFS Matrix. While it seems that sparse DSI matrix is similar to GFS matrix proposed in [16], sparse DSI matrix has two advantages over GFS matrix. Firstly, GFS matrix only exists for even order while our DSI matrix exists for all sizes, thus we can achieve improvements on some parameters that was not achievable by GFS matrix. Secondly, the technique mentioned in Sect. 4.3 could not be applied to GFS matrix due to the nature of its construction, thus losing the advantage that LFS and DSI matrices have.

6.2   Optimal Serial-Type Matrix of Order 4

It is natural to wonder if it is possible to achieve even lower fixed cost by considering other serial type matrix structure. Here, we prove that it is not possible for serial-type matrices of order 4. Before that, we state some lemmas that are useful for our proof.

Lemma 1. *If diffusion matrix of order k is MDS, then for every component u_i of the output vector $u \in [\mathrm{GF}(2^n)]^k$, it is some linear combination of all the input components v_i's.*

Proof. Suppose there is an output component u_y that is a linear combination of all input components except v_x. I.e. $u_y = \sum_{i=1}^{k} a_i \cdot v_i$, where $a_i \in GF(2^n)$ and $a_x = 0$. An input vector with all components zero except v_x nonzero has an output vector with at most $k-1$ nonzero components (since u_y is zero), which contradicts that the diffusion matrix is MDS.

---

[4] https://eprint.iacr.org/2017/1084.

Using Lemma 1, we can have the following necessary condition for a serial-type matrices.

1. A necessary condition for serial-type matrices to be MDS when raised to some power q is that every output components is some linear combination of all the input components after q iterations.

The following is a special case of Proposition 2 for serial-type matrices.

Lemma 2. *For any permutation matrices P, the branch numbers of these two matrices M and $P^{-1}MP$ are the same when raised to some power q.*

Proof. When raised to the power of q, we have M^q and $P^{-1}M^qP$. By Proposition 2, they have the same branch number.

For sparse DSI matrices of order 4 over $GF(2^n)$, there are 2 rows with 2 nonzero components, meaning there is a fixed cost of $2n$ XOR count. To achieve lower fixed cost, one has to consider some serial-type matrix structure with only 1 row with 2 nonzero components, denoted as One XOR Serial (OXS) matrices. In addition, when raised to the power of $q \leq 8$, OXS matrices have to be potentially MDS[5].

In a nutshell, we want to prove the following theorem:

Theorem 4. *There does not exist OXS matrix of order 4 that is q-MDS, where $q \leq 8$.*

Proof. As seen in Sect. 4.2, serial-type matrices can be described as some bit permutation followed by an XOR layer. Without loss of generality, we consider the general circuit structure of OXS matrices as in Fig. 4a.

Among the 4! possible bit permutations, there are only two permutations that satisfy Condition 1 when $q \leq 8$, namely $(1\ 2\ 3\ 4)$[6] and $(1\ 2\ 4\ 3)$. Note that they are related by permutation $P = (3\ 4)$, as shown in the following:

$$\begin{pmatrix} b & 0 & 0 & a \\ c & 0 & 0 & 0 \\ 0 & d & 0 & 0 \\ 0 & 0 & e & 0 \end{pmatrix} = \begin{pmatrix} 1 & 0 & 0 & 0 \\ 0 & 1 & 0 & 0 \\ 0 & 0 & 0 & 1 \\ 0 & 0 & 1 & 0 \end{pmatrix} \begin{pmatrix} * & 0 & * & 0 \\ * & 0 & 0 & 0 \\ 0 & 0 & 0 & * \\ 0 & * & 0 & 0 \end{pmatrix} \begin{pmatrix} 1 & 0 & 0 & 0 \\ 0 & 1 & 0 & 0 \\ 0 & 0 & 0 & 1 \\ 0 & 0 & 1 & 0 \end{pmatrix},$$

where $*$ is nonzero entry.

By Lemma 2, they have the same branch number. Therefore, we only need to analyse the first permutation, see Fig. 4b for the circuit.

To show that it is not q-MDS where $q \leq 8$, we show that there exists some nonzero input and output vectors pair which has at most 4 nonzero components. The vectors are expressed in terms of the nonzero entries of the OXS matrix.

---

[5] Given that sparse DSI matrices of order 4 can be 4-MDS, having $q > 8$ would be a bad trade-off between area and clock cycle.

[6] $(1\ 2\ 3\ 4)$ is a cycle permutation expression, where the component in the 1st position goes to 2nd position, 2nd to 3rd, 3rd to 4th, and finally the component in the last position goes to the 1st position.

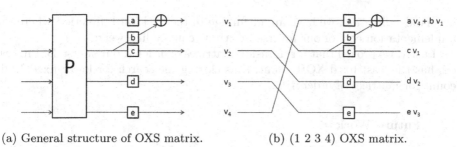

(a) General structure of OXS matrix.   (b) (1 2 3 4) OXS matrix.

Fig. 4. OXS matrix circuit structure, where P is bit permutation and a, b, c, d, e are field multiplications.

For $q \leq 7$, consider the input vector $(0, 1, b^{-1}d, 0)^T$. The resultant vectors after each iteration are

$$
\begin{pmatrix} 0 \\ 1 \\ b^{-1}d \\ 0 \end{pmatrix} \xrightarrow{i=1} \begin{pmatrix} 0 \\ 0 \\ d \\ b^{-1}de \end{pmatrix} \xrightarrow{i=2} \begin{pmatrix} ab^{-1}de \\ 0 \\ 0 \\ de \end{pmatrix} \xrightarrow{i=3} \begin{pmatrix} 0 \\ * \\ 0 \\ 0 \end{pmatrix} \xrightarrow{i=4} \begin{pmatrix} 0 \\ 0 \\ * \\ 0 \end{pmatrix} \xrightarrow{i=5} \begin{pmatrix} 0 \\ 0 \\ 0 \\ * \end{pmatrix} \xrightarrow{i=6} \begin{pmatrix} * \\ 0 \\ 0 \\ 0 \end{pmatrix} \xrightarrow{i=7} \begin{pmatrix} * \\ * \\ 0 \\ 0 \end{pmatrix}.
$$

By Definition 1, it is not MDS when raised to the power of up to 7.

For $q = 8$, consider the input vector

$$(0, a^{-2}b^{-1}c^{-1}d^{-2}e^{-2} + a^{-3}b^3c^{-2}d^{-3}e^{-3}, a^{-3}b^2c^{-2}d^{-2}e^{-3}, 0)^T.$$

After 8 iterations, we obtain $(0, b^{-1}c, 0, a^{-1}b)$.

By Definition 1, it is not MDS when raised to the power of 8.

This concludes that our sparse DSI of order 4 has the least fixed XOR count.

7   Conclusion and Future Work

7.1   Conclusion

In this paper, we have proposed a new class of matrices, DSI matrices, and presented several properties and results of these matrices. We also proposed a specific form of DSI matrices, in particular sparse DSI matrices, that have a favourable trade-off of area with throughput (we gain more reduction in hardware area than the increment in the clock cycle).

Using the newly introduced RI property, we can show that the inverse of the serial-type matrices can be of the same cost as the forward direction. This is particularly useful for scenarios where the decryption process is needed as one do not have to pay more for implementing the backward direction of the diffusion matrix.

We presented new lightweight sparse DSI and LFS k-MDS matrices that outperform existing lightweight matrices. Not only do our matrices perform better in forward direction, we have an advantage in the backward direction where the implementation cost of our inverse matrix is equally lightweight.

Lastly, we proved that for diffusion matrices of order 4, our sparse DSI matrices has the least fixed XOR count, thus closing the search for lower fixed XOR count for matrices of order 4.

7.2 Future Work

In the future, we aim to further optimise the search for higher-order sparse DSI k-MDS matrices. It is still an open problem whether such a matrix exists but if it does, we think it will be competitive against existing MDS matrix construction by virtue of having a lower fixed XOR count. Another direction is to search for DSI matrix with invertible binary matrices as entries, which might yield better results.

We also aim to find minimal fixed XOR count for serial-type matrix structure of higher order. We believe that sparse DSI matrices might also be the least fixed cost serial-type matrices for order larger than 4.

References

1. Shannon, C.E.: Communication theory of secrecy systems. Bell Syst. Tech. J. **28**(4), 656–715 (1949)
2. Daemen, J., Rijmen, V.: The Design of Rijndael: AES - The Advanced Encryption Standard. Information Security and Cryptography. Springer, Heidelberg (2002). https://doi.org/10.1007/978-3-662-04722-4
3. Aoki, K., Ichikawa, T., Kanda, M., Matsui, M., Moriai, S., Nakajima, J., Tokita, T.: *Camellia*: a 128-bit block cipher suitable for multiple platforms — design and analysis. In: Stinson, D.R., Tavares, S. (eds.) SAC 2000. LNCS, vol. 2012, pp. 39–56. Springer, Heidelberg (2001). https://doi.org/10.1007/3-540-44983-3_4
4. Guo, J., Peyrin, T., Poschmann, A., Robshaw, M.J.B.: The LED block cipher. In: CHES, pp. 326–341 (2011)
5. Guo, J., Peyrin, T., Poschmann, A.: The PHOTON family of lightweight hash functions. In: Rogaway, P. (ed.) CRYPTO 2011. LNCS, vol. 6841, pp. 222–239. Springer, Heidelberg (2011). https://doi.org/10.1007/978-3-642-22792-9_13
6. Sim, S.M., Khoo, K., Oggier, F., Peyrin, T.: Lightweight MDS involution matrices. Cryptology ePrint Archive, Report 2015/258 (2015). http://eprint.iacr.org/2015/258
7. Liu, M., Sim, S.M.: Lightweight MDS generalized circulant matrices (full version). Cryptology ePrint Archive, Report 2016/186 (2016). http://eprint.iacr.org/2016/186
8. Beierle, C., Kranz, T., Leander, G.: Lightweight multiplication in $GF(2^n)$ with applications to MDS matrices. Cryptology ePrint Archive, Report 2016/119 (2016). http://eprint.iacr.org/2016/119
9. Li, Y., Wang, M.: On the construction of lightweight circulant involutory MDS matrices. In: Peyrin, T. (ed.) FSE 2016. LNCS, vol. 9783, pp. 121–139. Springer, Heidelberg (2016). https://doi.org/10.1007/978-3-662-52993-5_7

10. Vaudenay, S.: On the need for multipermutations: cryptanalysis of MD4 and SAFER. In: Preneel, B. (ed.) FSE 1994. LNCS, vol. 1008, pp. 286–297. Springer, Heidelberg (1995). https://doi.org/10.1007/3-540-60590-8_22
11. Mattson Jr., H.F.: The theory of error-correcting codes (F. J. MacWilliams and N. J. A. Sloane). SIAM Rev. **22**(4), 513–519 (1980)
12. Khoo, K., Peyrin, T., Poschmann, A.Y., Yap, H.: FOAM: searching for hardware-optimal SPN structures and components with a fair comparison. Cryptology ePrint Archive, Report 2014/530 (2014). http://eprint.iacr.org/2014/530
13. Jean, J., Peyrin, T., Sim, S.M.: Optimizing implementations of lightweight building blocks. Cryptology ePrint Archive, Report 2017/101 (2017). http://eprint.iacr.org/2017/101
14. Sarkar, S., Syed, H.: Lightweight diffusion layer: importance of toeplitz matrices. IACR Trans. Symmetric Cryptol. **2016**(1), 95–113 (2016)
15. Gupta, K.C., Ray, I.G.: On constructions of MDS matrices from companion matrices for lightweight cryptography. Cryptology ePrint Archive, Report 2013/056 (2013). http://eprint.iacr.org/2013/056
16. Wu, S., Wang, M., Wu, W.: Recursive diffusion layers for (lightweight) block ciphers and hash functions. In: Knudsen, L.R., Wu, H. (eds.) SAC 2012. LNCS, vol. 7707, pp. 355–371. Springer, Heidelberg (2013). https://doi.org/10.1007/978-3-642-35999-6_23
17. Sarkar, S., Syed, H., Sadhukhan, R., Mukhopadhyay, D.: Lightweight design choices for LED-like block ciphers. In: Patra, A., Smart, N.P. (eds.) INDOCRYPT 2017. LNCS, vol. 10698, pp. 267–281. Springer, Cham (2017). https://doi.org/10.1007/978-3-319-71667-1_14

Two Simple Composition Theorems
with H-coefficients

Jacques Patarin$^{(\boxtimes)}$

Laboratoire de Mathématiques de Versailles, UVSQ, CNRS,
Université Paris-Saclay, 78035 Versailles, France
`jpatarin@club-internet.fr`

Abstract. We will present two new and simple theorems that show that when we compose permutation generators with independent keys, then the "quality" of CCA security increases. These theorems (Theorems 2 and 5 of this paper) are written in terms of H-coefficients (which are nothing else, up to some normalization factors, than transition probabilities). Then we will use these theorems on the classical analysis of Random Feistel Schemes (i.e. Luby-Rackoff constructions) and we will compare the results with the coupling technique. Finally, we will show an interesting difference between 5 and 6 Random Feistel Schemes. With 5 rounds on $2n$ bits $\rightarrow 2n$ bits, when the number of q queries satisfies $\sqrt{2^n} \ll q \ll 2^n$, we have some "holes" in the H-coefficient values, i.e. some H values are much smaller than the average value of H. This property for 5 rounds does not exist any more on 6 rounds.

1 Introduction

Security amplification results for block ciphers typically state that cascading (i.e. composing with independent keys) two, or more, block ciphers gives a new block cipher that offers better security against some classes of adversaries. One of the most important composition results is the so-called "two weak make one strong" theorem. This theorem was first established up to logarithmic terms by Maurer and Pietrzak [11]. It was later tightened by Maurer et al. [12]. In 2010, Cogliati et al. have obtained simpler proofs of this result by using the so-called "H-coefficient technique" (cf. [2]). In this paper, we will prove two new, and relatively simple, composition theorems: Theorems 2 and 5 of this paper.

These theorems are written directly in term of "H-coefficients", i.e. in term of the number of generic keys that send some plaintexts on some ciphertexts. (This is the same, up to some normalization factors, than transition probabilities). We will then show how the new theorems can be useful in term of classical cryptographic security (such as CCA: adaptive chosen plaintext and ciphertext attack).

We work here in term of information theory for security, i.e. the adversary can ask only for a limited number q of queries, but the number of his (or her) computations is not limited. Interestingly, Tessaro has obtained [20] very similar

© Springer International Publishing AG, part of Springer Nature 2018
A. Joux et al. (Eds.): AFRICACRYPT 2018, LNCS 10831, pp. 72–86, 2018.
https://doi.org/10.1007/978-3-319-89339-6_5

composition results in term of improved security. However, Tessaro works with complexity theory (instead of information theory), so the results and the proofs of [20] are in fact very different from the results and the proofs of this paper. Then we will apply our new theorems on random Feistel schemes, and show an interesting difference between 5 and 6 rounds.

2 A Simple Mathematical Property

Theorem 1. *Let $x_1, \ldots, x_n$ and $y_1, \ldots, y_n$ be real numbers and let α and β be real numbers, $\alpha \geq 0$, $\beta \geq 0$ such that:*

- $\sum_{i=0}^{n} x_i = 0$.
- $\sum_{i=0}^{n} y_i = 0$.
- $\forall i,\ 1 \leq i \leq n,\ x_i \geq -\alpha$.
- $\forall i,\ 1 \leq i \leq n,\ y_i \geq -\beta$.

Then: $\sum_{i=1}^{n} x_i y_i \geq -n\alpha\beta$.

Proof.

$$\sum_{i=1}^{n} (x_i + \alpha)(y_i + \beta) \geq 0$$

$$\sum_{i=1}^{n} x_i y_i + \beta \sum_{i=1}^{n} x_i + \alpha \sum_{i=1}^{n} y_i + n\alpha\beta \geq 0$$

Now since $\sum_{i=1}^{n} x_i = 0$ and $\sum_{i=1}^{n} y_i = 0$, we obtain $\sum_{i=1}^{n} x_i y_i \geq -n\alpha\beta$. □

3 A Composition Theorem in CCA with H-coefficients

Definition 1. *Let G be a permutation generator that generates permutations from $\{0,1\}^N$ to $\{0,1\}^N$ from a set of parameters K. The values of K will be called "keys". Let q be an integer (called the "number of queries"). Let $a = (a_i)$, $1 \leq i \leq q$, be q pairwise distinct elements of $\{0,1\}^N$, and similarly let $b = (b_i)$, $1 \leq i \leq q$, be q pairwise distinct elements of $\{0,1\}^N$. Then, by definition, $H(a,b)$ denotes the number of keys $k \in K$ such that: $\forall i,\ 1 \leq i \leq q,\ G_k(a_i) = b_i$.*

Remark 1. The set K that we will use will generally be much larger than usual sets of cryptographic keys. Then G will be considered as a "generic generator".

Remark 2. $H(a,b)$ is simply denoted by H when there is no risk of confusion about the values of a and b, or when we want to speak of all these coefficients $H(a,b)$.

Definition 2. *With the same notations as above, if there exist pairwise distinct values (a_i) and pairwise distinct values (b_i), $1 \leq i \leq q$, such that $H(a,b)$ (for these a and b) is much smaller than the average value of H, then we say that there is a "Hole" in the H-coefficient values with q queries.*

Theorem 2. *Let α_1 and α_2 be two real numbers. Let G_1 and G_2 be two permutation generators (with the same key space K) such that:
For all sequences of pairwise distinct elements a_i, $1 \leq i \leq q$, and for all sequences of pairwise distinct elements b_i, $1 \leq i \leq q$, we have: $H_1 \geq \frac{|K|}{2^N(2^N-1)\ldots(2^N-q+1)}(1-\alpha_1)$ and similarly $H_2 \geq \frac{|K|}{2^N(2^N-1)\ldots(2^N-q+1)}(1-\alpha_2)$ where H_1 denotes the H coefficient for G_1 and H_2 the H coefficient for G_2.
Then:
If we compose 2 such generators G_1 and G_2 with random independent keys, for the composition generator $G' = G_2 \circ G_1$, we have: for all sequences of pairwise distinct elements a_i, $1 \leq i \leq q$, and for all sequences of pairwise distinct elements b_i, $1 \leq i \leq q$, $H' \geq \frac{|K|^2}{2^N(2^N-1)\ldots(2^N-q+1)}(1-\alpha_1\alpha_2)$, where H' denotes the H coefficient for G'.*

Proof. Let $\tilde{H}_1$ (respectively $\tilde{H}_2$) denote the mean value of H_1 (respectively H_2). We have:

$$\tilde{H}_1 = \tilde{H}_2 = \frac{|K|}{2^N(2^N-1)\ldots(2^N-q+1)}.$$

Let denote by $\tilde{H}'$ the mean value of H for $G' = G_2 \circ G_1$. We have

$$\tilde{H}' = \frac{|K|^2}{2^N(2^N-1)\ldots(2^N-q+1)}.$$

Let $a = (a_1, \ldots, a_q)$ be q pairwise distinct plaintexts, and $b = (b_1, \ldots, b_q)$ be q ciphertexts of G'. Let J be the set of all $(t_1, \ldots, t_q)$ pairwise distinct values of $\{0,1\}^N$. We have $|J| = 2^N(2^N-1)\ldots(2^N-q+1)$. For $G' = G_2 \circ G_1$, we have:

$$H(a,b) = \sum_{t \in J} H_1(a,t)H_2(t,b).$$

We also have $\sum_{t \in J} H_1(a,t) = |K|$ and $\sum_{t \in J} H_2(t,b) = |K|$ since each key sends a value a to a specific value t. We also have $|K| = \tilde{H}_1 \cdot |J| = \tilde{H}_2 \cdot |J|$. By hypothesis, we also have:

$$\forall t \in J, H_1(a,t) \geq \tilde{H}_1(1-\alpha_1) \text{ and } H_2(a,t) \geq \tilde{H}_2(1-\alpha_2).$$

$\forall t \in J$, let $x_t = \frac{H_1(a,t)}{\tilde{H}_1} - 1$ and $y_t = \frac{H_2(t,b)}{\tilde{H}_2} - 1$. $\forall t \in J$, we have $x_t \geq -\alpha_1$, and $y_t \geq -\alpha_2$, $\sum_{t \in J} x_t = 0$ and $\sum_{t \in J} y_t = 0$. Therefore, from Theorem 1, we have $\sum_{t \in J} x_t y_t \geq -|J|\alpha_1\alpha_2$. For $G' = G_2 \circ G_1$, we have:

$$\begin{aligned}
H(a,b) &= \sum_{t \in J} H_1(a,t) \cdot H_2(t,b) \\
&= \sum_{t \in J} \left(\tilde{H}_1 x_t + \tilde{H}_1\right)\left(\tilde{H}_2 y_t + \tilde{H}_2\right) \\
&= \sum_{t \in J} \tilde{H}_1 \tilde{H}_2 x_t y_t + \tilde{H}_1 \tilde{H}_2 y_t + \tilde{H}_1 \tilde{H}_2 x_t + \tilde{H}_1 \tilde{H}_2 \\
&\geq -\tilde{H}_1 \tilde{H}_2 |J|\alpha_1\alpha_2 + |J|\tilde{H}_1 \tilde{H}_2.
\end{aligned}$$

Moreover $\tilde{H}' = \frac{|K|^2}{|J|} = |J|\tilde{H}_1\tilde{H}_2$. We have proved: $H(a,b) \geq \tilde{H}'(1-\alpha_1\alpha_2)$ as claimed.

$\square$

Theorem 3. *(H-coefficient technique, sufficient condition for security against CCA)*

Let α and β be real numbers, $\alpha > 0$ and $\beta > 0$

If: There exists a subset E of $(\{0,1\}^{qN})^2$ such that

(1a) For all $(a,b) \in E$, we have:

$$H(a,b) \geq \frac{|K|}{2^{Nq}}(1-\alpha)\,\overset{\circ}{1}$$

with

$$\overset{\circ}{1} \overset{déf}{=} \frac{1}{(1-\frac{1}{2^N})(1-\frac{2}{2^N})\dots(1-\frac{q-1}{2^N})}.$$

(1b) For all CCA acting on a random permutation f of $\mathcal{P}_N$, the probability that $(a,b) \in E$ is $\geq 1 - \beta$ where (a,b) denotes here the successive $b_i = f(a_i)$ or $a_i = f^{-1}(b_i)$, $1 \leq i \leq q$, that will appear.

Then

(2) For every CCA with q queries (i.e. q chosen plaintexts or ciphertexts) we have: $\mathbf{Adv}^{PRP} \leq \alpha + \beta$ where $\mathbf{Adv}^{PRP}$ denotes the probability to distinguish $G(f_1, \dots, f_r)$ when $(f_1, \dots, f_r) \in_R K$ from a permutation $f \in_R \mathcal{P}_N$.

Proof. This theorem is proved in [16,17].   □

Corollary 1. *From Theorem 3 (H-coefficients in CCA) with $\beta = 0$, we see that we have: $\mathbf{Adv}^{PRP} \leq \alpha_1 \alpha_2$ where $\mathbf{Adv}^{PRP}$ denotes the advantage in CCA to distinguish $G_2 \circ G_1$ (when the keys are independently and randomly chosen) from a permutation $f \in_R \mathcal{P}_n$.*

By induction, we see:

Theorem 4. *Let q and k be two integers. Let $\alpha_1, \dots, \alpha_k$ be k real values. Let $G_1, \dots, G_k$ be k permutation generators such that: for all sequences of pairwise distinct elements a_i, and for all sequences of pairwise distinct elements b_i, $1 \leq i \leq q$, we have:*

$$H \geq \frac{|K|}{2^N(2^N-1)\dots(2^N-q+1)}(1-\alpha_j).$$

If we compose k such generators $G_1, \dots, G_k$ with random and independent keys, for the composition generator $G' = G_k \circ \dots \circ G_1$, we have: for all sequences of pairwise distinct elements a_i, $1 \leq i \leq q$ and for all sequences of pairwise distinct elements b_i, $1 \leq i \leq q$, $H \geq \frac{|K|}{2^N(2^N-1)\dots(2^N-q+1)}(1-\alpha_1 \dots \alpha_k)$. Therefore, from Theorem 3 with $\beta = 0$, we see that we have: $\mathbf{Adv}^{PRP} \leq \alpha_1 \dots \alpha_k$.

4   A Composition Theorem to Eliminate a "hole"

J denotes, as above, the set of all q pairwise distinct values of $\{0,1\}^N$.

Theorem 5. *Let G_1 and G_2 be two permutation generators with the same key space K. Let H_1 (respectively H_2) denotes the H-coefficients for G_1 (respectively G_2).*

If:

(1) *For all sequences of pairwise distinct elements a_i, $1 \leq i \leq q$, and for all sequences of pairwise distinct $b_i \in E_1$, $1 \leq i \leq q$, we have*

$$H_1 \geq \frac{|K|}{2^N(2^N - 1)\ldots(2^N - q + 1)}(1 - \alpha_1)$$

with $|E_1| \geq |J|(1 - \epsilon_1)$.

(2) *For all sequences of pairwise distinct elements a_i, $1 \leq i \leq q$, and for all sequences of pairwise distinct $b_i \in E_2$, $1 \leq i \leq q$, we have*

$$H_2 \geq \frac{|K|}{2^N(2^N - 1)\ldots(2^N - q + 1)}(1 - \alpha_2)$$

with $|E_2| \geq |J|(1 - \epsilon_2)$.

Then: for the composition generator $G_2^{-1} \circ G_1$, for all sequences of pairwise distinct elements a_i, and for all sequences of pairwise distinct b_i, we have

$$H' \geq \frac{|K|^2}{2^N(2^N - 1)\ldots(2^N - q + 1)}(1 - \epsilon_1 - \epsilon_2)(1 - \alpha_1)(1 - \alpha_2)$$

where H' denotes the H-coefficients for $G_2^{-1} \circ G_1$ (we have no hole). Moreover, if $E_1 = E_2$, then

$$H' \geq \frac{|K|^2}{2^N(2^N - 1)\ldots(2^N - q + 1)}(1 - \epsilon_1)(1 - \alpha_1)(1 - \alpha_2)$$

Proof. For $G' = G_2^{-1} \circ G_1$, we have: $H'(a, b) = \sum_{t \in J} H_1(a, t)H_2(t, b)$, with $\sum_{t \in J} H_1(a, t) = |K|$ and $\sum_{t \in J} H_2(t, b) = |K|$. Let $\tilde{H}_1 = \frac{|K|}{|J|}$, $\tilde{H}_2 = \frac{|K|}{|J|}$, and $\tilde{H}' = \frac{|K|^2}{|J|} = \tilde{H}_1 \tilde{H}_2 |J|$. We have: $|J| = 2^N(2^N - 1)\ldots(2^N - q + 1)$. Let $P_1 = J \backslash E_1$ and $P_2 = J \backslash E_2$. Then

$$H'(a, b) \geq \sum_{t \in J \backslash P_1 \backslash P_2} H_1(a, t)H_2(t, b)$$

$$\geq \sum_{t \in J \backslash P_1 \backslash P_2} \tilde{H}_1(1 - \alpha_1)\tilde{H}_2(1 - \alpha_2)$$

$$\geq |J \backslash P_1 \backslash P_2|\tilde{H}_1(1 - \alpha_1)\tilde{H}_2(1 - \alpha_2)$$

$$\geq |J|(1 - \epsilon_1 - \epsilon_2)\tilde{H}_1(1 - \alpha_1)\tilde{H}_2(1 - \alpha_2)$$

$$\geq \frac{|K|^2}{|J|}(1 - \epsilon_1 - \epsilon_2)(1 - \alpha_1)(1 - \alpha_2)$$

as claimed.   □

5 Comments About the Composition Theorems

These very simple theorems of composition (Theorems 2 and 5) are not very well known because the classical theorems of composition (with more difficult proofs) usually do not consider hypothesis in term of the values on the H coefficients. (Sometimes, as in [2], H-coefficients are used for the proofs of the Theorems, but not in the terms of the Theorems). For example, the famous "two weak make one strong" theorem of Maurer and Pietrzak [9,12] says that if F and G are NCPA secure (Non Adaptive Chosen Plaintext Attacks), then the composition $G^{-1} \circ F$ is CCA secure. This result only holds in the information-theoretic setting, not in the computational setting (cf. [15,19]). Another example is this theorem of [2]:

Theorem 6. *(i.e. [2] Theorem 5 p.17)*
Let E, F and G be 3 block ciphers with the same message space M. Denote $\epsilon_E = \mathbf{Adv}_E^{NCPA}(q)$, $\epsilon_F = \mathbf{Adv}_F^{NCPA}(q)$, $\epsilon_{F^{-1}} = \mathbf{Adv}_{F^{-1}}^{NCPA}(q)$ and $\epsilon_{G^{-1}} = \mathbf{Adv}_{G^{-1}}^{NCPA}(q)$, where q is the number of queries. We have:

$$\mathbf{Adv}_{G \circ F \circ E}^{CCA}(q) \leq \epsilon_E \epsilon_F + \epsilon_E \epsilon_{G^{-1}} + \epsilon_{F^{-1}} \epsilon_{G^{-1}} + \min\{\epsilon_E \epsilon_F, \epsilon_E \epsilon_{G^{-1}}, \epsilon_{F^{-1}} \epsilon_{G^{-1}}\}$$

Why do we have 3 rounds in this theorem and only 2 rounds in Theorem 2 for the product of the advantages? (Moreover Theorem 6 was also proved by using the H-coefficient technique [2]). This is because in Theorem 2, we used the additional property that there are no "holes" in the hypothesis that H is greater than or equal to the mean value $H(1 - \epsilon)$, i.e. that this property was true for any q pairwise distinct inputs and q pairwise distinct outputs.

It is also interesting to compare our new Theorem 4 ($\mathbf{Adv}^{PRP} \leq \alpha_1 \ldots \alpha_k$) with these theorems of [2]:

Theorem 7. *(i.e. [2] Theorem 2 p. 10)*
Let $E_1, \ldots, E_n$ be n block ciphers with the same message space M. For any integer q, one has

$$\mathbf{Adv}_{E_n \circ \cdots \circ E_1}^{CCA}(q) \leq 2^{n-1} \max_{1 \leq i \leq n} \left(\prod_{1 \leq j \leq i-1} \mathbf{Adv}_{E_j}^{NCPA}(q) \times \prod_{i+1 \leq j \leq n} \mathbf{Adv}_{E_j^{-1}}^{NCPA}(q) \right).$$

Corollary 2. *(i.e. [2] Corollary 1 p.11)*
Let $E_1, \ldots, E_n$ be n block ciphers with the same message space M. Fix $q \geq 1$. For $i = 1, \ldots, n$, let $\epsilon_i = \max\{\mathbf{Adv}_{E_i}^{NCPA}(q), \mathbf{Adv}_{E_i^{-1}}^{NCPA}(q)\}$. Then one has

$$\mathbf{Adv}_{E_n \circ \cdots \circ E_1}^{CCA}(q) \leq 2^{n-1} \max_{1 \leq i \leq n} \prod_{\substack{1 \leq j \leq n \\ j \neq i}} \epsilon_j.$$

We see that with our new Theorem 4, we do not have the coefficient 2^{n-1}, and also we do not loose one of the n products. Therefore, if all the $\epsilon_i = \epsilon$ for example, we will get $\mathbf{Adv}^{CCA} \leq \epsilon^n$ instead of $\mathbf{Adv}^{CCA} \leq 2^{n-1} \epsilon^{n-1}$. However, in order to use our new Theorem 4, we need two conditions that were not in Theorem 7: the fact that we have "no hole" and an expression of ϵ directly in terms of the H-coefficients instead of $\mathbf{Adv}^{CCA}$. Therefore our Theorems and the theorems of [2] are both useful.

6   Application to Feistel Ciphers

We denote by Ψ^k a generic balanced Feistel Cipher with k rounds, i.e. a balanced Feistel cipher from $\{0,1\}^{2n}$ to $\{0,1\}^{2n}$ with k rounds, where the round functions are k random functions from $\{0,1\}^n$ to $\{0,1\}^n$. Ψ^k is also called a Luby-Rackoff's construction. We will show here how our new theorems can be useful for cryptographic security results on Ψ^k. (However, our new theorems are also interesting independently of these problems). The generic security problem has been intensively studied by many authors (for example [3,10,18]) since Luby and Rackoff major paper [8]. In [10], it was proved that when $k \to +\infty$, we have CCA security on Ψ^k when the number of queries q satisfies $q \ll 2^n$, and some explicit bounds for the Advantage in CCA are given. These bounds were later improved and at present, the best security bounds are obtained via the "H-coefficient technique", or via the coupling technique. These two techniques are very different and, interestingly, they give slightly different results.

Results with the H-coefficient Technique
A general view of the H-coefficient technique is given in [16,17] with the connections between these H-coefficients and various cryptographic securities (KPA, CPA, CCA,...). In 2016, in [4], another general H-coefficient theorem for CCA was proved. Essentially, the idea (of the results of [4]) is that, instead of introducing some sets E with good or bad properties (as in [17]), a computation of the mean value (computed with the probability on random permutations) is introduced. This is called the "Expectation Method" in [4].

In [18], the H-coefficient technique was used to study the security of Ψ^k. The main result was that we have CCA security for $q \ll 2^n$ not only when $k \to \infty$, but already after a finite number of rounds. More precisely, this property occurs for Ψ^k when $k \geq 5$ and an explicit bound for the Advantage in CCA is given in [18] for Ψ^6. In [1], the H-coefficient technique was used to obtain tight security bounds on Even-Mansour Cipers. From [18] (Theorem 6 p. 8), we have:

Theorem 8. *For all pairwise distinct* $[L_i, R_i]$, $1 \leq i \leq q$ *and for all pairwise distinct* $[S_i, T_i]$, $1 \leq i \leq q$ *the number H of* $(f_1, f_2, f_3, f_4, f_5, f_6) \in F_n^6$ *such that* $\forall i$, $1 \leq i \leq q$,

$$\Psi^6(f_1, f_2, f_3, f_4, f_5, f_6)[L_i, R_i] = [S_i, T_i]$$

satisfies $H \geq \frac{|F_n|^6}{2^{2nq}}(1 - \alpha)$ *where α can be chosen* $\alpha = \frac{8q}{2^n}$ *if* $q \leq \frac{2^n}{67n}$.

From this and Theorem 3, we obtain:

Theorem 9. *When* $q \leq \frac{2^n}{67n}$,

$$\mathbf{Adv}^{CCA}(\Psi^6) \leq \frac{8q}{2^n} + \frac{q^2}{2 \cdot 2^{2n}}.$$

Proof.

$$2^N(2^N - 1)\ldots(2^N - q + 1) \geq 2^{qN}\left(1 - \frac{1 + 2 + \ldots + (q-1)}{2^N}\right) \geq 2^{qN}\left(1 - \frac{q(q-1)}{2 \cdot 2^N}\right).$$

Therefore, for Ψ^6, when $q \leq \frac{2^n}{67n}$,

$$H \geq \frac{|\mathcal{F}_n|^6}{2^{2n}(2^{2n} - 1)\ldots(2^{2n} - q + 1)}\left(1 - \frac{q^2}{2 \cdot 2^{2n}}\right)\left(1 - \frac{8q}{2^n}\right)$$

where $\mathcal{F}_n$ denotes the set of all functions from $\{0, 1\}^n$ to $\{0, 1\}^n$.

$$H \geq \frac{|\mathcal{F}_n|^6}{2^{2n}(2^{2n} - 1)\ldots(2^{2n} - q + 1)}\left(1 - \frac{q^2}{2 \cdot 2^{2n}} - \frac{8q}{2^n}\right).$$

Now from this and Theorem 3 (with $\beta = 0$), we obtain:

$$\mathbf{Adv}^{CCA}(\Psi^6) \leq \frac{8q}{2^n} + \frac{q^2}{2 \cdot 2^{2n}}$$

as claimed.

Results with the Coupling Technique

The coupling technique is a major tool from the theory of Markov chains that allows to conveniently upper bound the so-called mixing time of a chain, i.e. the number of steps it takes for the chain, starting from any distribution, to be at statistical distance at most ϵ from its stationary distribution. The first use of coupling in cryptography is due to Mironov [13], who used it to analyse the RC4 stream cipher. It was first applied to (maximally unbalanced) Feistel ciphers by Morris et al. [14]. This was generalized to other types of Feistel ciphers (including the balanced Feistel Ψ^k) by Hoang and Rogaway [3]. Subsequently, the coupling technique was used to analyze the iterated Even-Mansour Cipher [5], tweakable block ciphers constructions [6] and Feistel schemes where the round functions are of the form: $x \to F(x \oplus k)$ where F is a random oracle and k the secret key [7].

From [3], we have

Theorem 10. *With $k' = \lfloor \frac{(k-1)}{2} \rfloor$, we have:*

$$\mathbf{Adv}^{NCPA}(\Psi^k) \leq \frac{2^{k'}}{k' + 1} \cdot \frac{q^{k'+1}}{2^{k'n}}$$

and

$$\mathbf{Adv}^{CCA}(\Psi^{2k-1}) \leq \frac{2^{k'}}{k' + 1} \cdot \frac{q^{k'+1}}{2^{k'n}}.$$

From Theorem 10, we see that with the coupling technique, we obtain:

NCPA: Ψ^3 has security when $q \ll 2^{n/2}$
Ψ^5 has security when $q \ll 2^{2n/3}$
Ψ^7 has security when $q \ll 2^{3n/4}$
etc.

CCA: Ψ^5 has security when $q \ll 2^{n/2}$
Ψ^7 has security when $q \ll 2^{2n/3}$
Ψ^9 has security when $q \ll 2^{3n/4}$
etc.

Therefore, in terms of queries, Theorem 2 (from H-coefficient technique) gives a better bound than Theorem 3 (from the coupling technique), since it gives CCA security for Ψ^6 when $q \ll 2^n$ (and therefore for Ψ^k, for all $k \geq 6$). However:

1. The proofs of Theorems 8 and 9 are much more complex than the proof of Theorem 10.
2. For a fixed value q, the **Adv** given in Theorem 10 is bounded by term that can be as small as wanted when k increases, unlike Theorem 2 where **Adv** is fixed when q and n are fixed.

Results with Our New Theorems

In a way from our new Theorem 4, we can get "the best of the two worlds", since from it and Theorem 8, we obtain:

Theorem 11. *For all integer $k \geq 1$, when $q \leq \frac{2^n}{67n}$, we have:*

$$\mathbf{Adv}^{CCA}(\Psi^{6k}) \leq \left(\frac{8q}{2^n} + \frac{q^2}{2.2^{2n}} \right)^k.$$

Proof. In the proof of Theorem 9, we have seen that for Ψ^6, we have, when $q \leq \frac{2^n}{67n}$,

$$H \geq \frac{|\mathcal{F}_n|^6}{2^{2n}(2^{2n}-1)\ldots(2^{2n}-q+1)} \left(1 - \frac{8q}{2^n} - \frac{q^2}{2.2^{2n}} \right).$$

Therefore, from our new composition Theorem 4, we obtain that for Ψ^{6k}, when $q \leq \frac{2^n}{67n}$,

$$H \geq \frac{|\mathcal{F}_n|^{6k}}{2^{2n}(2^{2n}-1)\ldots(2^{2n}-q+1)} \left(1 - \left(\frac{8q}{2^n} + \frac{q^2}{2.2^{2n}} \right)^k \right).$$

Theorem 11 is now obtained from this and Theorem 3 with $\beta = 0$.

This is the best bound known at present on Ψ^k: when $q \ll 2^n$, it gives CCA security, and when q and n are fixed such that $\frac{8q}{2^n} + \frac{q^2}{2.2^{2n}} < 1$, the bound can be as small as wanted by increasing k.

7 Other CCA Bounds on Ψ^k

Worse Bounds, But Simpler Proofs
When we look at the (difficult) proof of Theorem 8 on Ψ^6, we see that security when $q \ll 2^{3n/2}$ can easily be done. The security when $q \ll 2^{3n/4}$ is also relatively easy, and $q \ll 2^{4n/5}$ is a bit more complex.

Therefore, it is possible to stop the proof at, say, $q \ll 2^{4n/5}$ and then to use the coupling technique from Ψ^6 (instead of Ψ^3) or to use our new Theorem 4 in order to obtain a security bound. This bound will not be as good as the bound of Theorem 11, but the proof will be much simpler: we see that we have many possible trade-offs between the quality of the bounds and the simplicity of the proofs.

Better Bounds
Our Theorem 11 is the best explicit bound known at present on Ψ^k. However, it is expected that this bound can still be improved (not in term of queries: the bound $q \ll 2^n$ already obtained on Ψ^k is optimal in information complexity, but this bound can be improved in term of smaller value for $\mathbf{Adv}^{CCA}$). One way to obtain better bounds would be to analyse Ψ^{5k} instead of Ψ^{6k}. Ψ^5 is CCA secure when $q \ll 2^n$ (cf. [18]), but in Ψ^5 (unlike Ψ^6), we have "holes" when $\sqrt{2^n} \ll q \ll 2^n$ (cf. Appendix B of this paper). Therefore, we cannot use our new composition Theorem 4 on Ψ^{5k} (unlike what we did on Ψ^{6k}). However, Theorem 7 and Corollary 2 of [2] can be used on Ψ^{5k}. Due to the coefficient 2^{n-1} and to the fact that we loose one term ϵ_i of the product in Theorem 7 and Corollary 2 (see Sect. 5) we expect our results on Ψ^{6k} to be better than the results on $\Psi^{5k'}$ (obtained from Theorem 7) for small values of k and k'. However, for large values of k and k', the results on $\Psi^{5k'}$ should be better. We will not do it in this paper more precisely since we do not have an explicit bound for CCA security on Ψ^5 (but just the fuzzy bound $q \ll 2^n$). Moreover, in this paper, we study CCA security of Ψ^6 mainly to illustrate our new composition results.

A   An Exact Formula for the H-coefficient for $\Psi^k, 1 \leq k \leq 5$

The aim of this Appendix A is to prove Theorem 16, i.e. to obtain an exact formula H for Ψ^5. (A similar formula was already mentioned in [18]). We will need this Theorem 16 in Appendix B.

Definition of Ψ^k
We recall the definition of the balanced Feistel Schemes, i.e. the classical Feistel schemes. Let $\mathcal{P}_{2n}$ be the set of all permutations from $\{0, 1\}^{2n}$ to $\{0, 1\}^{2n}$. Let $\mathcal{F}_n$ be the set of all functions from $\{0, 1\}^n$ to $\{0, 1\}^n$. Let L, R, S and T be four n-bit strings in $\{0, 1\}^n$. Let $\Psi(f_1)$ denotes the permutation of $\mathcal{P}_{2n}$ such that:

$$\Psi(f_1)[L, R] = [S, T] \stackrel{\text{def}}{\Leftrightarrow} \begin{cases} S = R \\ T = L \oplus f_1(R) \end{cases}$$

More generally if $f_1, f_2, \ldots, f_k$ are k functions of $\mathcal{F}_n$, let $\Psi^k(f_1, \ldots, f_k)$ denotes the permutation of $\mathcal{P}_{2n}$ such that:

$$\Psi^k(f_1, \ldots, f_k) = \Psi(f_k) \circ \cdots \circ \Psi(f_2) \circ \Psi(f_1).$$

The permutation $\Psi^k(f_1, \ldots, f_k)$ is called a 'balanced Feistel scheme with k rounds' or shortly Ψ^k. When $f_1, \ldots, f_k$ are randomly and independently chosen in $\mathcal{F}_n$, then $\Psi^k(f_1, \ldots, f_k)$ is called a 'random Feistel scheme with k rounds' or a 'Luby-Rackoff construction with k rounds'.

Definition 3. Definition of H for Ψ^k
When $[L_i, R_i], [S_i, T_i], 1 \le i \le q$, is a given sequence of $2q$ values of $\{0,1\}^{2n}$, we will denote by $H_k(L, R, S, T)$ or in short by H_k, or simply by H, the number of k-tuples of functions $(f_1, \ldots f_k)$ of F_n^k such that:

$$\forall i, \ 1 \le i \le q, \ \Psi^k(f_1, \ldots, f_k)[L_i, R_i] = [S_i, T_i].$$

We will analyse the properties of these H values in order to obtain our security results.

Let $[L_i, R_i], [S_i, T_i], 1 \le i \le q$, be a given sequence of $2q$ values of $\{0,1\}^{2n}$. Let r be the number of independent equalities $R_i = R_j$, $i \ne j$, and let s be the number of independent equalities $S_i = S_j$, $i \ne j$.

Theorem 12. *The exact formula for H_1 (i.e. for Ψ^1) is:*

$$H_1 = 0 \ if \ (C) \ is \ not \ satisfied,$$

$$H_1 = \frac{|\mathcal{F}_n|}{2^{nq}} \cdot 2^{nr} \ if \ (C) \ is \ satisfied,$$

where (C) is this set of conditions:

1. $\forall i, \ 1 \le i \le q, \ R_i = S_i$
2. $\forall i, j \ 1 \le i \le q, \ 1 \le j \le q, \ R_i = R_j \Rightarrow T_i \oplus L_i = T_j \oplus L_j$.

Proof. For one round, we have $\Psi^1([L_i, R_i]) = [S_i, Y_i] \Leftrightarrow S_i = R_i$ and $T_i = L_i \oplus f_1(R_i)$. Therefore, if (C) is not satisfied, $H_1 = 0$. Now if (C) is satisfied, then f_1 is fixed on exactly $q - r$ points by $f_1(R_i) = T_i \oplus L_i$, and we obtain Theorem 12 as claimed.

$\square$

Theorem 13. *The exact formula for H_2 (i.e. for Ψ^2) is:*

$$H_2 = 0 \ if \ (C) \ is \ not \ satisfied,$$

$$H_2 = \frac{|\mathcal{F}_n|^2}{2^{2nq}} \cdot 2^{n(r+s)} \ if \ (C) \ is \ satisfied,$$

where (C) is this set of conditions:

1. $\forall i,j\, 1 \le i \le q,\, 1 \le j \le q,\, R_i = R_j \Rightarrow L_i \oplus L_j = S_i \oplus S_j$
2. $\forall i,j\, 1 \le i \le q,\, 1 \le j \le q,\, S_i = S_j \Rightarrow R_i \oplus R_j = T_i \oplus T_j$.

Proof. For two rounds we have $\psi^2([L_i, R_i]) = [S_i, T_i] \Leftrightarrow S_i = L_i \oplus f_1(R_i)$ and $T_i = R_i \oplus f_2(S_i)$. Therefore if (C) is not satisfied, $H_2 = 0$. Now if (C) is satisfied then (f_1, f_2) is fixed on exactly $2q - r - s$ points, and we obtain Theorem 13 as claimed. □

Definition 4. *(Framework for Ψ^3)*
For 3 rounds, Ψ^3, we define a "framework" as a set of equations $X_i = X_j$. We will say that two frameworks are equal if they imply exactly the same set of equations in X.

Theorem 14. *The exact formula for H_3 (i.e. for Ψ^3) is:*

$$H_3 = \frac{|\mathcal{F}_n|^3 \cdot 2^{n(r+s)}}{2^{3nq}} \sum_{\substack{all\ frameworks\ \mathcal{F} \\ that\ satisfy\ (F1)}} 2^{nx}[Number\ of\ X_i\ satisfying\ (C1)]$$

where:

- *x is the number of independent equalities $X_i = X_j$ for a framework $\mathcal{F}$.*
- *$(F1): X_i = X_j$ is in $\mathcal{F} \Rightarrow S_i \oplus S_j = R_i \oplus R_j$*

$$(C_1): \begin{cases} R_i = R_j \Rightarrow X_i \oplus X_j = L_i \oplus L_j \\ S_i = S_j \Rightarrow X_i \oplus X_j = T_i \oplus T_j \\ \textit{The only equations } X_i = X_j, i < j, \textit{ are exactly those implied by } \mathcal{F}. \end{cases}$$

Proof. We write $\Psi^3 = \Psi \cup \Psi^2$ with $\Psi^2([L_i, R_i]) = [X_i, S_i]$ and $\Psi([X_i, S_i]) = [S_i, T_i]$. For Ψ^2, we obtain from Theorem 13, $2^{n(r+x)}\frac{|\mathcal{F}_n|^2}{2^{2nq}}$ solutions when $(C1)$ is satisfied. For Ψ, we obtain from Theorem 12, $2^{ns}\frac{|\mathcal{F}_n|}{2^{nq}}$ solutions when $(C1)$ is satisfied. Thus, we obtain Theorem 14 as claimed. □

Definition 5. *(Framework for Ψ^4)*
For 4 rounds, Ψ^4, let us define a "framework" as a set of equations $X_i = X_j$ or $Y_i = Y_j$. We will say that two frameworks are equal if they imply exactly the same set of equalities in X and Y. For a framework $\mathcal{F}$, we denote by x the number of independent equalities $X_i = X_j$, and by y the number of independent equalities $Y_i = Y_j$.

Theorem 15. *The exact formula for H_4 (i.e. for Ψ^4) is:*

$$H_4 = \frac{|\mathcal{F}_n|^4 \cdot 2^{n(r+s)}}{2^{4nq}} \sum_{all\ frameworks\ \mathcal{F}} 2^{n(x+y)}[Number\ of\ X_i\ satisfying\ (C1)]$$

$$\cdot [Number\ of\ Y_i\ satisfying\ (C2)]$$

where

$$(C_1): \begin{cases} R_i = R_j \Rightarrow X_i \oplus X_j = L_i \oplus L_j \\ Y_i = Y_j \textit{ is in } \mathcal{F} \Rightarrow X_i \oplus X_j = S_i \oplus S_j \\ \textit{The only equations } X_i = X_j, i < j, \textit{ are exactly those implied by } \mathcal{F}. \end{cases}$$

$$(C_2) : \begin{cases} S_i = S_j \Rightarrow Y_i \oplus Y_j = T_i \oplus T_j \\ X_i = X_j \text{ is in } \mathcal{F} \Rightarrow Y_i \oplus Y_j = R_i \oplus R_j \\ \text{The only equations } Y_i = Y_j, i < j, \text{ are exactly those implied by } \mathcal{F}. \end{cases}$$

Proof. We write $\psi^4 = \Psi \circ \Psi^3$ with $\Psi^3([L_i, R_i]) = [Y_i, S_i]$ and $\Psi([Y_i, S_i]) = [S_i, T_i]$, and we sum over all possible Y. Then from Theorems 12 and 14, we obtain Theorem 15. $\square$

Definition 6. *(Framework for Ψ^5)*
For 5 rounds, Ψ^5, a "framework" is a set of equations $X_i = X_j$ or $Y_i = Y_j$, or $Z_i = Z_j$. We will say that two frameworks are equal if they imply exactly the same set of equalities in X, Y and Z. For a framework $\mathcal{F}$, we denote by x the number of independent equalities $X_i = X_j$, by y the number of independent equalities $Y_i = Y_j$, and by z the number of independent equalities $Z_i = Z_j$.

Theorem 16. *The exact formula for H_5 (i.e. for Ψ^5) is:*

$$H_5 = \frac{|\mathcal{F}_n|^5 \cdot 2^{n(r+s)}}{2^{5nq}} \sum_{\text{all frameworks } \mathcal{F}} 2^{n(x+y+z)}[Number \ of \ X_i, Z_i \ satisfying \ (C1)]$$
$$\cdot [Number \ of \ Y_i \ satisfying \ (C2)]$$

where

$$(C_1) : \begin{cases} R_i = R_j \Rightarrow X_i \oplus X_j = L_i \oplus L_j \\ Y_i = Y_j \text{ is in } \mathcal{F} \Rightarrow X_i \oplus X_j = Z_i \oplus Z_j \\ S_i = S_j \Rightarrow Z_i \oplus Z_j = T_i \oplus T_j \\ \text{The only equations } X_i = X_j, i < j, \text{ are exactly those implied by } \mathcal{F}. \\ \text{The only equations } Z_i = Z_j, i < j, \text{ are exactly those implied by } \mathcal{F}. \end{cases}$$

$$(C_2) : \begin{cases} X_i = X_j \text{ is in } \mathcal{F} \Rightarrow Y_i \oplus Y_j = R_i \oplus R_j \\ Z_i = Z_j \text{ is in } \mathcal{F} \Rightarrow Y_i \oplus Y_j = S_i \oplus S_j \\ \text{The only equations } Y_i = Y_j, i < j, \text{ are exactly those implied by } \mathcal{F}. \end{cases}$$

Proof. We write $\Psi^5 = \Psi \circ \Psi^4$ with $\Psi^4([L_i, R_i]) = [Z_i, S_i]$ and $\Psi([Z_i, S_i]) = [S_i, T_i]$, and we sum over all possible Z. Then from Theorems 12 and 15, we obtain Theorem 16. $\square$

B   "Holes" on Ψ^5 when $\sqrt{2^n} \ll q \ll 2^n$

We will present here a "structural" difference between Ψ^5 and Ψ^6: in Ψ^5, we have "holes" when $\sqrt{2^n} \ll q \ll 2^n$ (but not in Ψ^6: cf. Theorem 8).

5 Rounds

For Ψ^5, with $q \simeq \sqrt{2^n}$, we can choose all the R_i with the same value, all the S_i with the same value and the property: $\forall i, j,\ 1 \le i \le q,\ 1 \le j \le q,\ T_i \oplus T_j \ne L_i \oplus L_j$. For example, the first $\frac{n}{2}$ bits of the L_i values are always 0 and the last $\frac{n}{2}$ bits of the T_i values are always 0. Since all the R_i values are equal, then all the L_i values are pairwise distinct (because we want pairwise distinct $[L_i, R_i]$) and all the X_i values are pairwise distinct (because $R_i = R_j \Rightarrow X_i \oplus X_j = L_i \oplus L_j$. Similarly, since all the S_i values are equal, then all the T_i values are distinct (because we want pairwise distinct $[S_i, T_i]$) and all the Z_i values are pairwise distinct (because $S_i = S_j \Rightarrow Z_i \oplus Z_j = T_i \oplus T_j$). Moreover all the Y_i values are also pairwise distinct, because $Y_i = Y_j \Rightarrow X_i \oplus X_j = Z_i \oplus Z_j \Rightarrow L_i \oplus L_j = T_i \oplus T_j$, but we always have: $L_i \oplus L_j \ne T_i \oplus T_j$.

We know (cf. Appendix A, Theorem 16) that the exact formula for H is:

$$H_5 = \frac{|\mathcal{F}_n|^5 \cdot 2^{n(r+s)}}{2^{5nq}} \sum_{all\ frameworks\ \mathcal{F}} 2^{n(x+y+z)}[Number\ of\ X_i, Z_i\ satisfying\ (C1)]$$
$$\cdot [Number\ of\ Y_i\ satisfying\ (C2)].$$

Here we have only one framework (all the X_i are pairwise distinct, Y_i pairwise distinct, Z_i pairwise distinct) with $r = q-1, s = q-1, x = y = z = 0$, [Number of X_i satisfying (C1)] $= 2^n$, [Number of Z_i satisfying (C1)] $= 2^n$, and [Number of Y_i satisfying (C2)] $= 2^n(2^n - 1) \ldots (2^n - q + 1)$. we obtain:

$$H_5 = \frac{|\mathcal{F}_n|^5}{2^{2nq}} \cdot \left(1 - \frac{1}{2^n}\right)\left(1 - \frac{2}{2^n}\right) \ldots \left(1 - \frac{q-1}{2^n}\right) \ll \frac{|F_n|^5}{2^{2nq}}$$

when $q \ll \sqrt{2^n}$. However $\tilde{H}_5 = \frac{|\mathcal{F}_n|^5}{(2^n)(2^n-1)\ldots(2^n-q+1)} \simeq \frac{|\mathcal{F}_n|^5}{2^{2nq}}$. Therefore here we have $H_5 \ll \tilde{H}_5$, i.e. a "hole" of length $\sqrt{2^n}$.

This result is not in contradiction with the act that Ψ^5 is CCA secure when $q \ll 2^n$ because it is not possible in a CCA attack with q queries to obtain $R_1 = R_2 = \ldots = R_m$ and $S_1 = S_2 = \ldots = S_m$ with $m \simeq \sqrt{2^n}$.

References

1. Chen, S., Steinberger, J.: Tight security bounds for key-alternating ciphers. In: Nguyen, P.Q., Oswald, E. (eds.) EUROCRYPT 2014. LNCS, vol. 8441, pp. 327–350. Springer, Heidelberg (2014). https://doi.org/10.1007/978-3-642-55220-5_19
2. Cogliati, B., Patarin, J., Seurin, Y.: Security amplification for the composition of block ciphers: simpler proofs and new results. In: Joux, A., Youssef, A. (eds.) SAC 2014. LNCS, vol. 8781, pp. 129–146. Springer, Cham (2014). https://doi.org/10.1007/978-3-319-13051-4_8
3. Hoang, V.T., Rogaway, P.: On generalized Feistel networks. In: Rabin, T. (ed.) CRYPTO 2010. LNCS, vol. 6223, pp. 613–630. Springer, Heidelberg (2010). https://doi.org/10.1007/978-3-642-14623-7_33
4. Hoang, V.T., Tessaro, S.: Key-alternating ciphers and key-length extension: exact bounds and multi-user security. In: Robshaw, M., Katz, J. (eds.) CRYPTO 2016. LNCS, vol. 9814, pp. 3–32. Springer, Heidelberg (2016). https://doi.org/10.1007/978-3-662-53018-4_1

5. Lampe, R., Patarin, J., Seurin, Y.: An asymptotically tight security analysis of the iterated Even-Mansour cipher. In: Wang, X., Sako, K. (eds.) ASIACRYPT 2012. LNCS, vol. 7658, pp. 278–295. Springer, Heidelberg (2012). https://doi.org/10.1007/978-3-642-34961-4_18

6. Lampe, R., Seurin, Y.: Tweakable blockciphers with asymptotically optimal security. In: Moriai, S. (ed.) FSE 2013. LNCS, vol. 8424, pp. 133–151. Springer, Heidelberg (2014). https://doi.org/10.1007/978-3-662-43933-3_8

7. Lampe, R., Seurin, Y.: Security analysis of key-alternating Feistel ciphers. In: Cid, C., Rechberger, C. (eds.) FSE 2014. LNCS, vol. 8540, pp. 243–264. Springer, Heidelberg (2015). https://doi.org/10.1007/978-3-662-46706-0_13

8. Luby, M., Rackoff, C.: How to construct pseudo-random permutations from pseudorandom functions. SIAM J. Comput. **17**, 373–386 (1988)

9. Maurer, U.: Indistinguishability of random systems. In: Knudsen, L.R. (ed.) EUROCRYPT 2002. LNCS, vol. 2332, pp. 110–132. Springer, Heidelberg (2002). https://doi.org/10.1007/3-540-46035-7_8

10. Maurer, U., Pietrzak, K.: The security of many-round Luby-Rackoff pseudorandom permutations. In: Biham, E. (ed.) EUROCRYPT 2003. LNCS, vol. 2656, pp. 544–561. Springer, Heidelberg (2003). https://doi.org/10.1007/3-540-39200-9_34

11. Maurer, U., Pietrzak, K.: Composition of random systems: when two weak make one strong. In: Naor, M. (ed.) TCC 2004. LNCS, vol. 2951, pp. 410–427. Springer, Heidelberg (2004). https://doi.org/10.1007/978-3-540-24638-1_23

12. Maurer, U., Pietrzak, K., Renner, R.: Indistinguishability amplification. In: Menezes, A. (ed.) CRYPTO 2007. LNCS, vol. 4622, pp. 130–149. Springer, Heidelberg (2007). https://doi.org/10.1007/978-3-540-74143-5_8

13. Mironov, I.: (Not so) random shuffles of RC4. In: Yung, M. (ed.) CRYPTO 2002. LNCS, vol. 2442, pp. 304–319. Springer, Heidelberg (2002). https://doi.org/10.1007/3-540-45708-9_20

14. Morris, B., Rogaway, P., Stegers, T.: How to encipher messages on a small domain. In: Halevi, S. (ed.) CRYPTO 2009. LNCS, vol. 5677, pp. 286–302. Springer, Heidelberg (2009). https://doi.org/10.1007/978-3-642-03356-8_17

15. Myers, S.: Black-box composition does not imply adaptive security. In: Cachin, C., Camenisch, J.L. (eds.) EUROCRYPT 2004. LNCS, vol. 3027, pp. 189–206. Springer, Heidelberg (2004). https://doi.org/10.1007/978-3-540-24676-3_12

16. Patarin, J.: Étude des Générateurs de Permutations Pseudo-aléatoires basés sur le schéma du D.E.S., Ph.D., November 1991

17. Patarin, J.: The "coefficients H" technique. In: Avanzi, R.M., Keliher, L., Sica, F. (eds.) SAC 2008. LNCS, vol. 5381, pp. 328–345. Springer, Heidelberg (2009). https://doi.org/10.1007/978-3-642-04159-4_21

18. Patarin, J.: Security of balanced and unbalanced Feistel schemes with linear non equalities. Cryptology ePrint Archive: Report 2010/293 (2010)

19. Pietrzak, K.: Composition does not imply adaptive security. In: Shoup, V. (ed.) CRYPTO 2005. LNCS, vol. 3621, pp. 55–65. Springer, Heidelberg (2005). https://doi.org/10.1007/11535218_4

20. Tessaro, S.: Security amplification for the cascade of arbitrarily weak PRPs: tight bounds via the interactive hardcore lemma. In: Ishai, Y. (ed.) TCC 2011. LNCS, vol. 6597, pp. 37–54. Springer, Heidelberg (2011). https://doi.org/10.1007/978-3-642-19571-6_3

Improved Related-Tweakey Boomerang Attacks on Deoxys-BC

Yu Sasaki[(⊠)]

NTT Secure Platform Laboratories,
3-9-11, Midori-cho Musashino-shi, Tokyo 180-8585, Japan
sasaki.yu@lab.ntt.co.jp

Abstract. This paper improves previous distinguishers and key recovery attacks against Deoxys-BC that is a core primitive of the authenticated encryption scheme Deoxys, which is one of the remaining candidates in CAESAR. We observe that previous attacks by Cid et al. published from ToSC 2017 have a lot of room to be improved. By carefully optimizing attack procedures, we reduce the complexities of 8- and 9-round related-tweakey boomerang distinguishers against Deoxys-BC-256 to 2^{28} and 2^{98}, respectively, whereas the previous attacks require 2^{74} and 2^{124}, respectively. The distinguishers are then extended to 9-round and 10-round boomerang key-recovery attacks with a complexity 2^{112} and 2^{170}, respectively, while the previous rectangle attacks require 2^{118} and 2^{204}, respectively. The optimization techniques used in this paper are conceptually not new, yet we believe that it is important to know how much the attacks are optimized by considering the details of the design.

Keywords: CAESAR · Cryptanalysis · Deoxys-BC
Boomerang attack

1 Introduction

Authenticated encryption (AE) schemes are symmetric-key cryptographic algorithms that provide both confidentiality and authenticity of data in a single primitive. AE schemes offer several advantages when compared with the use of two separate algorithms. For example, it simplifies security arguments and key management, which avoids the risk of misuse of the schemes by non-experts of cryptography. It also offers better efficiency by sharing a part of the computation for confidentiality and authenticity. In the present time, CAESAR [2] is organized by the international cryptologic research community to identify a portfolio of AE schemes that offer advantages over GCM [15].

Deoxys [11] is one of the CAESAR third-round candidates. Its design is based on the tweakable block cipher Deoxys-BC, which is an AES [19] based tweakable block cipher using the tweakey framework [10]. Tweakable block ciphers (TBC) were first introduced and formalized by Liskov et al. [13], and in addition to the two standard inputs, a plaintext and a key, it takes an additional input called

A. Joux et al. (Eds.): AFRICACRYPT 2018, LNCS 10831, pp. 87–106, 2018.
https://doi.org/10.1007/978-3-319-89339-6_6

a tweak. The Deoxys AE scheme makes use of two versions of the cipher as its internal primitive: Deoxys-BC-256 and Deoxys-BC-384.

The tweakey framework unifies the vision of key and tweak as the *tweakey*. An n-bit block cipher using the framework will take a k-bit key and a t-bit tweak, and a dedicated *tweakey schedule* will use the $(k + t)$-bit tweakey to produce the n-bit *round subtweakeys*. This approach allows designers to claim full security of the tweakable block cipher.

The number of existing public security analysis of the Deoxys-BC is limited. The designers provided a few analyses [11]. As the cipher uses the AES round function, with the only differences to AES being the number of rounds (14 for Deoxys-BC-256 and 16 Deoxys-BC-384) and the tweakey schedule, much of the analysis leverages the existing analysis of the AES.

The work by Cid et al. [7] recently published from ToSC 2017 is the only third-party analysis so far. Cid et al. developed automated differential trail search method using the mixed integer linear programming (MILP) [17] to show that the lower bound of the number of active S-boxes is higher than the original expectation by the designers in the related-tweakey setting. Cid et al. then constructed boomerang attacks [20] by combining two short differential trails discovered by their tool. This leads to 8- and 9-round distinguishers against Deoxys-BC-256 with complexity of 2^{74} and 2^{124}, respectively, and 10- and 11-round distinguishers against Deoxys-BC-384 with complexity of 2^{44} and 2^{122}, respectively. Those are further extended to related-tweakey rectangle attacks for recovering key against 9-round and 10-round Deoxys-BC-256 and 12-round and 13-round Deoxys-BC-384. The summary of the previous attacks are given in Table 1.

We noticed that after the submission of this paper, Mehrdad et al. uploaded their analysis that studies related-tweakey impossible differential attacks against Deoxys-BC-256 [16]. One of their focuses is the related-tweak single-key model that is not covered in this paper but the number of attacked rounds is at most 8. Under the same (related-tweak related-key) model as ours, their attack reaches 9 rounds with complexity $(Time, Data, Memory) = (2^{118}, 2^{118}, 2^{114})$.

Our Contributions. In this paper, we present the best cryptanalysis against Deoxys-BC block cipher in the present time. Our attacks utilize the differential trails for boomerang-like attacks found by Cid et al. [7]. We observe that the automated differential trail search in [7] is very optimized, whereas the utilization of the detected trails in the attack procedure is not well-optimized, thus there is a lot of room to be improved. This is perhaps the main innovation of [7] is the development of new MILP models for automated differential search method. Yet we think that optimizing the attack complexity is important especially considering that Deoxys is one of the remaining candidates in CAESAR. For example, to compare security margin of several designs, known cryptanalytic results should be optimized as much as possible for all of the designs.

The optimization techniques used in our paper are conceptually not entirely new, e.g. changing differential trail to truncated differential trail in one of two pairs in the boomerang quartet, reducing the data complexity by using structure,

Table 1. Comparison of the Attacks against Deoxys-BC. SK, RK, KR, and dist stand for single-key, related-key, key-recovery and distinguisher, respectively.

Deoxys-BC-256

Rounds	Model	Approach	Goal	Time	Data	Mem.	Size set up	Ref.
8/14	SK	MitM	KR	$< 2^{128}$	–	–	$t = 128, k = 128$	[11]
8/14	SK	differential	KR	$< 2^{128}$	–	–	$t = 128, k = 128$	[11]
8/14	RK	boomerang	dist	2^{74}	2^{74}	negl.	$t = 128, k = 128$	[7]
				2^{28}	2^{28}	2^{27}	$t = 128, k = 128$	Ours
9/14	RK	boomerang	dist	2^{124}	2^{124}	negl.	$t = 128, k = 128$	[7]
				2^{98}	2^{98}	2^{17}	$l = 128, k = 128$	Ours
9/14	RK	boomerang	KR	2^{118}	2^{117}	2^{117}	$t = 128, k = 128$	[7]
				2^{112}	2^{98}	2^{17}	$t = 128, k = 128$	Ours
10/14	RK	rectangle	KR	2^{204}	$2^{127.58}$	$2^{127.58}$	$t < 52, k > 204$	[7]
		boomerang	KR	2^{170}	2^{170}	2^{17}	$t < 86, k > 170$	Ours
		boomerang		2^{170}	2^{98}	2^{98}	$t < 86, k > 170$	Ours

Deoxys-BC-384

Rounds	Model	Approach	Goal	Time	Data	Mem.	Size set up	Ref.
8/16	SK	MitM	KR	$< 2^{256}$	–	–	$t = 128, k = 256$	[11]
10/16	RK	boomerang	dist	2^{44}	2^{44}	negl.	$t = 128, k = 256$	[7]
				2^{22}	2^{22}	2^{17}	$t = 128, k = 256$	Ours
11/16	RK	boomerang	dist	2^{122}	2^{122}	negl.	$t = 128, k = 256$	[7]
				2^{100}	2^{100}	2^{17}	$t = 128, k = 256$	Ours
12/16	RK	rectangle	KR	2^{127}	2^{127}	2^{125}	$t = 128, k = 256$	[7]
		boomerang	KR	2^{148}	2^{148}	2^{17}	$t = 128, k = 256$	Ours
		boomerang		2^{148}	2^{100}	2^{100}	$t = 128, k = 256$	Ours
13/16	RK	rectangle	KR	2^{270}	2^{127}	2^{144}	$t < 114, k > 270$	[7]

and choosing the best way to append the key-recovery round. However applying a lot of optimization attempts including failure attempts that cannot be included in the paper and considering many details of the computation structure require hard work and significant amount of time. After the careful analysis, the attack complexity against Deoxys-BC-256 with respect to $\min(Time, Data, Memory)$ is improved by a factor of 2^{26} and 2^{34} for the longest distinguishing and key-recovery attacks, respectively. The improved complexities are listed in Table 1.

Finally, we provide a discussion toward developing an automated differential search tool such that the impact of the key recovery attack is taken into account.

Paper Outline. The remaining of this paper is organized as follows. Section 2 describes the specification of Deoxys-BC. Section 3 recalls the previous attacks by Cid et al. Sects. 4 and 5 discuss the improved attacks on Deoxys-BC-256 and Deoxys-BC-384, respectively. We give a discussion toward an improved differential search tool and conclude this paper in Sect. 6.

2   Specification of Deoxys-BC

Deoxys-BC-256 and Deoxys-BC-384 are AES-based tweakable block ciphers [11]. Both versions adopt 128-bit block sizes which besides a plaintext P (or a ciphertext C) and a key K, also take a *tweak* T. The concatenation of the key and tweak states is called the *tweakey* state. For Deoxys-BC-256 the tweakey size is 256 bits, while for Deoxys-BC-384 it is 384 bits. The breakdown of the key and tweak sizes in the tweakey can be chosen by the user, as long as the key size is greater or equal to the block size, i.e. 128 bits.

Deoxys-BC is an AES-like design. It transforms the initial plaintext (viewed as a 4×4 two-dimension array of bytes) using the AES round function. Deoxys-BC-256 and Deoxys-BC-384 have 14 and 16 rounds, respectively.

Deoxys-BC Round Function. Similarly to the AES, one round of Deoxys-BC has the following four transformations applied in the order specified below:

- AddRoundTweakey – XOR the 128-bit round subtweakey to the state.
- SubBytes – Apply the 8-bit AES S-box S to each byte in parallel.
- ShiftRows – Rotate the 4-byte i-th row left by i positions.
- MixColumns – Multiply the state by the 4×4 constant MDS matrix of AES.

MixColumns is not omitted in the last round. After the last round, a final AddRoundTweakey operation is performed to produce the ciphertext.

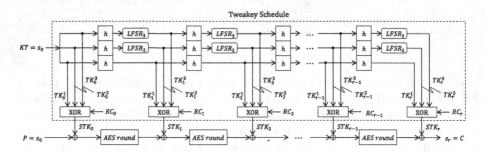

Fig. 1. Encryption of Deoxys-BC-384.

Definition of Subtweakeys. The *tweakey* state is composed of the key K and the tweak T. The tweakey state is divided into 128-bit words denoted by $TK_1, TK_2, \cdots$. More precisely, the tweakey state in Deoxys-BC-256 is composed of TK_1 and TK_2, and the tweakey state in Deoxys-BC-384 is composed of TK_1, TK_2, and TK_3. Finally, we denote by STK_i the 128-bit *subtweakey* that is added to the state at round i during the AddRoundTweakey operation. For Deoxys-BC-256, a subtweakey is defined as $STK_i = TK_i^1 \oplus TK_i^2 \oplus RC_i$, whereas for Deoxys-BC-384 it is defined as: $STK_i = TK_i^1 \oplus TK_i^2 \oplus TK_i^3 \oplus RC_i$.

The 128-bit words TK_i^1, TK_i^2, TK_i^3 are outputs produced by a special *tweakey schedule* algorithm, initialised with $TK_0^1 = W_1$ and $TK_0^2 = W_2$ for Deoxys-BC-256 and with $TK_0^1 = W_1$, $TK_0^2 = W_2$ and $TK_0^3 = W_3$ for Deoxys-BC-384. The tweakey schedule algorithm is defined as

$$TK_{i+1}^1 = h(TK_i^1),$$
$$TK_{i+1}^2 = h(LFSR_2(TK_i^2)),$$
$$TK_{i+1}^3 = h(LFSR_3(TK_i^3)),$$

where the byte permutation h is defined as

$$\begin{pmatrix} 0 & 1 & 2 & 3 & 4 & 5 & 6 & 7 & 8 & 9 & 10 & 11 & 12 & 13 & 14 & 15 \\ 1 & 6 & 11 & 12 & 5 & 10 & 15 & 0 & 9 & 14 & 3 & 4 & 13 & 2 & 7 & 8 \end{pmatrix},$$

numbered by the usual AES byte ordering.

The $LFSR_2$ and $LFSR_3$ functions are simply the application of an LFSR to each on the 16 bytes of a 128-bit tweakey word. The two LFSRs used are given in Table 2 (x_0 stands for the LSB of the cell).

Table 2. $LFSR_2$ and $LFSR_3$.

$LFSR_2$	$(x_7\|\|x_6\|\|x_5\|\|x_4\|\|x_3\|\|x_2\|\|x_1\|\|x_0) \rightarrow (x_6\|\|x_5\|\|x_4\|\|x_3\|\|x_2\|\|x_1\|\|x_0\|\|x_7 \oplus x_5)$
$LFSR_3$	$(x_7\|\|x_6\|\|x_5\|\|x_4\|\|x_3\|\|x_2\|\|x_1\|\|x_0) \rightarrow (x_0 \oplus x_6\|\|x_7\|\|x_6\|\|x_5\|\|x_4\|\|x_3\|\|x_2\|\|x_1)$

Finally, RC_i denotes the key schedule round constants. We omit the details of constant because it does not impact to the attacks. Encryption of Deoxys-BC-384 is illustrated in Fig. 1.

3 Previous Attacks on Deoxys-BC

Our attacks are based on the related-tweakey boomerang distinguishers and related-tweakey rectangle key-recovery attacks by Cid et al. [7]. In this section, we first briefly recall the framework of the related-tweakey boomerang-like attacks in Sect. 3.1. Then, in Sect. 3.2, we introduce the attacks by Cid et al. that are the main target of this paper.

3.1 Brief Introduction of Boomerang Attacks

Boomerang attacks and variants combine short differential trails with high probability. Here we briefly introduce the framework of the boomerang attack.

Boomerang and Rectangle Attacks. Boomerang attack [20] regards the target cipher as a composition of two sub-ciphers E_0 and E_1. The first sub-cipher is supposed to have a differential $\alpha \to \beta$, and the second one to have a differential $\gamma \to \delta$, with probabilities p and q, respectively. The basic boomerang attack requires an adaptive chosen plaintext/ciphertext scenario, and plaintext pairs result in a right quartet with probability $p^2 q^2$. The amplified boomerang attack (also called the rectangle attack) works in a chosen-plaintext scenario and a right quartet is obtained with probability $p^2 q^2 2^{-n}$ [12]. Further, it was pointed out in [3,4] that any value of β and γ is allowed as long as $\beta \neq \gamma$. As a result, the probability of the right quartet is increased to $2^{-n} \hat{p}^2 \hat{q}^2$, where

$$\hat{p} = \sqrt{\sum_i \mathrm{Pr}^2(\alpha \to \beta_i)} \text{ and } \hat{q} = \sqrt{\sum_j \mathrm{Pr}^2(\gamma_j \to \delta)}.$$

Boomerang and rectangle attacks under related-key setting were formulated in [5]. Let ΔK and ∇K be the key differences for the first and second sub-ciphers, respectively. The attack needs access to four related-key oracles with $K_1 \in \mathbb{K}$, where $\mathbb{K}$ is the key space, $K_2 = K_1 \oplus \Delta K$, $K_3 = K_1 \oplus \nabla K$ and $K_4 = K_1 \oplus \Delta K \oplus \nabla K$. In the related-key boomerang attack, paired plaintexts P_1, P_2 such that $P_1 \oplus P_2 = \alpha$ are queried to K_1 encryption oracle and K_2 encryption oracle, and the attacker receives ciphertexts C_1 and C_2. Then C_3 and C_4 are calculated by $C_3 = C_1 \oplus \delta$ and $C_4 = C_2 \oplus \delta$, and then queried to K_3 decryption oracle and K_4 decryption oracle. The resulting plaintext difference $P_3 \oplus P_4$ equals to α with probability $\hat{p}^2 \hat{q}^2$. The distinguishing game can be described more formally in an algorithmic form as Algorithm 1. The game returns a distinguishing bit $b \in \{0, 1\}$ that is set to 1 if the oracle is a target algorithm and 0 if the oracle is an ideal permutation. Algorithm 1 is $(\hat{p}\hat{q})^{-2}$ many iterations of 2 chosen-plaintext and 2 adaptively chosen-ciphertext queries. Hence the attack complexity is $(time, data, memory) = (4 \cdot (\hat{p}\hat{q})^{-2}, 4 \cdot (\hat{p}\hat{q})^{-2}, negligible)$.

Algorithm 1. Basic Procedure of Related-Key Boomerang Distinguishers

---

Input: $\alpha, \delta, K_1, K_2, K_3, K_4, \hat{p}\hat{q}$
Output: $b \in \{0, 1\}$
1: **for** $i \leftarrow 1, 2, \ldots, (\hat{p}\hat{q})^{-2}$ **do**
2:     Choose distinct input P_1. Set $P_2 \leftarrow P_1 \oplus \alpha$.
3:     Obtain $C_1 = E_{K_1}(P_1)$ and $C_2 = E_{K_2}(P_2)$ by making encryption queries.
4:     Set $C_3 \leftarrow C_1 \oplus \delta$ and $C_4 \leftarrow C_2 \oplus \delta$.
5:     Obtain $P_3 = D_{K_3}(C_3)$ and $P_4 = D_{K_4}(C_4)$ by making decryption queries.
6:     **if** $P_3 \oplus P_4 = \alpha$ **then**
7:         **return** 1
8:     **end if**
9: **end for**
10: **return** 0

In the attacks against full AES-192 and AES-256 [6], Biryukov and Khovratovich introduced *the boomerang switch* in order to gain free rounds at the boundary of two trails. The idea was to optimize the transition between the sub-trails of E_0 and E_1 in order to minimize the overall complexity of the distinguisher. In the previous boomerang and rectangle attacks against Deoxys-BC by Cid et al. [7], the following two types of switch techniques are exploited.

Ladder switch. A cipher is decomposed into rounds by default. However, decomposition regarding smaller operations, like columns and bytes, may lead to better distinguishers.

S-box switch. Suppose E_0 ends with an S-box and the output difference of this S-box is Δ. If the same difference Δ comes from the path of E_1, then the propagation through this S-box is for free in one of the directions.

The theoretical explanation behind those techniques were later formalized as the sandwich framework [8,9].

3.2 Previous Boomerang and Rectangle Attacks on Deoxys-BC

Cid et al. [7] presented related-tweakey boomerang distinguishers and related-tweakey rectangle key-recovery attacks against reduced rounds of Deoxys-BC. In short, Cid et al. [7] developed a new MILP-based differential search method for related-tweakey boomerang or rectangle attacks. Their tool has the following two advantages; (1) it takes into account incompatibility of linear relations between independently chosen subtweakey differences and (2) it optimizes the active-byte positions by taking into account the gain from the ladder switch technique.

Consequently, Cid et al. found 8- and 9-round related-tweakey boomerang trails against Deoxys-BC-256 with probability $\hat{p}\hat{q} = 2^{-36}$ and 2^{-61}, respectively and 10- and 11-round trails against Deoxys-BC-384 with probability $\hat{p}\hat{q} = 2^{-21}$ and 2^{-60}, respectively. The 8-round trail for Deoxys-BC-256 is presented in Table 3. In Table 3, the first column show the round number, the second, third, fourth, and fifth columns are the difference before AddRoundTweakey, the subtweakey difference, the difference before SubBytes and the difference before MixColumns, respectively. The sixth column is the probability of the total differential propagation during SubBytes in each round. The middle two rounds (rounds 4 and 5) are included in both of E_0 and E_1 due to the ladder switch technique. Namely, the boundary of E_0 and E_1 is defined byte-wise or column-wise instead of state-wise, thus some part of the state belongs to E_0 and the other part belongs to E_1. In round 1, the plaintext should have differences in 5 bytes, and one of them is canceled by the subtweakey difference. Then, each non-zero difference is converted to the specific output difference with probability 2^{-6}, thus the total probability in round 1 is $2^{-6\times4} = 2^{-24}$. The other rounds can be explained similarly.

The other related-tweakey boomerang trails can be found in Tables 4, 5 and 6 in Appendix A. Note that Cid et al. also showed similar trails for more rounds

Table 3. 8-round distinguisher of Deoxys-BC-256

$\Delta T K_0^1$: 00 00 00 00 00 00 00 00 00 00 00 00 00 00 00 46
$\Delta T K_0^2$: 00 00 00 00 00 00 00 00 00 00 00 00 00 00 00 d1
$\nabla T K_0^1$: 00 00 02 00 00 00 00 b3 00 00 00 00 00 00 00 00
$\nabla T K_0^2$: 00 00 a8 00 00 00 00 96 00 00 00 00 00 00 00 00

R	before ATK	ΔSTK	before SB	before MC	p_r
1	00 b9 00 00 00 00 d1 00 00 00 00 ab 61 00 00 97	00 00 00 00 00 00 00 00 00 00 00 00 00 00 00 97	00 b9 00 00 00 00 d1 00 00 00 00 ab 61 00 00 00	00 35 00 00 00 5d 00 00 00 01 00 00 00 8c 00 00	2^{-24}
2	00 00 00 00 00 00 00 00 00 e5 00 00 00 00 00 00	00 00 00 00 00 00 00 00 00 e5 00 00 00 00 00 00	00 00 00 00 00 00 00 00 00 00 00 00 00 00 00 00	00 00 00 00 00 00 00 00 00 00 00 00 00 00 00 00	1
3	00 00 00 00 00 00 00 00 00 00 00 00 00 00 00 00	00 00 00 00 00 00 00 00 00 00 00 00 00 00 00 00	00 00 00 00 00 00 00 00 00 00 00 00 00 00 00 00	00 00 00 00 00 00 00 00 00 00 00 00 00 00 00 00	1
4	00 00 00 00 00 00 00 00 00 00 00 00 00 00 00 00	ca 00 00 00 00 00 00 00 00 00 00 00 00 00 00 00	00 00 00 00 00 00 00 00 00 00 00 00	00 00 00 00 00 00 00 00 00 00 00 00	1
5	00 00 00 00 00 00 00 00 00 00 00 00	00 00 00 00 00 00 00 00 00 00 00	00 00 00 00 00 00 00 00 00 00 00	00 00 00 00 00 00 00 00 00 00 00	1

4			00
			  00
			    00
			      00
				00
				00
				00
				00
					1

5	00
	00
	00
	00
		00
		00
		00
		00 00
			00
			00
			00
			00 00
				00
				      00
				   00
				  00 00
					1

6	00 00 00 00 00 03 00 00 00 6a 00 00 00 00 00 00	00 00 00 00 00 03 00 00 00 6a 00 00 00 00 00 00	00 00 00 00 00 00 00 00 00 00 00 00 00 00 00 00	00 00 00 00 00 00 00 00 00 00 00 00 00 00 00 00	1
7	00 00 00 00 00 00 00 00 00 00 00 00 00 00 00 00	00 00 00 00 00 00 00 00 00 00 00 00 00 00 00 00	00 00 00 00 00 00 00 00 00 00 00 00 00 00 00 00	00 00 00 00 00 00 00 00 00 00 00 00 00 00 00 00	1
8	00 00 00 00 00 00 00 00 00 00 00 00 00 00 00 00	d5 00 00 00 00 00 00 00 00 00 00 00 00 00 06 00	d5 00 00 00 00 00 00 00 00 00 00 00 00 00 06 00	60 00 00 00 00 00 00 00 00 00 00 00 00 00 00 0c	2^{-12}

but with much lower probability. Because how to utilize them in the attack is unclear and we do not use them in this paper, we omit those trails.

As the last remarks, in the boomerang-type attacks, the attackers need to be very careful about the compatibility of two independently chosen short trails because such two independent trails may not be connected [18]. Cid et al. did the experimental verification (sometimes by reducing the number of rounds for each trail) to show that the two trails can be connected with the probability evaluated by them.

4 New Attacks on Deoxys-BC-256

In this section, we improve the distinguisher and key recovery attacks by Cid et al. [7] against Deoxys-BC-256. Considering that the differential search method in [7] is fairly optimized, we focus our attention on how to utilize the discovered boomerang trails rather than finding new trails.

4.1 Improved Boomerang Distinguishers

Truncating the Differential Trail. The boomerang distinguishers in [7] are the straightforward applications of Algorithm 1 to their boomerang trails. As shown in Tables 3 and 4, the trails have $(\hat{p}\hat{q}) = 2^{-36}$ and 2^{-61} for 8 rounds and 9 rounds, respectively, thus the data complexities are 2^{74} and 2^{124}, respectively. Hereafter, we first discuss the improvement for the 8-round distinguisher, and will later apply the improvement to 9 rounds.

The first improving point is Step 6 in Algorithm 1 that checks the match between the n-bit computed difference and α. It may be sufficient to match a part of differences as long as the number of matched bits is sufficient to discard all the wrong quartets. Recall the first half of the differential trail in the 8-round distinguisher in Table 3. In the previous attack, the attacker matches 128-bits of differences of the form

$$00\ 00\ 00\ 01\ \ b9\ 00\ 00\ 00\ \ 00\ d1\ 00\ 00\ \ 00\ 00\ ab\ 97$$

at Step 6 in Algorithm 1. We now ignore the match of differences for 4 active bytes before the active S-boxes in the first round, thus only check whether or not 12 bytes have the following difference.

$$00\ 00\ 00\ *\ \ *\ 00\ 00\ 00\ \ 00\ *\ 00\ 00\ \ 00\ 00\ *\ 97$$

Here, 97 in the last byte of the plaintext difference comes from `AddRoundTweakey` in the first round, which XORs subtweakey difference 97 to the zero-difference byte. Hence, we basically check whether S-boxes in 12 bytes are active or inactive. This saves us the probability of satisfying the differential transition through S-boxes in the first round, which increases the probability of the distinguisher from 2^{-72} to 2^{-48}. Hence, with this effort, the complexity of the distinguisher becomes $(time, data, memory) = (2^{50}, 2^{50}, negligible)$.

It should be noted that the probability that an ideal permutation satisfies the property also increases: $2^{-8 \times 12} = 2^{-96}$. Since this is smaller than 2^{-48}, the 8-round distinguisher can work.

Structure Technique. The data complexity of the above distinguisher can be further reduced by constructing the plaintext structure. This requires the use of additional memory, but the total memory amount is still practical.

In the differential trail in Table 3, we need the 4-byte difference of the following form before the MixColumns in the first round:

$$\text{00 00 00 00 35 5d 01 8c 00 00 00 00 00 00 00 00}$$

The corresponding plaintext difference does not have to be the one specified in Table 3 but can be any difference as long as the desired 4-byte difference can be generated with non-zero probability. Let $\mathcal{I}_{35}$ be a set of differences defined as follows.

$$\mathcal{I}_{35} \triangleq \{\Delta \in \{0,1\}^8 \mid \exists x \in \{0,1\}^8 \; s.t. \; \mathcal{S}(x) \oplus \mathcal{S}(x \oplus \Delta) = \text{35}\}.$$

The size of $\mathcal{I}_{35}$ is 126. Similarly, $\mathcal{I}_{5d}$, $\mathcal{I}_{01}$ and $\mathcal{I}_{8c}$ can be defined and the size of each set is 126.

To generate the structure, we generate two sets of 2^{32} plaintexts $\mathcal{P}_1$ and $\mathcal{P}_2$, where $\mathcal{P}_1$ (resp. $\mathcal{P}_2$) contains plaintexts to be queried to the oracle with K_1 (resp. K_2). In each set, all possible values are contained for four active bytes in the first round and the other 12 bytes are fixed to some specified value. To be more precise, 12 byte-values $c_i \in \{0,1\}^8, 0 \le i \le 15, i \ne 3, 4, 9, 14$ are fixed, and all the 2^{32} values are collected in the other 4 bytes. $\mathcal{P}_1$ and $\mathcal{P}_2$ are defined as follows. Note that we need to make difference 97 in the last byte to cancel the first subtweakey difference.

$$\mathcal{P}_1 \triangleq \{c_0, c_1, c_2, * \; *, c_5, c_6, c_7 \; c_8, *, c_{10}, c_{11}, \; c_{12}, c_{13}, *, c_{15}\},$$
$$\mathcal{P}_2 \triangleq \{c_0, c_1, c_2, * \; *, c_5, c_6, c_7 \; c_8, *, c_{10}, c_{11}, \; c_{12}, c_{13}, *, c_{15} \oplus 97\}.$$

To utilize $\mathcal{P}_1$ and $\mathcal{P}_2$ in the boomerang attack framework, each of the 2^{32} plaintexts in $\mathcal{P}_1$ is queried to the encryption oracle with K_1, then δ is XORed to the resulting ciphertext, and finally the generated ciphertext is queried to the decryption oracle with K_3. Namely the attacker performs the following process and stores the results in $\mathcal{P}_3$:

$$P_3^i \leftarrow D_{K_3}\big(E_{K_1}(P_1^i) \oplus \delta\big),$$

where P_1^i for $i = 0, 1, \cdots, 2^{32} - 1$ is each plaintext in $\mathcal{P}_1$.

The attacker then computes $P_4^i \leftarrow D_{K_4}\big(E_{K_2}(P_2^i) \oplus \delta\big)$ for each plaintext in $\mathcal{P}_2$, and checks the match of 12-byte difference between P_4^i and $\mathcal{P}_3$ (for Step 6 in Algorithm 1) along with another check if 4-byte difference between P_1^i and P_2^i are included in $\mathcal{I}_{35}$, $\mathcal{I}_{5d}$, $\mathcal{I}_{01}$ and $\mathcal{I}_{8c}$.

Time Complexity and Optimization. In the single structure, $4 \cdot 2^{32}$ queries are made, thus the data complexity is 2^{34}. The number of pairs that can be made from $\mathcal{P}_1$ and $\mathcal{P}_2$ is $2^{32*2} = 2^{64}$, of which $2^{64} \cdot \frac{126}{255}^4 \approx 2^{60}$ pairs satisfy the constraint for P_1 and P_2 (included in $\mathcal{I}_{35}$, $\mathcal{I}_{5d}$, $\mathcal{I}_{01}$ and $\mathcal{I}_{8c}$) and there should be $2^{60-48} = 2^{12}$ pairs satisfying the boomerang trail with probability 2^{-48}. This is sufficient to distinguish 8-round Deoxys-BC-256 from an ideal permutation.

One may note that generating 2^{12} quartets is too much for the attack. Indeed, the attack works by setting the size of $\mathcal{P}_1$ and $\mathcal{P}_2$ to 2^{26}. Then among 2^{52} possible pairs, about $2^{52-4-48} = 1$ pair will satisfy the boomerang trail. Overall, the data complexity is $4 \cdot 2^{26} = 2^{28}$ queries and the time complexity is 2^{28} memory access. The attacker needs to store 2^{26} plaintexts in $\mathcal{P}_1$ and in $\mathcal{P}_3$, thus the memory complexity is 2^{27} plaintexts.

Application to 9-Round Distinguisher. Recall the differential trail for the 9-round distinguisher in Table 4. Differently from the 8-round distinguisher, there is no active S-box in the first round. Hence, to apply the similar improvement, we need to change the attack model to the opposite direction i.e. chosen-ciphertext and adaptively chosen-plaintext attack. Note that Deoxys does not omit Mix-Columns in the last round but it is well-known that having such linear operation in the last round does not change the impact of the differential cryptanalysis. Indeed, the attacker can do analysis by considering $\texttt{MixColumns}^{-1}(\Delta C)$ instead of ΔC in general.

The rest is similar as the 8-round distinguisher, thus we only give a summary.

- By using the truncation of the differential trail, we can avoid the probability loss of 2^{-12}. Hence, the probability of the boomerang trail becomes $2^{-122+12} = 2^{-110}$. Note that the probability that an ideal permutation provides a pair with zero difference in 14 bytes is 2^{-112}, which is smaller than 2^{-110} in the boomerang trail.
- By using the structure, the attacker can define two sets of 2^{16} ciphertexts $\mathcal{C}_1$ and $\mathcal{C}_3$. 2^{32} pairs can be generated and $2^{32} \cdot \frac{126}{255} \approx 2^{30}$ pairs satisfy the ciphertext difference in the last round.
- After generating 2^{80} structures by changing the constant in 14 bytes of the ciphertext, the number of pairs reaches 2^{110}, thus the attacker can expect to find 1 quartet satisfying the boomerang trail. The data complexity is $4 * 2^{16} = 2^{18}$ per structure, thus 2^{98} in total. The time complexity is 2^{98} memory access. The attacker needs to store 2^{16} ciphertexts in $\mathcal{C}_1$ and $\mathcal{C}_2$, thus the required memory amount is 2^{17}.

Remarks to Increase Distinguishing Advantage. One may think that the gap of the probabilities between the actual cipher and an ideal permutation (2^{-110} vs 2^{-112}) is too small. We argue that the distinguishing advantage can be significantly increased with negligible cost.

The idea is after Step 6 of Algorithm 1 is passed, we inject another check whether the generated pair actually follows the boomerang trail. If so, the distinguishing game returns $b = 1$, otherwise it continues the algorithm. Suppose that a boomerang quartet C_1, C_2, C_3, C_4 is generated. The attacker then modifies C_1 and C_3 to C_1' and C_3' so that the two active S-boxes in the last round will not be modified and obtains the corresponding C_2' and C_4'. If C_1, C_2, C_3, C_4 follows the trail, the differential transitions through the two S-boxes in the last round are already satisfied, hence C_1', C_2', C_3', C_4' should form another boomerang quartet with probability $2^{-110+12} = 2^{-98}$. Thus after generating 2^{98} pairs of C_1' and C_3', the false positive can be eliminated. Note that 2^{98} pairs of C_1' and C_3' can be generated by using the structure technique, thus the complexity of this additional check is 2^{82} with the memory of size 2^{17}.

4.2   Improved Key Recovery Attacks

Cid et al. [7] discussed related-tweakey rectangle attacks. In [7], they directly applied the general complexity analysis in [14] for related-tweakey rectangle attack against SKINNY [1]. Hence, it is of interest to optimize the attack by taking into account the structure of Deoxys-BC. Indeed, we show that the attack complexity can be improved by using boomerang attacks instead of rectangle attacks.

Note that in the 9-round attack, we assume the default setting by the designers in which the 256-bit tweakey consists of 128-bit tweak and 128-bit key.

9-Round Attacks Using 9-Round Distinguisher. Our 9-round attack is very simple but effective. We do not append extra key-recovery round to the distinguisher, but recovers the key inside the distinguisher. We first run the 9-round distinguisher explained in Sect. 4.1 with complexity $(Time, Data, Memory) = (2^{98}, 2^{98}, 2^{17})$ to find a quartet of texts satisfying the boomerang trail. Due to the truncation of the differential trail, we did not pay attention to the output difference of the active S-boxes in the last round to identify the quartet. We use those information for key recovery.

As shown in Table 4, the input differences to the two active S-boxes in the last round are e3 and 0c. The output differences can be computed by MixColumns$^{-1}(\Delta C)$. From the property of the S-box, the actual values in those S-boxes can be reduced to about 2 choices per byte. Those immediately reveal 2-byte information of the last subkey STK_9 converted by inverse MixColumns and ShiftRows, namely ShiftRows$^{-1} \circ$ MixColumns$^{-1}(STK_9)$. Because we have 2 pairs in a quartet, the 2-byte information of STK_9 is uniquely identified. Because STK_9 is an XOR of tweak and key and tweak is known to he attacker, 2-byte information of the master key can be obtained.

The remaining is a simple exhaustive search on the other 14 bytes, which requires 2^{112} computations. Thus the total complexity of the 9-round key recovery is $(Time, Data, Memory) = (2^{112}, 2^{98}, 2^{17})$.

10-Round Attacks Using 9-Round Distinguisher. In this attack, we append 1 round to the end of the 9-round distinguisher in Table 4, which is illustrated in Fig. 2. Note that appending 1-round before the plaintext is hard because of too many active bytes in the initial state of the 8-round distinguisher.

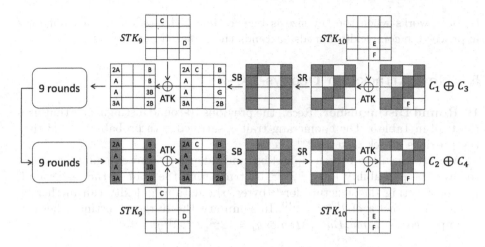

Fig. 2. Key recovery for 10-round Deoxys-BC-256. 'A', 'B', 'C', 'D', 'E' and 'F' are uniquely fixed difference by the boomerang trail and 'G' is $3B \oplus D$.

As discussed before, MixColumns in the last round does not have any impact to the attack. To simplify the discussion, we describe the attack by omitting the MixColumns in the last round.

In Fig. 2, the upper part is the computations for the first pair (C_1 and C_3). We need to ensure the exact difference of the distinguisher's input (in inverse direction). After P_1 and P_3 are obtained, P_2 and P_4 are generated and encryption queries are made to obtain C_2 and C_4, which is illustrated in the bottom half. Because the output of the distinguisher is truncated, we only know that 2 bytes are active (and then expanded to 2 columns after MixColumns in round 9).

As clearly illustrated in Fig. 2, the partial computation from the ciphertext to 9 active bytes through AddRoundTweakey^{-1}, ShiftRows^{-1}, SubBytes^{-1} involves 9 bytes of STK_{10}. By guessing those 9 bytes, we can compute the values of active bytes at the end of distinguisher from the ciphertext, which is enough to construct the structure for the remaining 9 rounds. Besides, for each obtained C_2 and C_4, we can compute back to the difference of the distinguisher's output.

In summary, by exhaustively guessing 9 bytes of STK_{10}, we can apply the 9-round distinguisher, which returns a valid boomerang quartet only when the guess of STK_{10} is correct. The attack is 2^{72} repetitions of the 9-round distinguisher that requires 2^{98} data and time complexities with 2^{17} memory, thus $(Time, Data, Memory) = (2^{170}, 2^{170}, 2^{17})$.

Note that during 2^{72} iterations of the 9-round distinguisher, 2^{98} queried data can be reused. (For different guess, only the order to make pairs changes.) Thus by storing 2^{98} queried data in the memory, the attack complexity can be $(Time, Data, Memory) = (2^{98}, 2^{170}, 2^{98})$.

In both cases, the attack is faster than the exhaustive search only if the key size in 256-bit tweakey is bigger than 170 bits. Given that the previous attack

[7] only works when the key size is bigger than 204 bits, our attack not only improves the complexity but also extends the attacked parameters.

5   New Attacks on Deoxys-BC-384

10-Round Distinguisher. Recall the previous 10-round distinguisher that uses the trail in Table 5. The boomerang trail is satisfied with probability 2^{-42} thus the previous attack requires 2^{44} queries.

We attack in the chosen-ciphertext and adaptively chosen-plaintext model to save the probability loss of 2^{-12} by truncating the trail in the last round. By constructing the structure for 2 bytes, the data complexity can further be reduced by a factor of $2^{12-2} = 2^{10}$. In summary, the 10-round distinguisher can be improved to $(Time, Data, Memory) = (2^{22}, 2^{22}, 2^{17})$.

11-Round Distinguisher. Recall the previous 11-round distinguisher that uses the trail in Table 6. The boomerang trail is satisfied with probability 2^{-120} thus the previous attack requires 2^{122} queries.

We attack in the chosen-ciphertext and adaptively chosen-plaintext model to save the probability loss of 2^{-12} by truncating the trail in the last round. By exploiting the structure for 2 bytes, the 11-round distinguisher can be improved to $(Time, Data, Memory) = (2^{100}, 2^{100}, 2^{17})$.

12-Round Key Recovery. We append 1 round to the end of 11-round distinguisher in Table 6, which is illustrated in Fig. 3. Differently from the 10-round

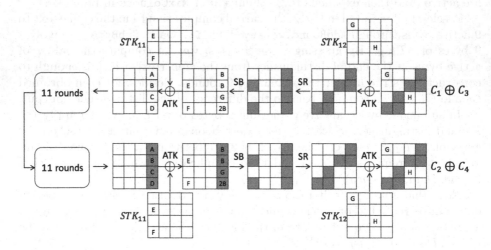

Fig. 3. Key recovery for 12-round Deoxys-BC-384.

key recovery attack against Deoxys-BC-256, the appended round only involves 6 bytes of STK_{12}.

Because the attack is the iteration for the 11-round distinguisher for exhaustive guesses of 6 subtweakey bytes in the key-recovery part, the attack complexity becomes $(Time, Data, Memory) = (2^{148}, 2^{148}, 2^{17})$ or $(2^{148}, 2^{100}, 2^{100})$.

6   Discussion and Conclusion

Discussion. The following features can be extracted by comparing the attacks in Sects. 4 and 5.

- Active byte positions at the input and output of the distinguisher significantly impact to the complexity of the key-recovery. If multiple active bytes locate in the same column in subsequent MixColumns like Fig. 3 rather than Fig. 2, the complexity of key recovery is much smaller.
- The attack complexity is reduced if the positions of subtweakey differences for subsequent AddRoundTweakey overlap with active bytes in the state.
- The existence of probabilistic propagation in the first and the last round of the distinguisher allows the attacker to optimize the attack. In contrast, it is hard to exploit probabilistic propagation in middle rounds.

The differential search by Cid et al. [7] did not consider those features and they found a lot of the best trails with the same score. Developing a new automated search method considering those features is a promising future research direction, which may allow us to identify the really best differential trail.

Concluding Remarks. In this paper, we showed how the attacks on Deoxys-BC can be optimized by considering the design details. Our attacks are based on the boomerang trails discovered by Cid et al. [7], but the attack procedures are carefully chosen to reduce the complexity. In particular, the improvement is big for Deoxys-BC-256. The complexity improvement with respect to max$(Time, Data, Memory)$ is from 2^{74} to 2^{28} for the 8-round distinguisher, from 2^{124} to 2^{98} for the 9-round distinguisher, from 2^{118} to 2^{112} for the 9-round key recovery, and from 2^{204} to 2^{170} for the 10-round key recovery. We believe that the presented analyses provide better understanding of Deoxys-BC.

A   Details of Boomerang Trails

Table 4. 9-round distinguisher of Deoxys-BC-256

```
ΔTK₀¹ : 00 7f 00 00   00 ff 00 00   0b 00 f1 00   00 00 00 7c
ΔTK₀² : 00 cf 00 00   00 3f 00 00   70 00 5e 00   00 00 00 be
∇TK₀¹ : 00 00 00 00   00 a1 00 04   00 00 00 00   00 00 00 00
∇TK₀² : 00 00 00 00   00 bf 00 a8   00 00 00 00   00 00 00 00
```

R	before ATK	ΔSTK	before SB	before MC	p_r
1	00 00 7b 00	00 00 7b 00	00 00 00 00	00 00 00 00	1
	b0 c0 00 00	b0 c0 00 00	00 00 00 00	00 00 00 00	
	00 00 af 00	00 00 af 00	00 00 00 00	00 00 00 00	
	61 00 00 c2	00 00 00 c2	00 00 00 00	00 00 00 00	
2	00 00 00 00	e0 80 00 00	e0 80 00 00	b4 c9 00 00	2^{-28}
	00 00 00 00	00 4d 00 00	00 4d 00 00	21 00 00 00	
	00 00 00 00	00 00 00 00	00 00 00 00	00 00 00 00	
	00 00 00 00	00 00 00 ea	00 00 00 ea	73 00 00 00	
3	63 89 00 00	00 89 00 00	63 00 00 00	8d 00 00 00	2^{-14}
	85 c9 00 00	85 00 00 00	00 c9 00 00	8c 00 00 00	
	00 c9 00 00	00 c9 00 00	00 00 00 00	00 00 00 00	
	00 40 00 00	00 40 00 00	00 00 00 00	00 00 00 00	
4	8e 00 00 00	8e 00 00 00	00 00 00 00	00 00 00 00	1
	8e 00 00 00	8e 00 00 00	00 00 00 00	00 00 00 00	
	01 00 00 00	01 00 00 00	00 00 00 00	00 00 00 00	
	00 00 00 00	00 00 00 00	00 00 00 00	00 00 00 00	
5	00 00 00 00	00 00 00 00	00 00 00	00 00 00	1
	00 00 00 00	00 00 80 03	00 00	00 00	
	00 00 00 00	13 00 00 00	00 00 00	00 00 00	
	00 00 00 00	00 98 00 00	00 00 00	00 00 00	
6	00 00	00 07	00	00	1
	00 00	00 35	00	00	
	00 00	00 b4	00	00	
	00 00	00 00	00 00	00 00	
5			00	00	1
			00 00	00 00	
			00	00	
			00	00	
6	00 00	00 00	00 00 00	00 00 00	2^{-7}
	32 00	00 00	32 00 00	2f 00 00	
	05 00	05 00	00 00 00	00 00 00	
	00 00	00 00	00 00	00 00	
7	00 00 00 00	00 00 00 00	00 00 00 00	00 00 00 00	1
	06 00 00 00	06 00 00 00	00 00 00 00	00 00 00 00	
	00 00 00 00	00 00 00 00	00 00 00 00	00 00 00 00	
	71 00 00 00	71 00 00 00	00 00 00 00	00 00 00 00	
8	00 00 00 00	00 00 00 00	00 00 00 00	00 00 00 00	1
	00 00 00 00	00 00 00 00	00 00 00 00	00 00 00 00	
	00 00 00 00	00 00 00 00	00 00 00 00	00 00 00 00	
	00 00 00 00	00 00 00 00	00 00 00 00	00 00 00 00	
9	00 00 00 00	00 00 00 00	00 00 00 00	00 00 00 00	2^{-12}
	00 00 00 00	00 e3 00 00	00 e3 00 00	72 00 00 00	
	00 00 00 00	00 00 00 00	00 00 00 00	00 00 00 00	
	00 00 00 00	00 0c 00 00	00 0c 00 00	00 00 9d 00	

Table 5. 10-round distinguisher of Deoxys-BC-384. The S-box switch is used in round 6 (lower) for the S-box at position (1,1).

$$\Delta TK_0^1 : 00\ 00\ 8b\ 00\ /\ 00\ 00\ 00\ 90\ /\ 90\ 00\ 00\ 00\ /\ 00\ 1b\ 00\ 00$$
$$\Delta TK_0^2 : 00\ 00\ 21\ 00\ /\ 00\ 00\ 00\ 63\ /\ 63\ 00\ 00\ 00\ /\ 00\ 42\ 00\ 00$$
$$\Delta TK_0^3 : 00\ 00\ 34\ 00\ /\ 00\ 00\ 00\ 7d\ /\ 7d\ 00\ 00\ 00\ /\ 00\ 49\ 00\ 00$$
$$\nabla TK_0^1 : 00\ 00\ 00\ 00\ /\ 00\ 00\ 00\ 6e\ /\ 00\ 00\ 00\ 00\ /\ b1\ 00\ 00\ 00$$
$$\nabla TK_0^2 : 00\ 00\ 00\ 00\ /\ 00\ 00\ 00\ 42\ /\ 00\ 00\ 00\ 00\ /\ f5\ 00\ 00\ 00$$
$$\nabla TK_0^3 : 00\ 00\ 00\ 00\ /\ 00\ 00\ 00\ b3\ /\ 00\ 00\ 00\ 00\ /\ d3\ 00\ 00\ 00$$

R	before ATK	ΔSTK	before SB	before MC	p_r
1	00 00 8e 00 a3 00 00 10 9e 00 00 00 00 8e 00 00	00 00 8e 00 00 00 00 10 9e 00 00 00 00 8e 00 00	00 00 00 00 a3 00 00 00 00 00 00 00 00 00 00 00	00 00 00 00 00 00 00 69 00 00 00 00 00 00 00 00	2^{-6}
2	00 00 00 bb 00 00 00 d2 00 00 00 69 00 00 00 69	00 00 00 bb 00 00 00 d2 00 00 00 69 00 00 00 69	00 00 00 00 00 00 00 00 00 00 00 00 00 00 00 00	00 00 00 00 00 00 00 00 00 00 00 00 00 00 00 00	1
3	00 00 00 00 00 00 00 00 00 00 00 00 00 00 00 00	00 00 00 00 00 00 00 00 00 00 00 00 00 00 00 00	00 00 00 00 00 00 00 00 00 00 00 00 00 00 00 00	00 00 00 00 00 00 00 00 00 00 00 00 00 00 00 00	1
4	00 00 00 00 00 00 00 00 00 00 00 00 00 00 00 00	00 00 00 00 00 00 00 00 00 00 00 00 00 00 00 00	00 00 00 00 00 00 00 00 00 00 00 00 00 00 00 00	00 00 00 00 00 00 00 00 00 00 00 00 00 00 00 00	1
5	00 00 00 00 00 00 00 00 00 00 00 00 00 00 00 00	69 00 00 00 00 bb 00 00 00 00 d2 00 00 00 00 69	00 00 00 00 00 00 00 00 00 00 00 00	00 00 00 00 00 00 00 00 00 00 00 00	1
6	00 00 00 00 00 00 00 00 00 00 00 00	10 00 00 9e 00 00 8e 00 00 8e 00 00	00 00 9e 00 00 00 00 00 00	00 00 00 00 00 00 00 00	1
5			00 00 00 00	00 00 00 00	1
6	00 00 00 00	00 00 00 00	00 00 00 9e 00 00 00 00	00 00 00 00 68 00 00 00 01 00 00 00 b9 00 00 00	2^{-6}
7	00 00 00 00 6a 00 00 00 ba 00 00 00 00 00 00 00	00 00 00 00 6a 00 00 00 ba 00 00 00 00 00 00 00	00 00 00 00 00 00 00 00 00 00 00 00 00 00 00 00	00 00 00 00 00 00 00 00 00 00 00 00 00 00 00 00	1
8	00 00 00 00 00 00 00 00 00 00 00 00 00 00 00 00	00 00 00 00 00 00 00 00 00 00 00 00 00 00 00 00	00 00 00 00 00 00 00 00 00 00 00 00 00 00 00 00	00 00 00 00 00 00 00 00 00 00 00 00 00 00 00 00	1
9	00 00 00 00 00 00 00 00 00 00 00 00 00 00 00 00	00 00 00 00 00 00 00 00 00 00 00 00 00 00 00 00	00 00 00 00 00 00 00 00 00 00 00 00 00 00 00 00	00 00 00 00 00 00 00 00 00 00 00 00 00 00 00 00	1
10	00 00 00 00 00 00 00 00 00 00 00 00 00 00 00 00	00 00 00 00 00 00 00 00 00 00 00 6a ba 00 00 00	00 00 00 00 00 00 00 00 00 00 00 6a ba 00 00 00	00 00 00 00 00 00 00 00 00 61 00 00 00 97 00 00	2^{-12}

Table 6. 11-round distinguisher of Deoxys-BC-384

ΔTK_0^1 : 00 8b 00 00 c4 00 00 00 7a 00 c5 a6 00 00 00 00
ΔTK_0^2 : 00 ad 00 00 c4 00 00 00 73 00 21 d8 00 00 00 00
ΔTK_0^3 : 00 a3 00 00 9a 00 00 00 3b 00 0d 2e 00 00 00 00
∇TK_0^1 : 00 00 02 00 00 00 00 00 d7 00 00 00 00 00 00 00
∇TK_0^2 : 00 00 99 00 00 00 00 00 bc 00 00 00 00 00 00 00
∇TK_0^3 : 00 00 0c 00 00 00 00 00 f1 00 00 00 00 00 00 00

R	before ATK	ΔSTK	before SB	before MC	p_r
1	00 9a 32 00 85 00 00 00 00 00 e9 00 00 00 50 00	00 9a 32 00 85 00 00 00 00 00 e9 00 00 00 50 00	00 00 00 00 00 00 00 00 00 00 00 00 00 00 00 00	00 00 00 00 00 00 00 00 00 00 00 00 00 00 00 00	1
2	00 00 00 00 00 00 00 00 00 00 00 00 00 00 00 00	00 00 00 00 00 00 00 00 00 00 00 00 00 00 00 00	00 00 00 00 00 00 00 00 00 00 00 00 00 00 00 00	00 00 00 00 00 00 00 00 00 00 00 00 00 00 00 00	1
3	00 00 00 00 00 00 00 00 00 00 00 00 00 00 00 00	00 00 00 00 00 00 00 4f f1 7a 00 00 00 57 00 00	00 00 00 00 00 00 00 4f f1 7a 00 00 00 57 00 00	00 00 00 00 00 00 2a 00 00 00 15 a6 00 00 6b 00	2^{-28}
4	00 00 00 a6 00 00 00 f1 00 00 bd 57 00 00 e9 a6	00 00 00 a6 00 00 00 f1 00 00 00 57 00 00 e9 00	00 00 00 00 00 00 00 00 00 00 bd 00 00 00 00 a6	00 00 00 00 00 00 00 00 19 00 00 00 2b 00 00 00	2^{-13}
5	32 00 00 00 00 00 00 00 4f 00 00 00 4f 00 00 00	32 00 00 00 00 00 00 00 4f 00 00 00 4f 00 00 00	00 00 00 00 00 00 00 00 00 00 00 00 00 00 00 00	00 00 00 00 00 00 00 00 00 00 00 00 00 00 00 00	1

6	00 00 00 00
	00 00 00 00
	00 00 00 00
	00 00 00 00
		00 00 85 00
		00 00 00 b9
		00 00 00 00
		9a 34 00 00
			00 00 00
			00 00 00
			  00 00 00
			  00 00
				00 00
				00 00
				00 00
				00 00
					1

7	00 00 00 00 00 00 00 00	00 08 00 00 00 09 00 1b	00 00 00 00 00	00 00 00 00 00 00	1
6			00 00 00 00 00	cb 00 ff 00 1a 00 00 00	1
7	8d 00 00 00 00 00 a3 00	8d 00 00 00 00 00 00 00	00 00 00 00 00 00 00 00 a3 00 00	00 00 00 00 00 00 00 00 00 b5 00	2^{-7}
8	00 00 00 00 00 00 c4 00 00 00 00 00 00 00 05 00	00 00 00 00 00 00 c4 00 00 00 00 00 00 00 05 00	00 00 00 00 00 00 00 00 00 00 00 00 00 00 00 00	00 00 00 00 00 00 00 00 00 00 00 00 00 00 00 00	1
9	00 00 00 00 00 00 00 00 00 00 00 00 00 00 00 00	00 00 00 00 00 00 00 00 00 00 c4 00 00 00 00 00	00 00 00 00 00 00 00 00 00 00 00 00 00 00 00 00	00 00 00 00 00 00 00 00 00 00 00 00 00 00 00 00	1
10	00 00 00 00 00 00 00 00 00 00 00 00 00 00 00 00	00 00 00 00 00 00 00 00 00 00 00 00 00 00 00 00	00 00 00 00 00 00 00 00 00 00 00 00 00 00 00 00	00 00 00 00 00 00 00 00 00 00 00 00 00 00 00 00	1
11	00 00 00 00 00 00 00 00 00 00 00 00 00 00 00 00	00 00 00 05 00 00 00 00 00 c4 00 00 00 00 00 00	00 00 00 05 00 00 00 00 00 c4 00 00 00 00 00 00	00 00 00 08 00 00 00 00 00 00 00 7f 00 00 00 00	2^{-12}

References

1. Beierle, C., et al.: The SKINNY family of block ciphers and its low-latency variant MANTIS. In: Robshaw, M., Katz, J. (eds.) CRYPTO 2016. LNCS, vol. 9815, pp. 123–153. Springer, Heidelberg (2016). https://doi.org/10.1007/978-3-662-53008-5_5
2. Bernstein, D.: CAESAR competition (2013). http://competitions.cr.yp.to/caesar.html
3. Biham, E., Dunkelman, O., Keller, N.: The rectangle attack – rectangling the serpent. In: Pfitzmann, B. (ed.) EUROCRYPT 2001. LNCS, vol. 2045, pp. 340–357. Springer, Heidelberg (2001). https://doi.org/10.1007/3-540-44987-6_21
4. Biham, E., Dunkelman, O., Keller, N.: New results on boomerang and rectangle attacks. In: Daemen, J., Rijmen, V. (eds.) FSE 2002. LNCS, vol. 2365, pp. 1–16. Springer, Heidelberg (2002). https://doi.org/10.1007/3-540-45661-9_1
5. Biham, E., Dunkelman, O., Keller, N.: Related-key boomerang and rectangle attacks. In: Cramer, R. (ed.) EUROCRYPT 2005. LNCS, vol. 3494, pp. 507–525. Springer, Heidelberg (2005). https://doi.org/10.1007/11426639_30
6. Biryukov, A., Khovratovich, D.: Related-key cryptanalysis of the full AES-192 and AES-256. In: Matsui, M. (ed.) ASIACRYPT 2009. LNCS, vol. 5912, pp. 1–18. Springer, Heidelberg (2009). https://doi.org/10.1007/978-3-642-10366-7_1
7. Cid, C., Huang, T., Peyrin, T., Sasaki, Y., Song, L.: A security analysis of deoxys and its internal tweakable block ciphers. IACR Trans. Symmetric Cryptol. 2017(3), 73–107 (2017)
8. Dunkelman, O., Keller, N., Shamir, A.: A practical-time related-key attack on the KASUMI cryptosystem used in GSM and 3G telephony. In: Rabin, T. (ed.) CRYPTO 2010. LNCS, vol. 6223, pp. 393–410. Springer, Heidelberg (2010). https://doi.org/10.1007/978-3-642-14623-7_21
9. Dunkelman, O., Keller, N., Shamir, A.: A practical-time related-key attack on the KASUMI cryptosystem used in GSM and 3G telephony. J. Cryptol. 27(4), 824–849 (2014)
10. Jean, J., Nikolić, I., Peyrin, T.: Tweaks and keys for block ciphers: the TWEAKEY framework. In: Sarkar, P., Iwata, T. (eds.) ASIACRYPT 2014. LNCS, vol. 8874, pp. 274–288. Springer, Heidelberg (2014). https://doi.org/10.1007/978-3-662-45608-8_15
11. Jean, J., Nikolić, I., Peyrin, T., Seurin, Y.: Deoxys v1.41. Submitted to CAESAR, October 2016
12. Kelsey, J., Kohno, T., Schneier, B.: Amplified boomerang attacks against reduced-round MARS and Serpent. In: Goos, G., Hartmanis, J., van Leeuwen, J., Schneier, B. (eds.) FSE 2000. LNCS, vol. 1978, pp. 75–93. Springer, Heidelberg (2001). https://doi.org/10.1007/3-540-44706-7_6
13. Liskov, M., Rivest, R.L., Wagner, D.: Tweakable block ciphers. In: Yung, M. (ed.) CRYPTO 2002. LNCS, vol. 2442, pp. 31–46. Springer, Heidelberg (2002). https://doi.org/10.1007/3-540-45708-9_3
14. Liu, G., Ghosh, M., Ling, S.: Security analysis of SKINNY under related-tweakey settings (long paper). IACR Trans. Symmetric Cryptol. 2017(3), 37–72 (2017). https://doi.org/10.13154/tosc.v2017.i3.37-72
15. McGrew, D.A., Viega, J.: The security and performance of the Galois/Counter Mode (GCM) of operation. In: Canteaut, A., Viswanathan, K. (eds.) INDOCRYPT 2004. LNCS, vol. 3348, pp. 343–355. Springer, Heidelberg (2004). https://doi.org/10.1007/978-3-540-30556-9_27

16. Mehrdad, A., Moazami, F., Soleimany, H.: Impossible differential cryptanalysis on Deoxys-BC-256. Cryptology ePrint Archive, Report 2018/048 (2018). https://eprint.iacr.org/2018/048

17. Mouha, N., Wang, Q., Gu, D., Preneel, B.: Differential and linear cryptanalysis using mixed-integer linear programming. In: Wu, C.-K., Yung, M., Lin, D. (eds.) Inscrypt 2011. LNCS, vol. 7537, pp. 57–76. Springer, Heidelberg (2012). https://doi.org/10.1007/978-3-642-34704-7_5

18. Murphy, S.: The return of the cryptographic boomerang. IEEE Trans. Inf. Theory **57**(4), 2517–2521 (2011). https://doi.org/10.1109/TIT.2011.2111091

19. National Institute of Standards and Technology: Federal Information Processing Standards Publication 197: Advanced Encryption Standard (AES). NIST, November 2001

20. Wagner, D.: The boomerang attack. In: Knudsen, L. (ed.) FSE 1999. LNCS, vol. 1636, pp. 156–170. Springer, Heidelberg (1999). https://doi.org/10.1007/3-540-48519-8_12

SCA-Resistance for AES: How Cheap Can We Go?

Ricardo Chaves[1]([⊠]), Łukasz Chmielewski[2], Francesco Regazzoni[3], and Lejla Batina[4]

[1] INESC-ID, IST, Universidade de Lisboa, Lisbon, Portugal
ricardo.chaves@inesc-id.pt
[2] Riscure BV, Delft, The Netherlands
[3] ALaRI - University of Lugano, Lugano, Switzerland
[4] Digital Security Group - ICIS, Radboud University Nijmegen,
Nijmegen, The Netherlands

Abstract. This paper introduces a novel AES structure capable of improving the robustness against power analysis attacks while allowing for a very compact structure with a potentially negligible area and performance impact. The proposed design is based on a low entropy masking scheme, where half of the time the true value and half of the time the complemented value are used to mask the power consumption variation. The obtained experimental results suggest that the area overhead for the protection against power analysis is as low as 5% LUT increase with a performance degradation of about 10%. When compared with the state of the art supported on FPGAs, efficiency improvements above 6 times and a throughput improvement of at least two times higher are achieved.

1 Introduction

Modern society is strongly dependent on electronic devices. Smart phones and smart devices pervaded every aspect of our lives, handling a large amount of private and sensitive information. As these smart devices become increasingly connected together to form the Internet of Things, they become crucial components of our critical infrastructure. To allow the safe deployment and operation of these devices, designers must rely on secure primitives.

Unfortunately, mathematically strong cryptographic algorithms are not sufficient to guarantee the security of devices when computers are pervasive. Contrary to few years ago, nowadays target devices are potentially "in the hands" of the attackers, which can exploit more efficient and effective ways to extract secret information. The most powerful way to gain access to secret data is to exploit the weaknesses of the implementation rather than to target the mathematical structure of the algorithm itself. These attacks are called physical attacks as they exploit the physical weaknesses of the computing device. One of the most powerful physical attacks is power analysis [11], which exploits the relation between the power consumed by the device and the data being processed.

© Springer International Publishing AG, part of Springer Nature 2018
A. Joux et al. (Eds.): AFRICACRYPT 2018, LNCS 10831, pp. 107–123, 2018.
https://doi.org/10.1007/978-3-319-89339-6_7

Countermeasures against power analysis attacks, were already mentioned in the seminal work of Kocher et at. [11]. Power analysis attacks infer the secret key exploiting the dependence between the power consumed by a device and the data being processed (which, in the case of cryptographic primitives, might have to be kept secret). To avoid these attacks it is thus necessary to remove the dependence between the secret data and the power consumed during the computation.

Countermeasures are usually classified using the approach followed for achieving the protection. The first approach consists in breaking the link between the actual data that is processed by the device and the data on which the computation is performed. It is usually called masking, originally proposed by Messerges et al. [12] exploiting the principle of secret sharing [3]. It often consist of randomizing the secret data by adding a random value to them. The value has to be removed at the end of the computation to obtain the correct result. The second approach consist in breaking the link between the data computed by the device and the power consumed by the computations. It is called hiding, and generally consist in the "hiding" of the power consumed by the computation of secret data within the power trace. One way to achieve hiding is by flattening the power consumption of a device: if all the computation consume the same amount of power, the power consumed will not be dependent on the secret data any more. Hiding is typically implemented using logic styles more robust against Side-Channel Attacks (SCA) such as SABL [21], WDDL [22], or MCML [16].

Both approaches have some issues, for instance the early propagation effect [20], which affect the security of the overall implementation. Additionally, their overhead in terms of area, performance, complexity of design and power/energy consumption can be too high for low cost and battery operated devices. As a result, often, designers have to trade performance and area utilization with resistance against power analysis attacks.

In this work, we propose a compact implementation of the AES algorithm, targeting reconfigurable devices, capable of reaching high throughputs while at the same time improving the robustness against power analysis attacks.

To achieve this result, we consider the use of low entropy masking schemes [14]. The main idea is to use two representations for each value, such that every value has the same average power consumption. In this case we consider the true and the complemented representation of each value. Moreover, we ensure that, on average, the usage of the true and complemented representations follow a uniform distribution. In this way, we mask the power consumption variation, reducing the information that an attacker can obtain, while collecting the several power traces needed to successful complete the attack. The representation of the value is controlled by XORing it with the appropriate mask value, randomly selected and updated at each cycle. While low entropy masking schemes, as the one herein considered, do not fully protect against SCA, the simplicity of this approach allows for a compact and high performance AES design. Experimental results suggest a significantly higher resistance against first order CPA at a potentially negligible area and performance cost, demonstrating the potential of the proposed approach.

The rest of the paper is organized as follows: Sect. 2 summarizes the state of the art AES designs and countermeasures implemented using reconfigurable hardware. Section 3 presents the proposed approach and details the resulting AES structure. Section 4 reports performance and area figures as well as the security analysis carried out using a SAKURA-G board as the test platform.

2 Countermeasures Against Power Analysis Attacks

Both approaches, masking and hiding, were proposed and explored for software and hardware, concentrating in the second case on both ASIC and reconfigurable devices. FPGAs have been initially used for prototyping and for low volume production, as they allow to limit the non recurring engineering costs. However, state of the art FPGAs have reached a size that is sufficient to fit in a complex System-on-chip, making them also an attractive platform for large scale consumer electronics. For this reason, we focus on countermeasures applied to reconfigurable logic. In the remaining part of this section, we concentrate on previous research efforts proposing countermeasures to power analysis attacks suitable for FPGAs.

Initial works proposing hiding for FPGAs attempted to adapt to reconfigurable hardware concepts previously proposed for ASIC. One example of this is dual rail precharge, proposed for ASIC [22]. It consists of gates where the computation is carried out in two phases: a precharge, where a refreshing wave is produced, and an evaluation, where both a true and a complemented value of the same operation are computed. This approach should, in theory, result in an identical amount of transitions (thus also in the same power consumption) regardless of the data processed. One of the first works proposing dual rail for FPGAs is the one of Yu and Schaumont [25]. The authors showed how to implement WDDL and how to improve its security on FPGA. Higher security was achieved by duplicating the placed and routed WDDL netlist. However, the area overhead is significant and the logic style itself suffers from the so called early propagation effect [20].

A recent improvement on hiding was reported by Wild et al. [23]. The authors propose GliFreD, a technique aiming at solving the early propagation issue, while avoiding glitches and mitigating imbalanced routing as well. The approach was evaluated protecting an implementation of the AES S-box as proposed by Canright [2]. The security evaluation shows a reduction in the perceived information. However, the area overhead is significantly larger: the protected S-box occupies approximately 30 times more slices, 2 times more LUTs, and 100 times more flip-flops.

Several masking countermeasures (and a combination of them) were explored by Güneysu and Moradi [8]. The authors demonstrated, how noise generation, clock randomization, and memory scrambling can defeat first order differential power analysis. They reported results on protecting an implementation of the AES algorithm based on a T-box approach. They further showed that by combining several countermeasures one can further increase the resistance to side-channel attacks. However, the area required by the protected version is approximately 2300 LUTs and 1100 Registers larger than the unprotected core. Similarly, the throughput is reduced by a factor 3.77. Despite these improvements in regard to the remaining state of the art, the cost of this protection is still excessively high for meeting the constraints of several applications.

The memory scrambling proposed in that work was further improved by Sasdrich et al. [19]. The authors propose to update the mask only before each encryption (keeping the same mask during the whole encryption process). To avoid information leakage caused by two values consecutively stored in a register with the same mask, each S-box is surrounded by two registers to interleave the computation of real data with the computation of dummy values. Reported results show a significant improvement compared to the previously proposed scrambling approach of Güneysu and Moradi. However, the area overhead is still significant and the security of the proposed approach, when using RAM, is reduced due to internal architecture of the distributed blocks. The design is much more secure when it is implemented using BRAMs, however the area overhead and the limitation of using a single mask per encryption still persist.

Regazzoni et al. [17] proposed to exploit the larger size of state of the art Xilinx FPGAs, which nicely fit look up tables of 8 bit inputs, for implementing a compact AES accelerator. To do so, the authors adapted to reconfigurable devices a masking scheme largely based on 4 and 8 bit tables, originally designed to be placed in the memory of micro-controllers [15]. Despite the higher throughput, area overhead was still considerably high (depending on the size of the datapath, it was reported to be approximately two to three times the size of the unprotected reference designs).

The concept of low entropy masking, herein considered when limiting the amount of possible masks, was introduced by Nassar et al. [13]. The authors present a study on the use of low entropy masking, i.e. using a limited subset of possible mask values. In their proposed approach, each S-box performs the byte substitution using a specific fixed predefined mask. The randomness of this approach is in the choice of each S-box at the beginning of the round computation. These masks $(m[i])$ are then used in a chaining scheme where $m_{out}[i] = m_{in}[i + 1 \ mod16]$. The authors also evaluate the impact of using a small subset of masks in their solution in terms of leakage, particularly high order leakage. The limited number of masks allows to obtain a more compact structure, at a cost of lower protection [24]. However, the performance (34% slower) and area impact (48% more LUTs) of this solution is still significant [14].

Overall, from the security point of view, the designs proposed so far suggest resistance up to at least first order attacks. However, they suffer from high area overhead as well as from relatively limited performance.

3   Proposed Low Entropy Masking

In this section we firstly describe the proposed approach, followed by the description of the resulting AES structure. The implemented AES structure is based on the unprotected T-box AES implementation, with a datapath of 128 bits, presented in [5], computing a 128 data block each 10 clock cycles.

3.1   Power Consumption Hiding with Low Entropy Masking

The proposed approach strives at obfuscating the relation between the key dependent data and the power consumption with a low area and performance impact. Rather than using dedicated logic, such as dual rail logic, which continuously hides the key dependent power consumption, we mask the key dependent power consumption by using a low entropy masking scheme to influence the average power consumption value.

This is done by randomly using the value or its complement, i.e. the value 1 can be represented by '1' if not-complemented or by '0' if complemented. Similarly, the value '0' can be '0' (not-complemented) or '1' (complemented). Selection between complemented and not-complemented is done randomly, following a uniform distribution of the random values. Ensuring that the complement of the value is used 50% of the time, the average power consumption will be the same for both 1 and 0 binary values. Herein, a more pragmatical approach is used by applying the complement or non-complement at the byte level. To implement this, low entropy masking is used [13]. In particular, a set of two masks are used such that the masks are the complement of each other. In this design we consider the simplest masks, namely "11111111" and "00000000". With these two mask values, the hiding is performed by:

$$S_i \cap M^i = S_i \cap 11111111 = \bar{S}_i, \tag{1}$$

if the mask status is '1' or:

$$S_i \oplus M^i = S_i \oplus 00000000 = S_i, \tag{2}$$

if the mask status is '0'. S_i represent byte i of the state and M^i the mask used on that byte. In practice, this correspond to the complemented or non-complemented value of the value itself. Once more, for the masking to work properly $M^i = 11111111$, 50% of the time in a random manner.

Unlike the approach proposed in [14] where each S-box implements a specific mask and, since the S-boxes are addressed by the masked data, two barrel shifters are required, the proposed approach has almost no overhead other than the memory needed to store the masked values.

With this solution all S-boxes must be able to perform the computation for the values affected by any of the used masks. In this particular case, the input is the value or its complement, depending on the mask status (M_{in}). Independent of the input mask, the generated output will have a different, random, mask status (M_{out}). Note that each byte of the AES 16 byte state has its own random mask status. In this approach, each S-box receives a different random value, thus the output of each S-box is masked independently.

In this design, a T-box based implementation is considered. Given this approach and the two considered masks, each T-box must be able to receive the complemented or non-complemented input value and generate a complemented or non-complemented output value, according to the input and output mask status. For this, two random bits are used for each byte of the round value (M_{in}^i and M_{out}^i). Considering S and $T(S)$ as the unmasked input and output values, respectively, each T-box needs to be able to compute $T(S)$, $T(\bar{S})$, $\bar{T}(S)$, and $\bar{T}(\bar{S})$, as illustrated in Fig. 1. When implemented with lookup tables, this leads to a 4 times larger lookup table.

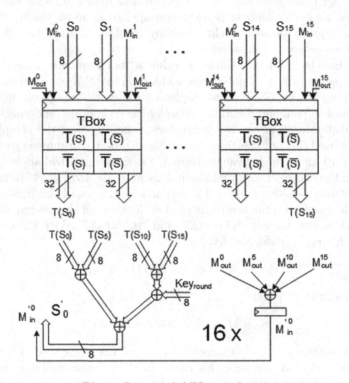

Fig. 1. Protected AES main loop.

To assure the correct mask status of the obtained results, one needs to compute the resulting mask status. This is very simple to compute, since the resulting values are either complemented or not complemented.

In regard to the remaining operations performed to compute the AES algorithm, no additional care needs to be taken, since these operations consist of linear operations, namely shifts and XOR operations that do not change the mask status.

The resulting mask status is given by the XOR of the mask status of all the involved values, as exemplified by the following:

$$S_0' \oplus M_{in}^0 = T(S_0) \oplus M_{out}^0 \oplus \cdots \oplus T(S_{15}) \oplus M_{out}^{15}. \qquad (3)$$

Given the linearity of the XOR operation, the value of the state (S) and the mask (M) can be computed separately as:

$$S'_0 = T(S_0) \oplus T(S_5) \oplus T(S_{10}) \oplus T(S_{15}); \quad (4)$$

$$M^0_{in} = M^0_{out} \oplus M^5_{out} \oplus M^{10}_{out} \oplus M^{15}_{out}, \quad (5)$$

where $T(S)$ represents the computation of the T-box operation over one byte of the state S.

In this way, there are no issues related to the "mask correction" as this is built into our scheme intrinsically. Figure 1 depicts the resulting round structure given the proposed masking approach, using a dual port lookup table for the T-box implementation. With this approach 16 random values per round are needed in order to define the mask status (M^i_{out}) of the output of each T-box.

The above description only considers the masking during the round computation. However, the first key addition (performed for each input block before the round computation itself) also needs to be protected. To protect the first key addition with the input data, the same masking approach is deployed, where each input byte is masked (by taking its complement or not), computing:

$$S' = Data_{in} \oplus M_{in} \oplus Key_0; \quad (6)$$

where $Data_{in}$ represents the 16 bytes of the input block, Key_0 represents the first 16 bytes of the expanded key, and M_{in} represents the 16 random bits of the first mask status. The resulting structure for this operation is shown at the top of Fig. 2.

Regarding the conclusion of the block cipher process, the AES algorithm has the particularity that in the last round the MixColumn operation is not computed. The result is obtained directly through the S-box. Three main solutions are used to deal with this property. The first is to perform the MixColumn on a separate logic block, not using T-boxes, and bypassing this operation in the last round using a multiplexer. This solution tends to result in more complex and costly structures, particularly on FPGAs. The second solution takes into account that for encryption the output of the T-box is:

$$T(S) = 1 \times S_{BOX}(S) \| 1 \times S_{BOX}(S) \| 2 \times S_{BOX}(S) \| 3 \times S_{BOX}(S), \quad (7)$$

where $\|$ corresponds to the concatenation of bytes and $S_{BOX}(S)$ corresponds to the S-box operation over one byte of the state S. Thus, the needed S-box operation $(S_{BOX}(S))$ can be obtained directly from $T(S)$. However, when performing the inverse MixColumn operation, in the decryption, the value $S^{-1}_{BOX}(S)$ is not outputted. As such, an additional entry in the lookup table is needed in order to provide the computation of $S^{-1}_{BOX}(S)$ for the decryption, requiring more memory space. The third solution recombines the 4 bytes outputted from the T-box to generate the S-box output [5]. This is possible since the XOR of the multiplication coefficients of the MixColumn operation results in 1. In the case of encryption:

$$1 \oplus 1 \oplus 2 \oplus 3 = 1, \quad (8)$$

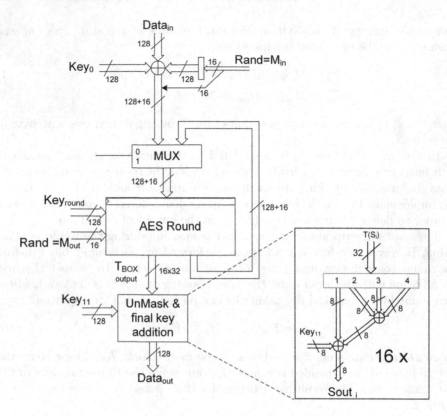

Fig. 2. Protected AES structure.

while in the case of decryption:

$$9 \oplus B_h \oplus D_h \oplus E_h = 1. \tag{9}$$

Thus, by XORing the 4 bytes of the T-box, both for encryption and decryption, the MixColumn operation is annulled. This option avoids the use of additional memory or a more complex data path to compute the S-box operation separately. However, it requires the use of additional XOR operations to compute (8) and (9).

This last approach is the one herein considered. As such, the output of T-box i is affected by the Mask M_{out}^i. Thus, the output of the S-box can be computed by:

$$S(S_i) = T_1(S_i) \oplus M_{out}^i \oplus T_2(S_i) \oplus M_{out}^i \oplus T_3(S_i) \oplus M_{out}^i \oplus T_4(S_i) \oplus M_{out}^i, \tag{10}$$

where T_1, T_2, T_3, and T_4 correspond to the first, second, third, and forth bytes outputted by the T-box, as detailed in (8) and (9). However, by performing this operation over these 4 bytes (all affected by the same mask) results in the output no longer being affected by the mask. Following this last operation, the final output value (S_{out}) would be obtained by XORing the S-box output with the last round key. However, has shown in (10), this computation would no longer be protected by the mask.

To solve this, the last key addition and the recombination of the T-box output must be performed together in such a way that the mask is only removed at the end, ensuring that the final key addition is performed with a masked value. This can be accomplished by:

$$(tmp_i \oplus M_{out}^i) = (T_2(S_i) \oplus M_{out}^i) \oplus (T_3(S_i) \oplus M_{out}^i) \oplus (T_4(S_i) \oplus M_{out}^i); \quad (11)$$

$$Sout_i = (tmp_i \oplus M_{out}^i) \oplus (T_1(S_i) \oplus M_{out}^i) \oplus Key_{last}, \quad (12)$$

where Key_{last} corresponds to the last round key. Note that for this approach to work properly, 3 (or more) input XOR operators must be available.

The resulting structure for the computation of each of the output bytes (S_{out_i}) of the state is depicted at the bottom left side of Fig. 2. With this approach the mask value is automatically removed, without the need to know the status of the mask (M_{out}), resulting in a relatively compact structure to remove the mask and to perform the last round computation.

3.2   FPGA Based Implementation Details

While the proposed structure is technology agnostic, the developed prototype considered in the following section was implemented on an FPGA based technology, in particular the Xilinx SPARTAN-6 technology. The more recent Xilinx FPGAs support 6 input LookUp Tables (LUT) and embedded RAM Blocks (BRAMs) ranging from 18 to 36 kbits of capacity.

As depicted at the bottom of Fig. 1, the key addition and MixColumn operation is computed by XORing 5 values, resulting in the next state value (S'). This entire operation can be mapped into a single LUT (per bit). Identically, the final round key addition and unmask operation (5 input XOR), depicted at the bottom left side of Fig. 2, can also be entirely mapped into a single LUT (per bit), thus assuring that no intermediate unmasked values exists during the key addition.

The T-box lookup operation is mapped into a BRAM. Considering only encryption or decryption, the unmasked operation corresponds to an 8 bit input with a 32 bit output operation. Given this, the total memory requirement (per T-box) is:

$$2^8 \times 32 = 8 \; kbits. \quad (13)$$

As such, in the proposed approach each T-box needs to compute 4 different combinations of complemented or non-complemented values (as illustrated in Fig. 1). A total amount of memory of 32 kbits per T-box is needed. This T-box can be mapped into a single 36 kbit BRAM (on VIRTEX 5 to 7 devices) or into two 18 kbit BRAMs on SPARTAN 6 devices. When supporting both encryption and decryption, twice as much memory is needed, i.e. 64 kbits.

Since the same mask is used for all T-boxes and the fact that the BRAMs are dual ported, each group of BRAMs is able to compute two T-boxes, one on each port of the BRAM.

Note that, when mapping one T-box into multiple BRAMs, care should be taken in order to assure that, for example, $T(S)$ and $\bar{T}(S)$ do not go into one BRAM and that $T(\bar{S})$ and $\bar{T}(\bar{S})$ to another BRAM, since this might result in additional leakage. One should place all combinations into a single BRAM, having each BRAM output fewer bits of the output result.

4   Experimental Results and Evaluation

In order to properly evaluate the proposed approach, the resulting structure was implemented on a SAKURA-G platform [9], with a Xilinx SPARTAN-6 LX75 FPGA. The implementation results were obtained using the Xilinx ISE Design Suite (v14.5) with the design described using VHDL. The presented implementation results were obtained after P&R using the default parameters of the tool.

For the required random values, two 16-bit Linear Feedback Shift Registers (LFSR) are herein used during the SCA evaluation to generate the pseudo random values, two for each byte. These LFSR are implemented using the polynomials $x^{16} + x^{14} + x^{13} + x^{11} + x^1$ and $x^{16} + x^{15} + x^{13} + x^4 + x^1$, initialized with the hexadecimal values $(\text{A376})_{\text{h}}$ and $(\text{7A1B})_{\text{h}}$, respectively. The state of each LFSR is used to set the status of the M_{in} mask for the first key addition and for the round masks M_{out}. Note that, in a real world implementation, true random number generators should be used. The results obtained are based on the LFSR specified above. For the leakage evaluation, the amplified output of the SAKURA-G board, which is connected to a shunt resistor which in turn connected in serial to the target FPGA. The power traces are obtained using a LeCroy WaveRunner 610Zi oscilloscope set at 1 GS/s using the full bandwidth of the scope.

4.1   Side-Channel Analysis Evaluation

As the implementation proposed in this work only claims security against first order side channel attacks that exploit the Hamming weight of the SBox output, we have chosen to analyze the acquired traces through TVLA with chosen input method [1] aimed at exploiting the SBox Hamming weight model (so-called HW model). The first group for TVLA contains traces for which all SBox outputs in round 5 are set to have Hamming weight equal to 0, 1, or 2; the second group contains traces without any limitations on the SBox outputs. We acquired 200 000 traces for the unprotected implementation (for which the PRNG is turned off) and 200 000 traces for the protected implementation (for which the PRNG is turned on).

Figure 3 presents a comparison of t-values for the unprotected and protected AES implementations for the rounds from 3 to 7; the maximum t-values values are marked. We do not present the results for other rounds since they do not show leakage (because we fix the SBox hamming weight only in round 5). We can observe leakage, namely a peak above the 4.5 threshold, for both the unprotected and protected implementations; however, the peak for the unprotected implementation is 25 times greater than for the protected one[1]. Therefore, we can notice a significant security improvement in the protected case.

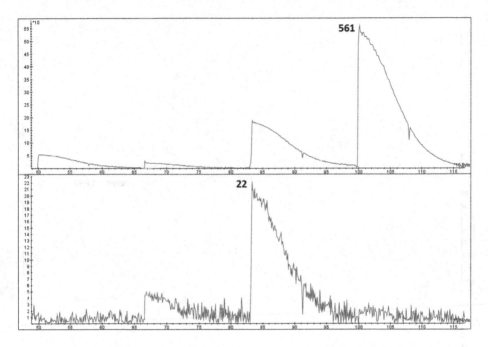

Fig. 3. t-values for the unprotected (top) and protected (bottom) AES implementations for the rounds from 3 to 7.

We have also performed a fixed vs. random TVLA analysis [7], but we have achieved very similar results: the peak for the unprotected implementation is approximately 30 times greater than for the protected one.

Subsequently, to further analyze the security of our solution we conducted a second experiment. We have chosen to analyze traces through classical DPA aimed at exploiting the HW model. Additionally, for sake of completeness, we aim at exploiting another common model: the SBox input-output Hamming distance model (i.e., a Hamming weight of the xor of the SBox output and the SBox input); we call the second model, the HD model. For this analysis 100 000 traces were collected for the unprotected implementation. We have collected 27

---

[1] We can notice that the strongest leakage for the unprotected implementation happens slightly later than for the protected one, but we do not have an explanation of this situation.

million traces for the protected implementation. Figure 4 presents the results of the side channel analysis aimed at recovering all 16 bytes of the key.

As it is visible in the top plot of Fig. 4, when the random generator is turned off (LFSRs initialized with all zeros), the key entropy is reduced to less than 15

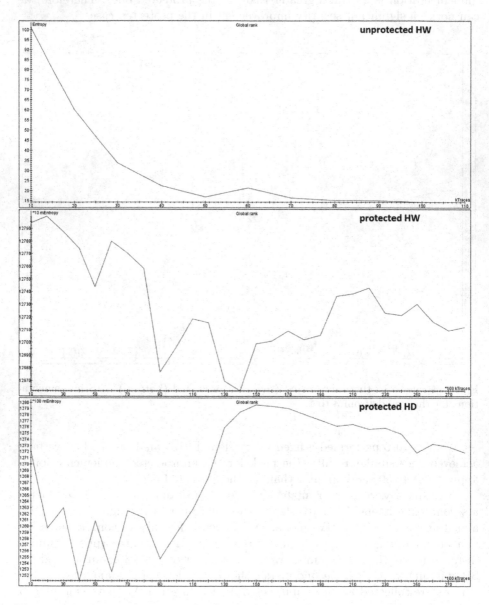

Fig. 4. Key convergence for the unprotected AES implementation for the HW model (top), key convergence of the protected AES implementation for the HW model (middle) and the HD model (bottom).

bits with 100 000 traces; only 2 out of 16 bytes do not reach the full convergence. Furthermore, the entropy is reduced to less than 23 bits, which can be efficiently brute-forced, already with 40 000 traces. We only present the results for the HW model as the attack using HD does not yield successful results.

When the random generator is active, we cannot reduce the search key space with 27 million traces, as visible in the key convergence plots in Fig. 4. In both models the remaining key entropy is approximately 127 bits. Therefore, we conclude that it seems to not be possible to mount a classical first order CPA with the collected 27 million traces. This also confirms that the leakage detected using TVLA for the protected implementation is most likely caused by the real device leakage model being non-linear (for example, some SBox output bits might be leaking in combination). We note that it might be possible to exploit this leakage using more complex side channel attacks, like, linear regression analysis [6], template attacks [4], or attacks on low entropy masking schemes [24]; we leave that as future work.

We perform the evaluation using Riscure's Inspector software package[2].

4.2   Implementation Results Analysis

In order to evaluate the impact of the proposed solution, in terms of area cost and performance, the resulting structure is herein compared with the equivalent unprotected AES structure, proposed in [5], and with the most relevant solution in the state of the art. To better compare with the state of the art, the proposed structure was also implemented on a Xilinx VIRTEX-5. The obtained results are depicted in Table 1.

The implementation results on a SPARTAN-6 suggest that the proposed structure requires a total of 603 LUTs and 55 Registers and 32 BRAMs, and is able to run at 110 MHz. Considering as an efficiency metric the achievable throughput per used LUTs, and achieving an encryption/decryption throughput of 1.4 Gbps, a efficiency of 2.3 throughput per LUT is achieved by the proposed solution.

When compared with the unprotected version of the AES structure [5], requiring 586 LUTs and achieving a throughput of 1.7 Gbps, the proposed protected solution requires 3% more LUTs, 37 more Registers and 2 to 4 times the number of BRAMs, depending if decryption is also supported. The extra LUTs and Registers are mainly due to the two 16-bit LFSR used to generate the Pseudo Random values. The actual cost of the proposed solution is basically in the needed extra BRAMs, since the SPARTAN BRAMs are relatively smaller and in the achievable throughput, being 20% slower. The throughput degradation is mostly due to the more complex routing, given the higher BRAM usage, since the datapath is basically the same.

This impact results on an efficiency degradation of 1.23 times. When considering an implementation supporting only encryption, requiring 16 BRAMs

---

[2] http://www.riscure.com/.

Table 1. DPA resistant AES implementations

	Device	Enc/dec	Logic		Freq.	Throughput	Efficiency
			LUT	BRAMs	[MHz]	[Mbps]	[Mbps/LUT]
[10]	XC3S500	n.a.	4888[a]	0	n.a.	n.a.	n.a.
[8]	SAKURA-G	Enc	2888[b]	16	147	35.4	0.01
[18]	SAKURA-G	Enc	1284	8	148	68.6	0.05
Ours	SAKURA-G	Enc	525	16	148	1894	3.6
Ours	SAKURA-G	Both	603	32	110	1400	2.3
[5]	SAKURA-G	Both	586	8	136	1740	3
[17]	XC5vlx50	Enc	1429	0	100	290	0.2
[17]	XC5vlx50	Enc	4772	0	100	1163	0.2
[5]	XC5vlx30	Enc	518	8	210	2688	5.2
Ours	XC5vlx50	Enc	547	8	187	2393	4.3
Ours	XC5vlx50	Both	548	16	157	1843	3.4

[a]Only Slice values are presented. The depicted value considers that 1 slice has 4 LUTs available.
[b]The value listed is for the AES core only. It does not include the mask generation structure.

(twice the original number of BRAMs), a throughput of 1.9 Gbps is achieved.

When targeting a VIRTEX-5 device, supporting larger BRAMs, and only performing encryption, the resulting structure only requires 8 BRAMs, the same as in the unprotected implementation. In this particular case, it can be stated that the proposed solution does not impose any additional BRAM cost. Performance-wise the implementation supporting only encryption allows to reduce the number of needed BRAMs and consequently a simpler routing can be achieved, resulting on a throughput of 2.4 Gbps, 10% slower than the non protected reference design.

When compared with the solution proposed in [18], only supporting encryption, the solution herein proposed requires less than half the number of LUTs and is able to achieve a 27 times higher throughput. The solution proposed in [18] requires 8 BRAMs, considering a 64-bit datapath. If the solution proposed in [18] implements a 128-bit datapath, it will also require 16 BRAMs, one for each SBOX. This is due to the fact that one of the dual ports of each BRAM needs to be reserved for the mask update. In this case it requires the same amount of BRAMs as for the solution herein proposed. Note that the results presented in [18] only consider the cost of the AES core, without the mask generation hardware, which substantially contributes to higher area costs.

In [17], a structure considering a more traditional approach to masking is proposed, for a 32 and 128 bit datapath. The authors implemented a masked design for the AES algorithm, which is heavily based on 4 and 8 bit look-up-tables, targeting the existing LUTs on the state of the art Xilinx FGPAs. With this approach no BRAMs are required. The obtained results [17] suggest a cost of 4772 LUTs and 904 Registers, achieving a throughout of 1.2 Gbps. When compared with their reference design [17], this solution imposes a cost of 3 times the amount of LUTs and achieves a throughput 2.5 times slower. When comparing the solution herein proposed with this one [17], the proposed solution requires 8 times fewer LUTs and achieves 2 times the throughput. However, the solution proposed in [17] does not require BRAMs so a direct comparison cannot be made. Notwithstanding, the structure herein proposed for encryption can have a almost no area cost and a 10% performance degradation on a VIRTEX-5, in regard to the reference design, while the structure in [17] imposes a area increase between 2 to 3 time, in regard to the reference design.

While Altera Stratix-II values were not obtained to compare with the structure presented in [14], proposing the low entropy masking scheme, it is possible to evaluate the overhead imposed by each approach. The results presented for the encryption structure presented in [14] suggest a overhead cost of 48% and 40% more LUTs and memory blocks, respectively, with a performance degradation of 34%. While the resulting structure supporting encryption on a VIRTEX-5 has a negligible area and performance impact.

Overall, when compared with the existing state of the art, the proposed solution suggests an efficiency improvement above 6 times with throughputs above 2 Gbps. Depending on the device and encryption support, the resulting structure can have a negligible cost increase and a minimum performance degradation.

To allow for further and independent evaluation, the implemented AES core is available at: http://sips.inesc-id.pt/~rjfc/cores/AES_DPA2018.

5 Conclusion

This paper introduced a novel AES design that improves the robustness against power analysis attacks by using low entropy masking. In the considered approach, the computed byte values are represented by either the actual value or by its complement, masking the average power consumption. The representation of each AES state byte is controlled by XORing it with the appropriate mask value, randomly selected and updated at each cycle, both at the input and output of the T-boxes. While low entropy masking schemes are known for not fully protecting against SCA, the simplicity of this approach enables an extreme compactness, reaching an almost negligible area cost, and very high performance.

Experimental results suggest a significantly higher resistance against first order CPA (suggesting not to be possible to mount a classical first order CPA with 27 million traces) at a potentially negligible area and performance cost. When compared with the state of the art, efficiency improvements above 6 times are expected with a throughput of at least two times higher than the best protected state of the art. When compared with the reference design on a VIRTEX-5, performing encryption, the obtained results suggest a 5% LUT increase and 10% performance degradation, which can be considered negligible and within the tools margin of error.

Acknowledgements. This work was partially supported by national funds through Fundação para a Ciência e a Tecnologia (FCT) with reference UID/CEC/50021/2013 and upon work from COST Action IC1403 CRYPTACUS, supported by COST (European Cooperation in Science and Technology).

References

1. Becker, G., Cooper, J., DeMulder, E., Goodwill, G., Jaffe, J., Kenworthy, G., Kouzminov, T., Leiserson, A., Marson, M., Rohatgi, P., Saab, S.: Test vector leakage assessment (TVLA) methodology in practice. In: International Cryptographic Module Conference, vol. 1001, p. 13 (2013)
2. Canright, D.: A very compact S-box for AES. In: Rao, J.R., Sunar, B. (eds.) CHES 2005. LNCS, vol. 3659, pp. 441–455. Springer, Heidelberg (2005). https://doi.org/10.1007/11545262_32
3. Chari, S., Jutla, C.S., Rao, J.R., Rohatgi, P.: Towards sound approaches to counteract power-analysis attacks. In: Wiener, M. (ed.) CRYPTO 1999. LNCS, vol. 1666, pp. 398–412. Springer, Heidelberg (1999). https://doi.org/10.1007/3-540-48405-1_26
4. Chari, S., Rao, J.R., Rohatgi, P.: Template attacks. In: Kaliski, B.S., Koç, K., Paar, C. (eds.) CHES 2002. LNCS, vol. 2523, pp. 13–28. Springer, Heidelberg (2003). https://doi.org/10.1007/3-540-36400-5_3
5. Chaves, R., Kuzmanov, G., Vassiliadis, S., Sousa, L.: Reconfigurable memory based AES co-processor. In: 20th International Parallel and Distributed Processing Symposium 2006, IPDPS 2006, pp. 8–pp. IEEE (2006)
6. Doget, J., Prouff, E., Rivain, M., Standaert, F.X.: Univariate side channel attacks and leakage modeling. J. Cryptograph. Eng. **1**(2), 123–144 (2011)
7. Gilbert Goodwill, B.J., Jaffe, J., Rohatgi, P.: A testing methodology for side-channel resistance validation (2011)
8. Güneysu, T., Moradi, A.: Generic side-channel countermeasures for reconfigurable devices. In: Preneel, B., Takagi, T. (eds.) CHES 2011. LNCS, vol. 6917, pp. 33–48. Springer, Heidelberg (2011). https://doi.org/10.1007/978-3-642-23951-9_3
9. Guntur, H., Ishii, J., Satoh, A.: Side-channel attack user reference architecture board SAKURA-G. In: 2014 IEEE 3rd Global Conference on Consumer Electronics (GCCE), pp. 271–274, October 2014
10. Kaps, J., Velegalati, R.: DPA resistant AES on FPGA using partial DDL. In: 2010 18th IEEE Annual International Symposium on Field-Programmable Custom Computing Machines (FCCM), pp. 273–280. IEEE (2010)
11. Kocher, P., Jaffe, J., Jun, B.: Differential power analysis. In: Wiener, M. (ed.) CRYPTO 1999. LNCS, vol. 1666, pp. 388–397. Springer, Heidelberg (1999). https://doi.org/10.1007/3-540-48405-1_25
12. Messerges, T.S.: Securing the AES finalists against power analysis attacks. In: Goos, G., Hartmanis, J., van Leeuwen, J., Schneier, B. (eds.) FSE 2000. LNCS, vol. 1978, pp. 150–164. Springer, Heidelberg (2001). https://doi.org/10.1007/3-540-44706-7_11
13. Nassar, M., Guilley, S., Danger, J.-L.: Formal analysis of the entropy/security trade-off in first-order masking countermeasures against side-channel attacks. In: Bernstein, D.J., Chatterjee, S. (eds.) INDOCRYPT 2011. LNCS, vol. 7107, pp. 22–39. Springer, Heidelberg (2011). https://doi.org/10.1007/978-3-642-25578-6_4

14. Nassar, M., Souissi, Y., Guilley, S., Danger, J.L.: RSM: a small and fast counter-measure for AES, secure against 1st and 2nd-order zero-offset SCAs. In: Design, Automation and Test in Europe Conference and Exhibition (DATE), pp. 1173–1178. IEEE (2012)

15. Oswald, E., Schramm, K.: An efficient masking scheme for AES software implementations. In: Song, J.-S., Kwon, T., Yung, M. (eds.) WISA 2005. LNCS, vol. 3786, pp. 292–305. Springer, Heidelberg (2006). https://doi.org/10.1007/11604938_23

16. Regazzoni, F., Eisenbarth, T., Poschmann, A., Großschädl, J., Gürkaynak, F.K., Macchetti, M., Deniz, Z.T., Pozzi, L., Paar, C., Leblebici, Y., Ienne, P.: Evaluating resistance of MCML technology to power analysis attacks using a simulation-based methodology. Trans. Comput. Sci. 4, 230–243 (2009)

17. Regazzoni, F., Wang, Y., Standaert, F.X.: FPGA implementations of the AES masked against power analysis attacks. Proc. COSADE 2011, 56–66 (2011)

18. Sasdrich, P., Mischke, O., Moradi, A., Güneysu, T.: Side-channel protection by randomizing look-up tables on reconfigurable hardware. In: Mangard, S., Poschmann, A.Y. (eds.) COSADE 2014. LNCS, vol. 9064, pp. 95–107. Springer, Cham (2015). https://doi.org/10.1007/978-3-319-21476-4_7

19. Sasdrich, P., Moradi, A., Mischke, O., Güneysu, T.: Achieving side-channel protection with dynamic logic reconfiguration on modern FPGAs. In: IEEE International Symposium on Hardware Oriented Security and Trust, HOST 2015, Washington, DC, USA, 5–7 May 2015, pp. 130–136 (2015)

20. Suzuki, D., Saeki, M.: Security evaluation of DPA countermeasures using dual-rail pre-charge logic style. In: Goubin, L., Matsui, M. (eds.) CHES 2006. LNCS, vol. 4249, pp. 255–269. Springer, Heidelberg (2006). https://doi.org/10.1007/11894063_21

21. Tiri, K., Verbauwhede, I.: Securing encryption algorithms against DPA at the logic level: next generation smart card technology In: Walter, C.D., Koç, Ç.K., Paar, C. (eds.) CHES 2003. LNCS, vol. 2779, pp. 125–136. Springer, Heidelberg (2003). https://doi.org/10.1007/978-3-540-45238-6_11

22. Tiri, K., Verbauwhede, I.: A logic level design methodology for a secure DPA resistant ASIC or FPGA implementation. In: 2004 Design, Automation and Test in Europe Conference and Exposition (DATE 2004), Paris, France, 16–20 February 2004, pp. 246–251 (2004)

23. Wild, A., Moradi, A., Güneysu, T.: Glifred: glitch-free duplication - towards power-equalized circuits on FPGAs. IACR Cryptology ePrint Archive 2015, 124 (2015)

24. Ye, X., Eisenbarth, T.: On the vulnerability of low entropy masking schemes. In: Francillon, A., Rohatgi, P. (eds.) CARDIS 2013. LNCS, vol. 8419, pp. 44–60. Springer, Cham (2014). https://doi.org/10.1007/978-3-319-08302-5_4

25. Yu, P., Schaumont, P.: Secure FPGA circuits using controlled placement and routing. In: Proceedings of the 5th International Conference on Hardware/Software Codesign and System Synthesis, CODES + ISSS 2007, Salzburg, Austria, 30 September–3 October 2007, pp. 45–50 (2007)

Cryptanalysis of 1-Round KECCAK

Rajendra Kumar[1][(✉)], Mahesh Sreekumar Rajasree[1], and Hoda AlKhzaimi[2]

[1] Center for Cybersecurity, Indian Institute of Technology Kanpur, Kanpur, India
{rjndr,mahesr}@iitk.ac.in
[2] Center for Cyber Security, New York University, Abu Dhabi, Abu Dhabi, UAE
hoda.alkhzaimi@nyu.edu

Abstract. In this paper, we give the first pre-image attack against 1-round KECCAK-512 hash function, which works for all variants of 1-round KECCAK. The attack gives a preimage of length less than 1024 bits by solving a system of 384 linear equations. We also give a collision attack against 1-round KECCAK using similar analysis.

Keywords: Cryptanalysis · KECCAK · SHA-3 · Preimage · Collision

1 Introduction

Hash functions are used in digital signatures, message integrity and authentication. In 2006, NIST announced the "NIST hash function competition" which received 64 proposals from around the world. In October 2012, KECCAK designed by Bertoni et al. [1], was selected as the winner of the competition and in 2015, it was standardized as a "Secure Hash Algorithm 3" [2].

The KECCAK hash family is based on the sponge construction [3]. Sponge construction has the property to generate an output of any length and because of this property, SHA3 standards include two extendable output functions which are SHAKE128 and SHAKE256. These can also be used as a pseudo-random generator. Due to its vast applications, a lot of security analysis is being performed on the KECCAK hash family.

In 2010, Bernstein [4] gave an idea for second preimage of KECCAK variants and in 2014, Chang et al. [5] improved the time complexity for 1st and 2nd preimage attack on 7-round Keccak-224, 8-round Keccak-256/384 and 9-round Keccak-512. Morawiecki et al. [6] gave a theoretical preimage attack up to 4 rounds of KECCAK by using a technique called as rotational cryptanalysis. Morawiecki and Srebrny [7] performed a preimage analysis of round reduced KECCAK by using toolkit CryptLogVer and SAT solver PrecoSAT. Naya-Plasencia et al. [8]

R. Kumar and M. S. Rajasree—Supported by the Center for Cyber Security, New York University AbuDhabi and Center for Cybersecurity and Cyber Defence of Critical Infrastructure, IIT Kanpur.
H. AlKhzaimi—Supported by the Center for Cyber Security, New York University AbuDhabi.

© Springer International Publishing AG, part of Springer Nature 2018
A. Joux et al. (Eds.): AFRICACRYPT 2018, LNCS 10831, pp. 124–137, 2018.
https://doi.org/10.1007/978-3-319-89339-6_8

gave a preimage attack on 2-round for KECCAK-224 and KECCAK-256 by using the meet in middle approach. In 2016 Guo et al. [9] gave preimage attack for 2 round for KECCAK-224, 256, 384 and 512. The complexity of attack [9] for KECCAK-384 is 2^{129} and for KECCAK-512 is 2^{384}. They extended this upto 4 round for small hash length. Dinur et al. [10,11] gave a collision attack upto 4 rounds using differential and algebraic techniques, and later improved upto 5 rounds using generalized internal differential [12]. Later Qiao et al. [13] gave the first collision attack on 5 round of SHAKE-128 by extending the framework developed by Dinur et al. [10]. By further analysing the KECCAK S-Box, Song et al. [14] gave the first practical collision attack on 5 round KECCAK-224. Apart from the above-mentioned attacks, there are several other attacks against KECCAK.

Our Contribution: In this paper, we give the first practical preimage attack against 1 round KECCAK-512. The only computation required in this attack is solving 384 linear equations. It is based on exploiting the degree of freedom in the equations between hash values and message bits, and converting these equations to simple assignments of values to message variables. Using this method, we can find a message of length less than 1024 bits corresponding to every hash value. Also, the time complexity of this attack is constant.

Organization: The rest of the paper contains the following sections. In Sect. 2, we briefly describe the structure of KECCAK. In Sect. 3, we show the cryptanalysis of 1 round KECCAK-512. Section 4 contains the implementation results and description of the collision attack. Section 5 contains conclusion and future works.

2   Structure of KECCAK

KECCAK hash function has 3 parameters: r is the bitrate, c is the capacity and n is the output length. It is based on sponge construction [3] which uses a padding function pad, a bitrate parameter r and a permutation function f as shown in Fig. 1.

2.1   Sponge Construction

The sponge construction has two phases - absorbing and squeezing. The sponge construction begins by applying the padding function pad on the input string M which produces M' whose length is a multiple of r. M' under goes the absorbing phase as follows.

1. M' is split into blocks of r bits namely $m_1, m_2, ...m_k$.
2. There is an initial string(o_0) which is a b bit string initialized to zero.
3. The initial r bits of o_0 is XORed with first block m_1 and is given as input to f. The output produced by f is denoted by o_1.
4. Similarly, the initial r bits of o_i is XORed with the m_{i+1} and given to f.
5. Finally, the output of the absorbing phase is o_k.

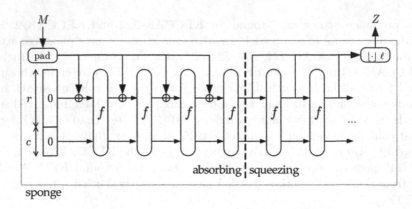

Fig. 1. Sponge function [3]

The squeezing phase consists of obtaining the output which can be of any length. Let n be the required output length such that $l = \alpha r + \beta$ where $\beta < r$.

1. Apply the f function α more times such that $o_{k+i} = f(o_{k+i-1})$.
2. Let O be the concatenation of the first r bits of each o_{k+i} where $0 \leq i \leq \alpha$.
3. The output of the sponge construction is the first l bits of O.

In case of SHA-3 hash family, f is a KECCAK-f[1600] permutation, and the *pad* function appends 10*1 to input M. KECCAK-f is a specialization of KECCAK-p permutation.

$$\text{KECCAK-}f[b] = \text{KECCAK-p}[b, 12 + 2\gamma]$$

where $\gamma = log_2(b/25)$.

2.2 KECCAK-p Permutation

KECCAK-p permutation is denoted by KECCAK-p$[b, n_r]$, where b is length of input string which is called the width of the permutation, n_r is number of rounds of internal transformation where $b \in \{25, 50, 100, 200, 400, 800, 1600\}$ and n_r being any positive integer. We can define two more quantities $w = b/25$ and $\gamma = log_2(b/25)$. For KECCAK-512, the number of rounds of internal transformation n_r is 24 and $b = 1600$. The b bit input string can be represented as a $5 \times 5 \times w$ 3-dimensional array known as state as shown in Fig. 2. A lane in a state S is denoted by $S[x][y]$ which is the substring $S[x][y][0]|S[x][y][1]|\ldots|S[x][y][w-1]$ where $|$ is the concatenation function.

The internal transformation consists of 5 step mappings θ, ρ, π, χ and ι which acts on a state. We give a brief description of each of these step mappings with A and A' being the state before and after applying a step mappings.

1. θ:

$$A'[x][y][z] = A[x][y][z] \oplus CP[(x+1) \bmod 5][(z-1) \bmod 64]$$
$$\oplus CP[(x-1) \bmod 5][z]$$

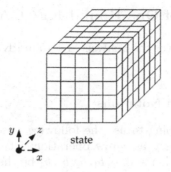

Fig. 2. KECCAK state [15]

where $CP[x][z]$ is the parity of a column, i.e,

$$CP[x][z] = A[x][0][z] \oplus A[x][1][z] \oplus A[x][2][z] \oplus A[x][3][z] \oplus A[x][4][z]$$

2. ρ:

$$A'[x][y] = A[x][y] << r[x][y]$$

where $<<$ means bitwise rotation towards MSB of the 64-bit word. The values of $r[x][y]$ are given in the table below.

4	18	2	61	56	14
3	41	45	15	21	8
2	3	10	43	25	39
1	36	44	6	55	20
0	0	1	62	28	27
$y \backslash x$	0	1	2	3	4

3. π:

$$A'[y][2x + 3y] = A[x][y]$$

π interchanges the lanes of the state A.

4. χ:

$$A'[x][y][z] = A[x][y][z] \oplus ((A[(x + 1) \bmod 5][y][z] \oplus 1)$$
$$.A[(x + 2) \bmod 5][y][z])$$

χ is the only non-linear operation among the 5 step mappings.

5. ι:

$$A'[0][0] = A[0][0] \oplus RC_i$$

where RC_i is a constant which depends on i where i is the round number.

3   Cryptanalysis of One-Round KECCAK

In this section, we will cover the analysis of 1 round KECCAK for the different preimage message size.

3.1   Preliminaries and Notations

In our analysis, we are going to use the following observations of the χ and θ operation [9]. Considering χ as a row operation, let a_0, a_1, a_2, a_3, a_4 be the 5 input bits to the χ operation and b_0, b_1, b_2, b_3, b_4 be the 5 output bits.

Observation 1: In χ operation, if all output bits b_0, b_1, b_2, b_3, b_4 are known, then we can exactly determine the input bits a_0, a_1, a_2, a_3, a_4 using

$$a_i = b_i \oplus (b_{i+1} \oplus 1).(b_{i+2} \oplus (b_{i+3} \oplus 1).b_{i+4})$$

Observation 2: In χ operation, if any 3 non-consecutive input bits are known, then all the output bits can be written as linear combinations of input bits.

Observation 3: In χ operation, given b_0, b_1, b_2 and $a_3 = 1$, we can exactly determine the values of a_0, a_1 and a_2.

$$a_2 = b_2$$

$$a_1 = b_1 \oplus (b_2 \oplus 1)$$

$$a_0 = b_0 \oplus (b_1 \oplus b_2).b_2$$

Observation 4: Let d_0, d_1, d_2, d_3, d_4 be the elements of a column. Then, the parity of column can be fixed to a constant c by choosing for any $i \in \{0, 1, 2, 3, 4\}$

$$d_i = c \oplus (\bigoplus_{j=1}^{j=4} d_{i+j})$$

In the rest of the paper, all the message variables and hash values are represented in the form of lanes (array) of length 64 and we will use $+$ symbol in place of $\oplus$. In all the equations and Figures, the value inside the brackets '()' indicates the offset by which the lane is shifted. For example, $x_i(k)$ denotes lane x_i rotated by an offset of k, whereas $x_i[k]$ denotes the kth bit of lane x_i. Every operation between two lanes are bitwise.

3.2   General Description of the Attack

We now give the generic description of the attack.

1. The given hash value uses the first 8 lanes of a state and we ignore the values in the rest of the 17 lanes.

2. Invert the ι operation by XORing the $(0,0)$ lane with the Round constant RC.
3. Invert the χ operation by using the above given observations. Let's call this state as I.
4. Apply the necessary operations on the message block to reach state I. For making the operations linear, use the above observations.
5. Check for the dependencies among the linear equations. If they are independent, then solve the system of linear equations.

3.3 Analysis of Preimage Attack by Using 1 Message Block

In this section, we are going to show that by using only 1 message block it is not possible to find the preimage for all the hash values of KECCAK-512. In the Subsect. 3.4, we will also characterize the hash values whose preimage can be found by using 1 message block. In KECCAK-512, we have $n = 512$, $c = 1024$ and $r = 576$. So, the hash value occupies 8 lanes and message block is of 9 lanes. Let $A = a_0a_1a_2a_3a_4a_5a_6a_7a_8$ be the message block of 576 bit length where each a_i is an array of 64 bits. Figure 3 shows the state after applying θ, ρ and π on A where $d_i[k] = CP[i-1][k] + CP[i+1][k-1]$ and CP represents the column parity.

Suppose $H = h_0h_1h_2h_3h_4h_5h_6h_7$ is the 512-bit hash value where each h_i is of 64 bits. We know that we can invert the last row of H and obtain the exact values of h'_0, h'_1, h'_2, h'_3 and h'_4 (shown in Fig. 4) using the formula given in Sect. 3.1. The same cannot be done for the second last row.

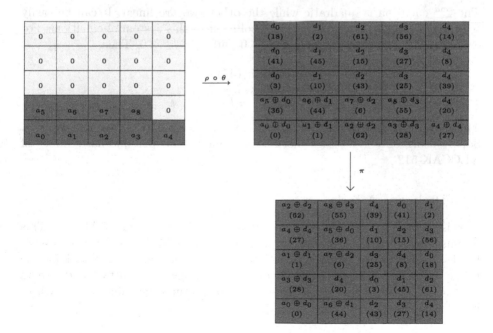

Fig. 3. State after applying θ, ρ, π

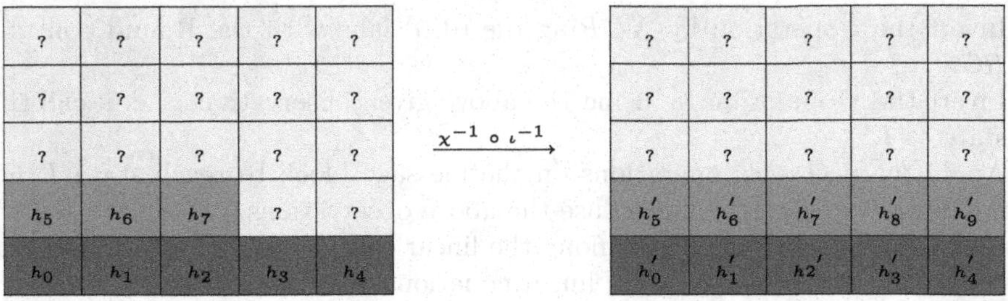

Fig. 4. Inverse operation on hash values

By equating the 3rd state of Fig. 3 and 2nd state of Fig. 4, we get the exact values of d_2, d_3, d_4 and two linear equations

$$a_0 + d_0 = h_0'$$

$$a_6 + d_1 = h_1'$$

By applying χ on the 3rd state of Fig. 3, we have the following equations

$$a_3(28) + d_3(28) + (d_4(20) + 1)d_0(3) = h_5$$

$$d_4(20) + (d_0(3) + 1)d_1(45) = h_6$$

$$d_0(3) + (d_1(45) + 1)d_2(61) = h_7$$

The 2nd equation is quadratic while the other two are linear. It can be easily seen that for many cases, there isn't a solution to this system of equations. For example, take the case where $d_4 = h_4' = 0$ and $d_2 = h_2' = 0$. Then,

$$(d_0(3) + 1)d_1(45) = h_6$$

$$d_0(3) = h_7$$

The above equations cannot be solved simultaneously if $h_7 = 1$ and $h_6 = 1$. So, by using only 1 message block we cannot get all possible hash values of KECCAK-512.

3.4   Preimage Attack

In this section, we give the preimage attack to one round KECCAK-512. This preimage attack gives a message of length less than 1024 bits, i.e two message blocks. In each of the following subsection, we describe a preimage attack for one round KECCAK-512 by considering different settings for the attack and give an analysis on it. We will be considering $h_0, ..., h_7$ as the hash value where each h_i is of length 64 bits.

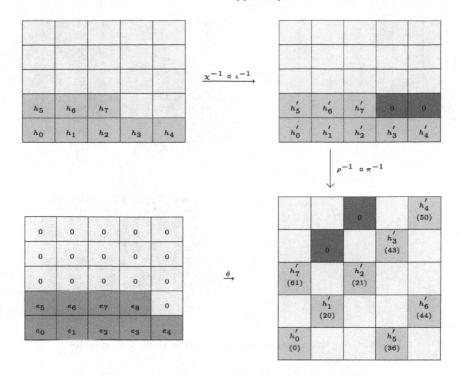

Fig. 5. Using one message block and keeping θ as identity

Using One Message Block and Keeping θ as Identity: We first invert the hash values by applying $\chi^{-1} \circ \iota^{-1}$. To do this, we make the lanes at $(3,1)$ and $(4,1)$ of the inverted state as 0 (refer Fig. 5). We further invert this state through π and ρ. $e_0, ..., e_8$ is the message block represented in 9 lanes. Since we are keeping θ as identity, we have only four free lane variables. Also, we must keep the last bit of the message block as 1 inorder to satisfy the padding rule, so the last bit of e_8(which is equal to e_3) should be 1. Therefore, we can assign

$$e_0 = h'_0(0), e_3 = h'_5(36), e_6 = h'_1(20)$$

Therefore, we can successfully find the preimage for hash values of the form $h_2 = h_6 = h_7 = 0$ and both h_0 and h_1 can take any arbitary values whereas h_5 can have arbitary values except for a single bit which must be 1 because $h_5 = h'_5 = e_3(28)$. Also, h_4 must be equal to $\overline{h_0}h_1$ and $h_3 = h_0$. Hence for 2^{191} hash values we can find preimage by using 1 message block and keeping θ as identity.

Using One Message Block Without Making θ as Identity: We first invert the hash values by applying $\chi^{-1} \circ \iota^{-1}$, but this time keeping the lane at $(3,1)$ as 1. So, now we have $h_7 = h'_7$. In Fig. 6, p_i denotes the value added to an element

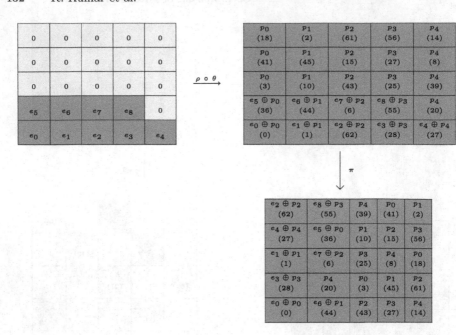

Fig. 6. Using one message block without making θ as identity

in i^{th} column by the θ function. By comparing the 3rd state in Fig. 6 and the state obtained by inverting the hash values, we use the following assignments.

$$e_0(0) = h'_0(0) + h'_7(61) \text{ because } p_0(3) = h'_7(0)$$

$$e_6(44) = h'_1(0) + 1 \text{ because } p_1(45) = 1$$

$$e_3(28) = h'_5(0) + h'_3(1) \text{ because } p_3(27) = h'_3(0)$$

Lanes (4,0) and (1,1) are rotations of each other. From 320 linear equations in 320 variables, there are only 319 linearly independent equations. Therefore, for at most 2^{383} hash values, we can find the preimage by solving these equations.

Therefore, hash values with $h_6 = h_7(0) \oplus h_4(6) \oplus \overline{h_0(6)}.(h_1(6) \oplus \overline{h_2(6)}.$ $h_3(6)) \oplus 1$, we can find the preimage using 1 message block.

Using Two Message Blocks and Making both θ Operation as Identity: By using the same idea used above, we are going to invert the hash values by applying $\rho^{-1} \circ \pi^{-1} \circ \chi^{-1} \circ \iota^{-1}$. We are going to make θ operation as identity by using the 5 lane variables of message block E. So, from second message block we are left with only 4 free lane variables (Fig. 7).

For the first message block we are using the message block

$$D = d_0, d_1, d_2, d_3, 0, d_0, d_1, d_2, d_3$$

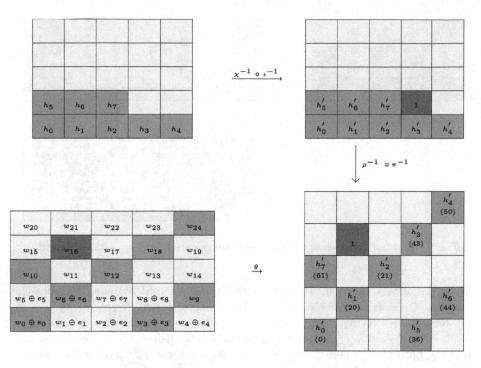

Fig. 7. Using two message blocks and making both θ operation as identity

$d_2(62)$	$d_3(55)$	0	$d_2(62)$	$d_2(62)d_3(55)$
0	$d_0(36)$	0	0	$d_0(36)$
$d_1(1)$	$d_2(6)$	0	$d_1(1)$	$\overline{d_1(1)}d_2(6)$
$d_3(28)$	0	0	$d_3(28)$	0
$d_0 \oplus RC_0$	$d_1(44)$	0	d_0	$\overline{d_0}d_1(44)$

Fig. 8. State W

This makes the θ operation identity. Figure 8 represents the state W which is obtained after applying a KECCAK-p permutation on message block D.

Substituting w_i, we get the following equations

$$h_0' = d_0 + RC_0 + e_0, \quad h_1'(20) = e_6$$

$$h_2'(21) = 0, \quad h_3'(43) = 0, \quad h_4'(50) = \overline{d_2(62)}d_3(55)$$

$$h_5'(36) = e_3 + d_0, \quad h_6'(44) = 0$$

$$h_7'(61) = d_1(1), \quad 1 = d_0(36)$$

w_{20}	w_{21}	w_{22}	w_{23}	w_{24}
w_{15}	w_{16}	w_{17}	w_{18}	w_{19}
w_{10}	w_{11}	w_{12}	w_{13}	w_{14}
$w_5 \oplus e_5$	$w_6 \oplus e_6$	$w_7 \oplus e_7$	$w_8 \oplus e_8$	w_9
$w_0 \oplus e_0$	$w_1 \oplus e_1$	$w_2 \oplus e_2$	$w_3 \oplus e_3$	$w_4 \oplus e_4$

$\xrightarrow{\rho \circ \theta}$

$w_{20} \oplus p_0$ (18)	$w_{21} \oplus p_1$ (2)	$w_{22} \oplus p_2$ (61)	$w_{23} \oplus p_3$ (56)	$w_{24} \oplus p_4$ (14)
$w_{15} \oplus p_0$ (41)	$w_{16} \oplus p_1$ (45)	$w_{17} \oplus p_2$ (15)	$w_{18} \oplus p_3$ (27)	$w_{19} \oplus p_4$ (8)
$w_{10} \oplus p_0$ (3)	$w_{11} \oplus p_1$ (10)	$w_{12} \oplus p_2$ (43)	$w_{13} \oplus p_3$ (25)	$w_{14} \oplus p_4$ (39)
$e_5 \oplus w_5 \oplus p_0$ (36)	$e_6 \oplus w_6 \oplus p_1$ (44)	$e_7 \oplus w_7 \oplus p_2$ (6)	$e_8 \oplus w_8 \oplus p_3$ (55)	$w_9 \oplus p_4$ (20)
$e_0 \oplus w_0 \oplus p_0$ (0)	$e_1 \oplus w_1 \oplus p_1$ (1)	$e_2 \oplus w_2 \oplus p_2$ (62)	$e_3 \oplus w_3 \oplus p_3$ (28)	$e_4 \oplus w_4 \oplus p_4$ (27)

$\downarrow \pi$

$e_2(62) \oplus w_2(62) \oplus p_2(62)$	$e_8(55) \oplus w_8(55) \oplus p_3(55)$	$w_{14}(39) \oplus p_4(39)$	$w_{15}(41) \oplus p_0(41)$	$w_{21}(2) \oplus p_1(2)$
$e_4(27) \oplus w_4(27) \oplus p_4(27)$	$e_5(36) \oplus w_5(36) \oplus p_0(36)$	$w_{11}(10) \oplus p_1(10)$	$w_{17}(15) \oplus p_2(15)$	$w_{23}(56) \oplus p_3(56)$
$e_1(1) \oplus w_1(1) \oplus p_1(1)$	$e_7(6) \oplus w_7(6) \oplus p_2(6)$	$w_{13}(25) \oplus p_3(25)$	$w_{19}(8) \oplus p_4(8)$	$w_{20}(18) \oplus p_0(18)$
$e_3(28) \oplus w_3(28) \oplus p_3(28)$	$w_9(20) \oplus p_4(20)$	$w_{10}(3) \oplus p_0(3)$	$w_{16}(45) \oplus p_1(45)$	$w_{22}(61) \oplus p_2(61)$
$e_0(0) \oplus w_0(0) \oplus p_0(0)$	$e_6(44) \oplus w_6(44) \oplus p_1(44)$	$w_{12}(43) \oplus p_2(43)$	$w_{18}(21) \oplus p_3(21)$	$w_{24}(14) \oplus p_4(14)$

Fig. 9. By using two message block and keeping only first θ operation as identity

From the above equation, we have to assign $d_0 = 1$ and by using the message lanes e_0, e_6, e_3, d_1, d_2 and d_3 we can get any values for $h'_0, h'_1, h'_4, h'_5, h'_7$. Hence, for hash values $h_0, h_1, h_2, h_3, h_4, h_5, h_6, h_7$ with constraints $h_3 = \overline{h_2}h_0$, $h_4 = h_2 + \overline{h_0}h_1$, $h_7 = \overline{h_6}$, preimage can be found by using 2 message block and keeping both the θ operation as identity. So, for total 2^{320} hash values we can find preimage by using this analysis.

By Using Two Message Block and Keeping only First θ Operation as Identity: We make the first θ operation applied to the message block D as identity. So, we are left with only 4 message lanes d_0, d_1, d_2, d_3. After applying a KECCAK-p permutation on message block D we get the state W which is same as the one shown above.

For the second message, we are not putting any constraints.

After applying $\pi \circ \rho \circ \theta$ over the state $W \oplus E$ and equating this state to the state we got after applying $\chi^{-1} \circ \iota^{-1}$ on the state of the hash value, we get 9 lane equation (576 equation) over the message block D and E (Fig. 9).

$$h'_0 = e_0(0) + d_0(0) + RC(0) + p_0(0), \quad h'_1 = e_6(44) + p_1(44)$$

$$h'_2 = p_2(43), \quad h'_3 = p_3(21), \quad h'_4 = \overline{d_2(12)}d_3(5) + p_4(14)$$

$$h'_5 = e_3(28) + d_0(28) + p_3(28), \quad h'_6 = p_4(20)$$

$$h'_7 = d_1(4) + p_0(3), \quad 1 = d_0(17) + p_1(45)$$

These equations are not linear because the column parities p_0 and p_3 contains the terms $\overline{d_0(0)}d_1(44), \overline{d_1(1)}d_2(6)$, and $\overline{d_2(62)}d_3(55)$. To make these equations linear we assigned $d_0 = 0$ and $d_2 = 0$. By this, we also get assignment of e_3, e_6 and d_3.

$$e_3(28) = h'_5(0) + h'_3(7) \text{ because } d_0 = 0 \text{ and } h'_3(0) = p_3(21)$$

$$e_6(44) = h_1'(0) + 1 \text{ because } d_0 = 0 \text{ and } d_0(17) + p_1(45) = 1$$

$$d_3(5) = h_4'(0) + h_6'(6) \text{ because } d_2 = 0 \text{ and } h_6' = p_4(20)$$

The remaining linear equation are

$$h_0' = e_0(0) + RC(0) + d_1(44) + d_3(55) + e_4(0) + d_1(43) + d_3(54) + e_1(63) + e_6(63)$$

$$h_2' = d_1(23) + d_3(34) + e_1(43) + e_6(43) + d_1(43) + d_3(6) + e_3(42) + e_8(42)$$

$$h_3' = e_2(21) + e_7(21) + d_1(0) + d_3(11) + e_4(20)$$

$$h_6' = d_3(48) + d_1(21) + e_3(20) + e_8(20) + d_1(20) + d_3(47) + RC(19) + e_0(19) + e_5(19)$$

$$h_7' = d_1(1) + d_1(47) + d_3(58) + e_4(3) + d_1(46) + d_3(57) + e_1(2) + e_6(2)$$

$$1 = RC(45) + d_3(9) + d_1(46) + e_0(45) + e_5(45) + e_2(44) + e_7(44)$$

We assign e_7 to 0 and assign the last bit of e_8 to 1 to satisfy the padding condition while the rest of the bits of e_8 are assigned to 0. This is done so that the preimage length is minimized. Now we are left with total 384 linear equation in 384 variables. All of these linear equations are linearly independent. Applying Gaussian elimination, we can completely find the message block D and E that gives the required hash value on application of 1 round of KECCAK-512.

4 Results and Extension to Collision Attack

The above preimage attack was implemented in C++ using the NTL library [16] from Victor Shoup. The code was executed on a laptop with Intel Core i5-7200 processor and 16 GB RAM giving the preimage in less than 0.005 s. In the analysis given in Sect. 3.4, if we randomly choose e_7 and e_8 while also keep the last bit of e_8 as 1, we can get 2^{127} preimages for the same hash value, thus giving us a collision attack.

The following tables describe the characterization of the hash values that can be found using the preimage analysis done in Sect. 3.4 (Table 1).

Table 1. Characterization of hash values

Type of attack	Number of hash values	Characterization of hash values
1 message block, θ as identity	2^{191}	$h_2 = h_6 = h_7 = 0, h_5[35] = 1, h_4 = \overline{h_0}h_1, h_3 = h_0$
1 message block, θ not identity	2^{447}	$h_6 = h_7(0) \oplus h_4(6) \oplus \overline{h_0(6)}.(h_1(6) \oplus \overline{h_2(6)}.h_3(6)) \oplus 1$
2 message blocks, both θ as identity	2^{320}	$h_3 = \overline{h_2}.h_0, h_4 = h_2 \oplus \overline{h_0}.h_1, h_7 = \overline{h_6}$
2 message blocks, first θ as identity	2^{512}	All possible hash values

5   Conclusion and Future Works

Our approach gives a preimage and collision attack to all the variants of 1 round KECCAK hash functions. These are currently the fastest attacks known. These attacks does not pose a threat to the security of 24-round KECCAK. In future, we need to find whether this idea can be extended to 2 rounds KECCAK-384 and KECCAK-512.

References

1. Bertoni, G., Daemen, J., Peeters, M., Van Assche, G.: Keccak specifications. Submission to NIST (Round 2) (2009)
2. Dworkin, M.J.: SHA-3 standard: permutation-based hash and extendable-output functions. Federal Information Processing Standard (NIST FIPS)-202 (2015)
3. Bertoni, G., Daemen, J., Peeters, M., Van Assche, G.: Cryptographic sponges (2011). http://sponge.noekeon.org
4. Bernstein, D.J.: Second preimages for 6 (7?(8??)) rounds of Keccak. NIST mailing list (2010)
5. Chang, D., Kumar, A., Morawiecki, P., Sanadhya, S.K.: 1st and 2nd preimage attacks on 7, 8 and 9 rounds of Keccak-224, 256, 384, 512. In: SHA-3 Workshop, August 2014
6. Morawiecki, P., Pieprzyk, J., Srebrny, M.: Rotational cryptanalysis of round-reduced KECCAK. In: Moriai, S. (ed.) FSE 2013. LNCS, vol. 8424, pp. 241–262. Springer, Heidelberg (2014). https://doi.org/10.1007/978-3-662-43933-3_13
7. Morawiecki, P., Srebrny, M.: A sat-based preimage analysis of reduced Keccak hash functions. Inf. Process. Lett. **113**(10–11), 392–397 (2013)
8. Naya-Plasencia, M., Röck, A., Meier, W.: Practical analysis of reduced-round KECCAK. In: Bernstein, D.J., Chatterjee, S. (eds.) INDOCRYPT 2011. LNCS, vol. 7107, pp. 236–254. Springer, Heidelberg (2011). https://doi.org/10.1007/978-3-642-25578-6_18
9. Guo, J., Liu, M., Song, L.: Linear structures: applications to cryptanalysis of round-reduced KECCAK. In: Cheon, J.H., Takagi, T. (eds.) ASIACRYPT 2016. LNCS, vol. 10031, pp. 249–274. Springer, Heidelberg (2016). https://doi.org/10.1007/978-3-662-53887-6_9
10. Dinur, I., Dunkelman, O., Shamir, A.: New attacks on Keccak-224 and Keccak-256. In: Canteaut, A. (ed.) FSE 2012. LNCS, vol. 7549, pp. 442–461. Springer, Heidelberg (2012). https://doi.org/10.1007/978-3-642-34047-5_25
11. Dinur, I., Dunkelman, O., Shamir, A.: Improved practical attacks on round-reduced Keccak. J. Cryptol. **27**(2), 183–209 (2014)
12. Dinur, I., Dunkelman, O., Shamir, A.: Collision attacks on up to 5 rounds of SHA-3 using generalized internal differentials. In: Moriai, S. (ed.) FSE 2013. LNCS, vol. 8424, pp. 219–240. Springer, Heidelberg (2014). https://doi.org/10.1007/978-3-662-43933-3_12
13. Qiao, K., Song, L., Liu, M., Guo, J.: New collision attacks on round-reduced Keccak. In: Coron, J.-S., Nielsen, J.B. (eds.) EUROCRYPT 2017. LNCS, vol. 10212, pp. 216–243. Springer, Cham (2017). https://doi.org/10.1007/978-3-319-56617-7_8

14. Song, L., Liao, G., Guo, J.: Non-full sbox linearization: applications to collision attacks on round-reduced KECCAK. In: Katz, J., Shacham, H. (eds.) CRYPTO 2017. LNCS, vol. 10402, pp. 428–451. Springer, Cham (2017). https://doi.org/10.1007/978-3-319-63715-0_15
15. Bertoni, G., Daemen, J., Peeters, M., Assche, G.: The Keccak reference (2011). http://keccak.noekeon.org/keccak-reference-3.0.pdf
16. Shoup, V.: NTL: a library for doing number theory (2001). www.shoup.net/ntl/

Asymmetric Cryptography

Performing Computations on Hierarchically Shared Secrets

Giulia Traverso[✉], Denise Demirel, and Johannes Buchmann

Technische Universität Darmstadt, Darmstadt, Germany
gtraverso@cdc.informatik.tu-darmstadt.de

Abstract. Hierarchical secret sharing schemes distribute a message to a set of shareholders with different reconstruction capabilities. In distributed storage systems, this is an important property because it allows to grant more reconstruction capability to better performing storage servers and vice versa. In particular, Tassa's conjunctive and disjunctive hierarchical secret sharing schemes are based on Birkhoff interpolation and perform equally well as Shamir's threshold secret sharing scheme. Thus, they are promising candidates for distributed storage systems. A key requirement is the possibility to perform function evaluations over shared data. However, practical algorithms supporting this have not been provided yet with respect to hierarchical secret sharing schemes. Aiming at closing this gap, in this work, we show how additions and multiplications of shares can be practically computed using Tassa's conjunctive and disjunctive hierarchical secret sharing schemes. Furthermore, we provide auditing procedures for operations on messages shared hierarchically, which allow to verify that functions on the shares have been performed correctly. We close this work with an evaluation of the correctness, security, and efficiency of the protocols we propose.

Keywords: Hierarchical secret sharing · Birkhoff interpolation
Verifiable secret sharing · Auditing · Multi-party computation
Distributed storage systems · Cloud computing

1 Introduction

In this work, we provide procedures allowing to evaluate functions on shares that have been generated by using a hierarchical secret sharing scheme. The primary focus of this paper is the application of secret sharing to distributed storage systems [23]. That is, shares of a document are generated and distributed to storage servers owned by multiple storage providers. Shamir's threshold secret sharing scheme [29] and Tassa's conjunctive and disjunctive hierarchical secret sharing schemes [31] are viable solutions for distributed storage systems. In particular, Shamir's threshold secret sharing scheme generates shares that are all equivalent in their reconstruction capability. Thus, to protect the confidentiality of data, the number of storage providers deployed must be larger than the reconstructing threshold. Otherwise, storage providers would have enough shares to retrieve

© Springer International Publishing AG, part of Springer Nature 2018
A. Joux et al. (Eds.): AFRICACRYPT 2018, LNCS 10831, pp. 141–161, 2018.
https://doi.org/10.1007/978-3-319-89339-6_9

the data within the storage servers they own. Instead, Tassa's conjunctive and disjunctive hierarchical secret sharing schemes generate shares with different reconstruction capabilities but that have all the same length. This allows for more flexibility because the reconstruction capability of the storage servers can be arranged such that no storage provider has enough information to retrieve the document. Thus, for the same reconstructing threshold, more shares can be distributed to less storage providers without breaking confidentiality. Clearly, if users can rely on less storage providers for a given reconstructing threshold, then this allow for a better trade-off between data protection and storage cost.

This paper shows how to practically compute additions and multiplications over hierarchically shared data when Tassa's conjunctive and disjunctive secret sharing schemes are used. So far solutions to perform operations on shared messages have only been instantiated for Shamir's threshold secret sharing schemes and have been generalized for any linear secret sharing scheme in [10]. Thus, in this work we fill this gap by introducing procedures allowing to evaluate functions on shares that have been generated using a hierarchical secret sharing scheme. More precisely, we show how to perform linear operations and multiplications on messages that have been shared and need to be reconstructed using the Birkhoff interpolation formula. Tassa's conjunctive and disjunctive hierarchical secret sharing schemes are based on Birkhoff interpolation and are linear schemes. Thus, we adapt to our setting the general procedure for computations over linear secret sharing schemes introduced in [10]. This is not trivial because in practice multiplications are split in a preprocessing and an on-line phase which both have to be adapted to the hierarchical setup. Furthermore, we prove that these procedures compute the outcome of functions correctly and provide perfect secrecy, i.e. only qualified subsets are able to retrieve the input messages and the result of computations. Moreover, we provide an audit procedure for computations over messages shared hierarchically. Lastly, we discuss security and efficiency of the algorithms introduced. The rest of the paper is organized as follows. First, the related work and the preliminaries are discussed in Sect. 2 and Sect. 3, respectively. Then, our contribution is presented. More precisely, in Sect. 4 it is shown how to perform operations over messages shared using Birkhoff interpolation-based hierarchical secret sharing schemes. Furthermore, it is proven that those procedures compute the outcome of functions correctly and provide perfect secrecy. Since multiplications on hierarchical shares require larger changes on the preprocessing phase we detail this process in Sect. 5. In Sect. 6, it is described how to perform the auditing procedure. Security and efficiency of the proposed protocols are discussed in Sect. 7. Conclusions can be found in Sect. 8.

2   Related Work

Independently introduced by Shamir [29] and Blakley [4], threshold secret sharing is a cryptographic primitive enabling a dealer to share a message equally among a set of players, called shareholders. The message can be reconstructed by subsets of a certain amount of shareholders while subsets smaller than the threshold do not learn any information about the data shared. Shamir's threshold secret sharing scheme is the best known solution and is based on polynomials and on Lagrange interpolation. It has been shown in [21] how shares can be periodically refreshed. Based on [12], it has been shown in [19] how to modify the definition of eligible subsets of shareholders for the reconstruction of the message. In [25], it has been shown how to add shareholders. Furthermore, it is possible to perform operations over shared messages [18]. This enables general multi-party computation, as discussed in [3,8,16]. Furthermore, in [28] it is shown how to perform an auditing procedure for computations over shared messages, which is based on the work done in [1] and in [11]. So called hierarchical secret sharing schemes [14] address scenarios where the shareholders are not equal in their reconstruction capability. Brickell in [7] and Simmons in [30] presented a solution where each shareholder receives only one share which is of equal size, but with different reconstruction capabilities. However, the reconstruction process is highly expensive. Ghodosi et al. showed in [17] how to construct efficient schemes for specific instantiations. Tassa solved these problems by introducing in [31] two schemes based on polynomials and Birkhoff interpolation (a generalization of Lagrange interpolation) for the reconstruction of the message. These are called conjunctive and disjunctive hierarchical secret sharing schemes, depending on which subsets of shareholders are eligible to access the shared message. It has been proven in [32] that Tassa's conjunctive and disjunctive hierarchical secret sharing schemes achieve the same flexibility as Shamir's threshold secret sharing scheme. More precisely, algorithms based on Birkhoff interpolation have been designed that allow Tassa's schemes to add shareholders, to periodically refresh the shares, and to modify the definition of eligible subsets for the reconstruction of the message. According to the notion of dynamic secret sharing[1] specified in [32], both Shamir's and Tassa's secret sharing schemes are dynamic. The last step to show that hierarchical secret sharing achieves the same functionalities as Shamir's threshold secret sharing is to prove that Tassa's schemes support the same operations over shared messages, i.e. linear combinations and multiplication. Conditions on the access structure allowing for multiplication have been investigated in [22]. However, they lead to schemes with either an increased length of the shares (which is not optimal for our application to distributed storage systems) or with stronger conditions on the access structure deviating from the original schemes proposed by Tassa. Furthermore, practical and ready to be used algorithms for linear operations and multiplications over Tassa's conjunctive and disjunctive hierarchical secret sharing schemes and for performing auditing over such computations were not proposed. And this is what we provide in this work.

---

[1] Note that this is different from the notion of fully dynamic secret sharing discussed in [5], where one scheme supports different access structures for different secrets.

3 Preliminaries

Secret sharing schemes are used to share a message $m \in \mathbb{F}_q$ across a set $S = \{s_1, \ldots, s_n\}$ of n shareholders. More precisely, a dealer generates shares $\sigma_1, \ldots, \sigma_n \in \mathbb{F}_q$ of message m and distributes each share $\sigma_i \in \mathbb{F}_q$ to the respective shareholder $s_i \in S$. Only specific subsets $A \subset S$ of shareholders can reconstruct the message provided that certain requirements are fulfilled. Instead, subsets $U \subset S$ not fulfilling such requirements cannot reconstruct the message and get no information about it. These subsets are called *authorized* and *unauthorized*, respectively. Denoted by $\mathcal{P}(S)$ the partition of set S, the *access structure* $\Gamma \subset \mathcal{P}(S)$ determines both sets, i.e. $A \in \Gamma$ and $U \notin \Gamma$. More formally, secret sharing is a pair of algorithms (Share, Reconstruct). Algorithm Share takes as input a message $m \in \mathbb{F}_q$ and the unique ID $i \in \mathcal{I}$ of shareholder $s_i \in S$ and outputs its share $\sigma_i \in \mathbb{F}_q$, for $i = 1, \ldots, n$. Algorithm Reconstruct takes as input a subset $R \subset S$ and outputs the message m if $R \in \Gamma$ and $\perp$ otherwise. Adapting the definition provided in [2] to the purpose of this paper, in the following we formalize the notions of correctness and perfect secrecy restricted to ideal secretsharing schemes, where the length of the message equals the length of the shares.

Definition 1. *Given the set* $\mathbb{F}_q$ *of messages and the set* $S = \{s_1, \ldots, s_n\}$ *of shareholders, the pair of algorithms* (Share, Reconstruct) *is a secret sharing scheme realizing access structure* $\Gamma \subset \mathcal{P}(S)$ *if the following two requirements hold.*

(1) Correctness: *if shares held by shareholders of an authorized set* $A \in \Gamma$ *are given as input to algorithm* Reconstruct, *then algorithm* Reconstruct *retrieves the message* m *shared during algorithm* Share, *for every message* $m \in \mathbb{F}_q$.
(2) Perfect secrecy: *if shares held by shareholders of an unauthorized set* $U \notin \Gamma$ *are given as input to algorithm* Reconstruct, *then algorithm* Reconstruct *leaks no information about the message* m *shared during algorithm* Share, *for every message* $m \in \mathbb{F}_q$.

Linear threshold secret sharing schemes are amongst the most studied schemes also due to their usage in practical scenarios. The first (t, n)-threshold secret sharing scheme is proposed by Shamir in [29] and it is based on interpolation of polynomials. More precisely, a message m is shared using a polynomial $f(x) = a_0 + a_1 x + \cdots + a_{t-1} x^{t-1}$ of degree $\deg(f(x)) = t - 1$, where $a_0 := m$ and coefficients $a_1, \ldots, a_{t-1} \in \mathbb{F}_q$ are chosen uniformly at random. Algorithm Share computes share $\sigma_i \in \mathbb{F}_q$ for shareholder $s_i \in S$ as a point on polynomial $f(x)$, i.e. $\sigma_i := f(i)$, where $i \in \mathcal{I}$ is the ID of shareholder s_i. Algorithm Reconstruct is based on Lagrange interpolation of polynomials. Thus, on the one hand, authorized subsets $A \subset S$ are composed of t or more shareholders, that is $|A| \geq t$. In fact, when t or more points of polynomial $f(x)$ are collected, it is possible to correctly interpolate polynomial $f(x)$ and message m is retrieved as $f(0) = a_0$. On the other hand, unauthorized subsets $U \subset S$ are composed of $t - 1$ or less shareholders, that is $|U| \leq t - 1$. In fact, when only $t - 1$ or less points are collected, polynomial $f(x)$ cannot be reconstructed and no information about message $m \in \mathbb{F}_q$ is leaked.

The so called *conjunctive* and *disjunctive* schemes proposed by Tassa in [31] are the first hierarchical secret sharing schemes based on Birkhoff interpolation of polynomials. More precisely, shares are either points on a polynomial or points on one of the derivatives of such polynomial. More precisely, a hierarchy is composed of levels $L_0, \ldots, L_\ell$, where L_0 is the highest level, L_ℓ the lowest, and $\ell \leq n$. The cardinality of each level L_h is denoted by n_h and each shareholder is assigned to one level only. In addition, a threshold t_h is associated with each level L_h, for $h \in 0, \ldots, \ell$, such that $0 < t_0 < \cdots < t_\ell$. Tassa individuated two types of access structures, defining, respectively the conjunctive and the disjunctive hierarchical secret sharing. On the one hand, the conjunctive access structure determines that a subset $A \subset S$ is authorized if, *for all levels* L_h, it contains t_h shareholders assigned to levels equal or higher than L_h, for $h = 0, \ldots, \ell$. On the other hand, the disjunctive access structure specifies that a subset $A \subset S$ is authorized if, *for at least one level* L_h, it contains t_h shareholders assigned to levels equal or higher than L_h, for $h = 0, \ldots, \ell$. In the following, we write information relating to disjunctive hierarchical secret sharing in brackets. For conjunctive (disjunctive) hierarchical secret sharing schemes the unique ID of shareholder $s_{i,j} \in S$ is a pair $(i, j) \in \mathcal{I} \times \mathcal{I}$, where $i = 1, \ldots, n_h$ and $j := t_{h-1}$ $(j := t_\ell - t_h)$, for $h = 0, \ldots, \ell$ with $t_{-1} := 0$ and $t := t_\ell$. The algorithms Share and Reconstruct of the conjunctive (disjunctive) hierarchical secret sharing are as follows.

Share. The algorithm takes as input a message $m \in \mathbb{F}_q$ and generates a polynomial $f(x) = a_0 + a_1 x + \cdots + a_{t-1} x^{t-1}$ of degree $\deg(f(x)) = t - 1$, where $a_0 := m$ $(a_{t-1} := m)$ and the coefficients $a_1, \ldots, a_{t-1} \in \mathbb{F}_q$ $(a_0, \ldots, a_{t-2} \in \mathbb{F}_q)$ are chosen uniformly at random. It outputs share $\sigma_{i,j} \in \mathbb{F}_q$ for shareholder $s_{i,j} \in S$ computed as $\sigma_{i,j} := f^j(i)$, where $f^j(x)$ is the j-th derivative of polynomial $f(x)$ and pair $(i, j) \in \mathcal{I} \times \mathcal{I}$ is the unique ID of shareholder $s_{i,j} \in S$, for $i = 1, \ldots, n_h$ and $h = 0, \ldots, \ell$.

Reconstruct. The algorithm takes as input a set of shares held by a subset $R \subset S$ of shareholders. If R is unauthorized, i.e. $R \notin \Gamma$, then it outputs $\perp$. If R is authorized, i.e. $R \in \Gamma$, then it reconstructs polynomial $f(x)$ using Birkhoff interpolation and outputs $m = a_0$ $(m = a_{t-1})$.

The Birkhoff interpolation problem is a generalization of the Lagrange interpolation problem and describes the problem of finding a polynomial $f(x) = a_0 + a_1 x + \cdots + a_{t-1} x^{t-1}$ satisfying the equalities $f^j(i) = \sigma_{i,j}$. Given an authorized set $R \in \Gamma$ of shareholders for conjunctive (disjunctive) hierarchical secret sharing schemes, the Birkhoff interpolation problem can be solved as follows. The *interpolation matrix* associated to set R is a binary matrix E where entry $e_{i,j}$ is set to '1' if shareholder $s_{i,j}$ participates with share $\sigma_{i,j}$ and '0' otherwise. Let us denote by $I(E) = \{(i, j)$ such that $e_{i,j} = 1\}$ the set containing the entries of E in lexicographic order, i.e. the pair (i, j) precedes the pair (i', j') if and only if $i < i'$ or $i = i'$ and $j < j'$. The elements of $I(E)$ are denoted by $(i_1, j_1), (i_2, j_2), \ldots, (i_r, j_r)$, where $r := |R|$. Furthermore, we set

$\varphi := \{\phi_0, \phi_1, \phi_2, \ldots, \phi_{t-1}\} = \{1, x, x^2, \ldots, x^t\}$ and denote by ϕ_k^j the j-the derivative of ϕ_k, for $k = 0, \ldots, t-1$. Then the matrix $A(E, X, \varphi)$ is defined as follows:

$$A(E, X, \varphi) = \begin{pmatrix} \phi_0^{j_1}(i_1) & \phi_1^{j_1}(i_1) & \phi_2^{j_1}(i_1) & \cdots & \phi_{t-1}^{j_1}(i_1) \\ \phi_0^{j_2}(i_2) & \phi_1^{j_2}(i_2) & \phi_2^{j_2}(i_2) & \cdots & \phi_{t-1}^{j_2}(i_2) \\ \vdots & \vdots & \vdots & \cdots & \vdots \\ \phi_0^{j_r}(i_r) & \phi_1^{j_r}(i_r) & \phi_2^{j_r}(i_r) & \cdots & \phi_{t-1}^{j_r}(i_r) \end{pmatrix}.$$

Polynomial $f(x)$ can be reconstructed in distributed fashion by computing

$$f(x) = \sum_{k=0}^{t-1} a_k x^k = \sum_{k=0}^{t-1} \sum_{l=1}^{r} a_{l,k} x^k,$$

where $a_{l,k} := \sigma_{i_l, j_l} (-1)^{l-1+k} \frac{\det(A_{l-1,k}(E,X,\varphi))}{\det(A(E,X,\varphi))}$ is computed locally by shareholder $s_{i_l, j_l} \in R$, for $l = 1, \ldots, r$, and matrix $A_{l-1,k}(E, X, \varphi)$ results from matrix $A(E, X, \varphi)$ by removing the l-th row and the $(k+1)$-th column (see [32], Theorem 1 for a formal proof). Necessary and sufficient requirements for Birkhoff interpolation problem to have a unique solution can be found in [31]. Examples of Birkhoff interpolation problems can be found in [26].

4   Operations on Messages Distributed Through Hierarchical Secret Sharing Schemes

In this section, we prove that Tassa's conjunctive and disjunctive hierarchical secret sharing schemes, based on Birkhoff interpolation, allow to perform operations over shared messages. More precisely, a message can be reconstructed which is the result of operations performed over previously shared messages. The operations supported are the sum of messages, the multiplication of a message by a scalar, and the product of messages.

4.1   Setting

Messages $m_1, m_2 \in \mathbb{F}_q$ are distributed to a set S of n shareholders according to the following assumptions.

(A1) The underlying access structure Γ remains the same for both messages m_1, m_2. More precisely, both polynomials $f(x)$ and $h(x)$ used to share m_1 and m_2, respectively, have the same degree. Furthermore, shareholder $s_{i,j}$ with unique ID (i, j) holds share $\sigma_{i,j}(m_1) := f^j(i)$ and $\sigma_{i,j}(m_2) := h^j(i)$.

(A2) The degree $t - 1$ of polynomials $f(x)$ and $h(x)$ is chosen such that $2t \le n$, where n is the total number of shareholders.

(A3) The ID (i, j) of each shareholder $s_{i,j} \in S$ is chosen such that index $i \in \mathcal{I}$ is selected once within the whole hierarchy and such that the corresponding Birkhoff interpolation problem has a unique solution. The requirements to achieve this can be found in [31].

(A4) The user communicates with the shareholders and the shareholders among each other using private channels.

(A5) A tamper-proof bulletin board is available to allow exchanging data during the preprocessing phase of the multiplication procedure. Note that this is a common assumption for auditable multi-party computation and a more formal definition can be found in [20].

Let us recall that index $j \in \mathcal{I}$ of the unique identity ID of shareholder $s_{i,j} \in S$ is defined as $j := t_{h-1}$ ($j := t_\ell - t_h$), for $h = 0, \ldots, \ell$ and $t_{-1} := 0$ (see Sect. 3). Algorithm Share defined in Sect. 3 is run separately to share and distribute message m_1 and message m_2 to the n shareholders of set S. More precisely, to share message m_1, algorithm Share selects a polynomial $f(x) = a_0 + a_1 x + \cdots + a_{t-1} x^{t-1}$, where $a_0 := m_1$ ($a_{t-1} := m_1$) and $a_1, \ldots, a_{t-1} \in \mathbb{F}_q$ ($a_0, \ldots, a_{t-2} \in \mathbb{F}_q$) are chosen uniformly at random. It distributes to each shareholder $s_{i,j} \in S$ share $\sigma_{i,j}(m_1) = f^j(i)$. To share message m_2, algorithm Share generates a polynomial $h(x) = b_0 + b_1 x + \cdots + b_{t-1} x^{t-1}$, where $b_0 := m_2$ ($b_{t-1} := m_2$) and $b_1, \ldots, b_{t-1} \in \mathbb{F}_q$ ($b_0, \ldots, b_{t-2} \in \mathbb{F}_q$) are chosen uniformly at random. It distributes to each shareholder $s_{i,j} \in S$ share $\sigma_{i,j}(m_2) = h^j(i)$. Afterwards, algorithms Linear and Multiply are run by each shareholder individually to perform linear operations and multiplications on their shares of messages m_1 and m_2. Finally, the result $m \in \mathbb{F}_q$ of these operations on m_1, m_2 can be reconstructed by running algorithm Reconstruct defined in Sect. 3 on the shares computed by each shareholder.

4.2 Linear Operations

In this section, algorithm Linear is presented, which computes share $\sigma_{i,j}(m) \in \mathbb{F}_q$ for shareholder $s_{i,j} \in S$, to be used as input for algorithm Reconstruct to retrieve message $m = \lambda_1 \cdot m_1 + \lambda_2 \cdot m_2$, for scalars $\lambda_1, \lambda_2 \in \mathbb{F}_q$.

Linear. The algorithm takes as input shares $\sigma_{i,j}(m_1), \sigma_{i,j}(m_2) \in \mathbb{F}_q$ held by shareholder $s_{i,j} \in S$, and scalars $\lambda_1, \lambda_2 \in \mathbb{F}_q$. It outputs share $\sigma_{i,j}(m) := \lambda_1 \cdot \sigma_{i,j}(m_1) + \lambda_2 \cdot \sigma_{i,j}(m_2) \in \mathbb{F}_q$ for shareholder $s_{i,j} \in S$.

Theorem 1. *The algorithm* Linear *for conjunctive (disjunctive) hierarchical secret sharing introduced above computes the shares correctly. More precisely, on input shares $\sigma_{i,j}(m_1), \sigma_{i,j}(m_2)$ and scalars λ_1, λ_2, the shares computed by* Linear *reconstruct to message m, where $m = \lambda_1 \cdot m_1 + \lambda_2 \cdot m_2$. Furthermore, perfect secrecy, according to Definition 1, is maintained while performing* Linear.

Proof. Let $\sigma_{i,j}(m) \in \mathbb{F}_q$ be the shares computed by shareholders $s_{i,j} \in R$ using algorithm Linear, where $R \in \Gamma$ is an authorized set. To prove correctness, we have to show that algorithm Reconstruct outputs message $m = \lambda_1 \cdot m_1 + \lambda_2 \cdot m_2$ when it takes as input shares $\sigma_{i,j}(m) \in \mathbb{F}_q$. More precisely, we have to show that the shares interpolate to a polynomial $p(x) = c_0 + c_1 x + \cdots + c_{t-1} x^{t-1}$ of degree $\deg(p(x)) = t - 1$, where $c_0 = \lambda_1 \cdot m_1 + \lambda_2 \cdot m_2$ ($c_{t-1} = \lambda_1 \cdot m_1 + \lambda_2 \cdot m_2$).

To prove perfect secrecy, we have to show, first, that algorithm Linear computes shares for message $m = \lambda_1 \cdot m_1 + \lambda_2 \cdot m_2$ without leaking information about the shares for message m_1 and message m_2. Second, we have to show that any unauthorized set $U \notin \Gamma$ gets no information about $m = \lambda_1 \cdot m_1 + \lambda_2 \cdot m_2$. In order to do that, we have to show that polynomial $p(x) = c_0 + c_1 x + \cdots + c_{t-1} x^{t-1}$ can be computed in distributed fashion by each shareholder $s_{i,j} \in R$. That is, correctness and perfect secrecy hold if each shareholder can compute a term $p_{(i,j),k}$ without leaking information to any other shareholder and such that:

$$p(x) = \sum_{k=0}^{t-1} c_k x^k = \sum_{k=0}^{t-1} \sum_{s_{i,j} \in R} p_{(i,j),k} x^k,$$

where $c_0 = \lambda_1 \cdot m_1 + \lambda_2 \cdot m_2 (c_{t-1} = \lambda_1 \cdot m_1 + \lambda_2 \cdot m_2)$.

Let us recall that message $m_1 \in \mathbb{F}_q$ is shared using polynomial $f(x) = a_0 + a_1 x + \cdots + a_{t-1} x^{t-1}$. Due to Birkhoff interpolation resolution formula (see Sect. 3), coefficient a_k of polynomial $f(x)$ can be computed as:

$$a_k = \sum_{l=1}^{r} a_{l,k} = \sum_{l=1}^{r} \sigma_l(m_1)(-1)^{l-1+k} \frac{\det(A_{l-1,k}(E, X, \varphi))}{\det(A(E, X, \varphi))},$$

for $k = 0, \ldots, t-1$, where $\sigma_l(m_1)$, for $l = 1, \ldots, r$, are the shares $\sigma_{i,j}(m_1)$ in lexicographic order ((i,j) precedes the pair (i',j') if $i < i'$ or $i = i'$ and $j < j'$). Similarly, message $m_2 \in \mathbb{F}_q$ is shared through polynomial $h(x) = b_0 + b_1 x + \cdots + b_{t-1} x^{t-1}$. Due to Birkhoff interpolation resolution formula, coefficient b_k of polynomial $h(x)$ can be computed as:

$$b_k = \sum_{l=1}^{r} b_{l,k} = \sum_{l=1}^{r} \sigma_l(m_2)(-1)^{l-1+k} \frac{\det(A_{l-1,k}(E, X, \varphi))}{\det(A(E, X, \varphi))},$$

for $k = 0, \ldots, t-1$, where $\sigma_l(m_2)$, for $l = 1, \ldots, r$, are the shares $\sigma_{i,j}(m_2)$ in lexicographic order. Because of the homomorphic property of polynomials, polynomial $p(x)$ can be computed as the linear combination of polynomial $f(x)$ and polynomial $h(x)$ with scalars $\lambda_1, \lambda_2 \in \mathbb{F}_q$. That is, $p(x) = \lambda_1 \cdot f(x) + \lambda_2 \cdot h(x)$. Therefore,

$$p(x) = \sum_{k=0}^{t-1} \lambda_1 \cdot a_k + \lambda_2 \cdot b_k = \sum_{k=0}^{t-1} \sum_{l=1}^{r} \lambda_1 \cdot a_{l,k} + \lambda_2 \cdot b_{l,k}.$$

This shows that the terms $p_{l,k} = p_{(i,j),k} := \lambda_1 \cdot a_{l,k} + \lambda_2 \cdot b_{l,k}$ computed by the shareholders $s_{i,j} \in R$ interpolate to polynomial $p(x)$ and correctness is provided. Regarding perfect secrecy, the computation of $p_{l,k}$ is performed solely by shareholder $s_l \in R$ using the information it has and without leaking $a_{l,k}$ nor $b_{l,k}$. Thus, no information about shares $\sigma_l(m_1), \sigma_l(m_2)$ is leaked. Moreover, being polynomial $p(x)$ of degree $\deg(p(x)) = t - 1$, the original access structure Γ is maintained: subsets $U \subset S$ of shareholders such that $U \notin \Gamma$ not only cannot reconstruct $m = \lambda_1 \cdot m_1 + \lambda_2 \cdot m_2$, but also do not get any information about m_1 nor m_2. Thus, perfect secrecy of the underlying conjunctive (disjunctive) hierarchical secret sharing is still maintained even if algorithm Linear is run and the shares computed by this algorithm are used as input for algorithm Reconstruct.

4.3 Multiplication

In this section, algorithm Multiply is presented, which computes share $\sigma_{i,j}(m)$ for shareholder $s_{i,j} \in S$. Share $\sigma_{i,j}(m)$ is used as input for algorithm Reconstruct to retrieve message $m = m_1 \cdot m_2$. Algorithm Multiply uses algorithm Linear (see Sect. 4.2) to compute message m as linear combinations of the shares for message m_1 and message m_2. More precisely, it builds on the multiplication algorithm discussed in [11] and the triplet generation presented in [1], requiring for each multiplication a preprocessing phase in which the shareholders jointly compute shares $\sigma_{i,j}(\alpha), \sigma_{i,j}(\beta), \sigma_{i,j}(\gamma)$ to messages $\alpha, \beta, \gamma \in \mathbb{F}_q$ such that $\alpha \cdot \beta = \gamma$. Note that, according to Assumption (A1) in Sect. 4.1, for algorithm Multiply to work the values α, β, and γ have to be shared according to the access structure Γ. More details about how to achieve this are provided in Sect. 5.

Multiply. The algorithm selects a triple (α, β, γ) generated during the preprocessing phase and it takes as input shares $\sigma_{i,j}(m_1), \sigma_{i,j}(m_2) \in \mathbb{F}_q$ and shares $\sigma_{i,j}(\alpha), \sigma_{i,j}(\beta), \sigma_{i,j}(\gamma) \in \mathbb{F}_q$ held by shareholder $s_{i,j} \in S$. It outputs share $\sigma_{i,j}(m) \in \mathbb{F}_q$ for message $m = m_1 \cdot m_2$, which is computed performing the following steps.

First, shareholder $s_{i,j}$ computes share $\sigma_{i,j}(\delta) := \sigma_{i,j}(m_1) - \sigma_{i,j}(\alpha)$ and share $\sigma_{i,j}(\varepsilon) := \sigma_{i,j}(m_2) - \sigma_{i,j}(\beta)$ using algorithm Linear. Second, shareholders from an authorized set $R \in \Gamma$ run algorithm Reconstruct with shares $\sigma_{i,j}(\delta), \sigma_{i,j}(\varepsilon)$ as input to publicly reconstruct values δ, ε using the bulletin board. Third, shareholder $s_{i,j} \in S$ computes the share $\sigma_{i,j}(m) := \sigma_{i,j}(\gamma) + \varepsilon \cdot \sigma_{i,j}(m_1) + \delta \cdot \sigma_{i,j}(m_2) - \delta\varepsilon$ using algorithm Linear.

Theorem 2. *The algorithm* Multiply *for conjunctive (disjunctive) hierarchical secret sharing introduced above computes the shares correctly. More precisely, on input shares $\sigma_{i,j}(m_1), \sigma_{i,j}(m_2)$, the shares computed by* Multiply *reconstruct to message m, where $m = m_1 \cdot m_2$. Furthermore, perfect secrecy, according to Definition 1, is maintained while performing* Multiply.

Proof. The correctness relies on the correctness of algorithm Linear, presented in Sect. 4.2. In fact, share $\sigma_{i,j}(m)$ is defined as the linear combination of shares $\sigma_{i,j}(\gamma), \sigma_{i,j}(m_1), \sigma_{i,j}(m_2)$ for messages γ, m_1, m_2, respectively, and scalars δ, ε. More precisely, in the first step the scalars δ and ε are computed in distributed fashion using algorithm Linear, such that $\delta = m_1 - \alpha$ and $\varepsilon = m_2 - \beta$. After those values have been reconstructed in the second step, in the third step each shareholder computes a share to message m by computing $\sigma_{i,j}(m) = \sigma_{i,j}(\gamma) + \varepsilon \cdot \sigma_{i,j}(m_1) + \delta \cdot \sigma_{i,j}(m_2) - \delta\varepsilon$ using algorithm Linear. Therefore, if algorithm

Reconstruct takes as input shares $\sigma_{i,j}(m) \in \mathbb{F}_q$ held by shareholders $s_{i,j} \in R$, where $R \in \Gamma$ is an authorized set, then it retrieves:

$$m = \gamma + \varepsilon \cdot m_1 + \delta \cdot m_2 - \delta\varepsilon$$

$$= \gamma + (m_2 - \beta) \cdot m_1 + (m_1 - \alpha) \cdot m_2 - (m_2 - \beta)(m_1 - \alpha)$$

$$= \gamma + m_1 \cdot m_2 - \beta \cdot \alpha$$

Since $\alpha \cdot \beta = \gamma$ this leads to

$$m = m_1 \cdot m_2,$$

showing that algorithm Multiply is correct. Thus, algorithm Reconstruct interpolates to a polynomial $p(x) = c_0 + c_1 x + \cdots + c_{t-1} x^{t-1}$ of degree $\deg(p(x)) = t - 1$ and retrieves message $m_1 \cdot m_2$ as $c_0(c_{t-1})$. The perfect secrecy of algorithm Multiply is implied by the perfect secrecy of algorithm Linear (proven in Sect. 4.2) and by the perfect secrecy of the preprocessing phase, which is discussed in Sect. 5.

5 Preprocessing Phase

In this section, we introduce the preprocessing phase enabling the multiplication between two shared messages (see Sect. 4.3). Preprocessing has been common practice for multi-party computation since it has been introduced by Beaver in [1], because it lowers the communication complexity of the algorithm Multiply. More precisely, during the preprocessing phase a triple (α, β, γ) is generated such that the following conditions hold.

- $\alpha \cdot \beta = \gamma$.
- Assumption (1) of Sect. 4.1 holds, i.e. each shareholder $s_{i,j} \in S$ with ID $(i, j) \in \mathcal{I} \times \mathcal{I}$ holds shares $\sigma_{i,j}(\alpha) := f_\alpha^j(i), \sigma_{i,j}(\beta) := f_\beta^j(i)$, and $\sigma_{i,j}(\gamma) := f_\gamma^j(i)$, where $f_\alpha(x), f_\beta(x)$, and $f_\gamma(x)$ are the polynomials of degree $t-1$ sharing α, β, and γ, respectively.

In [11] it is shown how to generate such triples, but it is assumed that Shamir's threshold secret sharing scheme is used. Thus, here we present a preprocessing phase for Tassa's conjunctive (disjunctive) hierarchical secret sharing scheme.

PreMult. The algorithm outputs for each shareholder $s_{i,j} \in S$ a triple of shares $\sigma_{i,j}(\alpha), \sigma_{i,j}(\beta), \sigma_{i,j}(\gamma) \in \mathbb{F}_q$, such that for each triple it holds that $\sigma_{i,j}(\gamma) = \sigma_{i,j}(\alpha\beta)$. This is done in three main steps.

First, each shareholder $s_{i,j}$ randomly chooses a pair of shares $\sigma_{i,j}(\alpha), \sigma_{i,j}(\beta)$, as shown in Appendix A. Second, shareholders $s_1, \ldots, s_r \in R$ from an authorized set $R \in \Gamma$ compute for each shareholder $s_{i,j}$ terms $\delta_{l,(i,j)}$ and $\varepsilon_{l,(i,j)}$. Third, using $\delta_{l,(i,j)}$ and $\varepsilon_{l,(i,j)}$ each shareholder $s_{i,j} \in S$ computes its share $\sigma_{i,j}(\gamma) \in \mathbb{F}_q$.

More precisely, in the second step each shareholder $s_l \in R$, for $l = 1, \ldots, r$, computes the input $\delta_{l,(i,j)}$ and $\varepsilon_{l,(i,j)}$ for $s_{i,j}$ by performing the following steps.

First, shareholder $s_l \in R$ uses its shares $\sigma_l(\alpha)$ and $\sigma_l(\beta)$ and the unique ID (i,j) of shareholder $s_{i,j}$ to compute the values $\lambda_{l,(i,j)}$ and $\mu_{l,(i,j)}$ defined as:

$$\lambda_{l,(i,j)} := \sigma_l(\alpha) \sum_{k=j-1}^{t-1} \frac{k!}{(k-j+1)!} (-1)^{l-1+k} \frac{\det(A_{l-1,k}(E,X,\varphi))}{\det(A(E,X,\varphi))} i^{k-j+1}$$

and

$$\mu_{l,(i,j)} := \sigma_l(\beta) \sum_{k=j-1}^{t-1} \frac{k!}{(k-j+1)!} (-1)^{l-1+k} \frac{\det(A_{l-1,k}(E,X,\varphi))}{\det(A(E,X,\varphi))} i^{k-j+1},$$

where $A(E,X,\varphi)$ and $A_{l-1,k}(E,X,\varphi)$ are the matrices defined in Sect. 3. Then, it randomly splits $\lambda_{l,(i,j)}$ and $\mu_{l,(i,j)}$ into r values, i.e. $\lambda_{l,(i,j)} = \lambda_{1,l,(i,j)} + \cdots + \lambda_{r,l,(i,j)}$ and $\mu_{l,(i,j)} = \mu_{1,l,(i,j)} + \cdots + \mu_{r,l,(i,j)}$ and sends $\lambda_{m,l,(i,j)}$ and $\mu_{m,l,(i,j)}$ to shareholder $s_m \in R$, for $m = 1,\ldots,r$ and $m \neq l$, using a private channel. Afterwards, it collects all values $\lambda_{l,m,(i,j)}$ and $\mu_{l,m,(i,j)}$ received from shareholder $s_m \in R$, for $m = 1,\ldots,r$ and $m \neq l$, and computes $\delta_{l,(i,j)} := \sum_{m=1}^{r} \lambda_{l,m,(i,j)}$ and $\varepsilon_{l,(i,j)} := \sum_{m=1}^{r} \mu_{l,m,(i,j)}$. Finally, it sends $\delta_{l,(i,j)}$ and $\varepsilon_{l,(i,j)}$ to shareholder $s_{i,j}$ using a private channel.

In the third step, all shareholders within the set S compute their shares. More precisely, each shareholder $s_{i,j} \in S$ computes share $\sigma_{i,j}(\gamma)$ using the values $\delta_{l,(i,j)}$ and $\varepsilon_{l,(i,j)}$ received from shareholder $s_l \in R$, for $l = 1,\ldots,r$, as

$$\sigma_{i,j}(\gamma) := \sigma_{i,j}(\alpha\beta) = \left(\sum_{l=1}^{r} \delta_{l,(i,j)} \right) \cdot \sigma_{i,j}(\beta) + \sigma_{i,j}(\alpha) \cdot \left(\sum_{l=1}^{r} \varepsilon_{l,(i,j)} \right).$$

Theorem 3. *The algorithm* PreMult *for conjunctive (disjunctive) hierarchical secret sharing introduced above computes the multiplicative triples correctly. More precisely, on input the shares $\sigma_{i,j}(\alpha)$ and $\sigma_{i,j}(\beta)$, the shares computed by algorithm* PreMult *reconstructs to γ, where $\gamma = \alpha\beta$. Furthermore, perfect secrecy, according to Definition 1, is maintained while performing* PreMult.

Proof. Let $\sigma_{i,j}(\alpha\beta)$ be the share computed by shareholder $s_{i,j} \in R$ using algorithm PreMult, where $R \in \Gamma$ is an authorized set. Correctness of algorithm PreMult is provided if the shares held by shareholders in R it outputs interpolate to a polynomial $p(x) = c_0 + c_1 x + \cdots + c_{2(t-1)} x^{2(t-1)}$, where $c_0 = \alpha\beta (c_{2(t-1)} = \alpha\beta)$. Polynomial $p(x)$ is defined as $p(x) = f_\alpha(x) \cdot f_\beta(x)$, given that α is shared using polynomial $f_\alpha(x)$ and β is shared using polynomial $f_\beta(x)$. We have to show that, for each share $\sigma_{i,j}(\gamma)$ computed by algorithm PreMult, it holds that $\sigma_{i,j}(\gamma) = \sigma_{i,j}(\alpha\beta)$, where $\sigma_{i,j}(\alpha)$ and $\sigma_{i,j}(\beta)$ were randomly selected from shareholder $s_{i,j}$. In this case $\sigma_{i,j}(\gamma)$ can be written as:

$$\sigma_{i,j}(\alpha\beta) = p^j(i) = [f_\alpha(i) \cdot f_\beta(i)]^j = f_\alpha^j(i) \cdot f_\beta^{j-1}(i) + f_\alpha^{j-1}(i) \cdot f_\beta^j(i).$$

The terms $f_\alpha^j(i)$ and $f_\beta^j(i)$ constitute the random values $\sigma_{i,j}(\alpha)$ and $\sigma_{i,j}(\beta)$ selected by shareholder $s_{i,j} \in S$. It is left to check that $\sum_{l=1}^{r} \delta_{l,(i,j)}$ and

$\sum_{l=1}^{r} \varepsilon_{l,(i,j)}$ correspond to $f_\alpha^{j-1}(i)$ and $f_\beta^{j-1}(i)$, respectively. From the second step, we recall that $\delta_{l,(i,j)} = \sum_{m=1}^{r} \lambda_{l,m,(i,j)}$. Thus, it follows that:

$$\sum_{l=1}^{r} \delta_{l,(i,j)} = \sum_{l=1}^{r} \sum_{m=1}^{r} \lambda_{l,m,(i,j)} = \sum_{l=1}^{r} f_{\alpha,l}^{j-1}(i) = f_\alpha^{j-1}(i),$$

where polynomial $f_{\alpha,l}^{j-1}(x)$ is the $(j-1)$-th derivative of polynomial $f_{\alpha,l}(x) = \sum_{k=0}^{t-1} \alpha_{l,k} x^k$, where $\alpha_{l,k}$ is the reconstructing term of Birkhoff interpolation formula (see Sect. 3). Note that the last equality of the expression above holds because the coefficients of $f_\alpha(x)$ can be computed in distributed fashion, see Theorem 2 in [32]. The equality $\sum_{l=1}^{r} \varepsilon_{l,(i,j)} = f_\beta^{j-1}(i)$ can be shown analogously. Moreover, since polynomial $p(x) = c_0 + c_1 x + \cdots + c_{2(t-1)} x^{2(t-1)}$ is the product of polynomials $f_\alpha(x)$ and $f_\beta(x)$, then $c_0 = a_0 b_0 = \alpha\beta (c_{2(t-1)} = a_{t-1} b_{t-1} = \alpha\beta)$. Thus, correctness holds. To prove perfect secrecy, we have to show that no information is leaked when share $\sigma_{i,j}(\alpha\beta)$ is generated for shareholder $s_{i,j} \in S$. Regarding the terms $\sum_{l=1}^{r} \delta_{l,(i,j)}$ and $\sum_{l=1}^{r} \varepsilon_{l,(i,j)}$, we have to show that they do not leak information about shares $\sigma_l(\alpha)$ and $\sigma_l(\beta)$ of shareholder $s_l \in R$, respectively. That is the case because shareholder $s_l \in R$ uses additive secret sharing [13] to split $\lambda_{l,(i,j)}$ and $\mu_{l,(i,j)}$ into r random values $\lambda_{m,l,(i,j)}$ and $\mu_{m,l,(i,j)}$, respectively. Furthermore, perfect secrecy holds also because index $i \in \mathcal{I}$ of each identity ID $(i,j) \in \mathcal{I} \times \mathcal{I}$ is used once, as required by Assumption (A3) of Sect. 4.1. Otherwise, points $f_\alpha^{j-1}(i)$ and $f_\beta^{j-1}(i)$ might correspond to already existing shares $\sigma_{i,j-1}(\alpha)$ and $\sigma_{i,j-1}(\beta)$ for α and β, respectively, already computed for shareholder $s_{i,j-1} \in S$. Moreover, because each share $\dot{\sigma}_{i,j}(\gamma)$ is a point on polynomial $p(x)$ or on one of its derivatives, the underlying conjunctive (disjunctive) hierarchical secret sharing scheme ensures that unauthorized subsets gain no information about α, β, γ.

6   Auditing Procedure for Computations over Hierarchically Shared Messages

Before presenting the auditing procedure for the algorithms Linear, PreMult, and Multiply for conjunctive (disjunctive) hierarchical secret sharing schemes we recall verifiable secret sharing. *Verifiable secret sharing* was introduced in [9] to allow shareholders to check the consistency of shares received from the message dealer. More precisely, audit data are generated that allow the shareholders to check whether the shares of each authorized subset of shareholders lead to the same message during the reconstruction algorithm. To provide verifiable secret sharing usually *commitment schemes* are used, which come with two properties. First, bindingness ensures that it is not possible to change the message committed to. Second, hidingness ensures that no information about the message is leaked. Furthermore, there are several commitment schemes with homomorphic properties available, i.e. operations performed on the values committed to can be transferred to operations performed on the commitments. Verifiable secret sharing uses Feldman commitment [15], which is unconditionally binding and computationally hiding, or Pedersen commitment [27], which is computationally binding and unconditionally hiding. In the following, we use Feldmann commitment for the sake of simplicity, but our solutions work with both schemes. In the following, we recall the definition of Feldman commitment and Pedersen commitment (in brackets).

Definition 2 ([15, 27]). *Feldman (Pedersen) commitment scheme is a triple* (Setup, Commit, Open) *of the following algorithms.*

Setup. *It takes as input a security parameter λ and it outputs a prime q, a group $\mathbb{G}$ of order q, and a generator $g \in \mathbb{G}$ (distinct generators $g, h \in \mathbb{G}$).*

Commit. *It takes as input a message $m \in \mathbb{F}_q$ (and randomness $r \in \mathbb{F}_q$) and it outputs commitment $c = g^m$ ($c = g^m h^r$).*

Open. *It takes as input a commitment $c \in \mathbb{G}$, a message $m \in \mathbb{F}_q$ (and randomness $r \in \mathbb{F}_q$) and it outputs '1' if $c = g^m$ (if $c = g^m h^r$) and '0' otherwise.*

6.1 Auditing Procedure for Conjunctive (Disjunctive) Hierarchical Secret Sharing Schemes

In this section, we present auditing procedures for computations on messages shared hierarchically by using Tassa's conjunctive (disjunctive) hierarchically secret sharing schemes, based on Birkhoff interpolation. More precisely, first, we present algorithms Audit.Setup and Audit.Share, which describes the steps to be performed during the setup phase and after algorithm Share, respectively. Then, we present algorithm Audit.Linear which is run after algorithm Linear to verify the correctness of linear operations. Finally, we present algorithms Audit.PreMult and Audit.Multiply, which allow auditing of multiplications.

Setup and Share. Algorithm Audit.Setup sets up the cryptographic primitives, i.e. commitment schemes and bilinear maps,[2] needed for the auditing procedures. This can be run by any party. However, the parameters must be made publicly available for the dealer of the input messages and the auditor running the auditing procedures. Then, to allow operations to be audited, the dealer commits to messages shared by running Audit.Share.

Audit.Setup. The algorithm takes as input a security parameter λ and it outputs two large primes p, q such that $q|(p-1)$. It also outputs a generator g of the q-th order subgroup $\mathbb{F}_q$ of $\mathbb{F}_p^*$.

Audit.Share. The dealer of messages $m_1, m_2 \in \mathbb{F}_q$ calls algorithm Commit.Share during algorithm Share and computes commitment $c(m_1) := g^{m_1} \mod p$ to message m_1 and commitment $c(m_2) := g^{m_2} \mod p$ to message m_2. It publishes the commitments on the bulletin board.

---

[2] For a formal definition of bilinear maps we refer to [6].

Linear Operations. In the following, algorithm Audit.Linear run by the auditor to verify the result of linear operations over shared messages is presented. We assume that either the shareholders or the message dealer published the used scalars $\lambda_1, \lambda_2 \in \mathbb{F}_q$ on the bulletin board.

Audit.Linear. The algorithm takes as input the commitments to the input values $c(m_1), c(m_2)$ and the scalars $\lambda_1, \lambda_2 \in \mathbb{F}_q$ from the bulletin board and the claimed result m. If $g^m = c(m_1)^{\lambda_1} \cdot c(m_2)^{\lambda_2}$ it returns '1' and '0' otherwise.

Multiplication. In the following, the auditing procedure for products over shared messages is presented. More precisely, first algorithm Audit.PreMult is introduced, which computes commitments to the multiplicative triples generated during algorithm PreMult of Sect. 5. Second, algorithm Audit.PreMult showing the auditing procedure for algorithm Multiply is presented.

Note that, algorithm PreMult is performed in distributed fashion by the shareholders of an authorized set $R \in \Gamma$. That is, each shareholder $s_{i,j} \in S$ receives input from each shareholder contained in R to compute share $\sigma_{i,j}(\alpha\beta)$. If one of the inputs is not valid, then shareholder $s_{i,j}$ cannot compute a valid share for $\alpha\beta$. This also affects the correctness of algorithm Multiply. In the following, it is explained what audit data have to be generated such that shareholder $s_{i,j}$ can detect inconsistent input sent by other malicious shareholders during algorithm PreMult of Sect. 5 performing the preprocessing phase.

Audit.PreMult. The algorithm is run by the auditor to verify whether the shares $\sigma_{i,j}(\alpha\beta)$, output of algorithm PreMult, have been computed correctly. The algorithm takes as input from the bulletin board commitments $c_{k,\alpha}, c_{k,\beta}$, for $k = 0, \ldots, t-1$, to the coefficients of the polynomials $f_\alpha(x), f_\beta(x)$ sharing α and β, respectively. Appendix B shows how commitments $c_{k,\alpha}$ and $c_{k,\beta}$ are computed. Then, each shareholder $s_{i,j} \in S$ has valid input $\delta_{l,i,j}$ and $\varepsilon_{l,i,j}$, for $l = 1, \ldots, r$, to compute share $\sigma_{i,j}(\alpha\beta)$ if and only if

$$g^{\sum_{l=1}^{r} \delta_{l,i,j}} \equiv \prod_{k=j-1}^{t-1} c_{k,\alpha}^{\frac{k!}{(k-j+1)!} i^{k-j+1}} = g^{f_\alpha^{(j-1)}(i)},$$

and if and only if

$$g^{\sum_{l=1}^{r} \varepsilon_{l,i,j}} \equiv \prod_{k=j-1}^{t-1} c_{k,\beta}^{\frac{k!}{(k-j+1)!} i^{k-j+1}} = g^{f_\beta^{(j-1)}(i)}.$$

If one of the both equalities is not satisfied, then it outputs '0' and aborts. Otherwise, each shareholder $s_{i,j} \in S$ holding shares $\sigma_{i,j}(\alpha), \sigma_{i,j}(\beta), \sigma_{i,j}(\gamma)$ computes commitments $c_{i,j}(\alpha) := g^{\sigma_{i,j}(\alpha)}, c_{i,j}(\beta) := g^{\sigma_{i,j}(\beta)}$, and $c_{i,j}(\gamma) := g^{\sigma_{i,j}(\gamma)}$ for $\sigma_{i,j}(\alpha), \sigma_{i,j}(\beta)$, and $\sigma_{i,j}(\gamma)$, respectively. It publishes $c_{i,j}(\alpha), c_{i,j}(\beta)$, and $c_{i,j}(\gamma)$ on the bulletin board and outputs '1'.

Audit.Multiply. The algorithm takes as input the values δ, ε, the commitments to the shares of the multiplicative triple, i.e. $c_{i,j}(\alpha), c_{i,j}(\beta)$, and $c_{i,j}(\gamma)$, for $s_{i,j} \in S$, the commitments to the input values, i.e. $c(m_1), c(m_2)$, and the claimed result m. Then, it first audits that the equation $\alpha\beta = \gamma$ was fulfilled and then that m has been computed correctly performing the following steps.

First, the auditor computes the reconstruction vector $(w_1, \ldots, w_r)$[3] for shareholders $s_1, \ldots, s_r \in R$, with $R \in \Gamma$ authorized set, which computed the input for γ during PreMult. Then, it computes the following commitments:

$$c(\alpha) := \prod_{l=1}^{r} c_l(\alpha)^{w_l}; \quad c(\beta) := \prod_{l=1}^{r} c_l(\beta)^{w_l}; \quad c(\gamma) := \prod_{l=1}^{r} c_l(\gamma)^{w_l},$$

where $c_l(\alpha), c_l(\beta), c_l(\gamma)$, for $l = 1, \ldots, r$, are commitments $c_{i,j}(\alpha), c_{i,j}(\beta), c_{i,j}(\gamma)$, respectively, in lexicographic order. The multiplicative triple (α, β, γ) was correct if and only if $e(c(\alpha), c(\beta)) = e(c(\gamma), g)$.[4] If the equation does not hold it outputs '0' and aborts the algorithm. Otherwise, the auditor takes from the bulletin board commitments $c(m_1), c(m_2)$ and the values δ, ε reconstructed during algorithm Multiply. If it holds that $c(\alpha)^{-1} \cdot c(m_1) = g^\delta$ and $c(\beta)^{-1} \cdot c(m_1) = g^\varepsilon$ and $g^m = c(\gamma) \cdot c(m_1)^\varepsilon \cdot c(m_2)^\delta \cdot g^{-\delta\varepsilon}$ it returns '1' and '0' otherwise.

7   Security and Efficiency

Security. We have proven that algorithm Linear of Sect. 4.2, algorithm Multiply of Sect. 4.3, and algorithm PreMult of Sect. 5 do not compromise the perfect secrecy and correctness of the underlying conjunctive (disjunctive) hierarchical secret sharing scheme. The adversary these algorithms can cope with is active, i.e. not only it knows data private to shareholders (like the passive adversary), but also it can make them deviate from the protocols. More precisely, assumptions (A1)–(A4) of Sect. 4.1 set requirements for, respectively, the access structure, the threshold, the identities of the shareholders, and the channels through which shareholders communicate. These assumptions together with verifiable secret sharing ensure that a honest majority of shareholders is able to correctly reconstruct the message, while maintaining the secrecy of their shares, even if all other shareholders are corrupted by the adversary and cheat. Assumption (5) prevents the adversary from tampering the bulletin board and, together with the auditing procedure, ensures correctness when operations on data are performed. As it is shown in [32], conjunctive (disjunctive) hierarchical secret sharing schemes support proactive secret sharing [21]. This means that, provided that the shares are refreshed periodically, our protocols can cope with a mobile adversary, which is only bounded in the amount of shareholders it can corrupt within a certain time interval, but not over time. Furthermore, we provide an auditing procedure in Sect. 6 allowing to detect misbehaviors. The protocols described use Feldman commitment, which ensures only computationally hidingness. However, the

---

[3] For conjunctive (disjunctive) hierarchical secret sharing schemes the interpolation vector is composed of the entries $w_l := (-1)^{l-1} \frac{\det(A_{l-1,0}(E,X,\varphi))}{\det(A(E,X,\varphi))}$ $\left(w_l := (-1)^{l+t-2} \frac{\det(A_{l-1,t-1}(E,X,\varphi))}{\det(A(E,X,\varphi))} \right)$ according to the notation of Sect. 3.

[4] Here the definition of bilinear maps is used.

auditing procedure can be easily adapted to Pedersen commitment to achieve unconditionally hidingness, which preserves even perfect secrecy of the underlying conjunctive (disjunctive) hierarchical secret sharing scheme.

Efficiency. With respect to efficiency, the algorithms Share, Reconstruct, Linear, Multiply, and PreMult for conjunctive (disjunctive) hierarchical secret sharing perform equally well as Shamir's threshold secret sharing. Besides polynomials' evaluation, algorithm Share requires also to compute up to $t - 1$ polynomials' derivatives. However, the additional multiplications due to derivation are balanced by the fewer multiplications needed when evaluating derivatives of polynomials. Algorithm Recostruct is the most expensive algorithm and requires in both Tassa's and Shamir's scheme to perform Gaussian elimination to find a solution to a system of t linear equations. Algorithm Linear and Multiply require that the shareholders perform steps very similar to the corresponding algorithms for Shamir's secret sharing (see for instance [3,28]). Algorithm PreMult requires more work with respect to the preprocessing phase compared to Shamir's threshold secret sharing. In fact, algorithm PreMult is computed in distributed fashion because additional information is needed to compute the shares. Despite the fact that only additions and polynomials' evaluation are performed to compute such additional information, algorithm PreMult increases the communication cost and requires secure channels. For Shamir's threshold secret sharing scheme this additional information needs not to be computed and the communication complexity is, thus, lower. For the same reasons, the auditing procedure during the on-line phase of Tassa's schemes has computational complexity similar to the one for Shamir's scheme while the auditing procedure during the off-line phase is more expensive. In fact, to perform algorithms Audit.Linear and Audit.Multiply, the auditor takes steps very similar to the corresponding auditing procedure for Shamir's secret sharing schemes, because algorithms Linear and Multiply are defined similarly. Instead, algorithm Audit.PreMult requires the computation of commitments in a distributed fashion, which increases the communication and the computation cost. However, we recall that the preprocessing phase is off-line and can be performed in advance. Regarding the on-line phase, which is the time critical phase, the schemes of both Shamir and Tassa perform equally well.

8   Conclusion

In this work, we showed how to practically compute linear operations and multiplications over shared messages when Tassa's conjunctive and disjunctive hierarchical secret sharing schemes are used. Together with the property of modifying the access structure and changing the set of shareholders shown in [32], we proved that Birkhoff interpolation-based secret sharing schemes allow for the same functionalities as Shamir's secret sharing scheme, which is based on Lagrange interpolation. Furthermore, we showed how to perform the preprocessing phase enabling to reconstruct the product of two shared messages and provided auditing procedures to check that the operations were performed correctly. Moreover, the protocols we proposed do not lower the overall security of the underlying conjunctive and disjunctive hierarchical secret sharing scheme and do not increase in the on-line phase the computation overhead with respect to the same protocols for Shamir's secret sharing scheme. From a theoretical point of view, this result can be inferred from the approach presented in [10], which shows how secure multi-party computation can be built from linear secret sharing schemes. From a practical point of view, this result is more interesting because it shows the exact procedures for achieving secure multi-party computation specifically for Tassa's conjunctive and disjunctive secret sharing schemes. Furthermore, this result impacts the framework of cloud computing and distributed storage systems. More precisely, the possibility to perform operations over hierarchically shared messages sets Tassa's conjunctive and disjunctive hierarchical secret sharing schemes as promising candidates for distributed storage systems, where the storage servers are granted with different reconstruction capabilities depending on their performance [24,33]. In fact, Tassa's conjunctive and disjunctive hierarchical secret sharing schemes together with the auditing procedure we presented would allow computations on documents outsourced to the cloud and stored in distributed fashion.

Acknowledgments. The authors thank Lucas Schabüser and Denis Butin for useful discussions. This work was in part funded by the European Commission through grant agreement no. 644962 (PRISMACLOUD). Furthermore, it received funding from the DFG as part of project S6 within the CRC 1119 CROSSING.

Appendix

A   Computation of Shares $\sigma_{i,j}(\alpha), \sigma_{i,j}(\beta)$

Algorithm RandShares computes random shares $\sigma_{i,j}(\alpha), \sigma_{i,j}(\beta)$ reconstructing to messages α, β, respectively. It is the first step of algorithm PreMult of Sect. 5. We present RandShares to compute shares $\sigma_{i,j}(\alpha)$ for α, but it can be run analogously to generate shares $\sigma_{i,j}(\beta)$ for β.

RandShares. The algorithm takes as input values $\alpha_{i,j} \in \mathbb{F}_q$ chosen uniformly at random by shareholders $s_{i,j} \in S$. It outputs shares $\sigma_{i,j}(\alpha)$ of message $\alpha \in \mathbb{F}_q$ for shareholders $s_{i,j} \in S$. To do that, each shareholder $s_{i,j} \in S$ has to perform the following steps.

(1) It chooses a secret message $\alpha_{i,j} \in \mathbb{F}_q$ uniformly at random.
(2) It runs algorithm Share to generate a polynomial $f_{\alpha_{i,j}}(x)$ of degree $t-1$ defined as $f_{\alpha_{i,j}}(x) := a_{0,(i,j)} + a_{1,(i,j)}x + \cdots + a_{t-1,(i,j)}x^{t-1}$, where $a_{0,(i,j)} = \alpha_{i,j}$ $(a_{t-1,(i,j)} = \alpha_{i,j})$ and coefficients $a_{1,(i,j)}, \ldots, a_{t-1,(i,j)} \in \mathbb{F}_q$ $(a_{0,(i,j)}, \ldots, a_{t-2,(i,j)} \in \mathbb{F}_q)$ are chosen uniformly at random. Shares $\sigma_{i',j'}(\alpha_{i,j})$ for shareholders $s_{i',j'} \in S$ with ID $(i',j') \neq (i,j)$ are computed as $\sigma_{i',j'}(\alpha_{i,j}) := f_{\alpha_{i,j}}^{j'}(i')$. Share $\sigma_{i,j}(\alpha_{i,j})$ for shareholder $s_{i,j}$ itself is computed as $\sigma_{i,j}(\alpha_{i,j}) := f_{\alpha_{i,j}}^{j}(i)$.

(3) It sends shares $\sigma_{i',j'}(\alpha_{i,j})$ to shareholders $s_{i',j'} \in S$ with ID $(i',j') \neq (i,j)$ using a private channel and keeps share $\sigma_{i,j}(\alpha_{i,j})$.

(4) It runs algorithm Linear of Sect. 4.2 to compute share $\sigma_{i,j}(\alpha)$ using share $\sigma_{i,j}(\alpha_{i,j})$ and all the shares $\sigma_{i,j}(\alpha_{i',j'})$ received from shareholders $s_{i',j'}$ as
$$\sigma_{i,j}(\alpha) := \sum_{(i',j') \neq (i,j)} \sigma_{i,j}(\alpha_{i',j'}) + \sigma_{i,j}(\alpha_{i,j}).$$

In the following, we prove correctness of algorithm RandShares and we show that perfect secrecy, according to Definition 1, is provided.

Theorem 4. *The algorithm* RandShares *for conjunctive (disjunctive) hierarchical secret sharing introduced above computes the shares $\sigma_{i,j}(\alpha)$ correctly. More precisely, on input random secret messages $\alpha_{i,j}$, the shares computed by algorithm* RandShares *reconstruct to a common value α. Furthermore, perfect secrecy, according to Definition 1, is maintained while performing* RandShares.

Proof. Let $\sigma_{i,j}(\alpha) \in \mathbb{F}_q$ be the shares computed using algorithm RandShares and held by shareholders $s_{i,j} \in R$, where $R \in \Gamma$ is an authorized set. To prove correctness, we have to show that algorithm Reconstruct outputs a message α when it takes as input shares $\sigma_{i,j}(\alpha)$ held by shareholders of an authorized set R. This means that correctness holds provided that algorithm Reconstruct can be successfully run by shareholders of any authorized set. This is implied by the correctness of algorithm Linear, presented in Sect. 4.2. In fact, each share $\sigma_{i,j}(\alpha)$ is computed as a sum of shares $\sigma_{i,j}(\alpha_{i',j'})$ and share $\sigma_{i,j}(\alpha_{i,j})$. Thus, for the homomorphic property of polynomials, shares $\sigma_{i,j}(\alpha)$ is either a point of polynomial $f_\alpha(x) := a_{0,\alpha} + a_{1,\alpha}x + \cdots + a_{t-1,\alpha}x^{t-1} = \sum_{(i,j)} f_{\alpha_{i,j}}(x)$ or a point on one of its derivatives, where $a_{0,\alpha} = \sum_{(i,j)} \alpha_{i,j}(a_{t-1,\alpha} = \sum_{(i,j)} \alpha_{i,j})$. Because of the underlying conjunctive (disjunctive) hierarchical secret sharing scheme, any authorized set R of shareholders can run algorithm Reconstruct over their shares and retrieve message $\alpha := \sum_{(i,j)} \alpha_{i,j}$. This proves correctness. With respect to perfect secrecy, the underlying conjunctive (disjunctive) hierarchical secret sharing scheme guarantees that shares $\sigma_{i,j}(\alpha)$ are computed without leaking information about the secret messages $\alpha_{i,j}$. Furthermore, this implies that unauthorized sets of shareholders not only cannot successfully run algorithm Reconstruct to retrieve α, but also no information about it is gained.

B   Computation of Commitments $c_{k,\alpha}, c_{k,\beta}$

In this section, algorithm Audit.RandShares is presented, which computes commitments $c_{k,\alpha}, c_{k,\beta}$ to the coefficients of the polynomials sharing messages α, β, respectively. Algorithm Audit.RandShares constitutes the first step of algorithm Audit.PreMult of Sect. 6.1. More precisely, commitments $c_{k,\alpha}, c_{k,\beta}$, for $k = 0, \ldots, t-1$, are used to check the validity of terms $\delta_{l,i,j}$ and $\varepsilon_{l,i,j}$ for the computation of shares $\sigma_{i,j}(\alpha\beta)$. Note that commitments $c_{k,\alpha}, c_{k,\beta}$ can be correctly computed provided that an auditing procedure verifying the validity of shares $\sigma_{i,j}(\alpha), \sigma_{i,j}(\beta)$ for shareholders $s_{i,j}$ is performed, where shares $\sigma_{i,j}(\alpha), \sigma_{i,j}(\beta)$ are the output of algorithm RandShares of Appendix A. For consistency with algorithm Audit.PreMult, Feldman commitment is used. However, the algorithm can be easily adapted to Pedersen commitment. In the following, we present algorithm Audit.RandShares to compute commitment $c_{k,\alpha}$, for $k = 0, \ldots, t-1$. Algorithm Audit.RandShares can be run analogously to generate commitment $c_{k,\beta}$, for $k = 0, \ldots, t-1$.

Audit.RandShares. The algorithm is run by an auditor to verify that shares $\sigma_{i,j}(\alpha)$ was computed correctly. This is performed in the following steps.

(1) Each shareholder $s_{i,j} \in S$ running algorithm Share to share the secret message $\alpha_{i,j} \in \mathbb{F}_q$ among all other shareholders $s_{i',j'} \in S$ for $(i', j') \neq (i, j)$ calls algorithm Commit.Share and computes commitments $c_{k,\alpha_{i,j}} := g^{a_{k,(i,j)}}$ mod p, to coefficient $a_{k,(i,j)}$ of polynomial $f_{\alpha_{i,j}}(x)$, for $k = 0, \ldots, t-1$. It publishes the commitments on the bulletin board.

(2) Each shareholder $s_{i,j} \in S$ has valid input $\sigma_{i,j}(\alpha_{i',j'})$, for $(i', j') \neq (i, j)$, to compute share $\sigma_{i,j}(\alpha)$ if and only if

$$g^{\sigma_{i,j}(\alpha_{i',j'})} \equiv \prod_{k=j}^{t-1} c_{k,\alpha_{i',j'}}^{\frac{k!}{(k-j)!} i^{k-j}} = g^{f_{\alpha_{i',j'}}^{j}(i)}.$$

If the above equality is not satisfied, then it outputs '0' and aborts. Otherwise, it publishes '1' on the bulletin board and Step (3) can be performed.

(3) The auditor uses commitments $c_{k,\alpha_{i,j}}$ published by shareholders $s_{i,j} \in S$ on the bulletin board to compute commitments $c_{k,\alpha} := \prod_{(i,j)} c_{k,\alpha_{i,j}}$, for $k = 0, \ldots, t-1$. It publishes the commitments on the bulletin board.

References

1. Beaver, D.: Efficient multiparty protocols using circuit randomization. In: Feigenbaum, J. (ed.) CRYPTO 1991. LNCS, vol. 576, pp. 420–432. Springer, Heidelberg (1992). https://doi.org/10.1007/3-540-46766-1_34
2. Beimel, A.: Secret-sharing schemes: a survey. In: Chee, Y.M., Guo, Z., Ling, S., Shao, F., Tang, Y., Wang, H., Xing, C. (eds.) IWCC 2011. LNCS, vol. 6639, pp. 11–46. Springer, Heidelberg (2011). https://doi.org/10.1007/978-3-642-20901-7_2
3. Ben-Or, M., Goldwasser, S., Wigderson, A.: Completeness theorems for non-cryptographic fault-tolerant distributed computation. In: STOC 1988 (1988)
4. Blakley, G.R., et al.: Safeguarding cryptographic keys. In: Proceedings of the National Computer Conference (1979)
5. Blundo, C., Cresti, A., De Santis, A., Vaccaro, U.: Fully dynamic secret sharing schemes. In: Stinson, D.R. (ed.) CRYPTO 1993. LNCS, vol. 773, pp. 110–125. Springer, Heidelberg (1994). https://doi.org/10.1007/3-540-48329-2_10
6. Boneh, D., Franklin, M.: Identity-based encryption from the Weil pairing. In: Kilian, J. (ed.) CRYPTO 2001. LNCS, vol. 2139, pp. 213–229. Springer, Heidelberg (2001). https://doi.org/10.1007/3-540-44647-8_13
7. Brickell, E.F.: Some ideal secret sharing schemes. In: Quisquater, J.-J., Vandewalle, J. (eds.) EUROCRYPT 1989. LNCS, vol. 434, pp. 468–475. Springer, Heidelberg (1990). https://doi.org/10.1007/3-540-46885-4_45

8. Chaum, D., Crépeau, C., Damgård, I.: Multiparty unconditionally secure protocols. In: STOC 1988 (1988)
9. Chor, B., Goldwasser, S., Micali, S., Awerbuch, B.: Verifiable secret sharing and achieving simultaneity in the presence of faults (extended abstract). In: FOCS (1985)
10. Cramer, R., Damgård, I., Maurer, U.: General secure multi-party computation from any linear secret-sharing scheme. In: Preneel, B. (ed.) EUROCRYPT 2000. LNCS, vol. 1807, pp. 316–334. Springer, Heidelberg (2000). https://doi.org/10. 1007/3-540-45539-6_22
11. Damgård, I., Nielsen, J.B.: Scalable and unconditionally secure multiparty computation. In: Menezes, A. (ed.) CRYPTO 2007. LNCS, vol. 4622, pp. 572–590. Springer, Heidelberg (2007). https://doi.org/10.1007/978-3-540-74143-5_32
12. Desmedt, Y., Jajodia, S.: Redistributing secret shares to new access structures and its applications. Technical report ISSE TR-97-01, George Mason University (1997)
13. Doganay, M.C., Pedersen, T.B., Saygin, Y., Savas, E., Levi, A.: Distributed privacy preserving k-means clustering with additive secret sharing. In: PAIS (2008)
14. Farràs, O., Padró, C.: Ideal hierarchical secret sharing schemes. In: TCC (2010)
15. Feldman, P.: A practical scheme for non-interactive verifiable secret sharing. In: 28th Annual Symposium on Foundations of Computer Science (1987)
16. Gennaro, R., Rabin, M.O., Rabin, T.: Simplified VSS and fact-track multiparty computations with applications to threshold cryptography. In: PODC 1998 (1998)
17. Ghodosi, H., Pieprzyk, J., Safavi-Naini, R.: Secret sharing in multilevel and compartmented groups. In: Boyd, C., Dawson, E. (eds.) ACISP 1998. LNCS, vol. 1438, pp. 367–378. Springer, Heidelberg (1998). https://doi.org/10.1007/BFb0053748
18. Goldreich, O., Micali, S., Wigderson, A.: How to play any mental game or a completeness theorem for protocols with honest majority. In: STOC 1990 (1990)
19. Gupta, V., Gopinath, K.: G_{its}^2 VSR: an information theoretical secure verifiable secret redistribution protocol for long-term archival storage. In: SISW 2007 (2007)
20. Heather, J., Lundin, D.: The append-only web bulletin board. In: Degano, P., Guttman, J., Martinelli, F. (eds.) FAST 2008. LNCS, vol. 5491, pp. 242–256. Springer, Heidelberg (2009). https://doi.org/10.1007/978-3-642-01465-9_16
21. Herzberg, A., Jarecki, S., Krawczyk, H., Yung, M.: Proactive secret sharing or: how to cope with perpetual leakage. In: Coppersmith, D. (ed.) CRYPTO 1995. LNCS, vol. 963, pp. 339–352. Springer, Heidelberg (1995). https://doi.org/10.1007/3-540-44750-4_27
22. Käsper, E., Nikov, V., Nikova, S.: Strongly multiplicative hierarchical threshold secret sharing. In: Desmedt, Y. (ed.) ICITS 2007. LNCS, vol. 4883, pp. 148–168. Springer, Heidelberg (2009). https://doi.org/10.1007/978-3-642-10230-1_13
23. Loruenser, T., Happe, A., Slamanig, D.: ARCHISTAR: towards secure and robust cloud based data sharing. In: CloudCom 2015 (2015)
24. Nojoumian, M., Stinson, D.R.: Social secret sharing in cloud computing using a new trust function. In: PST 2012 (2012)
25. Nojoumian, M., Stinson, D.R., Grainger, M.: Unconditionally secure social secret sharing scheme. Inf. Secur. IET **4**, 202–211 (2010)
26. Pakniat, N., Eslami, Z., Nojoumian, M.: Ideal social secret sharing using Birkhoff interpolation method. IACR 2014 (2014)
27. Pedersen, T.P.: Non-interactive and information-theoretic secure verifiable secret sharing. In: Feigenbaum, J. (ed.) CRYPTO 1991. LNCS, vol. 576, pp. 129–140. Springer, Heidelberg (1992). https://doi.org/10.1007/3-540-46766-1_9
28. Schabhüser, L., Demirel, D., Buchmann, J.A.: An unconditionally hiding auditing procedure for computations over distributed data. In: CNS 2016 (2016)

29. Shamir, A.: How to share a secret. Commun. ACM **22**, 612–613 (1979)
30. Simmons, G.J.: How to (really) share a secret. In: Goldwasser, S. (ed.) CRYPTO 1988. LNCS, vol. 403, pp. 390–448. Springer, New York (1990). https://doi.org/ 10.1007/0-387-34799-2_30
31. Tassa, T.: Hierarchical threshold secret sharing. J. Cryptology **20**, 237–264 (2007)
32. Traverso, G., Demirel, D., Buchmann, J.: Dynamic and verifiable hierarchical secret sharing. In: Nascimento, A.C.A., Barreto, P. (eds.) ICITS 2016. LNCS, vol. 10015, pp. 24–43. Springer, Cham (2016). https://doi.org/10.1007/978-3-319-49175-2_2
33. Traverso, G., Demirel, D., Habib, S.M., Buchmann, J.A.: As³: adaptive social secret sharing for distributed storage systems. In: PST 2016 (2016)

Development of a Dual Version
of DeepBKZ and Its Application
to Solving the LWE Challenge

Masaya Yasuda[1](✉), Junpei Yamaguchi[2], Michiko Ooka[3],
and Satoshi Nakamura[3]

[1] Institute of Mathematics for Industry, Kyushu University,
744 Motooka Nishi-ku, Fukuoka 819-0395, Japan
yasuda@imi.kyushu-u.ac.jp
[2] Graduate School of Mathematics, Kyushu University, Fukuoka, Japan
[3] Faculty of Mathematics, Kyushu University, Fukuoka, Japan

Abstract. Lattice basis reduction is a strong tool in cryptanalysis. In 2017, DeepBKZ was proposed as a new variant of BKZ, and it calls LLL with deep insertions (DeepLLL) as a subroutine alternative to LLL. In this paper, we develop a dual version of DeepBKZ (which we call "Dual-DeepBKZ"), to reduce the dual basis of an input basis. For Dual-DeepBKZ, we develop a dual version of DeepLLL, and then combine it with the dual enumeration by Micciancio and Walter. It never computes the dual basis of an input basis, and it is as efficient as the primal DeepBKZ. We also demonstrate that Dual-DeepBKZ solves several instances in the TU Darmstadt LWE challenge. We use Dual-DeepBKZ in the bounded distance decoding (BDD) approach for solving an LWE instance. Our experiments show that Dual-DeepBKZ reduces the cost of Liu-Nguyen's BDD enumeration more effectively than BKZ. For the LWE instance of $(n, \alpha) = (40, 0.015)$ (resp., $(n, \alpha) = (60, 0.005)$), our results are about 2.2 times (resp., 4.0 times) faster than Xu et al.'s results, for which they used BKZ in the fplll library and the BDD enumeration with extreme pruning while we used linear pruning in our experiments.

Keywords: Lattice basis reduction · Dual lattices
LLL with deep insertions · BKZ · LWE (Learning with Errors)

1 Introduction

The security of lattice-based cryptography relies on the hardness of lattice problems such as the shortest vector problem (SVP), the closest vector problem (CVP), and the LWE problem by Regev [19]. From a basis of a lattice L, *lattice basis reduction* finds a new basis of L with short and nearly orthogonal basis vectors. It can be easier to solve lattice problems over a more reduced basis, and hence it is important to develop strong reduction algorithms for security evaluation of lattice-based cryptography. The most famous reduction is LLL [14], and

© Springer International Publishing AG, part of Springer Nature 2018
A. Joux et al. (Eds.): AFRICACRYPT 2018, LNCS 10831, pp. 162–182, 2018.
https://doi.org/10.1007/978-3-319-89339-6_10

its blockwise generalization is the block Korkine-Zolotarev (BKZ) algorithm by Schnorr and Euchner [21]. Recently, BKZ 2.0 [7], terminating-BKZ [12], and progressive-BKZ [2] have been developed as efficient variants of BKZ, and some of them have been implemented in software. In particular, the fplll library [23] includes fast implementations of floating-point reduction algorithms including BKZ 2.0, and it has been often used to solve lattice problems. In 2017, Deep-BKZ [26] was proposed as a new variant of BKZ, which calls DeepLLL [21] as a subroutine alternative to LLL. For the SVP challenge [9], DeepBKZ with block-sizes $\beta \approx 40$ found a number of new solutions (that is, shorter lattice vectors) in dimensions from 102 to 125 within a few months over a PC (cf., BKZ 2.0 with $\beta = 75$ and 20%-pruning [11] had found short lattice vectors in dimensions from 90 to 112 [7, Sect. 5.2]).

The *duality* of a lattice helps to develop a new reduction algorithm (see [16] for dual lattices). For example, the primal-dual reduction [13], the slide reduction [10], and Self-Dual BKZ [18] make use of the duality. In this paper, we develop a dual version of DeepBKZ. To develop it, we develop a dual version of DeepLLL (Dual-DeepLLL), in which we consider a reordered basis given by

$$\widehat{\sigma}_{k,\ell}(\mathbf{B}) = [\mathbf{b}_1, \ldots, \mathbf{b}_{k-1}, \mathbf{b}_{k+1}, \ldots, \mathbf{b}_\ell, \mathbf{b}_k, \mathbf{b}_{\ell+1}, \ldots, \mathbf{b}_n] \qquad (1)$$

for a basis $\mathbf{B} = [\mathbf{b}_1, \ldots, \mathbf{b}_n]$ and $k \leq \ell$. This is opposite to the deep insertion in the primal DeepLLL [21]. By performing the basis transformation $\mathbf{B} \leftarrow \widehat{\sigma}_{k,\ell}(\mathbf{B})$ recursively, we reduce the dual basis $\mathbf{D} = (\mathbf{B}^{-1})^\top = [\mathbf{d}_1, \ldots, \mathbf{d}_n]$. In Dual-DeepLLL, it requires to recompute the Gram-Schmidt orthogonalization (GSO) information for the reordered basis $\widehat{\sigma}_{k,\ell}(\mathbf{B})$. We give an explicit formula to keep track of the GSO information. This makes Dual-DeepLLL to run practically like LLL. To develop Dual-DeepBKZ, we combine Dual-DeepLLL with the dual enumeration by Micciancio and Walter [18, Sect. 7], which finds a short dual lattice vector. As well as the primal DeepBKZ [26], in Dual-DeepBKZ with blocksize β, every call of Dual-DeepLLL reduces the total number of calls of the dual enumeration over local projected blocks $\mathbf{B}_{[h,j]}$ for $2 \leq j \leq n$ with $h = \max(j - \beta + 1, 1)$. For an input basis, Dual-DeepBKZ never computes the dual basis, and it is as efficient as the primal DeepBKZ [26]. While forward GSO vectors become shorter in processing of DeepBKZ, *backward* GSO vectors $\mathbf{b}_i^*$ become *longer* in processing of Dual-DeepBKZ (equivalently, corresponding dual-GSO vectors $\mathbf{d}_i^\dagger$ become shorter).

We demonstrate that Dual-DeepBKZ and DeepBKZ [26] solve several instances of the LWE challenge [6,9], which have been published since 2016 to test algorithms for solving the (search-)LWE problem. There are two approaches for solving the search-LWE problem (see [1,3] for details); the BDD approach and the embedding approach. The BDD approach requires to solve a particular case of CVP, and dual HKZ reduction is suitable for solving CVP (e.g., Blömer [4] improved an algorithm for solving CVP over a dual HKZ reduced basis). Since Dual-DeepBKZ is a local block version of dual HKZ reduction, we adopt it in the BDD approach. On the other hand, DeepBKZ is a local block version of primal HKZ reduction, and it is suitable for the embedding approach. We implement both Dual-DeepBKZ and DeepBKZ, and report experimental results on their running time for solving several LWE instances. In particular, we show some experimental evidences that Dual-DeepBKZ reduces the cost of Liu-Nguyen's BDD enumeration [15] more effectively than BKZ in solving the LWE challenge.

Notation. The symbols $\mathbb{Z}$ and $\mathbb{R}$ denote the ring of integers and the field of real numbers, respectively. Throughout this paper, we basically represent all vectors in column format. For a vector $\mathbf{a} = (a_1, \ldots, a_n)^\top \in \mathbb{R}^n$, let $\|\mathbf{a}\|$ denote its Euclidean norm defined by $\|\mathbf{a}\|^2 = \sum_{i=1}^n a_i^2$. For two vectors $\mathbf{a} = (a_1, \ldots, a_n)^\top$ and $\mathbf{b} = (b_1, \ldots, b_n)^\top \in \mathbb{R}^n$, we let $\langle \mathbf{a}, \mathbf{b} \rangle$ denote the inner product $\sum_{i=1}^n a_i b_i$.

2   Preliminaries

We briefly review lattices and dual lattices, and the GSO for their bases. We also present DeepLLL [21] and DeepBKZ [26].

2.1   Lattices and Bases

For a positive integer n, linearly independent vectors $\mathbf{b}_1, \ldots, \mathbf{b}_n \in \mathbb{R}^n$ define the (full-rank) *lattice*

$$\mathcal{L}(\mathbf{B}) := \left\{ \sum_{i=1}^n x_i \mathbf{b}_i : x_i \in \mathbb{Z} \text{ for all } 1 \leq i \leq n \right\}$$

of dimension n with basis $\mathbf{B} = [\mathbf{b}_1, \ldots, \mathbf{b}_n] \in \mathbb{R}^{n \times n}$. Every lattice has infinitely many bases; If $\mathbf{B}_1$ and $\mathbf{B}_2$ are two bases such that $\mathcal{L}(\mathbf{B}_1) = \mathcal{L}(\mathbf{B}_2)$, there exists a unimodular matrix $\mathbf{V} \in \mathrm{GL}_n(\mathbb{Z})$ satisfying $\mathbf{B}_1 = \mathbf{B}_2 \mathbf{V}$. For a basis $\mathbf{B}$ of a lattice L, the *volume* of L is defined as $\mathrm{vol}(L) = |\det(\mathbf{B})| > 0$, which is independent of the choice of bases.

The GSO for a basis $\mathbf{B}$ is the orthogonal family $\mathbf{B}^* = [\mathbf{b}_1^*, \ldots, \mathbf{b}_n^*] \in \mathbb{R}^{n \times n}$, recursively defined by $\mathbf{b}_1^* := \mathbf{b}_1$ and

$$\mathbf{b}_i^* := \mathbf{b}_i - \sum_{j=1}^{i-1} \mu_{i,j} \mathbf{b}_j^*, \ \mu_{i,j} := \frac{\langle \mathbf{b}_i, \mathbf{b}_j^* \rangle}{\|\mathbf{b}_j^*\|^2} \text{ for } 1 \leq j < i \leq n. \tag{2}$$

We note that a basis must be regarded as an *ordered* set for its GSO. Set $\mathbf{U} = (\mu_{i,j}) \in \mathbb{R}^{n \times n}$, where we set $\mu_{i,i} = 1$ for all i and $\mu_{i,j} = 0$ for all $j > i$. Then

$$\mathbf{B} = \mathbf{B}^* \mathbf{U}^\top \text{ and } \mathrm{vol}(L) = \prod_{i=1}^n \|\mathbf{b}_i^*\|.$$

For each $2 \leq \ell \leq n$, the orthogonal projection from $\mathbb{R}^n$ over the orthogonal supplement of the $\mathbb{R}$-vector space $\langle \mathbf{b}_1, \ldots, \mathbf{b}_{\ell-1} \rangle_{\mathbb{R}}$ is defined as (we set $\pi_1 = \mathrm{id}$)

$$\pi_\ell : \mathbb{R}^n \to \langle \mathbf{b}_1, \ldots, \mathbf{b}_{\ell-1} \rangle_{\mathbb{R}}^\perp = \langle \mathbf{b}_\ell^*, \ldots, \mathbf{b}_n^* \rangle, \ \pi_\ell(\mathbf{x}) = \sum_{i=\ell}^n \frac{\langle \mathbf{x}, \mathbf{b}_i^* \rangle}{\|\mathbf{b}_i^*\|^2} \mathbf{b}_i^*.$$

2.2   Dual Lattices and Dual Bases

The *dual* of a lattice L is defined as

$$\widehat{L} := \{\mathbf{x} \in \operatorname{span}_{\mathbb{R}}(L) : \langle \mathbf{x}, \mathbf{y} \rangle \in \mathbb{Z} \text{ for } \forall \mathbf{y} \in L\},$$

where $\operatorname{span}_{\mathbb{R}}(L)$ denotes the $\mathbb{R}$-vector space spanned by the vectors of L (that is, $\operatorname{span}_{\mathbb{R}}(L) \simeq L \otimes_{\mathbb{Z}} \mathbb{R}$). The dual of a full-rank lattice $L = \mathcal{L}(\mathbf{B})$ with basis $\mathbf{B}$ has a basis $\mathbf{D} = \left(\mathbf{B}^{-1}\right)^{\top}$. Write $\mathbf{B} = [\mathbf{b}_1, \ldots, \mathbf{b}_n]$ and $\mathbf{D} = [\mathbf{d}_1, \ldots, \mathbf{d}_n]$. Then the relation $\mathbf{D}^{\top}\mathbf{B} = \mathbf{I}_n$ is maintained, where $\mathbf{I}_n$ denotes the identity matrix of size n (that is, $\langle \mathbf{d}_i, \mathbf{b}_j \rangle = \delta_{ij}$ where δ_{ij} denotes the Kronecker delta). This tells how the dual basis $\mathbf{D}$ changes with respect to changes of the primal basis $\mathbf{B}$.

Now define the GSO for the dual basis $\mathbf{D}$ as in case of the primal basis, but going through the basis vectors *in reverse order*; $\mathbf{d}_n^{\dagger} := \mathbf{d}_n$ and

$$\mathbf{d}_j^{\dagger} := \mathbf{d}_j - \sum_{i=j+1}^{n} \widehat{\mu}_{j,i} \mathbf{d}_i^{\dagger}, \ \widehat{\mu}_{j,i} := \frac{\langle \mathbf{d}_j, \mathbf{d}_i^{\dagger} \rangle}{\|\mathbf{d}_i^{\dagger}\|^2} \text{ for } 1 \le j < i \le n. \tag{3}$$

Set $\widehat{\mu}_{j,j} = 1$ for all $1 \le j \le n$. For each $1 \le \ell \le n-1$, let

$$\tau_{\ell} : \mathbb{R}^n \to \langle \mathbf{d}_{\ell+1}, \ldots, \mathbf{d}_n \rangle_{\mathbb{R}}^{\perp} = \langle \mathbf{d}_1^{\dagger}, \ldots, \mathbf{d}_{\ell}^{\dagger} \rangle_{\mathbb{R}}, \ \tau_{\ell}(\mathbf{x}) = \sum_{i=1}^{\ell} \frac{\langle \mathbf{x}, \mathbf{d}_i^{\dagger} \rangle}{\|\mathbf{d}_i^{\dagger}\|^2} \mathbf{d}_i^{\dagger}.$$

We also let $\tau_n = \text{id}$. For a basis $\mathbf{B} = [\mathbf{b}_1, \ldots, \mathbf{b}_n]$ and $1 \le i \le j \le n$, we denote by $\mathbf{B}_{[i,j]}$ the local projected block basis $[\pi_i(\mathbf{b}_i), \pi_i(\mathbf{b}_{i+1}), \ldots, \pi_i(\mathbf{b}_j)]$. Then its dual basis is given by $[\tau_j(\mathbf{d}_i), \ldots, \tau_j(\mathbf{d}_j)]$. The particular case $i = j$ shows

$$\frac{\mathbf{b}_i^{*}}{\|\mathbf{b}_i^{*}\|} = \frac{\mathbf{d}_i^{\dagger}}{\|\mathbf{d}_i^{\dagger}\|} \text{ and } \|\mathbf{b}_i^{*}\| \cdot \|\mathbf{d}_i^{\dagger}\| = 1 \tag{4}$$

for all $1 \le i \le n$.

2.3   DeepLLL [21]

Schnorr and Euchner [21] proposed DeepLLL, an improvement of LLL [14]. In LLL, only adjacent basis vectors $\mathbf{b}_{\ell-1}$ and $\mathbf{b}_{\ell}$ can be swapped for a basis $\mathbf{B} = [\mathbf{b}_1, \ldots, \mathbf{b}_n]$. In DeepLLL, non-adjacent basis vectors can be changed; For a reduction parameter $\frac{1}{4} < \delta < 1$, a basis vector $\mathbf{b}_{\ell}$ is inserted between $\mathbf{b}_{k-1}$ and $\mathbf{b}_k$ for $k < \ell$ if the *deep exchange condition*

$$\|\pi_k(\mathbf{b}_{\ell})\|^2 < \delta \|\mathbf{b}_k^{*}\|^2 \tag{5}$$

is satisfied. In this case, the new GSO vector at the k-th position is given by $\pi_k(\mathbf{b}_{\ell})$, strictly shorter than the old GSO vector $\mathbf{b}_k^{*}$.

Definition 1. *For a reduction parameter* $\frac{1}{4} < \delta < 1$, *we say that a basis* $\mathbf{B} = [\mathbf{b}_1, \ldots, \mathbf{b}_n]$ *is δ-DeepLLL-reduced if the following two conditions are satisfied;*

(i) The basis $\mathbf{B}$ is size-reduced, namely, $|\mu_{i,j}| < 1/2$ for all $1 \leq j < i \leq n$.
(ii) We have $\|\pi_k(\mathbf{b}_\ell)\|^2 \geq \delta\|\mathbf{b}_k^*\|^2$ for all $1 \leq k < \ell \leq n$ (The case $\ell = k+1$ is just Lovász' condition [14] between $\mathbf{b}_k$ and $\mathbf{b}_{k+1}$).

We note that $\mathbf{B}$ is said to be δ-LLL-reduced if it satisfies (i) and Lovász' condition between $\mathbf{b}_k$ and $\mathbf{b}_{k+1}$ for $1 \leq k \leq n-1$.

Every DeepLLL-reduced basis has a local property; If a basis $\mathbf{B}$ is δ-DeepLLL-reduced, then the local block $\mathbf{B}_{[i,j]}$ is also δ-DeepLLL-reduced for all $i \leq j$. Let $\mathfrak{S}_n$ denote the group of permutations among n elements. For $\sigma \in \mathfrak{S}_n$ and $\mathbf{B} = [\mathbf{b}_1, \ldots, \mathbf{b}_n]$, we let $\sigma(\mathbf{B}) := [\mathbf{b}_{\sigma(1)}, \ldots, \mathbf{b}_{\sigma(n)}]$ denote the reordered basis. For $1 \leq k < \ell \leq n$, we define $\sigma_{k,\ell} \in \mathfrak{S}_n$ as $\sigma_{k,\ell}(i) = i$ for $1 \leq i < k$ or $\ell < i \leq n$, $\sigma_{k,\ell}(k) = \ell$, and $\sigma_{k,\ell}(i) = i-1$ for $k+1 \leq i \leq \ell$. Then

$$\sigma_{k,\ell}(\mathbf{B}) = [\mathbf{b}_1, \ldots, \mathbf{b}_{k-1}, \mathbf{b}_\ell, \mathbf{b}_k, \ldots, \mathbf{b}_{\ell-1}, \mathbf{b}_{\ell+1}, \ldots, \mathbf{b}_n],$$

which is obtained by inserting $\mathbf{b}_\ell$ between $\mathbf{b}_{k-1}$ and $\mathbf{b}_k$ (i.e., a *deep insertion*). DeepLLL takes a basis $\mathbf{B}$ of a lattice L and a reduction parameter $\frac{1}{4} < \delta < 1$ as input, and outputs a δ-DeepLLL-reduced basis of L (see [5, Fig. 5.1] or [8, Algorithm 2.6.3] for procedures of DeepLLL). In the below, we present the GSO formula [26, Theorem 1] for the reordered basis $\sigma_{k,\ell}(\mathbf{B})$, which makes DeepLLL practical (see [26, Algorithm 4] for their GSO update algorithm):

Theorem 1 ([26]). *Let* $\mathbf{B} = [\mathbf{b}_1, \ldots, \mathbf{b}_n]$ *be a basis, and* $\mathbf{B}^* = [\mathbf{b}_1^*, \ldots, \mathbf{b}_n^*]$ *its GSO with coefficients* $\mu_{i,j}$ *and* $B_i = \|\mathbf{b}_i^*\|^2$. *For* $1 \leq k < \ell \leq n$, *let* $\mathbf{C} = \sigma_{k,\ell}(\mathbf{B}) = [\mathbf{c}_1, \ldots, \mathbf{c}_n]$, *and* $\mathbf{C}^* = [\mathbf{c}_1^*, \ldots, \mathbf{c}_n^*]$ *its GSO. Then we have* $\mathbf{c}_i^* = \mathbf{b}_i^*$ *for* $1 \leq i \leq k-1$ *and* $\ell+1 \leq i \leq n$, $\mathbf{c}_k^* = \pi_k(\mathbf{b}_\ell)$, *and*

$$\mathbf{c}_i^* = \frac{D_i^{(\ell)}}{D_{i-1}^{(\ell)}}\mathbf{b}_{i-1}^* - \frac{\mu_{\ell,i-1}B_{i-1}}{D_{i-1}^{(\ell)}}\sum_{h=i}^{\ell}\mu_{\ell,h}\mathbf{b}_h^*$$

for $k+1 \leq i \leq \ell$, *where set* $D_j^{(\ell)} = \|\pi_j(\mathbf{b}_\ell)\|^2$ *for* $1 \leq j \leq \ell$. *With respect to the squared lengths* $C_i = \|\mathbf{c}_i^*\|^2$, *we have* $C_k = D_k^{(\ell)}$ *and*

$$C_i = \frac{D_i^{(\ell)}B_{i-1}}{D_{i-1}^{(\ell)}}$$

for $k+1 \leq i \leq \ell$.

2.4 DeepBKZ [26]

For a basis $[\mathbf{b}_1, \ldots, \mathbf{b}_n]$ and $1 \leq j \leq k \leq n$, we denote by $L_{[j,k]}$ the lattice spanned by the local block basis $\mathbf{B}_{[j,k]}$ of dimension $k - j + 1$. A basis $\mathbf{B}$ is called (δ, β)-*BKZ-reduced* [21] with blocksize $2 \leq \beta \leq n$ and factor $\frac{1}{4} < \delta < 1$ if it is δ-LLL-reduced and it satisfies $\|\mathbf{b}_j^*\| = \lambda_1(L_{[j,k]})$ for all $1 \leq j \leq n$ with $k = \min(j + \beta - 1, n)$, where $\lambda_1(L)$ denotes the first successive minimum of a lattice L. We simply call the basis β-*BKZ-reduced* when δ is unconscious. From an input basis of a lattice L, BKZ [21, Sect. 6] finds a β-BKZ-reduced basis of L. For higher blocksizes β, BKZ outputs a more reduced basis than LLL and DeepLLL in practice (see [10] for their experimental results).

The original BKZ [21] uses LLL as a subroutine to reduce local bases $\mathbf{B}_{[j,k]}$ before enumeration (e.g., see [11] for enumeration) for finding a shortest vector over $L_{[j,k]}$ (cf., BKZ 2.0 [7], an updated version of BKZ, calls aborted-BKZ with small blocksizes for local blocks $\mathbf{B}_{[j,k]}$ for higher blocksizes $\beta \geq 50$). In contrast, DeepBKZ [26, Algorithm 3] uses DeepLLL instead of LLL. From a basis of a lattice L, it finds a DeepBKZ-reduced basis of L, defined as follows:

Definition 2. *Let $\frac{1}{4} < \delta < 1$ and $\beta \geq 2$. A basis is called (δ, β)-DeepBKZ-reduced if it is both δ-DeepLLL-reduced and β-BKZ-reduced.*

A basis $\mathbf{B} = [\mathbf{b}_1, \ldots, \mathbf{b}_n]$ of a lattice L is called *HKZ-reduced* if the following two conditions are satisfied; (i) The basis $\mathbf{B}$ is size-reduced. (ii) We have $\|\mathbf{b}_i^*\| = \lambda_1(\pi_i(L))$ for all $1 \leq i \leq n$. The notion of BKZ-reduction is a local block version of HKZ-reduction (see [16, Definition 7.8] for HKZ-reduction). It is clear that any HKZ-reduced basis is also (δ, β)-DeepBKZ-reduced for any $\frac{1}{4} < \delta < 1$ and $\beta \geq 2$. Namely, DeepBKZ-reduction is a middle notion between BKZ-reduction and HKZ-reduction.

3 Development of Dual-DeepBKZ

In this section, we develop Dual-DeepBKZ, a dual version of DeepBKZ [26].

3.1 Dual-DeepLLL

Here we develop Dual-DeepLLL, a dual version of DeepLLL, which we shall embed into Dual-DeepBKZ as a main subroutine in the next subsection. Let $\mathbf{B} = [\mathbf{b}_1, \ldots, \mathbf{b}_n]$ be a basis of a lattice L. For $1 \leq k < \ell \leq n$, we define $\widehat{\sigma}_{k,\ell} \in \mathfrak{S}_n$ by $\widehat{\sigma}_{k,\ell}(i) = i$ for $1 \leq i < k$ or $\ell < i \leq n$, $\widehat{\sigma}_{k,\ell}(\ell) = k$, and $\widehat{\sigma}_{k,\ell}(i) = i + 1$ for $k \leq i \leq \ell - 1$ (cf., $\sigma_{k,\ell} \in \mathfrak{S}_n$). The reordered basis $\widehat{\sigma}_{k,\ell}(\mathbf{B})$ is given by (1), in which the basis vector $\mathbf{b}_k$ is inserted between $\mathbf{b}_\ell$ and $\mathbf{b}_{\ell+1}$. In this paper, we call the basis transformation $\mathbf{B} \leftarrow \widehat{\sigma}_{k,\ell}(\mathbf{B})$ a *dual deep insertion*.

GSO Formula. To keep track of the GSO information of a new basis after a dual deep insertion, we give an explicit formula for the GSO of $\mathbf{C} = \widehat{\sigma}_{k,\ell}(\mathbf{B})$ like Theorem 1. Let $\mathbf{D} = [\mathbf{d}_1, \ldots, \mathbf{d}_n]$ be the dual basis of $\mathbf{B}$. Let $\mathbf{D}' = [\mathbf{d}_1', \ldots, \mathbf{d}_n']$ denote the basis obtained by changing the order of basis vectors of $\mathbf{D}$ reversely (i.e., $\mathbf{d}_i' = \mathbf{d}_{n-i+1}$ for $1 \leq i \leq n$). Consider the deep insertion $\sigma_{n-\ell+1, n-k+1}$ for $\mathbf{D}'$, and set $\mathbf{E}' = \sigma_{n-\ell+1, n-k+1}(\mathbf{D}') = [\mathbf{e}_1', \ldots, \mathbf{e}_n']$. In the same manner, let $\mathbf{E} = [\mathbf{e}_1, \ldots, \mathbf{e}_n]$ denote the basis obtained by changing the order of basis vectors of $\mathbf{E}'$ reversely. Then $\mathbf{E} = \widehat{\sigma}_{k,\ell}(\mathbf{D})$, and hence $\mathbf{E}^\top \mathbf{C} = \mathbf{I}_n$ since $\mathbf{D}^\top \mathbf{B} = \mathbf{I}_n$. Therefore $\mathbf{E}$ is the dual basis of $\mathbf{C}$ (this is why we call $\widehat{\sigma}_{k,\ell}$ a dual deep insertion):

$$
\begin{array}{ccc}
\mathbf{B} = [\mathbf{b}_1,\ldots,\mathbf{b}_n] & \xrightarrow{\text{dual deep insertion}} & \mathbf{C} = \widehat{\sigma}_{k,\ell}(\mathbf{B}) = [\mathbf{c}_1,\ldots,\mathbf{c}_n] \\
\downarrow{\text{dual}} & & \text{dual}\uparrow \\
\mathbf{D} = [\mathbf{d}_1,\ldots,\mathbf{d}_n] & & \mathbf{E} = [\mathbf{e}_1,\ldots,\mathbf{e}_n] = \widehat{\sigma}_{k,\ell}(\mathbf{D}) \\
\downarrow{\text{reverse order}} & & \text{reverse order}\uparrow \\
\mathbf{D}' = [\mathbf{d}'_1,\ldots,\mathbf{d}'_n] & \xrightarrow{\text{deep insertion}} & \mathbf{E}' = \sigma_{n-\ell+1,n-k+1}(\mathbf{D}') = [\mathbf{e}'_1,\ldots,\mathbf{e}'_n]
\end{array}
$$

We remark that dual GSO process (3) for $\mathbf{D}$ (resp., $\mathbf{E}$) coincides with primal GSO process (2) for $\mathbf{D}'$ (resp., $\mathbf{E}'$) by the reverse order of GSO vectors. By applying Theorem 1 to the pair $(\mathbf{D}', \mathbf{E}')$, we can obtain an explicit GSO formula for $\mathbf{E}$, and hence for $\mathbf{C}$ as follows:

Theorem 2. *Let* $\mathbf{B} = [\mathbf{b}_1,\ldots,\mathbf{b}_n]$ *be a basis, and* $\mathbf{B}^* = [\mathbf{b}_1^*,\ldots,\mathbf{b}_n^*]$ *its GSO with coefficients* $\mu_{i,j}$ *and* $B_i = \|\mathbf{b}_i^*\|^2$. *Let* $\mathbf{D} = (\mathbf{B}^{-1})^\top = [\mathbf{d}_1,\ldots,\mathbf{d}_n]$ *denote the dual basis of* $\mathbf{B}$, *and* $\mathbf{D}^\dagger = [\mathbf{d}_1^\dagger,\ldots,\mathbf{d}_n^\dagger]$ *its GSO with coefficients* $\widehat{\mu}_{j,i}$. *For* $1 \le k < \ell \le n$, *set* $\mathbf{C} = \widehat{\sigma}_{k,\ell}(\mathbf{B}) = [\mathbf{c}_1,\ldots,\mathbf{c}_n]$, *and let* $\mathbf{C}^* = [\mathbf{c}_1^*,\ldots,\mathbf{c}_n^*]$ *denote its GSO. Then*

$$
\mathbf{c}_j^* = \begin{cases}
\mathbf{b}_j^* & (1 \le j \le k-1 \text{ or } \ell+1 \le j \le n), \\[2mm]
\mathbf{b}_{j+1}^* - \dfrac{\widehat{\mu}_{k,j+1}}{\widehat{D}_j^{(k)}} \displaystyle\sum_{h=k}^{j} \dfrac{\widehat{\mu}_{k,h}}{B_h}\mathbf{b}_h^* & (k \le j \le \ell-1), \\[4mm]
\dfrac{\tau_\ell(\mathbf{d}_k)}{\widehat{D}_\ell^{(k)}} & (j = \ell),
\end{cases}
$$

where we set $\widehat{D}_i^{(k)} := \|\tau_i(\mathbf{d}_k)\|^2$ *for* $1 \le k \le i \le n$. *For* $C_j = \|\mathbf{c}_j^*\|^2$, *we have*

$$
C_j = \begin{cases}
B_j & (1 \le j \le k-1 \text{ or } \ell+1 \le j \le n), \\[2mm]
\dfrac{\widehat{D}_{j+1}^{(k)} B_{j+1}}{\widehat{D}_j^{(k)}} & (k \le j \le \ell-1), \\[4mm]
\dfrac{1}{\widehat{D}_\ell^{(k)}} & (j = \ell).
\end{cases}
$$

Proof. Here we prove the formula for $C_j = \|\mathbf{c}_j^*\|^2$ only. By Theorem 1, we have $\|\mathbf{e}'^*_{n-\ell+1}\|^2 = \|\pi_{n-\ell+1}(\mathbf{d}'_{n-k+1})\|^2$ and

$$
\|\mathbf{e}'^*_{n-j+1}\|^2 = \frac{\|\pi_{n-j+1}(\mathbf{d}'_{n-k+1})\|^2 \cdot \|\mathbf{d}'^*_{n-j}\|^2}{\|\pi_{n-j}(\mathbf{d}'_{n-k+1})\|^2}
$$

for $k \le j \le \ell - 1$. By using the notation for $\mathbf{D}$ and $\mathbf{E}$, we can rewrite these equations as $\|\mathbf{e}_\ell^\dagger\|^2 = \|\tau_\ell(\mathbf{d}_k)\|^2 = \widehat{D}_\ell^{(k)}$ and

$$\|\mathbf{e}_j^\dagger\|^2 = \frac{\|\tau_j(\mathbf{d}_k)\|^2 \cdot \|\mathbf{d}_{j+1}^\dagger\|^2}{\|\tau_{j+1}(\mathbf{d}_k)\|^2} = \frac{\widehat{D}_j^{(k)} \cdot \|\mathbf{d}_{j+1}^\dagger\|^2}{\widehat{D}_{j+1}^{(k)}}$$

for $k \le j \le \ell - 1$. By the duality for pairs $(\mathbf{B}, \mathbf{D})$ and $(\mathbf{C}, \mathbf{E})$, we have $B_i = \|\mathbf{d}_i^\dagger\|^{-2}$ and $C_i = \|\mathbf{e}_i^\dagger\|^{-2}$ from (4) for $1 \le i \le n$. This completes the proof. □

Computation of $\widehat{\mu}_{k,j}$ and $\widehat{D}_i^{(k)}$ In Theorem 2, the dual basis $\mathbf{D}$ of $\mathbf{B}$ is required in computing the GSO information of $\mathbf{C} = \widehat{\sigma}_{k,\ell}(\mathbf{B})$. However, computation of the dual basis is costly since it involves matrix inversion. Here we give a method to compute $\widehat{\mu}_{k,j}$ and $\widehat{D}_i^{(k)}$ without computing the dual basis; By (4), for any $1 \le k \le i \le n$, we have

$$\widehat{D}_i^{(k)} = \sum_{j=k}^{i} \widehat{\mu}_{k,j}^2 \|\mathbf{d}_j^\dagger\|^2 = \sum_{j=k}^{i} \frac{\widehat{\mu}_{k,j}^2}{B_j}.$$

By this, it is sufficient to compute all $\widehat{\mu}_{k,j}$ to obtain $\widehat{D}_i^{(k)}$. It follows from (4) that $\widehat{\mu}_{k,j} = \langle \mathbf{d}_k, \mathbf{b}_j^* \rangle$ for any $k \le j \le n$. For $j = k$, we have $\widehat{\mu}_{k,k} = 1$ by definition. For $j = k + 1$, we have $\widehat{\mu}_{k,k+1} = \langle \mathbf{d}_k, \mathbf{b}_{k+1} \rangle - \sum_{h=1}^{k} \mu_{k+1,h} \langle \mathbf{d}_k, \mathbf{b}_h^* \rangle = -\mu_{k+1,k}$ from $\mathbf{b}_{k+1}^* = \mathbf{b}_{k+1} - \sum_{h=1}^{k} \mu_{k+1,h} \mathbf{b}_h^*$ and $\langle \mathbf{d}_k, \mathbf{b}_i \rangle = \delta_{ki}$ (we remark that each $\mathbf{b}_h^*$ is included in the space $\langle \mathbf{b}_1, \ldots, \mathbf{b}_h \rangle_\mathbb{R}$). In the same manner, we can compute all $\widehat{\mu}_{k,j}$ recursively from the GSO coefficients $\mu_{i,j}$ of $\mathbf{B}$ as $\widehat{\mu}_{k,k} = 1$ and

$$\widehat{\mu}_{k,j} = -\sum_{h=k}^{j-1} \mu_{j,h} \langle \mathbf{d}_k, \mathbf{b}_h^* \rangle = -\sum_{h=k}^{j-1} \mu_{j,h} \widehat{\mu}_{k,h} \tag{6}$$

for $k + 1 \le j \le n$.

Algorithm. Here we present a new reduction algorithm using dual deep insertions, which we call "Dual-DeepLLL". In the following, we define a dual notion of DeepLLL-reduction:

Definition 3. *Given a reduction parameter $\frac{1}{4} < \delta < 1$, we say that a basis is δ-Dual-DeepLLL-reduced if its dual basis is δ-DeepLLL-reduced.*

Algorithm 1 is our Dual-DeepLLL. It takes a basis $\mathbf{B} = [\mathbf{b}_1, \ldots, \mathbf{b}_n]$ of a lattice L and a reduction parameter $\frac{1}{4} < \delta < 1$ as input, and outputs a δ-Dual-DeepLLL-reduced basis of L. Dual-DeepLLL performs simple unimodular transformations only over the primal basis $\mathbf{B}$ until its dual basis $\mathbf{D} = [\mathbf{d}_1, \ldots, \mathbf{d}_n]$ is δ-DeepLLL-reduced. In particular, it involves no matrix inversion, and it is as efficient as the primal DeepLLL [21]. In the following, we describe several key procedures in Dual-DeepLLL (we use the same notation as in Theorem 2):

Algorithm 1. Dual-DeepLLL

Input: A basis $\mathbf{B} = [\mathbf{b}_1, \ldots, \mathbf{b}_n]$ of a lattice L and a reduction parameter $\frac{1}{4} < \delta < 1$
Output: A δ-Dual-DeepLLL-reduced basis $\mathbf{B}$ of L
1: Compute $\mathbf{B}^* = [\mathbf{b}_1^*, \ldots, \mathbf{b}_n^*]$ of $\mathbf{B}$ with coefficients $\mu_{i,j}$ and $B_i = \|\mathbf{b}_i^*\|^2$ (set $\mu_{i,i} = 1$)
2: $\widehat{\mu}_{n,n} = 1$ and $k \leftarrow n - 1$ /* $\widehat{\mu}_{j,i}$ are the GSO coefficients of the dual basis $\mathbf{D}$ */
3: **while** $k \geq 1$ **do**
4:    $\widehat{\mu}_{k,k} = 1$
5:    **for** $j = k + 1$ to n **do**
6:       $\widehat{\mu}_{k,j} \leftarrow -\sum_{h=k}^{j-1} \mu_{j,h}\widehat{\mu}_{k,h}$ and $q = \lceil \widehat{\mu}_{k,j} \rfloor$ /* see (6) for computation of $\widehat{\mu}_{k,j}$ */
7:       **if** $q \neq 0$ **then**
8:          $\mathbf{b}_j \leftarrow \mathbf{b}_j + q\mathbf{b}_k$ /* size-reduce $\mathbf{D} = [\mathbf{d}_1, \ldots, \mathbf{d}_n]$ over $\mathbf{B}$ */
9:          $\widehat{\mu}_{k,\ell} \leftarrow \widehat{\mu}_{k,\ell} - q\widehat{\mu}_{j,\ell}$ for $j \leq \ell \leq n$ /* update $\widehat{\mu}_{k,\ell}$ */
10:          $\mu_{j,h} \leftarrow \mu_{j,h} + q\mu_{k,h}$ for $1 \leq h \leq k$ /* update $\mu_{j,h}$ */
11:       **end if**
12:    **end for**
13:    $D \leftarrow \sum_{j=k}^{n} \frac{\widehat{\mu}_{k,j}^2}{B_j}$ and $\ell \leftarrow n$ /* $D = \widehat{D}_n^{(k)} = \|\tau_n(\mathbf{d}_k)\|^2$ */
14:    **while** $\ell \geq k + 1$ **do**
15:       **if** $B_\ell \cdot D < \delta$ **then**
16:          $\mathbf{B} \leftarrow \widehat{\sigma}_{k,\ell}(\mathbf{B})$ and update its GSO /* a dual deep insertion */
17:          $k \leftarrow \min(\ell, n - 1) + 1$
18:       **else**
19:          $D \leftarrow D - \frac{\widehat{\mu}_{k,\ell}^2}{B_\ell}$ and $\ell \leftarrow \ell - 1$ /* update $D = \widehat{D}_\ell^{(k)} = \|\tau_\ell(\mathbf{d}_k)\|^2$ */
20:       **end if**
21:    **end while**
22:    $k \leftarrow k - 1$
23: **end while**

(a) *Dual deep exchange condition*: In Dual-DeepLLL, a dual deep insertion $\widehat{\sigma}_{k,\ell}$ for $\mathbf{B}$ is performed only if $B_\ell \cdot \widehat{D}_\ell^{(k)} < \delta$, which we call the *dual deep exchange condition* (see Step 15 in Algorithm 1). By (4), this can be rewritten as $\|\tau_\ell(\mathbf{d}_k)\|^2 < \delta\|\mathbf{d}_\ell^\dagger\|^2$, which is just the deep exchange condition (5) for $\mathbf{D}$. This implies that the dual basis of any output basis by Dual-DeepLLL satisfies condition (ii) in Definition 1. To the contrary to the original DeepLLL, the new GSO vector at the ℓ-th position over the primal basis $\mathbf{B}$ after a dual deep insertion is strictly *longer* than the old GSO vector $\mathbf{b}_\ell^*$ in Dual-DeepLLL (over the dual basis $\mathbf{D}$, the new dual-GSO vector is strictly shorter than the old dual-GSO vector $\mathbf{d}_\ell^\dagger$ as in DeepLLL).

(b) *Size-reducing the dual basis*: In Step 8 of Algorithm 1, computation of $\mathbf{b}_j \leftarrow \mathbf{b}_j + q\mathbf{b}_k$ over the primal basis $\mathbf{B}$ corresponds to that of $\mathbf{d}_k \leftarrow \mathbf{d}_k - q\mathbf{d}_j$ over the dual basis $\mathbf{D}$ with $q = \lceil \widehat{\mu}_{k,j} \rfloor$ since $\mathbf{D}^\top \mathbf{B} = \mathbf{I}_n$ is maintained. This makes the dual basis $\mathbf{D}$ size-reduced. By combining this with the argument in (a), we see that the dual basis of any output basis by Dual-DeepLLL satisfies both (i) and (ii) in Definition 1 (that is, any output basis is δ-Dual-DeepLLL-reduced).

(c) *Efficient GSO update*: In Step 16 of Algorithm 1, it requires to update certain GSO information of the primal basis **B** after every dual deep insertion. From Theorem 2, we can construct an algorithm to update the GSO information (see the next subsection). Such algorithm makes Dual-DeepLLL practical.

Remark 1. The insertion restriction technique [21, Comments in Sect. 3] for DeepLLL can be adopted for Dual-DeepLLL; For a parameter $\varepsilon > 0$ (e.g., $\varepsilon = 20$), a dual deep insertion $\mathbf{B} \leftarrow \widehat{\sigma}_{k,\ell}(\mathbf{B})$ is performed only in case of either $\ell \geq n - \varepsilon + 1$ or $\ell \leq k + \varepsilon$. This restriction accelerates Dual-DeepLLL in performance, but the output basis is not guaranteed to be Dual-DeepLLL-reduced.

Efficient GSO Update Algorithm. Here we give an efficient algorithm to update some GSO information of the reordered basis $\mathbf{C} = \widehat{\sigma}_{k,\ell}(\mathbf{B})$ by a dual deep insertion. This algorithm can be adopted as a subroutine in Step 16 of Algorithm 1. We use the same notation as in Theorem 2. For the GSO vectors $\mathbf{C}^* = [\mathbf{c}_1^*, \ldots, \mathbf{c}_n^*]$, we let

$$\xi_{i,j} = \frac{\langle \mathbf{c}_i, \mathbf{c}_j^* \rangle}{\|\mathbf{c}_j^*\|^2} \text{ for } 1 \leq j < i \leq n.$$

The GSO vectors $\mathbf{c}_j^*$ and their squared lengths $C_j = \|\mathbf{c}_j^*\|^2$ are obtained from Theorem 2. We can also compute the GSO coefficients $\xi_{i,j}$ directly as follows:

Proposition 1. *The GSO coefficients $\xi_{i,j}$ are as follows:*

(A) *For $j = \ell$, we have $\xi_{i,\ell} = \sum_{h=k}^{\ell} \widehat{\mu}_{k,h}\mu_{i,h}$ for $\ell + 1 \leq i \leq n$.*

(B) *For $k \leq j \leq \ell - 1$, we have*

$$\xi_{i,j} = \begin{cases} \dfrac{\mu_{i+1,j+1}\widehat{D}_j^{(k)}}{\widehat{D}_{j+1}^{(k)}} - \dfrac{\widehat{\mu}_{k,j+1}}{\widehat{D}_{j+1}^{(k)}B_{j+1}} \displaystyle\sum_{h=k}^{j} \widehat{\mu}_{k,h}\mu_{i+1,h} & (j+1 \leq i \leq \ell - 1), \\[4mm] -\dfrac{\widehat{\mu}_{k,j+1}}{\widehat{D}_{j+1}^{(k)}B_{j+1}} & (i = \ell), \\[4mm] \dfrac{\mu_{i,j+1}\widehat{D}_j^{(k)}}{\widehat{D}_{j+1}^{(k)}} - \dfrac{\widehat{\mu}_{k,j+1}}{\widehat{D}_{j+1}^{(k)}B_{j+1}} \displaystyle\sum_{h=k}^{j} \widehat{\mu}_{k,h}\mu_{i,h} & (\ell + 1 \leq i \leq n). \end{cases}$$

(C) *For $1 \leq j \leq k - 1$, we have $\xi_{i,j} = \mu_{i+1,j}$ for $k \leq i \leq \ell - 1$ and $\xi_{\ell,j} = \mu_{k,j}$.*
(D) *For the other indices $1 \leq j < i \leq n$, we have $\xi_{i,j} = \mu_{i,j}$.*

Proof. It follows from Theorem 2. □

In Dual-DeepLLL, it is sufficient to update the GSO coefficients $\xi_{\ell,j}$ and the squared lengths C_j. In Algorithm 2, we give an algorithm to efficiently update some GSO information in Dual-DeepLLL. This algorithm is based on results of Theorem 2 and Proposition 1.

Algorithm 2. Update of some GSO information in Dual-DeepLLL

Input: Indices $1 \leq k < \ell \leq n$, GSO information $(\mu_{i,j})$ and $B_i = \|\mathbf{b}_i^*\|^2$ of a basis $\mathbf{B}$, and $\widehat{\mu}_{k,h}$ for $k \leq h \leq n$ and $\widehat{D}_i^{(k)}$ for $k \leq i \leq n$

Output: Updated GSO information $(\mu_{i,j})$ and B_i of the new basis $\mathbf{B} \leftarrow \widehat{\sigma}_{k,\ell}(\mathbf{B})$

1: Copy $(\xi_{i,j}) \leftarrow (\mu_{i,j})$

2: **for** $i = \ell + 1$ **to** n: $\xi_{i,\ell} \leftarrow \sum\limits_{h=k}^{\ell} \widehat{\mu}_{k,h}\mu_{i,h}$; /* by Proposition 1 (A) */

3: /* by Proposition 1 (B) */

4: **for** $j = k$ **to** $\ell - 1$ **do**

5:     **for** $i = j + 1$ **to** $\ell - 1$: $\xi_{i,j} \leftarrow \dfrac{\mu_{i+1,j+1}\widehat{D}_j^{(k)}}{\widehat{D}_{j+1}^{(k)}} - \dfrac{\widehat{\mu}_{k,j+1}}{\widehat{D}_{j+1}^{(k)}B_{j+1}} \sum\limits_{h=k}^{j} \widehat{\mu}_{k,h}\mu_{i+1,h}$;

6:     $\xi_{\ell,j} \leftarrow -\dfrac{\widehat{\mu}_{k,j+1}}{\widehat{D}_{j+1}^{(k)}B_{j+1}}$

7:     **for** $i = \ell + 1$ **to** n: $\xi_{i,j} \leftarrow \dfrac{\mu_{i,j+1}\widehat{D}_j^{(k)}}{\widehat{D}_{j+1}^{(k)}} - \dfrac{\widehat{\mu}_{k,j+1}}{\widehat{D}_{j+1}^{(k)}B_{j+1}} \sum\limits_{h=k}^{j} \widehat{\mu}_{k,h}\mu_{i,h}$;

8: **end for**

9: **for** $j = 1$ **to** $k - 1$ **do**

10:     **for** $i = k$ **to** $\ell - 1$: $\xi_{i,j} \leftarrow \mu_{i+1,j}$; $\xi_{\ell,j} \leftarrow \mu_{k,j}$ /* by Proposition 1 (C) */

11: **end for**

12: Copy $(\mu_{i,j}) \leftarrow (\xi_{i,j})$

13: **for** $j = k$ **to** $\ell - 1$: $B_j \leftarrow \dfrac{\widehat{D}_{j+1}^{(k)}B_{j+1}}{\widehat{D}_j^{(k)}}$; $B_\ell \leftarrow \dfrac{1}{D_\ell^{(k)}}$ /* by Theorem 2 */

3.2 Dual-DeepBKZ

We define a dual notion of DeepBKZ-reduction as follows:

Definition 4. *For $\frac{1}{4} < \delta < 1$ and $2 \leq \beta \leq n$, a basis $\mathbf{B} = [\mathbf{b}_1, \ldots, \mathbf{b}_n]$ is called (δ, β)-Dual-DeepBKZ-reduced if its dual basis is (δ, β)-DeepBKZ-reduced, that is, it is both δ-DeepLLL-reduced and β-BKZ-reduced.*

Algorithm 3 is our Dual-DeepBKZ. It takes as input a basis $\mathbf{B} = [\mathbf{b}_1, \ldots, \mathbf{b}_n]$ of a lattice L, a reduction parameter $\frac{1}{4} < \delta < 1$ and a blocksize $2 \leq \beta \leq n$. It outputs a (δ, β)-Dual-DeepBKZ-reduced basis of L. The main components of Dual-DeepBKZ are Dual-DeepLLL (Algorithm 1) and Dual-Enumeration by Micciancio and Walter [18, Sect. 7]. In the following, we describe several key procedures of Dual-DeepBKZ:

(a) *Call of Dual-Enumeration*: For a search bound $A > 0$, Dual-Enumeration enumerates all vectors $\mathbf{x} = (x_1, \ldots, x_n)^\top \in \mathbb{Z}^n$ over a basis $\mathbf{B} = [\mathbf{b}_1, \ldots, \mathbf{b}_n]$ of a lattice L such that it satisfies $\|\mathbf{v}\|^2 \leq A$ for the dual lattice vector $\mathbf{v} \in \widehat{L}$ with $x_i = \langle \mathbf{v}, \mathbf{b}_i \rangle$ for all $1 \leq i \leq n$ (for any $\mathbf{z} \in \widehat{L}$, it satisfies $\langle \mathbf{z}, \mathbf{b}_i \rangle \in \mathbb{Z}$ for all $1 \leq i \leq n$). In Step 6 of Algorithm 3, we call Dual-Enumeration over the local block $\mathbf{B}_{[h,j]}$ for $2 \leq j \leq n$ with $h = \max(j - \beta + 1, 1)$, to find a

---

Algorithm 3. Dual-DeepBKZ

Input: A basis $\mathbf{B} = [\mathbf{b}_1, \ldots, \mathbf{b}_n]$ of a lattice L and a reduction parameter $\frac{1}{4} < \delta < 1$, and a blocksize $2 \leq \beta \leq n$

Output: A (δ, β)-Dual-DeepBKZ-reduced basis $\mathbf{B}$ of L

1: $\mathbf{B} \leftarrow$ Dual-DeepLLL$(\mathbf{B}, \delta)$ and flag $\leftarrow 1$ /* compute $\mu_{i,\ell}$ and $\|\mathbf{b}_i^*\|^2$ */
2: **while** flag ≥ 1 **do**
3:     flag $\leftarrow 0$
4:     **for** $j = n$ downto 2 **do**
5:         $h \leftarrow \max(j - \beta + 1, 1)$
6:         $\mathbf{x} \leftarrow$ Dual-Enum$(\mu_{[h,j]}, \|\mathbf{b}_h^*\|^2, \ldots, \|\mathbf{b}_j^*\|^2, A)$ /* over the local block $\mathbf{B}_{[h,j]}$, enumerate all coefficient vectors $\mathbf{x} = (x_h, \ldots, x_j) \in \mathbb{Z}^{j-h+1}$ of $\mathbf{v} \in \widehat{L}$ with $\|\tau_j(\mathbf{v})\|^2 \leq A$ for a search bound A (e.g., set $A = 0.99/\|\mathbf{b}_j^*\|^2$) */
7:         **if** $\mathbf{x} \neq (0, \ldots, 0, 1)$ **then**
8:             flag $\leftarrow$ flag $+ 1$
9:             Insert $\mathbf{v} \in \widehat{L}$ into the dual basis of $\mathbf{B}$ at the j-th position to obtain a new basis $\mathbf{B}$ /* see [19, Sect. 7] for details */
10:            $\mathbf{B} \leftarrow$ Dual-DeepLLL$(\mathbf{B}, \delta)$ at stage j
11:         **end if**
12:     **end for**
13: **end while**

---

short dual lattice vector $\mathbf{v} \in \widehat{L}$ satisfying $\|\tau_j(\mathbf{v})\|^2 < 1/\|\mathbf{b}_j^*\|^2$, equivalently, $\|\tau_j(\mathbf{v})\|^2 < \|\mathbf{d}_j^\dagger\|^2$ by (4) for the dual basis $\mathbf{D} = [\mathbf{d}_1, \ldots, \mathbf{d}_n]$ of $\mathbf{B}$.

(b) *Insertion of dual lattice vectors*: In Step 9 of Algorithm 3, we insert such a short vector $\mathbf{v} \in \widehat{L}$ into $\mathbf{D}$ at the j-th position to obtain a new basis of L. This is achieved by certain unimodular transformation over a primal basis [18, Sect. 7]. The dual lattice of the new basis has $\tau_j(\mathbf{v})$ as the j-th dual-GSO vector, strictly shorter than the old dual-GSO vector $\mathbf{d}_j^\dagger$.

(c) *Call of Dual-DeepLLL*: In Steps 1 and 10 in Algorithm 3, we call Dual-DeepLLL to reduce every local block $\mathbf{B}_{[h,j]}$ before Dual-Enumeration. Since the dual basis $[\tau_j(\mathbf{d}_h), \ldots, \tau_j(\mathbf{d}_j)]$ of $\mathbf{B}_{[h,j]}$ is δ-DeepLLL-reduced, any dual basis vector $\mathbf{d}_i$ can not be found by Dual-Enumeration over $\mathbf{B}_{[h,j]}$ if we set $\delta \approx 1$ (we used $\delta = 0.99$ in our experiments). In other words, every short dual basis vector $\mathbf{d}_i$ is inserted into the dual basis $\mathbf{D}$ in Dual-DeepLLL. Like the primal DeepBKZ [26], this reduces the total number of calls of Dual-Enumeration.

Remark 2. Dual-DeepBKZ terminates if the dual-GSO vector $\mathbf{d}_j^\dagger$ is the shortest over the dual basis of the local block $\mathbf{B}_{[h,j]}$ for all $2 \leq j \leq n$ with $h = \max(j - \beta + 1, 1)$. Hence the dual basis of any output basis by Dual-DeepBKZ is (δ, β)-DeepBKZ-reduced, that is, the primal basis is (δ, β)-Dual-DeepBKZ-reduced. In a tour, Dual-DeepBKZ calls Dual-Enumeration over every block $\mathbf{B}_{[h,j]}$ backward from $j = n$ to 2. Hence, in processing of Dual-DeepBKZ, backward dual-GSO vectors $\mathbf{d}_j^\dagger$ become shorter, equivalently, backward GSO vectors $\mathbf{b}_j^*$ of the primal basis become *longer*. Conversely, forward GSO vectors $\mathbf{b}_j^*$ become shorter since $\mathrm{vol}(L) = \prod_{i=1}^n \|\mathbf{b}_i^*\|$ is constant (see right-side of Figs. 1 and 2 below).

4   Application to Solving the LWE Challenge

Since 2016, sample LWE instances have been published in the web page of [9] to test algorithms that solve the (search-)LWE problem proposed by Regev [19] (see also [6] for details on the LWE challenge). In this section, we apply both Dual-DeepBKZ (Algorithm 3) and DeepBKZ [26] for solving the LWE challenge, and report experimental results on their total running time.

4.1   The LWE Challenge and BDD Strategy

Here we describe the parameter setting of the LWE challenge [6,9], and present the BDD strategy [1, Sect. 4.2], which is useful to solve the LWE problem.

Parameter Setting of the LWE Challenge. Let n be a security parameter, q an odd prime modulus parameter, and $\chi = D_{\mathbb{Z},\sigma}$ denote the discrete Gaussian distribution over $\mathbb{Z}$ with mean 0 and standard deviation $\sigma > 0$. We let $\mathbb{Z}_q$ denote a set of representatives of integers modulo q in the interval $(-q/2, q/2)$, that is, $\mathbb{Z}_q = \mathbb{Z} \cap (-q/2, q/2)$ (this notation is not standard in mathematics, but seems specific in cryptography). The *search-LWE problem* with limited number m of LWE samples is to recover a secret vector $\mathbf{s} \in \mathbb{Z}_q^n$ from an LWE instance $(\mathbf{A}, \mathbf{b})$, where $\mathbf{A} = [\mathbf{a}_1, \ldots, \mathbf{a}_m]$ is an $n \times m$ matrix over $\mathbb{Z}_q$ and $\mathbf{b} = (b_1, \ldots, b_m)^\top$ is a vector of length m over $\mathbb{Z}_q$ with

$$\mathbf{b} \equiv \mathbf{A}^\top \mathbf{s} + \mathbf{e} \bmod q \tag{7}$$

for an error vector $\mathbf{e} = (e_1, \ldots, e_m)^\top \in \mathbb{Z}^m$ (i.e., it satisfies $b_i \equiv \langle \mathbf{a}_i, \mathbf{s} \rangle + e_i \bmod q$ for all $1 \leq i \leq m$). Here all entries of both $\mathbf{A}$ and $\mathbf{s}$ are uniformly random over $\mathbb{Z}_q$, while every entry of $\mathbf{e}$ is sampled from the distribution χ. In the LWE challenge [6,9], every LWE instance $(\mathbf{A}, \mathbf{b})$ is characterized by a pair (n, α) with $40 \leq n \leq 120$ and $0.005 \leq \alpha \leq 0.070$ (different from the notation in this paper, all vectors are represented in row format in the web page of [9]). Each pair (n, α) determines three parameters m, q, σ; (i) $m = n^2$. (ii) q is the smallest prime number exceeding m. (iii) $\sigma = \alpha q$.

BDD Strategy. This is to regard the search-LWE problem as the BDD problem [1, Sect. 4.2]. As seen from previous records in the web page of [9], the BDD strategy seems the most suitable for solving the LWE challenge among a number of strategies to solve the search-LWE problem (see [1,3] for strategies). Given an LWE instance $(\mathbf{A}, \mathbf{b})$ with parameters q, m, n, let

$$\Lambda_q(\mathbf{A}) := \left\{ \mathbf{x} \in \mathbb{Z}^m : \mathbf{x} \equiv \mathbf{A}^\top \mathbf{z} \bmod q \text{ for some } \mathbf{z} \in \mathbb{Z}_q^n \right\}$$

denote the m-dimensional q-ary lattice (see [17, Sect. 2] for q-ary lattices). We can regard $(\mathbf{A}, \mathbf{b})$ as a BDD instance over $\Lambda_q(\mathbf{A})$; We regard $\mathbf{b}$ as a target vector bounded in distance from the lattice vector $\mathbf{v} := \mathbf{A}^\top \mathbf{s} \in \Lambda_q(\mathbf{A})$. The

BDD strategy is successful if we could find the lattice vector $\mathbf{v}$ close to $\mathbf{b}$ with distance $\|\mathbf{b} - \mathbf{v}\|$ equal to $\|\mathbf{e}\|$, which is bounded by sizes of m and σ (we can easily recover the secret vector $\mathbf{s}$ from $\mathbf{v}$).

There are two approaches in the BDD strategy; (A) The *decoding approach* (or the *BDD approach*) [1, Sect. 5.4] is to find the lattice vector $\mathbf{v}$ over $\Lambda_q(\mathbf{A})$ using an approximate-CVP method such as Babai's nearest plane algorithm (see Subsect. 4.2 below). (B) The *embedding approach* [1, Sect. 5.5] reduces the BDD problem to unique-SVP [16, p. 191] by embedding $\mathbf{v}$ as a shortest lattice vector over a certain lattice (see Subsect. 4.3 below).

4.2 Decoding Approach and Dual-DeepBKZ

Here we adopt Dual-DeepBKZ in the decoding approach of the BDD strategy for solving the LWE challenge, and show several experimental results.

Procedures. Given an LWE instance $(\mathbf{A}, \mathbf{b})$ with parameters q, m, n. For the $n \times m$ matrix $\mathbf{A} = [\mathbf{a}_1, \dots, \mathbf{a}_m]$, we use only the first d vectors $\mathbf{a}_1, \dots, \mathbf{a}_d$ for $d \le m$ (more generally, we can extract d column vectors freely from $\mathbf{A}$). Suitable d shall be chosen in our experiments (see Table 1 below). Procedures of the decoding approach for recovering the secret vector $\mathbf{s} \in \mathbb{Z}_q^n$ are the following three steps:

1. For the sub-matrix $\mathbf{A}_d = [\mathbf{a}_1, \dots, \mathbf{a}_d]$ of $\mathbf{A}$, construct a $d \times (d + n)$ matrix

$$\mathbf{C} = \left(q\mathbf{I}_d \mid \mathbf{A}_d^\top \right).$$

   Note that the columns of $\mathbf{C}$ form a system of generators of the d-dimensional q-ary lattice $L := \Lambda_q(\mathbf{A}_d)$. Compute a basis $\mathbf{B}$ of L by performing Hermite normal form (HNF) or modified-LLL for $\mathbf{C}$ (see [8, Chap. 2] for details).
2. Reduce $\mathbf{B}$ by lattice basis reduction.
3. For the sub-vector $\mathbf{b}_d = (b_1, \dots, b_d)^\top$ of $\mathbf{b}$ of length d, it satisfies $\mathbf{b}_d \equiv \mathbf{B}\mathbf{z} + \mathbf{e}_d \bmod q$ for some $\mathbf{z} \in \mathbb{Z}^d$, where $\mathbf{e}_d$ denotes the sub-vector of the error vector $\mathbf{e} \in \mathbb{Z}^m$ of length d. Then solve the BDD instance $(\mathbf{B}, \mathbf{b}_d)$ over $L = \mathcal{L}(\mathbf{B})$ to recover $\mathbf{e}_d$. Since by (7) we have

$$\mathbf{b}_d \equiv \mathbf{A}_d^\top \mathbf{s} + \mathbf{e}_d \bmod q,$$

we can also recover the secret vector $\mathbf{s} \in \mathbb{Z}_q^n$ from the triple $(\mathbf{A}_d, \mathbf{b}_d, \mathbf{e}_d)$.

Our Implementation. We implemented the above procedures for solving the LWE challenge in C++ programs with the NTL library [22]. For Step 1, we used LLL in the NTL library to obtain a basis $\mathbf{B}$ of the lattice L. For Step 2, we used BKZ_FP with blocksize 20 (floating point implementation of BKZ) in the NTL library as a preprocessing, and then called Dual-DeepBKZ with blocksizes $\beta \ge 20$ to reduce $\mathbf{B}$. In particular, we used $\varepsilon = 20$ as a parameter of the insertion restriction for Dual-DeepLLL, a subroutine of Dual-DeepBKZ (see Remark 1 for the restriction). For Step 3, we adopted Liu-Nguyen's BDD enumeration [15] for the BDD instance $(\mathbf{B}, \mathbf{b}_d)$ to find the error vector $\mathbf{e}_d$ of length d. For a bounding function $R_1^2 \leq \cdots \leq R_d^2$, the BDD enumeration finds a lattice vector $\mathbf{v} \in \mathcal{L}(\mathbf{B})$ satisfying $\|\pi_{d+1-k}(\mathbf{v} - \mathbf{b})\| \leq R_k$ for all $1 \leq k \leq d$. For two parameters c and p, we set

$$R_i^2 = cR^2 \cdot \min\left\{\frac{i+p}{d}, 1\right\} \text{ for } 1 \leq i \leq d \tag{8}$$

with $R^2 = \sigma^2 d = (\alpha q)^2 d$, which is linear pruning extended by p. In our experiments, we fixed $p = 5$ and used $c \approx 1.0$ (note that $\|\mathbf{e}_d\|^2 \approx R^2$ since every entry of $\mathbf{e}_d$ should have been sampled from the distribution $\chi = D_{\mathbb{Z},\sigma}$).

For our experiments, we implemented Dual-DeepBKZ (Algorithm 3) and the BDD enumeration [15, Algorithm 4] in C++ programs with help of the NTL library. In Dual-DeepBKZ, we did not use any pruning technique [11] for Dual-Enumeration (namely, we used Dual-Enumeration with full enumeration setting). In our implementation, we used the int data type for the lattice basis $\mathbf{B}$, and the long double for its GSO information. We also used the gcc 6.4.0 compiler with option O3 -std=c++11. Furthermore, we used a single thread of a 64-bit PC with Intel Xeon CPU E3-1225 v5@3.30 GHz and 4.0 GB RAM.

Experimental Results. In Table 1, we summarize our experimental results on the total running time to solve several instances in the LWE challenge [6,9] by the decoding approach. In our experiments, for $\alpha = 0.005$, we set $d \approx 3n$ for $40 \leq n \leq 60$ to reduce a basis $\mathbf{B}$ effectively by Dual-DeepBKZ with blocksizes up to $\beta \approx 40$ (choice of suitable d depends on lattice basis reduction). For larger α, we used somewhat larger d than $3n$. Furthermore, we raised a blocksize of Dual-DeepBKZ one by one from 20 up to the β written in Table 1 so that the error vector $\mathbf{e}_d$ of length d is included in the range of extended linear pruning (8) of BDD enumeration for some $1.0 \leq c \leq 1.2$. In our experiments, we sampled a number of *pseudo error vectors* $\mathbf{e}_d'$ of length d from the distribution $\chi = D_{\mathbb{Z},\sigma}$, and verify whether most of $\mathbf{e}_d'$ satisfy $\|\pi_{d+1-k}(\mathbf{e}_d')\| \leq R_k$ for all $1 \leq k \leq d$ with bounding function $R_1^2 \leq \cdots \leq R_d^2$ given by (8). If so, we estimate that the target error vector $\mathbf{e}_d$ would also satisfy the same condition with high probability.

Comparison with [25]. At ACNS 2017, Xu et al. [25] reported their experimental results on solving almost the same LWE instances as in Table 1 by the decoding approach. They used BKZ in the fplll library [23] and their parallelized Liu-Nguyen's BDD enumeration [15] with extreme pruning. They chose d so that the running costs of lattice basis reduction and the BDD enumeration are almost equal in order to minimize the total running cost. In the following, we compare our results (Table 1) with their results [25, Table 2] for large LWE instances:

(i) For $(n, \alpha) = (40, 0.015)$, they used $d = 120$, and $\beta = 18$ for a blocksize of BKZ. It took 12 and 10 s respectively for BKZ and the BDD enumeration with extreme pruning, but it required 819 trials to find the error vector $\mathbf{e}_d$ of length d (extreme pruning is very fast, but the probability to find the desired vector is very low). According to their results [25, Table 2], it took 18403 s $\approx$ 5.1 h ($> (12 + 10) \times 819$ s) in total for solving this LWE instance

Table 1. Total running time to solve several instances in the LWE challenge [6,9] by the decoding approach (In a preprocessing, we used BKZ_FP with blocksize 20 in the NTL library [22]. We also used Dual-DeepBKZ (Algorithm 3) with blocksizes up to β to obtain a reduced lattice basis, and the BDD enumeration [15, Algorithm 4] with extended linear pruning (8) to recover the error vector e_d of length d)

n	α	d	BKZ_FP	Dual-DeepBKZ	BDD Enum.	Total time
40	0.005	120	6 s	5 s ($\beta = 20$)	< 0.01 s ($c = 1.2$)	11 s
	0.010	130	9 s	4 s ($\beta = 20$)	0.03 s ($c = 1.0$)	13 s
	0.015	140	15 s	8,076 s ($\beta = 37$)	240 s ($c = 1.0$)	8,331 s $\approx$ 2.3 h
45	0.005	140	13 s	31 s ($\beta = 20$)	< 0.01 s ($c = 1.0$)	44 s
	0.010	140	14 s	453 s ($\beta = 30$)	476 s ($c = 1.1$)	943 s $\approx$ 15.7 m
50	0.005	150	18 s	29 s ($\beta = 20$)	0.02 s ($c = 1.2$)	47 s
55	0.005	160	19 s	383 s ($\beta = 28$)	1.95 s ($c = 1.1$)	404 s $\approx$ 6.7 m
60	0.005	180	34 s	44,394 s ($\beta = 36$)	1,001 s ($c = 1.1$)	45,429 s $\approx$ 12.6 h

(over a single thread of a desktop with Intel Core i7@3.60 GHz CPU and 32 GB 1600 MHz DDR3 memory). In contrast, we used $d = 140$, and up to $\beta = 37$ for blocksizes of Dual-DeepBKZ. It took about 15, 8076, and 240 s respectively for BKZ_FP (with blocksize 20), Dual-DeepBKZ and the BDD enumeration with extended linear pruning (8) for $c = 1.0$ (cf., $c = 0.8$ was used in [25] for efficiency). Since only one trial is required in our case, it took $8,331$ s $\approx$ 2.3 h in total, about 2.2 times faster than [25].

(ii) For $(n, \alpha) = (60, 0.005)$, Xu et al. [25] used $d = 140$. It took about 27 and 24 hours respectively for BKZ with blocksize $\beta = 28$ and the BDD enumeration with extreme pruning (they used 720 threads on the Amazon EC2 platform, but the running time is converted over a single thread). Therefore it took about 51 h in total for solving this LWE instance. In contrast, we used $d = 180$, and up to $\beta = 36$ for blocksizes of Dual-DeepBKZ. It took 34, 44394, and 1001 s respectively for BKZ_FP (with blocksize 20), Dual-DeepBKZ, and the BDD enumeration with extended linear pruning (8) for $c = 1.1$ (cf., $c = 0.8$ was used in [25]). Therefore it took about $45,429$ s $\approx$ 12.6 h in total, about 4.0 times faster than [25].

Cost of full BDD Enumeration. Here we give experimental evidences that Dual-DeepBKZ can reduce the BDD enumeration cost more efficiently than BKZ for LWE instances. The cost of the BDD enumeration over a basis $\mathbf{B} = [\mathbf{b}_1, \ldots, \mathbf{b}_d]$ with full enumeration setting $R_1^2 = \cdots = R_d^2 = R^2$ is approximately given by

$$N = \sum_{k=1}^{d} H_k \text{ with } H_k = \frac{V_k(R)}{\prod_{i=d+1-k}^{d} \|\mathbf{b}_i^*\|} \text{ for } 1 \leq k \leq d, \tag{9}$$

where $V_k(R)$ denotes the volume of the k-dimensional ball with radius $R > 0$ [15, Sect. 4]. In Figs. 1 and 2, we show experimental results on transition of the cost

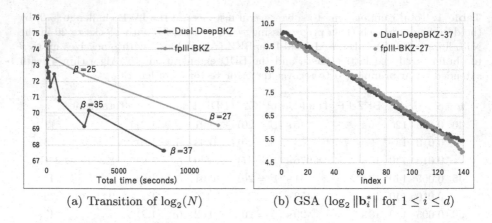

(a) Transition of $\log_2(N)$ (b) GSA ($\log_2 \|\mathbf{b}_i^*\|$ for $1 \leq i \leq d$)

Fig. 1. Transition of $\log_2(N)$ and GSA by Dual-DeepBKZ and the fplll implementation of BKZ with blocksizes $\beta \geq 20$ for the basis $\mathbf{B} = [\mathbf{b}_1, \ldots, \mathbf{b}_d]$ in the decoding approach for the LWE challenge by $(n, \alpha) = (40, 0.015)$ with $d = 140$, where N denotes the cost of full BDD enumeration (9) for squared radius $R^2 = (\alpha q)^2 d$

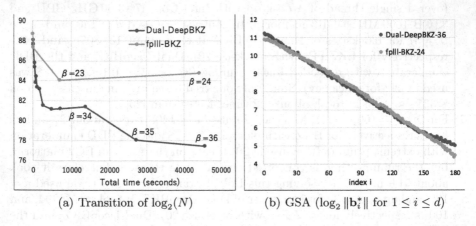

(a) Transition of $\log_2(N)$ (b) GSA ($\log_2 \|\mathbf{b}_i^*\|$ for $1 \leq i \leq d$)

Fig. 2. Same as Fig. 1, but for $(n, \alpha) = (60, 0.005)$ with $d = 180$

of the full BDD enumeration with $R^2 = (\alpha q)^2 d$ by Dual-DeepBKZ and the fplll implementation of BKZ for the basis $\mathbf{B}$ in the decoding approach for large LWE instances of $(n, \alpha) = (40, 0.015)$ and $(60, 0.005)$:

- As seen from left-side of Figs. 1 and 2, for the same blocksize β, Dual-DeepBKZ and the fplll implementation of BKZ might reduce the cost N by the same degree. However, BKZ requires a huge amount of time even for small blocksizes $\beta \approx 25$. In other words, Dual-DeepBKZ runs much faster than BKZ for blocksizes $\beta \geq 25$, and hence Dual-DeepBKZ reduces the cost N more effectively than BKZ within the same time (since the q-ary lattice

$\Lambda_q(\mathbf{A}_d)$ includes many short lattice vectors of length q, it might take a long time to run BKZ over the lattice).

- In right-side of Figs. 1 and 2, we present the GSA (Geometric Series Assumption [20]) shape of bases $\mathbf{B}$ output by Dual-DeepBKZ and BKZ with different blocksizes. As described in Remark 2, backward GSO vectors by Dual-DeepBKZ are longer than by BKZ (conversely, forward GSO vectors by BKZ are shorter). We see from the form of (9) that such GSA shape can reduce the cost N of full BDD enumeration effectively.

4.3 Embedding Approach and DeepBKZ [26]

In this subsection, we adopt DeepBKZ [26] in the embedding approach for solving the LWE challenge, and show several experimental results. While Dual-DeepBKZ is useful to reduce the BDD enumeration cost, DeepBKZ is useful to find a short lattice vector, and it is suitable for the embedding approach.

Procedures. Given an LWE instance $(\mathbf{A}, \mathbf{b})$ with parameters q, m, n. For the $n \times m$ matrix $\mathbf{A} = [\mathbf{a}_1, \dots, \mathbf{a}_m]$, we use only the first d vectors $\mathbf{a}_1, \dots, \mathbf{a}_d$ for $d \le m$ as in the decoding approach (we can extract d column vectors freely from $\mathbf{A}$). Procedures of the embedding approach are the following two steps:

1. As in Step 1 of the decoding approach, from the sub-matrix $\mathbf{A}_d = [\mathbf{a}_1, \dots, \mathbf{a}_d]$ of $\mathbf{A}$, compute a basis $\mathbf{B}$ of the d-dimensional q-ary lattice $\Lambda_q(\mathbf{A}_d)$. Furthermore, for the sub-vector $\mathbf{b}_d = (b_1, \dots, b_d)^\top$ of $\mathbf{b}$ of length d, construct a $(d+1) \times (d+1)$ matrix

$$\mathbf{T} = \begin{pmatrix} \mathbf{B} & \mathbf{b}_d \\ \mathbf{0}_d & 1 \end{pmatrix},$$

where let $\mathbf{0}_d$ denote the row vector of length d with all entries 0. Let $M := \mathcal{L}(\mathbf{T})$ be the lattice spanned by the columns of $\mathbf{T}$, and its dimension is $d+1$. For the error vector $\mathbf{e}_d$ of length d, the lattice M includes very short vectors $\pm \mathbf{w}$ where we set

$$\mathbf{w} := \begin{pmatrix} \mathbf{e}_d \\ 1 \end{pmatrix} \equiv \begin{pmatrix} \mathbf{b}_d \\ 1 \end{pmatrix} - \begin{pmatrix} \mathbf{A}_d^\top \mathbf{s} \\ 0 \end{pmatrix} \bmod q \in \mathbb{Z}_q^{d+1}.$$

2. Reduce $\mathbf{T}$ by lattice basis reduction to find short lattice vectors $\pm \mathbf{w} \in M$. Then we can recover $\mathbf{e}_d$, and hence $\mathbf{s}$ as in Step 3 of the decoding approach.

Our Implementation. For Step 1, we used LLL in the NTL libary to obtain a basis $\mathbf{T}$ of the lattice M. For Step 2, we used BKZ_FP with blocksize 20 in a preprocessing, and called DeepBKZ [26] with blocksizes $\beta \ge 20$ to reduce $\mathbf{T}$. We implemented DeepBKZ [26, Algorithm 3] in C++ programs. Our implementation for DeepBKZ is almost the same as in the decoding approach for Dual-DeepBKZ. In particular, we did not use any pruning [11] for SVP enumeration over every local block. As in Dual-DeepBKZ, we used the insertion restriction with parameter $\varepsilon = 20$ for DeepLLL [21], a main subroutine in DeepBKZ.

Table 2. Total running time to solve the same LWE instances as in Table 1 by the embedding approach (We used the same d as in Table 1. In a preprocessing, we used BKZ_FP with blocksize 20 in the NTL library [22]. We used DeepBKZ [26] with blocksizes up to β to find very short lattice vectors $\pm \mathbf{w} \in M$)

n	α	d	BKZ_FP	DeepBKZ [26]	Total time
40	0.005	120	7 s	1 s ($\beta = 20$)	8 s
	0.010	130	9 s	13 s ($\beta = 23$)	22 s
	0.015	140	15 s	74 s ($\beta = 25$)	89 s
45	0.005	140	13 s	4 s ($\beta = 20$)	17 s
	0.010	140	15 s	838 s ($\beta = 28$)	853 s $\approx$ 14.2 m
50	0.005	150	18 s	13 s ($\beta = 22$)	31 s
55	0.005	160	19 s	79 s ($\beta = 25$)	98 s
60	0.005	180	34 s	2,152 s ($\beta = 26$)	2,186 s $\approx$ 36.4 m

Experimental Results. In Table 2, we summarize our experimental results on the total running time to solve the same LWE instances as in Table 1 by the embedding approach. We used the same d as in Table 1 (for such d, lattice vectors $\pm \mathbf{w}$ are the shortest over the lattice M). In our experiments, we raised a blocksize of DeepBKZ one by one from 20 up to the β in Table 2.

(i) For $(n, \alpha) = (40, 0.015)$, we used DeepBKZ with blocksizes up to $\beta = 25$. It took about 15 and 74 s for BKZ_FP and DeepBKZ respectively, and only 89 s in total.

(ii) For $(n, \alpha) = (60, 0.005)$, we used DeepBKZ with blocksizes up to $\beta = 26$. It took about 34 and 2152 s for BKZ_FP and DeepBKZ respectively, and 2186 s $\approx$ 36.4 min in total.

Compared to Table 1, the embedding approach (Table 2) is much faster for these LWE instances. This seems due to the difference of approaches (in our experiments for the decoding approach, DeepBKZ was slower than Dual-DeepBKZ).

Remark 3. In Wang et al. [24] estimated the average and the minimum runtime of progressive-BKZ [2] in the embedding approach for solving every instance (n, α) of the LWE challenge with $\alpha = 0.005$, by extrapolating their experimental data over Intel Xeon CPU E5-2697 v2@2.70 GHz with 24 cores (over-clocked to 3.50 GHz and hyperthreads to 48 threads);

$$\begin{cases} \log_2(\text{Average Runtime (seconds)}) = 0.0153n^2 - 1.17n + 27.6, \\ \log_2(\text{Minimum Runtime (seconds)}) = 0.00584n^2 - 0.208n + 2.21, \end{cases} \quad (10)$$

which are converted over a single thread [24, Sect. 4 and Fig. 2]. From their estimates (10) for $n = 60$, we have $2^{12.48}$ s on average and $2^{10.754}$ on minimum. In contrast, from Table 2, DeepBKZ required $2186 \approx 2^{11.094}$ s in our experiments. This shows that DeepBKZ is as competitive as progressive-BKZ. But for large $n \geq 65$, DeepBKZ required a larger amount of time than progressive-BKZ in our experiments (this might be due to our implementation for such large cases with lattice dimensions $d \geq 200$).

5 Conclusion

In this paper, we have reported experimental results on the total running time for solving several instances in the LWE challenge [6,9] (see Tables 1 and 2). We called Dual-DeepBKZ (Algorithm 3) and DeepBKZ [26] in the decoding approach and the embedding approach [1, Sects. 5.4 and 5.5], respectively. Our results were obtained over a general-purpose 64-bit PC (Intel Xeon CPU E3-1225 v5@3.30 GHz and 4.0 GB RAM) with non-optimal implementation in C++ programs with the NTL library [22]. We hope that our results would be a benchmark to develop new reduction algorithms for solving the LWE problem [19].

Acknowledgments. This work was supported by JST CREST Grant Number JPMJCR14D6, Japan. This work was also supported by JSPS KAKENHI Grant Number 16H02830.

References

1. Albrecht, M.R., Player, R., Scott, S.: On the concrete hardness of learning with errors. J. Math. Cryptol. **9**(3), 169–203 (2015)
2. Aono, Y., Wang, Y., Hayashi, T., Takagi, T.: Improved progressive BKZ algorithms and their precise cost estimation by sharp simulator. In: Fischlin, M., Coron, J.-S. (eds.) EUROCRYPT 2016. LNCS, vol. 9665, pp. 789–819. Springer, Heidelberg (2016). https://doi.org/10.1007/978-3-662-49890-3_30. http://www2.nict.go.jp/security/pbkzcode/
3. Bindel, N., Buchmann, J., Göpfert, F., Schmidt, M.: Estimation of the hardness of the learning with errors problem with a restricted number of samples, IACR ePrint 2017/140 https://eprint.iacr.org/2017/140 (2017)
4. Blömer, J.: Closest vectors, successive minima, and dual HKZ-bases of lattices. In: Montanari, U., Rolim, J.D.P., Welzl, E. (eds.) ICALP 2000. LNCS, vol. 1853, pp. 248–259. Springer, Heidelberg (2000). https://doi.org/10.1007/3-540-45022-X_22
5. Bremner, M.R.: Lattice Basis Reduction: An Introduction to the LLL Algorithm and Its Applications. CRC Press, Boca Raton (2011)
6. Buchmann, J., Büscher, N., Göpfert, F., Katzenbeisser, S., Krämer, J., Micciancio, D., Siim, S., van Vredendaal, C., Walter, M.: Creating cryptographic challenges using multi-party computation: the LWE challenge. In: International Workshop on ASIA Public-Key Cryptography-ASIAPKC 2016, pp. 11–20. ACM (2016)
7. Chen, Y., Nguyen, P.Q.: BKZ 2.0: better lattice security estimates. In: Lee, D.H., Wang, X. (eds.) ASIACRYPT 2011. LNCS, vol. 7073, pp. 1–20. Springer, Heidelberg (2011). https://doi.org/10.1007/978-3-642-25385-0_1
8. Cohen, H.: A Course in Computational Algebraic Number Theory. Graduate Texts in Mathematics, vol. 138. Springer, Heidelberg (1993). https://doi.org/10.1007/978-3-662-02945-9
9. T. U. Darmstadt, Lattice Challenge. http://www.latticechallenge.org/svp-challenge/

10. Gama, N., Nguyen, P.Q.: Finding short lattice vectors within Mordell's inequality. In: Symposium on the Theory of Computing, STOC 2008, pp. 207–216. ACM (2008)
11. Gama, N., Nguyen, P.Q., Regev, O.: Lattice enumeration using extreme pruning. In: Gilbert, H. (ed.) EUROCRYPT 2010. LNCS, vol. 6110, pp. 257–278. Springer, Heidelberg (2010). https://doi.org/10.1007/978-3-642-13190-5_13
12. Hanrot, G., Pujol, X., Stehlé, D.: Analyzing blockwise lattice algorithms using dynamical systems. In: Rogaway, P. (ed.) CRYPTO 2011. LNCS, vol. 6841, pp. 447–464. Springer, Heidelberg (2011). https://doi.org/10.1007/978-3-642-22792-9_25
13. Koy, H.: Primal/duale segment-reduktion von Gitterbasen, Lecture Universität Frankfurt (2000)
14. Lenstra, A.K., Lenstra, H.W., Lovász, L.: Factoring polynomials with rational coefficients. Math. Ann. **261**(4), 515–534 (1982)
15. Liu, M., Nguyen, P.Q.: Solving BDD by enumeration: an update. In: Dawson, E. (ed.) CT-RSA 2013. LNCS, vol. 7779, pp. 293–309. Springer, Heidelberg (2013). https://doi.org/10.1007/978-3-642-36095-4_19
16. Micciancio D., Goldwasser, S.: Complexity of Lattice Problems: A Cryptographic Perspective. Springer Science & Business Media, Heidelberg (2012). https://doi.org/10.1007/978-1-4615-0897-7
17. Micciancio, D., Regev, O.: Lattice-based cryptography. In: Bernstein, D.J., Buchmann, J., Dahmen, E. (eds.) Post-Quantum Cryptography, pp. 147–191. Springer, Heidelberg (2009). https://doi.org/10.1007/978-3-540-88702-7_5
18. Micciancio, D., Walter, M.: Practical, predictable lattice basis reduction. In: Fischlin, M., Coron, J.-S. (eds.) EUROCRYPT 2016. LNCS, vol. 9665, pp. 820–849. Springer, Heidelberg (2016). https://doi.org/10.1007/978-3-662-49890-3_31
19. Regev, O.: On lattices, learning with errors, random linear codes, and cryptography. In: Symposium on the Theory of Computing, STOC 2005, pp. 84–93. ACM (2005)
20. Schnorr, C.P.: Lattice reduction by random sampling and birthday methods. In: Alt, H., Habib, M. (eds.) STACS 2003. LNCS, vol. 2607, pp. 145–156. Springer, Heidelberg (2003). https://doi.org/10.1007/3-540-36494-3_14
21. Schnorr, C.P., Euchner, M.: Lattice basis reduction: improved practical algorithms and solving subset sum problems. Math. Program. **66**, 181–199 (1994)
22. Shoup, V.: NTL: A Library for doing Number Theory. http://www.shoup.net/ntl/
23. The FPLLL development team, fplll, a lattice reduction library (2016). https://github.com/fplll/fplll
24. Wang, Y., Aono, Y., Takagi, T.: An experimental study of Kannan's embedding technique for the search LWE problem. In: International Conference on Information and Communication Security, ICICS 2017 (2017, to appear)
25. Xu, R., Yeo, S.L., Fukushima, K., Takagi, T., Seo, H., Kiyomoto, S., Henricksen, M.: An experimental study of the BDD approach for the search LWE problem. In: Gollmann, D., Miyaji, A., Kikuchi, H. (eds.) ACNS 2017. LNCS, vol. 10355, pp. 253–272. Springer, Cham (2017). https://doi.org/10.1007/978-3-319-61204-1_13
26. Yamaguchi, J., Yasuda, M.: Explicit formula for Gram-Schmidt vectors in LLL with deep insertions and its applications. In: Kaczorowski, J., Pieprzyk, J., Pomykała, J. (eds.) NuTMiC 2017. LNCS, vol. 10737, pp. 142–160. Springer, Heidelberg (2017). https://doi.org/10.1007/978-3-319-76620-1_9

Unified Formulas for Some Deterministic Almost-Injective Encodings into Hyperelliptic Curves

Michel Seck$^{(\boxtimes)}$ and Nafissatou Diarra

Department of Mathematics and Computer Science,
Cheikh Anta Diop University, Dakar, Senegal
{michel.seck,nafissatou.diarra}@ucad.edu.sn

Abstract. Recently, efficient deterministic and invertible encodings on some hyperelliptic curves in genus 1 and 2 using the technique in Elligator 2 (ACM CCS 2013) have been proposed. We have successfully generalized their encodings for hyperelliptic curves of genus 3, 4 and 5. We have found unified formulas (using Mersenne numbers) for the encodings into the hyperelliptic curves of genus $g \leq 5$: $\mathbb{H}_g : y^2 = f_g(x) = x^{(2g+1)} + a_{(2g-1)}x^{(2g-1)} + a_{(2g-3)}x^{(2g-3)} + \ldots + a_1 x + a_0$. We have conjectured that our method works on arbitrary genus.

Keywords: Deterministic encoding · Injective encoding
Elliptic curves-based cryptography · Hyperelliptic curves · Elligator
Random bit-string

1 Introduction

For the construction of cryptographic protocols or schemes [2,4] in (hyper)elliptic curves-based cryptography, it is sometimes necessary to be able to represent a bit-string as a point of an (hyper) elliptic curve [10,12,14]. In Elligator 2 (designed by Bernstein et al.: ACM CCS 2013 [1]), uniform elliptic curves-points can be represented by uniform random strings of bits. Many authors have studied the problem of designing deterministic encodings into (hyper) elliptic curves. In the last decade, many deterministic encodings have been proposed for certain families of elliptic curves and hyperelliptic curves.

- In 2006, Shallue and van de Woestijne [15] published the first type of encoding function to ordinary elliptic curves (curves given by an equation of the form E $: y^2 = x^3 + ax + b$). Ulas [16], in 2007, generalized and simplified the encoding of Shallue and van de Woestijne by encoding in the curves $C : y^2 = x^n + ax + b$ and $C' : y^2 = x^n + ax^2 + bx$. They were the first to publish an encoding to a certain family of hyperelliptic curves in any genus.
- At CRYPTO 2009, Icart [8] defined a deterministic encoding function into the elliptic curve $E : y^2 = x^3 + ax + b$ over finite fields $\mathbb{F}_q$ such that $q \equiv 2 \mod 3$.

© Springer International Publishing AG, part of Springer Nature 2018
A. Joux et al. (Eds.): AFRICACRYPT 2018, LNCS 10831, pp. 183–202, 2018.
https://doi.org/10.1007/978-3-319-89339-6_11

Kammerer et al. [9] have introduced in 2010 a series of new encodings based on same principles as Icart's function, namely solving curve equations in radicals. They proposed an encoding into the Hessian curve $E : x^3 + y^3 + 1 = 3dxy, d \neq 1$ over $\mathbb{F}_q$ and the hyperelliptic curve $H_{1,a,b} : y^2 = (x^3 + 3ax + 2)^2 + 8bx^3$ over $\mathbb{F}_q$ with $q \equiv 2 \mod 3$.

- In 2013, Fouque et al. [5] proposed a new, essentially optimal geometric construction for a large class of curves like the hyperelliptic curve $H_d^\lambda : y^2 = \lambda ax^5 + (c^2 + 1/c^2)x^3 + x$ over $\mathbb{F}_q$. In the same year, Bernstein et al. [1] proposed two encodings namely Elligator 1 and Elligator 2. In Elligator 1, they introduced an encoding into the Edwards curve $E : y^2 + x^2 = 1 + dx^2y^2$ over $\mathbb{F}_q$, and in Elligator 2, they proposed an encoding into the curve $E : y^2 = x^3 + Ax^2 + Bx$ with $AB(A^2 - 4B) \neq 0$ over $\mathbb{F}_q$ where $q = p^n, p > 2$.

- In 2015, He et al. [7] proposed two deterministic encodings from $\mathbb{F}_q$ to generalized Huff curves. Yu et al. [11], in 2016, also proposed a deterministic encoding from a finite field $\mathbb{F}_q$ to a twisted Edwards curve E when $q \equiv 2 \mod 3$.

- In 2017, at Africacrypt-2017, Seck et al. [3] have proposed three encoding functions into three different families of hyperelliptic curves by using the technique in Elligator 2 of Bernstein et al. [1]. They showed that one can use their encodings to design indifferentiable and deterministic hash functions into the Jacobian of certain families of hyperelliptic curves using the result of Farashahi et al. [6].

Contributions: The main results of this paper are based on the work of Bernstein et al. [1] in Elligator 2 and of Seck et al. [3].

Our first contribution is the construction of four deterministic almost-injective encoding functions $\psi_i : \mathcal{R}_i \subset \mathbb{F}_q \to \mathbb{H}_i$ for $i = 1, 3, 4, 5$, where:

$$\mathbb{H}_1 : y^2 = f_1(x) = x^3 + a_1 x + a_0;$$

$$\mathbb{H}_3 : y^2 = f_3(x) = x^7 + a_5 x^5 + a_3 x^3 + a_1 x + a_0;$$

$$\mathbb{H}_4 : y^2 = f_4(x) = x^9 + a_7 x^7 + a_5 x^5 + a_3 x^3 + a_1 x + a_0;$$

$$\mathbb{H}_5 : y^2 = f_5(x) = x^{11} + a_9 x^9 + a_7 x^7 + a_5 x^5 + a_3 x^3 + a_1 x + a_0.$$

Their almost-injectivity means that any point in the co-domain $\mathbb{H}_g$ have exactly two pre-images $(r, -r)$ in the domain $\mathbb{F}_q$. Note that in case q is a prime, one can restrict the domain to $\{0, \ldots, (q-1)/2\}$ in order to have an injective encoding for each $\mathbb{H}_g$. We show that one can invert these encodings under suitable conditions.

Our second contribution is an unified formula of the above encodings. We design a deterministic almost-injective encoding function $\psi_g : \mathcal{R}_g \subset \mathbb{F}_q \to \mathbb{H}_g$ where g is a nonzero integer less than or equal to five. This encoding generalizes the encoding in [3] $\psi_2 : \mathcal{R}_2 \subset \mathbb{F}_q \to \mathbb{H}_2$ where $\mathbb{H}_2 : y^2 = f_2(x) = x^5 + a_3 x^3 + a_1 x + a_0$ and our four encoding functions $\psi_i, i = 1, 3, 4, 5$.

Note that all these encodings depend on a parameter s that satisfies the second degree equation $\alpha_g s^2 + \beta_g s - \gamma_g = 0$ where α_g, β_g and γ_g only depend on the genus g of the hyperelliptic curve $\mathbb{H}_g$. The main motivation of the construction of the encoding ψ_5 is that after encoding into the hyperelliptic curves $\mathbb{H}_i$ for $i = 3, 4$, we note that $\alpha_2 = 3$ is prime, $\alpha_3 = 31$ is prime and $\alpha_4 = 127$ is also a prime integer. We first conjectured that α_g is prime for any genus $g \geq 2$. Unfortunately $\alpha_5 = 511$ is not prime. We remark that $\alpha_g = 2^{2g-1} - 1$ is a Mersenne number for $g \in \{1, 2, 3, 4, 5\}$.

Based on these constructions, we conjectured that our method can be extended for arbitrary genus g even if for cryptography use in case of Discrete Logarithm Problem (DLP), one must restrict to $g \leq 4$. So our encoding is only for theoretical interest for $g \geq 5$. Therefore the importance of our results lies more on the theoretical side in case of hyperelliptic curves-based on DLP.

Organization of the paper: This paper is organised as follows.

In Sect. 2: We give some preliminaries such as definition of the square root function and of a quadratic character in finite fields, and some results from the encoding into the hyperelliptic curve $\mathbb{H}_2$ of genus 2 of Seck *et al.* [3].

In Sect. 3: We give our new encodings over the hyperelliptic curves $\mathbb{H}_i$, $i = 1, 3, 4, 5$. We show in this section under what conditions our encodings are invertible.

In Sect. 4: We give a generalization of all encoding functions into the hyperelliptic curves $\mathbb{H}_i$, $i = 1, 2, 3, 4, 5$. And we conclude in Sect. 5.

In the **Appendix**, we give an implementation of our unified encoding using the Sage computer-algebra system [13].

2 Preliminaries

2.1 Square Root Function

Let $\mathbb{F}_q$ be the finite field of q elements with $q \equiv 3 \mod 4$, and set $A = \mathbb{F}_q^2 = \{x^2,\ x \in \mathbb{F}_q\}$. Define the square root function $\sqrt{\cdot}$ on A as follows:

$$\sqrt{\cdot} : A \to \mathbb{F}_q : a \mapsto \sqrt{a} = a^{(q+1)/4}$$

Then $\sqrt{a}$ is called the **principal square root of** a. Also note that if q is an odd prime, one can take $\sqrt{A} = \{0, 1, \ldots, (q-1)/2\}$.

2.2 Quadratic Character

Fix a prime power $q \equiv 3 \mod 4$. We say that a in the finite field $\mathbb{F}_q$ is a quadratic residue, if a is a square in $\mathbb{F}_q$ i.e. if there is $m \in \mathbb{F}_q$ such that $a = m^2$. One then defines the quadratic character as follows:

$$\chi(a) = \left(\frac{a}{q}\right) = \begin{cases} 0, & \text{if } a = 0 \text{ in } \mathbb{F}_q \\ 1, & \text{if } a \text{ is a nonzero square} \\ -1, & \text{if } a \text{ is not a square.} \end{cases}$$

More generally, $\chi(a) = a^{\frac{q-1}{2}}$, $\chi(am) = \chi(a)\chi(m)$, $\chi(\frac{1}{a}) = \chi(a) = \frac{1}{\chi(a)}$ if $a \neq 0$. If a is a square then $a^{\frac{q+1}{4}}$ is a square root of a, precisely the principal square root of a and its square is $a^{\frac{q+1}{2}} = \chi(a)a = a$. Any square root m of a satisfies $m = \chi(m)a^{\frac{q+1}{4}}$.

2.3   An Almost-Injective Encoding on $\mathbb{H}_2$

Let us recall some results of Seck *et al.* [3] about injective encoding on a class of hyperelliptic curves of genus 2.

Let $\mathbb{F}_q$ be a finite field with $\mathrm{char}(\mathbb{F}_q) = p \neq 2, 5$, $q = p^n$ is an odd prime power. We assume that $q \equiv 7 \mod 8$, then 2 is a square.

Let $s \in \mathbb{F}_q^*$ such that $7s^2 + 20s - 100 = 0$:

- If $p \neq 7$ and $q \equiv 7 \mod 8$, we have $\Delta_s = 3200 = 2 \times 4^2 \times 10^2$ which is a square, then $s = \dfrac{-10 \pm 20\sqrt{2}}{7}$.
- If $p = 7$ and $q \equiv 7 \mod 8$, then $s = 5$.

Let $w \in \mathbb{F}_q^*$ be an arbitrary parameter. Let $\mathbb{H}_2 : y^2 = f_2(x) = x^5 + a_3 x^3 + a_1 x + a_0$, with $a_3 = sw^2$, $a_1 = \dfrac{sw^4}{2}$, $a_0 = \dfrac{s - 10}{10} w^5$ be an hyperelliptic curve of genus 2 over $\mathbb{F}_q$ with the previous conditions on q. Let u be a parameter such that $\chi(u) = -1$ and define the set $\mathcal{R}_2 = \{r \in \mathbb{F}_q^*, f_2([ur^2(-50 - 35s) - 1]) \neq 0\}$.

(**Algorithm 3** in [3])
Input: The hyperelliptic curve $\mathbb{H}_2$, an element $r \in \mathcal{R}_2$
Output: A point (x, y) on $\mathbb{H}_2$
$v := w[ur^2(-50 - 35s) - 1];$
$\varepsilon := \chi(v^5 + a_3 v^3 + a_1 v + a_0);$
$x := \dfrac{1 + \varepsilon}{2} v + \dfrac{1 - \varepsilon}{2}\left(\dfrac{w(-v + w)}{v + w}\right);$
$y := -\varepsilon\sqrt{x^5 + a_3 x^3 + a_1 x + a_0};$
return (x, y).

Algorithm 1. Genus2-Encoding1

Definition 1. *(Definition 2 in* [3] *) In the situation of Algorithm 1, the encoding function for the hyperelliptic curve $\mathbb{H}_2$ is the function $\psi_2 : \mathcal{R}_2 \to \mathbb{H}_2 : r \mapsto \psi_2(r) = (x, y)$.*

Theorem 1. *(Theorem 3 in* [3]*) Algorithm 1 computes a deterministic almost-injective encoding $\psi_2 : \mathcal{R}_2 \to \mathbb{H}_2 : r \mapsto \psi_2(r) = (x, y)$, in time $\mathcal{O}(\log^{2 + o(1)} q)$, where $Z_2 = \mathbb{F}_q \setminus \mathcal{R}_2$ is a subset of $\mathbb{F}_q$ of at most 10 elements.*

The inverse of the encoding function is given by the following theorem.

Theorem 2. *(Theorem 4 in* [3]*) In the situation of Theorem 1 and Definition 1, we have the following.*

1. *Let (x, y) be a point of the hyperelliptic curve $\mathbb{H}_2$, then $(x, y) \in \mathrm{Im}(\psi_2)$ if and only if $uw(x + w)(-50 - 35s)$ is a nonzero square in $\mathbb{F}_q$.*
2. *Let $(x, y) \in \mathrm{Im}(\psi_2)$ and define $\bar{r}$ as follows:*
   $\bar{r} = \sqrt{\dfrac{x + w}{uw(-50 - 35s)}}$ *if $y \notin \sqrt{\mathbb{F}_q^2}$ and $\bar{r} = \sqrt{\dfrac{2w}{u(x + w)(-50 - 35s)}}$ if $y \in \sqrt{\mathbb{F}_q^2}$.*
   Then $\bar{r} \in \mathcal{R}_2$ and $\psi_1(\bar{r}) = (x, y)$.

3   New Almost-Injective and Invertible Encodings into Hyperelliptic Curves

In this section, we propose four almost-injective encoding functions into four families of hyperelliptic curves $\mathbb{H}_3, \mathbb{H}_4, \mathbb{H}_5$ and $\mathbb{H}_1$ using the approach of Bernstein et al. [1] in Elligator 2 for elliptic curves. We use the same approach as Seck et al. ([3] Sect. 3) in order to find unified formulas of our encodings and those of Seck et al. [3]. As mentioned in [3], our new encodings have the same asymptotic complexity, namely $\mathcal{O}(\log^{2+\circ(1)} q)$.

We suppose, in this section, that

- $\mathbb{F}_q$ is a finite field with $\mathrm{char}(\mathbb{F}_q) = p$ and $q = p^n$ is an odd prime power. We assume that $q \equiv 7 \mod 8$, then 2 is a square;
- $w \in \mathbb{F}_q^*$ is an arbitrary parameter;
- $u \in \mathbb{F}_q$ is a parameter such that $\chi(u) = -1$.

3.1   An Almost-Injective Encoding in Genus $g = 3$

In this subsection, we propose an almost-injective encoding into hyperelliptic curves of genus 3.

Assume that $\mathrm{char}(\mathbb{F}_q) = p \neq 2, 3, 7$. Let $s \in \mathbb{F}_q^*$ such that $31s^2 + 42s - 441 = 0$:

- If $p \neq 31$ and $q \equiv 7 \mod 8$, we have $\Delta_s = 56448 = 2^7 \times 3^2 \times 7^2$ which is a square, then $s = \frac{-21 \pm 84\sqrt{2}}{31}$.
- If $p = 31$ and $q \equiv 7 \mod 8$, then $s = \frac{21}{?}$.

Let $\mathbb{H}_3 : y^2 = f_3(x) = x^7 + a_5 x^5 + a_3 x^3 + a_1 x + a_0$, with $a_5 = sw^2$, $a_1 = \frac{sw^6}{3}$, $a_3 = \frac{5sw^4}{3}$ and $a_0 = \frac{s-21}{21} w^7$, be an hyperelliptic curve of genus 3 over $\mathbb{F}_q$ with the previous conditions on q. Define the set $\mathcal{R}_3 = \{r \in \mathbb{F}_q^*, f_3(w[ur^2(-651s - 441) - 1]) \neq 0\}$.

Input: The hyperelliptic curve $\mathbb{H}_3$, an element $r \in \mathcal{R}_3$
Output: A point (x, y) on $\mathbb{H}_3$
$v := w[ur^2(-651s - 441) - 1]$;
$\varepsilon := \chi(v^7 + a_5 v^5 + a_3 v^3 + a_1 v + a_0)$;
$x := \dfrac{1+\varepsilon}{2} v + \dfrac{1-\varepsilon}{2} \left(\dfrac{w(-v+w)}{v+w} \right)$;
$y := -\varepsilon\sqrt{x^7 + a_5 x^5 + a_3 x^3 + a_1 x + a_0}$;
return (x, y).

Algorithm 2. Genus3-Encoding2

Definition 2. *In the situation of Algorithm 2, the encoding function for the hyperelliptic curve $\mathbb{H}_3$ is the function $\psi_3 : \mathcal{R}_3 \to \mathbb{H}_3 : r \mapsto \psi_3(r) = (x, y)$.*

Theorem 3. *Algorithm 2 computes a deterministic almost-injective encoding $\psi_3 : \mathcal{R}_3 \to \mathbb{H}_3 : r \mapsto \psi_3(r) = (x, y)$, in time $\mathcal{O}(\log^{2+\circ(1)} q)$, where $Z_3 = \mathbb{F}_q \setminus \mathcal{R}_3$ is a subset of $\mathbb{F}_q$ of at most 15 elements.*

Proof. 1. $f_3(v) \neq 0$ by definition of $\mathcal{R}_3$. Therefore $\varepsilon = \chi(v^7 + a_5 v^5 + a_3 v^3 + a_1 v + a_0) \neq 0$.

2. x is well defined since $v + w = 0 \Leftrightarrow r = 0$ and $0 \notin \mathcal{R}_3$.

3. Let us prove that $f_3(x)$ is nonzero square.

   - If $\varepsilon = 1$ i.e $f_3(v)$ is a nonzero square and $x = v$ then $f_3(x)$ is a nonzero square.

   - If $\varepsilon = -1$ then we have $x = \left(\frac{w(-v+w)}{v+w}\right)$ and $f_3(x) = \frac{1}{(v+w)^7}\left[w^7(-v+w)^7 + a_5 w^5(-v+w)^5(v+w)^2 + a_3 w^3(-v+w)^3(v+w)^4 + a_1 w(-v+w)(v+w)^6 + a_0(v+w)^7\right]$. Using $a_5 = sw^2$, $a_1 = \frac{sw^6}{3}$, $a_3 = \frac{5sw^4}{3}$ $a_0 = \frac{s-21}{21}w^7$, after some computations, yields, the following: $f_3(x) = \frac{(\frac{-62}{21}sw^7 - 2w^7)v^7 + (2sw^9 - 42w^9)v^5 + (\frac{10}{3}sw^{11} - 70w^{11})v^3 + (\frac{2}{3}sw^{13} - 14w^{13})v + \frac{64}{21}sw^{14}}{(v+w)^7}$

Define $\beta_7 = (\frac{-62}{21}sw^7 - 2w^7)$, $\beta_5 = (2sw^9 - 42w^9)$, $\beta_3 = (\frac{10}{3}sw^{11} - 70w^{11})$, $\beta_1 = (\frac{2}{3}sw^{13} - 14w^{13})$ and $\beta_0 = \frac{64}{21}sw^{14}$.

Then $f_3(x) = \frac{\beta_7}{(v+w)^7}\left[v^7 + \frac{\beta_5}{\beta_7}v^5 + \frac{\beta_3}{\beta_7}v^3 + \frac{\beta_1}{\beta_7}v + \frac{\beta_0}{\beta_7}\right]$. We have $\frac{\beta_5}{\beta_7} = \frac{21(2sw^9 - 42w^9)}{-62sw^7 - 42w^7} = \frac{w^2(21s - 441)}{(-31s - 21s)}$. Since $31s^2 + 42s - 441 = 0$,

then $21s - 441 = -31s^2 - 21s$. So $\frac{\beta_5}{\beta_7} = \frac{w^2(-31s^2 - 21s)}{-3ss - 21} = sw^2 = a_5$.

$\frac{\beta_3}{\beta_7} = \frac{(\frac{10}{3}sw^{11} - 70w^{11})}{(\frac{-62}{21}sw^7 - 2w^7)} = \frac{10sw^{11} - 210w^{11}}{\frac{3}{21}(-62sw^7 - 42w^7)} = \frac{5}{3}w^4\left(\frac{21(2s - 42)}{-62s - 42}\right) = \frac{5}{3}w^4\left(\frac{(21s - 441)}{-31s - 21}\right) = \frac{5}{3}w^4\left(\frac{-31s^2 - 21}{-31s - 21}\right)$. So $\frac{\beta_3}{\beta_7} = \frac{5}{3}sw^4 = a_5$.

$\frac{\beta_1}{\beta_7} = \frac{(\frac{2}{3}sw^{13} - 14w^{13})}{(\frac{-62}{21}sw^7 - 2w^7)} = \frac{1}{3}\frac{21(2sw^{13} - 42w^{13})}{-62sw^7 - 42w^7} = \frac{w^6}{3}\frac{(21s - 441)}{-62s - 441} = \frac{w^6}{3}\frac{(-31s^2 - 21s)}{-31s - 21} = \frac{1}{3}sw^6 = a_1$.

$\frac{\beta_0}{\beta_7} = \frac{\frac{64}{21}sw^{14}}{(\frac{-62}{21}sw^7 - 2w^7)} = \frac{64sw^7}{-62s - 42} = \frac{32sw^7}{-31s - 21}$. We have

$$31s + 42s - 441 = 0 \Leftrightarrow -31s - 42s + 441 = 0$$
$$\Leftrightarrow -31s^2 + 630s + 441 = 672s$$
$$\Leftrightarrow (s - 21)(-31s - 21) = 32s * 21$$
$$\Leftrightarrow \frac{32sw^7}{-31s - 21} = \frac{s - 21}{21}w^7$$

So $\frac{\beta_0}{\beta_7} = \frac{32sw^7}{-31s - 21} = \frac{s-21}{21}w^7 = a_0$.

We prove that $f_3(x) = \dfrac{\beta_7}{(v+w)^7} \cdot f_2(v)$. This implies that $\chi(f_3(x)) = \chi(\beta_7)\chi(v+w)\chi(f_3(v)) = -\chi(\beta_7(v+w))$ since $f_3(v)$ is a nonzero nonsquare. But, we have $\beta_7(v+w) = \omega^7 \frac{-31s-21}{21}\left(wur^2(-651s-441)\right) = uw^8 r^2(-31s-21)^2 = u\left(rw^4(-31s-21)\right)^2$. Since $r \neq 0$ in $\mathcal{R}_3$, then $\chi(\beta_7(v+w)) = \chi(u) = -1$. Hence $\chi(f_3(x)) = 1$, therefore $f_3(x)$ is a nonzero square, we deduce that $y = -\varepsilon\sqrt{f_3(x)}$ is well-defined.

$\square$

Theorem 4. *In the situation of Theorem 3 and Definition 2, we have the following.*

1. *Let (x,y) be a point of the hyperelliptic curve $\mathbb{H}_3$, then $(x,y) \in \mathrm{Im}(\psi_3)$ if and only if $uw(x+w)(-441-651s)$ is a nonzero square in $\mathbb{F}_q$.*
2. *Let $(x,y) \in \mathrm{Im}(\psi_3)$ and define $\bar{r}$ as follows:*
$\bar{r} = \sqrt{\dfrac{x+w}{uw(-441-651s)}}$ *if* $y \notin \sqrt{\mathbb{F}_q^2}$ *and* $\bar{r} = \sqrt{\dfrac{2w}{u(x+w)(-441-651s)}}$ *if* $y \in \sqrt{\mathbb{F}_q^2}$.
Then $\bar{r} \in \mathcal{R}_3$ and $\psi_3(\bar{r}) = (x,y)$.

Proof. 1.   – Assume that $(x,y) \in \mathrm{Im}(\psi_3)$.
- If $\varepsilon = 1$ then $x = v$. Hence $x + w = 0 \Leftrightarrow v + w = 0 \Leftrightarrow r = 0$ but we know that $0 \notin \mathcal{R}_3$. Now, we have $uw(x+w)(-441-651s) = uw(v+w)(-441-651s) = uw[ur^2w(-441-651s)](-441-651s) = u^2w^2r^4(-441-651s)^2$.
- If $\varepsilon = -1$ then $x = \frac{w(-v+w)}{v+w}$, Hence $x + w = 0 \Leftrightarrow \frac{-vw+w^2}{v+w} = -w \Leftrightarrow w = 0$ but we know that $w \in \mathbb{F}_q^*$. Now we have $uw(x+w)(-441-651s) = uw[\frac{w(-v+w)}{v+w} + w](-441-651s) = \frac{uw}{v+w}(2w^2)(-441-651s) = \frac{2w^2}{r^2}$, since $v+w = uwr^2(-441-651s)$ by Theorem 3, 2 is a square when $q \equiv 7 \mod 8$.

We conclude that $uw(x+w)(-441-651s)$ is a nonzero square.

– Conversely assume that $uw(x+w)(-441-651s)$ is a nonzero square in $\mathbb{F}_q$. Let us prove that $(x,y) \in \mathrm{Im}(\psi_3)$. Put $\bar{r} = \sqrt{\dfrac{x+w}{uw(-441-651s)}}$ if $y \notin \sqrt{\mathbb{F}_q^2}$ and $\bar{r} = \sqrt{\dfrac{2w}{u(x+w)(-441-651s)}}$ if $y \in \sqrt{\mathbb{F}_q^2}$. By above assumptions $\dfrac{x+w}{uw(-441-651s)}$ and $\dfrac{2w}{u(x+w)(-441-651s)}$ are well-defined and are nonzero square, then $\bar{r}$ is always well-defined.

Now, we are going to prove that $\bar{r} \in \mathcal{R}_3$ and $(x,y) \in \mathrm{Im}(\psi_3)$. Define $\bar{v}, \bar{\varepsilon}, \bar{x}, \bar{y}$ as in Algorithm 2. If $y \notin \sqrt{\mathbb{F}_q^2}$ then $\bar{r} = \sqrt{\dfrac{x+w}{uw(-441-651s)}} \Longrightarrow \bar{v} = w[u\bar{r}^2(-441-651s) - 1] = w[\frac{x+w}{w} - 1] = x$. So we have $\bar{\varepsilon} = \chi(\bar{v}^7 + a_5\bar{v}^5 + a_3\bar{v}^3 + a_1\bar{v} + a_0) = \chi(f_3(\bar{v})) = 1$. Hence $\bar{x} = \frac{1+\bar{\varepsilon}}{2}\bar{v} + \frac{1-\bar{\varepsilon}}{2}\left(\frac{w(-\bar{v}+w)}{\bar{v}+w}\right) = \bar{v} = x$ and $\bar{y} = -\bar{\varepsilon}\sqrt{x^7 + a_5x^5 + a_3x^3 + a_1x + a_0} = -\sqrt{x^7 + a_5x^5 + a_3x^3 + a_1x + a_0} = y$. Now if $y \in \sqrt{\mathbb{F}_q^2}$ then $\bar{r} = \sqrt{\dfrac{2w}{u(x+w)(-441-651s)}}$, since $\bar{v} = w[u\bar{r}^2(-441-651s) - 1]$ then $\bar{v} = w\frac{w-x}{x+w}$.

Now, after some computations, we have: $\bar{\varepsilon} = \chi(\bar{v}^7 + a_5\bar{v}^5 + a_3\bar{v}^3 + a_1\bar{v} + a_0) = \chi\left(\left(\frac{\frac{-62}{21}sw^7 - 2w^7}{(x+w)^7}\right)(x^7 + a_5x^5 + a_3x^3 + a_1x + a_0)\right) = \chi(2 \times 21 \times w(x+w)(-31s - 21)) = \chi(w(x+w)(-651s - 441)) = -1$ because $uw(x+w)(-441 - 651s)$ is a nonzero square and $\chi(u) = -1$. Since $\bar{\varepsilon} = -1$ then $\bar{x} = \frac{w(-\bar{v}+w)}{\bar{v}+w} = x$ and $\bar{y} = -\bar{\varepsilon}\sqrt{x^7 + a_5x^5 + a_3x^3 + a_1x + a_0} = \sqrt{x^7 + a_5x^5 + a_3x^3 + a_1x + a_0} = y$. In both cases we have $\bar{x} = x$ and $\bar{y} = y$. Since for all $\bar{v}$, we have $\bar{v}^7 + a_5\bar{v}^5 + a_3\bar{v}^3 + a_1\bar{v} + a_0 \neq 0$, then $f_3(\bar{v}) \neq 0$, thus $\bar{r} \in \mathcal{R}_3$.

2. Follows from the previous proof.

□

3.2 An Almost-Injective Encoding in Genus $g = 4$

Similarly to the above subsection, in this subsection, we propose an almost-injective encoding into hyperelliptic curves of genus 4.

We assume that $\text{char}(\mathbb{F}_q) = p \neq 2, 3$. Let $s \in \mathbb{F}_q^*$ such that $127s^2 + 72s - 1296 = 0$:

- If $p \neq 127$ and $q \equiv 7 \mod 8$, we have $\Delta_s = 663552 = 2^{13} \times 3^4$ which is a square, then $s = (-36 \pm 288\sqrt{2})/127$.
- If $p = 127$ and $q \equiv 7 \mod 8$, then $s = 18$.

Let $\mathbb{H}_4 : y^2 = f_4(x) = x^9 + a_7x^7 + a_5x^5 + a_3x^3 + a_1x + a_0$, with $a_7 = sw^2$, $a_5 = \frac{7sw^4}{2}$, $a_3 = \frac{7sw^6}{3}$, $a_1 = \frac{sw^8}{4}$, $a_0 = \frac{s-36}{36}w^9$ be an hyperelliptic curve of genus 4 over $\mathbb{F}_q$ with the previous conditions on q. Define the set $\mathcal{R}_4 = \{r \in \mathbb{F}_q^*, f_4(w[ur^2(-2286s - 648) - 1]) \neq 0\}$.

Input: The hyperelliptic curve $\mathbb{H}_4$, an element $r \in \mathcal{R}_4$
Output: A point (x, y) on $\mathbb{H}_4$
$v := w[ur^2(-2286s - 648) - 1]$;
$\varepsilon := \chi(v^9 + a_7v^7 + a_5v^5 + a_5v^5 + a_3v^3 + a_1v + a_0)$;
$x := \dfrac{1+\varepsilon}{2}v + \dfrac{1-\varepsilon}{2}\left(\dfrac{w(-v+w)}{v+w}\right)$;
$y := -\varepsilon\sqrt{x^9 + a_7x^7 + a_5x^5 + a_3x^3 + a_1x + a_0}$;
return (x, y).

Algorithm 3. Genus4-Encoding3

Definition 3. *In the situation of Algorithm 3, the encoding function for the hyperelliptic curve $\mathbb{H}_4$ is the function $\psi_4 : \mathcal{R}_4 \to \mathbb{H}_4 : r \mapsto \psi_4(r) = (x, y)$.*

Theorem 5. *Algorithm 3 computes a deterministic almost-injective encoding $\psi_4 : \mathcal{R}_4 \to \mathbb{H}_4 : r \mapsto \psi_4(r) = (x, y)$, in time $\mathcal{O}(\log^{2+o(1)} q)$, where $Z_4 = \mathbb{F}_q \setminus \mathcal{R}_4$ is a subset of $\mathbb{F}_q$ of at most 19 elements.*

Proof. 1. $f_4(v) \neq 0$ by definition of $\mathcal{R}_4$. Therefore $\varepsilon = \chi(v^9 + a_7v^7 + a_5v^5 + a_5v^5 + a_3v^3 + a_1v + a_0) \neq 0$
2. x is well defined since $v + w = 0 \Leftrightarrow r = 0$ and $0 \notin \mathcal{R}_4$.

3. Let us prove that $f_4(x)$ is nonzero square.

   – If $\varepsilon = 1$ i.e $f_4(v)$ is a nonzero square and $x = v$ then $f_4(x)$ is a nonzero square.

   – If $\varepsilon = -1$ then we have $x = \left(\frac{w(-v+w)}{v+w}\right)$ and $f_4(x) = \frac{g_4(v)}{(v+w)^9}$ with

$$g_4(v) = \omega^9(-v+\omega)^9 + a_7\omega^7(-v+\omega)^7(v+\omega)^2 + a_5\omega^5(-v+\omega)^5(v+\omega)^4 + a_3\omega^3(-v+\omega)^3(v+\omega)^6 + a_1\omega(-v+\omega)(v+\omega)^8 + a_0(v+\omega)^7.$$

Using $a_7 = sw^2$, $a_1 = \frac{sw^8}{4}$, $a_3 = \frac{7sw^6}{3}$, $a_5 = \frac{7sw^4}{2}$ $a_0 = \frac{s-36}{36}w^9$, after some computations, yields, the following:

$$f_4(x) = \frac{\gamma_9 v^9 + \gamma_7 v^7 + \gamma_5 v^5 + \gamma_3 v^3 + \gamma_1 v + \gamma_0}{(v+w)^9} \text{ with } \gamma_9 = -\frac{127}{18}sw^9 -$$

$2w^9$; $\gamma_7 = 2sw^{11} - 72w^{11}$; $\gamma_5 = 7sw^{13} - 252w^{13}$; $\gamma_3 = \frac{14}{3}sw^{15} - 168w^{15}$; $\gamma_1 = \frac{1}{2}sw^{17} - 18w^{17}$ and $\gamma_0 = \frac{64}{9}sw^{18}$.

This implies that $f_4(x) = \frac{\gamma_9}{(v+w)^9}\left(v^9 + \frac{\gamma_7}{\gamma_9}v^7 + \frac{\gamma_5}{\gamma_9}v^5 + \frac{\gamma_3}{\gamma_9}v^3 + \frac{\gamma_1}{\gamma_9}v + \frac{\gamma_0}{\gamma_9}\right)$.

Now let us prove that $\frac{\gamma_7}{\gamma_9} = a_7$, $\frac{\gamma_5}{\gamma_9} = a_5$, $\frac{\gamma_3}{\gamma_9} = a_3$, $\frac{\gamma_1}{\gamma_9} = a_1$ and $\frac{\gamma_0}{\gamma_9} = a_0$.

$\frac{\gamma_7}{\gamma_9} = \frac{2sw^{11} - 72w^{11}}{-\frac{127}{18}sw^9 - 2w^9} = \frac{(36s - 1296)w^2}{-127s - 36}w^2$. We have $127s^2 + 72s -$

$1296 = 0 \Leftrightarrow 36s - 1296 = -127s^2 - 36s$; this implies that $\frac{\gamma_7}{\gamma_9} =$

$\frac{(-127s^2 - 36s)}{-127s - 36}w^2 = sw^2$. $\frac{\gamma_5}{\gamma_9} = \frac{7sw^{13} - 252w^{13}}{-\frac{127}{18}sw^9 - 2w^9} = \frac{7(18s - 648)}{-127s - 36}w^4 =$

$\frac{7}{2}\frac{(36s - 1296)}{-127s - 36}w^4 = \frac{7}{2}\frac{-127s^2 - 36s}{-127s - 36}w^4 = \frac{7}{2}sw^4 = a_5$.

$\frac{\gamma_3}{\gamma_9} = \frac{\frac{14}{3}sw^{15} - 168w^{15}}{-\frac{127}{18}sw^9 - 2w^9} = \frac{6(14s - 504)}{-127s - 36}w^6 = \frac{7(12s - 432)}{-127s - 36}w^6 =$

$\frac{7}{3}\frac{36s - 1296}{-127s - 36}w^6 = \frac{7}{3}\frac{-127s^2 - 36s}{-127s - 36} = \frac{7}{3}sw^6 = a_3$.

$\frac{\gamma_1}{\gamma_9} = \frac{\frac{1}{2}sw^{17} - 18w^{17}}{-\frac{127}{18}sw^9 - 2w^9} = \frac{9(s - 36)}{-127s - 36}w^8 = \frac{1}{4}\frac{36s - 1296}{-127s - 36}w^8 = \frac{sw^8}{4} = a_1$.

$\frac{\gamma_0}{\gamma_9} = \frac{\frac{64}{9}sw^{18}}{-\frac{127}{18}sw^9 - 2w^9} = \frac{128sw^9}{-127s - 36}$. Now we know that $127s^2 + 72s -$

$1296 = 0$, we are going to use this equation to prove that $\frac{128s}{-127s - 36} = \frac{s - 36}{36}$.

$$127s^2 + 72s - 1296 = 0 \Leftrightarrow 4608s = -127s^2 + 4536s + 1296$$

$$\Leftrightarrow 36 \times 128s = (s - 36)(-127s - 36)$$

$$\Leftrightarrow \frac{128s}{-127s - 36} = \frac{s - 36}{36}$$

So $\frac{\gamma_0}{\gamma_9} = \frac{128sw^9}{-127s - 36} = \frac{s - 36}{36}w^9 = a_0$.

We prove that $f_4(x) = \dfrac{\gamma_9}{(v+w)^9} \cdot f_4(v)$. This implies that $\chi(f_4(x)) = \chi(\gamma_9)\chi(v+w)\chi(f_4(v)) = -\chi(\gamma_9(v+w))$ since $f_4(v)$ is a nonzero non-square. But, we have $\gamma_9(v+w) = \omega^9 \frac{-127s-36}{18}\left(wur^2(-2286s-648)\right) = uw^{10}r^2(-127s-36)^2 = u\left(rw^5(-127s-36)\right)^2$. Since $r \neq 0$ in $\mathcal{R}_4$, then $\chi(\gamma_9(v+w)) = \chi(u) = -1$. Hence $\chi(f_4(x)) = 1$, therefore $f_4(x)$ is a nonzero square, we deduce that $y = -\varepsilon\sqrt{f_4(x)}$ is well-defined.

$\square$

Theorem 6. *In the situation of Theorem 5 and Definition 3, we have the following.*

1. *Let (x,y) be a point of the hyperelliptic curve $\mathbb{H}_4$, then $(x,y) \in \mathrm{Im}(\psi_4)$ if and only if $uw(x+w)(-2286s-648)$ is a nonzero square in $\mathbb{F}_q$.*
2. *Let $(x,y) \in \mathrm{Im}(\psi_4)$ and define $\bar{r}$ as follows:*
   $\bar{r} = \sqrt{\dfrac{x+w}{uw(-2286s-648)}}$ *if* $y \notin \sqrt{\mathbb{F}_q^2}$ *and* $\bar{r} = \sqrt{\dfrac{2w}{u(x+w)(-2286s-648)}}$ *if* $y \in \sqrt{\mathbb{F}_q^2}$.
   Then $\bar{r} \in \mathcal{R}_4$ and $\psi_4(\bar{r}) = (x,y)$.

Proof. Similar to the proof of Theorem 4.

$\square$

3.3   An Almost-Injective Encoding on Genus $g = 5$

We propose here an almost-injective encoding into hyperelliptic curves of genus 5.
    We assume that $\mathrm{char}(\mathbb{F}_q) = p \neq 2,5,11$. Let $s \in \mathbb{F}_q^*$ such that $511s^2 + 110s - 3025 = 0$:

- If $p \nmid 511$ and $q \equiv 7 \mod 8$, we have $\Delta_s = 6195200 = 2^{11} \times 5^2 \times 11^2$ which is
  a square, then $s = \dfrac{-55 \pm 880\sqrt{2}}{511}$.
- If $p \mid 511$ and $q \equiv 7 \mod 8$, then $s = \frac{55}{2}$.

Let $\mathbb{H}_5 : y^2 = f_5(x) = x^{11} + a_9x^9 + a_7x^7 + a_5x^5 + a_3x^3 + a_1x + a_0$, with $a_9 = sw^2$, $a_7 = 6sw^4$, $a_5 = \dfrac{42sw^6}{5}$, $a_3 = 3sw^8$, $a_1 = \dfrac{sw^{10}}{5}$ and $a_0 = \dfrac{s-55}{55}w^{11}$, be an hyperelliptic curve of genus 5 over $\mathbb{F}_q$ with the previous conditions on q. Define the set $\mathcal{R}_5 = \{r \in \mathbb{F}_q^*, f_5(w[ur^2(-28105s - 3025) - 1]) \neq 0\}$.

Input: The hyperelliptic curve $\mathbb{H}_5$, an element $r \in \mathcal{R}_5$
Output: A point (x,y) on $\mathbb{H}_5$
$v := w[ur^2(-28105s - 3025) - 1]$;
$\varepsilon := \chi(v^9 + a_9v^9 + a_7v^7 + a_5v^5v^3 + a_5v^5 + a_1v + a_0)$;
$x := \dfrac{1+\varepsilon}{2}v + \dfrac{1-\varepsilon}{2}\left(\dfrac{w(-v+w)}{v+w}\right)$;
$y := -\varepsilon\sqrt{x^{11} + a_9x^9 + a_7x^7 + a_5x^5 + a_3x^3 + a_1x + a_0}$;
return (x,y).

Algorithm 4. Genus5-Encoding4

Definition 4. *In the situation of Algorithm 4, the encoding function for the hyperelliptic curve* $\mathbb{H}_5$ *is the function* $\psi_5 : \mathcal{R}_5 \to \mathbb{H}_5 : r \mapsto \psi_5(r) = (x, y)$.

Theorem 7. *Algorithm 4 computes a deterministic almost-injective encoding* $\psi_5 : \mathcal{R}_5 \to \mathbb{H}_5 : r \mapsto \psi_5(r) = (x, y)$, *in time* $\mathcal{O}(\log^{2+o(1)} q)$, *where* $Z_5 = \mathbb{F}_q \setminus \mathcal{R}_5$ *is a subset of* $\mathbb{F}_q$ *of at most* 23 *elements.*

Proof. 1. $f_5(v) \neq 0$ by definition of $\mathcal{R}_5$. Therefore $\varepsilon = \chi(v^9 + a_9 v^9 + a_7 v^7 + a_5 v^5 v^3 + a_5 v^5 + a_1 v + a_0) \neq 0$

2. x is well defined since $v + w = 0 \Leftrightarrow r = 0$ and $0 \notin \mathcal{R}_5$

3. Let us prove that $f_5(x)$ is nonzero square.
   - If $\varepsilon = 1$ i.e $f_5(v)$ is a nonzero square and $x = v$ then $f_5(x)$ is a nonzero square.
   - If $\varepsilon = -1$ then we have $x = \left(\frac{w(-v+w)}{v+w}\right)$ and $f_4(x) = \frac{g_5(v)}{(v+w)^{11}}$. with

   $g_5(v) = \omega^{11}(-v + w)^{11} + a_9\omega^9(-v + w)^9(v + w)^2 + a_7\omega^7(-v + w)^7(v + w)^4 + a_5\omega^5(-v+w)^5(v+w)^6 + a_3\omega^3(-v+w)^3(v+w)^8 + a_1\omega(-v+w)(v+w)^{10} + a_0(v + w)^{11}$.

   Using $a_9 = sw^2$, $a_7 = 6sw^4$, $a_5 = \dfrac{42sw^6}{5}$, $a_3 = 3sw^8$, $a_1 = \dfrac{sw^{10}}{5}$, $a_0 = \dfrac{s - 55}{55}w^{11}$, after some computations, yields, the following:

   $$f_5(x) = \frac{\eta_{11}v^{11} + \eta_9 v^9 + \eta_7 v^7 + \eta_5 v^5 + \eta_3 v^3 + \eta_1 v + \eta_0}{(v + w)^9} \text{ with}$$

   $\eta_{11} = -\frac{1022}{55}sw^{11} - 2w^{11}$, $\eta_9 = 2sw^{13} - 110w^{13}$; $\eta_7 = 12sw^{15} - 660w^{15}$; $\eta_5 = \frac{84}{5}sw^{17} - 924w^{17}$; $\eta_3 = 6sw^{19} - 330w^{19}$; $\eta_1 = \frac{y}{5}sw^{21} - 22w^{21}$ and $\eta_0 = \frac{1024}{55}sw^{22}$. The expression of the function f_5 becomes:

   $$f_5(x) = \frac{\eta_{11}}{(v + w)^{11}}\left(v^{11} + \frac{\eta_9}{\eta_{11}}v^9 + \frac{\eta_7}{\eta_{11}}v^7 + \frac{\eta_5}{\eta_{11}}v^5 + \frac{\eta_3}{\eta_{11}}v^3 + \frac{\eta_1}{\eta_{11}}v + \eta_0\right).$$

   Now our main goal is to prove that $\frac{\eta_9}{\eta_{11}} = a_9$; $\frac{\eta_7}{\eta_{11}} = a_7$; $\frac{\eta_5}{\eta_{11}} = a_5$; $\frac{\eta_3}{\eta_{11}} = a_3$; $\frac{\eta_1}{\eta_{11}} = a_1$ and $\frac{\eta_0}{\eta_{11}} = a_0$.

   $\dfrac{\eta_9}{\eta_{11}} = \dfrac{2sw^{13} - 110w^{13}}{-\frac{1022}{55}sw^{11} - 2w^{11}} = \dfrac{55s - 3025}{-511s - 55}w^2$. Now since $511s^2 + 110s - 3025 = 0$, we have $55s - 3025 = 511s^2 - 55s$. This implies that $\dfrac{\eta_9}{\eta_{11}} = \dfrac{-511s^2 - 55s}{-511s - 55}w^2 = sw^2 = a_9$. $\dfrac{\eta_7}{\eta_{11}} = \dfrac{12sw^{15} - 660w^{15}}{-\frac{1022}{55}sw^{11} - 2w^{11}} = \dfrac{55(6s - 55)}{-511s - 55}w^4 = \dfrac{6(55s - 3025)}{-511s - 55}w^4 = 6 \times \dfrac{-511s^2 - 55s}{-511s - 55}w^4 = 6sw^4 = a_7$.

   $\dfrac{\eta_5}{\eta_{11}} = \dfrac{\frac{84}{5}sw^{17} - 924w^{17}}{-\frac{1022}{55}sw^{11} - 2w^{11}} = \dfrac{55}{5} \cdot \dfrac{42s - 2310}{-511s - 55}w^6 = \dfrac{42}{5} \cdot \dfrac{55s - 3025}{-511s - 55}w^6 = \dfrac{42}{5} \cdot \dfrac{-511s^2 - 55s}{-511s - 55}w^6 = \dfrac{42}{5}sw^6 = a_5$.

   $\dfrac{\eta_3}{\eta_{11}} = \dfrac{6sw^{19} - 330w^{19}}{-\frac{1022}{55}sw^{11} - 2w^{11}} = \dfrac{55(3s - 165)}{-511s - 55}w^8 = \dfrac{3(55s - 3025)}{-511s - 55}w^8 = a_3$.

$$\frac{\eta_1}{\eta_{11}} = \frac{\frac{2}{5}sw^{21} - 22w^{21}}{-\frac{1022}{55}sw^{11} - 2w^{11}} = \frac{55}{5} \times \frac{s - 55}{-511s - 210}w^{10} = \frac{sw^{10}}{5} = a_1.$$

$$\frac{\eta_0}{\eta_{11}} = \frac{\frac{1024}{55}sw^{22}}{-\frac{1022}{55}sw^{11} - 2w^{11}} = \frac{512s}{-511s - 55}w^{11}.$$

$$511s^2 + 110s - 3025 = 0 \Leftrightarrow 28160s = -511s^2 + 28050s + +3025$$

$$\Leftrightarrow 55 \times 512s = (s - 55)(-511s - 55)$$

$$\Leftrightarrow \frac{512s}{-511s - 55} = \frac{s - 55}{55}$$

So $\dfrac{\eta_0}{\eta_{11}} = \dfrac{512s}{-511s - 55}w^{11} = \dfrac{s - 55}{55}w^{11} = a_0$.

We prove that $f_5(x) = \dfrac{\eta_{11}}{(v + w)^{11}}.f_5(v)$. This implies that $\chi(f_5(x)) = \chi(\eta_{11})\chi(v + \omega))\chi(f_5(v)) = -\chi(\eta_{11}(v + w))$ since $f_5(v)$ is a nonzero non-square.

But, we have $\eta_{11}(v + w) = \eta_{11}\frac{-127s - 36}{18}\left(wur^2(-28105s - 3025)\right) = uw^{10}r^2(-511s - 55)^2 = u\left(rw^6(-511s - 55)\right)^2$. Since $r \neq 0$ in $\mathcal{R}_5$, then $\chi(\eta_{11}(v + w)) = \chi(u) = -1$. Hence $\chi(f_5(x)) = 1$, therefore $f_5(x)$ is a nonzero square, we deduce that $y = -\varepsilon\sqrt{f_5(x)}$ is well-defined.

$\square$

Theorem 8. *In the situation of Theorem 7 and Definition 4, we have the following.*

1. *Let (x, y) be a point of the hyperelliptic curve $\mathbb{H}_5$, then $(x, y) \in \text{Im}(\psi_5)$ if and only if $uw(x + w)(-28105s - 3025)$ is a nonzero square in $\mathbb{F}_q$.*
2. *Let $(x, y) \in \text{Im}(\psi_5)$ and define $\bar{r}$ as follows:*
$\bar{r} = \sqrt{\dfrac{x + w}{uw(-28105s - 3025)}}$ *if $y \notin \sqrt{\mathbb{F}_q^2}$ and $\bar{r} = \sqrt{\dfrac{2w}{u(x + w)(-28105s - 3025)}}$ if $y \in$*
$\sqrt{\mathbb{F}_q^2}$. *Then $\bar{r} \in \mathcal{R}_5$ and $\psi_5(\bar{r}) = (x, y)$.*

Proof. Similar to the proof of Theorem 4.

$\square$

3.4   Encoding in Genus $g = 1$ Using Our Technique

In this subsection, we show how one can encode into an elliptic curve given by $E = \mathbb{H}_1 : y^2 = x^3 + a_1x + a_0$ over a finite field $\mathbb{F}_q$ where $q \equiv 7 \mod 8$ using the same approach as in the previous subsections.

We assume that $\text{char}(\mathbb{F}_q) = p \neq 2, 3$. Let $s \in \mathbb{F}_q^*$ such that $s^2 + 6s - 9 = 0$. Since $q \equiv 7 \mod 8$, we have $\Delta_s = 72 = 2^3 \times 3^2$ which is a square, then $s = -3 \pm 3\sqrt{2}$. Let $E = \mathbb{H}_1 : y^2 = f_1(x) = x^3 + a_1x + a_0$, with $a_1 = sw^2$ and

$a_0 = \dfrac{s-3}{3}w^3$, be an elliptic curve over $\mathbb{F}_q$ with the previous conditions on q.
Define the set $\mathcal{R}_1 = \{r \in \mathbb{F}_q^*, f_1(w[ur^2(-3s-9)-1]) \neq 0\}$.

Input: The elliptic curve $E = \mathbb{H}_1$, an element $r \in \mathcal{R}_1$
Output: A point (x, y) on E
$v := w[ur^2(-3s-9)-1]$;
$\varepsilon := \chi(v^3 + a_1 v + a_0)$;
$x := \dfrac{1+\varepsilon}{2}v + \dfrac{1-\varepsilon}{2}\left(\dfrac{w(-v+w)}{v+w}\right)$;
$y := -\varepsilon\sqrt{x^3 + a_1 x + a_0}$;
return (x, y).

Algorithm 5. Genus1-Encoding5

Definition 5. *In the situation of Algorithm 5, the encoding function for the elliptic curve E is the function $\psi_1 : \mathcal{R}_1 \to E : r \mapsto \psi_1(r) = (x, y)$.*

Theorem 9. *Algorithm 5 computes a deterministic almost-injective encoding $\psi_1 : \mathcal{R}_1 \to E : r \mapsto \psi_1(r) = (x, y)$, in time $\mathcal{O}(\log^{2+o(1)} q)$, where $Z_1 = \mathbb{F}_q \setminus \mathcal{R}_1$ is a subset of $\mathbb{F}_q$ of at most 9 elements.*

Proof. 1. $f_1(v) \neq 0$ by definition of $\mathcal{R}_1$. Therefore $\varepsilon = \chi(v^3 + a_1 v + a_0) \neq 0$
2. x is well defined since $v + w = 0 \Leftrightarrow r = 0$ and $0 \notin \mathcal{R}_1$.
3. Let us prove that $f_1(x)$ is nonzero square.

- If $\varepsilon = 1$ i.e $f_1(v)$ is a nonzero square and $x = v$ then $f_1(x)$ is a nonzero square.
- If $\varepsilon = -1$ then we have $x = \left(\dfrac{w(-v+w)}{v+w}\right)$ and $f_1(x) = \dfrac{1}{(v+w)^3}\Big[w^3(-v + w)^3 + a_1 w(-v+w)(v+w)^2 + a_0(v+w)^3\Big]$. Using $a_1 = sw^2$, $a_0 = \dfrac{s-3}{3}w^3$, we have $f_1(x) = \dfrac{(-2sw^3/3 - 2w^3)v^3 + (2sw^5 - 6w^5)v + 4sw^6/3}{(v+w)^3}$

$f_1(x) = \dfrac{(-2sw^3/3 - 2w^3)}{(v+w)^3}\left(v^3 + \dfrac{(2sw^5 - 6w^5)}{(-2sw^3/3 - 2w^3)}v + \dfrac{4sw^6/3}{(-2sw^3/3 - 2w^3)}\right)$.

We have $\dfrac{(2sw^5 - 6w^5)}{(-2sw^3/3 - 2w^3)} = \dfrac{3s-9}{-s-3}w^2 = sw^2 = a_1$ since $3s - 9 = -s^2 - 3s$

and $\dfrac{4sw^6/3}{(-2sw^3/3 - 2w^3)} = \dfrac{s-3}{3}w^3 = a_0$ since $s^2 + 6s - 9 = 0 \Leftrightarrow 6s = -s^2 + 9 \Leftrightarrow \dfrac{2s}{-s-3} = \dfrac{s-3}{3}$. We prove that $f_1(x) = \dfrac{(-2sw^3/3 - 2w^3)}{(v+w)^3} \cdot f_1(v)$.

This implies that $\chi(f_1(x)) = \chi(-2sw^3/3 - 2w^3)\chi(v+w)\chi(f_1(v)) = -\chi(w(-3s-9s)(v+w))$ since $f_1(v)$ is a nonzero non-square. But, we have $w(-3s-9s)(v+w) = w(-3s-9s)(wur^2(-3s-9)) = uw^2r^2(-3s-9s)^2 = u(rw(-3s-9))^2$. Since $r \neq 0$ in $\mathcal{R}_1$, then $\chi(w(-3s-9s)(v+w)) = \chi(u) = -1$. Hence $\chi(f_1(x)) = 1$, therefore $f_1(x)$ is a nonzero square, we deduce that $y = -\varepsilon\sqrt{f_1(x)}$ is well-defined.

$\square$

Remark 1. We emphasize that we construct an encoding function into the elliptic curve $E = \mathbb{H}_1 : y^2 = f_1(x) = x^3 + a_1 x + a_0$ with $a_1 = sw^2$ $a_0 = \dfrac{s-3}{3} w^3$ in order to find unified formulas in genus $g \leq 5$ even if the family of these elliptic curves is small.

Theorem 10. *In the situation of Theorem 9 and Definition 5, we have the following.*

1. *Let (x, y) be a point of the elliptic curve E, then $(x, y) \in \mathrm{Im}(\psi_1)$ if and only if $uw(x + w)(-3s - 9)$ is a nonzero square in $\mathbb{F}_q$.*
2. *Let $(x, y) \in \mathrm{Im}(\psi_1)$ and define $\bar{r}$ as follows:*
$$\bar{r} = \sqrt{\frac{x+w}{uw(-3s-9)}} \ \text{if } y \notin \sqrt{\mathbb{F}_q^2} \ \text{and } \bar{r} = \sqrt{\frac{2w}{u(x+w)(-3s-9)}} \ \text{if } y \in \sqrt{\mathbb{F}_q^2}. \ \text{Then}$$
$\bar{r} \in \mathcal{R}_1$ *and* $\psi_1(\bar{r}) = (x, y)$.

Proof. Similar to the proof of Theorem 4. □

4 Unified Formulas for the Five Encodings

Our main goal in this section is to find some formulas in order to unify the five Algorithms [1, 2, 3, 4 and 5] and the Theorems [1, 4, 6, 8 and 10] (Tables 1, 2 and 3).

Table 1. Different families of hyperelliptic curves considered in this paper

Genus g	Curve
1	$\mathbb{H}_1 = E : y^2 = f_1(x) = x^3 + a_3 x + a_0$
2	$\mathbb{H}_2 : y^2 = f_1(x) = x^5 + a_3 x^3 + a_1 x + a_0$
3	$\mathbb{H}_3 : y^2 = f_2(x) = x^7 + a_5 x^5 + a_3 x^3 + a_1 x + a_0$
4	$\mathbb{H}_4 : y^2 = f_3(x) = x^9 + a_7 x^7 + a_5 x^5 + a_3 x^3 + a_1 x + a_0$
5	$\mathbb{H}_5 : y^2 = f_4(x) = x^{11} + a_9 x^9 + a_7 x^7 + a_5 x^5 + a_3 x^3 + a_1 x + a_0$

Table 2. The fundamental second degree equation and the different values of v defined in Algorithms 1, 2, 3, 4 and 5.

Genus g	Second degree equation	Value of v
1	$s^2 + 6s - 9 = 0$	$v = w[ur^2(-3s - 9) - 1]$
2	$7s^2 + 20s - 100 = 0$	$v = w[ur^2(-35s - 50) - 1]$
3	$31s^2 + 42s - 441 = 0$	$v = w[ur^2(-651s - 441) - 1]$
4	$127s^2 + 72s - 1296 = 0$	$v = w[ur^2(-2286s - 648) - 1]$
5	$511s^2 + 110s - 3025 = 0$	$v = w[ur^2(-28105s - 3025) - 1]$

Remark 2. 1. The parameter $s \in \mathbb{F}_q^*$ satisfies the equation $\alpha_g s^2 + \beta_g s - \gamma_g = 0$ where $\alpha_g = 2^{2g-1} - 1$; $\beta_g = 2 \times g \times \deg(f_g) = 4g^2 + 2g$ and $\gamma_g = (g \times \deg(f_g))^2 = (2g^2 + g)^2$.

2. Note that $\alpha_g = 2^{2g-1} - 1$ is a Mersenne number and $M_2 = 3$, $M_3 = 7$, $M_4 = 127$ are respectively the second, third and fourth prime Mersenne numbers.

Remark 3. $v = v(g) = w[ur^2(-m_g s - n_g) - 1]$ where

- $m_g = \dfrac{1}{2} \times \alpha_g \times \beta_g$ if g is odd and $m_g = \dfrac{1}{4} \times \alpha_g \times \beta_g$ if g is even.

- $n_g = (g \times \deg(f_g))^2 = (2g^2 + g)^2$ if the genus g is odd and $n_g = \dfrac{1}{2} \times (g \times \deg(f_g))^2 = \dfrac{1}{2} \times (2g^2 + g)^2$ if g is even.

Table 3. The relationship between the genus g and the values of the coefficients a_0, a_1, $a_{(2g-1)}$ and a_3 in the different hyperelliptic curves $\mathbb{H}_g$.

Genus g	a_1	$a_{(2g-1)}$	a_0	$a_3, g \geq 3$
1	$\frac{sw^2}{1}$	sw^2	$\frac{s-3}{3}w^3$	-
2	$a_1 = \frac{sw^4}{2}$	sw^2	$\frac{s-10}{10}w^5$	-
3	$a_1 = \frac{sw^6}{3}$	sw^2	$\frac{s-21}{21}w^7$	$\frac{5sw^4}{3}$
4	$a_1 = \frac{sw^8}{4}$	sw^2	$\frac{s-36}{36}w^9$	$\frac{7sw^6}{3}$
5	$a_1 = \frac{sw^{10}}{5}$	sw^2	$\frac{s-55}{55}w^{11}$	$3sw^8 = \frac{9}{3}sw^8$

Remark 4. Note that for any genus $y \leq 5$, $a_0 = \dfrac{\left(s - (2g^2 + g)\right)}{(2g^2 + g)} w^{(2g+1)}$, $a_1 = \frac{sw^{2g}}{g}$, $a_{(2g-1)} = sw^2$ and $a_3 = \frac{2g-1}{3} sw^{2g-2}$ for $g \geq 3$.

4.1 An Almost-Injective Encoding on $\mathbb{H}_g$

Let $y \in \{1, 2, 3, 4, 5\}$. We assume that $\text{char}(\mathbb{F}_q) = p$, $p \neq 2$ and $p \nmid (2g^2 + g)$. Let $s \in \mathbb{F}_q^*$ such that $\alpha_g s^2 + \beta_g s - \gamma_g = 0$ where $\alpha_g = 2^{2g-1} - 1$; $\beta_g = 4g^2 + 2g$ and $\gamma_g = (2g^2 + g)^2$. If $p | \alpha_g$ then $s = \gamma_g / \beta_g$ otherwise $p \nmid \alpha_g$; we have $\Delta_s = \beta_g^2 + 4 \times \alpha_g \times \gamma_g$ and then $s = (-\beta_g \pm \sqrt{\Delta_s})/(2 * \alpha_g)$.

Let $\mathbb{H}_g : y^2 = h_g(x) = x^{(2g+1)} + a_{(2g-1)} x^{(2g-1)} + a_{(2g-3)} x^{(2g-3)} + \ldots + a_1 x + a_0$ be an hyperelliptic curve of genus g over $\mathbb{F}_q$ with the previous conditions on q where $a_0 = \dfrac{\left(s - (2g^2 + g)\right)}{(2g^2 + g)} w^{(2g+1)}$, $a_{(2g-1)} = sw^2$, $a_1 = \frac{sw^{2g}}{g}$ for $g \geq 1$, $a_3 = \frac{2g-1}{3} sw^{2g-2}$ for $g \geq 3$, $a_5 = \frac{7sw^4}{2}$ if $g = 4$ and $a_7 = 6sw^4$, $a_5 = \frac{42sw^6}{5}$ if $g = 5$. Define

- $\mathcal{R}_g = \{r \in \mathbb{F}_q^*, h_g(w[ur^2(-m_g s - n_g) - 1]) \neq 0\}$;

- $m_g = \frac{1}{2} \times \alpha_g \times \beta_g$ if the genus g is odd and $m_g = \frac{1}{4} \times \alpha_g \times \beta_g$ if g is even where $\alpha_g = 2^{2g-1} - 1$ and $\beta_g = 4g^2 + 2g$;

- $n_g = (2g^2 + g)^2$ if g is odd and $n_g = \dfrac{1}{2} \times (2g^2 + g)^2$ if g is even.

The following algorithm generalizes Algorithms 1, 2, 3, 4 and 5.

Input: The hyperelliptic curve $\mathbb{H}_g$, an element $r \in \mathcal{R}_g$
Output: A point (x, y) on $\mathbb{H}_g$
$v := v(g) = w[ur^2(-m_g s - n_g) - 1]$;
$\varepsilon := \chi(v^{(2g+1)} + a_{(2g-1)} v^{(2g-1)} + a_{(2g-3)} v^{(2g-3)} + \ldots + a_1 v + a_0)$;
$x := \dfrac{1+\varepsilon}{2} v + \dfrac{1-\varepsilon}{2} \left(\dfrac{w(-v+w)}{v+w} \right)$;
$y := -\varepsilon \sqrt{x^{(2g+1)} + a_{(2g-1)} x^{(2g-1)} + a_{(2g-3)} x^{(2g-3)} + \ldots + a_1 x + a_0}$;
return (x, y).

Algorithm 6. Genus-g-Encoding6-Generalization

Definition 6. *In the situation of Algorithm 6, the encoding function for the hyperelliptic curve $\mathbb{H}_g$ is the function $\psi_g : \mathcal{R}_g \to \mathbb{H}_g : r \mapsto \psi_g(r) = (x, y)$.*

Theorem 11. *Algorithm 6 computes a deterministic almost-injective encoding $\psi_g : \mathcal{R}_g \to \mathbb{H}_g : r \mapsto \psi_g(r) = (x, y)$, in time $\mathcal{O}(\log^{2+o(1)} q)$, where $Z_g = \mathbb{F}_q \setminus \mathcal{R}_g$ is a subset of $\mathbb{F}_q$ of at most $(2g + 1)^2 + 1$ elements.*

Proof. Follows from the Remarks 2, 3 and the Theorems 3, 5, 7, 9. □

Lemma 1. *In the situation of Theorem 11 and Definition 6, we have $\phi_g(r) = \phi_g(-r)$, $\forall r \in \mathcal{R}_g$ and $\#(\phi_g^{-1}(\phi_g(r))) = 2$, $\forall r \in \mathcal{R}_g$ (where $\#(f)$ means the cardinal of f).*

Proof. Similar to the proof of **Lemma 1** in [3]. □

Theorem 12. *In the situation of Theorem 11 and Definition 6, we have the following.*

1. *Let (x, y) be a point of the hyperelliptic curve $\mathbb{H}_g$, then $(x, y) \in \text{Im}(\psi_g)$ if and only if $uw(x + w)(-n_g - m_g s)$ is a nonzero square in $\mathbb{F}_q$.*
2. *Let $(x, y) \in \text{Im}(\psi_g)$ and define $\bar{r}$ as follows:*
   $$\bar{r} = \sqrt{\frac{x+w}{uw(-n_g - m_g s)}} \ \text{ if } y \notin \sqrt{\mathbb{F}_q^2} \ \text{ and } \ \bar{r} = \sqrt{\frac{2w}{u(x+w)(-n_g - m_g s)}} \ \text{ if } y \in \sqrt{\mathbb{F}_q^2}.$$
   Then $\bar{r} \in \mathcal{R}_g$ and $\psi_g(\bar{r}) = (x, y)$.

Proof. Follows from the Remark 3 and the Theorems 4, 6, 8, 10. □

4.2   Almost-Injective Encodings on $\mathbb{H}_g$, $g \in \{6, 7, 8, 9\}$

Using the results in the previous subsection (Subsect. 4.1), we verify that Algorithm 6, Definition 6 and Theorems 11 and 12 can be extended to the families of hyperelliptic curves $\mathbb{H}_g : y^2 = h_g(x) = x^{(2g+1)} + a_{(2g-1)} x^{(2g-1)} + a_{(2g-3)} x^{(2g-3)} + \ldots + a_1 x + a_0$ of genus $g \in \{6, 7, 8, 9\}$ where the coefficients of $\mathbb{H}_g$ are given in the following table (Table 4).

Table 4. Coefficients of $\mathbb{H}_g$, $6 \leq g \leq 9$

Genus g = 6	$a_0 = \dfrac{(s - 78)}{78}w^{13}$, $a_1 = \dfrac{sw^{12}}{6}$, $a_3 = \dfrac{11}{3}sw^{10}$, $a_5 = \dfrac{33}{2}sw^8$, $a_7 = 22sw^6$, $a_9 = \dfrac{55}{6}sw^4$, $a_{11} = sw^2$
Genus g = 7	$a_0 = \dfrac{(s - 105)}{105}w^{15}$, $a_1 = \dfrac{sw^{14}}{7}$, $a_3 = \dfrac{13}{3}sw^{12}$, $a_5 = \dfrac{143}{5}sw^{10}$, $a_7 = \dfrac{429}{7}sw^8$, $a_9 = \dfrac{143}{3}sw^3$, $a_{11} = 13sw^4$, $a_{13} = sw^2$
Genus g = 8	$a_0 = \dfrac{(s - 136)}{136}w^{17}$, $a_1 = \dfrac{sw^{16}}{8}$, $a_3 = \dfrac{15}{3}sw^{14}$, $a_5 = \dfrac{91}{2}sw^{12}$, $a_7 = 143sw^{10}$, $a_9 = \dfrac{715}{4}sw^8$, $a_{11} = 91sw^8$, $a_{13} = \dfrac{35}{2}sw^4$, $a_{15} = sw^2$
Genus g = 9	$a_0 = \dfrac{(s - 171)}{171}w^{19}$, $a_1 = \dfrac{sw^{18}}{9}$, $a_3 = \dfrac{17}{3}sw^{16}$, $a_5 = 68sw^{14}$, $a_7 = \dfrac{884}{3}sw^{12}$, $a_9 = \dfrac{4862}{9}sw^{10}$, $a_{11} = 442sw^8$, $a_{13} = \dfrac{476}{3}sw^6$, $a_{15} = \dfrac{68}{3}sw^4$, $a_{17} = sw^2$

5 Conclusion

We have successfully constructed four deterministic almost-injective encodings $\phi_i, i = 1, 3, 4, 5$ into four families of hyperelliptic curves $\mathbb{H}_1, \mathbb{H}_3, \mathbb{H}_4$ and $\mathbb{H}_5$ of genus $g = 1, 3, 4, 5$ respectively. We have also constructed an unified deterministic encoding into an hyperelliptic curve of genus $g \leq 5$ that generalizes our four encodings and those of Seck *et al.* In each case, we have showed in what conditions one can invert the encoding function. We think that our encoding in genus $g \leq 5$ can be extended to any genus.

Appendix: Implementation of Our Unified Encoding ψ_g (Subsect. 4.1) Using the Sage Computer-Algebra System [13] Available on GitHub [17]

```
class EncodingValidationOfParameters():
    def __init__(self, q, u, w, g = 2, s=None):
        self.R = FiniteField(q,"a")
        self.a = self.R.gen()
        self.poly = PolynomialRing(self.R,"x")
        self.x = self.poly.gen()
        self.q = q
        self.u = self.value2Fq(u)
        self.w = self.value2Fq(w)
        self.s = s
        self.g = g # g=genus of the curve
        self.alpha_g = 2^(2*g-1)-1
        self.beta_g = 4*g^2+2*g
        self.gamma_g = (2*g^2+g)^2
        self.mg = self.valueOfMg()
        self.ng = self.valueOfNg()
        #verification of the parameters
        self._chekingOfParameters()
        self._checkingValueOfTheParameterS()
        self.coefs = self.coefficients()
```

```
        self.f = self.function()
        self._chekingIfCurveIsHyperelliptic()

    def __repr__(self):
        eq = "y^2="+str(self.f)
        return "Hyperelliptic curve defined by {} over finite field".format(eq)+""\
            +" F_{}/< {} >".format(self.R.characteristic(),
                                   str(self.R.modulus()).replace("x","a"))
    def function(self):
        g, R = self.g, self.R
        t0, tn = [R(self.coefs[0])], [self.x^(2*g+1)]
        poly_l = t0+[R(self.coefs[i])*self.x^(2*i-1) for i in range(1, g+1)]+tn
        return sum(poly_l)
    def valueOfMg(self):
        if self.g % 2 == 0: return (1/4)*self.alpha_g*self.beta_g
        else : return (1/2)*self.alpha_g*self.beta_g
    def valueOfNg(self):
        if self.g % 2 == 0: return (1/2)*(2*self.g^2+self.g)^2
        else : return (2*self.g^2+self.g)^2
    def coefficients(self):
        g, s, w, R = self.g, self.s, self.w, self.R
        coefs = [(R(s-(2*g^2+g))/R(2*g^2+g))*w^(2*g+1),
                 (s*w^(2*g))/R(g), R((2*g-1)/3)*s*w^(2*g-2)]
        if g >= 3: coefs.append(s*w^2)
        if g == 4: coefs.insert(3, R(7/2)*s*w^4)
        if g == 5:
            coefs.insert(3, R(42/5)*s*w^6)
            coefs.insert(4, R(6)*s*w^4)
        return coefs[:]
    def value2Fq(self, value):
        import re
        search = re.compile("[a-zA-Z]+")
        if isinstance(value, str):
            return self.R(eval(search.sub("self.a",value).replace("^","**")))
        else: return self.R(value)
    def _chekingOfParameters(self):
        """ We check if the parameters  u,w,g,q satisfy the required conditions
        """
        p, g = self.R.characteristic(), self.g
        if (p% 2 == 0) or ((2*g^2+g)%p == 0):
            raise ValueError("The characteristic of F{}".format(self.q)+""\
                +" divise {}".format((2*g^2+g)))
        if (self.q%8 != 7):
            raise ValueError("q is different to 7 modulo 8".format(self.q))
        if self.w.is_zero() or self.u.is_zero(): raise ValueError("w = 0 or u = 0 in Fq ")
        if self.u.is_square(): raise ValueError("u is square in Fq")
        if self.g not in range(1,6): raise ValueError("The genus g out of range(1,5)")


    def _checkingValueOfTheParameterS(self):
        p, g = self.R.characteristic(), self.g
        alpha_g, beta_g, gamma_g = self.alpha_g, self.beta_g, self.gamma_g
        if self.s is None:
            if alpha_g % p == 0: self.s = gamma_g/beta_g
            else:
                delta_s = beta_g^2+4*alpha_g*gamma_g
                self.s = self.R((-beta_g+self.R(delta_s).square_root())/(2*alpha_g))
    def _chekingIfCurveIsHyperelliptic(self):
        """ We check if f(x) doesn't have a double root"""
        solution_f, solution_fprime = self.f.roots(), self.f.derivative().roots()
        f_roots = [root[0] for root in solution_f]
        fprime_roots = [root[0] for root in solution_fprime]
        if (set(f_roots) & set(fprime_roots)) != set():
            raise ValueError("The function f={}".format(self.f)+" has double roots")

class EncodingAndInvertGenusg(EncodingValidationOfParameters):
    def __init__(self, q, u, w, g=2, s = None):
        EncodingValidationOfParameters.__init__(self,q, u, w, g = g, s=s)
```

```
def _quadraticCharacter(self, value):
    if self.R(value).is_zero(): return 0
    elif self.R(value).is_square(): return 1
    else: return -1
def valuesNotInDomainOfTheEncoding(self):
    R, w, s, u, x = self.R, self.w, self.s, self.u, self.x
    roots = self.f(w*(u*x^2*(R(-self.mg)*s+R(-self.ng))+R(-1))).roots()
    return set([R(0)]) | set([root[0] for root in roots if root !=[]])
def encode(self, value):
    """ The encoding function psi(r)=(x,y)"""
    R, w, s, u, poly, a = self.R, self.w, self.s, self.u, self.poly, self.a
    r = self.value2Fq(value)
    if r in self.valuesNotInDomainOfTheEncoding():
        raise ValueError("The encoding function is not defined at r={}".format(r))
    v = w*(u*r^2*(R(-self.mg)*s+R(-self.ng))+R(-1))
    e = epsilon = self._quadraticCharacter(self.f(v))
    x = R((1+e)/2)*v+R((1-e)/2)*R(w*(-v+w)/(v+w))
    y = R(-e)*R(self.f(x)).square_root()
    return (x,y)
def decode(self, point):
    """ The inverse of the encoding function"""
    x,y,ng,mg = self.value2Fq(point[0]), self.value2Fq(point[1]), self.ng,self.mg
    R, w, s, u, poly, a = self.R, self.w, self.s, self.u, self.poly, self.a
    if not (y^2-self.f(x)).is_zero():
        raise ValueError("The given value is not a point of the hyperelliptic curve")
    if not (u*w*(x+w)*(R(-ng)+R(-mg)*s)).is_square():
        raise Exception("u*w*(x+w)*(-ng-mg*s) is not a square in Fq")
    r1 = ((x+w)/(u*w*(R(-ng)+R(-mg)*s))).square_root()
    r2 = (R(2)*w/(u*w*(x+w)*(R(-ng)+R(-mg)*s))).square_root()
    return "The preimages of ({} , {}) by the encoding function".format(x,y)+""\
        +" are equal to ({} , {}) or ({} , {})".format(r1, R(-r1),r2, R(-r2))


#First example
q = 2^521-1
fe = EncodingAndInvertGenusg(q=q,u=3,w=5,g=2); print(fe)
pt = fe.encode(121); print("\n (x,y) = "+str(pt)+"\n")
dc = fe.decode(pt); print("\n"+str(dc)+"\n")
# Second example . we change the genus of the curve
ge = EncodingAndInvertGenusg(q=q,u=3,w=5,g=3); print(ge)
pt2 = ge.encode(121); print("\n (x,y) = "+str(pt2)+"\n")
dc2 = ge.decode(pt2); print("\n"+str(dc2)+"\n")
```

References

1. Bernstein, D.J., Hamburg, M., Krasnova, A., Lange, T.: Elligator: elliptic-curve points indistinguishable from uniform random strings. In: Gligor, V., Yung, M. (eds.) CCS. ACM (2013)

2. Boneh, D., Franklin, M.: Identity-based encryption from the weil pairing. In: Kilian, J. (ed.) CRYPTO 2001. LNCS, vol. 2139, pp. 213–229. Springer, Heidelberg (2001). https://doi.org/10.1007/3-540-44647-8_13

3. Seck, M., Boudjou, H., Diarra, N., Khlil, A.Y.O.C.: On indifferentiable hashing into the Jacobian of hyperelliptic curves of genus 2. In: Joye, M., Nitaj, A. (eds.) AFRICACRYPT 2017. LNCS, vol. 10239, pp. 205–222. Springer, Cham (2017). https://doi.org/10.1007/978-3-319-57339-7_12

4. Choon, J.C., Hee Cheon, J.: An identity-based signature from gap Diffie-Hellman groups. In: Desmedt, Y.G. (ed.) PKC 2003. LNCS, vol. 2567, pp. 18–30. Springer, Heidelberg (2003). https://doi.org/10.1007/3-540-36288-6_2

5. Fouque, P.-A., Joux, A., Tibouchi, M.: Injective encodings to elliptic curves. In: Boyd, C., Simpson, L. (eds.) ACISP 2013. LNCS, vol. 7959, pp. 203–218. Springer, Heidelberg (2013). https://doi.org/10.1007/978-3-642-39059-3_14

6. Farashahi, R.R., Fouque, P.A., Shparlinski, I.E., Tibouchi, M., Voloch, J.F.: Indifferentiable deterministic hashing to elliptic and hyperelliptic curves. Math. Comput. **82**(281), 491–512 (2013)
7. He, X., Yu, W., Wang, K.: Hashing into generalized huff curves. In: Lin, D., Wang, X.F., Yung, M. (eds.) Inscrypt 2015. LNCS, vol. 9589, pp. 22–44. Springer, Cham (2016). https://doi.org/10.1007/978-3-319-38898-4_2
8. Icart, T.: How to hash into elliptic curves. In: Halevi, S. (ed.) CRYPTO 2009. LNCS, vol. 5677, pp. 303–316. Springer, Heidelberg (2009). https://doi.org/10.1007/978-3-642-03356-8_18
9. Kammerer, J.G., Lercier, R., Renault, G.: Encoding points on hyperelliptic curves over finite fields in deterministic polynomial time. CoRR, abs/1005.1454 (2010)
10. Koblitz, N.: Hyperelliptic cryptosystems. J. Cryptol. **1**(3), 139–150 (1989)
11. Yu, W., Wang, K., Li, B., He, X., Tian, S.: Deterministic encoding into twisted Edwards curves. In: Liu, J.K., Steinfeld, R. (eds.) ACISP 2016. LNCS, vol. 9723, pp. 285–297. Springer, Cham (2016). https://doi.org/10.1007/978-3-319-40367-0_18
12. Menezes, A.J., Wu, Y.-H., Zuccherato, R.J.: An elementary introduction to hyperelliptic curves. In: Koblitz, N. (ed.) Algebraic Aspects of Cryptography. Algorithms and Computation in Mathematics, vol. 3, pp. 155–178. Springer, Heidelberg (1998). https://doi.org/10.1007/978-3-662-03642-6
13. The Sage Developers: SageMath, the Sage Mathematics Software System (Version 7.4) (2017). http://www.sagemath.org
14. Scholten, J., Vercauteren, F.: An introduction to elliptic and hyperelliptic curve cryptography and the NTRU cryptosystem (2008)
15. Shallue, A., van de Woestijne, C.E.: Construction of rational points on elliptic curves over finite fields. In: Hess, F., Pauli, S., Pohst, M. (eds.) ANTS 2006. LNCS, vol. 4076, pp. 510–524. Springer, Heidelberg (2006). https://doi.org/10.1007/11792086_36
16. Ulas, M.: Rational points on certain hyperelliptic curves over finite fields. Bull. Pol. Acad. Sci. Math. **55**(2), 97–104 (2007)
17. Seck, M.: Sage Code for Generalization of Encodings into Hyperelliptic Curves, February 2018. Available on GitHub at https://gist.github.com/MichelSeck/50ca60e7ef4acb8196e3af78aa5ef2a1

HILA5 Pindakaas:[†] On the CCA Security of Lattice-Based Encryption with Error Correction

Daniel J. Bernstein[1](✉), Leon Groot Bruinderink[2](✉),
Tanja Lange[2](✉), and Lorenz Panny[2](✉)

[1] Department of Computer Science, University of Illinois at Chicago,
Chicago, IL 60607-7045, USA
djb@cr.yp.to
[2] Department of Mathematics and Computer Science,
Technische Universiteit Eindhoven,
P.O. Box 513, 5600 MB Eindhoven, The Netherlands
l.groot.bruinderink@tue.nl, tanja@hyperelliptic.org, lorenz@yx7.cc

Abstract. We show that the NISTPQC submission HILA5 is not secure against chosen-ciphertext attacks. Specifically, we demonstrate a key-recovery attack on HILA5 using an active attack on reused keys. The attack works around the error correction in HILA5. The attack applies to the HILA5 key-encapsulation mechanism (KEM), and also to the public-key encryption mechanism (PKE) obtained by NIST's procedure for combining the KEM with authenticated encryption. This contradicts the most natural interpretation of the IND-CCA security claim for HILA5.

Keywords: Post-quantum cryptography · KEM · RLWE
Reaction attack

1 Introduction

HILA5 [13] is a public-key scheme designed by Saarinen and published at SAC 2017. HILA5 was submitted as a "Key Encapsulation Mechanism and Public Key Encryption Algorithm" [12] to NIST's call [10] for post-quantum proposals. HILA5's design is based on Ring Learning With Errors (RLWE) over NTRU NTT rings. HILA5 takes the same ring parameters as New Hope [2] and changes the reconciliation method by which Alice and Bob achieve the same key to get a much lower chance of decryption failures.

The HILA5 submission [12] states

[†] "Helaas pindakaas" is a Dutch expression meaning "Oh well, too bad".

[*] Author list in alphabetical order; see https://www.ams.org/profession/leaders/culture/CultureStatement04.pdf. This work was supported in part by the Commission of the European Communities through the Horizon 2020 program under project number 645622 (PQCRYPTO), project number 643161 (ECRYPT-NET), and project number 645421 (ECRYPT-CSA); and by the U.S. National Science Foundation under grant 1314919. Date of this document: 2018.02.27.

A. Joux et al. (Eds.): AFRICACRYPT 2018, LNCS 10831, pp. 203–216, 2018.
https://doi.org/10.1007/978-3-319-89339-6_12

This design also provides IND-CCA secure KEM-DEM [CS03] public key encryption if used in conjunction with an appropriate AEAD [Rog02] such as NIST approved AES256-GCM [FIP01, Dwo07].

In this paper we show that HILA5 is not CCA secure: We compute Alice's secret key by sending her multiple encapsulation messages and using her answers to determine whether her decapsulated shared secret matches a certain guess or not. Our attack works independently of whether an AEAD is used or not and despite the error correcting code introduced in HILA5.

We have fully implemented our attack and experimentally verified that it works with high probability. We use the HILA5 reference implementation for Alice's part and also to verify that the retrieved secret key works for decryption. We use a slightly modified version of the same software for computations on the attacker's side; of course the attacker need not follow the computations an honest party would.

Acknowledgement. We thank Christine van Vredendaal for helpful discussions.

1.1 Related Work

Ajtai–Dwork [1] and NTRU [7] are the oldest lattice-based encryption systems. In 1999 Hall, Goldberg, and Schneier [6] developed a reaction attack which recovers the Ajtai–Dwork private key by observing decryption failures for suitably crafted encryptions to the public key. They wrote "We feel that the existence of these attacks effectively limits these ciphers to theoretical considerations only. That is, any implementation of the ciphers will be subject to the attacks we present and hence not safe."

Hoffstein and Silverman [8] adapted the attack to NTRU. As a defense, they suggested modifying NTRU to use the Fujisaki–Okamoto transform [5]. For a system without decryption failures, this transform turns a CPA-secure system into a CCA-secure one. At the same time this complicates and slows down the cryptosystem. For NTRU, the transform turns out to still allow attacks that exploit occasional decryption failures induced by *valid* ciphertexts; see [9].

New Hope [2] is a key-encapsulation mechanism (KEM), presented as a key-exchange protocol. It allows occasional decryption failures for valid ciphertexts, and explicitly avoids the "changes" that would be required for the Fujisaki–Okamoto transform. To prevent reaction attacks and other chosen-ciphertext attacks by a malicious Bob, New Hope requires using ephemeral keys, meaning keys that change with every execution of the protocol. The New Hope paper warns that reusing a public key in multiple protocol runs ("key caching") would be "disastrous for security", although it does not describe an attack.

Fluhrer [4] showed the details of how to attack key reuse in a similar key-exchange protocol. Followup work [3] extended the attack to more key-exchange protocols.

HILA5 is similar to New Hope, and still does not use the Fujisaki–Okamoto transform. HILA5 includes an error-correction method that practically eliminates decryption failures for valid ciphertexts. HILA5 does not warn against key caching: on the contrary, the most natural interpretation of the HILA5 security claims is that HILA5 is secure against chosen-ciphertext attacks. See Sect. 5. We published our results in December 2017; as of February 2018, the designer of HILA5 has not proposed an alternative interpretation of the security claims.

2   Data Flow in the Attack

A KEM is defined by three algorithms. Key generation produces a secret key and a public key. Encapsulation produces a ciphertext and a session key, given a public key. Decapsulation produces a session key or failure, given a ciphertext and a secret key. The HILA5 submission document [12] gives details and reference code for a particular KEM, the "HILA5 KEM".

Our attack is a key-recovery attack against the HILA5 KEM: the attacker, evil Bob, ends up computing the secret key of a target Alice. This secret key gives the attacker the ability to run the decapsulation algorithm using Alice's secret key, and thus the ability to immediately decrypt legitimate ciphertexts sent by other users to Alice.

Our attack is a chosen-ciphertext attack: evil Bob chooses ciphertexts to provide to Alice (different from the legitimate ciphertexts), and learns something from observing the outputs of Alice decapsulating those ciphertexts. Formally, the attack shows that the HILA5 KEM does not provide IND-CCA2 security.

There are two important ways that the attack does not need the full power of a CCA2 decapsulation oracle. First, the attack is what is called a "reaction attack" in [6] or a "sloppy Alice attack" in [14]: evil Bob has a guess for the output of each decapsulation, and learns whether Alice's actual decapsulation output matches this guess. Evil Bob does not need any further information.

Second, evil Bob chooses all of his ciphertexts, and learns the secret key from Alice's reactions, before seeing the legitimate ciphertexts to decrypt. Formally, the attack shows not only that the HILA5 KEM does not provide IND-CCA2 security, but also that it does not provide IND-CCA1 security.

2.1   Hashing the Secret Key Does Not Stop the Attack

One can easily stop key-recovery attacks by defining HILA5Hash as follows. HILA5Hash key generation computes a uniform random 32-byte string s, and then runs HILA5 key generation to obtain a public key, hashing s to generate all randomness used in HILA5 key generation. The HILA5Hash secret key is s. HILA5Hash encapsulation is the same as HILA5 encapsulation. HILA5Hash decapsulation reconstructs the HILA5 secret key from s (again running the HILA5 key-generation algorithm; alternatively, the HILA5 secret key can be cached), and then runs the HILA5 decapsulation algorithm.

Unless the hash function is easy to invert, a key-recovery attack against HILA5 does not produce a key-recovery attack against HILA5Hash. However, this hashing does not prevent the attacker from decrypting legitimate ciphertexts sent by other users to Alice.

2.2   AEAD Does Not Stop the Attack

A PKE is defined by three algorithms. Key generation produces a secret key and a public key, as in a KEM. Encryption produces a ciphertext, given a plaintext and a public key. Decryption produces a plaintext or failure, given a ciphertext and a secret key.

The subtitle of the HILA5 submission is "Key Encapsulation Mechanism (KEM) and Public Key Encryption Algorithm". The submission document does not include a definition of a PKE, but NIST had already stated before submission that it would automatically convert each submitted KEM to a PKE using the following "standard conversion technique": "appending to the KEM ciphertext, an AES-GCM ciphertext of the plaintext message" where the AES-GCM key is "the symmetric key output by the encapsulate function". This is the standard Cramer–Shoup "KEM-DEM" construction, using AES-GCM as the DEM. We write "HILA5 PKE" for the PKE that NIST will automatically produce in this way from the HILA5 KEM.[1]

Breaking the IND-CCA2 security of a KEM does not necessarily imply breaking the IND-CCA2 security of a PKE obtained in this way. IND-CCA2 attacks against the KEM can see session keys produced by decapsulation, whereas IND-CCA2 attacks against the PKE are merely able to see the result of AES-GCM decryption using those keys.

However, our attack against the HILA5 KEM is also a key-recovery attack against the HILA5 PKE. It is important here that the attack is a reaction attack: what evil Bob needs to know is merely whether a guessed session key is correct. Starting from this guessed session key, evil Bob produces a valid AES-GCM ciphertext using this guess as an AES key. If decapsulation in fact produces this session key then AES-GCM decryption succeeds and produces the plaintext that evil Bob started with. If decapsulation produces a different session key then AES-GCM decryption is practically guaranteed to fail (anything else would be a surprising security flaw in AES-GCM), so evil Bob sees a decryption failure from the PKE.

To summarize, evil Bob sees decryption failures from the PKE, and learns from this which guesses were correct, which is the same information that evil Bob obtains from the KEM. Evil Bob then computes the secret key from this information. Consequently, the HILA5 PKE does not provide IND-CCA2 security, and does not even provide IND-CCA1 security.

2.3   Black Holes Would Stop the Attack

Like other chosen-ciphertext attacks, our attack is inapplicable to scenarios where the results of decapsulation and decryption are hidden from the attacker.

---

[1] NIST actually deviates slightly from the KEM-DEM construction: it specifies a "randomly generated IV" for AES-GCM, while Cramer and Shoup use a deterministic DEM. For consistency with the ciphertext sizes mentioned in [12], we actually define "HILA5 PKE" to be the Cramer–Shoup construction using AES-GCM with an all-zero IV. Switching to NIST's construction would expand ciphertext sizes by 12 bytes using the default IV sizes for AES-GCM, and would not affect our attack.

For example, if ciphertexts are sent to NSA's public key, and if NSA hides the results of applying its secret key to those ciphertexts, then an attacker outside NSA cannot use our attack to compute NSA's secret key. However, if NSA reacts to those results in a way that leaks to the attacker which ciphertexts were valid, then the attacker can compute NSA's secret key.

2.4   The Fujisaki–Okamoto Transform Would Stop the Attack

We briefly outline a more radical change to HILA5, which we call "HILA5FO". HILA5FO ciphertexts are slightly larger than HILA5 ciphertexts, decapsulation is more complicated, and decapsulation is extrapolated (from reported HILA5 benchmarks) to be several times slower, but HILA5FO would stop our attack.

The idea of the HILA5FO KEM is to reapply the encapsulation algorithm as part of decapsulation, and check whether the resulting ciphertext is identical to the received ciphertext. This is not a new idea: it is used in many other submissions to NIST (with various differences in details), typically with credit to Fujisaki and Okamoto [5].

HILA5 does not provide any easy way to reconstruct the randomness used in encapsulation (most importantly Bob's b), so the HILA5FO KEM computes this randomness as a hash of a plaintext recovered as part of decapsulation. The HILA5 KEM does not transmit a plaintext, so the HILA5FO KEM is instead built from the HILA5 PKE.

Encapsulation in the HILA5FO KEM thus chooses a random plaintext, and encrypts this plaintext using the HILA5 PKE (the HILA5 KEM producing a session key for AES-GCM) using a hash of the plaintext to compute all randomness used inside the PKE. Decapsulation applies HILA5 PKE decryption (HILA5 KEM decapsulation producing a session key for AES-GCM decryption), and checks that the resulting plaintext produces the same ciphertext.

Deriving a PKE from the HILA5FO KEM would involve two layers of AES-GCM, which can be compressed to one layer as follows: place 32 bytes of randomness at the beginning of the user-supplied plaintext, and then encrypt this plaintext using the HILA5 PKE, again using a hash of the plaintext to compute all randomness used inside the PKE. The overall ciphertext size is the original plaintext size, plus 32 bytes (the randomness), plus the HILA5 KEM ciphertext size, plus 16 bytes (the AES-GCM authenticator), i.e., 32 bytes more than the HILA5 PKE. The main cost in HILA5FO decryption (for short messages) is reapplying HILA5 KEM encapsulation, which according to [12, Table 1] is five times slower than HILA5 KEM decapsulation.

3   Preliminaries

This section describes the HILA5 scheme and Fluhrer's attack on RLWE schemes.

3.1   The HILA5 Scheme

We describe the scheme as given in [12, Sect. 4.9] but leave out formatting and NTT conversions. These are used in the attack implementation to interface with the reference implementation but do not contribute to the security and hamper readability.

The major computations take place in the ring $R = \mathbb{Z}_q[x]/(x^n + 1)$, where $n = 1024$ and $q = 12289$. Alice's secret key is a small, random polynomial $a \in R$, where small (here and in the following) means that the coefficients are chosen from a narrow distribution around zero, more precisely the discrete binomial distribution Ψ_{16} which has integer values in $[-16, 16]$. To compute the public key she picks another small random polynomial $e \in R$ and a random $g \in R$ and computes $A = ga + e$. She publishes (g, A) and keeps a as her secret.

An honest Bob picks two random small polynomials $b, e' \in R$ and computes $B = gb + e'$ and $y = Ab$. Bob sends B to Alice. The second value

$$y = Ab = (ga + e)b = gab + eb \approx gab$$

is very close to what Alice can compute using her secret:

$$x = aB = a(gb + e') = gab + e'a \approx gab,$$

because a, b, e, e' are all small.

A simple rounding operation to achieve a shared secret, such as taking the top bits of each coefficient, will induce differences between Alice's and Bob's version with too high probability. For example, Bob could take $k[i] = \lfloor 2\, y[i]/q \rfloor$ and Alice could take $k'[i] = \lfloor 2\, x[i]/q \rfloor$, where we use $t[i]$ to denote the ith coefficient of polynomial or vector t, but for indices with $(gab)[i] \approx 0$ (or $q/2$) the error-terms can cause the values to flip to a different bit, i.e., $k[i] \neq k'[i]$. For this rounding operation, we call elements of $\{0, q/2\}$ the "edges", as these are the values for which it is probable that errors occur.

This is why Bob sends a second vector, a binary reconciliation vector c, to help Alice recover the same k as Bob. Basically, this means that the scheme uses two pairs of edges. If $y[i]$ was close to one edge of a certain pair, Bob will choose the other pair of edges, so that Alice can still successfully recover the shared secret. In previous work [11], the reconciliation vector achieves a successful shared secret with high probability, as long as $|x[i] - y[i]| < q/8$.

HILA5 differs in how these reconciliation bits are computed. For each coefficient $y[i]$ of y Bob computes $k[i] = \lfloor 2\, y[i]/q \rfloor$, $c[i] \equiv \lfloor 4\, y[i]/q \rfloor \bmod 2$, and

$$d[i] = \begin{cases} 1 & \text{if } |(y[i] \bmod \lfloor q/4 \rfloor) - \lfloor q/8 \rfloor| \leq \beta \\ 0 & \text{otherwise,} \end{cases}$$

where $\beta = 799$. He then selects the first 496 positions i for which $d[i] = 1$ and restarts with fresh b and e' if there are fewer. Positions with $d[i] = 1$ are those for which it is likely that Alice and Bob recover the same value. In other words, for these indices the value $(gab)[i]$ is likely to be far away from an edge, thus further reducing the probability of errors in the shared secret. (Note that the description suggests to discard some positions if there are more than 496 such positions while the code deterministically discards the later ones by setting $d[j] = 0$ for them.)

The encapsulation consists of B, d, c, and an extra part r described below; here d covers the full n positions while c can be compressed to those positions i where $d[i] = 1$.

Alice recovers the $k[i]$ at the selected 496 positions by computing

$$k'[i] = \lfloor 2\,(x[i] - c[i] \cdot \lfloor q/4 \rfloor + \lfloor q/8 \rceil \bmod q)/q \rfloor.$$

The HILA5 submission shows that $k'[i] = k[i]$ with probability $1 - 2^{-36}$. Let k (resp. k') be the 496-bit string given by the concatenation of the $k[i]$ (resp. $k'[i]$).

The role of r is not well described but the HILA5 design overview says that is an encrypted encoding of a part of k. It is computed by splitting k as $k = m\|z$, where m gets the first 256 bits and z the remaining 240 bits. HILA5 uses a custom-designed error-correcting code XE5 that corrects at least 5 errors to compute a 240-bit checksum s of m and then computes $r = s \oplus z$, where $\oplus$ denotes bitwise addition (XOR).

Alice computes $k' = m'\|z'$, the checksum s' on m', and applies the XE5 error correction to m', s', z' and r to correct m' to m.

3.2 Fluhrer's Attack

The chosen-ciphertext attack on HILA5 that we are going to present is a variant of the following attack against key reuse in RLWE-based key exchange protocols presented by Fluhrer in 2016 [4]. This section assumes that Bob computes the $c[i]$ and $k[i]$ in a way similar to the previous section. The $d[i]$ were added in HILA5 and will be considered in the next section.

Recall that Alice's version of the shared secret key is

$$gab + e'a,$$

where g is some large public generator element, a and b are Alice's and Bob's small private keys, and c' is a small noise vector chosen by Bob. This version of the shared secret differs from Bob's by some small error, hence they need to employ a reconciliation mechanism to arrive at the same secret bit string.

The general strategy of an evil Bob is to artificially force one (say, the first) coefficient of gab to be close to the edge M between the intervals that are mapped to bits 0 and 1 during reconciliation. An honest user would set the reconciliation bit $c[0]$ in that case, so Alice would use another mapping that is less likely to produce an error; but evil Bob does not. Since evil Bob proceeds honestly except for the first bit, he knows two possibilities for Alice's key, hence he can query Alice with one of these guesses and distinguish between 0 and 1 based on her reaction. If we assume for the moment that evil Bob can choose, hence knows, $(gab)[0]$, this tells him that $(e'a)[0]$ lies in a certain interval.

After a few queries using binary search with varying values for $(gab)[0]$, evil Bob knows the exact distance of $(e'a)[0]$ from the edge, and if he sets $e' = 1$, this distance is nothing but the first coefficient of Alice's secret key a. Note that in Fluhrer's setting the edge M is at zero and he uses b with $(gab)[0] = 1$, hence evil Bob can just multiply that b by small distances to obtain a prescribed $(gab)[0]$ when searching for $(e'a)[0]$. In our adaptation of the attack to HILA5, this step is more involved; see Sect. 4.2.

One could apply this method individually to each coefficient to extract Alice's full secret key. However, being able to recover the coefficient at one position is enough: due to the structure of the underlying ring, evil Bob can shift the ith coefficient of a into the constant term of $e'a$ by setting e' to $-x^{n-i}$, i.e., a vector with one entry of -1 and 0 elsewhere.

We now come back to the assumption made above. Notice that evil Bob does not a priori know a vector $b \in R$ such that $(gab)[0] = 1$, but he can still reasonably guess one: Alice's public key is $ga + e$ for small vectors a and e, hence if b is a small low-weight vector such that $(b \cdot (ga + e))[0]$ is close to 1, there is a good chance that in fact $(gab)[0] = 1$. Thus, while evil Bob does not have a deterministic method to find an "evil" b, he can still just make educated guesses based on Alice's public key until he finds one that works. Finding $b \in R$ with $(b \cdot (ga + e))[0]$ close to 1 is an offline computation using only Alice's public key; testing for $(gab)[0] = 1$ requires interaction with Alice.

There are several follow-ups to Fluhrer's paper, e.g. the recently posted [3], but a small and new generalization of Fluhrer's attack is sufficient to attack HILA5.

4   Chosen-Ciphertext Attack on HILA5

In this section, we describe how we circumvent the error-correction code and how to adapt Fluhrer's attack to the HILA5 case.

4.1   Working Around Error Correction

The HILA5 construction includes XE5 as an error-correcting code that is applied to the shared secret after decapsulation. Both Alice and Bob compute their version of a redundancy check, which will help Alice to correct up to 5 errors in the shared secret. The redundancy part r is divided into ten subcodewords $r = r_0, \ldots, r_9$ of variable sizes. For the purpose of the attack, these sizes do not matter, but we use the same notation L_i for the size, as in the HILA5 paper. This means we can index each $r_i = r_{(i,0)} \cdots r_{(i,L_i-1)}$ for $i \in \{0, \ldots, 9\}$.

Bob first computes his part of the HILA5 encapsulation, i.e., he computes his version of the shared secret, selects the indices that are safe to use by Alice and computes the reconciliation vector. The last 240 bits of Bob's shared secret are used in XE5 error-correction. From these bits, Bob constructs his redundancy check r', and sends this as part of the ciphertext.

Upon receiving Bob's ciphertext, Alice first computes her part of the HILA5 decapsulation, i.e., she computes her version of the shared secret. Then she computes her own redundancy check r and computes the distance r^Δ with Bob's r' from the ciphertext:

$$r^\Delta = r' \oplus r$$

To determine which bits in the shared secret are erroneous, Alice determines a weight $w_k^\Delta \in [0, 10]$ for each of the 256 bits by the following formula:

$$w_k^\Delta = r_{0,\lfloor k/16 \rfloor}^\Delta + \sum_{j=1}^{9} r_{j,k \bmod L_j}^\Delta$$

Now, if a single bit k of Alice's shared secret is flipped, it means $w_k^\Delta = 10$ [12, Lemma 2], and it is therefore detectable and correctable by Alice. Moreover, it is shown that XE5 corrects bit k as long as $w_k^\Delta \geq 6$ [12, Theorem 1], which means XE5 can correct at least 5 bits in the shared secret. This means that applying Fluhrer's original attack directly to HILA5 will not work, as Fluhrer's original attack depends crucially on the attacker's ability to detect single-bit errors in Alice's version of the shared secret. Thus, to apply Fluhrer's attack, we have to work around these error-correction abilities.

In the attack described in the next section, we focus on inducing errors only in the first bit $k = 0$ of the shared secret. This means the attacker evil Bob needs to force w_0^Δ to be less than 6, as this means XE5 is no longer capable of correcting the first bit. However, evil Bob needs to leave the remaining error-correction in place, otherwise he still does not know if the first bit was the only flipped bit. In order to do that, evil Bob needs to change his redundancy check r' to do exactly that. As w_0^Δ is obtained by summing up the first bits of the subcodeword distances r_i^Δ, he can flip any 5 of the bits labeled $r'_{(0,0)}$ through $r'_{(9,0)}$ to force $w_0^\Delta < 6$. Our attack flips the first 5 of these bits. This means in the following section we consider the issue of error-correction solved and can directly apply a modification of Fluhrer's attack.

4.2 Details of the Attack

This section elaborates evil Bob's approach to recover Alice's secret key. As mentioned before, the general procedure mimics Fluhrer's attack (Sect. 3.2). The major steps are:

1. Guess a small low-weight secret b_0 such that $(gab_0)[0]$ is at the edge M.
2. For each $\delta \in \{-16, \ldots, 16\}$, compute b_δ such that $(gab_\delta)[0] = M + \delta$.
3. For each target coefficient of Alice's secret:
   (a) Choose e' such that $(e'a)[0]$ is the target coefficient.
   (b) Perform a binary search using the b_δ to recover the target coefficient. (Alice's coefficient $(gab_\delta + e'a)[0]$ maps to a 1 bit iff $(-e'a)[0] > \delta$.)
4. If the results look "bad" after recovering a few coefficients in this way, the guess for b_0 was probably wrong and evil Bob should start over at step 1.

Note that for each oracle query, i.e., for every interaction with Alice, Bob proceeds honestly except for using specially crafted b_δ and e', setting $d_0 = c_0 = 1$, and flipping a few bits in the error correction as described in Sect. 4.1. We now explain and analyze the steps above in more detail.

Forcing Coefficients Near the Edge. In HILA5's reconciliation mechanism, there is no edge at zero for any choice of reconciliation bit, hence Fluhrer's attack does not apply without modifications. We chose to set the reconciliation bit c_0 to 1 and attack the edge at

$$M = \lfloor q/8 \rceil = 1536.$$

To perform the binary search for Alice's secret coefficients in the attack, we need to find small low-weight vectors b_δ such that

$$(gab_\delta)[0] = M + \delta$$

for all δ with $|\delta| \leq 16$. (As mentioned in Sect. 3.2, Fluhrer's evil Bob attacked $M = 0$, thus he could guess b_1 based on Alice's public key and set $b_\delta = \delta \cdot b_1$.) One could of course try to guess each b_δ individually based on Alice's public key, but as we want to get all b_δ right at the same time, this has exponentially low success probability. Instead, we make use of a special property of the M used in HILA5: The inverse

$$M^{-1} \bmod q = -8$$

is small.[2] Hence, as soon as evil Bob successfully guessed b_0, he may simply set

$$b_\delta = (1 + \delta M^{-1} \bmod q) \cdot b_0.$$

In our case, we choose b_0 with only two non-zero coefficients from $\{\pm 1\}$, thus b_δ will have only two non-zero coefficients bounded by $1 + 8\delta$. This property is necessary to make sure evil Bob can actually know what Alice's version of the shared secret will be (except for the target bit that leaks information): If the coefficients of b_δ are too large, the error $eb - e'a$ between Alice's and Bob's shared secrets becomes too large to recover from and their secrets will mismatch no matter what the value of the attacked bit is. In theory, with these parameters we still expect a tiny possibility of unintended errors, but this happens so rarely that it is not an issue in practice. If it ever does occur, Bob can detect that his recovered secret key is wrong and simply start over with a new b_0.

When evil Bob chooses a random b_0 with two non-zero coefficients in $\{\pm 1\}$ and with $(Ab_0)[0] = M$, the probability that in fact $(gab_0)[0] = M$ holds is just the probability that two Ψ_{16}-distributed values sum to zero:

$$\sum_{i=0}^{32} \binom{32}{i}^2 / 2^{64} \approx 9.9\%,$$

hence he can expect to find a good b_0 after about 10 tries. Since A can be approximated by a uniformly distributed sequence over $\mathbb{Z}_q$, the expected number of ± 1-combinations of two coefficients of A which equal M is

$$\binom{1024}{2} \cdot 4/q \approx 170.$$

---

[2] Note that this also holds for some other "natural" choices of M as rounded fractions of q, but it is not automatically true for any conceivable M.

Hence, the probability that evil Bob exhausts this pool of choices without finding a good b_0 is roughly 2^{-25}.

(If this ever happens, then evil Bob can still try a larger interval, i.e., search for b_0 with $|(Ab_0)[0] - M| \leq K$ for some small K. This would in theory work for a wider range of keys, but the expected number of wrong guesses grows slightly. One could also choose three non-zero coefficients in b_0, although this increases the chance of unintended errors in Alice's shared secret. We have not had any problems with $K = 0$ in practice.)

Detecting Bad Guesses. After choosing b_0 based on Alice's public key as described above, evil Bob may just go ahead and try to recover Alice's secret key using that b_0. If it is correct, he will of course find a sequence that looks like it was sampled from the Ψ_{16} distribution. If b_0 is bad, say, $(gab_0)[0] = M + \gamma$ for some small $\gamma \neq 0$, then

$$(gab_\delta)[0] = M + \delta + \gamma - 8\delta\gamma,$$

hence typically $(gab_\delta)[0]$ is considerably smaller than M if $\delta > 0$ and considerably larger if $\delta < 0$; in both cases Alice's secret $(e'a)[0]$ is dominated by $\delta + \gamma - 8\delta\gamma$, which means the oracle output does not depend on the secret. This implies the binary search will always converge to 0 or -1 when b_0 is bad. (For $\delta = 0$, the behavior *does* depend on $(e'a)[0]$ since γ is small, so both cases really occur.) Evil Bob can detect this failure mode by determining a few coefficients and checking whether all of them are in $\{0, -1\}$. If this is the case, evil Bob simply starts over with a new b_0. The probability that an actual secret key starts with a sequence of k coefficients from $\{0, -1\}$ is about 0.27^k, hence setting $k = 8$ reduces the probability of a false negative to roughly 2^{-15}. There is a small probability of false positives if evil Bob uses only this heuristic (e.g., when $|\gamma| = 1$), but this can easily can be detected using statistical methods (the recovered sequence will not be Ψ_{16}-distributed) or by simply testing the obtained secret key in the end and running the attack again if it failed. In practice the heuristic works fine.

The Number of Queries. Assuming we already have a good b_0, the binary search needs an expected $5 + \varepsilon$ queries to the oracle to recover one coefficient.[3] Since evil Bob decides whether he has a good b_0 based on the first few coefficients that he obtains using that b_0, he usually wastes a few hundred queries on guesses for b_0 that turn out to be useless: If he looks at the first 8 coefficients obtained from each b_0 as suggested above, this adds expected ≈ 400 queries to the 5120 needed to recover all the coefficients. In summary, evil Bob will with overwhelming probability recover Alice's secret key in less than 6000 queries.

Evil Bob can trade computation for a smaller number of queries: retrieve some coefficients, and reduce the original lattice problem to low enough dimension to solve by computation.

---

[3] The ε arises from the fact that Ψ_{16} samples from $33 > 2^5$ distinct values, but the extremal values occur so rarely that $\varepsilon \approx 2^{-27}$.

4.3   Implementation

We implemented a proof of concept of the attack in Python, reusing portions of the HILA5 reference implementation via the `ctypes` library. The only modifications we made to the reference implementation were making some functions non-`static` to be able to call them from within Python, and adding extra parameters to the encapsulation function (not used by Alice) such that evil Bob can override his private values b and e'. The complete attack script can be found at https://helaas.org/hila5-20171218.tar.gz. As expected, we have never observed the attack script failing to recover Alice's key. The empirical number of queries matches the theoretical prediction made above.

5   HILA5 Security Claims

In this section, we discuss our interpretation of security claims made by both the paper and NIST submission of HILA5, which motivated this paper.

NIST does not require IND-CCA2 security for KEM and PKE submissions. Instead it requires submissions to say whether they are aiming for IND-CCA2 security or merely for IND-CPA security.

IND-CPA security is adequate in the context of key exchange in TLS, if a new public key is generated for each TLS session. For example, New Hope [2] appears to be safe for use in TLS. New Hope does not aim for IND-CCA2 security, and specifically warns against using a key more than once: "No key caching ... it is crucial that both parties use fresh secrets for each instantiation".

We emphasize that our attack does not break the IND-CPA security of HILA5. If HILA5 were clearly labeled as aiming merely for IND-CPA security then our attack would merely be a cautionary note, showing the importance of not reusing keys.

However, HILA5 went beyond claiming IND-CPA security. There are some undefined words in the HILA5 security claims, but the most natural interpretation of the security claims is that the HILA5 PKE provides IND-CCA2 security. There is certainly a high risk of the claims being interpreted in this way by potential users. Our attack shows that the HILA5 PKE does not provide IND-CCA2 security.

There is even a risk of users thinking that the HILA5 KEM is being claimed to provide IND-CCA2 security.[4] The HILA5 submission document does not say that the HILA5 KEM security target is merely IND-CPA. Our attack shows that the HILA5 KEM does not provide IND-CCA2 security.

We give four quotes from [12] to explain why the HILA5 security claims are most naturally interpreted as claiming IND-CCA2 security for the HILA5 PKE. We have not found anything in [12] or [13] indicating a different interpretation.

---

[4] Adam Langley posted an online table of speeds for announced KEMs submitted to NIST. He wrote "I only want to list CCA-secure KEMs here". He listed HILA5, and accepted a correction from the HILA5 author regarding the speed of HILA5. After the correction, HILA5 had the fastest decapsulation in the entire table.

[12, Section 1]: *The HILA5 KEM can be adopted for public key encryption in straightforward fashion. We recommend using the AES-256-GCM AEAD [FIP01, Dwo07] in conjunction with the KEM when public key encryption functionality is desired.*

The details of this "conjunction" are not formally defined. The most natural interpretation is that this is the HILA5 PKE, using the session key produced by the HILA5 KEM as the AES-GCM key.

[12, Section 4.1]: *NIST requires at least IND-CPA [BDPR98] security from a KEM scheme (Section 1.6). ... The design also provides IND-CCA secure KEM-DEM [CS03] public key encryption if used in conjunction with an appropriate AEAD [Rog02] such as NIST approved AES256-GCM [FIP01, Dwo07]. These properties are derived from [Pei14].*

This is a claim of IND-CCA security for a PKE. "IND-CCA" in the literature usually means IND-CCA2, although sometimes it means merely IND-CCA1. The PKE is not formally defined, but again the most natural interpretation is simply that the session key produced by the HILA5 KEM is the AES-GCM key used to encrypt a user-supplied plaintext. Our attack shows that this PKE does not even provide IND-CCA1 security, let alone IND-CCA2 security.

Our attack does not work against what we call the HILA5FO PKE (see Sect. 2.4), a more complicated PKE using the Fujisaki–Okamoto transformation. This transformation is also mentioned in "[Pei14]" as a way to achieve IND-CCA security. It is conceivable that the HILA5 submission was alluding to a PKE of this type. However, this interpretation does not appear to be compatible with the statement "Ciphertext size: 2012 Byte expansion (KEM) + payload + MAC" in [12, Sect. 6]; the HILA5FO ciphertext size is 32 bytes larger than this.

[12, Section 4.9]: *For active security we suggest that K is used as keying material for an AEAD (Authenticated Encryption with Associated Data) [Rog02] scheme such as AES256-GCM [Dwo07, FIP01] or Keyak [BDP+16] in order to protect message integrity.*

Here "K" is defined as the session key produced by the HILA5 KEM. In the context of KEMs and PKEs, "active security" is normally interpreted as IND-CCA2 security, although it might have other interpretations. The authentication in AES-GCM prevents modifications to the message encrypted by AES-GCM, but this is not enough to stop active attacks, since it does not protect the underlying KEM.

[12, Section 6.1]: *HILA5 is essentially drop-in compatible with current public key encryption applications. There are no practical usage restrictions.*

Security against chosen-ciphertext attacks is essential for a wide range of current PKE applications, so this would appear to include a claim of CCA security for the HILA5 PKE. However, our attack retrieves the secret key from the HILA5 PKE.

References

1. Ajtai, M., Dwork, C.: A public-key cryptosystem with worst-case/average-case equivalence. In: STOC, pp. 284–293. ACM (1997)
2. Alkim, E., Ducas, L., Pöppelmann, T., Schwabe, P.: Post-quantum key exchange - a new hope. In: USENIX Security Symposium, pp. 327–343. USENIX Association (2016)
3. Ding, J., Alsayigh, S., Saraswathy, R.V., Fluhrer, S.R., Lin, X.: Leakage of signal function with reused keys in RLWE key exchange. In: ICC, pp. 1–6. IEEE (2017)
4. Fluhrer, S.R.: Cryptanalysis of ring-LWE based key exchange with key share reuse. IACR Cryptology ePrint Archive 2016/085 (2016). https://ia.cr/2016/085
5. Fujisaki, E., Okamoto, T.: Secure integration of asymmetric and symmetric encryption schemes. In: Wiener, M. (ed.) CRYPTO 1999. LNCS, vol. 1666, pp. 537–554. Springer, Heidelberg (1999). https://doi.org/10.1007/3-540-48405-1_34
6. Hall, C., Goldberg, I., Schneier, B.: Reaction attacks against several public-key cryptosystem. In: Varadharajan, V., Mu, Y. (eds.) ICICS 1999. LNCS, vol. 1726, pp. 2–12. Springer, Heidelberg (1999). https://doi.org/10.1007/978-3-540-47942-0_2
7. Hoffstein, J., Pipher, J., Silverman, J.H.: NTRU: a ring-based public key cryptosystem. In: Buhler, J.P. (ed.) ANTS 1998. LNCS, vol. 1423, pp. 267–288. Springer, Heidelberg (1998). https://doi.org/10.1007/BFb0054868
8. Hoffstein, J., Silverman, J.H.: Reaction attacks against the NTRU public key cryptosystem. NTRU Cryptosystems Technical report 015, version 2 (2000). https://web.archive.org/web/20000914041434/http://www.ntru.com:80/NTRUF TPDocsFolder/NTRUTech015.pdf
9. Howgrave-Graham, N., Nguyen, P.Q., Pointcheval, D., Proos, J., Silverman, J.H., Singer, A., Whyte, W.: The impact of decryption failures on the security of NTRU encryption. In: Boneh, D. (ed.) CRYPTO 2003. LNCS, vol. 2729, pp. 226–246. Springer, Heidelberg (2003). https://doi.org/10.1007/978-3-540-45146-4_14
10. National Institute of Standards and Technology: Announcing request for nominations for public-key post-quantum cryptographic algorithms (2016). https://csrc.nist.gov/news/2016/public-key-post-quantum-cryptographic-algorithms
11. Peikert, C.: Lattice cryptography for the internet. In: Mosca, M. (ed.) PQCrypto 2014. LNCS, vol. 8772, pp. 197–219. Springer, Cham (2014). https://doi.org/10.1007/978-3-319-11659-4_12
12. Saarinen, M.-J.O.: HILA5: key encapsulation mechanism (KEM) and public key encryption algorithm (2017). Submission to NIST: https://github.com/mjosaarinen/hila5/blob/master/Supporting_Documentation/hila5spec.pdf
13. Saarinen, M.-J.O.: HILA5: on reliability, reconciliation, and error correction for ring-LWE encryption. In: Adams, C., Camenisch, J. (eds.) SAC 2017. LNCS, vol. 10719, pp. 192–212. Springer, Cham (2018). https://doi.org/10.1007/978-3-319-72565-9_10
14. Verheul, E.R., Doumen, J.M., van Tilborg, H.C.A.: Sloppy Alice attacks! Adaptive chosen ciphertext attacks on the McEliece public-key cryptosystem. In: Blaum, M., Farrell, P.G., van Tilborg, H.C.A. (eds.) Information, Coding and Mathematics. ECS(CIT), vol. 687, pp. 99–119. Springer, Boston (2002). https://doi.org/10.1007/978-1-4757-3585-7_7

Large FHE Gates from Tensored Homomorphic Accumulator

Guillaume Bonnoron[1($\boxtimes$)], Léo Ducas[2], and Max Fillinger[2]

[1] Chair of Naval Cyber Defense & Lab-STICC/CID/IRIS, Brest, France
guillaume.bonnoron@telecom-bretagne.eu
[2] CWI, Amsterdam, The Netherlands

Abstract. The main bottleneck of all known Fully Homomorphic Encryption schemes lies in the bootstrapping procedure invented by Gentry (STOC'09). The cost of this procedure can be mitigated either using Homomorphic SIMD techniques, or by performing larger computation per bootstrapping procedure.

In this work, we propose new techniques allowing to perform more operations per bootstrapping in FHEW-type schemes (EUROCRYPT'13). While maintaining the quasi-quadratic $\tilde{O}(n^2)$ complexity of the whole cycle, our new scheme allows to evaluate gates with $\Omega(\log n)$ input bits, which constitutes a quasi-linear speed-up. Our scheme is also very well adapted to large threshold gates, natively admitting up to $\Omega(n)$ inputs. This could be helpful for homomorphic evaluation of neural networks.

Our theoretical contribution is backed by a preliminary prototype implementation, which can perform 6-to-6 bit gates in less than 10 s on a single core, as well as threshold gates over 63 input bits even faster.

Keywords: Fully Homomorphic Encryption · Large gates
Threshold gates · Ideal lattices

1 Introduction

Since the first scheme of Gentry [1,2] a lot of effort has been made to push Fully Homomorphic Encryption (FHE) toward practicality. A first line of research followed the initial approach of Gentry, by bootstrapping FHE from a Somewhat Homomorphic Encryption (SHE) scheme supporting arbitrary circuits of bounded depth. This bootstrapping step consists in homomorphically evaluating the decryption procedure, to refresh ciphertexts. After successive theoretical and practical improvements [3–7], this bootstrapping procedure has been made feasible in practice, but remains quite expensive, taking several minutes on a single core. Fortunately, this cost can be mitigated thanks to SIMD techniques, allowing to perform the same homomorphic computation on several data sets for the price of one.

G. Bonnoron—Funded and supported by Ecole Navale, IMT Atlantique, Naval Group and Thales.

L. Ducas is supported by a Veni Innovational Research Grant from NWO under project number 639.021.645.

© Springer International Publishing AG, part of Springer Nature 2018
A. Joux et al. (Eds.): AFRICACRYPT 2018, LNCS 10831, pp. 217–251, 2018.
https://doi.org/10.1007/978-3-319-89339-6_13

A second line of FHE schemes arose from the SHE scheme of Gentry-Sahai-Waters [8]. This SHE scheme supports a different class of functions, including branching programs, and this was also proved sufficient to bootstrap it to FHE via Barrington's theorem [9,10]. Interestingly, this approach theoretically allows obtaining FHE from a weaker version of the LWE assumption (namely the approximation factor decreases from super-polynomial to polynomial). On the efficiency front, Alperin-Sheriff and Peikert [11] showed how to avoid the costly use of Barrington's transformation by implementing the homomorphic decryption procedure more directly. Then, Ducas and Micciancio [12] adapted the construction to the ring-setting. Providing parameters and implementation, they demonstrated this approach to be feasible with a proof of concept scheme (FHEW): the bootstrapping procedure could be run in under a second on a single core. While their parameters allow one binary gate per bootstrapping, they noted it should be possible in principle to perform slightly larger gates, such as the add-with-carry gate (3-inputs, 2-outputs). This idea was implemented in [13].

Further improvements and generalization were proposed in [14,15], leading to a scheme named TFHE. In particular they contributed two improvements of the bootstrapping step, accelerating it by a polylog factor. In practice, this leads to a bootstrapping in less than 0.1 s, allowing the same bootstrapped gates as in FHEW [12].

FHE from Homomorphic Accumulator. The core idea in FHE schemes from this second line is to tailor the SHE scheme precisely to the decryption procedure. Namely, the decryption procedure of an LWE ciphertext $\mathbf{c} = (\mathbf{a}, b) \in \mathbb{Z}_q^{n+1}$ under key $\mathbf{s} \in \mathbb{Z}_q^n$ for a plaintext space $\mathbb{Z}_t$ is given by:

$$m = \lfloor t(b - \langle \mathbf{a}, \mathbf{s} \rangle)/q \rceil \bmod t \in \mathbb{Z}_t.$$

Given the ciphertext $\mathbf{c}$, this procedure can be split into a $\mathbb{Z}_q$-linear step $L_{\mathbf{c}}$: $\mathbf{s} \mapsto b - \langle \mathbf{a}, \mathbf{s} \rangle$, followed by a non-linear function $N : \mathbb{Z}_q \to \mathbb{Z}_t$. Note that one can embed an arbitrary post-decryption transformation $f : \mathbb{Z}_t \mapsto \mathbb{Z}_t$ by setting $N_f : x \mapsto f(\lfloor tx/q \rceil \bmod t)$.

Assume that we have an SHE scheme that precisely supports the class of functions that can be written as $N_f \circ L_{\mathbf{c}}$ (a notion formalized as a homomorphic accumulator in [12]), and such that the output is again an LWE ciphertext. Then, taking $t = 4$ one can construct an FHE scheme, performing any binary gate g over encryptions of bits (b_1, b_2) for each bootstrap operation. Indeed, using the linearity of LWE ciphertexts, one can compute an encryption of $m = b_1 + 2b_2$, and construct the appropriate function f such that $f(m) = g(b_1, b_2)$.

In more detail, messages m are encoded as powers of a q-th root of unity X^m. With such an encoding, the linear step $L_{\mathbf{c}}$ is performed by sequential ciphertext multiplications. The non-linear part N_f is performed by computing a subset-sum of the coefficients of the polynomial $E = X^m = \sum e_i X^i$, by exploiting the identity $f(m) = \sum f(i)e_i$.

As the useful computation is provided by the function $f : \mathbb{Z}_t \to \mathbb{Z}_t$, a larger plaintext modulus t allows to perform more computation between each bootstrap operation. Namely, one can build arbitrary k-bit to 1-bit gates if $t \geq 2^k$, and, if we restrict to certain classes of gates, even larger ones (e.g. threshold gates only require $t \geq k + 1$). For most k-to-1 bit functions, this corresponds to a speed up of $\Omega(2^k / \log k) = \tilde{O}(t)$, according to the classical circuit lower-bound of Riordan and Shannon [16]. It is therefore worth increasing the size of the plaintext modulus t in order to perform much more computations per bootstrap operation.

Parameter Constraints and Efficiency. In the set-up of [12,13,15], the constraints for correctness impose asymptotically that $t \leq O(q/n)$.[1] Taking $q = \Theta(n)$, this gives a quasi-quadratic runtime for the whole process, but allows quite small plaintext size: $t \leq O(1)$. In practice, this t cannot be made much larger than 4, maybe up to 6 as done in [13].

Looking more precisely at the complexity of each step, we note an imbalance between the cost of the linear and non-linear steps. Indeed, the linear part requires $\tilde{\Theta}(n)$ operations over $\mathcal{R}_q$, while the non-linear part requires only $\Theta(\log n)$ such operations.

This Work. We aim to improve the performance of this line of FHE schemes by increasing the plaintext modulus t. Having remarked the imbalance of the costs of the linear and non-linear steps, we proceed to increase the cost of the non-linear step while maintaining the overall quasi-quadratic complexity.

Our approach consists in choosing a ciphertext modulus of the form pq for co-primes p, q, and to perform the linear-step $L_{\mathbf{c}}$ in a CRT fashion. During this linear-step, our SHE scheme only works with the rings $\mathcal{R}_p = \mathbb{Z}[X]/(X^p - 1)$ and $\mathcal{R}_q = \mathbb{Z}[Y]/(Y^q - 1)$ separately, for a cost of $\tilde{O}(n(p+q))$. Then we proceed to a CRT reconstruction by tensoring the two rings: $\mathcal{R}_p \otimes \mathcal{R}_q \simeq \mathcal{R}_{pq} = \mathbb{Z}[Z]/(Z^{pq}-1)$, noting that $X^a \otimes Y^b = Z^{aq+pb \bmod pq}$. This raises the cost of the non-linear part to $\tilde{\Theta}(pq)$. Setting $p, q = \Theta(n)$ we maintain the quasi-quadratic complexity, but reach a larger plaintext-modulus $t = \Theta(n)$. This is somehow a reminiscence of the approach of [11], adapted to the ring-setting.

One (not so) novel technical aspect is that we choose in this work to use convolution rings $\mathbb{Z}[X]/(X^p - 1)$, as in the NTRU schemes [17] rather than cyclotomic ones. The reason is that we need to use some non-power of 2 roots of unity to ensure co-primality of p and q. Indeed, if (say) p is prime, the fact that $X^{p-1} = -1 - X - \cdots - X^{p-2}$ in the p-th cyclotomic ring $\mathbb{Z}(X)/(\Phi_p(X))$ makes the non-linear step described above quite problematic.[2] Yet, we show that the switch to convolution rings can be done without affecting security, by formalizing what we call the *NTRU trick*.[3] More precisely, an appropriately defined version

---

[1] More precisely, $t \leq q/\sqrt{n \cdot \log 1/p_{\text{fail}}}$, where p_{fail} is the failure probability. In this paper, we will always aim for exponentially small failure probability.

[2] And maybe even impossible due to dimensionality constraints.

[3] We wish to clarify that our scheme does not require the NTRU assumption, namely the assumption that $f/g \bmod q$ is indistinguishable from random even for small f and g. Up to the usual circular-security assumption, our scheme is based on a ring-LWE type of assumption.

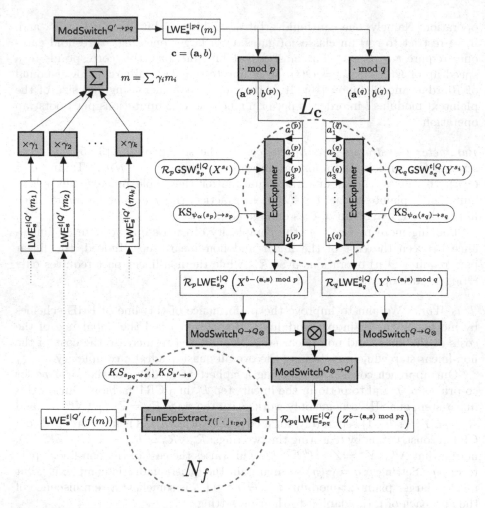

On the left side, there are the k input bits $m_1, \cdots, m_k$ that get combined into $m \in \mathbb{Z}_t$. On the right side we have the two Homomorphic Accumulator ExtExpInner, which perform the linear part $L_\mathbf{c}$ of the bootstrapped computation in a CRT fashion. After tensoring it is fed to the non-linear part of the computation $N_f : x \mapsto f(\lfloor tx/q \rceil \bmod t)$, i.e. FunExpExtract, where f is the function to be homomorphically evaluated. The computation is intrinsically done with the bootstrapping process, so the final output can directly be used as input.

Grey boxes represent operations, white square boxes represent ciphertexts, and rounded white boxes represent key material. The linear step $L_\mathbf{c}$ and the non-linear step N_f discussed in introduction are highlighted by dashed red circles.

Fig. 1. Scheme overview.

of Ring-LWE over convolution rings is as secure as the usual cyclotomic version of Ring-LWE from [18].

Our work also relies on one of the improvements of [15], namely, the use of an "external multiplication" $\mathsf{GSW} \times \mathsf{LWE} \to \mathsf{LWE}$ replacing the $\mathsf{GSW} \times \mathsf{GSW} \to \mathsf{GSW}$

operation used in [8, 11–13], which saves a log factor on time and memory. It turns out that the trick of [14, 15] of implementing a mux-gate, is not compatible with our circulant ring set-up, but we instead propose to exploit the Galois action for a similar logarithmic speed-up.

In addition, we propose to use an alternative Gadget matrices based on the Chinese Remainder Theorem, an idea already presented in [19] for different purposes. We show that such gadgets permit a logarithmic speed-up when dealing with gadget inversions of tensored ciphertexts; this contribution may find theoretical and practical applications in other contexts.

To summarize our theoretical construction, we provide schematics in Fig. 1, omitting some extra tweaks for practical efficiency that are deferred to Appendix F. We hope this overview may guide the reader through our paper.

Circular Security. We recall that all the FHE literature, including our work, relies on (sometimes implicit) circular-security assumptions [2], that may be different from one scheme to the next. Understanding those assumptions is arguably the most important theoretical question in this field.

One particular property of our scheme is that this circular security assumption can not be avoided even when relaxing the scheme to a leveled FHE scheme [2]. Indeed, the careful reader may notice that "External Inner-product in the Exponent" step (ExtExpInner, Sect. 4.3) requires circular encryption.

Instantiation and Implementation. To attest to the feasibility of our approach, we also provide an instantiation supporting 6-to-6 bit gates, at a security level of about 100 bits. Its current implementation runs this 6-to-6 bits bootstrapped gate in about 10 s.

Related Work. Recently Chillotti et al. [20] also proposed the construction of large homomorphic gates, using a quite different approach. They claim impressive performances, such as a 16-to-8 bit homomorphic gate running in about 2 s. Admittedly, our current implementation is significantly slower.

Impact. Our implementation should certainly not be understood as publicity for the practical efficiency of this overall design. It nevertheless serves the purpose of demonstrating that our new building blocks can be used inside a reasonable scheme. It is therefore plausible that our contributions are not only of theoretical interest, but may as well find some use in future practical FHE designs.

Plan. We begin in Sect. 2 with preliminary results and notations. Then we introduce the underlying encryption schemes at hand in Sect. 3. Section 4 presents in detail the building blocks of the gate, leading to the overall description in Sect. 5. Finally Sect. 6 reports implementation details and performances.

All proofs are deferred to appendices. Moreover, Appendix F provides several useful optimization of our scheme for its concrete efficiency.

2   Preliminaries

2.1   Subgaussian Random Variables

Definition 1. *We say that a real random variable X is* subgaussian *with parameter δ (or δ-subgaussian) if $\mathbb{E}[X] = 0$, and for all t, $\mathbb{E}[\exp(tX)] \leq \exp(t^2\delta^2/2)$.*

Subgaussian random variables have the following well known properties (see [21,22]):

Theorem 1. *Let X_1 and X_2 be subgaussian random variables with parameters δ_1 and δ_2, respectively.*

- *$X_1 + X_2$ is $(\delta_1 + \delta_2)$-subgaussian.*
- *If X_1 and X_2 are independent, $X_1 + X_2$ is $\sqrt{\delta_1^2 + \delta_2^2}$-subgaussian.*
- *aX_1 is $(|a|\delta_1)$-subgaussian.*
- *Subgaussian tail estimate: $P(|X_1| \geq \sqrt{2\lambda}\delta_1) \leq 2\exp(-\lambda)$.*

Note that [21] also defines non-centered subgaussian variables. However, in this work, we only consider centered ones, i.e. with $\mathbb{E}[X] = 0$.

2.2   Rings

Our FHE scheme uses *circulant convolution rings* (or, for short, *circulant rings*). Circulant rings of degree d will be denoted with indeterminate T: $\mathcal{R}_d = \mathbb{Z}[T]/(T^d - 1)$. We fix two distinct odd primes p and q. When speaking specifically of rings $\mathcal{R}_p$, $\mathcal{R}_q$, and $\mathcal{R}_{pq}$ we shall use indeterminates X, Y and Z, respectively. We write $\tilde{\mathcal{R}}_d$ for the cyclotomic ring $\mathbb{Z}[\tilde{T}]/\Phi_d(\tilde{T})$ where $\Phi_d(\tilde{T})$ is the d-th cyclotomic polynomial; if d is prime, $\Phi_d(\tilde{T}) = 1 + \tilde{T} + \tilde{T}^2 + \ldots + \tilde{T}^{d-1}$. We identify a ring element $a \in \mathcal{R}_d$ with its lowest degree representative $a_0 + a_1T + \ldots + a_{d-1}T^{d-1} \in \mathbb{Z}[T]$ and call $a_0, \ldots, a_{d-1}$ the coefficients of a. We identify $a \in \mathcal{R}_d/Q\mathcal{R}_d$ with its lowest degree representative with coefficients $a_0, \ldots, a_{d-1} \in [-Q/2, Q/2)$. We define the following norms for ring elements:

Definition 2. *Let $a \in \mathcal{R}_d$ (or $\mathcal{R}_d/Q\mathcal{R}_d$). We define the* coefficient norm *of a as $\|a\| = \|(a_0, \ldots, a_{d-1})\| = \sqrt{\sum a_i^2}$.*

Definition 3. *Let $a \in \mathcal{R}_d$ (or $\mathcal{R}_d/Q\mathcal{R}_d$). We define the* operator norm *of a as $|a| = \max_{b \in \mathcal{R}\setminus\{0\}} \|ab\|/\|b\|$. We expand this notion to vectors $\mathbf{x} \in \mathcal{R}_d^n$ by maximizing $\mathbf{y}$ over $\mathcal{R}^n \setminus \{0\}$ and replacing the multiplication with the inner product over $\mathcal{R}_d$.*

Definition 4. *We define the (normalized)* trace function[4] *as follows: We let $\mathrm{Tr}^*_{\mathcal{R}_d/\mathbb{Z}} : \mathcal{R}_d \to \mathbb{Z}, a \mapsto a_0$. If d is clear from context, we simply write this function as Tr^*. We let $\mathrm{Tr}^*_{\mathcal{R}_{pq}/\mathcal{R}_p} : \mathcal{R}_{pq} \to \mathcal{R}_p$ be the linear function defined by*

$$\mathrm{Tr}^*_{\mathcal{R}_{pq}/\mathcal{R}_p}(Z^k) = \begin{cases} X^{k/q} & \text{if } q|k \\ 0 & \text{otherwise} \end{cases}$$

---

[4] This is simply a special case of the usual definition of the trace function, but we do not need the general definition here.

The following property is easy to see:

Lemma 1. $\mathrm{Tr}^*_{\mathcal{R}_d/\mathbb{Z}}$ and $\mathrm{Tr}^*_{\mathcal{R}_{pq}/\mathcal{R}_p}$ are linear, and $\mathrm{Tr}^*_{\mathcal{R}_p/\mathbb{Z}} \circ \mathrm{Tr}^*_{\mathcal{R}_{pq}/\mathcal{R}_p} = \mathrm{Tr}^*_{\mathcal{R}_{pq}/\mathbb{Z}}$.

Definition 5. A random variable $A \in \mathcal{R}_d$ is δ-subgaussian if, for every $b \in \mathcal{R}_d \setminus \{0\}$, $\mathrm{Tr}^*(Ab)/\|b\|$ is δ-subgaussian.

Finally, we show that if we trace down a subgaussian random variable over $\mathcal{R}_{pq}$ down to $\mathcal{R}_p$, the result is a subgaussian random variable over $\mathcal{R}_p$.

Lemma 1. Let A be a δ-subgaussian random variable over $\mathcal{R}_{pq}$. Then $\mathrm{Tr}^*_{\mathcal{R}_{pq}/\mathcal{R}_p}(A)$ is δ-subgaussian as well.

2.3   Gadgets

Throughout this exposition we use a binary *decomposition* operation on ring elements, and the reverse. For simplicity we adopt the notation of gadget vector and matrix.

Definition 6. The gadget vector $\mathbf{g}^T$ of size K is set to $\left(1\ 2\ 2^2\ \cdots\ 2^{K-1}\right) \in \mathcal{R}_d^K$. Reciprocally, we define $\mathbf{g}^{-T}$ as a function such that, for $\mathbf{w} \in \mathcal{R}_d^n$, $\mathbf{V} = \mathbf{g}^{-T}(\mathbf{w})$ is a $(K \times n)$-matrix whose entries are ring elements with coefficients in $\{0, 1\}$ such that $\mathbf{g}^T\mathbf{V} = \mathbf{w}$.

Definition 7. For some integer $n \geq 1$, the gadget matrix $\mathbf{G}_n$ is defined by $\mathbf{G}_n = \mathbf{I}_{n+1} \otimes \mathbf{g} \in \mathcal{R}_d^{(n+1)K \times (n+1)}$.

$$\mathbf{G}_n^T = \begin{pmatrix} 1\ 2\ \cdots\ 2^{K-1}\ 0\ 0\ \cdots\ & 0 & \cdots\ 0\ 0\ \cdots\ & 0 \\ 0\ 0\ \cdots\ & 0 & 1\ 2\ \cdots\ 2^{K-1}\ \cdots\ 0\ 0\ \cdots\ & 0 \\ \vdots & & \vdots\ \qquad\ \vdots & \vdots \\ 0\ 0\ \cdots\ & 0 & 0\ 0\ \cdots\ 0 & \cdots\ 1\ 2\ \cdots\ 2^{K-1} \end{pmatrix}$$

We define $\mathbf{G}_n^{-1}$ similarly to $\mathbf{g}^{-T}$: for $\mathbf{a} \in \mathcal{R}_d^{n+1}$, we let $\mathbf{d} = \mathbf{G}_n^{-1}(\mathbf{a}) \in \mathcal{R}_d^{(n+1)K}$ be the vector whose entries have coefficients in $\{0, 1\}$ such that $\mathbf{d}^T \cdot \mathbf{G} = \mathbf{a}$. For convenience we write $\mathbf{G}_n = \mathbf{G}$ as n is typically clear from context.

2.4   Circulant LWE and Reduction to Ring-LWE

It is well known that the naive decisional version of Ring-LWE is insecure over circulant rings, simply by exploiting the CRT decomposition. Say that d is prime, and note that $\mathcal{R}_d/Q\mathcal{R}_d \simeq \tilde{\mathcal{R}}_d/Q\tilde{\mathcal{R}}_d \times \mathbb{Z}/Q\mathbb{Z}$ if Q is coprime to d, so one may mount an attack on the $\mathbb{Z}/Q\mathbb{Z}$ part (projecting to this part corresponds to evaluate the polynomial at 1, and therefore maintain smallness of the error). However, this does not mean that such rings are inherently insecure: the NTRU cryptosystems [17,23] use circulant rings, choosing the secret key and errors that evaluate to a fixed known value (say 0) at 1.

This suggests a strategy to construct a variant of Ring-LWE over circulant rings that would be as secure as the cyclotomic Ring-LWE, simply by lifting all elements $\tilde{x} \in \tilde{\mathcal{R}}_d/Q\tilde{\mathcal{R}}_d$ to $x \simeq (\tilde{x}, 0)$, yet this reverse CRT operation may not keep small elements small. In Appendix E.1 we show how to circumvent this obstacle, and discuss error sampling in practice in Appendix E.2.

3   Encryption Schemes

3.1   LWE Encryption

We recall the definition of the most basic LWE symmetric encryption scheme (see [24–26]). LWE symmetric encryption is parametrized by a dimension n, a message modulus $t \geq 2$, a ciphertext modulus $Q = n^{O(1)}$ and an error distribution χ. The message space of the scheme is $\mathbb{Z}_t$. (Typically, $e \leftarrow \chi$ satisfies the condition $|e| < Q/2t$, and $t = 2$ is used to encrypt message bits.) The (secret) key of the encryption scheme is a vector $\mathbf{s} \in \mathbb{Z}_Q^n$, which may be chosen uniformly at random, or as a random short vector. The encryption of a message $m \in \mathbb{Z}_t$ under key $\mathbf{s} \in \mathbb{Z}_Q^n$ is

$$\mathbf{c} = (\mathbf{a}, \langle \mathbf{a}, \mathbf{s} \rangle + e + \lfloor Q/t \rfloor \, m \bmod Q) \in \mathbb{Z}_Q^{n+1} \tag{1}$$

where $\mathbf{a} \leftarrow \mathbb{Z}_Q^n$ is chosen uniformly at random. A ciphertext $(\mathbf{a}, b)$ is decrypted by computing

$$m' = \lfloor t(b - \langle \mathbf{a}, \mathbf{s} \rangle)/Q \rceil \bmod t \in \mathbb{Z}_t. \tag{2}$$

We write $\mathbf{c} \in \mathsf{LWE}_{\mathbf{s}}^{t|Q}(m)$ to denote that $\mathbf{c}$ is an LWE-encryption of m, and $\mathbf{c} \in \mathsf{LWE}_{\mathbf{s}}^{t|Q}(m; E)$ if $\mathbf{c}$ is a random LWE-ciphertext such that $\mathbf{c} = (\mathbf{a}, \langle \mathbf{a}, \mathbf{s} \rangle + \lfloor Q/t \rfloor \, m + e)$ where e is a subgaussian random variable with parameter E. The error of $\mathbf{c} = (\mathbf{a}, b) \in \mathsf{LWE}_{\mathbf{s}}^{t|Q}(m)$ is $\mathsf{err}(\mathbf{c}) = (b - \langle \mathbf{a}, \mathbf{s} \rangle - \lfloor Q/t \rfloor \, m) \bmod Q$, reduced modulo Q to the centered interval $[-Q/2, Q/2)$.

Notice that the error $\mathsf{err}(\mathbf{a}, b)$ depends not just on $(\mathbf{a}, b)$, but also on $\mathbf{s}, Q, t$ and m. By the subgaussian tail estimate, if $e = \mathsf{err}(\mathbf{c})$ is subgaussian with parameter E, then $|e| < \sqrt{2\lambda}E$ except with probability at most $2\exp(-\lambda)$. Thus, if t divides Q and $E \leq Q/(2t\sqrt{2\lambda})$, the decryption procedure recovers the encrypted message with high probability:

$$\lfloor t(b - \langle \mathbf{a}, \mathbf{s} \rangle)/Q \rceil \bmod t = \left\lfloor \frac{t}{Q} \cdot \left(\frac{Q}{t}m + e \right) \right\rceil = \left\lfloor m + \frac{t}{Q}e \right\rceil = m \bmod t$$

because $\frac{t}{Q}|e| < 1/2$ except with probability $2\exp(-\lambda)$.

3.2   CLWE and CGSW Encryption Schemes

Below, we describe two encryption schemes, Circulant-LWE and Circulant-GSW (Circulant variant of [8]), which we need for our *homomorphic accumulator* (see Sect. 4). We do not specify any decryption procedures since these are not needed for the homomorphic accumulator.

Definition 8. *We let $\mathcal{R}$, $\tilde{\mathcal{R}}$, d, and Q be as in Sect. 2.2. Let $t \geq 2$ be the plaintext modulus. The Circulant-LWE scheme over $\mathcal{R}$ consists of the following algorithms:*

- KeyGen: *Output a uniformly random element s of $\tilde{\mathcal{R}}$.*

- $\mathsf{Enc}_s(m)$ *for* $m \in \mathcal{R}/t\mathcal{R}$: *Let* (a, b) *be a sample from the Circulant-LWE distribution over* $\mathcal{R}$ *with secret* s *and output* $(a, b' = b + \lfloor Q/t \rceil \cdot m)$.

We also define an n-*dimensional variant of the scheme where the key is* $\mathbf{s} \in \mathcal{R}^n$, $\mathbf{a}$ *is a random vector in* $\mathcal{R}^n$ *and the product* $a \cdot s$ *is replaced by the inner product over* $\mathcal{R} \langle \mathbf{a}, \mathbf{s} \rangle = \sum_{i=1}^n \mathbf{a}_i \cdot \mathbf{s}_i$.

Lemma 2. *If the decisional* $\tilde{\mathcal{R}}$-*LWE problem is hard, then the Circulant-LWE scheme is CPA-secure for messages of the form* $m = X^k$.

Definition 9. *We let* $\mathcal{R}, \tilde{\mathcal{R}}, d,$ *and* Q *be as in Sect. 2.2 and* $\mathbf{G}$ *as in Definition 7. Furthermore, let* $t \geq 2$ *be the plaintext modulus and* B *an integer* ≥ 2, *let* K *be the smallest integer such that* $B^K \geq Q$.

   The Circulant-GSW scheme is described by the following algorithms:

- KeyGen: *Sample a uniformly random* s *from* $\tilde{\mathcal{R}}$.
- $\mathsf{Enc}_s(m)$ *for* $m \in \mathcal{R}/t\mathcal{R}$: *Generate a matrix* $\mathbf{A} \in \mathcal{R}^{2K \times 2}$ *where each row is a sample from the Circulant-LWE distribution with secret* s. *Output* $\mathbf{A} + \lfloor Q/t \rceil \cdot m\mathbf{G}$.

We also define a n-*dimensional variant of the scheme where* $\mathbf{A} \in \mathcal{R}^{(n+1)K \times (n+1)}$ *whose rows are samples from the* n-*dimensional Circulant-LWE and where* $\mathbf{G}_1$ *is replaced by* $\mathbf{G}_n$.

Lemma 3. *If the decisional* $\tilde{\mathcal{R}}$-*LWE problem is hard, then the Circulant-GSW scheme is CPA-secure.*

   Finally, we define the following notations for various ciphertext spaces:

- We write $\mathbf{c} \in \mathcal{R}_d\mathsf{LWE}_{\mathbf{s}}^{t|Q}(m, E)$ if $\mathbf{c} = (\mathbf{a}, \mathbf{a}^t\mathbf{s} + \left\lfloor \frac{Q}{t} \right\rceil m + \mathbf{e})$ for some random error vector $\mathbf{e}$ that is E-subgaussian. We extend the notation to $\mathbf{C} \in \mathcal{R}_d\mathsf{LWE}_{\mathbf{s}}^{t|Q}(\mathbf{m}^T, E)$ for message $\mathbf{m} \in \mathcal{R}_t^k$ that are vectors, meaning that the i-th column $\mathbf{C}_i$ of $\mathbf{C}$ is in $\mathcal{R}_d\mathsf{LWE}_{\mathbf{s}}^{t|Q}(m_i, E)$. Furthermore, we write $\mathsf{err}(\mathbf{c})$ for the error term e in $\mathbf{c}$.
- We write $\mathbf{C} \in \mathcal{R}_d\mathsf{GSW}_s^{t|Q}(m, E)$ if $\mathbf{C} = (\mathbf{a}, \mathbf{a}s + \mathbf{e}) + \left\lfloor \frac{Q}{t} \right\rceil \cdot m\mathbf{G}$, and the components of $\mathbf{e}$ are independent E-subgaussian variables. We write $\mathsf{err}(\mathbf{C})$ for the error vector $\mathbf{e}$ in $\mathbf{C}$.

4 Homomorphic Operations

Most of the operations presented below are meaningful both in the ring/circulant-setting or over the integers. We consider the $\mathcal{R}\mathsf{LWE}$ problem over rings $\mathcal{R}_d = \mathbb{Z}[X]/(X^d - 1)$ with d prime and over $\mathcal{R} = \mathbb{Z}$ (i.e., simply the LWE problem). However, most of the results presented in this section also hold for cyclotomic rings. We assume that coefficients of ring elements in $\mathcal{R}/Q\mathcal{R}$ can be added and multiplied in constant time since, in our implementation, each coefficient fits into a machine word. Thus, adding two ring elements takes time $O(d)$ and multiplying them takes time $O(d \log d)$ using FFT.

4.1   Known Building Blocks

Let us first recall, within our formalism, known building blocks from the literature. The only novelty is in this section concerns the FunExpExtract function: while this was already constructed in previous work, in our set-up we will need to apply a trick from [27] to improve its efficiency.

Linearity.

> **Key Material**: None
> **Runtime**: $O(nd)$ for addition, $O(nd \log d)$ for multiplication
> **Signature**:
>
> $$\mathsf{Add} : \mathcal{R}_d \mathsf{LWE}_{\mathbf{s}}^{t|Q}(m;\ E) \times \mathcal{R}_d \mathsf{LWE}_{\mathbf{s}}^{t|Q}(m';\ E')$$
>
> $$\to \mathcal{R}_d \mathsf{LWE}_{\mathbf{s}}^{t|Q}\left(m + m';\ \sqrt{E^2 + E'^2}\right) \tag{3}$$
>
> $$x \in \mathcal{R}_d, \mathsf{Mult}_x : \mathcal{R}_d \mathsf{LWE}_{\mathbf{s}}^{t|Q}(m;\ E) \to \mathcal{R}_d \mathsf{LWE}_{\mathbf{s}}^{t|Q}(xm;\ |x|E)$$
>
> The error term in the result of Add holds when the error terms in the input ciphertexts are independent. Otherwise, it is $E + E'$.
>
> The Add operations are computed by simply adding the ciphertexts component-wise. The Mult_x operations work by scalar multiplication with x.

Modulus Switching.

> **Key Material**: None
> **Runtime**: $O(d)$
> **Signature**: $\mathsf{ModSwitch}^{Q \to Q'}$:
>
> $$\mathcal{R}_d \mathsf{LWE}_{\mathbf{s}}^{t|Q}(m;\ E) \to \mathcal{R}_d \mathsf{LWE}_{\mathbf{s}}^{t|Q'}\left(m;\ \sqrt{(kE)^2 + 1 + \sum_i |\mathbf{s}_i|^2}\right) \tag{4}$$
>
> where $\mathbf{s} \in \mathcal{R}_d^n$ and $k = \lfloor Q'/t \rceil / \lfloor Q/t \rceil \approx Q'/Q$.

The basic idea of modulus switching is to multiply the ciphertext with Q'/Q, or rather $\lfloor Q'/t \rceil / \lfloor Q/t \rceil$. However, since this factor is not necessarily an integer, we instead use a randomized rounding function $[x] = \lfloor x \rfloor + B_r$ where B_r is a Bernoulli random variable with $\Pr[B_r = 1] = x - \lfloor x \rfloor$. The rounding error $r = [x] - x$ is subgaussian with parameter 1. Let us write $k = \lfloor Q'/t \rceil / \lfloor Q/t \rceil$. Applying the rounding function component-wise to $k \cdot (\mathbf{a}, \langle \mathbf{a}, \mathbf{s} \rangle + \lfloor Q/t \rceil m + e)$, we obtain

$$(k\mathbf{a}+\mathbf{r}, k\langle \mathbf{a}, \mathbf{s} \rangle + \lfloor Q'/t \rceil m + ke + r') = (k\mathbf{a}+\mathbf{r}, \langle k\mathbf{a}+\mathbf{r}, \mathbf{s} \rangle + \lfloor Q'/t \rceil m + ke + r' - \langle \mathbf{r}, \mathbf{s} \rangle)$$

where $\mathbf{r}$ is the vector of rounding errors for $k\mathbf{a}$ and r' is the rounding error for b. Thus, the error term of the modulus-switched ciphertext is $ke + r - \langle \mathbf{r}, \mathbf{s} \rangle$. For each i, $\mathbf{r}_i \mathbf{s}_i$ is $|\mathbf{s}_i|$-subgaussian. Since all terms in the sum are independent, the error parameter is $\sqrt{(kE)^2 + 1 + \sum_i |\mathbf{s}_i|^2}$.

Remark 1. We only use modulus switching in the following two cases: when the dimension of the key is $n = 1$, and for short keys in $\mathbb{Z}^n$, i.e., n-dimensional keys where $|s_i| \leq 1$. In the first case, the error parameter simplifies to $\sqrt{(kE)^2 + 1 + |s|^2}$, in the second case to $\sqrt{(kE)^2 + n + 1}$.

Key switching.

> **Key Material:** $\mathbf{S} = [\mathbf{S}_i]_{i \in [n]}$ where $\mathbf{S}_i \in \mathcal{R}_d\mathsf{LWE}_{s'}^{Q|Q}(s_i \cdot \mathbf{g}^T; \sigma)$ (Size: $O(nd \log^2 Q)$)
> **Runtime:** $O(d \log dn \log Q)$
> **Signature:** $\mathsf{KeySwitch}_{\mathbf{S}}^{s \to s'}$:
>
> $$\mathcal{R}_d\mathsf{LWE}_s^{t|Q}(m; E) \to \mathcal{R}_d\mathsf{LWE}_{s'}^{t|Q}\left(m; \sqrt{E^2 + \sigma^2 d^2 nK}\right). \tag{5}$$
>
> where $\mathbf{s} \in \mathcal{R}_d^n$, $s' \in \mathcal{R}_d$.

Algorithm 1. $\mathsf{KeySwitch}_{\mathbf{S}}^{s \to s'}(\mathbf{c})$: Transform an $\mathcal{R}_d\mathsf{LWE}$ ciphertext under key $\mathbf{s}$ into a ciphertext under s'.

Require:
$\mathbf{S} = [\mathbf{S}_i]_{i \in [n]}$ where $\mathbf{S}_i \in \mathcal{R}_d\mathsf{LWE}_{s'}^{Q|Q}(s_i \cdot \mathbf{g}^T; \sigma)$.
A ciphertext $(\mathbf{a}, b) \in \mathcal{R}_d\mathsf{LWE}_s^{t|Q}(m; E)$ for some $m \in \mathcal{R}/t\mathcal{R}$.
Ensure: A ciphertext $c \in \mathcal{R}_d\mathsf{LWE}_{s'}^{t|Q}\left(m; \sqrt{E^2 + \sigma^2 d^2 nK}\right)$ if the error terms in $\mathbf{c}$ and $\mathbf{S}$ are independent.

> **return** $(\mathbf{0}_{n'}, b) - \mathbf{g}^{-T}(\mathbf{a}) \cdot \mathbf{S}$

Lemma 4. *Algorithm 1 is correct. Furthermore, if $e = \mathsf{err}(\mathbf{c})$ and $\mathbf{e}_i = \mathsf{err}(\mathbf{S}_i)$, then the error term of the output ciphertext is $e + \sum_{i=1}^n \mathbf{d}_i^T \mathbf{e}_i$, where each $\mathbf{d}_i$ is a vector whose entries have operator norm at most d.*

Remark 2. In practice, the choice of the basis decomposition B for the gadget is important. It allows to trade off key size and running time against error growth. We use

$$S = \left[\mathcal{R}_d\mathsf{LWE}_{s'}^{1;Q}(B^j s_i; \sigma)\right]_{i=1\ldots n, j=0\ldots K-1}, \text{ with } K = \lceil \log_B Q \rceil$$

as key material. The key size decreases to $O(nn'dK \log Q)$, and the running time decreases to $O(d \log dnn'K)$, while the output error parameter also increases to $\sqrt{E^2 + \sigma^2 d^2 B^2 nK}$.

External Multiplication.

> **Key Material:** None
> **Runtime:** $O(Kd\log d)$
> **Signature:** ExtMult :
>
> $$\mathcal{R}_d\mathsf{LWE}_s^{t|Q}(T^m; E) \times \mathcal{R}_d\mathsf{GSW}_s^{t|Q}(T^{m'}; E')$$
> $$\rightarrow \mathcal{R}_d\mathsf{LWE}_s^{t|Q}\left(T^{m+m'}; \sqrt{E^2 + 2Kd^2E'^2}\right) \quad (6)$$
>
> for $s \in \mathcal{R}$ if $\lfloor Q/t \rceil$ is invertible modulo Q.

Algorithm 2. ExtMult$(\mathbf{c}, \mathbf{C})$: Multiply an $\mathcal{R}_d\mathsf{LWE}$ ciphertext and a $\mathcal{R}_d\mathsf{GSW}$ ciphertext into a $\mathcal{R}_d\mathsf{LWE}$ ciphertext.

Require: A ciphertext $\mathbf{c} \in \mathcal{R}_d\mathsf{LWE}_s^{t|Q}(T^m; E)$, and a ciphertext $\mathbf{C} \in \mathcal{R}_d\mathsf{GSW}_s^{t|Q}(T^{m'}; E')$ with $\lfloor Q/t \rceil$ invertible modulo Q.
Ensure: A ciphertext $c \in \mathcal{R}_d\mathsf{LWE}_s^{t|Q}\left(T^{m+m'}; \sqrt{E^2 + 2Kd^2E'^2}\right)$.

> **return** $\mathbf{G}^{-1}\left(\lfloor Q/t \rceil^{-1} \cdot \mathbf{c}\right) \cdot \mathbf{C}$

Lemma 5. *Algorithm 2 is correct. Furthermore, for $e = \mathrm{err}(\mathbf{c})$ and $\mathbf{e} = \mathrm{err}(\mathbf{C})$, the error term of the output is $X^k \cdot e + \mathbf{d}^T\mathbf{e}$ for some k and a random vector $\mathbf{d} \in \mathcal{R}_d^{2K}$ independent of $\mathbf{e}$ with $\|\mathbf{d}_i\| \le d$ for every i.*

Exponent Function Extraction.

> **Key Material:** A key-switch key $\mathbf{S}$ from $\mathbf{s}^{(pq)} \in \mathcal{R}_{pq}^3$ to $s' = \sum_{i=0}^{p-1} \mathbf{s}_{i+1}$
> $X^i \in \mathcal{R}_p \subseteq \mathcal{R}_{pq}$ (Size: $O(p(q+n)K^2)$)
> **Runtime:** $O(pq\log(pq)K)$
> **Signature:** FunExpExtract$_{F,\mathbf{S}}^{\mathbf{s}^{(pq)}\rightarrow\mathbf{s}}$:
>
> $$\mathcal{R}_{pq}\mathsf{LWE}_{\mathbf{s}^{(pq)}}^{t|Q'}(Z^m; E) \rightarrow \mathsf{LWE}_s^{t|Q'}\left(F(m); |F|\sqrt{E^2 + 3\sigma^2p^2q^2K}\right) \quad (7)$$
>
> for some function $F : \mathbb{Z}_{pq} \rightarrow \mathbb{Z}_t$ where $|F| = \sum_{i\in\mathbb{Z}_{pq}} |F(i)|$ and $\mathbf{s} \in \mathbb{Z}^p$.

Let us first consider the function F_0 that maps $0 \mapsto 1$ and $k \mapsto 0$ for $k \ne 0$. If we can extract this function, we can extract *any* function by first multiplying the ciphertext with an appropriate polynomial.

This extraction is easily provided by the trace function $\mathrm{Tr}^* = \mathrm{Tr}^*_{\mathcal{R}_{pq}/\mathbb{Z}}$ (see Lemma 1). Indeed, if $(a,b) \in \mathcal{R}_{pq}\mathsf{LWE}_s(m)$, then $(\mathbf{a}, \mathrm{Tr}^*(b)) \in \mathsf{LWE}_\mathbf{s}(m_0)$, where $\mathbf{a}, \mathbf{s} \in \mathbb{Z}^{pq}$ are the vectors of coefficients of a and s.

However, this leads to an LWE ciphertext with quadratic dimension $pq = \Theta(n^2)$, that must be key-switched to a much smaller dimension $\Theta(n)$. Such a key-switch without any ring structure would require up to $\tilde{\Theta}(n^3)$ running time, and as much key-material.

To circumvent this issue, we exploit the intermediate ring, following one of the tricks of [28]. Namely, we choose a key in $\mathcal{R}_p$, which can also be viewed as an element of $\mathcal{R}_{pq}$. Switching to this key, exploiting the structure of $\mathcal{R}_{pq}$, requires only $\tilde{\Theta}(pq) = \tilde{\Theta}(n^2)$ operations. Then, one can trace a down to $\mathcal{R}_p$, and b down to $\mathbb{Z}$, and obtain the desired result.

Algorithm 3. $\mathsf{FunExpExtract}_{F,\mathbf{S}}^{\mathbf{s}^{(pq)}\to\mathbf{s}}$: Turn an $\mathcal{R}_{pq}\mathsf{LWE}$ encryption of Z^m into an LWE encryption of $F(m)$.

Require:

A ciphertext $\mathbf{c} \in \mathcal{R}_{pq}\mathsf{LWE}_{\mathbf{s}^{(pq)}}^{t|Q'}(Z^m; E)$,

A function $F : \mathbb{Z}_{pq} \to \mathbb{Z}_t$,

A key-switch key $\mathbf{S}$ from $\mathbf{s}^{(pq)}$ to $s' \in \mathcal{R}_p \subseteq \mathcal{R}_{pq}$, where $s' = \sum_{i=0}^{p-1} \mathbf{s}_{i+1}^{(pq)} X^i$.

Ensure: A ciphertext $c' \in \mathsf{LWE}_s^{t|Q'}\left(F(m); |F|\sqrt{E^2 + 3\sigma^2 p^2 q^2 K}\right)$.

$f \leftarrow \sum_{i\in\mathbb{Z}_{pq}} F(i)Z^{-i \bmod pq} \in \mathcal{R}_{pq}$

$\mathbf{c} \leftarrow \mathsf{KeySwitch}_{\mathbf{S}}^{\mathbf{s}^{(pq)}\to s'}(\mathbf{c})$ $\triangleright \in \mathcal{R}_{pq}\mathsf{LWE}_{s'}^{t|Q'}(Z^m)$

$\mathbf{c} \leftarrow \mathsf{Mult}_f(\mathbf{c})$ $\triangleright \in \mathcal{R}_{pq}\mathsf{LWE}_{s'}^{t|Q'}(\sum_{i\in\mathbb{Z}_{pq}} F(i)Z^{m-i \bmod pq})$

$(a,b) \leftarrow \mathrm{Tr}_{\mathcal{R}_{pq}/\mathcal{R}_p}^*(\mathbf{c})$ $\triangleright \in \mathcal{R}_p\mathsf{LWE}_{s'}^{t|Q'}(\sum_{i,\ \mathrm{st}\ q|(m-i)} F(i)X^{m-i \bmod pq})$

$\mathbf{a} \leftarrow (a_0, a_{p-1}, a_{p-2}, \ldots, a_1)$

$b \leftarrow \mathrm{Tr}_{\mathcal{R}_p/\mathbb{Z}}^*(b)$

return $(\mathbf{a}, b)$

Lemma 6. *Algorithm 3 is correct and runs in time* $O(pq \log(pq) \log Q')$.

Remark 3. Note that we could reduce the error parameter in Algorithm 3 by performing the multiplication before the key-switch. However, doing the key-switch first allows to amortize the cost of gates with multiple outputs, as we shall describe in Sect. F.3.

4.2 New Building Blocks

Exponent Multiplication by Galois Conjugation.

> **Key Material:** None
> **Runtime:** $O(nd)$
> **Signature:** Galois^α :
>
> $$\mathcal{R}_d\mathsf{LWE}_s^{t|Q}(T^m;\ E) \to \mathcal{R}_d\mathsf{LWE}_{\psi_\alpha(s)}^{t|Q}\left(T^{\alpha m};\ E\right). \qquad (8)$$
>
> where $\alpha \in \mathbb{Z}_d^*$ and ψ_α is the automorphism of $\mathcal{R}_d$ defined by $T \mapsto T^\alpha$.

Given a $\mathcal{R}_d$LWE-ciphertext $(a, as + \lfloor Q/t \rceil T^m + e)$, by applying ψ_α component-wise, we obtain $(\psi_\alpha(a), \psi_\alpha(a) \cdot \psi_\alpha(s) + \lfloor Q/t \rceil T^{\alpha m} + \psi_\alpha(e))$. Applying Galois$^\alpha$ does not change the error parameter because $\mathrm{Tr}^*(\psi_\alpha(e)b) = \mathrm{Tr}^*(\psi_\alpha(e\psi_\alpha^{-1}(b))) = \mathrm{Tr}^*(e\psi_\alpha^{-1}(b))$. The running time is $O(d)$ because for $x \in \mathcal{R}$, $\psi_\alpha(x)$ is computed simply by permuting the coefficients of x. Even if the ciphertext is in FFT representation, the runtime remains $O(d)$, as ψ_α also acts on those representations by permutation.

Exponent CRT by tensoring.

> **Key Material**: None
> **Runtime**: $O(pq)$
> **Signature**: ExpCRT:
>
> $$\mathcal{R}_p\mathsf{LWE}_{s_p}^{t|Q_\otimes}(X^{m_p}; E_p) \times \mathcal{R}_q\mathsf{LWE}_{s_q}^{t|Q_\otimes}(Y^{m_q}; E_q)$$
>
> $$\to \mathcal{R}_{pq}\mathsf{LWE}_{\mathbf{s}}^{t|Q_\otimes}\left(Z^m; \sqrt{E_p^2 + E_q^2} + t\sqrt{2\lambda}E_pE_q\right) \quad (9)$$
>
> if $t \cdot \lfloor Q_\otimes/t \rceil = 1 \bmod Q_\otimes$, and where $m = \alpha m_p + \beta m_q$ is such that $m_p = m \bmod p$ and $m_q = m \bmod q$ and $\mathbf{s} = (-\psi_\alpha(s_p) \otimes \psi_\beta(s_q), \psi_\alpha(s_p) \otimes 1, 1 \otimes \psi_\beta(s_q))$.

Note that the condition $t \cdot \lfloor Q_\otimes/t \rceil = 1$ can be easily satisfied in our bootstrapping scheme because we perform a modulus switch before and after ExpCRT.

Algorithm 4. ExpCRT$\left(\mathbf{c}^{(p)}, \mathbf{c}^{(q)}\right)$

Require: Ciphertexts $\mathbf{c}^{(p)} \in \mathcal{R}_p\mathsf{LWE}_{s_p}^{t|Q_\otimes}(X^{m_p}; E_p)$ and $\mathbf{c}^{(q)} \in \mathcal{R}_q\mathsf{LWE}_{s_q}^{t|Q_\otimes}(Y^{m_q}; E_q)$.
Ensure: A ciphertext $\mathbf{c} \in \mathcal{R}_{pq}\mathsf{LWE}_{\mathbf{s}}^{t|Q_\otimes}(Z^m; \sqrt{E_p^2 + E_q^2} + t\sqrt{2\lambda}E_pE_q)$ except with probability $2\min(p,q)\exp(-\lambda)$

$(a_p, b_p) \leftarrow \mathsf{Galois}^\alpha\left(\mathbf{c}^{(p)}\right)$ $\triangleright \in \mathcal{R}_p\mathsf{LWE}_{\psi_\alpha(s_p)}^{t|Q_\otimes}(X^{\alpha m_p}; E_p)$
$(a_q, b_q) \leftarrow \mathsf{Galois}^\beta\left(\mathbf{c}^{(q)}\right)$ $\triangleright \in \mathcal{R}_q\mathsf{LWE}_{\psi_\beta(s_q)}^{t|Q_\otimes}(Y^{\beta m_q}; E_q)$
$\mathbf{a} \leftarrow (a_p \otimes a_q, a_p \otimes b_q, b_p \otimes a_q)$
return $(t\mathbf{a}, tb_p \otimes b_q)$

We will need the following lemma to bound the tensor product of two subgaussian random variables.

Lemma 7. *Let A and B be independent subgaussian random variables on $\mathcal{R}_p$ and $\mathcal{R}_q$, respectively, with parameters γ and δ. Then, for every $\lambda \in \mathbb{R}$, $A \otimes B$ is subgaussian with parameter $\sqrt{2\lambda}\gamma\delta$ except with probability $2\min(p,q)\exp(-\lambda)$.*[5]

Lemma 8. *Algorithm 4 is correct and runs in time $\Theta(pq)$.*

---

[5] More formally, for some event E with $p(E) \leq 2\min(p,q)\exp(-\lambda)$, when conditioning on $\overline{E}$, $A \otimes B$ is subgaussian with parameter $\sqrt{2\lambda}\gamma\delta$.

4.3   Evaluating Inner Products in Exponents

This procedure allows evaluation of inner products in exponents with $\log d$ times less homomorphic additions in exponents than in FHEW, also less key material.

As a subroutine, we construct an (External) Multiply-and-Add operation in the exponent, for a public coefficient $\alpha \in \mathbb{Z}_d^*$. We defer the error analysis of this step to the Algorithm 6 with $\ell = 1$.

External Multiply-and-Add in the Exponent.

> **Key Material:** Key-switch keys $\mathbf{S}^\alpha$ (from $\psi_\alpha(s)$ to s) and $\mathbf{S}^\beta$ (from $\psi_\beta(s)$ to s), where $\beta = \alpha^{-1} \mod d$ (Size: $O(Kd \log Q)$)
>
> **Runtime:** $O(Kd \log d)$
>
> **Signature:** $\mathsf{ExtExpMultAdd}_{\mathbf{S}^\alpha, \mathbf{S}^\beta}^\alpha$:
>
> $$\mathcal{R}_d\mathsf{LWE}_s^{t|Q}(T^{m'}; E) \times \mathcal{R}_d\mathsf{GSW}_s^{t|Q}(T^m; E') \to \mathcal{R}_d\mathsf{LWE}_s^{t|Q}\left(T^{\alpha m + m'}; E''\right).$$
>
> where $E'' = \sqrt{E^2 + d^2 K(4\sigma^2 + E'^2)}$.

Algorithm 5. $\mathsf{ExtExpMultAdd}_{\mathbf{S}^\alpha, \mathbf{S}^\beta}^\alpha(\mathbf{c}, \mathbf{C})$

Require: $\alpha \in \mathbb{Z}_d^*$, with inverse $\beta = \alpha^{-1} \in \mathbb{Z}_d^*$
   A $\psi_\alpha(s) \to s$ Key-Switching key $\mathbf{S}^\alpha \in \mathcal{R}_d\mathsf{LWE}_s^{Q|Q}\left(\psi_\alpha(s) \cdot \mathbf{g}^T; \sigma\right)$
   A $\psi_\beta(s) \to s$ Key-Switching key $\mathbf{S}^\beta \in \mathcal{R}_d\mathsf{LWE}_s^{Q|Q}\left(\psi_\beta(s) \cdot \mathbf{g}^T; \sigma\right)$
   A ciphertext $\mathbf{c} \in \mathcal{R}_d\mathsf{LWE}_s^{t|Q}(T^{m'}; E)$. A ciphertext $\mathbf{C} \in \mathcal{R}_d\mathsf{GSW}_s^{t|Q}(T^m; E')$
Ensure: A ciphertext $\mathbf{c}' \in \mathcal{R}_d\mathsf{LWE}_s^{t|Q}(T^{\alpha m + m'}; E'')$.

   $\mathbf{c}_1 \leftarrow \mathsf{Galois}^\beta(\mathbf{c})$ $\triangleright \in \mathcal{R}_d\mathsf{LWE}_{\psi_\beta(s)}^{t|Q}(T^{\beta m'})$
   $\mathbf{c}_2 \leftarrow \mathsf{KeySwitch}_{\mathbf{S}^\beta}^{\psi_\beta(s) \to s}(\mathbf{c}_1)$ $\triangleright \in \mathcal{R}_d\mathsf{LWE}_s^{t|Q}(T^{\beta m'})$
   $\mathbf{c}_3 \leftarrow \mathsf{ExtMult}(\mathbf{C}, \mathbf{c}_2)$ $\triangleright \in \mathcal{R}_d\mathsf{LWE}_s^{t|Q}(T^{m + \beta m'})$
   $\mathbf{c}_4 \leftarrow \mathsf{Galois}^\alpha(\mathbf{c}_3)$ $\triangleright \in \mathcal{R}_d\mathsf{LWE}_{\psi_\alpha(s)}^{t|Q}(T^{\alpha m + m'})$
   $\mathbf{c}_5 \leftarrow \mathsf{KeySwitch}_{\mathbf{S}^\alpha}^{\psi_\alpha(s) \to s}(\mathbf{c}_4)$ $\triangleright \in \mathcal{R}_d\mathsf{LWE}_s^{t|Q}(T^{\alpha m + m'})$
   return $\mathbf{c}_5$.

Remark 4. A similar speed-up was obtained in [15] using a different technique, namely a *Mux* operation. We are unfortunately unable to use it in our circulant set-up, essentially because encryptions of 0 are not allowed: our IND-CPA-security guarantee (Lemma 2) only applies to encryptions of X^m for some $m \in \mathbb{Z}_d$. Yet our technique is more general, precisely, we do not restrict the secret input vector to have binary coefficients.

By chaining, this allows us to evaluate inner products $\langle \mathbf{x}, \mathbf{y} \rangle$ over $\mathbb{Z}_d$ in the exponent, given GSW encryptions $\mathcal{R}_d\mathsf{GSW}_s^{t|Q}(T^{x_i})$ and a public vector of coefficients $\mathbf{y} \in \mathbb{Z}_d^\ell$.

External Inner-product in the Exponent.

Key Material: Key-switch keys $\mathbf{S}^\alpha$ from $\psi_\alpha(s)$ to s, for every $\alpha \in \mathbb{Z}_d^*$. (Size: $O(d^2 \log^2 Q)$)

Runtime: $O(lKd \log d)$

Signature: $\mathsf{ExtExpInner}_{[\mathbf{S}^\alpha]_\alpha}^{\mathbf{y}}$:

$$\bigoplus_{i=1}^{\ell} \mathcal{R}_d \mathsf{GSW}_s^{t|Q}(T^{x_i}; E') \to \mathcal{R}_d \mathsf{LWE}_s^{t|Q}\left(T^{\langle \mathbf{x}, \mathbf{y}\rangle}; \sqrt{2K\ell^2 d^2\sigma^2 + 2K\ell d^2 E'^2}\right). \tag{10}$$

Algorithm 6. $\mathsf{ExtExpInner}_{[\mathbf{S}^\alpha]_\alpha}^{\mathbf{y}}([\mathbf{C}_i]_{i\in[l]})$

Require: A public vector $\mathbf{y} \in \mathbb{Z}_d^\ell$
  A $\psi_\alpha(s) \to s$ Key-Switching key $\mathbf{S}^\alpha \in \mathcal{R}_d \mathsf{LWE}_s^{Q|Q}\left(\psi_\alpha(s) \cdot \mathbf{g}^T; \sigma\right)$ for each $\alpha \in \mathbb{Z}_d^*$
  A ciphertext $\mathbf{C}_i \in \mathcal{R}_d \mathsf{GSW}_s^{t|Q}(T^{x_i}; E')$ for each $i \in [\ell]$
Ensure: A ciphertext $\mathbf{c} \in \mathcal{R}_d \mathsf{LWE}_s^{t|Q}\left(T^{\langle \mathbf{x}, \mathbf{y}\rangle}; \sqrt{4K\ell^2 d^2\sigma^2 + 2K\ell d^2 E'^2}\right)$

  $\mathbf{c} \leftarrow (0, T^0)$ $\triangleright \in \mathcal{R}_d \mathsf{LWE}_s^{t|Q}(T^0; 0)$
  for i from 1 to ℓ where $\mathbf{y}_i \neq 0$ **do**
    $\alpha = \mathbf{y}_i;\ \beta = \alpha^{-1} \bmod d$
    $\mathbf{c} \leftarrow \mathsf{ExtExpMultAdd}_{\mathbf{S}^\alpha, \mathbf{S}^\beta}^\alpha(\mathbf{c}, \mathbf{C}_i)$ $\triangleright \in \mathcal{R}_d \mathsf{LWE}_s^{t|Q}\left(T^{\sum_{j=1}^{i} x_j y_j}, \dots\right)$
  end for
  return $\mathbf{c}$

Theorem 9. *Algorithm 6 is correct and runs in time $\Theta(lKd \log d)$.*

Remark 5. The asymmetry in the error parameter $\sqrt{4K\ell^2 d^2\sigma^2 + 2K\ell d^2 E'^2}$ with ℓ^2 on the left-hand side and ℓ on the right is due to the fact that key-switch keys can be reused in multiple loop iterations. Thus, the error parameter that we state in Algorithm 6 represents the worst case where we have the same α in every loop iteration, and $\alpha = \alpha^{-1} \bmod d$. In practice, this will happen very rarely, so we can expect an error parameter close to $\sqrt{K\ell d^2(4\sigma^2 + 2E'^2)}$.

5   Joining the Building Blocks

In this section, we explain how the building blocks we described in Sect. 4 fit together to form the homomorphic evaluation and bootstrapping procedure EvalBootstrap. See Fig. 1 for a schematic overview. We build an algorithm that, given ciphertexts $\mathbf{c}_i \in \mathsf{LWE}_\mathbf{s}(m_i; E_{in})$, $i \in \{1, \dots, k\}$ with $\mathbf{s} \in \mathbb{Z}_{Q'}^p$ a short vector (i.e., $\mathbf{s}_i \in \{-1, 0, 1\}$ for all i), a function $f : \mathbb{Z}_t \to \mathbb{Z}_t$, and coefficients $\gamma_1, \dots, \gamma_k \in \mathbb{Z}_t$ such that $\sum_i |\gamma_i| \leq t$, produces $\mathbf{c} \in \mathsf{LWE}_\mathbf{s}(f(m); E_{out})$ where

$m = \sum_{i=1}^{k} \gamma_i m_i$. We do *not* assume that the error terms in the c_i are independent of each other, or independent of the key material used by EvalBootstrap: if an input c_i is the result of a previous application of EvalBootstrap, then its error term is not independent of the error terms in the bootstrapping/evaluation key material. We use the following parameters for the building blocks:

- n as the security parameter,
- $p, q = \Theta(n)$, $Q = \text{poly}(n)$, $K = \lceil \log Q \rceil = O(\log n)$, $t = \Theta(n)$ such that $t \leq \sqrt{pq}/4$,
- $\lambda = \Theta(n)$ such that $\lambda \leq q$ as the failure parameter; the decryption and homomorphic evaluation procedures should only fail with probability exponentially small in λ,
- σ as the error parameter used in the key material,
- $Q', Q_\otimes = O(Q/\sqrt{n^3 \sigma})$, with $t \cdot \lfloor Q_\otimes/t \rfloor = 1 \bmod Q_\otimes$.

For $m_i \in \{0, 1\}$, the algorithm can evaluate arbitrary k-bit gates if $t \geq 2^k$, using $\gamma_i = 2^{i-1}$ and an appropriately chosen f. We can compute a threshold gate if $t > k$ by setting $\gamma_i = 1$ for all i.

Theorem 10. *Algorithm 7 is correct and runs in time $\tilde{O}(n^2)$. Moreover, there exists $Q = O(\gamma'|f|n^{6.5}\sigma^{1.5})$ such that the output of EvalBootstrap can be used as input for another execution of EvalBootstrap with coefficients $\gamma'_1, \ldots, \gamma'_k$ such that $\gamma' = \sum_i |\gamma'_i|$ (with failure probability exponentially small in n).*

6   Implementation

In addition to the formal analysis, we developed a complete implementation of the scheme. Our objective was to make it efficient and usable. We present below the key techniques that enable us to evaluate a 6-bit gate in roughly 6.4 s.

6.1   Implementation Details

FFT. The most intensive computations throughout the scheme are the multiplications of ring elements. For efficiency this is classically done in the *frequency domain*. The cost for a multiplication decreases from $\Theta(n^c)$ down to $\Theta(n \log n)$, where $c = \log(3)$ in the case of Karatsuba algorithm for example. Since we are dealing with circulant ring elements, we may wish to run the FFT operation in the ring dimension exactly. But our ring dimensions are prime, which is the worst case for FFT efficiency. We ran some benchmarks and it turned out that it was much faster to use a bigger dimension (with small prime factors), and do the polynomial reduction afterwards. Also we do not meet the conditions to apply NTT (our moduli are not primes), so our choice was to stick with FFT computations and we use the FFTW library [29] for the forward and backward transforms.

More challenges arose with FFT computations since our biggest modulus is $Q = 2^{56}$ and the FFT works with *double precision* numbers (i.e. 53 bits

Algorithm 7. EvalBootstrap$_{\mathcal{S}}^{f,\gamma_1,\ldots,\gamma_k}(\mathbf{c}_1,\ldots,\mathbf{c}_k)$: Homomorphically evaluate a function and produce a bootstrapped encryption of the result.

Require: $\mathbf{c}_i \in \mathsf{LWE}_{\mathbf{s}}^{t|Q'}(m_i; E_{\mathrm{in}})$, $f : \mathbb{Z}_t \to \mathbb{Z}_t$, $\gamma_i \in \mathbb{Z}_t$ where $\gamma = \sum |\gamma_i|$ and $\gamma E_{\mathrm{in}} \leq T$ for a certain $T = \Theta(Q/(n^2\sqrt{\sigma}))$, and $\mathcal{S}$ is the required public key material consisting of:

- Bootstrapping keys $\mathbf{BK}_i^{(d)} \in \mathcal{R}_d\mathsf{LWE}_{\mathbf{s}^{(d)}}^{t|Q}(\mathbf{s}_i \bmod d; \sigma)$ for $i = 1,\ldots,n$ and $d = p, q$, where $|s^{(d)}| = O(n\sqrt{\sigma})$
- Key-switch keys $\mathbf{S}^{d,\alpha}$ from $\psi_\alpha(s)$ to s for $d \in \{p,q\}$ and $\alpha \in \mathbb{Z}_d^*$
- A key-switch key $\mathbf{S}$ from $\mathbf{s}^{(pq)}$ to s' where $\mathbf{s}^{(pq)} = \left(-\psi_\alpha(s^{(p)}) \otimes \psi_\beta(s^{(q)}), \psi_\alpha(s^{(p)}) \otimes 1, 1 \otimes \psi_\beta(s^{(q)})\right)$ for $\alpha = q^{-1} \bmod p$, and $\beta = p^{-1} \bmod q$, and $s' = \sum_{i=0}^{p-1} \mathbf{s}_{i+1}X^i$

Ensure: $\mathbf{c} \in \mathsf{LWE}_{\mathbf{s}}^{t|Q'}\left(f(\sum_{i=1}^k \gamma_i m_i); E_{\mathrm{out}}\right)$ where $E_{\mathrm{out}} = O(|f|n^{4.5}\sigma)$, except with probability exponentially small in n.

$\mathbf{c} \leftarrow \sum_{i=1}^k \gamma_i \mathbf{c}_i$ $\qquad\qquad\qquad\qquad\qquad\qquad\qquad \triangleright \in \mathsf{LWE}_{\mathbf{s}}^{t|Q'}(m; \gamma E)$

$\mathbf{c} \leftarrow \mathsf{ModSwitch}^{Q' \to pq}(\mathbf{c})$ $\qquad\qquad\qquad \triangleright \in \mathsf{LWE}_{\mathbf{s}}^{t|pq}(m; \sqrt{r^2\gamma^2E^2 + (p+1)^2})$ where $r = \lfloor pq/t \rfloor / \lfloor Q'/t \rfloor$

$\left(\mathbf{a}^{(p)}, b^{(p)}\right) \leftarrow \mathbf{c} \bmod p$

$\left(\mathbf{a}^{(q)}, b^{(q)}\right) \leftarrow \mathbf{c} \bmod q$

$\mathbf{c}^{(p)} \leftarrow X^{b^{(p)}} \cdot \mathsf{ExtExpInner}_{[\mathbf{S}^{p,\alpha}]_\alpha}^{-\mathbf{a}^{(p)}}\left([\mathbf{BK}_i^{(p)}]_i\right)$

$\qquad\qquad\qquad\qquad\qquad\qquad \triangleright \in \mathcal{R}_p\mathsf{LWE}_{\mathbf{s}}^{t|Q}\left(X^{b - \langle \mathbf{a},\mathbf{s}\rangle \bmod p}; O(n^{2.5}\sigma)\right)$

$\mathbf{c}^{(q)} \leftarrow Y^{b^{(q)}} \cdot \mathsf{ExtExpInner}_{[\mathbf{S}^{q,\alpha}]_\alpha}^{-\mathbf{a}^{(q)}}\left([\mathbf{BK}_i^{(q)}]_i\right)$

$\qquad\qquad\qquad\qquad\qquad\qquad \triangleright \in \mathcal{R}_q\mathsf{LWE}_{\mathbf{s}}^{t|Q}\left(Y^{b - \langle \mathbf{a},\mathbf{s}\rangle \bmod q}; O(n^{2.5}\sigma)\right)$

$\mathbf{c}^{(p)} \leftarrow \mathsf{ModSwitch}^{Q \to Q\otimes}(\mathbf{c}^{(p)})$ $\qquad \triangleright \in \mathcal{R}_p\mathsf{LWE}_{\mathbf{s}^{(p)}}^{t|Q\otimes}\left(X^{b - \langle \mathbf{a},\mathbf{s}\rangle \bmod p}; O(n\sqrt{\sigma})\right)$

$\mathbf{c}^{(q)} \leftarrow \mathsf{ModSwitch}^{Q \to Q\otimes}(\mathbf{c}^{(q)})$ $\qquad \triangleright \in \mathcal{R}_q\mathsf{LWE}_{\mathbf{s}^{(q)}}^{t|Q\otimes}\left(Y^{b - \langle \mathbf{a},\mathbf{s}\rangle \bmod q}; O(n\sqrt{\sigma})\right)$

$\mathbf{c}^{(pq)} \leftarrow \mathsf{ExpCRT}(\mathbf{c}^{(p)}, \mathbf{c}^{(q)})$ $\qquad\qquad \triangleright \in \mathcal{R}_{pq}\mathsf{LWE}_{\mathbf{s}^{(pq)}}^{t|Q\otimes}\left(Z^{b - \langle \mathbf{a},\mathbf{s}\rangle}; O(n^{3.5}\sigma)\right)$

$\mathbf{c}^{(pq)} \leftarrow \mathsf{ModSwitch}^{Q\otimes \to Q'}(\mathbf{c}^{(pq)})$ $\qquad \triangleright \in \mathcal{R}_{pq}\mathsf{LWE}_{\mathbf{s}^{(pq)}}^{t|Q'}\left(Z^{b - \langle \mathbf{a},\mathbf{s}\rangle}; O(n^{3.5}\sigma)\right)$

$F \leftarrow (x \mapsto f(\lfloor tx/q \rfloor \bmod t))$ $\qquad\qquad \triangleright F : \mathbb{Z}_{pq} \to \mathbb{Z}_t, |F| = |f|pq/t = O(|f|n)$

$\mathbf{c} \leftarrow \mathsf{FunExpExtract}_{F,\mathbf{S}}^{\mathbf{s}^{(pq)} \to \mathbf{s}}(\mathbf{c}^{(pq)})$ $\qquad\qquad \triangleright \in \mathsf{LWE}_{\mathbf{s}}^{Q'|t}\left(f(m); O(|f|n^{4.5}\sigma)\right)$

return c

---

mantissa). So we have to split the ring coefficients into two halves of 28 bits each and apply the FFT transformation on each to prevent rounding errors. We perform this splitting trick only when needed, i.e. when the ring element is not small. For example, in ExtMult products of ring element are computed where one of the operands is the output of a Gadget decomposition. This operand needs not be split before FFT forward transform because it is very small.

Pre-computations. In order to minimize the evaluation time of the gate, a maximum of heavy computations are done in the setup phase. Consequently all keys materials: bootstrapping keys, key-switching keys, among others, are computed ahead of time and in FFT domain. Our `CirculantRing` class allows to transparently manipulate ring element in FFT or coefficient representation which greatly contribute to both performance and code readability.

Further Optimization. The implementation has been done in C++11, using its most convenient and efficient features. For example, all classes are extensively defined with template parameters (dimension, moduli, basis decomposition...). This trick allows the computer to know, at compile time, the values of many variables. The compiler then produces dedicated and highly optimized binaries.

Open-Source. Many efforts have also been made for general availability and usability. The whole code is documented with Doxygen and many unitary tests are provided. With under 4,000 lines of code, it remains accessible to whoever wants to tweak or improve it. The implementation is open-source [6].

At the first start (and only then), heavy computations are performed by the FFTW components, in order to optimize the FFT for the current computer.

6.2   Parameters

For our first implementation, we targeted a 6-bit input gate. The parameters of the scheme are as follows:

- For 6 input bits, the plaintext modulus $t = 2^6$.
- The ring dimensions p and q are 1439 and 1447, so $pq = 2,077,892$. Hence the FFT dimensions are $d_1^{FFT} = 3072 = 3 \cdot 2^{10}$ for $\mathcal{R}_p, \mathcal{R}_q$ and $d_2^{FFT} = 4,194,304 = 2^{22}$ for $\mathcal{R}_{pq}$.
- The modulus in ExtExpInner and the LWE are $Q, Q' = 2^{56}$.
- Errors and secrets are sampled according to Sect. E.2. Secrets are ternary, one third of the coefficients are set to -1, another to 1 and the rest to 0. Errors have variance 4.

For ExpCRT we want a small inverse to $\lfloor Q_\otimes/t \rceil \mod Q_\otimes$. Hence we choose $Q_\otimes = (2^{19} - t + 1)^2$. Finally, for the gadget decomposition we use $B = 2^8$ and $K = 7$ for ExtExpInner and FunExpExtract and their key material.

We also have extra parameters related an to optimization presented in Appendix F.1. Namely, we apply an extra KeySwitch over LWE ciphertext to decrease the length l of the decryption inner-product from $l = p = 1439$ down to $l = 600$. This key-switch happens with modulus $Q = 2^{56}$, error standard deviation 2^{33}, and gadget parameters $B = 2^6$, $K = 10$.

Error Growth and Correctness. To choose the parameters, we simulated the error growth throughout the gate, using heuristic error propagation assumption, described in Appendix F.2. This simulation script is provided with the code as file `scripts/parameters.sage`. We compared the predicted variance of each

---

[6] https://github.com/gbonnoron/Borogrove.

step to the experimental one, and found them to be corroborated. From the final variance, and according to a central limit heuristic, we predict a failure probability of only 2^{-74} for the above parameter set. In practice we have tested our scheme hundreds of time on different inputs, and never observed failure.

Security. To estimate the concrete security of our parameter set, we use the `lwe-estimator` from Albrecht [30]. All the LWE instances behind our LWE, $\mathcal{R}_p$LWE, $\mathcal{R}_q$LWE ciphertexts given as part of the evaluation key offers at least 100 bits of security, according to the estimator as of commit `cc5f6e8`, which includes the latest result of [31] for small secrets. Therefore we feel safe to claim at least 80 bits of security.

6.3 Performances

We run our test on a punchy laptop: Core i7-6500U (2.50 GHz, 4 MB L2 cache), 16 GB RAM with a GNU/Linux Fedora 26 installed on a SSD. The computation is single-threaded and we got the following timings:

- FFTW *wisdom* computation (only once per computer): 68 min
- Key pre-processing (once per user key pair): 38 s
- 6-bit input, 1-bit output gate evaluation: 6.4 s

The gate time breaks down into: 0.60 s per ExtExpInner (the two could be run in parallel), 4.0 s for the KeySwitch in FunExpExtract and only 0.55 s for the output bit related operations. Consequently, computing another function (1 more output bit) on the same 6 input bits would add only 0.55 s, and so on. For 6-to-6 bit gate it yields just above 10 s. On the memory front, we need 9.2 GB of RAM to store all key materials for the computation.

Optimisations. This first implementation includes only those on ExtExpInner described in Sect. F.1. Over the total gate evaluation time, 60% (3.8 s) are spent on FFT forward and backward transforms. The 3.8 s break down into 0.9 sec for more than 350k FFT in dimension d_1^{FFT} ($\mathcal{R}_p$ and $\mathcal{R}_q$), and 2.9 s for only around 250 FFT in dimension d_2^{FFT} for $\mathcal{R}_{pq}$. We estimate that the optimisations of Appendix F.4 will bring these 2.9 s down to 1 or 1.5 s at most. This rough estimate is based on partial implementation, soon to be confirmed after complete integration. The overall gate time should drop below 6 s and the cost of additional output bits become negligible.

A   Proofs for Section 2 (Preliminaries)

Lemma 1. *Let A be a δ-subgaussian random variable over $\mathcal{R}_{pq}$. Then $\mathrm{Tr}^*_{\mathcal{R}_{pq}/\mathcal{R}_p}(A)$ is δ-subgaussian as well.*

Proof. Let $b \in \mathcal{R}_p$. Then, $\mathrm{Tr}^*_{\mathcal{R}_p/\mathbb{Z}}\big(\mathrm{Tr}^*_{\mathcal{R}_{pq}/\mathcal{R}_p}(Ab)\big)/\|b\| = \mathrm{Tr}^*(Ab)/\|b\|$ which is δ-subgaussian by assumption.

B   Proofs for Section 3 (Encryption Schemes)

Lemma 2. *If the decisional $\tilde{\mathcal{R}}$- LWE problem is hard, then the Circulant-LWE scheme is CPA-secure for messages of the form $m = X^k$.*

Proof. If $\tilde{\mathcal{R}}$- LWE is hard, then by Lemma 3, the Circulant-LWE distribution is indistinguishable from the uniform distribution over $\mathcal{S}_{d,Q}^2$. To prove CPA-security, it suffices to show that, for any $k \in \mathbb{Z}/d\mathbb{Z}$ and $u = \lfloor Q/t \rfloor$, we have $\mathcal{S}_{d,Q} + uX^k = \mathcal{S}_{d,Q} + u$. This then shows that a Circulant-LWE encryption of $m = X^k$ is indistinguishable from a uniformly random sample from $\mathcal{S}_{d,Q} \times (\mathcal{S}_{d,Q} + u)$. Indeed, $\mathcal{S}_{d,Q} + u = \{\sum_{i=0}^{d-1} a_i X^i \mid \sum a_i = u \bmod Q\} = \mathcal{S}_{d,Q} + uX^k$.

Lemma 3. *If the decisional $\tilde{\mathcal{R}}$- LWE problem is hard, then the Circulant-GSW scheme is CPA-secure.*

Proof. Let $\mathbf{C}$ be a Circulant-GSW ciphertext. Each row of $\mathbf{C}$ is of the form $(a, b) + (0, uB^i m)$ or $(a, b) + (uB^i m, 0)$ where $m = X^k$ and (a, b) is a Circulant-LWE sample, and thus indistinguishable from a random element of $\mathcal{S}_{d,Q}^2$. By the same argument as in the previous proof, each row of $\mathbf{C}$ is indistinguishable from a uniformly random samble from either $(\mathcal{S}_{d,Q} + uB^i) \times \mathcal{S}_{d,Q}$, or $\mathcal{S}_{d,Q} \times (\mathcal{S}_{d,Q} + uB^i)$ where i only depends on the row number, not on m.

C   Proofs for Section 4 (Homomorphic Operations)

Lemma 4. *Algorithm 1 is correct. Furthermore, if $e = \mathsf{err}(\mathbf{c})$ and $e_i = \mathsf{err}(\mathbf{S}_i)$, then the error term of the output ciphertext is $e + \sum_{i=1}^{n} \mathbf{d}_i^T e_i$, where each $\mathbf{d}_i$ is a vector whose entries have operator norm at most d.*

Proof. By definition of $\mathbf{g}^{-T}$, it is easy to see that the error term is $e - \sum_{i=1}^{n} \mathbf{g}^{-T}(\mathbf{a}_i) e_i$ and each component of $g^{-T}(\mathbf{a}_i)$ is in $\mathcal{R}_d / 2\mathcal{R}_d$. Thus, the second part of the lemma follows. The first part holds because for every i, $g^{-T}(\mathbf{a}_i) e_i$ is subgaussian with parameter at most $\sqrt{K} d\sigma$. If the error terms are independent, it follows that the error parameter is as stated in the algorithm.

Lemma 5. *Algorithm 2 is correct. Furthermore, for $e = \mathsf{err}(\mathbf{c})$ and $\mathbf{e} = \mathsf{err}(\mathbf{C})$, the error term of the output is $X^k \cdot e + \mathbf{d}^T \mathbf{e}$ for some k and a random vector $\mathbf{d} \in \mathcal{R}_d^{2K}$ independent of $\mathbf{e}$ with $\|\mathbf{d}_i\| \leq d$ for every i.*

Proof. Write $u = \lfloor Q/t \rfloor$, so $\mathbf{c} = (a, as + e + \lfloor Q/t \rfloor T^m)$ and $\mathbf{C} = (\mathbf{a}, \langle \mathbf{a}, \mathbf{s}\rangle + \mathbf{e}) + uT^{m'} \mathbf{G}$. Let $\mathbf{d} = \mathbf{G}^{-1}(u^{-1} \cdot \mathbf{c})$. We have:

$$\mathbf{d}^T \cdot \mathbf{C} = \mathbf{d}^T \cdot (\mathbf{a}, \mathbf{a}s + \mathbf{e}) + uT^{m'} \mathbf{d}^T \mathbf{G}$$

$$= (\mathbf{d}^T \mathbf{a}, \mathbf{d}^T \mathbf{a}s + \mathbf{d}^T \mathbf{e}) + uu^{-1}T^{m'}\left(a, as + e + \left\lfloor \frac{Q}{t}\right\rfloor T^m\right)$$

$$= \left(a', a's + e' + \left\lfloor \frac{Q}{t}\right\rfloor T^{m+m'}\right)$$

where $a' = \mathbf{d}^T \mathbf{a} + a T^{m'}$ and $e' = \mathbf{d}^T \mathbf{e} + e T^{m'}$. Each component of $\mathbf{e}$ is independent and subgaussian with parameter E', and $\mathbf{d}$ is a vector in $\mathcal{R}_d^{2K}$, where each entry has binary coefficients. Thus, for every i, we have $|\mathbf{d}_i| \leq d$. Using the following Lemma 2, the error parameter follows.

Lemma 2. *Let e be a γ-subgaussian variable over $\mathcal{R}_d$ and $\mathbf{e} = (\mathbf{e}_1, \ldots, \mathbf{e}_n)$ be a vector of independent δ-subgaussian random variables over $\mathcal{R}_d$. Let $\mathbf{d}$ be a random variable over $\mathcal{R}_d^n$ such that $|\mathbf{d}_i| \leq k$ for all i. If $\mathbf{d}$ and $\mathbf{e}$ are independent and e and $\mathbf{e}$ are independent, then $e + \langle \mathbf{d}, \mathbf{e} \rangle$ is $\sqrt{\gamma^2 + k^2 n \delta^2}$-subgaussian.*

We first consider the case where $e = 0$ and $\mathbf{d}$ is a fixed vector instead of a random variable. For every $b \in \mathcal{R}_d$ and every i, we have $\mathrm{Tr}(\mathbf{d}_i \mathbf{e}_i b)/\|b\| \leq k\mathrm{Tr}(\mathbf{e}_i(\mathbf{d}_i b))/\|\mathbf{d}_i b\|$ which is $(k\delta)$-subgaussian. From the independence of the $\mathbf{e}_i$, it follows that $\mathrm{Tr}(\langle \mathbf{d}, \mathbf{e} \rangle b)/\|b\|$ is $(\sqrt{n} k \delta)$-subgaussian.

If $\mathbf{d}$ and e are random variables independent of $\mathbf{e}$, it holds for every $b \in \mathcal{R}_d$ that

$$\mathbb{E}[\exp(t\mathrm{Tr}(eb + \langle \mathbf{d}, \mathbf{e} \rangle b)/\|b\|)]$$

$$= \sum_{e^*, \mathbf{d}^*} P[e = e^*, \mathbf{d} = \mathbf{d}^*] \cdot \mathbb{E}[\exp(t\mathrm{Tr}(eb + \langle \mathbf{d}, \mathbf{e} \rangle b)/\|b\|) \mid e = e^*, \mathbf{d} = \mathbf{d}^*]$$

$$= \sum_{e^*, \mathbf{d}^*} P[e = e^*, \mathbf{d} = \mathbf{d}^*] \cdot \exp(t\mathrm{Tr}(e^* b)/\|b\|) \cdot \mathbb{E}[\exp(t\mathrm{Tr}(\langle \mathbf{d}^*, \mathbf{e} \rangle b)/\|b\|)]$$

$$\leq \sum_{e^*, \mathbf{d}^*} P[e = e^*, \mathbf{d} = \mathbf{d}^*] \cdot \exp(t\mathrm{Tr}(e^* b)/\|b\|) \cdot \exp(t^2 n k^2 \delta^2 / 2)$$

$$= \mathbb{E}[t \exp(\mathrm{Tr}(eb)/\|b\|)] \cdot \exp(t^2 n k^2 \delta^2 / 2)$$

$$\leq \exp(t^2(\gamma^2 + n k^2 \delta^2)/2)$$

which concludes the proof.

Lemma 6. *Algorithm 3 is correct and runs in time $O(pq \log(pq) \log Q')$.*

Proof. We can compute $\mathrm{Tr}^*_{\mathcal{R}_{pq}/\mathcal{R}_p}(x)$ by examining p coefficients of x, and $\mathrm{Tr}^*_{\mathcal{R}_p/\mathbb{Z}}(x)$ is simply the constant term of x. Thus, the runtime is dominated by the key-switch, which runs in time $O(pq \log(pq) K)$. After the multiplication and key-switch, it holds that

$$c \in \mathcal{R}_{pq}\mathsf{LWE}_{\mathbf{s}(pq)}^{t|Q'}\left(\sum_{i \in \mathbb{Z}_{pq}} Z^{m-i \bmod pq}; |F|\sqrt{E^2 + 3\sigma^2 p^2 q^2 K} \right)$$

since $|f| \leq |F|$. Using Lemma 1, the linearity of the trace function, and the fact that $s' \in \mathcal{R}_p$, we conclude that after the trace,

$$(a, b) \in \mathcal{R}_p\mathsf{LWE}_{s'}^{t|Q'}\left(\mathrm{Tr}^*_{\mathcal{R}_{pq}/\mathcal{R}_p}\left(\sum_{i \in \mathbb{Z}_{pq}} F(i) Z^{m-i \bmod pq} \right); |F|\sqrt{E^2 + 3\sigma^2 p^2 q^2 K} \right)$$

It holds that

$$\mathrm{Tr}^*(b) = \mathrm{Tr}^*(a \cdot s') + \lfloor Q'/t \rfloor \, \mathrm{Tr}^*_{\mathcal{R}_{pq}/\mathbb{Z}}\left(\sum_{i \in \mathbb{Z}_{pq}} F(i) Z^{m-i \bmod pq}\right) + \mathrm{Tr}^*(e)$$

and by Lemma 1, $\mathrm{Tr}^*\left(\sum_{i \in \mathbb{Z}_{pq}} F(i) Z^{m-i \bmod pq}\right) = F(j)$ if $m = j$. Since $\mathrm{Tr}^*(as) = a_0 s_0 + \sum_{i=1}^{p-1} a_{p-i} s_i = \langle \mathbf{a}, \mathbf{s} \rangle$ and Tr^* does not increase the error parameter, the correctness of our algorithm follows.

Lemma 7. *Let A and B be independent subgaussian random variables on $\mathcal{R}_p$ and $\mathcal{R}_q$, respectively, with parameters γ and δ. Then, for every $\lambda \in \mathbb{R}$, $A \otimes B$ is subgaussian with parameter $\sqrt{2\lambda}\gamma\delta$ except with probability $2\min(p, q)\exp(-\lambda)$.*[7]

Proof. We want to show that for every $y \in \mathcal{R}_{pq} \setminus \{0\}$, $\mathrm{Tr}^*((A \otimes B)y)/\|y\|$ is subgaussian (except with a small probability). Let $y \in \mathcal{R}_{pq} \setminus \{0\}$. We can write $y = \sum_{i=0}^{q-1} y_i \otimes Y^i$. It holds that $\|y\| = \sqrt{\sum_i \|y_i\|^2}$. Thus,

$$\frac{\mathrm{Tr}^*((A \otimes B)y)}{\|y\|} = \sum_i \frac{\mathrm{Tr}^*(Ay_i \otimes BY^i)}{\|y\|} = \sum_i \frac{\mathrm{Tr}^*(Ay_i) \cdot \mathrm{Tr}^*(BY^i)}{\|y\|}$$

Let E_i be the event that $|\mathrm{Tr}^*(Ay_i)| \geq \sqrt{2\lambda}\gamma\|y_i\|$. Applying the subgaussian tail estimate, we conclude that for each i, $p(E_i) \leq 2\exp(-\lambda)$. By the union bound, it follows that, for $E = \bigcup_i E_i$, $p(E) \leq 2q\exp(-\lambda)$. We now proceed similarly to the proof of Lemma 2. For every fixed value $a \in \mathcal{R}_p$ such that $\mathrm{Tr}^*(ay_i) < \sqrt{2\lambda}\gamma\|y_i\|$ for all i, we have

$$\sum_i \frac{\mathrm{Tr}^*(ay_i) \cdot \mathrm{Tr}^*(BY^i)}{\|y\|} = \frac{\mathrm{Tr}^*(\sum_i B\mathrm{Tr}^*(ay_i)Y^i)}{\|y\|}$$

which is subgaussian with parameter

$$\frac{\|\sum_i \mathrm{Tr}^*(ay_i)Y^i\| \, \delta}{\|y\|} = \frac{\sqrt{\sum_i \mathrm{Tr}^*(ay_i)^2}\delta}{\sqrt{\sum_j \|y_j\|^2}} < \frac{\sqrt{2\lambda}\gamma\delta\sqrt{\sum_i \|y_i\|^2}}{\sqrt{\sum_j \|y_j\|^2}} = \sqrt{2\lambda}\gamma\delta$$

We can then use the independence of A and B to conclude that, conditioned on $\overline{E}$, $\mathrm{Tr}^*((A \otimes B)y)/\|y\|$ is $(\sqrt{2\lambda}\gamma\delta)$-subgaussian, as claimed.

Using a similar argument, this time writing $y = \sum_{i=0}^{p-1} X^i \otimes y_i$, it also follows that $\mathrm{Tr}^*((A \otimes B)y)/\|y\|$ is $(\sqrt{2\lambda}\gamma\delta)$-subgaussian except with probability $2p\exp(-\lambda)$. This proves our claim.

Lemma 8. *Algorithm 4 is correct and runs in time $\Theta(pq)$.*

---

[7] More formally, for some event E with $p(E) \leq 2\min(p, q)\exp(-\lambda)$, when conditioning on $\overline{E}$, $A \otimes B$ is subgaussian with parameter $\sqrt{2\lambda}\gamma\delta$.

Proof. Let $m' = \alpha q m_p + \beta p m_q \bmod pq$. It holds that $m' \bmod p = m_p$ and $m' \bmod q = m_q$. Thus, by the Chinese Remainder Theorem, $m' = m$. Let $s'_p = \psi_\alpha(s_p)$ and $s'_q = \psi_\beta(s_q)$. Let us write $b'_p = u X^{\alpha m_p} + e_p$ and $b'_q = Q_\otimes Y^{\beta m_q}/t + e_q$. We have

$$tb_p \otimes b_q = ta_p s_p \otimes b_q + tb'_p \otimes a_q s_q + tb'_p \otimes b'_q$$
$$= -ta_p s'_p \otimes a_q s'_q + ta_p s'_p \otimes b'_q + tb_p \otimes a_q s'_q + tb'_p \otimes b'_q$$

and $tb'_p \otimes b'_q = \lfloor Q_\otimes/t \rceil X^{\alpha m_p} \otimes Y^{\beta m_q} + X^{\alpha m_p} \otimes e_q + e_p \otimes Y^{\beta m_q} + te_p \otimes e_q$. Since $X^{\alpha m_p} \otimes Y^{\alpha m_q} = Z^m$, the error term is

$$e_{pq} = X^{\alpha m_p} \otimes e_q + e_p \otimes Y^{\beta m_q} + te_p \otimes e_q.$$

Since e_p and e_q are independent, the sum of the first two terms is subgaussian with parameter $\sqrt{E_p^2 + E_q^2}$. The third term is subgaussian with parameter $t\sqrt{2\lambda}E_p E_q$, except with probability $2\min(p,q)\exp(-\lambda)$ by Lemma 7. In total, e_{pq} is subgaussian with parameter $\sqrt{E_p^2 + E_q^2} + t\sqrt{2\lambda}E_p E_q$ except with probability $2\min(p,q)\exp(-\lambda)$.

Thus, with $\mathbf{a} = (a_p \otimes a_q, a_p \otimes b_q, b_p \otimes a_q)$ and $\mathbf{s} = (-\psi_\alpha(s_p) \otimes \psi_\beta(s_q), \psi_\alpha(s_p) \otimes 1, 1 \otimes \psi_\beta(s_q)) = (-s'_p \otimes s'_q, s'_p \otimes 1, 1 \otimes s'_q)$, an easy computation shows that $tb_p \otimes b_q - t\langle \mathbf{a}, \mathbf{s} \rangle = tb'_p \otimes b'_q = \lfloor Q_\otimes/t \rceil Z^m + e_{pq}$. The algorithm is correct.

The running time is dominated by the cost of tensoring the ring elements, which takes time $\Theta(pq)$.

Theorem 9. *Algorithm 6 is correct and runs in time $\Theta(lKd\log d)$.*

Proof. By induction, we prove that the error term of $\mathbf{c}$ in the i-th iteration of the for-loop is of the form $e_1 + e_2$ where e_1 is $(2id\sqrt{K}\sigma)$-subgaussian, and $e_2 = \sum_{j=1}^{i} \langle \mathbf{d}^{(j)}, \psi_{\mathbf{y}_j}(\mathbf{e}^{(j)}) \rangle$ with the following properties: $\mathbf{e}^{(j)}$ is the error vector of $\mathbf{C}_j$, and $\mathbf{d}^{(j)} \in \mathcal{R}_d^{2K}$ is a random vector with $|d_n^{(j)}| \leq d$ that is independent of $\mathbf{e}^{(k)}$ for all $k \geq j$.

Clearly, our claim holds prior to the loop (with $i = 0$) since $\mathbf{c}$ has no error term at this point. Suppose now that the claim holds for $i - 1$. Let $\alpha = \mathbf{y}_i$ and $\beta = \alpha^{-1} \bmod d$. During the ExtExpMultAdd operation, we first apply a Galois operation, which results in an error term of $\psi_\beta(e_1) + \psi_\beta(e_2)$. This is followed by a key-switch, which, by Lemma 4, changes the error to $\psi_\beta(e_1) + \psi_\beta(e_2) + e_{ks,1}$ where $e_{ks,1}$ is independent of $\mathbf{e}^{(j)}$ for all j, and subgaussian with parameter $\sqrt{K}d\sigma$. Next comes an ExtMult operation which changes it to $X^k\psi_\beta(e_1) + X^k\psi_\beta(e_2) + X^k e_{ks,1} + \langle \mathbf{d}, \mathbf{e}^{(i)} \rangle$ for some k, where $\mathbf{e}$ is the error in $\mathbf{C}_i$, and $\mathbf{d} \in \mathcal{R}_d^{2K}$ is a random vector independent of $\mathbf{e}^{(j)}$ for $j \geq i$ which satisfies $|d_n| \leq d$ for every n, by Lemma 5. After the second Galois and key-switch, the error term becomes $X^{\alpha k}e_1 + X^{\alpha k}e_2 + X^{\alpha k}\psi_\alpha(e_{ks,1}) + \psi_\alpha(\langle \mathbf{d}, \mathbf{e}^{(i)} \rangle) + \psi_\alpha(e_{ks,2})$ where $e_{ks,2}$ is again subgaussian with parameter $\sqrt{K}d\sigma$. We can reorder the error terms and write

$$\underbrace{X^{\alpha k}e_1 + X^{\alpha k}\psi_\alpha(e_{ks,1}) + \psi_\alpha(e_{ks,2})}_{e'_1} + \underbrace{X^{\alpha k}e_2 + \psi_\alpha(\langle \mathbf{d}, \mathbf{e}^{(i)} \rangle)}_{e'_2}$$

By the induction hypothesis and since $e_{ks,1}$ and $e_{ks,2}$ are subgaussian with parameter $d\sqrt{K}\sigma$, it follows that e_1' is $(2id\sqrt{K}\sigma)$-subgaussian (because we do not assume that e_1, $e_{ks,1}$ and $e_{ks,2}$ are independent). Finally, it holds that

$$X^{\alpha k} e_2 = \sum_{j=1}^{i-1} \left\langle X^{\alpha k} \mathbf{d}^{(j)}, \psi_{\mathbf{y}_j}\left(\mathbf{e}^{(j)}\right) \right\rangle$$

and thus, setting $\mathbf{d}'^{(j)} = X^{\alpha k} \mathbf{d}^{(j)}$ for $j < i$ and $\mathbf{d}'^{(i)} = \psi_{\mathbf{y}_i}(\mathbf{d})$, we have $e_2' = \sum_{j=1}^{i} \left\langle \mathbf{d}'^{(j)}, \psi_{\mathbf{y}_j}(\mathbf{e}^{(j)}) \right\rangle$ which completes the induction step. Finally, by repeated applications of Lemma 2, we conclude that the error term in the output is subgaussian with parameter $\sqrt{4K\ell^2 d^2\sigma^2 + 2K\ell d^2 E'^2}$.

It is easy to see that the algorithm has the claimed runtime by adding up the runtimes of the algorithms used in ExtExpMultAdd.

D   Proofs for Section 5 (Joining the Building Blocks)

Theorem 10. *Algorithm 7 is correct and runs in time $\tilde{O}(n^2)$. Moreover, there exists $Q = O(\gamma'|f|n^{6.5}\sigma^{1.5})$ such that the output of* EvalBootstrap *can be used as input for another execution of* EvalBootstrap *with coefficients $\gamma_1', \ldots, \gamma_k'$ such that $\gamma' = \sum_i |\gamma_i'|$ (with failure probability exponentially small in n).*

Proof. It is straighforward to verify the error parameters for each step in the comments of the algorithm. There are two steps where failures might occur: the ExpCRT step, and the FunExpExtract step. The failure probability for ExpCRT is $2\exp(-\lambda)$. FunExpExtract will not fail to extract the value of F, but if the error term in $\mathbf{c}$ is too large, the output might not be an encryption of $f(m)$. The subgaussian tail estimate guarantees that the failure probability is at most $2\exp(-\lambda)$ if $\sqrt{r^2\gamma^2 E_{in}^2 + p + 1} \le pq/(2t\sqrt{2\lambda})$ where $r = \lfloor pq/t \rfloor / \lfloor Q'/t \rfloor$. Since $t \le \sqrt{pq}/4$ and $\lambda \le q$, this condition is satisfied if $\sqrt{r^2\gamma^2 E_{in}^2 + p + 1} \le \sqrt{2p}$, or equivalently,

$$\gamma E_{in} \le \underbrace{\sqrt{\frac{p-1}{r^2}}}_{T} = \Theta\left(\sqrt{\frac{Q'^2}{pq^2}}\right) = \Theta\left(\frac{Q}{n^2\sqrt{\sigma}}\right)$$

The runtime is dominated by ExtExpInner and FunExpExtract, which run in time $O(nKd\log d)$ and $O(Kpq\log(pq))$, respectively. Given our asymptotic parameter choices, both of those are $\tilde{O}(n^2)$.

If we want to use outputs of EvalBootstrap as inputs for another execution of EvalBootstrap, where the absolute values of the coefficients sum up to γ', we require that $\gamma' E_{out} \le T$. From the asymptotic formulas for E_{out} and T, it is easy to see that this inequality can be satisfied by a Q in $O(|f|\gamma'n^{6.5}\sigma^{1.5})$.

E   More Details on Circulant LWE

E.1   Circulant LWE and Reduction to Ring-LWE

In all this subsection, we assume d to be prime. It is well known that the naive decisional version of Ring-LWE is insecure over circulant rings, simply by exploiting the CRT decomposition $\mathcal{R}_d/Q\mathcal{R}_d \simeq \tilde{\mathcal{R}}_d/Q\tilde{\mathcal{R}}_d \times \mathbb{Z}/Q\mathbb{Z}$ when Q is coprime to d, and mounting an attack on the $\mathbb{Z}/Q\mathbb{Z}$ part (projecting to this part corresponds to evaluating the polynomial at 1, and therefore maintain smallness of the error). However, this does not mean that such rings are inherently insecure: The NTRU cryptosystems [17,23] use circulant rings, choosing the secret key and errors that evaluate to a fixed known value (say 0) at 1.

This suggests a strategy to construct a variant of Ring-LWE over circulant rings that would be as secure as the cyclotomic Ring-LWE, simply by lifting all elements $\tilde{x} \in \tilde{\mathcal{R}}_d/Q\tilde{\mathcal{R}}_d$ to $x \simeq (\tilde{x}, 0)$, yet this reverse CRT operation may not keep small elements small.

Instead, one can construct such a lift without working modulo Q, in order to preserve smallness of coefficients (up to some reasonable distortion). We also note that such a lift should actually start from the co-different ideal $\tilde{\mathcal{R}}_d^\vee$, so as to match the Ring-LWE instances admitting worst-case hardness proofs [18], yet a reduction (with some loss on the error parameter) to Ring-LWE without the co-different was given in [33].

Because $1 - X$ and $\Phi_d(X)$ are *not coprime* over $\mathbb{Z}[X]$ (their gcd is d, not 1), we *do not* have a CRT decomposition of $\mathcal{R}_d$ as $\tilde{\mathcal{R}}_d \times \mathbb{Z}$. Yet, those polynomials are coprime over $\mathbb{Q}[X]$ which allows to write

$$K_d = \tilde{K}_d \times \mathbb{Q}$$

where $K_d = \mathbb{Q}[X]/(X^d - 1)$ and $\tilde{K}_d = \mathbb{Q}[X]/\Phi_d(X)$.[8] We write L the canonical inclusion map $L : \tilde{K}_d \to K_d$, which is explicitly given by

$$L : \sum_{i=0}^{d-1} a_i X^i \mapsto \sum_{i=0}^{d-1} a_i X^i - \frac{1}{d} \left(\sum_{i=0}^{d-1} a_i \right) \left(\sum_{i=0}^{d-1} X^i \right).$$

Note that the above formula can be extended to a $\mathbb{Q}$-linear map $K_d \to K_d$, viewing $\tilde{K}_d$ as a subspace of K_d according to the above isomorphism $K_d = \tilde{K}_d \times \mathbb{Q}$. This extension of L is the projection orthogonal to the all-1 vector in coefficient representation. Unfortunately the image $L(\tilde{\mathcal{R}}_d)$ is not included in $\mathcal{R}_d$: the projection does not maintain integrality of coefficients. Yet, one notes that a small ideal $\mathfrak{I} \subset \tilde{\mathcal{R}}_d$ does have an integer lift: namely, the ideal $\tilde{\mathfrak{I}} = (1 - X)\mathcal{R}_d$ satisfies $L(\tilde{\mathfrak{I}}) \subset \mathcal{R}_d$. Moreover, for $a \in \tilde{\mathfrak{I}}$, it holds that $\sum a_i = 0$, in particular L preserves sizes of elements of $\tilde{\mathfrak{I}}$.

Also consider the lift L taken modulo Q (assuming Q is coprime to d), simply replacing $\frac{1}{d} \in \mathbb{Q}$ by the inverse of d in $\mathbb{Z}/Q\mathbb{Z}$, denoted by L_Q. Consider a Ring-LWE sample as defined in [33]: $(\tilde{a}, \tilde{b} = \tilde{a}\tilde{s} + \tilde{e}) \in (\tilde{\mathcal{R}}/Q\tilde{\mathcal{R}})^2$ for small $\tilde{s}, \tilde{e} \in \mathcal{R}$.

---

[8] While $\tilde{K}_d$ is a field, K_d is only a ring, but we keep this notation for coherence.

We lift this sample to $\mathcal{R}/Q\mathcal{R}$:

$$a = L_Q(\tilde{a}), b = L_Q((1 - X)\tilde{b}). \tag{11}$$

We define $s = L((1 - X)\tilde{s})$ and $e = L((1 - X)\tilde{s})$, and it holds that $s = L_Q((1-X)\tilde{s}) \mod Q$ and $e = L_Q((1-X)\tilde{e}) \mod Q$ since s and e are integral. Therefore,

$$\begin{aligned}
b &= L_Q((1 - X)\tilde{a} \cdot \tilde{s} + (1 - X)\tilde{e}) \\
&= L_Q(\tilde{a}) \cdot L_Q((1 - X)\tilde{s}) + L_Q((1 - X)\tilde{e}) \\
&= L_Q(\tilde{a})s + e \mod Q \\
&= as + e \mod Q
\end{aligned}$$

We also note that s, e are still small since the operator norm of $1 - X$ is less than 2: these Circulant-LWE samples are useful.

It remains to explain what this transformation does to uniform samples $(\tilde{a}, \tilde{b}) \in (\tilde{\mathcal{R}}/Q\tilde{\mathcal{R}})^2$. Assume that Q is coprime to d, it then holds that Q and $(1 - X)$ are coprimes over the integral ring $\tilde{\mathcal{R}}_d$. Therefore, the multiplication by $1 - X$ over $(\tilde{\mathcal{R}}/Q\tilde{\mathcal{R}})$ is a bijection, so the sample $(\tilde{a}, (1 - X)\tilde{b}) \in (\tilde{\mathcal{R}}/Q\tilde{\mathcal{R}})^2$ is also uniform in $(\tilde{\mathcal{R}}/Q\tilde{\mathcal{R}})^2$. Finally, the lift L_Q is injective, so the final sample $(a, b) \in (\mathcal{R}/Q\mathcal{R})^2$ is uniform over $(L_Q(\tilde{\mathcal{R}}/Q\tilde{\mathcal{R}}))^2$. One easily characterizes the image $L_Q(\tilde{\mathcal{R}}/Q\tilde{\mathcal{R}})$ of L_Q as the set $\mathcal{S}_{d,Q} = \{\sum_{i=0}^{d-1} a_i X^i \mid \sum a_i = 0 \mod Q\}$ of elements of $\mathcal{R}/Q\mathcal{R}$ whose coefficients sums to 0 modulo Q.

Lemma 3 (Hardness of Circulant-LWE). *Assume that d is prime, and Q is coprime to d. If it is hard to distinguish samples $(\tilde{a}_i, \tilde{b}_i = \tilde{a}_i\tilde{s} + \tilde{e}_i) \in (\tilde{\mathcal{R}}/Q\tilde{\mathcal{R}})^2$ from uniform where $\tilde{e}_i$ are independent random variables drawn from a distribution ψ, then the samples $(a_i = L_Q(\tilde{a}_i), b_i = L_Q((1 - X)\tilde{b}_i) \in \mathcal{S}_{d,Q}^2 \subset (\mathcal{R}/Q\mathcal{R})^2$ are also hard to distinguish from uniform samples in $\mathcal{S}_{d,Q}^2$.*

E.2   Simpler Error Distribution in CLWE for Practice

In practice, most FHE schemes do not follow precisely the Ring-LWE problem definition admitting reduction to worst-case problem [18,34]. For example, HElib [7] uses Ring-LWE with spherical errors in the coefficient embedding, and very sparse ternary secrets, and ignoring the co-different ideal $\mathcal{R}^\vee$. The TFHE scheme [15] also relies on Ring-LWE with ternary secrets, which is not know to reduce to the regular Ring-LWE. Cutting such corners appears quite crucial to error growth management and therefore efficiency. We will follow this approach, and define adjust the distributions as follows.

- we proceed to sample secrets and error isotropically in $\mathcal{S}_{d,Q}$, while the above reduction leads to errors with a distortion factor $(1-X)$. This distortion seems to be an artefact of the proof, as it breaks symmetries: one could choose a different way of breaking those symmetries by replacing $1 - X$ by $1 - X^e$ for any e coprime to d. Respecting the symmetries seems a better idea in the light of recent analysis [32, 36].

This variant could also be proved secure (with a loss of a constant factor about $\sqrt{2}$ on the size of the error), simply by adding more noise to make it spherical again, using the convolution lemma of [35], but this would drag us away from the topic of this paper.

- we choose to use ternary secrets s, which, as in previous schemes leads to serious performance improvements due to smaller error growth. It has recently been showed that such choices make lattice attacks somewhat faster [31], especially when s is very sparse: we will account for this refined analysis when measuring the concrete security of our proposed parameters.

Sampling of a. We sample a uniform in $\mathcal{R}_d/(Q\mathcal{R}_d)$ under the constraint $a(1)$ mod $Q = 0$ by choosing all the coefficients a_i at random for $i \geq 1$, and setting $a_0 = -\sum_{i>0} a_i \bmod Q$.

Sampling of s. When d is prime, we sample a a ternary s of density $\delta = 2/3$ by choosing exactly $\lfloor \delta d/2 \rfloor$ coefficients set to 1 and $\lfloor \delta d/2 \rfloor$ coefficients set to -1. This implies that $s(1) = 0$, and $\|s\|^2 = 2\lfloor \delta d/2 \rfloor$. Indeed, we find it preferable to fix its length to avoid sampling sparse keys that would be subtentially weaker.

Sampling of e. We wish to sample errors e with variance σ in a way that ensures $e(1) = 0$. We set:

$$e = \sum_{i=0}^{\sigma^2 d/2} T^{a_i} - T^{b_i},$$

where the a_i's and b_i's' are independant uniform exponents modulo d. One note that this distribution is invariant by permutation over $\{1, T, \ldots, T^{d-1}\}$: we have preserved the symmetries of the ring. Note that this procedure would get rather slow for large σ, yet we won't exceed $\sigma \leq 8$ in our parameter choices.

Remark 6. The above procedure would not be adapted for composite degree d, as more care is required to construct a lift as done in Sect. E.1. Yet, while we will make use of circulant ring $\mathcal{R}_d$ with composite degree $d = pq$, we will never directly construct ciphertexts over that ring. Indeed, the ciphertext in $\mathcal{R}_d$ will be publicly constructed by tensoring two ciphertexts from $\mathcal{R}_p$ and $\mathcal{R}_q$, and are therefore no easier to decrypt than the original ciphertexts over $\mathcal{R}_p$ and $\mathcal{R}_q$.

F   Optimizations

In this section, we present some optimization of the scheme for practice. Our implementation does include the optimizations from Sects. F.1, F.2 and F.3. We left out the optimization from Sect. F.4, which requires substantial modifications to our code base.

F.1   Accelerating ExtExpInner

Factoring Galois-KeySwitch *Sequences.* We note that it is possible to factor some operations when chaining $\mathsf{ExtExpMultAdd}^\alpha$ and $\mathsf{ExtExpMultAdd}^{\alpha'}$, by applying $\mathsf{Galois}^{\alpha\beta'}$ rather than Galois^α followed by Galois^β (together with the appropriate Key Switches), cf. Fig. 2.

Furthermore, if $\mathbf{y} \in \mathbb{Z}_d^\ell$ contains repeated values, it is possible to re-index the inner product to make equal values contiguous, and skip useless Galois[1] operations. Those tricks also decrease the final error E by constant factors.

Pushing this trick to its limits, if ℓ is large enough, one could re-index the inner product so that the $\alpha\beta'$ all belong to a small[9] subset $\mathbb{Z}_d^*$, allowing to decrease the size of the key material. In combination with the following optimization, this should lead to reduce the overall key-size by a significant factor.

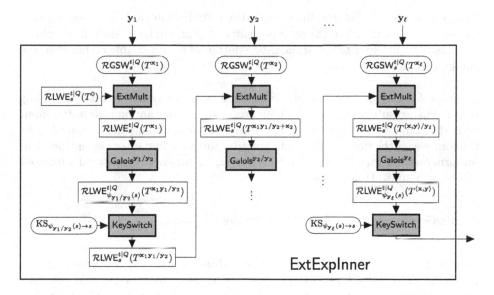

Fig. 2. Optimized ExtExpInner (external inner product in exponent) overview

Decreasing LWE *Dimension.* In our theoretical scheme, the homomorphic inner product in exponent operation is done over vectors of length $\ell = p + 1$ where p is the dimension of the secret in the LWE scheme.

In practice, we remark that this dimension is quite larger than needed for security, given the amount of noise and the modulus pq of those ciphertexts. We therefore proceed with an extra LWE key-switch just the combination of the LWE ciphertexts. In practice it allows to decrease the dimension by a factor between 2 and 3, which accelerates the ExtExpInner operations by the same factor. As a small added bonus, it also slightly decreases the error in the ciphertexts outputted by this function.

---

[9] Of size roughly $d/\ell + 2$ assuming the public vector $\mathbf{y} \in \mathbb{Z}_d^\ell$ is uniformly random.

F.2   Heuristic Error Propagation

Our theoretical analysis of the scheme used sub-gaussian analysis [21] to provide bounds on error propagation that are already significantly better than worst-case bounds. Yet those bounds are asymptotic, without explicit constants, and for some operations may not be perfectly tight. As in previous work [12,15], when it comes to choose practical parameters, we rely on a tighter but heuristic analysis of error propagation, essentially treating all random variables as independent gaussians. More precisely, considering that the critical random variable for correctness is obtained as the sum of many random variables, we only compute its variance as the sum of the variance of its terms, and treat this final result as Gaussian in accordance with the central limit theorem (which is formally not applicable due to potential dependencies).

Linear Operations. For the linear operations Add, Mult and Galois operations, we use the same Eqs. (3), (8) as in our sub-gaussian analysis, since it is tight in this case, but apply it to the standard deviation of each variable rather than the sub-gaussianity parameter.

Modulus Switching. For our analysis, we needed to randomize the rounding step to ensure sub-gaussianity without resorting to the randomness of the input ciphertext. Instead, in practice we use deterministic rounding and account for the randomness of the input ciphertext. Treating the rounding errors as independent uniform random variables in the interval $[-1/2, 1/2]$ allows to heuristically improve the error bound (4) down to

$$\mathsf{ModSwitch} : \mathcal{R}_d\mathsf{LWE}_\mathbf{s}^{t|Q}(m;\ E) \to \mathcal{R}_d\mathsf{LWE}_\mathbf{s}^{t|Q'}\left(m;\ \sqrt{\frac{Q'^2}{Q^2}E^2 + \frac{\|\mathbf{s}\|^2}{12}}\right) \quad (12)$$

Key Switching, External Multiplication and Inner Product in the Exponent. We first note that, according to Remark 2, the bounds given by (5) and (6) must be amended to account for the use of a Gadget matrix in base B rather than in base 2. Additionally, we note that this bound accounts for the worst output of $\mathbf{G}^{-1}$. Instead, we treat the output of $\mathbf{G}^{-1}$ as a uniform random vectors with coordinates uniform in the integer interval $I_B = \{-\lfloor\frac{B-1}{2}\rfloor, \ldots, \lceil\frac{B-1}{2}\rceil\}$. Each such coordinate has variance $V_B = \frac{1}{B}\sum_{i\in I_B} i^2 \approx B^2/12$.
   For our heuristic analysis, we therefore amend (5) to

$$\mathsf{KeySwitch} : \mathcal{R}_d\mathsf{LWE}_\mathbf{s}^{t|Q}(m;\ E) \to \mathcal{R}_d\mathsf{LWE}_{\mathbf{s}'}^{t|Q}\left(m;\ \sqrt{E^2 + \sigma^2 dnKV_B}\right). \quad (13)$$

Similarly, (6) is heuristically changed to

$$\mathsf{ExtMult} : \mathcal{R}_d\mathsf{LWE}_s^{t|Q}(T^m;\ E) \times \mathcal{R}_d\mathsf{GSW}_s^{t|Q}(T^{m'};\ E')$$
$$\to \mathcal{R}_d\mathsf{LWE}_s^{t|Q}\left(T^{m+m'};\ \sqrt{E^2 + E'^2 dKV_B}\right). \quad (14)$$

Note that assuming independence decreased the factor d^2 to a factor d. Similarly, a factor $4\ell^2$ can be decreased to 2ℓ, ignoring the potential dependences discussed in Remark 5. The trick described in Sect. F.1 further decreases this 2ℓ factor to ℓ.

In conclusion, the accumulated error in the error propagation of the whole ExtExpInner operation (10) is now heuristically given by:

$$\mathsf{ExtExpInner} : \bigoplus_{i=1}^{\ell} \mathcal{R}_d \mathsf{GSW}_s^{t|Q}(T^{x_i}; E') \to \mathcal{R}_d \mathsf{LWE}_s^{t|Q}\left(T^{\langle \mathbf{x}, \mathbf{y} \rangle}; \sqrt{dK\ell V(\sigma^2 + E'^2)}\right).$$

(15)

Tensoring. Looking only at the variance of individual coefficient, one may save the factor $\sqrt{2\lambda}$ in the error propagation of ExpCRT, namely, (9) becomes:

$$\mathsf{ExpCRT} : \mathcal{R}_p \mathsf{LWE}_{s_p}^{t|Q'}(X^{m_p}; E_p) \times \mathcal{R}_q \mathsf{LWE}_{s_q}^{t|Q'}(Y^{m_q}; E_q)$$

$$\to \mathcal{R}_{pq} \mathsf{LWE}_{\mathbf{s}}^{t|Q'}\left(Z^m; \sqrt{E_p^2 + E_q^2 + t^2 E_p^2 E_q^2}\right). \quad (16)$$

We could successfully confirm all these heuristic equations by measuring the actual errors in our implementation.

F.3   Amortising FunExpExtract

The costly steps of the FunExpExtract algorithm consist in computing

$$c^{(pq)} \mapsto \mathrm{Tr}^*_{\mathcal{R}_{pq}/\mathcal{R}_p}(f \cdot \mathbf{G}^{-T}(c^{(pq)}) \cdot \mathbf{S})$$

where f represent the function F to extract, $\mathbf{S}$ is a Key-Switching Key (See Fig. 1 and Algorithm 7). We note here that the most expensive part of the computation $\mathbf{G}^{-T}(c^{(pq)}) \cdot \mathbf{S}$ can be re-used for up to several different f's.

This amortization allows to extend our technique so that not only the input of the function is large, but also its output.

F.4   Accelerating FunExpExtract

As mentioned above, the practical cost of the FunExpExtract step as described in Sect. 4 is prohibitive. The costly steps consist in the computation of

$$\mathrm{Tr}^*_{\mathcal{R}_{pq}/\mathcal{R}_p}(f \cdot \mathbf{G}^{-T}(\mathbf{x} \otimes \mathbf{y}) \cdot \mathbf{S})$$

where f represent the function F to extract, $\mathbf{x}$, $\mathbf{y}$ are the ciphertexts outputted by ExtExpInner, and $\mathbf{S}$ is a Key-Switching Key. Naively, even using precomputations of f and $\mathbf{S}$, this operation would require $4K + 1$ FFT's in dimension pq: one forward FFT for each component of $\mathbf{G}^{-1}(\mathbf{c})$, and one FFT backward.[10] We here show how to get completely rid of those large FFT's, requiring only small FFT's (dimension p and q) and a few additions of vectors of dimension pq.

---

[10] This is assuming the FFT can handle numbers of bit-size $\Theta(\log(n))$. In practice more FFT at **double** precision will be needed to avoid numerical errors.

FFT of Pure Tensors. To tackle these costly FFT operations, one should first note that FFT and $\otimes$ can be commuted. Indeed, one may first rewrite $x \otimes y = (x \otimes 1) \cdot (1 \otimes y)$, and note that the FFT coefficients of $x \otimes 1 \in \mathcal{R}_{pq}$ are easily derived from the FFT coefficients of $x \in \mathcal{R}_p$ by simply repeating the coefficients q times (and similarly for $1 \otimes y$). This remark allows us to decrease the naive cost of the FFT operation over pure tensors from $\Theta(pq \log pq)$ to $\Theta(pq + p \log p + q \log q)$.

The CRT-Gadget. To provide an asymptotic improvement for gadget inversion of pure tensors, we need to rely on a different Gadget matrix construction, based on the Chinese-Remainder Theorem. We describe it over the integers $\mathbb{Z}$, yet it naturally extends coefficient-wise to any ring $\mathcal{R}_d$.

Consider a modulus Q such that we can write $Q = \prod_{i=1}^{K} q_i$ where the q_i are small coprime integers. Consider the CRT isomorphism $\mu : r \in \mathbb{Z}_Q \mapsto (r \bmod q_1, \ldots, r \bmod q_K)$, and let $\mathbf{g} \in \mathbb{Z}_Q^K$ be the vector of the *Bezout coefficients*, i.e., the coefficients such that $\mu^{-1}(\mathbf{x}) = \mathbf{x}^T \mathbf{g} \bmod Q$. This gadget also permits to efficiently find small pre-images. Indeed, define: $\mathbf{g}^{-T}(x) = (x_1, \ldots x_K) \in \mathbb{Z}^K$ where x_i is the representative of $x \bmod q_i$ in the range $(-q_i/2, q_i/2]$.

Gadget Inversion of Pure Tensors (in FFT Format). This new gadget has the advantage that gadget inversion is somewhat homomorphic. Let us write $\odot$ for the coefficient-wise product of vectors. While in general we have $\mathbf{g}^{-T}(xy) \neq \mathbf{g}^{-T}(x) \odot \mathbf{g}^{-T}(y)$, it nevertheless holds that

$$(\mathbf{g}^{-T}(x) \odot \mathbf{g}^{-T}(y))\mathbf{g} = xy \bmod Q.$$

It also hold that $\mathbf{g}^{-T}(x) \odot \mathbf{g}^{-T}(y)$ is rather small, namely, its i-th coefficient has absolute value less than $q_i^2/4$. This will allow us, at the cost of increased error propagation, to swap the gadget-inversion and the tensoring.

More precisely, we define

$$\mathbf{g}_{\otimes}^{-T}(x, y) = (\mathbf{g}^{-T}(x)_i \otimes \mathbf{g}^{-T}(y)_i)_{i=1\ldots k},$$

and note that it is a proper gadget inversion: $\mathbf{g}_{\otimes}^{-T}(x, y)\mathbf{g} = x \otimes y \bmod Q$, and the coefficients of $\mathbf{g}_{\otimes}^{-T}(x, y)_i$ are less than $q_i^2/4$.

For inputs $(x, y) \in \mathcal{R}_p \times \mathcal{R}_q$ One may compute $g_{\otimes}^{-T}(x, y)$ in FFT format in time $\Theta(Kpq + Kp \log p + Kq \log q)$, that is in time linear in the size of the output. Indeed, one may compute each $(\mathbf{g}^{-T}(x)_i, \mathbf{g}^{-T}(y)_i)$, convert them to FFT format, and then only perform the tensoring step using the remark above. In comparison, the naive algorithm would have cost $\Theta(Kpq \log pq)$: asymptotically, our new trick improves the complexity by a logarithmic factor $\Theta(\log pq)$. The impact in practice may quite substantial also considering the large hidden constants in FFT operations.

Tracing Down in the FFT Domain. At last, we note that the trace operation $\mathrm{Tr}^*_{\mathcal{R}_{pq}/\mathcal{R}_p}$ can also be performed directly in the FFT domain in time $\Theta(pq)$ by summing the appropriate FFT coefficients. The allows to replace the final large backward FFT (in dimension pq) by a cheap backward FFT in dimension p. The cost of this step decreases form $\Theta(pq \log pq)$ down to $\Theta(pq + p \log p)$.

References

1. Gentry, C.: Fully homomorphic encryption using ideal lattices. In: Mitzenmacher, M. (ed.) 41st ACM STOC, Bethesda, MD, USA, 31 May–2 June 2009, pp. 169–178. ACM Press (2009)
2. Gentry, C.: A fully homomorphic encryption scheme. Ph.D. thesis, Stanford University (2009). crypto.stanford.edu/craig
3. Smart, N.P., Vercauteren, F.: Fully homomorphic encryption with relatively small key and ciphertext sizes. In: Nguyen, P.Q., Pointcheval, D. (eds.) PKC 2010. LNCS, vol. 6056, pp. 420–443. Springer, Heidelberg (2010). https://doi.org/10.1007/978-3-642-13013-7_25
4. Brakerski, Z., Vaikuntanathan, V.: Efficient fully homomorphic encryption from (standard) LWE. In: Ostrovsky, R. (ed.) 52nd FOCS, Palm Springs, CA, USA, 22–25 October 2011, pp. 97–106. IEEE Computer Society Press (2011)
5. Gentry, C., Halevi, S., Smart, N.P.: Fully homomorphic encryption with polylog overhead. In: Pointcheval, D., Johansson, T. (eds.) EUROCRYPT 2012. LNCS, vol. 7237, pp. 465–482. Springer, Heidelberg (2012). https://doi.org/10.1007/978-3-642-29011-4_28
6. Brakerski, Z., Gentry, C., Vaikuntanathan, V.: (Leveled) fully homomorphic encryption without bootstrapping. In: Goldwasser, S. (ed.) ITCS 2012, Cambridge, MA, USA, 8–10 January 2012, pp. 309–325. ACM (2012)
7. Halevi, S., Shoup, V.: Bootstrapping for HElib. In: Oswald, E., Fischlin, M. (eds.) EUROCRYPT 2015, Part I. LNCS, vol. 9056, pp. 641–670. Springer, Heidelberg (2015). https://doi.org/10.1007/978-3-662-46800-5_25
8. Gentry, C., Sahai, A., Waters, B.: Homomorphic encryption from learning with errors: conceptually-simpler, asymptotically-faster, attribute-based. In: Canetti, R., Garay, J.A. (eds.) CRYPTO 2013, Part I. LNCS, vol. 8042, pp. 75–92. Springer, Heidelberg (2013). https://doi.org/10.1007/978-3-642-40041-4_5
9. Barrington, D.A.M.: Bounded-width polynomial-size branching programs recognize exactly those languages in NC^1. In: 18th ACM STOC, Berkeley, CA, USA, 28–30 May 1986, pp. 1–5. ACM Press (1986)
10. Brakerski, Z., Vaikuntanathan, V.: Lattice-based FHE as secure as PKE. In: Naor, M. (ed.) ITCS 2014, Princeton, NJ, USA, 12–14 January 2014, pp. 1–12. ACM (2014)
11. Alperin-Sheriff, J., Peikert, C.: Faster bootstrapping with polynomial error. In: Garay, J.A., Gennaro, R. (eds.) CRYPTO 2014, Part I. LNCS, vol. 8616, pp. 297–314. Springer, Heidelberg (2014). https://doi.org/10.1007/978-3-662-44371-2_17
12. Ducas, L., Micciancio, D.: FHEW: bootstrapping homomorphic encryption in less than a second. In: Oswald, E., Fischlin, M. (eds.) EUROCRYPT 2015, Part I. LNCS, vol. 9056, pp. 617–640. Springer, Heidelberg (2015). https://doi.org/10.1007/978-3-662-46800-5_24
13. Biasse, J.-F., Ruiz, L.: FHEW with efficient multibit bootstrapping. In: Lauter, K., Rodríguez-Henríquez, F. (eds.) LATINCRYPT 2015. LNCS, vol. 9230, pp. 119–135. Springer, Cham (2015). https://doi.org/10.1007/978-3-319-22174-8_7
14. Gama, N., Izabachène, M., Nguyen, P.Q., Xie, X.: Structural lattice reduction: generalized worst-case to average-case reductions and homomorphic cryptosystems. In: Fischlin, M., Coron, J.-S. (eds.) EUROCRYPT 2016, Part II. LNCS, vol. 9666, pp. 528–558. Springer, Heidelberg (2016). https://doi.org/10.1007/978-3-662-49896-5_19

15. Chillotti, I., Gama, N., Georgieva, M., Izabachène, M.: Faster fully homomorphic encryption: bootstrapping in less than 0.1 seconds. In: Cheon, J.H., Takagi, T. (eds.) ASIACRYPT 2016, Part I. LNCS, vol. 10031, pp. 3–33. Springer, Heidelberg (2016). https://doi.org/10.1007/978-3-662-53887-6_1

16. Riordan, J., Shannon, C.E.: The number of two-terminal series-parallel networks. Stud. Appl. Math. **21**(1–4), 83–93 (1942)

17. Hoffstein, J., Pipher, J., Silverman, J.H.: NTRU: a ring-based public key cryptosystem. In: Buhler, J.P. (ed.) ANTS 1998. LNCS, vol. 1423, pp. 267–288. Springer, Heidelberg (1998). https://doi.org/10.1007/BFb0054868

18. Lyubashevsky, V., Peikert, C., Regev, O.: On ideal lattices and learning with errors over rings. In: Gilbert, H. (ed.) EUROCRYPT 2010. LNCS, vol. 6110, pp. 1–23. Springer, Heidelberg (2010). https://doi.org/10.1007/978-3-642-13190-5_1

19. Halevi, S., Halevi, T., Shoup, V., Stephens-Davidowitz, N.: Implementing BP-obfuscation using graph-induced encoding. Cryptology ePrint Archive, Report 2017/104 (2017). http://eprint.iacr.org/2017/104

20. Chillotti, I., Gama, N., Georgieva, M., Izabachène, M.: Improving TFHE: faster packed homomorphic operations and efficient circuit bootstrapping. Cryptology ePrint Archive, Report 2017/430 (2017). http://eprint.iacr.org/2017/430

21. Vershynin, R.: Introduction to the non-asymptotic analysis of random matrices. In: Eldar, Y., Kutyniok, G. (eds.) Compressed Sensing, Theory and Applications, pp. 210–268. Cambridge University Press, Cambridge (2012)

22. Rivasplata, O.: Subgaussian Random Variables: An Expository Note (2012). https://sites.ualberta.ca/~omarr/publications/subgaussians.pdf

23. Hoffstein, J., Howgrave-Graham, N., Pipher, J., Silverman, J.H., Whyte, W.: NTRUSign: digital signatures using the NTRU lattice. In: Joye, M. (ed.) CT-RSA 2003. LNCS, vol. 2612, pp. 122–140. Springer, Heidelberg (2003). https://doi.org/10.1007/3-540-36563-X_9

24. Blum, A., Furst, M., Kearns, M., Lipton, R.J.: Cryptographic primitives based on hard learning problems. In: Stinson, D.R. (ed.) CRYPTO 1993. LNCS, vol. 773, pp. 278–291. Springer, Heidelberg (1994). https://doi.org/10.1007/3-540-48329-2_24

25. Regev, O.: On lattices, learning with errors, random linear codes, and cryptography. In: Gabow, H.N., Fagin, R. (eds.) 37th ACM STOC, Baltimore, MA, USA, 22–24 May 2005, pp. 84–93. ACM Press (2005)

26. Applebaum, B., Cash, D., Peikert, C., Sahai, A.: Fast cryptographic primitives and circular-secure encryption based on hard learning problems. In: Halevi, S. (ed.) CRYPTO 2009. LNCS, vol. 5677, pp. 595–618. Springer, Heidelberg (2009). https://doi.org/10.1007/978-3-642-03356-8_35

27. Gentry, C., Halevi, S., Peikert, C., Smart, N.P.: Ring switching in BGV-style homomorphic encryption. In: Visconti, I., De Prisco, R. (eds.) SCN 2012. LNCS, vol. 7485, pp. 19–37. Springer, Heidelberg (2012). https://doi.org/10.1007/978-3-642-32928-9_2

28. Gentry, C., Halevi, S., Peikert, C., Smart, N.P.: Field switching in BGV-style homomorphic encryption. Cryptology ePrint Archive, Report 2012/240 (2012). http://eprint.iacr.org/2012/240

29. Frigo, M., Johnson, S.G.: The design and implementation of FFTW3. Proc. IEEE **93**(2), 216–231 (2005). Special issue on "Program Generation, Optimization, and Platform Adaptation"

30. Albrecht, M.R., Player, R., Scott, S.: On the concrete hardness of learning with errors. Cryptology ePrint Archive, Report 2015/046 (2015). http://eprint.iacr.org/2015/046

31. Albrecht, M.R.: On dual lattice attacks against small-secret LWE and parameter choices in HElib and SEAL. In: Coron, J.-S., Nielsen, J.B. (eds.) EUROCRYPT 2017, Part II. LNCS, vol. 10211, pp. 103–129. Springer, Cham (2017). https://doi.org/10.1007/978-3-319-56614-6_4

32. Castryck, W., Iliashenko, I., Vercauteren, F.: Provably weak instances of ring-LWE revisited. In: Fischlin, M., Coron, J.-S. (eds.) EUROCRYPT 2016, Part I. LNCS, vol. 9665, pp. 147–167. Springer, Heidelberg (2016). https://doi.org/10.1007/978-3-662-49890-3_6

33. Ducas, L., Durmus, A.: Ring-LWE in polynomial rings. In: Fischlin, M., Buchmann, J., Manulis, M. (eds.) PKC 2012. LNCS, vol. 7293, pp. 34–51. Springer, Heidelberg (2012). https://doi.org/10.1007/978-3-642-30057-8_3

34. Lyubashevsky, V., Peikert, C., Regev, O.: A toolkit for ring-LWE cryptography. In: Johansson, T., Nguyen, P.Q. (eds.) EUROCRYPT 2013. LNCS, vol. 7881, pp. 35–54. Springer, Heidelberg (2013). https://doi.org/10.1007/978-3-642-38348-9_3

35. Peikert, C.: An efficient and parallel Gaussian sampler for lattices. In: Rabin, T. (ed.) CRYPTO 2010. LNCS, vol. 6223, pp. 80–97. Springer, Heidelberg (2010). https://doi.org/10.1007/978-3-642-14623-7_5

36. Peikert, C.: How (not) to instantiate ring-LWE. In: Zikas, V., De Prisco, R. (eds.) SCN 2016. LNCS, vol. 9841, pp. 411–430. Springer, Cham (2016). https://doi.org/10.1007/978-3-319-44618-9_22

Two-Face: New Public Key Multivariate Schemes

Gilles Macario-Rat[1]([✉]) [iD] and Jacques Patarin[2]

[1] Orange, Châtillon, France
gilles.macariorat@orange.com
[2] Université Versailles Saint-Quentin, Versailles, France
jpatarin@club-internet.fr

Abstract. We present here new multivariate schemes that can be seen as HFE generalization having a property called 'Two-Face'. Particularly, we present five such families of algorithms named 'Dob', 'Simple Pat', 'General Pat', 'Mac', and 'Super Two-Face'. These families have connections between them, some of them are refinements or generalizations of others. Notably, some of these schemes can be used for public key encryption, and some for public key signature. We introduce also new multivariate quadratic permutations that may have interest beyond cryptography.

Keywords: Multivariate cryptography · HFE generalization
New multivariate quadratic permutations
(=new DO permutation polynomials)

1 Introduction, the Two-Face Technique

In the search for post-quantum cryptography, multivariate schemes are still interesting options. Plenty of them have been proposed but unfortunately most of them were cryptographically broken, such as the Matsumoto Imai scheme C* or its variant SFLASH [1–3]. However, some of these schemes are still valid such as UOV or HFE with well chosen perturbations [4,5]. At present, it seems more difficult to build secure multivariate encryption scheme than multivariate signature schemes. In this paper, we present new families of public key multivariate schemes for encryption or signature, inspired by HFE.

We first recall here a simple description of the HFE scheme. See [6]. As generally in the multivariate schemes, the context is a finite field $\mathbb{F}_q$ (the ground field) and one of its extensions $\mathbb{F}_{q^n}$ of degree n. A natural isomorphism between $\mathbb{F}_q^n$ (or more precisely $\mathbb{F}_q[x]/g(x)$ for any irreducible polynomial g over $\mathbb{F}_q$ of degree n, see [7]) and $\mathbb{F}_{q^n}$ allows to consider simultaneously univariate and multivariate versions of polynomials. The starting point of the HFE scheme is a univariate polynomial $P(a)$ over $\mathbb{F}_{q^n}$, having the two following main properties.

© Springer International Publishing AG, part of Springer Nature 2018
A. Joux et al. (Eds.): AFRICACRYPT 2018, LNCS 10831, pp. 252–265, 2018.
https://doi.org/10.1007/978-3-319-89339-6_14

(1) Its multivariate version is a set of quadratic multivariate polynomials. This means that its univariate version has the following form.

$$P(a) = \sum_{i,j} \alpha_{i,j} a^{q^i + q^j} + \sum_i \beta_i a^{q^i} + \gamma.$$

Such polynomials are sometimes called (extended) Dembowski-Ostrom polynomials [8,9]. In this paper we will call them simply 'DO', or will refer to their multivariate counterparts as 'quadratic multivariate' polynomials.
(2) The degree of $P(a)$ in a is small.

From (1), with the help of two more secret affine polynomials S and T, the product $S \circ P \circ T$ is also DO, so it can be publicly output as a set of multivariate quadratic equations. Moreover, some "perturbations" can be applied to this set of equations, in order to increase the security of the HFE obtained. For example, some of the n equations can be kept secret, this is called the perturbation "$-$" (minus). From (2), the solutions in a of the equations $P(a) = b$ can be efficiently computed.

The so called Two-Face technique we present now, can be seen as a generalization of HFE in the sense that the two previously mentioned properties (1) and (2) are held by two different but related polynomials. More generally, we are interested in cases where it is possible to find two equivalent faces of polynomial equations, having the prescribed properties, thereafter described.

Face (1) $E_1(a) = b$ where E_1 is DO. Its role is to allow two additional permutations S and T to hide the inner structure of E_1 into a set of quadratic polynomial equations, multivariate version the composition product $S \circ E_1 \circ T(x) = y$. Unlike in HFE, the degree of E_1 is high.
Face (2) $E_2(a, b) = 0$. Its role is to allow the extraction of solutions in a, since its degree in a is low, even though its degree in b may be high. Conversely, Face 2 is not DO in a and cannot be used to output multivariate quadratic equations.

We will explain later on how E_1 and E_2 are related.
In this article, we will present:

- How to design a multivariate scheme named 'Dob' from the Dobbertin polynomial that resist as far as we know, all known attacks by introducing some "perturbations" in Sect. 2.
- More general "Two-Face" schemes where we use polynomials that are not necessarily permutations, named 'Simple Pat' and 'General Pat', in Sects. 3 and 4.
- Two-Face schemes where we use precisely permutation polynomials, named 'Mac', in Sect. 5.
- Generalization of the 'Two-Face' concept, in Sect. 6.

2   The "Dob" Schemes

2.1   Dobbertin Permutation

This is the original family from which we imagined the Two-face properties. Dobbertin in [10] proved that $P(x) = x^{2^m+1} + x^3 + x$ is a permutation polynomial over $\mathbb{F}_2^n$ for every odd n, where $n = 2m - 1$. The "Two-face" name comes from the fact that from the first equation

$$E_1(x) = x^{2^m+1} + x^3 + x = y, \tag{1}$$

we can get a second one:

$$E_2(x, y) = x^9 + x^6y + x^5 + x^4y + x^3(y^{2^m} + y^2) + xy^2 + y^3 = 0. \tag{2}$$

A proof that we can get (2) from (1) can be obtained by hand easily. Introduce an intermediate variable $z = x^{2^m}$. Use the fact that since $n = 2m - 1$, we get $z^{2^m} = x^{2^{2m}} = x^2$ (implicitly, polynomial computations over $\mathbb{F}_{q^n}$ are done modulo $x^{q^n} - x$). Then eliminate z between the two equations $y = xz + x^3 + x$ and $y^{2^m} = x^2z + z^3 + z$. This gives $(x^4 + x^2)(x^3 + x + y) + (x^3 + x + y)^3 + x^3y^{2^m} = 0$ and then (2). We see from (1) that we have a DO polynomial in x. However, its degree in x is high, which makes difficult to solve the equation in x directly. Nevertheless, from (2) it is possible to compute x knowing y, by solving a polynomial equation of degree 9 only.

2.2   Cryptanalysis of the 'nude Dob'

If we used directly (1) into a 'nude Dob' scheme i.e. without any perturbation, we would get a weak scheme, totally broken by Gröbner basis computation. More precisely the degree of regularity obtained in a Gröbner basis attack is always only 3 in the experiments we conducted. (The degree of regularity is the highest degree that must be used in order to the Gröbner basis computation to succeed). The reason is most probably related to the fact that from $E_1(x) = y$, one may derive equations of the kind $E(x, y) = 0$, linear in x, and of small degree in y. We have looked for equations of the kind $\sum \alpha_i x_i + \sum \beta_i y_i + \sum \gamma_{i,j} x_i y_j = 0$ that may be satisfied by the multivariate version of x and y, that is to say the kind of equations 'à la Patarin' (see [11]) used for the cryptanalysis of the Matsumoto-Imai C* scheme. We founded no such equations, nor equations in degree 2 in y, valid for the Dobbertin permutations (more precisely for $n \geq 11$, in fact some of them exist for $n \leq 10$). However, it is more likely that due to the simple form of the Dobbertin permutation, such equations with higher degree in y may exist. In practice, such equations are sufficient to retrieve x from y, since they are linear in x, and this explains why the 'Dob' scheme without perturbation is weak.

However, with adequate perturbations the modified scheme resists so far all the attacks we know. Precisely, we recommend the perturbations $+$, $\oplus$, $-$, $\widehat{v}$, described hereafter. They lead to what we call the "Dob" schemes.

2.3   Need for Perturbations

HFE is a well studied system. We will call 'nude HFE' the scheme with no perturbations. Today's best attacks on 'nude HFE' are quasi-polynomial. However, with some well chosen modifications, HFE seems much more strong. Similarly for Two-Face that is inspired from HFE, it seems reasonable to recommend a choice of perturbations that aim to thwart known attacks. Here are the main ones we would like to recommend.

"$\oplus$", **circle plus.** Let k be a small integer. Let $v_1, \ldots, v_k$ be k secret linear combinations of $x_1, \ldots, x_n$. This perturbation $\oplus$ adds n secret quadratic combinations of $v_1, \ldots, v_k$ to each variable $y_1, \ldots, y_n$. This can be removed when the secret key is known, by an exhaustive search on $v_1, \ldots, v_k$, at a cost in q^k.

"$+$", **plus.** Let k be a small integer. Let $q_1, \ldots, q_k$ be k secret quadratic combinations of $x_1, \ldots, x_n$. This perturbation $+$ adds n secret linear combinations of $q_1, \ldots, q_k$ to each variable $y_1, \ldots, y_n$. This can be removed when the secret key is known by an exhaustive search on $q_1, \ldots, q_k$, at a cost in q^k.

"$-$", **minus.** This is simply the forgetting operator that removes a small amount of k equations. This perturbation cost almost nothing in signature, but it has a cost in q^k in encryption, this is why it is more often used in signature.

"$\widehat{v}$", **circle v.** Let k be a small integer. Let $v_1, \ldots, v_k$ be k secret linear combinations of $x_1, \ldots, x_n$. This perturbation $\widehat{v}$ turns a multiplicative constant of the variable x in a vector of n random secret linear combinations of the k variables $v_1, \ldots, v_k$. This can be removed when the secret key is known, by an exhaustive search on $v_1, \ldots, v_k$, at a cost in q^k.

Since the introduction of perturbations is critical for the security, these perturbations must be considered as an essential part of the design of the scheme.

2.4   "Dob" Encryption Schemes

For the encryption schemes, we suggest the perturbations $+$ and $\oplus$. Perturbations $+$ and $\oplus$ combined thwart the Minrank attack and attacks against the kernels of the differential equations. See [12,13].

Formally the public polynomial is $Pub = S \circ P \circ T + H \circ R + U \circ L$, where

- R is a set of r random quadratic polynomials in n variables;
- H is a set of n random linear polynomials in r variables;
- L is a set of s random linear polynomials in n variables;
- U is a set of n random quadratic polynomials in s variables.

For encryption of a message x of n bits, compute and publish $y = Pub(x)$. For decryption of a message y of n bits, guess by exhaustive search two vectors p_1 and p_2 of respectively r and s bits. Solve in x the equation $S \circ P \circ T(x) = y - H(p_1) - U(p_2)$. Stop when $R(x) = p_1$ and $L(x) = p_2$.

Example of parameters. For example, the parameters $n = 129$, $r = s = 6$ give a very efficient scheme with a security level of 2^{80}. Decryption costs 2^{12} root computations of a 9 degree polynomial. At present we do not know any specific attack that could defeat it.

2.5 "Dob" Signature Schemes

For the signature schemes, we suggest the perturbation $-$. Formally the public polynomial is $Pub = (S \circ P \circ T)_{n-r}$, where $(.)_{n-r}$ are the first $n - r$ equations. For the signature of a message y of $n - r$ bits, expand the message to n bits in $y*$, solve in x the equation $S \circ P \circ T(x) = y*$, then publish the message and its signature (y, x). For the verification of a signed message (y, x) of $(n - r, n)$ bits, compute and check if $y = Pub(x)$.

We mention that the devastating attack based on a property of the differential of the central polynomial of SFLASH (see [14]) does not apply in our case. Indeed, since the Dobertin polynomial holds 2 quadratic monomials instead of one in the case of SFLASH, then the kernel of the public key has no exploitable expression. For the same reason, the attack based on another property of the differential (searching for multiplications) (see [15]) is also ineffective in the Dobbertin case.

Example of parameters. The example of parameters $n = 257$, $r = 129$ seems to be a possible implementation for a security level of 2^{128}, and again we do not know any specific attack that could apply.

Remark 1. In this section, we could have considered the polynomial $E_1(x) = x^{2^m+1} + x^3 + ax$ with $a \neq 1$, and then used the perturbation $\widehat{v}$ on a. However in this case, E_1 is generally not a permutation any more. We have preferred for 'Dob' to use other perturbations and keep the permutation property.

3   The (Simple) Pat Polynomial Family

This is the generic family that can be obtained from any suitable polynomial P using the Two-Face technique and generalizing the 'Dob' family. In this case, the degree n is odd, and as for the 'Dob' family and we note $n = 2m - 1$. The polynomial P has the particular following form.

$$E_1(x) = P(x) = x^{q^m+1} + \sum_{\substack{i=0,\ i=q^j,\ i=q^j+q^k}}^{i \leq d} \alpha_i x^i. \tag{1}$$

In other words, we have $P(x) = x^{q^m+1} + Q(x)$, where Q is DO ans its degree is bounded by a small value d. Using the same remark as for the 'Dob' family, we can derive also a second equation by eliminating an intermediate variable $z = x^{q^m}$ between $y = P(x)$ and $y^{q^m} = P(x)^{q^m}$. The elimination gives

$$E_2(x, y) = x^{d+q-1}(y - Q(x)) + \sum_{i=0}^{d} \alpha_i^{q^m} x^{d-i}(y - Q(x))^i - y^{q^m} x^d = 0. \tag{2}$$

We can also easily see that the degree in x of this equation is bounded by $\max(2d + q - 1, d^2)$.

From this polynomial P of the simple 'Pat' family, we can obviously define in the same way a Two-Face scheme, as with the 'Dob' family, using also the same kind of perturbations. However, since the polynomials of the 'Pat' family are not permutations in general, performance of the secret key is slowed since computation of roots of a polynomial may retrieve several values, up to the degree of the polynomial in theory, a small amount in practise, and so stays attractive. From a security point of view, none of the known attacks apply to the 'Pat' Two-Face schemes, nor the 'Dob' family, which is a special case of the 'Pat' family, however the bijective property of 'Dob' may become the target of future attacks. Therefore, it is good to have some options as backup.

Here are some examples.

Example 1.

$$q = 2, \quad d = 5, \quad B(x, z) = xz + x^5 + x^3$$
$$E_1(x) = B(x, x^{q^m}) = x^{2^m + 1} + x^5 + x^3$$
$$E_2(x, y) = x^{25} + x^{23} + x^{20}y + x^{13} + x^9 + x^8 y + x^7 y^2 + x^6 y + x^5 y^4 + x^5 y^2$$
$$\qquad + x^5 y^{2^m} + x^3 y^4 + x^2 y^3 + y^5$$

Example 2.

$$q = 2, \quad d = 6, \quad B(x, z) = xz + x^6 + x^5$$
$$E_1(x) = B(x, x^{q^m}) = x^{2^m + 1} + x^6 + x^5$$
$$E_2(x, y) = x^{36} + x^{34} + x^{32} + x^{31} + x^{27} + x^{26} + x^{25}y + x^{24}y^2 + x^{21}y + x^{20}y^2$$
$$\qquad + x^{13} + x^{12}y^4 + x^{12} + x^{10}y^4 + x^7 y^4 + x^7 y + x^6 y^4 + x^6 y^{2^m} + xy^5 + y^6$$

The examples above illustrate how E_1 and E_2 seem very different, yet related, since precisely solutions in x of $E_1(x) = y$ are by design solutions of $E_2(x, y) = 0$. The equation $E_2(x, y) = 0$ may have more solutions in x than $E_1(x) = y$ but they can be easily sorted out by simple test. The polynomial E_2 has many monomials with various degrees in x, and its multivariate counterpart has therefore a high degree. It is then reasonable to think that E_2 is useless for an attacker, yet essential to invert the scheme.

Experimental Results. We did some experiments, see Table 1: 'd2' is the degree in x of E_2, 'dreg' is the degree of regularity, 'deg' is the degree of the HFE polynomial. It seems that random 'Simple Pat' schemes with parameter d have roughly similar regularity degree as random HFE with parameter d^2. However, more simulations might be required to compare more precisely the two schemes. Moreover we shall also investigate in the future which factors should be tuned to increase the degree of regularity.

Table 1. Comparison 'Simple Pat' vs HFE

Simple Pat					Original HFE		
d	q	d2	n	dreg	deg	n	dreg
9	2	81	39	4	36	25	4
10	2	100	39	5	36	32	4
12	2	144	23	5	36	41	4
20	2	400	25	5	81	41	4
24	2	576	25	5	128	25	4
32	2	1024	25	5	129	25	5
33	2	1089	25	6	257	25	5
34	2	1156	25	6	513	25	6

4 The (General) Pat Polynomial Families

We generalize one step ahead the previous definition by selecting a polynomial B in two variables over $\mathbb{F}_{q^n}$, say x and z. We choose B to have the special form:

$$B(x,z) = \sum_{i=0,\ i=q^j,\ i=q^j+q^k}^{i \le d} \alpha_i x^i + \sum_{i=q^j,\ i=q^j+q^k}^{i \le d} \beta_i z^i + \sum_{i=q^k,\ j=q^l}^{i+j \le d} \gamma_{i,j} x^i z^j$$

That is, we require that B has an extended 'Dembowski-Ostrom' form in two variables, and its total degree is bounded by d. Again we choose an odd degree n and set m such that $n = 2m-1$. Then we define our Face (1) with the polynomial E_1 given by:

$$E_1(x) = B(x, x^{q^m}). \tag{1}$$

Then E_1 is by design DO. The special form of B has been chosen in such a way that we can also mimic the idea of the 'Dob' and simple 'Pat' family; that is introduce on purpose an intermediate variable $z = x^{q^m}$. Therefore we have $y = E_1(x) = B(x, z)$. This gives also $y^{q^m} = B(x, z)^{q^m}$. In this latter, we can replace each occurrence of x^{q^m} by z, and each occurrence of z^{q^m} by x^q. Formally, this is equivalent to replace z by x^{q^m} and x by $z^{q^{m-1}}$. Therefore we get $y^{q^m} = B(z^{q^{m-1}}, x^{q^m})^{q^m}$. Now, the same idea to get a second equation is to eliminate z between those two equations. It becomes difficult to get the result by hand, but the classical tool called 'Resultant' or 'Eliminant' (see [16,17]) does perfectly the job on a computer (see 'Resultant' on 'Magma', [18]). We use the notation Res for 'Resultant'. So our second equation is given by:

$$E_2(x,y) = \mathrm{Res}_z(B(x,z) - y, B(z^{q^{m-1}}, x^{q^m})^{q^m} - y^{q^m}) = 0. \tag{2}$$

One of the interests of (2) should be that its degree in x is small, otherwise it would be useless. It is possible to estimate this degree. Let us consider one generic monomial $x^i z^j$ of $B(x,z)$, then in $B' = B(z^{q^{m-1}}, x^{q^m})^{q^m}$, it becomes $x^{qj} z^i$. Since the degree of B is bounded by d, then the degree of B' is bounded by qd. The theory of resultants gives us that the degree in x of (2), that is $\mathrm{Res}_z(B(x,z) - y, B'(x,y) - y^{q^m})$, is bounded by qd^2.

Example 1.

$$q = 2 \quad d = 3 \quad n = 2m - 1$$
$$z = x^{2^m} \quad t = y^{2^m}$$
$$E_1(x) = B(x, z) = x^3 + xz + z^3$$
$$E_2(x, y) = x^{18} + x^{15} + x^{12}y + x^{12}t + x^{11} + x^9 + x^7 + x^6y^2 + x^6t^2 +$$
$$x^6t + x^5t + x^4y + x^3y^2 + x^3t^2 + x^3t + y^3 + y^2t + yt^2 + t^3$$

Example 2.

$$q = 2 \quad d = 5 \quad n = 2m - 1$$
$$z = x^{2^m} \quad t = y^{2^m}$$
$$E_1(x) = B(x, z) = x^4z + xz + x + z^5$$
$$E_2(x, y) = x^{50} + x^{40}t + x^{35} + x^{34}y + x^{34} + x^{33} + x^{32}y + x^{31} + x^{30}y + x^{29} +$$
$$x^{28}y + x^{28} + x^{27}y + x^{27} + x^{26}y + x^{26} + x^{25}y + x^{25}t + x^{25} +$$
$$x^{24}yt + x^{24}y + x^{24}t + x^{23}t + x^{23} + x^{22}yt + x^{22}y + x^{19}y +$$
$$x^{18}y^2 + x^{18}y + x^{18} + x^{17}y + x^{17}t + x^{17} + x^{16}yt + x^{16}y +$$
$$x^{15}t^2 + x^{15}t + x^{15} + x^{14}yt^2 + x^{14}yt + x^{14}y + x^{14} + x^{13}y +$$
$$x^{13}t^2 + x^{13} + x^{12}yt^2 + x^{11}y^2 + x^{11}y + x^{11}t^2 + x^{11}t +$$
$$x^{10}y^4 + x^{10}y^2 + x^{10}yt^2 + x^{10}yt + x^{10}y + x^{10}t^4 + x^{10}t +$$
$$x^9t^2 + x^8y^2t + x^8yt^2 + x^8yt + x^8y + x^8t^2 + x^7y^2 +$$
$$x^7yt^2 + x^6t^2 + x^6t + x^5yt^2 + x^5t^3 + x^4y^2t + x^4yt^3 +$$
$$x^4t + x^3t^3 + x^3 + x^2yt^3 + x^2y + xt + x + y + t^5$$

4.1 Scheme Construction

We describe how to construct a Two-Face cryptosystem, using the special families we have just introduced. The first step is the selection of the following parameters: the values of q, n, the polynomial B and two secret affine permutations of $\mathbb{F}_q^n$, S and T. For the perturbations, we can use "+", "$\oplus$", and "$\widehat{v}$" as defined above. Then we have to make public the coordinates of $P = S \circ E_1 \circ T$ over $\mathbb{F}_q$ as quadratic multivariate polynomials. Then as usual, the public key can be used either, given x, to compute y such that $P(x) = y$, or given (x, y), to check that $P(x) = y$. The secret key is used, given y, to compute x such that $P(x) = y$. To do so, one first uses S to translate the problem into the hidden space, then uses E_2 instead of E_1 to find a solution, then uses T to translate the solution back into the public space. One may argue here that E_2 may have several solutions. It is sufficient to consider that the number of solutions is bounded and in practice it is low, and therefore it is possible to enumerate them all and select the suitable one.

4.2 Practical Experiments

See Table 2.

Table 2. Comparison 'General Pat' vs HFE

		General MacPat			Original HFE		
d	q	deg	n	dreg	deg	n	dreg
9	2	162	25	5	36	25	4
10	2	200	25	5	36	32	4
14	2	200	25	5	36	41	4
16	2	512	25	5	81	41	4
17	2	578	25	6	128	25	4
17	2	578	29	6	129	25	5
17	2	578	31	6	257	25	5
17	2	578	33	6	513	25	6
18	2	648	25	6	1025	32	6
20	2	800	25	6	2049	33	6
30	2	1152	33	6	3072	33	6
50	2	4608	33	7	4097	33	7

5 The Mac Polynomial Family

This is the generalization of the Dobbertin family, and also the specialization of the general 'Pat' families, to special families for which the corresponding polynomial $P(x)$ is specially a permutation polynomial. For these families, we found that only $q = 2^p$ is possible. Indeed, we point out here that such permutation polynomials families are very sparse and the ones we give here were found by exhaustive search. Here are four examples of new quadratic permutations. This is an interesting part of this paper, since new quadratic permutations are difficult to find and may have interest beyond cryptography.

Example 1.

$$q = 2 \quad d = 4 \quad n = 2m - 1, \quad n \not\equiv 0 \pmod 3, \text{ and } n \not\equiv 0 \pmod 5$$
$$z = x^{2^m} \quad t = y^{2^m}$$
$$E_1(x) = B(x, z) = x^2 z^2 + x^2 z + xz$$
$$E_2(x, y) = x^4 y^2 + x^4 y + x^4 t + x^3 y + x^2 t + xy + xt + y^2 + t^2 + t$$

Example 2.

$$q = 2 \quad d = 6 \quad n = 2m - 1, \quad n \not\equiv 0 \pmod 7$$
$$z = x^{2^m} \quad t = y^{2^m}$$
$$E_1(x) = B(x, z) = x^4 z^2 + x^2 z + xz$$
$$E_2(x, y) = x^8 y + x^8 t^2 + x^8 t + x^7 t + x^6 y + x^6 t + x^5 y + x^4 y + x^3 y^2 +$$
$$x^3 y + x^2 y^2 + x^2 y + xy + y^4 + y^2 + t$$

Example 3.

$$q = 2 \quad d = 8 \quad n = 2m - 1, \quad n \not\equiv 0 \pmod{15}$$

$$z = x^{2^m} \quad t = y^{2^m}$$

$$E_1(x) = B(x, z) = x^4 z^4 + x^2 z + xz$$

$$E_2(x, y) = x^{16}y^4 + x^{16}y + x^{16}t + x^{15}y + x^{14}y^2 + x^{14}y + x^{13}y + x^{12}y^2 +$$
$$x^{12}y + x^{11}t + x^{10}y^2 + x^{10}y + x^{10}t + x^9 y^2 + x^9 t + x^8 y +$$
$$x^8 t + x^7 y + x^6 t^2 + x^6 t + x^4 y + x^4 t^2 + x^4 t + x^3 t + x^2 y +$$
$$x^2 t^2 + x^2 t + xy + xt^2 + y^2 + t^4 + t$$

Example 4.

$$q = 4 \quad d = 5 \quad n = 2m - 1, \quad n \not\equiv 0 \pmod{3}$$

$$z = x^{2^m} \quad t = y^{2^m}$$

$$f = \text{generator of } \mathbb{F}_4$$

$$E_1(x) = B(x, z) = fx^5 + x^4 z + xz^4 + f^2 z^5$$

$$E_2(x, y) = x^{100} + f^2 x^{97} + x^{80}y + fx^{80}t + fx^{76} + x^{73} + f^2 x^{68}y +$$
$$x^{68}t + fx^{60}yt + x^{57}yt + f^2 x^{54}yt + f^2 x^{52} + fx^{51}yt + fx^{49}$$
$$+ x^{48}yt + f^2 x^{45}yt + fx^{42}yt + fx^{40}y^2 t + f^2 x^{40}yt^2 +$$
$$x^{30}yt + f^2 x^{36}yt + f^2 x^{34}y^2 t + x^{34}yt^2 + fx^{33}yt +$$
$$f^2 x^{32}y + x^{32}t + x^{30}yt + x^{28} + f^2 x^{27}yt + f^2 x^{25} +$$
$$fx^{24}yt + x^{21}yt + x^{20}y^4 + fx^{20}y^3 t + f^2 x^{20}y^2 t^2 +$$
$$x^{20}yt^3 + fx^{20}y + fx^{20}t^4 + f^2 x^{20}t + f^2 x^{18}yt + f^2 x^{17}y^4 +$$
$$x^{17}y^3 t + fx^{17}y^2 t^2 + f^2 x^{17}yt^3 + x^{17}t^4 + f^2 x^{16}y^2 t +$$
$$x^{16}yt^2 + fx^{15}yt + x^{10}y^2 t + fx^{10}yt^2 + f^2 x^8 y^4 +$$
$$x^8 y^3 t + fx^8 y^2 t^2 + f^2 x^8 yt^3 + x^8 t^4 + fx^5 y^4 +$$
$$f^2 x^5 y^3 t + x^5 y^2 t^2 + fx^5 yt^3 + f^2 x^5 t^4 + y^5 + fy^4 t +$$
$$fyt^4 + ft^5$$

Remark 1. As for the proven case of Dobbertin's polynomial family, in the Mac cases (permutation polynomials), the two faces are equivalent, that is given y, $E_1(x) = y$ and $E_2(x, y) = 0$ have exactly the same solutions in x. This property was at least observed for the four previous example. A proper generalization of this result is beyond this article.

Remark 2. Example 3 presents a family of DO permutation polynomials for $q = 4$. This opens the possibility of finding other families of DO permutation polynomials over $\mathbb{F}_q$ for $q = 2^p$. This is by sure of cryptographic interest, since bigger q could lead to smaller public keys, and of mathematical interest as well.

6   Other Generalizations

6.1   Three or a Few More Blocks, 'Super Two-Face'

Taking back the idea of the 'Pat' schemes, let consider that the variable x is 'duplicated' more than twice, a small number of times, three times for instance. We then consider $B(x, z_1, z_2)$ a DO polynomial of small degree, in 3 variables. We can then define $E_1(x) = B(x, x^{q^m}, x^{q^{2m}})$. Let suppose that $n = 3m - 1$. We have then $x^{q^m} \circ x^{q^m} \circ x^{q^m} = x^{q^{3m}} = x^q$. Therefore, by letting $z_1 = x^{q^m}$, $z_2 = z_1^{q^m}$, we have also $x^q = z_2^{q^m}$. Then by eliminating z_1 and z_2 in the following system,

$$B(x, z_1, z_2) = y$$
$$B(z_1^{q^{2m-1}}, z_2^{q^{2m-1}}, x^{q^{2m}})^{q^m} = y^{q^m}$$
$$B(z_2^{q^{m-1}}, x^{q^m}, z_1^{q^m})^{q^{2m}} = y^{q^{2m}}$$

we get similarly $E_2(x, y) = 0$. We call this scheme 'Super Two-Face' as it shows that it can expand the family very largely. By this mean, we also discovered new DO permutation polynomials. Experiments are still undergoing.

6.2   More Blocks

Ultimately, by using a quadratic polynomial $B(x, z_1, \ldots, z_{n-1})$, and the implicit equations $z_1 = x^q$, $z_2 = z_1^q$, $\ldots$, $z_{n-1} = z_{n-2}^q$, $x = z_{n-1}^q$, one can define similarly $E_1(x) = B(x, x^q, x^{q^2}, \ldots, x^{q^{n-1}})$. An open problem is to find possible values of B such that finding E_2 is easy.

7   Conclusion

HFE [6] is one of the main multivariate schemes existing nowadays. In the state of the art of cryptanalysis, [19–21] 'nude' HFE (i.e. without perturbation) has a "quasi-polynomial" attack. With addition of well chosen perturbations, HFE seems very efficient (mostly in signature scheme), and no realistic attacks are known. In this article, we have largely widen the family of public-key schemes that can be created from multivariate polynomials close to HFE. For this we have introduced the 'Two-Face' concept, that is, we have split the equation of HFE, into two different but related ones, with separated roles, equations (1) and (2) in this article. From a cryptographic point of view, this is maybe the most important point in this article. This enabled us to design many variants ('Dob', 'Simple Pat', 'General Pat', 'Mac', 'Super Two-Face'...). We have then tested attacks by Gröbner basis computation on these variants. Unfortunately, as for HFE, most of these 'nude Two-Face' variants (without perturbation) show a small regularity degree very similar to the behaviour of 'nude HFE'. However, we still have many polynomials to test.

Nevertheless, as for HFE (and some others generalizations like 'Intermediate Field System' [22]) as soon as some appropriate perturbations are added, the regularity degree increases and then Gröbner basis attacks don't work any more.

We have started our study by the Dobbertin permutation polynomial family and our 'Dob' scheme. For cryptographic applications, the permutation property is not required and this led us to our 'Pat' schemes. Surprisingly, we were also able to discover new DO permutation polynomials. It led us to the 'Mac' schemes, and it seems that even more such polynomials could be found. This has a mathematical interest per se, because the probability that a random DO polynomial is a permutation is very small. Moreover, all those new DO permutation polynomials have like the Dobbertin one a generic form which makes them infinite families, i.e. for an infinity of values n, a quadratic polynomial with a given expression that depends on n, is a permutation of $\mathbb{F}_{2^n}$.

Permutations present also a cryptographic interest, since it speeds up the cryptographic computations, as there is only one root to compute. For example our scheme 'Dob' based on the Dobbertin permutation polynomials seems currently very efficient and resistant to all known attacks as soon as it includes perturbations.

We have also looked at the attacks against the Matsumoto-Imai C* scheme and its variant SFLASH [14,15] and explain why they can't a priori apply to 'Dob'. In this article we have also suggested some possible realistic parameters for our schemes.

Acknowledgements. We thank Ludovic Perret and Jean Charles Faugère, INRIA, for fruitful discussions and help for the experimental computations.

References

1. Gilbert, H., Minier, M.: Cryptanalysis of SFLASH. [36], pp. 288–298 (2002)
2. Fouque, P., Macario-Rat, G., Stern, J.: Key recovery on hidden monomial multivariate schemes. [37], pp. 19–30 (2008)
3. Ding, J., Dubois, V., Yang, B., Chen, C.O., Cheng, C.: Could SFLASH be repaired? IACR Cryptology ePrint Archive **2009**, 596 (2009)
4. Faugère, J., Perret, L.: On the security of UOV. IACR Cryptology ePrint Archive **2009**, 483 (2009)
5. Hamdi, O., Bouallegue, A., Harari, S.: Hidden field equations cryptosystem performances. In: AICCSA, pp. 308–311. IEEE Computer Society (2006)
6. Patarin, J.: Hidden fields equations (HFE) and isomorphisms of polynomials (IP): two new families of asymmetric algorithms. [34], pp. 33–48 (1996)
7. Lidl, R., Niederreiter, H.: Finite Fields. Encyclopedia of Mathematics and its Applications, 2nd edn. Cambridge University Press, Cambridge (1996)
8. Dembowski, P., Ostrom, T.G.: Planes of order n with collineation groups of order n^2. Math. Z. **103**(3), 239–258 (1968)
9. Ding, J., Yang, B.-Y.: Degree of regularity for HFEv and HFEv-. In: Gaborit, P. (ed.) PQCrypto 2013. LNCS, vol. 7932, pp. 52–66. Springer, Heidelberg (2013). https://doi.org/10.1007/978-3-642-38616-9_4

10. Dobbertin, H.: Almost perfect nonlinear power functions on $GF(2^n)$: the Welch case. IEEE Trans. Inf. Theory **45**(4), 1271–1275 (1999)
11. Patarin, J.: Cryptanalysis of the Matsumoto and Imai public key scheme of eurocrypt'98. Des. Codes Crypt. **20**(2), 175–209 (2000)
12. Fouque, P., Granboulan, L., Stern, J.: Differential cryptanalysis for multivariate schemes. [32], pp. 341–353 (2005)
13. Dubois, V., Granboulan, L., Stern, J.: Cryptanalysis of HFE with internal perturbation. [33]. pp. 249–265 (2007)
14. Bouillaguet, C., Fouque, P.-A., Macario-Rat, G.: Practical key-recovery for all possible parameters of SFLASH. In: Lee, D.H., Wang, X. (eds.) ASIACRYPT 2011. LNCS, vol. 7073, pp. 667–685. Springer, Heidelberg (2011). https://doi.org/10.1007/978-3-642-25385-0_36
15. Dubois, V., Fouque, P.-A., Shamir, A., Stern, J.: Practical cryptanalysis of SFLASH. In: Menezes, A. (ed.) CRYPTO 2007. LNCS, vol. 4622, pp. 1–12. Springer, Heidelberg (2007). https://doi.org/10.1007/978-3-540-74143-5_1
16. Salmon, G.: Lessons Introductory to the Modern Higher Algebra. Elibron Classics Series. Adegi Graphics LLC, Rye Brook (1999)
17. Geddes, K.O., Czapor, S.R., Labahn, G.: Algorithms for Computer Algebra. Kluwer Academic Publishers, Norwell (1992)
18. Bosma, W., Cannon, J., Playoust, C.: The Magma algebra system. I: the user language. J. Symb. Comput. **24**(3–4), 235–265 (1997). Computational algebra and number theory (London, 1993)
19. Faugère, J.-C., Joux, A.: Algebraic cryptanalysis of hidden field equation (HFE) cryptosystems using Gröbner bases. In: Boneh, D. (ed.) CRYPTO 2003. LNCS, vol. 2729, pp. 44–60. Springer, Heidelberg (2003). https://doi.org/10.1007/978-3-540-45146-4_3
20. Bettale, L., Faugère, J.-C., Perret, L.: Cryptanalysis of multivariate and odd-characteristic HFE variants. In: Catalano, D., Fazio, N., Gennaro, R., Nicolosi, A. (eds.) PKC 2011. LNCS, vol. 6571, pp. 441–458. Springer, Heidelberg (2011). https://doi.org/10.1007/978-3-642-19379-8_27
21. Bettale, L., Faugère, J., Perret, L.: Cryptanalysis of HFE, multi-HFE and variants for odd and even characteristic. IACR Cryptology ePrint Archive **2011**, 399 (2011)
22. Billet, O., Patarin, J., Seurin, Y.: Analysis of intermediate field systems. In: First Conference on Symbolic Computation and Cryptography, Beijing, China, 28–30 April 2008, pp. 110–117 (2008)
23. Goubin, L., Courtois, N.: Cryptanalysis of the TTM cryptosystem. [24], pp. 44–57 (2000)
24. Okamoto, T. (ed.) Advances in Cryptology - ASIACRYPT 2000. LNCS, vol. 1976. Springer, Heidelberg (2000). https://doi.org/10.1007/3-540-44448-3
25. Zhang, W., Tan, C.H.: A new perturbed Matsumoto-Imai signature scheme. [26], pp. 43–48 (2014)
26. Emura, K., Hanaoka, G., Zhao, Y. (eds.): Proceedings of the 2nd ACM Workshop on ASIA Public-Key Cryptography, ASIAPKC 2014, 3 June, 2014, Kyoto, Japan. ACM (2014)
27. Zhang, W., Tan, C.H.: MI-T-HFE, a new multivariate signature scheme. Cryptology ePrint Archive, Report 2015/890 (2015). http://eprint.iacr.org/2015/890
28. Ding, J., Gower, J.E., Schmidt, D., Wolf, C., Yin, Z.: Complexity estimates for the F4 attack on the perturbed Matsumoto-Imai cryptosystem. [29], pp. 262–277 (2005)
29. Smart, N.P. (ed.): Cryptography and Coding 2005. LNCS, vol. 3796. Springer, Heidelberg (2005). https://doi.org/10.1007/11586821

30. Ding, J.: A new variant of the Matsumoto-Imai cryptosystem through perturbation. [31], pp. 305–318 (2004)
31. Bao, F., Deng, R.H., Zhou, J. (eds.): Public Key Cryptography-PKC 2004. LNCS, vol. 2947. Springer, Heidelberg (2004). https://doi.org/10.1007/978-3-540-24632-9_22
32. Cramer, R. (ed.): Advances in Cryptology - EUROCRYPT 2005. vol.3494. LNCS, Springer, Heidelberg (2005). https://doi.org/10.1007/11426639_20
33. Okamoto, T., Wang, X. (eds.): Public Key Cryptography - PKC 2007. LNCS, vol. 4450. Springer, Heidelberg (2007). https://doi.org/10.1007/978-3-540-71677-8_17
34. Maurer, U.M. (ed.): Advances in Cryptology - EUROCRYPT 1996. LNCS, vol. 1070. Springer, Heidelberg (1996). https://doi.org/10.1007/3-540-68339-9_4
35. MacAulay, F.S.: Some formulæ in elimination. Proc. Lond. Math. Soc. s1−35(1), 3–27 (1902)
36. Knudsen, L.R. (ed.): Advances in Cryptology - EUROCRYPT 2002. LNCS, vol. 2332. Springer, Heidelberg (2002). https://doi.org/10.1007/3-540-46035-7
37. Smart, N.P. (ed.): Advances in Cryptology - EUROCRYPT 2008. LNCS, vol. 4965. Springer, Heidelberg (2008). https://doi.org/10.1007/978-3-540-78967-3_2
38. Hou, X.d.: Permutation polynomials over finite fields - a survey of recent advances. Finite Fields Appl. 32(C), 82–119 (2015)
39. Blokhuis, A., Coulter, R.S., Henderson, M., O'Keefe, C.M.: Permutations amongst the Dembowski-Ostrom polynomials. In: Jungnickel, D., Niederreiter, H. (eds.) Finite Fields and Applications, pp. 37–42. Springer, Heidelberg (2001). https://doi.org/10.1007/978-3-642-56755-1_4
40. Plût, J., Fouque, P., Macario-Rat, G.: Solving the "isomorphism of polynomials with two secrets" problem for all pairs of quadratic forms. CoRR abs/1406.3163 (2014)

Cryptanalysis of RSA Variants
with Modified Euler Quotient

Mengce Zheng[1](✉)![ORCID], Noboru Kunihiro[2], and Honggang Hu[1]

[1] CAS Key Laboratory of Electromagnetic Space Information,
University of Science and Technology of China, Hefei, China
mczheng@mail.ustc.edu.cn, hghu2005@ustc.edu.cn
[2] The University of Tokyo, Tokyo, Japan
kunihiro@k.u-tokyo.ac.jp

Abstract. The standard RSA scheme provides the key equation $ed \equiv 1$ (mod $\varphi(N)$) for $N = pq$, where $\varphi(N) = (p-1)(q-1)$ is Euler quotient (or Euler's totient function), e and d are the public and private keys, respectively. It has been extended to the following variants with *modified Euler quotient* $\omega(N) = (p^2 - 1)(q^2 - 1)$, which in turn indicates the *modified key equation* is $ed \equiv 1$ (mod $\omega(N)$).
  - An RSA-type scheme based on singular cubic curves $y^2 \equiv x^3 + bx^2$ (mod N) for $N = pq$.
  - An extended RSA scheme based on the field of Gaussian integers for $N = PQ$, where P, Q are Gaussian primes with $p = |P|$, $q = |Q|$.
  - A scheme working in quadratic field quotients using Lucas sequences with an RSA modulus $N = pq$.
In this paper, we investigate some key-related attacks on such RSA variants using lattice-based techniques. To be specific, small private key attack, multiple private keys attack, and partial key exposure attack are proposed. Furthermore, we provide the first results for multiple private keys attack and partial key exposure attack when analyzing the RSA variants with modified Euler quotient.

Keywords: RSA variants · Modified Euler quotient · Lattice
Multiple private keys attack · Partial key exposure attack

1 Introduction

1.1 Background

RSA [30] is currently one of the most widely used public key cryptosystems in the world. In the case of the standard RSA, a public modulus N is the product of two large primes p and q of the same bit-size, namely $N = pq$. The key equation is $ed \equiv 1$ (mod $\varphi(N)$), where $\varphi(N) = (p-1)(q-1)$ is Euler quotient (or Euler's totient function), (N, e) and (p, q, d) are called the public and private keys, respectively. In the encryption process, a message string is transformed into an integer M and then encrypted as $C = M^e$ (mod N). The decryption process

© Springer International Publishing AG, part of Springer Nature 2018
A. Joux et al. (Eds.): AFRICACRYPT 2018, LNCS 10831, pp. 266–281, 2018.
https://doi.org/10.1007/978-3-319-89339-6_15

computes C^d (mod N). Since e and d are always calculated as exponents in the encryption and decryption phases, they are called public and private exponents as well. In the following analyses, we further use α and δ for simplicity, whose values come from $e = N^\alpha$ and $d = N^\delta$.

The standard RSA cryptosystem has been generalized by various approaches such as modifying its modulus [35], modifying Euler quotient [13,23] and modifying the encryption/decryption process [15,28] for specific purposes. This paper focuses on the RSA variants with modified Euler quotient $\omega(N) = (p^2-1)(q^2-1)$ for $N = pq$. We provide the *modified key equation* used in such RSA variants, which shows the relation $ed \equiv 1$ (mod $\omega(N)$) between $\omega(N)$ and two integers e and d. It can be rewritten as

$$ed = k(p^2 - 1)(q^2 - 1) + 1, \qquad (1)$$

where k is an unknown positive integer. In the general cases, we have $0 < \alpha, \delta < 2$ since $0 < e, d < \omega(N) \approx N^2$. But, α and δ can be generated to exceed above range for some security considerations. Next, we briefly introduce three related schemes. One may refer to [7,13,23] for more details.

The First Variant. This RSA variant was introduced by Kuwakado et al. [23] in 1995. It is based on singular cubic curves with $y^2 \equiv x^3 + bx^2$ (mod N) for an RSA modulus $N = pq$ and $b \in \mathbb{Z}/N\mathbb{Z}$. The public exponent e and the private exponent d satisfy $\gcd(e, (p^2-1)(q^2-1)) = 1$ and $d \equiv e^{-1}$ (mod $(p^2-1)(q^2-1)$). Thus, we have $ed = k(p^2 - 1)(q^2 - 1) + 1$ for a positive integer k from the key generation algorithm.

The Second Variant. This variant was introduced by Elkamchouchi et al. [13] in 2002. It is based on the ring of Gaussian integers $\mathbb{Z}[i]$. A Gaussian integer $a + bi$ is a complex number for integers a, b and $i^2 = -1$, whose norm is defined by $|a + bi| = \sqrt{a^2 + b^2}$. The RSA cryptosystem can be extended over the domain of Gaussian integers because of the similar property and arithmetical operations. Let modulus N be the product of two Gaussian primes P, Q and let e, d be integers satisfying $d \equiv e^{-1}$ (mod $(|P|^2-1)(|Q|^2-1)$). Note that the key equation is $ed = k(|P|^2 - 1)(|Q|^2 - 1) + 1$ for a positive integer k. When denoting $|P|$ and $|Q|$ by p and q respectively, we have the same modified key equation as derived in the first variant.

The Third Variant. This variant was introduced by Castagnos [7] in 2007. It is based on an RSA modulus $N = pq$ and Lucas sequences working in quadratic field quotients. Let e be an integer satisfying $\gcd(e, (p^2-1)(q^2-1)) = 1$. Though the inverse $d = e^{-1}$ (mod $(p^2 - 1)(q^2 - 1)$) does not explicitly appear in this scheme, we can analyze its security by solving $ed = k(p^2 - 1)(q^2 - 1) + 1$ for small d.

Small Private Key Attack. In 1990, Wiener [40] showed that one can break the standard RSA scheme when the private key d is less than $\frac{1}{3}N^{0.25}$. Wiener's attack utilizes the continued fraction approach to deal with the key equation $ed = k(p-1)(q-1)+1$. If d is small enough, k/d will be one of the convergents of the continued fraction expansion of the public rational fraction e/N. Thus, k and d can be recovered by computing the continued fraction expansion. Furthermore, [6] presented a new improved attack on RSA based on Wiener's technique using continued fraction.

Later in 1999, Boneh and Durfee [3] introduced the small inverse problem and proposed an improved attack using Coppersmith's lattice-based techniques [10] that works for $d < N^{0.292}$. The aim is to find the small roots of the modular equation $x(y + A) + 1 \equiv 0 \pmod{e}$ with known A and e. Herrmann and May [17] presented an optimized algorithm to solve the same equation using the linearization technique, which is applied to obtain smaller dimensional lattices. Though the latter attack does not improve the insecure bound, it simplifies the lattice construction and reduces the practical consumption.

The small private key attacks on several RSA variants have also been studied in [31–33]. As for the RSA variants with modified Euler quotient $\omega(N) = (p^2 - 1)(q^2 - 1)$, Bunder et al. [5] proposed an attack using the continued fraction approach. They showed that when $d^2e < 2N^3 - 18N^2$, k/d can be found among the convergents of the continued fraction expansion of $e/(N^2 - \frac{9}{4}N + 1)$. Thus, the factorization of N, namely p and q can be deduced from k and d. Peng et al. [27] proposed a better lattice-based attack and improved the insecure bound to $\delta < 2 - \sqrt{\alpha}$ for $\alpha \geq 1$. The attack is reduced to solving small roots $(k, p^2 + q^2)$ of the modular equation $x(N^2 + 1 - y) + 1 \equiv 0 \pmod{e}$ using the linearization technique of [17]. Though Peng et al. gave a refinement on the insecure bound of the small private exponent, they did not present a complete range of solvable α.

Multiple Private Keys Attack. The security of RSA with multiple key pairs was first studied by Howgrave-Graham and Seifert [19] in 1999. In this case, where given n multiple key pairs $(e_1, d_1), \ldots, (e_n, d_n)$ for a common public modulus N such that $e_i d_i \equiv 1 \pmod{\varphi(N)}$ for all $i = 1, 2, \ldots, n$, the standard RSA can be viewed as the special case for $n = 1$. Similarly, the values of the public and private keys are estimated as N^α and N^δ, respectively.

Later, this attack type was improved by the lattice-based techniques in [1, 36]. The previous works confirm an intuitive inference that RSA becomes more vulnerable when there are more key pairs. Takayasu and Kunihiro [36] proposed the best attack so far that works for $\delta < 1 - \sqrt{2/(3n+1)}$ when given N and public keys $e_1, \ldots, e_n \approx N$. If there are even more key pairs, larger secret keys can be recovered, which indicates that full-size private keys i.e. $\delta = 1$ can be recovered with infinitely many key pairs.

The multiple private keys attack has been extended to other RSA variants in several papers like [26,41]. However, to attack the RSA variant with modified Euler quotient with multiple key pairs is not analyzed before.

Partial Key Exposure Attack. In 1998, Boneh et al. [4] proposed several attacks on RSA given a fraction of the private key bits with small public exponent *e*. Their attacks utilized some known most significant bits (MSBs) or some known least significant bits (LSBs) of the private exponent d. In practice, above partial key information can be captured using side channel attacks, e.g. cold boot attacks [16] and others [22,29]. Therefore, so-called partial key exposure attack has gradually become an important part when estimating the security of RSA.

Blömer and May [2] later improved partial key exposure attacks on RSA using Coppersmith's lattice-based techniques [10]. They showed that RSA is also vulnerable to larger public exponent e given some private key exposure. In 2005, Ernst et al. [14] presented several new attacks that work up to full-size exponents (i.e., $e \approx N$ or $d \approx N$) by three theorems under a common heuristic assumption. The best-known attack was proposed by Takayasu and Kunihiro [37,39], which can achieve Boneh and Durfee's bound [3] of the small private key attack.

In addition to the partial key exposure attacks on the standard RSA scheme, this attack type has been extended to other RSA variants in several papers like [34]. However, the partial key exposure attack on the RSA variant with modified Euler quotient is not considered before.

1.2   Our Contributions

In this paper, we first derive the crucial modular equation in our analyses from the modified key Eq. 1. We have $ed = k(p^2q^2 - p^2 - q^2 + 1) + 1$, which can be rewritten as $ed = k\left((N+1)^2 - (p+q)^2\right) + 1$. Thus, we are required to solve

$$x(y + A) + 1 \equiv 0 \pmod{e} \tag{2}$$

for $A := (N + 1)^2$ with small roots $x = k$ and $y = -(p + q)^2$. Note that our modular equation is slightly different compared with the root $y = p^2 + q^2$ used in [27].

Then we apply the lattice-based techniques [10] to solve the crucial modular Eq. 2 for some interesting cases. To be specific, we propose three key-related attacks on the RSA variants with modified Euler quotient. We reproduce the small private key attack as the result of [27] using the linearization technique [17] for an accurate range of solvable α.

Proposition 1. *Let $N = pq$ be an RSA modulus with two prime factors p, q of the same bit-size. Let $e = N^\alpha$ be a valid public key and $d = N^\delta$ be its corresponding private key such that $ed \equiv 1 \pmod{(p^2 - 1)(q^2 - 1)}$. Then modulus N of the RSA variants with modified Euler quotient can be efficiently factored if*

$$\delta < 2 - \sqrt{\alpha} \quad for \quad 1 \leq \alpha < 4.$$

We further provide the result of multiple private keys attack on the RSA variants with modified Euler quotient for the first time.

Proposition 2. *Let $N = pq$ be an RSA modulus with two prime factors p, q of the same bit-size. Let $e_i = N^\alpha$ be a valid public key and $d_i = N^\delta$ be its* *corresponding private key such that $e_i d_i \equiv 1 \pmod{(p^2 - 1)(q^2 - 1)}$ for $1 \leq i \leq n$. Then modulus N of the RSA variants with modified Euler quotient can be efficiently factored if*

$$\delta < 2 - \sqrt{\frac{4\alpha}{3n + 1}} \quad for \quad \frac{4}{3n + 1} < \alpha < 3n + 1.$$

When we have one single key pair, namely $n = 1$, the condition becomes $\delta < 2 - \sqrt{\alpha}$, which is identical to that in Proposition 1.

We also show the result of partial key exposure attack on the RSA variants with modified Euler quotient for the first time.

Proposition 3. *Let $N = pq$ be an RSA modulus with two prime factors p, q of the same bit-size. Let $e = N^\alpha$ be a valid public key and $d = N^\delta$ be its corresponding private key such that $ed \equiv 1 \pmod{(p^2 - 1)(q^2 - 1)}$. Given an approximation $\tilde{d}$ with known MSBs $d_M = N^{\gamma_M}$, LSBs $d_L = N^{\gamma_L}$ and unknown $\hat{d} = N^{\delta - \gamma}$ (for $\gamma = \gamma_M + \gamma_L$) such that $d = \tilde{d} + \hat{d}L = d_M M + \hat{d}L + d_L$ for $M := 2^{(\delta - \gamma_M) \log_2 N}$ and $L := 2^{\gamma_L \log_2 N}$. Then modulus N of the RSA variants with modified Euler quotient can be efficiently factored if*

$$\delta < \frac{3\gamma + 7 - 2\sqrt{3\alpha + 3\gamma + 1}}{3}.$$

We summarize our upper bounds with comparative cryptanalytic results on the standard RSA in Table 1. For simplicity, we set full-size public keys, namely $e \approx N$ in standard RSA and $e \approx N^2$ in RSA variants with $\omega(N)$ to show the respective conditions on δ. More precisely, n indicates the number of given key pairs in multiple private keys attack and γ (or N^γ) indicates the known key exposure in partial key exposure attack.

Table 1. Summary of three key-related attacks on RSA and its variant

	Standard RSA [30]	RSA variants [7, 13, 23]
Small private key attack	$\delta < 0.292$ [3]	$\delta < 0.585$
Multiple private keys attack	$\delta < 1 - \sqrt{\frac{2}{3n+1}}$ [36]	$\delta < 2 - \sqrt{\frac{8}{3n+1}}$
Partial key exposure attack	$\delta < \frac{\gamma+2-\sqrt{2-3\gamma^2}}{2}$ [37]	$\delta < \frac{3\gamma+7-2\sqrt{3\gamma+7}}{3}$

1.3 Organization

The rest of this paper is organized as follows. In Sect. 2, we review some facts and mathematical lemmas of lattice-based attacks. In Sect. 3, we present our small private key attack in details. In Sect. 4, we propose the multiple private keys attack on such RSA variants by applying Minkowski sum technique. In Sect. 5, we propose the partial key exposure attack for such RSA variants. We conclude the paper in Sect. 6.

2   Preliminaries

In this section, we introduce some notions of the lattice-based attacks, which include the LLL algorithm [24], Howgrave-Graham's lemma [18], Coppersmith's techniques [8,9]. One may refer to [10,25] for more details.

A lattice $\mathcal{L}$ spanned by linearly independent vectors $\boldsymbol{b}_1, \ldots, \boldsymbol{b}_w$ in $\mathbb{R}^n$ is the set of their integer linear combinations, which is denoted by $\mathcal{L}(\boldsymbol{b}_1, \ldots, \boldsymbol{b}_w) = \{\sum_{i=1}^{w} z_i \boldsymbol{b}_i : z_i \in \mathbb{Z}\}$. We call $(\boldsymbol{b}_1, \ldots, \boldsymbol{b}_w)$ a basis of $\mathcal{L}$ and w is the lattice dimension. If $w = n$, then $\mathcal{L}$ is called full-rank. In another way, $\boldsymbol{b}_i$'s can be regarded as row vectors to generate a basis matrix B. The lattice determinant is defined as $\det(\mathcal{L}) := \sqrt{\det(BB^{\mathrm{T}})}$, where B^{T} is a transpose of B. We have $\det(\mathcal{L}) = |\det(B)|$ for a full-rank lattice from the definition, which implies that B is a square matrix. Moreover, the determinant of a triangular basis matrix can be easily computed as the product of its diagonal entries.

In 1982, Lenstra et al. [24] proposed the so-called LLL algorithm that is practically used for finding approximately shortest lattice vectors, which plays an important role in the field of lattice-based cryptanalyses.

Lemma 1. *Let $\mathcal{L}$ be a lattice with determinant $\det(\mathcal{L})$ and vectors in $\mathbb{R}^n$. The LLL algorithm outputs a reduced basis $(\boldsymbol{v}_1, \boldsymbol{v}_2, \ldots, \boldsymbol{v}_w)$ in polynomial time in n, w and input length. For $1 \leq i \leq w$, the reduced vectors $\boldsymbol{v}_i$'s satisfy*

$$\|\boldsymbol{v}_i\| \leq 2^{\frac{w(w-1)}{4(w+1-i)}} \det(\mathcal{L})^{\frac{1}{w+1-i}}.$$

Howgrave-Graham [18] later showed how to judge whether the roots of a modular equation are also roots over the integers. This reformulation is more concise and straightforward compared with Coppersmith's original methods. For a given n-variate polynomial $g(x_1, \ldots, x_n) = \sum a_{i_1, \ldots, i_n} x_1^{i_1} \cdots x_n^{i_n}$, its norm is defined as $\|g(x_1, \ldots, x_n)\| := \sqrt{\sum |a_{i_1, \ldots, i_n}|^2}$. We provide the following lemma and then discuss the combination of Lemmas 1 and 2.

Lemma 2. *Let $g(x_1, \ldots, x_n) \in \mathbb{Z}[x_1, \ldots, x_n]$ be an integer polynomial that is a sum of at most w monomials. Suppose that*

1. *$g(x_1', \ldots, x_n') = 0 \pmod{R}$, where $|x_1'| < X_1, \ldots, |x_n'| < X_n$, and*
2. *$\|g(x_1 X_1, \ldots, x_n X_n)\| < R/\sqrt{w}$.*

Then $g(x_1', \ldots, x_n') = 0$ holds over the integers.

The main idea of the lattice-based attacks is to construct a set of shift polynomials modulo an integer R with the common roots and then reduce them to several equations over the integers by the LLL algorithm. The basis matrix consists of the shift polynomials' coefficient vectors, which come from a given modular equation. It spans a lattice of dimension w and we use the LLL algorithm to obtain short lattice vectors that correspond to the polynomial forms. If the norms of the polynomials are sufficiently small, these equations still hold over the integers. Eventually, we can efficiently extract the common roots by Gröbner bases computation or resultant computation. Notice that the linearization technique makes it easier to construct a triangular matrix and hence simplifies the whole analysis.

The above fundamental lemmas indicate the final condition, which can be roughly summarized as

$$\det(\mathcal{L}) < R^w. \tag{3}$$

We here do not discuss more how to solve integer polynomial equations since it makes use of the essential idea of solving modular equations by adding an auxiliary parameter. See Coron's reformulations [11,12] for the detail. We should note that solving multivariate equations is heuristic because the newly derived polynomials are not guaranteed to be algebraically independent. In this paper, we assume that the polynomials derived from the reduced vectors of the LLL algorithm are algebraically independent as discussed in the literature of lattice-based attacks on RSA and its variants [3,21]. In fact, there are barely works that contradict this assumption.

3 Small Private Key Attack

In this section, we aim to solve the crucial modular Eq. 2 for sufficient small private key d. Applying the linearization technique, we can reproduce the insecure bound on d for the RSA variants with modified Euler quotient.

In order to find all small roots (x, y) of the bivariate modular equation $xy + Ax + 1 \equiv 0 \pmod{e}$. We first transform the original polynomial $xy + Ax + 1$ into $Ax + z$ by letting $z := xy + 1$. The shift polynomials $g_{[i,j,k]}(x, y, z)$ are defined in the following form for $f(x, y, z) := Ax + z$,

$$g_{[i,j,k]}(x, y, z) := x^i y^j f^k(x, y, z) e^{s-k} = x^i y^j (Ax + z)^k e^{s-k},$$

where s is a fixed positive integer and $i, j, k \in \mathbb{N}$. We denote the set of shift polynomials by $\mathcal{G} \cup \mathcal{H}$ for

$$\mathcal{G} := \{g_{[i,j,k]}(x, y, z) : (i, j, k) \in \mathcal{I}_{\mathcal{G}}\},$$
$$\mathcal{H} := \{g_{[i,j,k]}(x, y, z) : (i, j, k) \in \mathcal{I}_{\mathcal{H}}\},$$

where two index sets $\mathcal{I}_{\mathcal{G}}$ and $\mathcal{I}_{\mathcal{H}}$ are defined by

$$\mathcal{I}_{\mathcal{G}} := \{(i, j, k) : j = 0; i = 0, \ldots, s; k = 0, \ldots, s - i\},$$
$$\mathcal{I}_{\mathcal{H}} := \{(i, j, k) : i = 0; k = 0, \ldots, s; j = 1, \ldots, \tau k\},$$

for a parameter $0 \leq \tau \leq 1$ to be optimized later. It is clear that all the shift polynomials share the small roots modulo e^s. The polynomial and monomial orders $\prec$ are defined as $g_{[i,j,k]} \prec g_{[i',j',k']}$ and $x^i y^j z^k \prec x^{i'} y^{j'} z^{k'}$, respectively if (1) $i + k < i' + k'$; or (2) $i + k = i' + k'$ and $k < k'$; or (3) $i = i'$, $k = k'$ and $j < j'$.

We can substitute each occurrence of xy by the term $z - 1$. The lattice basis matrix is generated by taking the coefficient vectors of $g_{[i,j,k]}(xX, yY, zZ)$ as row vectors, where X, Y and Z denote the upper bounds on the roots (x, y, z). Additionally, the rows and columns are arranged according to above orders $\prec$, which guarantees that the lattice basis matrix is triangular. Table 2 shows a toy example for two parameters $s = 2$ and $\tau = 1$, where symbols "–" indicate the non-zero off-diagonal entries, and f denotes $AxX + zZ$.

Table 2. A toy example of the lattice basis matrix for $s = 2$ and $\tau = 1$

		1	x	z	yz	x^2	xz	z^2	yz^2	y^2z^2
$g_{[0,0,0]}$	e^2	e^2								
$g_{[1,0,0]}$	xXe^2		e^2X							
$g_{[0,0,1]}$	fe		$-$	eZ						
$g_{[0,1,1]}$	yYf	$-$		$-$	YZ					
$g_{[2,0,0]}$	$(xX)^2e^2$					e^2X^2				
$g_{[1,0,1]}$	$xXfe$					$-$	eXZ			
$g_{[0,0,2]}$	f^2					$-$	$-$	Z^2		
$g_{[0,1,2]}$	yYf^2		$-$	$-$			$-$	$-$	YZ^2	
$g_{[0,2,2]}$	$(yY)^2f^2$	$-$		$-$	$-$			$-$	$-$	Y^2Z^2

Since we have $e = N^\alpha$ and $d = N^\delta$, we can figure out $X = N^{\alpha+\delta-2}, Y = N$ and $Z = N^{\alpha+\delta-1}$. We are able to compute the determinant $\det(\mathcal{L})$ by counting the numbers of X, Y, Z and e appearing in the diagonal entries respectively, which signify the contributions of the shift polynomials to $\det(\mathcal{L})$. We omit the rounding of τk since it is negligible in our asymptotic analysis for sufficiently large s.

We compute the dimension w of the full-rank lattice and the contributions of the shift polynomials denoted by n_X, n_Y, n_Z and n_e, respectively.

$$w = \sum_{(i,j,k)\in\mathcal{I}_\mathcal{G}\cup\mathcal{I}_\mathcal{H}} 1 = \sum_{i=0}^{s}\sum_{k=0}^{s-i}1 + \sum_{k=0}^{s}\sum_{j=1}^{\tau k}1 = \frac{1+\tau}{2}s^2 + o(s^2),$$

$$n_X = \sum_{(i,j,k)\in\mathcal{I}_\mathcal{G}\cup\mathcal{I}_\mathcal{H}} i = \sum_{i=0}^{s}\sum_{k=0}^{s-i}i = \frac{1}{6}s^3 + o(s^3),$$

$$n_Y = \sum_{(i,j,k)\in\mathcal{I}_\mathcal{G}\cup\mathcal{I}_\mathcal{H}} j = \sum_{k=0}^{s}\sum_{j=1}^{\tau k}j = \frac{\tau^2}{6}s^3 + o(s^3),$$

$$n_Z = \sum_{(i,j,k)\in\mathcal{I}_\mathcal{G}\cup\mathcal{I}_\mathcal{H}} k = \sum_{i=0}^{s}\sum_{k=0}^{s-i}k + \sum_{k=0}^{s}\sum_{j=1}^{\tau k}k = \frac{1+2\tau}{6}s^3 + o(s^3),$$

$$n_e = \sum_{(i,j,k)\in\mathcal{I}_\mathcal{G}\cup\mathcal{I}_\mathcal{H}} (s-k) = \sum_{i=0}^{s}\sum_{k=0}^{s-i}(s-k) + \sum_{k=0}^{s}\sum_{j=1}^{\tau k}(s-k) = \frac{2+\tau}{6}s^3 + o(s^3).$$

From above rough condition $3 \det(\mathcal{L}) < R^w$ for $\det(\mathcal{L}) = X^{n_X} Y^{n_Y} Z^{n_Z} e^{n_e}$ and $R = e^s$, we have

$$(\alpha + \delta - 2) + \tau^2 + (1 + 2\tau)(\alpha + \delta - 1) + (2 + \tau)\alpha < 3(1 + \tau)\alpha,$$

when dealing with the exponents and omitting other lower order terms of s. It can be simplified to

$$\tau^2 + (2\delta - 2)\tau + \alpha + 2\delta - 3 < 0.$$

The value of the left side reaches its minimum by setting $\tau = 1 - \delta$ and then the inequality becomes

$$\delta^2 - 4\delta - \alpha + 4 > 0.$$

Therefore, we obtain the final condition

$$\delta < 2 - \sqrt{\alpha}.$$

Note that $0 \leq \tau = 1 - \delta \leq 1$ and hence we have $0 \leq \delta \leq 1$. Combining it with $\alpha + \delta \geq 2$ and $\delta < 2 - \sqrt{\alpha}$, we have $1 \leq \alpha < 4$ that is our complete solvable range of α. Thus, we attain the bound of Proposition 1 as required.

4   Multiple Private Keys Attack

In this section, we propose the multiple private keys attack on the RSA variants with modified Euler quotient. To specify the analytic situation for given n key pairs, we define the following general multiple private keys attack scenario.

Let N be the product of two primes p, q of the same bit-size. Let $e_i = N^\alpha$ and $d_i = N^\delta$ for $1 \leq i \leq n$ such that $e_i d_i \equiv 1 \pmod{\omega(N)}$, where $\omega(N) = (p^2 - 1)(q^2 - 1)$. Given N and n key pairs (e_i, d_i) (for $1 \leq i \leq n$), the goal is to efficiently factor N.

In this case, we need to solve the simultaneous modular equations

$$\begin{cases} f_1(x_1, y) := x_1(y + A) + 1 \equiv 0 \pmod{e_1} \\ f_2(x_2, y) := x_2(y + A) + 1 \equiv 0 \pmod{e_2} \\ \quad \vdots \\ f_n(x_n, y) := x_n(y + A) + 1 \equiv 0 \pmod{e_n} \end{cases} \tag{4}$$

for $A := (N + 1)^2$ and the roots $(x_1, x_2, \ldots, x_n, y) = (k_1, k_2, \ldots, k_n, -(p + q)^2)$ whose values are bounded by $X_1 = \cdots = X_n = N^{\alpha + \delta - 2}$ and $Y = N$.

To deal with above simultaneous modular Eq. 4, Aono [1] proposed Minkowski sum based lattice constructions. We also apply this tool to provide the generation of the shift polynomials. The underlying shift polynomials are defined by

$$g_{i_k, j_k}^{(k)}(x_k, y) := x_k^{i_k - j_k} f_k^{j_k}(x_k, y) e_k^{s - j_k}$$

with $0 \leq j_k \leq i_k \leq s$ and $i_k, j_k \in \mathbb{N}$ for $1 \leq k \leq n$. It is clear that we have $g_{i_k, j_k}^{(k)}(x_k, y) \equiv 0 \pmod{e_k^s}$ for each k. We define the same Minkowski sum based shift polynomials as [1] by

$$g_{i_1, \ldots, i_n, j}(x_1, \ldots, x_n, y) := \sum_{j_1 + \cdots + j_n = j} a_{j_1, \ldots, j_n} g_{i_1, j_1}^{(1)} g_{i_2, j_2}^{(2)} \cdots g_{i_n, j_n}^{(n)}$$

for a particular $a_{j_1, \ldots, j_n}$ such that the corresponding diagonal entry in the basis matrix is

$$X_1^{i_1} \cdots X_n^{i_n} Y^j e_1^{s - \min\{i_1, j\}} \cdots e_n^{s - \min\{i_n, j\}}.$$

Thus, all the shift polynomials share the common roots $(x_1, x_2, \ldots, x_n, y) = (k_1, \ldots, k_n, -(p+q)^2)$ modulo $(e_1 \cdots e_n)^s$. We consider the shift polynomials with $\max\{i_1, \ldots, i_n\} \leq j$. Applying a useful criterion from [36], we compare the sizes of the diagonal entries with the size of the modulus to choose as many helpful polynomials as possible. It requires that

$$X_1^{i_1} \cdots X_n^{i_n} Y^j e_1^{s - i_1} \cdots e_n^{s - i_n} \leq (e_1 \cdots e_n)^s,$$

which leads to

$$(\alpha + \delta - 2) \sum_{k=1}^{n} i_k + j + \alpha n s - \alpha \sum_{k=1}^{n} i_k \leq \alpha n s.$$

That is $j \leq (2 - \delta) \sum_{k=1}^{n} i_k$. Therefore, we select the shift polynomials over the index set

$$\mathcal{I} := \{(i_1, \ldots, i_n, j) : 0 \leq i_1, i_2, \ldots, i_n \leq s; 0 \leq j \leq (2 - \delta) \sum_{k=1}^{n} i_k\}.$$

The lattice basis matrix is triangular as discussed in [1,36]. We follow a similar analysis in Sect. 3 (ignoring lower order terms of s) to compute the lattice dimension

$$w = \sum_{(i_1, \ldots, i_n, j) \in \mathcal{I}} 1 = \frac{n(2 - \delta)}{2} s^{n+1},$$

and respective contributions of the diagonal entries to the determinant that are denoted by n_{X_k}, n_Y and n_{e_k} for $1 \leq k \leq n$,

$$n_{X_1} = \cdots = n_{X_n} = \sum_{(i_1, \ldots, i_n, j) \in \mathcal{I}} i_k = \frac{(3n+1)(2-\delta)}{12} s^{n+2},$$

$$n_Y = \sum_{(i_1, \ldots, i_n, j) \in \mathcal{I}} j = \frac{n(3n+1)(2-\delta)^2}{24} s^{n+2},$$

$$n_{e_1} = \cdots = n_{e_n} = \sum_{(i_1, \ldots, i_n, j) \in \mathcal{I}} (s - \min\{i_n, j\}) = \frac{2 + (3n-1)(2-\delta)}{12} s^{n+2}.$$

We can find solutions of the simultaneous modular Eq. 4 if the condition 3 holds, that is

$$X_1^{n_{X_1}} \cdots X_n^{n_{X_n}} Y^{n_Y} e_1^{n_{e_1}} \cdots e_n^{n_{e_n}} < (e_1 \cdots e_n)^{sw},$$

which leads to

$$2n(3n+1)(2-\delta)(\alpha+\delta-2) + n(3n+1)(2-\delta)^2 + n(4-(6n+2)(2-\delta))\alpha < 0.$$

It can be reduced to

$$-(3n+1)(2-\delta)^2 + 4\alpha < 0.$$

Finally, we derive the condition for the multiple private keys attack scenario

$$\delta < 2 - \sqrt{\frac{4\alpha}{3n+1}}.$$

The range of solvable α is determined by $2 - \sqrt{\frac{4\alpha}{3n+1}} > 0$ and $\alpha + 2 - \sqrt{\frac{4\alpha}{3n+1}} > 2$, which imply

$$\frac{4}{3n+1} < \alpha < 3n+1$$

as claimed in Proposition 2.

5 Partial Key Exposure Attack

In this section, we propose the partial key exposure attack on the RSA variants with modified Euler quotient. To specify the analytic situation for given leakage of the private key, we define the following general partial key exposure attack scenario.

Let N be the product of two primes p, q of the same bit-size. Let $e = N^\alpha$ and $d = N^\delta$ such that $ed \equiv 1 \pmod{\omega(N)}$, where $\omega(N) = (p^2-1)(q^2-1)$. Given N, e and $\tilde{d}$ (i.e. MSBs d_M and LSBs d_L) that is a known approximation of d satisfying

$$d = \tilde{d} + \hat{d}L = d_M M + \hat{d}L + d_L$$

for $M := 2^{(\delta-\gamma_M)\log_2 N}$ and $L := 2^{\gamma_L \log_2 N}$, which implies that $|\hat{d}| < N^{\delta-\gamma}$ for $\gamma := \gamma_M + \gamma_L$, the target is to efficiently factor N.

Recall that the modified key Eq. 1 is $ed = k(p^2-1)(q^2-1) + 1$. Since $d = \tilde{d} + \hat{d}L$, we substitute it with its approximation and obtain

$$e(\tilde{d} + \hat{d}L) = k(p^2-1)(q^2-1) + 1.$$

We now focus on the integer equation

$$f(x, y, z) := 1 - e\tilde{d} + eLx + y((N+1)^2 + z) \tag{5}$$

with small roots $x = -\hat{d}$, $y = k$ and $z = -(p+q)^2$, whose values are bounded by $X = N^{\delta-\gamma}$, $Y = N^{\alpha+\delta-2}$ and $Z = N$, respectively. If we discover the small roots of $f(x, y, z)$, we can factor the RSA modulus N.

We turn to solving the integer polynomial 5 by applying Jochemsz and May's strategy [20]. A similar construction is also described in [39]. We first give the definition of the auxiliary parameter $W := \|f(xX, yY, zZ)\|_\infty$, namely l_∞-norm of a certain polynomial. For our integer polynomial 5, we have

$$W = \max\{|1 - e\tilde{d}|, |eLX|, |Y(N+1)^2|, |YZ|\} = N^{\alpha+\delta}.$$

We set a suitable integer $R := WX^{s-1}Y^{s-1}Z^{s-1+\tau s}$ (as a modulus) for a fixed positive integer s and $\tau \geq 0$ to be optimized later. We then perform a transformation on the original polynomial 4 by

$$f'(x, y, z) := (1 - e\tilde{d})^{-1} f(x, y, z) \pmod{R}.$$

The shift polynomials $g^{\mathcal{G}}_{[i,j,k]}(x, y, z)$ and $g^{\mathcal{H}}_{[i,j,k]}(x, y, z)$ are defined in the following forms,

$$g^{\mathcal{G}}_{[i,j,k]}(x, y, z) := x^i y^j z^k f'(x, y, z) X^{s-1-i} Y^{s-1-j} Z^{s-1+\tau s-k},$$
$$g^{\mathcal{H}}_{[i,j,k]}(x, y, z) := x^i y^j z^k R,$$

for $i, j, k \in \mathbb{N}$. We denote the set of shift polynomials by $\mathcal{G} \cup \mathcal{H}$, where

$$\mathcal{G} := \{g^{\mathcal{G}}_{[i,j,k]}(x, y, z) : (i, j, k) \in \mathcal{I}_{\mathcal{G}}\},$$
$$\mathcal{H} := \{g^{\mathcal{H}}_{[i,j,k]}(x, y, z) : (i, j, k) \in \mathcal{I}_{\mathcal{H}} \setminus \mathcal{I}_{\mathcal{G}}\},$$

for two index sets $\mathcal{I}_{\mathcal{G}}$ and $\mathcal{I}_{\mathcal{H}}$ defined by

$$\mathcal{I}_{\mathcal{G}} := \{(i, j, k) : i = 0, \ldots, s-1; j = 0, \ldots, s-1-i; k = 0, \ldots, j+\tau s\},$$
$$\mathcal{I}_{\mathcal{H}} := \{(i, j, k) : i = 0, \ldots, s; j = 0, \ldots, s-i; k = 0, \ldots, j+\tau s\}.$$

It is noticeable that all the shift polynomials share the common roots $(x, y, z) = (-\hat{d}, k, -(p+q)^2)$ modulo R. The polynomial and monomial orders are quite straightforward as mentioned in [20]. Therefore, we can construct a triangular basis matrix with diagonal entries $X^{s-1}Y^{s-1}Z^{s-1+\tau s}$ for $\mathcal{G}$ and $X^i Y^j Z^k R = WX^{s-1+i}Y^{s-1+j}Z^{s-1+\tau s+k}$ for $\mathcal{H}$. We then follow a similar analysis in Sect. 3 (ignoring lower order terms of s) to compute the lattice dimension

$$w = \sum_{(i,j,k)\in\mathcal{I}_{\mathcal{G}}} 1 + \sum_{(i,j,k)\in\mathcal{I}_{\mathcal{H}}\setminus\mathcal{I}_{\mathcal{G}}} 1 = \frac{1+3\tau}{6}s^3.$$

Recall that the rough condition 3 $\det(\mathcal{L}) < R^w$ indicates

$$\prod_{(i,j,k)\in\mathcal{I}_{\mathcal{G}}} X^{s-1}Y^{s-1}Z^{s-1+\tau s} \prod_{(i,j,k)\in\mathcal{I}_{\mathcal{H}}\setminus\mathcal{I}_{\mathcal{G}}} WX^{s-1+i}Y^{s-1+j}Z^{s-1+\tau s+k}$$
$$< \left(WX^{s-1}Y^{s-1}Z^{s-1+\tau s}\right)^w.$$

Thus, we can find solutions of the integer Eq. 5 when $X^{n_X} Y^{n_Y} Z^{n_Z} < W^{n_W}$ (ignoring lower order terms of s) for

$$n_X = \sum_{(i,j,k)\in\mathcal{I}_\mathcal{G}} (s-1) + \sum_{(i,j,k)\in\mathcal{I}_\mathcal{H}\setminus\mathcal{I}_\mathcal{G}} (s-1+i) - (s-1)w = \frac{1+3\tau}{6}s^3,$$

$$n_Y = \sum_{(i,j,k)\in\mathcal{I}_\mathcal{G}} (s-1) + \sum_{(i,j,k)\in\mathcal{I}_\mathcal{H}\setminus\mathcal{I}_\mathcal{G}} (s-1+j) - (s-1)w = \frac{2+3\tau}{6}s^3,$$

$$n_Z = \sum_{(i,j,k)\in\mathcal{I}_\mathcal{G}} (s-1+\tau s) + \sum_{(i,j,k)\in\mathcal{I}_\mathcal{H}\setminus\mathcal{I}_\mathcal{G}} (s-1+\tau s+k) - (s-1+\tau s)w$$

$$= \frac{1+3\tau+3\tau^2}{6}s^3,$$

$$n_W = w - \sum_{(i,j,k)\in\mathcal{I}_\mathcal{H}\setminus\mathcal{I}_\mathcal{G}} 1 = \sum_{(i,j,k)\in\mathcal{I}_\mathcal{G}} 1 = \frac{1+3\tau}{6}s^3.$$

Substituting them for the inequality, we obtain

$$(1+3\tau)(\delta-\gamma) + (2+3\tau)(\alpha+\delta-2) + (1+3\tau+3\tau^2) < (1+3\tau)(\alpha+\delta),$$

which leads to

$$3\tau^2 + (3\delta - 3\gamma - 3)\tau + \alpha + 2\delta - \gamma - 3 < 0.$$

The value of the left side reaches its minimum by setting $\tau = (1+\gamma-\delta)/2$ and we have

$$\delta < \frac{3\gamma + 7 - 2\sqrt{3\alpha + 3\gamma + 1}}{3}$$

as claimed in Proposition 3.

It is also possible to apply known bounds given in [20, Appendix B] to solve an integer polynomial of special forms including our integer polynomial 5. We provide a useful lemma as follows.

Lemma 3. Let $f(x_1, x_2, x_3) = a_0 + a_1 x_1 + x_2(a_2 + x_3) \in \mathbb{Z}[x_1, x_2, x_3]$ be an integer polynomial. Suppose that x_1, x_2, x_3 are bounded by X_1, X_2, X_3 respectively, and $W = \max\{|a_0|, |a_1|X_1, |a_2|X_2, X_2 X_3\}$. Then the roots can be found for an optimized $\tau \geq 0$ if

$$X_1^{1+3\tau} X_2^{2+3\tau} X_3^{1+3\tau+3\tau^2} < W^{1+3\tau}.$$

We directly apply Lemma 3 with $X_1 = N^{\delta-\gamma}$, $X_2 = N^{\alpha+\delta-2}$, $X_3 = N$ and $W = N^{\alpha+\delta}$ for our attack and have

$$(1+3\tau)(\delta-\gamma) + (2+3\tau)(\alpha+\delta-2) + (1+3\tau+3\tau^2) < (1+3\tau)(\alpha+\delta),$$

that is equivalent to

$$3\tau^2 + (3\delta - 3\gamma - 3)\tau + \alpha + 2\delta - \gamma - 3 < 0,$$

which gives the same result as stated in Proposition 3.

6 Concluding Remarks

We study some key-related attacks on the RSA variants with modified Euler quotient $\omega(N) = (p^2 - 1)(q^2 - 1)$ in this paper. Some interesting cases such as given more key pairs and given some key exposure are analyzed like previous works in the literature. We propose the multiple private keys attack that extends the small private key attack for n key pairs. Since the case of $n = 1$ corresponds to the small private key attack, it is a meaningful extension of the latter.

For the partial key exposure attack, a preliminary result is provided assuming we already know some most and least significant bits of the private key. However, there exist several methods to improve the results for given only the most significant bits or the least significant bits like [39]. A combined scenario i.e. partial key exposure attack with multiple key pairs has also been analyzed in [38]. To generalize partial key exposure attacks with only MSBs, LSBs or multiple key pairs on the RSA variants with modified Euler quotient remains as future work.

Acknowledgments. The authors would like to thank the anonymous reviewers for their valuable comments and suggestions. This work was partially supported by National Natural Science Foundation of China (Grant Nos. 61522210, 61632013).

References

1. Aono, Y.: Minkowski sum based lattice construction for multivariate simultaneous Coppersmith's technique and applications to RSA. In: Boyd, C., Simpson, L. (eds.) ACISP 2013. LNCS, vol. 7959, pp. 88–103. Springer, Heidelberg (2013). https://doi.org/10.1007/978-3-642-39059-3_7
2. Blömer, J., May, A.: New partial key exposure attacks on RSA. In: Boneh, D. (ed.) CRYPTO 2003. LNCS, vol. 2729, pp. 27–43. Springer, Heidelberg (2003). https://doi.org/10.1007/978-3-540-45146-4_2
3. Boneh, D., Durfee, G.: Cryptanalysis of RSA with private key d less than $N^{0.292}$. In: Stern, J. (ed.) EUROCRYPT 1999. LNCS, vol. 1592, pp. 1–11. Springer, Heidelberg (1999). https://doi.org/10.1007/3-540-48910-X_1
4. Boneh, D., Durfee, G., Frankel, Y.: An attack on RSA given a small fraction of the private key bits. In: Ohta, K., Pei, D. (eds.) ASIACRYPT 1998. LNCS, vol. 1514, pp. 25–34. Springer, Heidelberg (1998). https://doi.org/10.1007/3-540-49649-1_3
5. Bunder, M., Nitaj, A., Susilo, W., Tonien, J.: A new attack on three variants of the RSA cryptosystem. In: Liu, J.K., Steinfeld, R. (eds.) ACISP 2016. LNCS, vol. 9723, pp. 258–268. Springer, Cham (2016). https://doi.org/10.1007/978-3-319-40367-0_16
6. Bunder, M., Tonien, J.: New attack on the RSA cryptosystem based on continued fractions. Malays. J. Math. Sci. **11**(S3), 45–57 (2017)
7. Castagnos, G.: An efficient probabilistic public-key cryptosystem over quadratic fields quotients. Finite Fields Appl. **13**(3), 563–576 (2007)
8. Coppersmith, D.: Finding a small root of a bivariate integer equation; factoring with high bits known. In: Maurer, U. (ed.) EUROCRYPT 1996. LNCS, vol. 1070, pp. 178–189. Springer, Heidelberg (1996). https://doi.org/10.1007/3-540-68339-9_16

9. Coppersmith, D.: Finding a small root of a univariate modular equation. In: Maurer, U. (ed.) EUROCRYPT 1996. LNCS, vol. 1070, pp. 155–165. Springer, Heidelberg (1996). https://doi.org/10.1007/3-540-68339-9_14

10. Coppersmith, D.: Small solutions to polynomial equations, and low exponent RSA vulnerabilities. J. Cryptol. **10**(4), 233–260 (1997)

11. Coron, J.-S.: Finding small roots of bivariate integer polynomial equations revisited. In: Cachin, C., Camenisch, J.L. (eds.) EUROCRYPT 2004. LNCS, vol. 3027, pp. 492–505. Springer, Heidelberg (2004). https://doi.org/10.1007/978-3-540-24676-3_29

12. Coron, J.-S.: Finding small roots of bivariate integer polynomial equations: a direct approach. In: Menezes, A. (ed.) CRYPTO 2007. LNCS, vol. 4622, pp. 379–394. Springer, Heidelberg (2007). https://doi.org/10.1007/978-3-540-74143-5_21

13. Elkamchouchi, H., Elshenawy, K., Shaban, H.: Extended RSA cryptosystem and digital signature schemes in the domain of Gaussian integers. In: ICCS 2002, vol. 1, pp. 91–95. IEEE (2002)

14. Ernst, M., Jochemsz, E., May, A., de Weger, B.: Partial key exposure attacks on RSA up to full size exponents. In: Cramer, R. (ed.) EUROCRYPT 2005. LNCS, vol. 3494, pp. 371–386. Springer, Heidelberg (2005). https://doi.org/10.1007/11426639_22

15. Fiat, A.: Batch RSA. In: Brassard, G. (ed.) CRYPTO 1989. LNCS, vol. 435, pp. 175–185. Springer, New York (1990). https://doi.org/10.1007/0-387-34805-0_17

16. Halderman, J.A., Schoen, S.D., Heninger, N., Clarkson, W., Paul, W., Calandrino, J.A., Feldman, A.J., Appelbaum, J., Felten, E.W.: Lest we remember: cold-boot attacks on encryption keys. Commun. ACM **52**(5), 91–98 (2009)

17. Herrmann, M., May, A.: Maximizing small root bounds by linearization and applications to small secret exponent RSA. In: Nguyen, P.Q., Pointcheval, D. (eds.) PKC 2010. LNCS, vol. 6056, pp. 53–69. Springer, Heidelberg (2010). https://doi.org/10.1007/978-3-642-13013-7_4

18. Howgrave-Graham, N.: Finding small roots of univariate modular equations revisited. In: Darnell, M. (ed.) Cryptography and Coding 1997. LNCS, vol. 1355, pp. 131–142. Springer, Heidelberg (1997). https://doi.org/10.1007/BFb0024458

19. Howgrave-Graham, N., Seifert, J.-P.: Extending Wiener's attack in the presence of many decrypting exponents. CQRE 1999. LNCS, vol. 1740, pp. 153–166. Springer, Heidelberg (1999). https://doi.org/10.1007/3-540-46701-7_14

20. Jochemsz, E., May, A.: A strategy for finding roots of multivariate polynomials with new applications in attacking RSA variants. In: Lai, X., Chen, K. (eds.) ASIACRYPT 2006. LNCS, vol. 4284, pp. 267–282. Springer, Heidelberg (2006). https://doi.org/10.1007/11935230_18

21. Jochemsz, E., May, A.: A polynomial time attack on RSA with private CRT-exponents smaller than $N^{0.073}$. In: Menezes, A. (ed.) CRYPTO 2007. LNCS, vol. 4622, pp. 395–411. Springer, Heidelberg (2007). https://doi.org/10.1007/978-3-540-74143-5_22

22. Kocher, P.C.: Timing attacks on implementations of Diffie-Hellman, RSA, DSS, and other systems. In: Koblitz, N. (ed.) CRYPTO 1996. LNCS, vol. 1109, pp. 104–113. Springer, Heidelberg (1996). https://doi.org/10.1007/3-540-68697-5_9

23. Kuwakado, H., Koyama, K., Tsuruoka, Y.: New RSA-type scheme based on singular cubic curves $y^2 \equiv x^3 + bx^2 \pmod{n}$. IEICE Trans. Fundam. Electron. Commun. Comput. Sci. **E78–A**(1), 27–33 (1995)

24. Lenstra, A.K., Lenstra, H.W., Lovász, L.: Factoring polynomials with rational coefficients. Math. Ann. **261**(4), 515–534 (1982)

25. May, A.: Using LLL-reduction for solving RSA and factorization problems. In: Nguyen, P.Q., Vallée, B. (eds.) The LLL Algorithm - Survey and Applications. ISC, pp. 315–348. Springer, Heidelberg (2010). https://doi.org/10.1007/978-3-642-02295-1_10

26. Peng, L., Hu, L., Lu, Y., Sarkar, S., Xu, J., Huang, Z.: Cryptanalysis of variants of RSA with multiple small secret exponents. In: Biryukov, A., Goyal, V. (eds.) INDOCRYPT 2015. LNCS, vol. 9462, pp. 105–123. Springer, Cham (2015). https://doi.org/10.1007/978-3-319-26617-6_6

27. Peng, L., Hu, L., Lu, Y., Wei, H.: An improved analysis on three variants of the RSA cryptosystem. In: Chen, K., Lin, D., Yung, M. (eds.) Inscrypt 2016. LNCS, vol. 10143, pp. 140–149. Springer, Cham (2017). https://doi.org/10.1007/978-3-319-54705-3_9

28. Quisquater, J.J., Couvreur, C.: Fast decipherment algorithm for RSA public-key cryptosystem. Electron. Lett. **18**(21), 905–907 (1982)

29. Ristenpart, T., Tromer, E., Shacham, H., Savage, S.: Hey, you, get off of my cloud: exploring information leakage in third-party compute clouds. In: Al-Shaer, E., Jha, S., Keromytis, A.D. (eds.) ACM CCS 2009, pp. 199–212. ACM Press, Chicago (2009)

30. Rivest, R.L., Shamir, A., Adleman, L.: A method for obtaining digital signatures and public-key cryptosystems. Commun. ACM **21**(2), 120–126 (1978)

31. Sarkar, S.: Small secret exponent attack on RSA variant with modulus $N = p^r q$. Des. Codes Cryptogr. **73**(2), 383–392 (2014)

32. Sarkar, S.: Revisiting prime power RSA. Discrete Appl. Math. **203**, 127–133 (2016)

33. Sarkar, S., Maitra, S.: Cryptanalytic results on 'Dual CRT' and 'Common Prime' RSA. Des. Codes Cryptogr. **66**(1–3), 157–174 (2013)

34. Sarkar, S., Venkateswarlu, A.: Partial key exposure attack on CRT-RSA. In: Meier, W., Mukhopadhyay, D. (eds.) INDOCRYPT 2014. LNCS, vol. 8885, pp. 255–264. Springer, Cham (2014). https://doi.org/10.1007/978-3-319-13039-2_15

35. Takagi, T.: Fast RSA-type cryptosystem modulo $p^k q$. In: Krawczyk, H. (ed.) CRYPTO 1998. LNCS, vol. 1462, pp. 318–326. Springer, Heidelberg (1998). https://doi.org/10.1007/BFb0055738

36. Takayasu, A., Kunihiro, N.: Cryptanalysis of RSA with multiple small secret exponents. In: Susilo, W., Mu, Y. (eds.) ACISP 2014. LNCS, vol. 8544, pp. 176–191. Springer, Cham (2014). https://doi.org/10.1007/978-3-319-08344-5_12

37. Takayasu, A., Kunihiro, N.: Partial key exposure attacks on RSA: achieving the Boneh-Durfee bound. In: Joux, A., Youssef, A. (eds.) SAC 2014. LNCS, vol. 8781, pp. 345–362. Springer, Cham (2014). https://doi.org/10.1007/978-3-319-13051-4_21

38. Takayasu, A., Kunihiro, N.: Partial key exposure attacks on RSA with multiple exponent pairs. In: Liu, J.K., Steinfeld, R. (eds.) ACISP 2016. LNCS, vol. 9723, pp. 243–257. Springer, Cham (2016). https://doi.org/10.1007/978-3-319-40367-0_15

39. Takayasu, A., Kunihiro, N.: A tool kit for partial key exposure attacks on RSA. In: Handschuh, H. (ed.) CT-RSA 2017. LNCS, vol. 10159, pp. 58–73. Springer, Cham (2017). https://doi.org/10.1007/978-3-319-52153-4_4

40. Wiener, M.J.: Cryptanalysis of short RSA secret exponents. IEEE Trans. Inf. Theory **36**(3), 553–558 (1990)

41. Zheng, M., Hu, H.: Cryptanalysis of prime power RSA with two private exponents. Sci. China Inf. Sci. **58**(11), 1–8 (2015)

Saber: Module-LWR Based Key Exchange, CPA-Secure Encryption and CCA-Secure KEM

Jan-Pieter D'Anvers, Angshuman Karmakar$^{(\boxtimes)}$, Sujoy Sinha Roy, and Frederik Vercauteren

imec-COSIC, KU Leuven, Kasteelpark Arenberg 10, Bus 2452, 3001 Leuven-Heverlee, Belgium
{janpieter.danvers,angshuman.karmakar,sujoy.sinharoy, frederik.vercauteren}@esat.kuleuven.be

Abstract. In this paper, we introduce Saber, a package of cryptographic primitives whose security relies on the hardness of the Module Learning With Rounding problem (Mod-LWR). We first describe a secure Diffie-Hellman type key exchange protocol, which is then transformed into an IND-CPA encryption scheme and finally into an IND-CCA secure key encapsulation mechanism using a post-quantum version of the Fujisaki-Okamoto transform. The design goals of this package were simplicity, efficiency and flexibility resulting in the following choices: all integer moduli are powers of 2 avoiding modular reduction and rejection sampling entirely; the use of LWR halves the amount of randomness required compared to LWE-based schemes and reduces bandwidth; the module structure provides flexibility by reusing one core component for multiple security levels. A constant-time AVX2 optimized software implementation of the KEM with parameters providing more than 128 bits of post-quantum security, requires only 101K, 125K and 129K cycles for key generation, encapsulation and decapsulation respectively on a Dell laptop with an Intel i7-Haswell processor.

1 Introduction

The threat of quantum computers, which break most widely used public key cryptographic primitives, has sparked a rising interest in post-quantum cryptography. This is emphasized by organizations such as ETSI and NIST that are looking towards standardization of post-quantum cryptography [18]. Lattice based cryptography is one of the most promising candidates that are resilient to all known quantum attacks. Examples include NTRU based schemes [11,25,37] and protocols based on the (ring)-Learning With Errors (LWE) problem: Alkim et al. [4] presented 'A New Hope', based on the ring-LWE problem; Bos et al. [17] introduced an alternative scheme called 'Frodo' based solely on LWE, but suffers from higher bandwidth and computational complexity; Bhattacharya et al. [12] improved upon the bandwidth of 'Frodo', by basing their protocol on LWR

A. Joux et al. (Eds.): AFRICACRYPT 2018, LNCS 10831, pp. 282–305, 2018.
https://doi.org/10.1007/978-3-319-89339-6_16

whilst still avoiding the use of rings; Bos et al. [16] presented a CCA-secure Mod-LWE based key exchange called 'Kyber' which takes the middle road between 'Frodo' and 'a New Hope' by using modules. Concurrently to our work, Jin et al. described a generic key exchange for Ring-LWE, Mod-LWE, LWE and LWR in [29], and Baan et al. [8] described a LWR, Ring-LWR key exchange.

In this paper, we introduce Saber, a suite of cryptographic primitives based on the Mod-LWR problem. The choices we made for the underlying hard problem and also the actual parameters of the scheme were motivated by three design principles: simplicity of the scheme and its implementation, efficiency and flexibility:

- Learning with Rounding (LWR) [10]: schemes based on (variants of) LWE require sampling from noise distributions, which needs randomness. Furthermore, the noise is included in public keys and ciphertexts resulting in higher bandwidth. LWR based schemes naturally reduce the bandwidth while avoiding additional randomness for the noise since it is deterministically obtained.
- Choice of moduli: we choose all integer moduli in the scheme to be powers of 2. This eliminates the need for explicit modular reduction and complicated sampling routines such as rejection sampling. We also prove that using powers of two, the keys are unbiased and that there is no need for steps such as uplifting and randomization or decoding of the exchanged information. These advantages contribute to the simplicity of our design, and facilitate constant time implementations. The main disadvantage of using such moduli is that it excludes the use of the number theoretic transform (NTT) to speed up polynomial multiplication. We propose the use of a combination of Toom-Cook and Karatsuba polynomial multiplication to mitigate this disadvantage.
- Modules [16,31]: the module versions of the problems (see Sect. 2) allow to interpolate between the original pure LWE/LWR problems and their ring versions, lowering computational complexity and bandwidth compared to LWE/LWR, while introducing protection against attacks on the ring structure of Ring-LWE/LWR and flexibility to move to higher security levels without any need to change the underlying arithmetic.

A high-level constant-time software implementation of Saber is provided and has been placed in the public domain[1] as part of the submission to the NIST competition. The implementation has been optimized using AVX2 instructions available in modern Intel processors and uses a combination of Toom-Cook and Karatsuba polynomial multiplication algorithms.

The remainder of the paper is organised as follows: in Sect. 2 we review the necessary background; we present a secure Diffie-Hellman type key exchange scheme in Sect. 3, a CPA secure encryption scheme in Sect. 4 and a CCA secure key encapsulation mechanism in Sect. 5. A security analysis of the hardness on the underlying mod-LWR problem is given in Sect. 6.1, based on which three parameter sets are chosen in Sect. 6.2. Finally, specific implementation choices that speed up our protocols are discussed in Sect. 7 and our implementation results are compared with the state of the art in Sect. 8.

---

[1] Source codes available at https://github.com/Angshumank/SABER.

2   Preliminaries

2.1   Notation

We denote with $\mathbb{Z}_q$ the ring of integers modulo an integer q with representants in $[0, q)$ and for an integer z, we denote $z \bmod q$ the reduction of z in $[0, q)$. R_q is the quotient ring $\mathbb{Z}_q[X]/(X^n + 1)$ with n a fixed power of 2 (we only need $n = 256$). For any ring R, $R^{l \times k}$ denotes the ring of $l \times k$-matrices over R. For $p \mid q$, the mod p operator is extended to (matrices over) R_q by applying it coefficient-wise. Single polynomials are written without markup, vectors are bold lower case and matrices are denoted with bold upper case. $\mathcal{U}$ denotes the uniform distribution and β_μ is a centered binomial distribution with parameter μ and corresponding standard deviation $\sigma = \sqrt{\mu/2}$. If χ is a probability distribution over a set S, then $x \leftarrow \chi$ denotes sampling $x \in S$ according to χ. If χ is defined on $\mathbb{Z}_q$, $\boldsymbol{X} \leftarrow \chi(R_q^{l \times k})$ denotes sampling the matrix $\boldsymbol{X} \in R_q^{l \times k}$, where all coefficients of the entries in $\boldsymbol{X}$ are sampled from χ.

We use the part selection function $\texttt{bits}(x, i, j)$ with $j \leq i$ to access j consecutive bits of a positive integer x *ending* at the i-th index (assuming least significant bit in the 0-th index), producing an integer in $\mathbb{Z}_{2^j}$; i.e., written in standard C code the function returns $(x \gg (i - j))\&(2^j - 1)$, where $\gg$ is the right-shift operator. This is explained in Fig. 1. The part selection function is extended to polynomials and matrices by applying it coefficient-wise. Finally let $\lfloor\rceil$ denote rounding to the nearest integer, which can be extended to polynomials and matrices coefficient-wise.

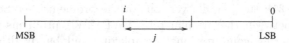

Fig. 1. The $\texttt{bits}(x, i, j)$ operator.

2.2   Cryptographic Definitions

Let KE be a Diffie-Hellman type key exchange protocol between two parties as illustrated in Protocol 1. KE is called $(1 - \delta)$-correct if after execution of the protocol $Pr[k' = k] \geqslant 1 - \delta$, where the probability is computed over the random coins used in Protocol 1. KE is called IND-RND secure if it is hard for an adversary to distinguish the real shared secret from random. More formally, we define the advantage of an adversary in distinguishing the key k from a uniformly random key $\hat{k} \leftarrow \mathcal{U}(\mathcal{K})$ as follows:

$$\text{Adv}_{\text{KE}}^{\text{ind-rnd}}(A) = \left| Pr\left[A(\mathbf{P}, \mathbf{A}, \mathbf{B}, k) = 1\right] - Pr\left[A(\mathbf{P}, \mathbf{A}, \mathbf{B}, \hat{k}) = 1\right] \right|.$$

A public key encryption scheme consists of a triple of functions PKE = (KeyGen, Enc, Dec), where KeyGen returns a secret key sk and a public key pk;

Public parameters P	
Alice	Bob
Choose secret a	
Compute $\mathbf{A}$ as function of $\mathbf{P}$ and a $\xrightarrow{\quad \mathbf{A} \quad}$	Choose secret b
	Compute $\mathbf{B}$ as function of $\mathbf{P}$ and b
$\xleftarrow{\quad \mathbf{B} \quad}$	
k = Derive key from $\mathbf{P}, a, \mathbf{B}$	k' = Derive key from $\mathbf{P}, b, \mathbf{A}$

Protocol 1: Diffie-Hellman type key exchange protocol

Enc takes a public key pk and a message $m \in \mathcal{M}$ to produce a ciphertext $c \in \mathcal{C}$, and Dec takes the secret key sk together with ciphertext c to output a message $m' \in \mathcal{M}$ or the symbol $\perp$ to denote rejection. The PKE is said to be $(1 - \delta)$-correct if $Pr[\text{Dec}(sk, \text{Enc}(pk, m)) = m] \geqslant 1 - \delta$, where the probability is taken over $(pk, sk) \leftarrow \text{KeyGen}$ and the random coins of Enc. We use the notion of indistinguishability under chosen plaintext attacks (IND-CPA) and define the advantage of an adversary A by:

$$\text{Adv}_{\text{enc}}^{\text{ind-cpa}}(A) = \left| Pr \left[b' = b : \begin{array}{c} (pk, sk) \leftarrow \text{KeyGen}(); \\ (m_1, m_2) \leftarrow A^{\text{Enc}}(pk); \ b \leftarrow \mathcal{U}(\{0, 1\}); \\ c \leftarrow \text{Enc}(pk, m_b); \ b' \leftarrow A^{\text{Enc}}(pk, c); \end{array} \right] - \frac{1}{2} \right|.$$

The weaker notion of one-wayness under chosen plaintext attacks (OW-CPA) is defined as:

$$\text{Adv}_{\text{enc}}^{\text{ow-cpa}}(A) = \left| Pr \left[m' = m : \begin{array}{c} (pk, sk) \leftarrow \text{KeyGen}(); \\ m \leftarrow \mathcal{M}; \ c \leftarrow \text{Enc}(pk, m); \\ m' \leftarrow A^{\text{Enc}}(pk, c); \end{array} \right] - \frac{1}{2} \right|.$$

A key-encapsulation mechanism KEM = (KeyGen, Encaps, Decaps) is a triple of probabilistic algorithms, where KeyGen returns a secret key sk and a public key pk, where Encaps takes a public key pk and produces a ciphertext c and a key $k \in \mathcal{K}$, and where Decaps takes the secret key sk, the public key pk and ciphertext c to return a key $k \in \mathcal{K}$ or the symbol $\perp$ to denote rejection. The KEM is said to be $(1-\delta)$-correct if $Pr[\text{Decaps}(sk, c) = k : (c, k) \leftarrow \text{Encaps}(pk)] \geqslant 1-\delta$, where the probability is taken over $(pk, sk) \leftarrow \text{KeyGen}$ and the random coins of Encaps. We use the notion of indistinguishability under chosen ciphertext attacks (IND-CCA) to define the advantage of an adversary A by:

$$\text{Adv}_{\text{KEM}}^{\text{ind-cca}}(A) = \left| Pr \left[b' = b : \begin{array}{c} (pk, sk) \leftarrow \text{KeyGen}(); \ b \leftarrow \mathcal{U}(\{0, 1\}); \\ (c, d, k_0) \leftarrow \text{Encaps}(pk); \\ k_1 \leftarrow \mathcal{K}; \ b' \leftarrow A^{\text{Decaps}}(pk, c, d, k_b); \end{array} \right] - \frac{1}{2} \right|.$$

The advantage of an adversary A in distinguishing a pseudorandom generator gen() with seed $seed_{\mathbf{A}} \leftarrow \mathcal{U}(\{0, 1\}^{256})$ from a uniformly random distribution is defined as follows:

$$\text{Adv}^{\text{prg}}_{\text{gen}()}(A) = \left| Pr \left[b' = 1 : \begin{array}{c} seed_A \leftarrow \mathcal{U}(\{0,1\}^{256}) \\ A \leftarrow \text{gen}(seed_A) \in R_q^{l \times l}; b' = A(A); \end{array} \right] \cdot \right.$$
$$\left. - Pr \left[b' = 1 : A \leftarrow \mathcal{U}(R_q^{m \times l}); b' = A(A); \right] \right| \tag{1}$$

2.3 LWE, LWR and Mod-LWR Problems

The learning with errors (LWE) problem was introduced by Regev [34] and its decisional version states that it is hard to distinguish uniform random samples $(a, u) \leftarrow \mathcal{U}(\mathbb{Z}_q^{l \times 1} \times \mathbb{Z}_q)$ from LWE-samples of the form

$$\left(a, b = a^T s + e \right) \in \mathbb{Z}_q^{l \times 1} \times \mathbb{Z}_q, \tag{2}$$

where the secret vector $s \leftarrow \beta_\mu(\mathbb{Z}_q^{l \times 1})$ is fixed for all samples, $a \leftarrow \mathcal{U}(\mathbb{Z}_q^{l \times 1})$ and $e \leftarrow \beta_\mu(\mathbb{Z}_q)$ is a small error. A module version of LWE, called Mod-LWE, was analyzed by Langlois and Stehlé [31] and essentially replaces the ring $\mathbb{Z}_q$ in the above samples by a quotient ring of the form R_q with corresponding error distribution $\beta_\mu(R_q^{l \times 1})$. The rank of the module is l and the dimension of the ring R_q is n. The case $l = 1$ corresponds to the ring-LWE problem introduced in [32].

The LWR problem was introduced by Banerjee et al. [10] and is a derandomized version of the LWE problem. In contrast to the LWE problem, the "noise" in the LWR problem is generated deterministically by scaling and rounding coefficients modulo q to modulo p (with $p < q$). In detail, an LWR sample is given by

$$\left(a, b = \left\lfloor \frac{p}{q}(a^T s) \right\rceil \right) \in \mathbb{Z}_q^{l \times 1} \times \mathbb{Z}_p \tag{3}$$

for a fixed $s \leftarrow \beta_\mu(\mathbb{Z}_q^{l \times 1})$ and uniform random $a \leftarrow \mathcal{U}(\mathbb{Z}_q^{l \times 1})$. The decisional LWR problem states that is it hard to distinguish samples from the LWR distribution from that of the uniform distribution. A reduction from the LWE problem to the LWR problem was given by Banerjee et al. [10], and further improved by Alwen et al. [6], Bogdanov et al. [15] and, Alperin-Sheriff and Daniel Apon [5].

The security of our protocol relies on the hardness of the module version of LWR (Mod-LWR), which is a straightforward generalization of Mod-LWE. A Mod-LWR sample is given by

$$\left(a, b = \left\lfloor \frac{p}{q}(a^T s) \right\rceil \right) \in R_q^{l \times 1} \times R_p \tag{4}$$

where the secret $s \leftarrow \beta_\mu(R_q^{l \times 1})$ is fixed for all samples and $a \leftarrow \mathcal{U}(R_q^{l \times 1})$.

The advantage of an adversary A in distinguishing m samples from a Mod-LWR distribution from that of a uniform distribution is defined as follows, where m, k, μ, q and p are positive integers with $q > p$:

$$\text{Adv}^{\text{Mod-LWR}}_{m,l,\mu,q,p}(A) = \left| Pr \left(b' = 1 : \begin{array}{c} A \leftarrow \mathcal{U}(R_q^{m \times l}); \ s \leftarrow \beta_\mu(R_q^{l \times 1}); \\ b' = A(A, \lfloor (p/q)As \rceil); \end{array} \right) \right. $$
$$\left. - Pr \left(b' = 1 : \begin{array}{c} A \leftarrow \mathcal{U}(R_q^{m \times l}); \ u \leftarrow \mathcal{U}(R_p^{l \times 1}); \\ b' = A(A, u); \end{array} \right) \right|. \tag{5}$$

3   Key Exchange

In Protocol 2 we describe a Diffie-Hellman type key exchange scheme Saber.KE based on the hardness of Mod-LWR problem. Unlike the Diffie-Hellman key exchange [22], in our scheme the two communicating parties sometimes fail to agree on the same key. As in previous works [12,23,33], we can make this failure probability negligibly small by sending some additional reconciliation data c.

	Alice		Bob
1	$seed_A \leftarrow \mathcal{U}(\{0,1\}^{256})$		
2	$A \leftarrow \text{gen}(seed_A) \in R_q^{l \times l}$		
3	$s \leftarrow \beta_\mu(R_q^{l \times 1})$		$s' \leftarrow \beta_\mu(R_q^{l \times 1})$
4	$b = \text{bits}(As + h, \epsilon_q, \epsilon_p) \in R_p^{l \times 1}$	$\xrightarrow{b,\, seed_A}$	$A \leftarrow \text{gen}(seed_A) \in R_q^{l \times l}$
5			$b' = \text{bits}(A^T s' + h, \epsilon_q, \epsilon_p) \in R_p^{l \times 1}$
6			$v' = b^T \text{bits}(s', \epsilon_p, \epsilon_p) \in R_p$
7	$v = b'^T \text{bits}(s, \epsilon_p, \epsilon_p) \in R_p$	$\xleftarrow{b',\, c}$	$c = \text{bits}(v' + h_1, \epsilon_p - 1, \epsilon_t) \in R_t$
8	$k = \text{bits}(v - 2^{\epsilon_p - \epsilon_t - 1} c + h_2, \epsilon_p, 1)$		$k' = \text{bits}(v' + h_1, \epsilon_p, 1)$
9	$key_{\text{Alice}} = \text{kdf}(k)$		$key_{\text{Bob}} = \text{kdf}(k')$

Protocol 2: Saber.KE key exchange

All moduli involved in the scheme are chosen to be powers of 2, in particular we choose $q = 2^{\epsilon_q}$, $p = 2^{\epsilon_p}$ and $t = 2^{\epsilon_t}$ with $\epsilon_q > \epsilon_p > (\epsilon_t + 1)$, so we have $2t \mid p \mid q$. In practice, our main parameter set will correspond to the case $\epsilon_q = 13$, $\epsilon_p = 10$ and $\epsilon_t = 3$. The secret vectors s and s' are sampled from $\beta_\mu(R_q^{l \times 1})$, with $\mu < p$, while the matrix $A \in R_q^{l \times l}$ is sampled using a pseudorandom generator $\text{gen}()$ initialized with $seed_A$. The session key is obtained by feeding the common secret $k = k' \in R_2$ into a key derivation function $\text{kdf}()$. The algorithm also uses three constants: a constant vector $h \in R_q^{l \times 1}$ consisting of polynomials all coefficients of which are set to the constant $2^{\epsilon_q - \epsilon_p - 1}$, a constant polynomial $h_1 \in R_q$ with all coefficients equal to $2^{\epsilon_q - \epsilon_p - 1}$, and a constant polynomial $h_2 \in R_q$ with all coefficients set equal to $(2^{\epsilon_p - 2} - 2^{\epsilon_p - \epsilon_t - 2} + 2^{\epsilon_q - \epsilon_p - 1})$. These constants are used to mimic rounding operations, which are necessary to reduce failure probability, while retaining the reduction to the underlying decisional Mod-LWR problem.

Note that the operations $\text{bits}(s, \epsilon_p, \epsilon_p)$ in line 6 and $\text{bits}(s', \epsilon_p, \epsilon_p)$ in line 7 simply mean we are considering $s \mod p$ and $s' \mod p$ as elements in R_p which is well defined since $p \mid q$.

Correctness: Using Saber.KE two communicating parties agree on a common random key with overwhelming probability. A tight bound on the failure probability can be obtained using following observations from Bos et al. [17]: the reconciliation between two integer values $v_i, v_i' \in \mathbb{Z}_p$ is correct if the distance between v_i and v_i' is smaller than $p/4(1 - 1/t)$, and fails if the distance is bigger than $p/4(1 + 1/t)$. In between these values, the probability of success decreases linearly from 1 to 0. Consequently, a tight bound on the failure probability given the distribution of $\Delta v_i = v_i' - v_i$ can be calculated by adding to Δv_i a discrete uniformly distributed error $e_r \in \mathbb{Z}_p$ with range $[-p/4t, p/4t]$. The success probability of the reconciliation between v_i and v_i' then equals $Pr[|\Delta v_i + e_r| < p/4]$. Using the above observation we can estimate a bound on the error probability:

Theorem 1. *Let A be a matrix in $R_q^{l \times l}$ and s, s' two vectors in $R_q^{l \times 1}$ sampled as in Protocol 2. Define e and e' as the rounding errors introduced by scaling and rounding As and $A^T s'$, i.e.* $\texttt{bits}(As + h, \epsilon_q, \epsilon_p) = \frac{p}{q}As + e$ *and* $\texttt{bits}(A^T s' + h, \epsilon_q, \epsilon_p) = \frac{p}{q}A^T s' + e'$. *Let $e_r \in R_q$ be a polynomial with uniformly distributed coefficients with range $[-p/4t, p/4t]$. If we set*

$$\delta = Pr[||(s'^T e - e'^T s + e_r) \mod p||_\infty > p/4]$$

then after executing the Saber.KE protocol, both communicating parties agree on a n-bit key with probability $1 - \delta$.

Proof. The polynomials v' and v calculated by Bob and Alice respectively in Protocol 2 are given as: $v' = (\frac{p}{q}s'^T As + s'^T e \mod p)$ and $v = (\frac{p}{q}s'^T As + e'^T s \mod p)$. Here, the coefficients of e, e' are the rounding errors and so are in $(-1/2, 1/2]$. It can be easily seen that the values calculated by the communicating parties differ by $\Delta v = ||(s'^T e - e'^T s) \mod p||$. Therefore, Bob and Alice agree on the same secret if $||\Delta v + e_r||_\infty \leq \frac{p}{4}$. Hence, for $\delta = Pr[||(s'^T e - e'^T s + e_r) \mod p||_\infty > p/4]$ the Saber.KE protocol is $(1 - \delta)$ correct. $\qquad \square$

Similar to Bos et al. [16], a tight upper bound on the value of δ is calculated using a Python script. To be able to practically compute the distribution of $\Delta v = v' - v \in R_p$, Bos et al. assume independence between the terms $s'^T e$ and $e'^T s$, which is not necessarily the case. Analogous to Theorem 5.2 from Jin and Zhao [29], one could argue that they are independent if conditioned on $s'^T As \equiv a \mod q/p$, where $a \in R_{q/p}$. The recommended parameter set described in Sect. 6.2 yields $\delta < 2^{-136}$.

Unbiased Keys: Since our moduli are powers of 2 and as such non-prime, there exists (negligibly small) exceptional sets for s and s' such that the common key is biased. The intuition is that if all coefficients of the polynomials in s or s' are divisible by a high power of 2, the same property will hold for As or $A^T s'$, and their scaled versions. The following theorem however shows that outside these sets, uniformity is attained.

Theorem 2. *Let S_{bad} denote the set of elements in $R_q^{l \times 1}$ for which none of the coefficients w satisfies $\gcd(w, q) | (q/p)$ and let S_{bad}' denote the set of elements in $R_q^{l \times 1}$ for which none of the coefficients w satisfies $\gcd(w, p) | (p/2)$. Let $s, s' \leftarrow \beta_\mu(R_q^{l \times 1})$ and let $A \leftarrow \mathcal{U}(R_q^{l \times l})$ and determine k as follows:*

1. $b = \texttt{bits}(As + h, \epsilon_q, \epsilon_p)$
2. $k = \texttt{bits}(b^T(s' \mod p) + h_1, \epsilon_p, 1)$

For $s \notin S_{bad}$ and $s' \notin S'_{bad}$, k is distributed uniformly for $A \leftarrow \mathcal{U}(R_q^{l \times l})$. This occurs with a probability $Pr[s \notin S_{bad}]Pr[s' \notin S'_{bad}]$.

Proof. Note that the multiplication of a uniformly distributed coefficient of A, by a coefficient w of s, is uniformly distributed in its ϵ_p most significant bits if $\gcd(w, q)|(q/p)$, which is equivalent to stating that $\lfloor pw/q \rceil$ is invertible in $\mathbb{Z}_p$.

The distribution of the coefficients of $b = \texttt{bits}(As + h, \epsilon_q, \epsilon_p)$ is as follows: since convolution of any distribution with a uniform distribution in $\mathbb{Z}_p$ results again in a uniform distribution in $\mathbb{Z}_p$, we need only one term of the summation step to be uniform in its p most significant bits. Therefore, the coefficients of b will be uniformly distributed if $s \notin S_{bad}$.

Finally note that the distribution of $k' = \texttt{bits}(b^T(s' \mod p) + h_1, \epsilon_p, 1)$ is uniform if b has a uniform distribution and if $s' \notin s'_{bad}$. As above, a multiplication of a uniformly distributed coefficient of b, with a coefficient w' of s is uniformly distributed in its most significant bit if $\gcd(w', p)|(p/2)$. Therefore, k will be uniform if the coefficients of b are uniformly distributed and if $s' \notin S'_{bad}$. The probability of a sampling s and s' so that k has a uniform distribution is thus $Pr[s \notin S_{bad}]Pr[s' \notin S'_{bad}]$. $\square$

Since in our setting s, s' are sampled from $\beta_\mu(R_q)$, the coefficients are small and thus the only sampleable vector in S_{bad} and S'_{bad} is the all zero vector which occurs with probability 2^{-1436}. In the rest of the paper, we assume that the secret vectors are not in the vector sets: $s \notin S_{bad}$ and $s' \notin S'_{bad}$.

Security: The security of Saber.KE can be reduced to the decisional Mod-LWR problem as shown by the following theorem.

Theorem 3. *For any adversary A, there exist three adversaries B_0, B_1 and B_2 such that $Adv_{Saber.KE}^{ind-rnd}(A) \leqslant Adv_{gen()}^{prg}(B_0) + Adv_{l,l,\mu,q,p}^{mod-lwr}(B_1) + Adv_{l+1,l,\mu,q,p}^{mod-lwr}(B_2)$, if $q/p \leqslant p/(2t)$.*

Proof. The IND-RND security of our key exchange can be expressed as the probability that an adversary A can distinguish between k and a uniformly random key $\hat{k} \leftarrow \mathcal{U}(\mathcal{K})$, given the public information A, b, b' and c. The proof proceeds by a sequence of games G_i, where $Adv_{G_i}(A) = |Pr[S_{A,i}] - 1/2|$, in which $S_{A,i}$ is the event that the adversary guesses correctly in game G_i. The sequence of games is depicted in Fig. 2.

The first game G_0 is the original game. In game G_1, the public matrix is no longer generated using the pseudorandom generator $\texttt{gen}()$, but is sampled from a uniformly random distribution. An adversary that can distinguish these two games, can also distinguish the matrix generated through the pseudorandom generator from a uniformly random matrix, and therefore $|Pr[S_{A,0}] - Pr[S_{A,1}]| \leqslant Adv_{gen()}^{prg}(B_0)$.

During the second game G_2, the vector b is generated uniformly random, so that (A, b) is a uniformly distributed sample, in contrast to the first game G_1, where (A, b) forms a Mod-LWR sample. An adversary that can distinguish

Game G_0:

1. $seed_A \leftarrow \mathcal{U}(\{0,1\}^{256})$
2. $A \leftarrow \text{gen}(seed_A)$
3. $s, s' \leftarrow \beta_\eta(\mathbb{R}_q^{l \times 1})$
4. $b = \text{bits}($
   $A \cdot s + h, \epsilon_q, \epsilon_p)$
5. $b' = \text{bits}($
   $A^T \cdot s' + h, \epsilon_q, \epsilon_p)$
6. $v' = b^T \cdot \text{bits}(s', \epsilon_p, \epsilon_p)$
7. $c = \text{bits}(v' + h_1, \epsilon_p - 1, \epsilon_t)$
8. $k' = \text{bits}(v' + h_1, \epsilon_p, 1)$
9. $\hat{k} \leftarrow \mathcal{U}(\mathbb{R}_2)$
10. $u \leftarrow \mathcal{U}(\{0,1\})$
11. if $u = 0$:
    $\text{return}(A, b, b', c, k')$
12. else:
    $\text{return}(A, b, b', c, \hat{k})$

Game G_1:

1.
2. $A \leftarrow \mathcal{U}(\mathbb{R}_q^{l \times l})$
3. $s, s' \leftarrow \beta_\eta(\mathbb{R}_q^{l \times 1})$
4. $b = \text{bits}($
   $A \cdot s + h, \epsilon_q, \epsilon_p)$
5. $b' = \text{bits}($
   $A^T \cdot s' + h, \epsilon_q, \epsilon_p)$
6. $v' = b^T \cdot \text{bits}(s', \epsilon_p, \epsilon_p)$
7. $c = \text{bits}(v' + h_1, \epsilon_p - 1, \epsilon_t)$
8. $k' = \text{bits}(v' + h_1, \epsilon_p, 1)$
9. $\hat{k} \leftarrow \mathcal{U}(\mathbb{R}_2)$
10. $u \leftarrow \mathcal{U}(\{0,1\})$
11. if $u = 0$:
    $\text{return}(A, b, b', c, k')$
12. else:
    $\text{return}(A, b, b', c, \hat{k})$

Game G_2:

1.
2. $A \leftarrow \mathcal{U}(\mathbb{R}_q^{l \times l})$
3. $s' \leftarrow \beta_\eta(\mathbb{R}_q^{l \times 1})$
4. $b \leftarrow \mathcal{U}(\mathbb{R}_p^{l \times 1})$
5. $b' = \text{bits}($
   $A^T \cdot s' + h, \epsilon_q, \epsilon_p)$
6. $v' = b^T \cdot \text{bits}(s', \epsilon_p, \epsilon_p)$
7. $c = \text{bits}(v' + h_1, \epsilon_p - 1, \epsilon_t)$
8. $k' = \text{bits}(v' + h_1, \epsilon_p, 1)$
9. $\hat{k} \leftarrow \mathcal{U}(\mathbb{R}_2)$
10. $u \leftarrow \mathcal{U}(\{0,1\})$
11. if $u = 0$:
    $\text{return}(A, b, b', c, k')$
12. else:
    $\text{return}(A, b, b', c, \hat{k})$

Game G_3:

2. $A \leftarrow \mathcal{U}(\mathbb{R}_q^{l \times l})$
3. $s' \leftarrow \beta_\eta(\mathbb{R}_q^{l \times 1})$
4. $b \leftarrow \mathcal{U}(\mathbb{R}_p^{l \times 1})$
5. $b' = \text{bits}($
   $A^T \cdot s' + h, \epsilon_q, \epsilon_p)$
6. $v' = b^T \cdot \text{bits}(s', \epsilon_p, \epsilon_p)$
7. $c = \text{bits}($
   $v' + h_1, \epsilon_p - 1, 2\epsilon_p - \epsilon_q - 1)$
8. $k' = \text{bits}(v' + h_1, \epsilon_p, 1)$
9. $\hat{k} \leftarrow \mathcal{U}(\mathbb{R}_2)$
10. $u \leftarrow \mathcal{U}(\{0,1\})$
11. if $u = 0$:
    $\text{return}(A, b, b', c, k')$
12. else:
    $\text{return}(A, b, b', c, \hat{k})$

Game G_4:

2. $A \leftarrow \mathcal{U}(\mathbb{R}_q^{l \times l})$
3. $s' \leftarrow \beta_\eta(\mathbb{R}_q^{l \times 1})$
4. $b \leftarrow \mathcal{U}(\mathbb{R}_q^{l \times 1})$
5. $b' = \text{bits}($
   $A^T \cdot s' + h, \epsilon_q, \epsilon_p)$
6. $v' = \text{bits}($
   $b^T \cdot s', \epsilon_q, \epsilon_p)$
7. $c = \text{bits}($
   $v' + h_1, \epsilon_p - 1, \epsilon_p - 1)$
8. $k' = \text{bits}(v' + h_1, \epsilon_p, 1)$
9. $\hat{k} \leftarrow \mathcal{U}(\mathbb{R}_2)$
10. $u \leftarrow \mathcal{U}(\{0,1\})$
11. if $u = 0$:
    $\text{return}(A, b, b', c, k')$
12. else:
    $\text{return}(A, b, b', c, \hat{k})$

Game G_5:

2. $A \leftarrow \mathcal{U}(\mathbb{R}_q^{l \times l})$
4. $b \leftarrow \mathcal{U}(\mathbb{R}_q^{l \times 1})$
5. $b' \leftarrow \mathcal{U}(\mathbb{R}_p^{l \times 1})$
6. $v' \leftarrow \mathcal{U}(\mathbb{R}_p^{l \times 1})$
7. $c = \text{bits}($
   $v' + h_1, \epsilon_p - 1, \epsilon_p - 1)$
8. $k' = \text{bits}(v' + h_1, \epsilon_p, 1)$
9. $\hat{k} \leftarrow \mathcal{U}(\mathbb{R}_2)$
10. $u \leftarrow \mathcal{U}(\{0,1\})$
11. if $u = 0$:
    $\text{return}(A, b, b', c, k')$
12. else:
    $\text{return}(A, b, b', c, \hat{k})$

Fig. 2. Sequence of games that are used in the proof of Theorem 3

between game G_1 and G_2 has also solved the decisional Mod-LWR problem on this sample, and therefore $|Pr[S_{A,1}] - Pr[S_{A,2}]| \leqslant \text{Adv}_{l,l,\mu,q,p}^{\text{mod-lwr}}(B_1)$.

In game G_2, the number of bits dropped in the calculation of b' and c is $\epsilon_q - \epsilon_p$ and $\epsilon_p - \epsilon_t - 1$ respectively, which is reduced to $\epsilon_q - \epsilon_p$ in game G_3. If we compare G_3 to G_2, since $(\epsilon_q - \epsilon_p) \leqslant (\epsilon_p - \epsilon_t - 1)$, the number of dropped bits is the same or less, and therefore the number of available bits to the adversary is at least the same. From this we conclude that G_2 is at least as hard as G_3: $\forall A, \exists A' : \text{Adv}_{G_2}(A) \leqslant \text{Adv}_{G_3}(A')$.

Up to game G_3, the coefficients of the inputs for the generation of b' and c are in $\mathbb{Z}_q$ and $\mathbb{Z}_p$ respectively. This is evened up to coefficients in $\mathbb{Z}_q$ for all of the calculations in game G_4. Using s' instead of $\text{bits}(s', \epsilon_p, \epsilon_p)$ does not change the result of the multiplication because $\mu < p$. Since $p \mid q$, generating b from $\mathcal{U}(\mathbb{R}_q^{l \times 1})$ instead of $\mathcal{U}(\mathbb{R}_p^{l \times 1})$ makes the advantage of the adversary in Game G_4 at least as big as in game G_3, as the adversary in Game G_4 can easily calculate the same value for c as in Game G_3. Cutting off the last $\epsilon_q - \epsilon_p$ bits of v' does not change the game since they are not used in the rest of the protocol. Thus we can state: $\forall A', \exists A'' : \text{Adv}_{G_3}(A') \leqslant \text{Adv}_{G_4}(A'')$.

Algorithm 1. Saber.KeyGen()

1 $seed_A \leftarrow \mathcal{U}(\{0,1\}^{256})$
2 $A \leftarrow \text{gen}(seed_A) \in R_q^{l \times l}$
3 $s \leftarrow \beta_\mu(R_q^{l \times 1})$
4 $b = \text{bits}(As + h, \epsilon_q, \epsilon_p) \in R_p^{l \times 1}$
5 return $(pk := (b, seed_A), sk := s)$

Analogous to game G_2, b' and c are replaced by a uniform random value in game G_5, so that the Mod-LWR samples (A, b') and (b, v'), which share secret key s', are replaced by uniformly random variables. Therefore, an adversary that can distinguish between these two games, can solve the corresponding Mod-LWR decisional problem and thus $|Pr[S_{A'',4}] - Pr[S_{A'',5}]| \leqslant \text{Adv}_{l+1,l,\mu,q,p}^{\text{mod-lwr}}(B_2)$.

In the resulting game G_5, the keys are independent of the values b, b' and v'. Moreover, since v' is uniformly distributed in $\mathbb{R}_p^{l \times 1}$, where q is a power of two, and since k' is generated as the first bit of v', k' is also uniformly distributed, and therefore $Pr[S_{A'',5}] = 1/2$. Working backwards from the probability of success in game G_5 to that in game G_0, and using the fact that $\text{Adv}_{G_i}(A) = |Pr[S_{A,i}] - 1/2|$, gives the desired result.   □

4   CPA Secure Encryption

The key exchange scheme of the previous section can be transformed into a CPA secure public-key encryption scheme Saber.PKE by using a similar transformation from Diffie-Hellman key exchange to ElGamal encryption, i.e. the messages sent by Alice now define her public key, and the encryption simply consists of an XOR with the common (pre)key.

The message space is $\mathcal{M} \in \{0,1\}^n$ and a message $m \in \mathcal{M}$ is represented as an element in R_q with coefficients in $\{0,1\}$. Algorithms 1 to 3 describe the public-key encryption scheme Saber.PKE=(KeyGen, Enc, Dec), where the setup parameters are the same as in the key-exchange scheme described before. If the optional parameter r is specified while calling Saber.ENC, it is used as a seed to generate the secret vector s'.

Security and Correctness: It is easily seen that the security and correctness of the encryption scheme are equivalent to that of the key exchange introduced in Sect. 3.

Theorem 4. *For any adversary A against Saber.PKE, there exists an adversary B against Saber.KE such that $\text{Adv}_{Saber.PKE}^{ind-cpa}(A) = \text{Adv}_{Saber.KE}^{ind-rnd}(B)$. Furthermore, Saber.PKE is $(1 - \delta)$ correct if and only if Saber.KE is $(1 - \delta)$ correct.*

Proof. The proof proceeds by showing the equivalence between Saber.PKE and the combination of Saber.KE with a one time pad of the message m with k'_{KE}. Note that the most significant bit of each coefficient of v' is equal to the corresponding (pre)key bits of k' in Saber.KE. Therefore, in line 5 of the Algorithm 2,

---

Algorithm 2. Saber.Enc($pk = (\boldsymbol{b}, seed_A), m \in \mathcal{M}; r$)

1 $\boldsymbol{A} \leftarrow \text{gen}(seed_A) \in R_q^{l \times l}$
2 $\boldsymbol{s}' \leftarrow \beta_\mu(R_q^{l \times 1})$
3 $\boldsymbol{b}' = \text{bits}(\boldsymbol{A}^T \boldsymbol{s}' + \boldsymbol{h}, \epsilon_q, \epsilon_p) \in R_p^{l \times 1}$
4 $v' = \boldsymbol{b}^T \text{bits}(\boldsymbol{s}', \epsilon_p, \epsilon_p) \in R_p$
5 $c_m = \text{bits}(v' + h_1 + 2^{\epsilon_p - 1} m, \epsilon_p, \epsilon_t + 1) \in R_{2t}$
6 **return** $c := (c_m, \boldsymbol{b}')$

Algorithm 3. Saber.Dec($sk = \boldsymbol{s}, c_m, \boldsymbol{b}'$)

1 $v = \boldsymbol{b}'^T \text{bits}(\boldsymbol{s}, \epsilon_p, \epsilon_p) \in R_p$
2 $m' = \text{bits}(v - 2^{\epsilon_p - \epsilon_t - 1} c_m + h_2, \epsilon_p, 1) \in R_2$
3 **return** m'

---

the addition is essentially a one time pad of the message bits m with the coefficients of the (pre)key k' in the key exchange scheme (Protocol 2). We can therefore conclude that the security of our encryption equals the security of our key exchange scheme for the same parameters. Similarly, it can be seen that Saber.PKE is correct if the keys k and k' are equal. Hence, the correctness of the encryption scheme is equivalent to the correctness of the key exchange in Protocol 2.   □

5   CCA Secure KEM

The CPA secure encryption scheme can be turned into a CCA secure KEM Saber.KEM = (Encaps, Decaps) using an appropriate transformation. Recently, several post-quantum versions [26,28,35,38] of the Fujisaki-Okamoto transform with corresponding security reductions have been developed. At this point, the FO$^{\not\perp}$ transformation in [26] with post-quantum reduction from Jiang et al. [28] gives the tightest reduction for schemes with non-perfect correctness. However, other transformations could be used to turn Saber.PKE into a CCA secure KEM.

Saber.KEM is described in detail in Algorithms 4 and 5. The functions $\mathcal{G} : \{0,1\}^* \rightarrow \{0,1\}^{l \times n}$ and $\mathcal{H} : \{0,1\}^* \rightarrow \{0,1\}^n$ are hash functions, z is a secret random seed used to return a pseudorandom response when the re-encryption fails, and the Saber.Enc and Saber.Dec functions are from the CPA secure asymmetric encryption described in Sect. 4.

Correctness: Following Hofheinz et al. [26], Saber.KEM is $(1 - \delta)$ correct if and only if Saber.PKE is $(1 - \delta)$ correct, and thus also if and only if Saber.KE is $(1 - \delta)$ correct.

Security: By modeling the hash functions $\mathcal{G}$ and $\mathcal{H}$ as random oracles, a lower bound on the CCA security can be proven. We use the security bounds of

---

Algorithm 4. Saber.Encaps($pk = (\boldsymbol{b}, seed_{\boldsymbol{A}})$)

1 $m \leftarrow \mathcal{U}(\{0,1\}^{256})$
2 $(\hat{K}, r) = \mathcal{G}(pk, m)$
3 $c = \mathsf{Saber.Enc}(pk, m; r)$
4 $K = \mathcal{H}(\hat{K}, c)$
5 **return** (c, K)

Algorithm 5. Saber.Decaps($sk = (\boldsymbol{s}, z), pk = (\boldsymbol{b}, seed_{\boldsymbol{A}}), c$)

1 $m' = \mathsf{Saber.Dec}(\boldsymbol{s}, c)$
2 $(\hat{K}', r') = \mathcal{G}(pk, m')$
3 $c' = \mathsf{Saber.Enc}(pk, m'; r')$
4 **if** $c = c'$ **then**
5   **return** $K = \mathcal{H}(\hat{K}', c)$
6 **else**
7   **return** $K = \mathcal{H}(z, c)$

Hofheinz et al. [26], which considers a KEM variant of the Fujisaki-Okamoto transform that can also handle a small failure probability δ of the encryption scheme. This failure probability should be cryptographically negligibly small for the security to hold. Using Theorems 3.2 and 3.4 from [26], we get the following theorems for the security and correctness of our KEM in the random oracle model:

Theorem 5 (ROM, Hofheinz et al. [26]). *For a IND-CCA adversary B, making at most $q_{\mathcal{H}}$ and $q_{\mathcal{G}}$ queries to respectively the random oracle $\mathcal{G}$ and $\mathcal{H}$, and q_D queries to the decryption oracle, there exists an IND-CPA adversary A such that:*

$$Adv_{Saber.KEM}^{ind\text{-}cca}(B) \leqslant 3Adv_{Saber.PKE}^{ind\text{-}cpa}(A) + q_{\mathcal{G}}\delta + \frac{2q_{\mathcal{G}} + q_{\mathcal{H}} + 1}{2^{256}}.$$

Jiang et al. [28] also provide a security reduction against a quantum adversary in the quantum random oracle model from IND-CCA security to OW-CPA security. IND-CPA with a sufficiently large message space implies OW-CPA [13,26]. Therefore, we can reduce the IND-CCA security of Saber.KEM to the IND.CPA security of the underlying public key encryption:

Theorem 6 (QROM, Jiang et al. [28]). *For any IND-CCA quantum adversary B, making at most $q_{\mathcal{H}}$ and $q_{\mathcal{G}}$ queries to respectively the random quantum oracle $\mathcal{G}$ and $\mathcal{H}$, and q_D many (classical) queries to the decryption oracle, there exists an adversary A such that:*

$$Adv_{Saber.KEM}^{ind\text{-}cca}(B) \leqslant 2q_{\mathcal{H}}\frac{1}{\sqrt{2^{256}}} + 4q_{\mathcal{G}}\sqrt{\delta} + 2(q_{\mathcal{G}} + q_{\mathcal{H}})\sqrt{Adv_{Saber.PKE}^{ind\text{-}cpa}(A)}$$

Multi Target Protection: As described in [16], hashing the public key into $\hat{K}$ has two beneficial effects: it makes sure that K depends on the input of both parties, and it offers multi-target protection. In this scenario, the adversary uses Grover's algorithm to precompute an m that has a relatively high failure probability. Hashing pk into $\hat{K}$ ensures that an attacker is not able to use precomputed 'weak' values of m.

6 Security Analysis and Parameter Selection

6.1 Security Analysis

Our security analysis is similar to the one in 'a New Hope' [4]. The hardness of Mod-LWR is analyzed as an LWE problem, since there are no known attacks that make use of the Module or LWR structure. A set of l LWR samples given by with $\boldsymbol{A} \leftarrow \mathcal{U}(R_q^{l \times l})$ and $\boldsymbol{s} \leftarrow \beta_\mu(R_q^{l \times 1})$, can be rewritten as an LWE problem in the following way:

$$\left(\boldsymbol{A}, \left\lfloor \frac{p}{q}(\boldsymbol{As} \mod q) \right\rceil \mod p\right) = \left(\boldsymbol{A}, \frac{p}{q}(\boldsymbol{As} \mod q) + \boldsymbol{e} \mod p\right)$$

We can lift this to a problem modulo q by multiplying by $\frac{q}{p}$:

$$\frac{q}{p}\boldsymbol{b} = \boldsymbol{As} + \frac{q}{p}\boldsymbol{e} \mod q,$$

where $q/p\boldsymbol{e}$ is the random variable containing the error introduced by the rounding operation, of which the coefficients are discrete and nearly uniformly distributed in $(-q/2p, q/2p]$.

BKW type of attacks [30] and linearization attacks [7] are not feasible, since the number of samples is at most double the dimension of the lattice. Moreover, the secret vectors $\boldsymbol{s}$ and $\boldsymbol{s}'$ are dense enough to avoid the sparse secret attack described by Albrecht [2]. As a result, we end up with two main type of attacks: the primal and the dual attack, that make use of BKZ lattice reduction [19,36].

Weighted Primal Attack: The primal attack constructs a lattice that has a unique shortest vector that contains the noise $\boldsymbol{e}$ and the secret $\boldsymbol{s}$. BKZ, with block dimension b, can be used to find this unique solution. An LWE sample $(\boldsymbol{A}, \boldsymbol{b} = \boldsymbol{As} + \boldsymbol{e}) \in \mathbb{Z}_q^{m \times n} \times \mathbb{Z}_q^m$ can be transformed to the following lattice: $\Lambda = \{\boldsymbol{v} \in \mathbb{Z}^{m+n+1} : (\boldsymbol{A}|\boldsymbol{I}_m| - \boldsymbol{b})\boldsymbol{v} = 0 \mod q\}$, with dimension $d = m + n + 1$ and volume q^m. The unique shortest vector in this lattice is $\boldsymbol{v} = (\boldsymbol{s}, \boldsymbol{e}, 1)$, and it has norm $\lambda \approx \sqrt{n\sigma_s^2 + m\sigma_e^2}$. Using heuristic models, the primal attack succeeds if [4]:

$$\sqrt{n\sigma_s^2 + m\sigma_e^2} < \delta^{2b-d-1}\mathrm{Vol}(\Lambda)^{\frac{1}{d}}$$

$$\text{where: } \delta = \left((\pi b)^{\frac{1}{d}}\frac{b}{2\pi e}\right)^{\frac{1}{2(b-1)}}$$

However, the vector $v = (s, e, 1)$ is unbalanced since $||s_i||$ is not necessarily equal to $||e_i||$. In our case, $||s_i|| < ||e_i||$, which can be exploited by the lattice rescaling method described by Bai and Galbraith [9], and further analysed in [21]. Analogous to [4], the primal attack is successful if the projected norm of the unique shortest vector on the last b Gram-Schmidt vectors is shorter than the $(d - b)^{\text{th}}$ Gram-Schmidt vector, or:

$$\sigma_s \sqrt{b} \leqslant \delta^{2b-d-1} \left(\frac{q}{\alpha} \right)^{\frac{m}{d}} .$$

Weighted Dual Attack: The dual attack tries to distinguish between an LWE sample $(A, b = As + e) \in \mathbb{Z}_q^{m \times n} \times \mathbb{Z}_q^m$ and a uniformly random sample by finding a short vector (v, w) in the lattice $\Lambda = \{(x, y) \in \mathbb{Z}^m \times \mathbb{Z}^n : A^T x = y \mod q\}$. This short vector is used to compute a distinguisher $z = vb$. If $b = As + e$, we can write $z = vAs + ve = ws + ve$, which is small and approximately Gaussian distributed. If b is generated uniformly, z will also be uniform mod q. Since in our case, $||s_i|| < ||e_i||$, we observe that the ws term will be smaller than the ve term. The weighted attack [9,21] optimizes the shortest vector so that these terms have a similar variance, by considering the weighted lattice $\Lambda' = \{(x, y') \in \mathbb{Z}^m \times (\alpha^{-1}\mathbb{Z})^n : (x, \alpha y') \in \Lambda \mod q\}$.

Following the strategy of [4], we can calculate the cost of the dual attack. The statistical distance between a uniformly distributed z and a Gaussian distributed z is bounded by $\epsilon = 4\exp(-2\pi^2\tau^2)$, where $\tau = ||u||\sigma_e/q$. Since the key is hashed, an advantage of ϵ is not sufficient and must be repeated at least $R = \max(1, 1/(2^{0.2075b}\epsilon^2))$ times. The cost of the dual attack is thus equal to:

$$\text{Cost}_{\text{dual}} = \text{Cost}_{\text{BKZ}} R = b2^{cb} R, .$$

6.2 Parameter Selection

We use a python script to choose parameters q, p and t for optimum usage of communication bandwidth, while achieving a quantum security level of 128 and failure probability 2^{-128}. Additional parameter sets are generated as Light and Fire versions of the Saber.KEM, a light and paranoid version respectively (Table 1).

We would like to remark that choosing p and q as primes facilitates the use of NTT based polynomial multiplications [3,16]. However, rounding from R_q to R_p introduces significant bias as $p \nmid q$. Bogdanov et al. [15] proved the pseudorandomness of the LWR problem for moduli p and q for general lattices but left it as open problem for the ring version. However by choosing p and q as a power-of-two, we can be assured of the pseudorandomness, which we also showed in Sect. 3.

Table 1. Security and correctness of Saber.KEM.

Sec cat	Fail prob	Attack	Classical	Quantum	pk (B)	sk (B)	Ciphertext (B)
LightSaber-KEM: $k = 2$, $n = 256$, $q = 2^{13}$, $p = 2^{10}$, $t = 2^2$, $\mu = 10$							
1	2^{-120}	Primal	126	115	672	1568	736
		Dual	126	115			
Saber-KEM: $k = 3$, $n = 256$, $q = 2^{13}$, $p = 2^{10}$, $t = 2^3$, $\mu = 8$							
3	2^{-136}	Primal	199	181	992	2304	1088
		Dual	198	180			
FireSaber-KEM: $k = 4$, $n = 256$, $q = 2^{13}$, $p = 2^{10}$, $t = 2^5$, $\mu = 6$							
5	2^{-165}	Primal	270	246	1312	3040	1472
		Dual	270	245			

7　Implementation

In this section, we describe a constant-time software implementation of Saber. Our implementation is relatively simpler than several existing lattice-based post-quantum key exchange schemes [4,16,17]. This is primarily due to the underlying LWR problem and our choice of power-of-two moduli. As the LWR problem inherently introduces errors, Saber can bypass error sampling operations unlike other LWE-based schemes. Our choice of power-of-two moduli results in faster arithmetic operations and does not require rejection sampling [4,16] for generating the random matrix A. In the remaining part of this section we describe the building blocks that are used to realize an efficient implementation of Saber.

Symmetric Primitives: The hash functions $\mathcal{G}$ and $\mathcal{H}$ in the CCA-secure Saber-KEM are implemented using SHA3-512 and SHA3-256 respectively, standardized in FIPS 202 [1]. For pseudorandom number generation, we use the extendable output function SHAKE-128 [1]. On parallel platforms, such as Intel processors that support 'single instruction multiple data' (SIMD), one can speedup pseudorandom number generation by using a vectorized implementation of SHAKE-128 and multiple seed values [16]. We decided to use SHAKE-128 serially to generate pseudorandom byte string of a required length from a given seed. This is mainly because of the fact that on majority of resource-constrained platforms (e.g., billions of IoT devices) SIMD would not be feasible, and hence multiple execution of SHAKE-128 would worsen performance (time and energy) because of the costly initialization operation [1] performed in each execution of SHAKE-128. Note that, it is essential for the correctness of the KEM, that all parties generate pseudorandomness in the same way.

Secret Polynomial Generation: Saber requires sampling of secret polynomials from an error distribution. Sampling from a centered binomial distribution can be performed easily [4] in constant time by comparing the Hamming weights of two random integers of same length. Hence we use a centered binomial distribution β_μ with the parameter $\mu = 8$ to sample the secret polynomials.

Matrix A Generation: Since A consists of 9 polynomials, each having 256 13-bit coefficients, we use SHAKE-128 to generate $9 \cdot 256 \cdot 13/8 = 3,744$ pseudo-random bytes. Next we pack these bytes into the 13-bit coefficients of A. Note that in our case no additional rejection sampling is required as in Kyber, due to their use of a prime moduli. The rejection sampling wastes a portion of the generated pseudorandom bytes.

Polynomial Arithmetic: Our protocols relies heavily on polynomial arithmetic in the ring R_q with modulus $q = 2^{13}$ and the irreducible polynomial $f(x) = x^{256} + 1$. While polynomial addition and subtraction are simple coefficient-wise addition and subtraction operations, polynomial multiplication is a costly operation. An optimized polynomial multiplication routine is crucial for an efficient implementation of Saber. Since q is not a prime, we cannot apply the Number Theoretic Transform (NTT) unlike the key exchange schemes such as 'New Hope' [4], Kyber [16] etc. The next best alternative is the Karatsuba method which does not require any special modulus. Hence we use the Karatsuba polynomial multiplication method in Saber. The Karatsuba polynomial multiplication has a higher asymptotic complexity of $O(n^{\log_2 3})$. Though we lose in asymptotic time complexity, we gain in modular arithmetic since modular reduction comes for free. Furthermore, we found that the Karatsuba polynomial multiplication method is relatively easier to vectorize in modern Intel processors that support AVX/AVX2 'single instruction multiple data' (SIMD) instructions.

The Karatsuba multiplication method follows a top-down recursive approach: a 256-coefficient polynomial multiplication is split into three 128-coefficient polynomial multiplications, next each 128-coefficient polynomial multiplication is split into three 64 coefficient polynomial multiplications, and so on. After several levels of recursive splitting, when the polynomial size becomes small enough, i.e., reaches a particular threshold, a quadratic-complexity polynomial multiplication such as the School-book method is used to compute the smallest polynomial multiplications. If we set the threshold value to 16, then a 256-coefficient Karatsuba polynomial multiplication calls the School-book polynomial multiplication routine 81 times.

However, we can improve this by using the Toom-Cook polynomial multiplication. The Toom-Cook method is a generalization of the Karatsuba method and can be used to split a 256-coefficient polynomial multiplication into seven 64-coefficient polynomial multiplications. This is called *four-way Toom-Cook* multiplication. The smaller multiplications can be computed using the Karatsuba method as described above. Thus using the four-way Toom-Cook multiplication, the total number of calls to the School-book multiplication routine reduces to only 63 for a 256-coefficient polynomial multiplication.

In the Toom-Cook multiplication the choice of the evaluation points affects the computation time. Following [14], we choose the set of evaluation points to be $\{0, \pm 1/2, \pm 1, 2, \infty\}$. In the interpolation phase multiplications and divisions by scalar constants are performed. Divisions by odd scalars are performed by computing multiplications by their respective inverses. However, the inverse of an even divisor does not exist when the modulus is a power of two, which is true for Saber. For an even divisor we compute the division in two steps: first, we multiply by the inverse of the odd factor, then we compute a true division (i.e. right shifting) by the power-of-two factor since we know beforehand the division has to be exact. In the four-way Toom-Cook multiplication, the maximum power-of-two factor we have is 8, which could result in a loss of precision of 3 bits. Hence, during the interpolation phase, we allow the intermediate coefficients to grow by 3 bits such that the extra bits can be used to calculate the divisions by 2, 4 and 8. Our choice of modulus $q = 2^{13}$ is especially helpful since we can use 16-bit data variables (short integers in C) to store the 13-bit coefficients. The steps are shown in Algorithm 6 in Appendix A.

AVX2 Implementation of Polynomial Multiplication: Starting from Sandy Bridge, Intel provides AVX/AVX2 SIMD instructions that support computation on 128/256-bit vectors. We utilize this feature to achieve fast polynomial multiplication inspired by the software implementations of NTRU Prime [11] and NTRU KEM [27]. In Algorithm 6 the interpolation phase is trivial to vectorize. However, the evaluation phase, where 64-coefficient polynomial multiplications are performed requires special care to take advantage of vectorized instructions. We explain this below.

Assume that we want to compute · 16 polynomial multiplications $C_0 \cdot D_0$, $C_1 \cdot D_1$, to $C_{15} \cdot D_{15}$ where each polynomial has 16 coefficients. Also assume that the polynomials are stored in two AVX2-arrays C_{AVX} and D_{AVX} as shown in Fig. 3. The i-th coefficients of all C_j (and D_j) polynomials reside in the same AVX2 vectors. With such an arrangement it is easy to compute the 16 polynomial multiplications in a batch by multiplying the elements of C_{AVX} and D_{AVX}. We design the polynomial multiplier routine with the aim to obtain such an arrangement of coefficients during the threshold School-book multiplications. This is explained below.

The seven 64-coefficient polynomial multiplications in Algorithm 6 require 63 School-book multiplications of 16-coefficient polynomials. Since a 16-coefficient polynomial fits in an AVX2 vector, the 63 School-book multiplications can be computed in 4 batches using vectorized instructions. However, the batching is not trivial to implement. In the Karatsuba recursion, we do not immediately compute a School-book multiplication every time the recursion reaches the threshold condition. Instead, a *lazy approach* is adapted. We keep two 'buckets' each of which is an array of 16 AVX2 vectors. These buckets are gradually filled with the 16-coefficient polynomials that are the multiplicands of the School-book

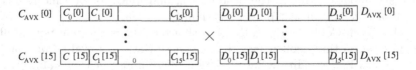

Fig. 3. Arrangement of coefficients for batch polynomial multiplication

multiplications. Once the buckets are full, each of them can be viewed as a 16×16 matrix, containing 256 coefficients. Next we transpose the matrices using a sequence of AVX2 operations to reach the arrangement as shown in Fig. 3. Now a batch multiplication is performed. The result is a collection of 31 vectors. This is again transposed to get the result of each 16-coefficient polynomial multiplication in two vectors. This lazy approach requires a bookkeeping which has a small overhead.

Table 2. Cycle count of the building blocks used in Saber and Kyber

Scheme	Operation	Cycles
Saber `AVX2 optimized`	Toom-Cook polynomial multiplication	3,439
	Sampling secret polynomial vector	13,656
	Generating random matrix A (serial SHAKE-128)	40,100
	Generating random matrix A (parallel SHAKE-128)[†]	25,300
Saber `C`	Toom-Cook polynomial multiplication	20,520
	Sampling secret polynomial vector	13,656
	Generating random matrix A	54,707

Kyber
`AVX2 + assembly`
`optimized`
	NTT	560

	Inverse NTT	489
	Sampling secret/error polynomial vector	10,545
	Generating random matrix A (parallel SHAKE-128)	32,601
Kyber `C`	NTT	16,431
	Inverse NTT	13,098
	Sampling secret/error polynomial vector	10,545
	Generating random matrix A	69,620

[†]Not used in Saber, see Sect. 7.

8   Results

In Table 3, we compare our software implementation of Saber with software implementations of other lattice based post-quantum key exchange and encryption schemes. We compiled the Saber software using `gcc-7.1` with optimization flags `-O3` and measured computation time using a single core of a Intel(R) Core(TM) i7-6600U processor running at 2.60 GHz with hyper-threading, Turbo-Boost, and multi-core support disabled on a Dell Latitude E7470 laptop with Ubuntu 16.04 operating system.

We remark that a totally fair comparison between the listed schemes and their software implementations is not possible since they are based on different

Table 3. Performance and comparison of lattice-based KEMs and public-key encryption schemes. Cycles for key generation, encapsulation/encryption, and decapsulation/decryption are represented by **K**, **E**, and **D** respectively in the 5th column. Sizes of secret key (sk), public key (pk) and ciphertext (c) are reported in the last column. Constant-time implementations are marked with ✓ in the column **ct?**. Performances are measured on the platform specified in the beginning of this section if not indicated otherwise.

Scheme	Problem	Security	ct?	Cycles	Bytes
Passively secure KEMs					
NewHope [4] AVX2 optimized	Ring-LWE	255	✓	**K:** 88,920[†]	**sk:** 1,792
				E: 110,986[†]	**pk:** 1,824
				D: 19,422[†]	**c:** 2,048
Frodo [17]	LWE	130	✓	**K:** 2,938,000[*]	**sk:** 11,280
				E: 3,484,000[*]	**pk:** 11,296
				D: 338,000[*]	**c:** 11,288
CCA-secure KEMs					
NTRU Prime [11]	NTRU	129	✓	**K:** 6,115,384[⊗]	**sk:** 1,600
				E: 59,600[⊗]	**pk:** 1,218
				D: 97,452[⊗]	**c:** 1,047
NTRU KEM [27] AVX2 optimized	NTRU	123	✓	**K:** 307,914[⊥]	**sk:** 1,422
				E: 48,646[⊥]	**pk:** 1,140
				D: 67,338[⊥]	**c:** 1,281
spLWE-KEM [20]	spLWE	128	?	**K:** 336,700[‡]	**sk:** ?
				E: 813,800[‡]	**pk:** ?
				D: 785,200[‡]	**c:** 804
Kyber [16] AVX2 + assembly optimized	Module-LWE	161	✓	**K:** 92,461	**sk:** 2400
				E: 120,280	**pk:** 1088
				D: 113,718	**c:** 1152
Kyber [16] C implementation	Module-LWE	161	✓	**K:** 251,856	**sk:** 2400
				E: 336,112	**pk:** 1088
				D: 435,836	**c:** 1152
Saber AVX2 optimized	Module-LWR	180	✓	**K:** 101,138	**sk:** 2,304
				E: 125,392	**pk:** 992
				D: 129,138	**c:** 1,088
Saber C implementation	Module-LWR	180	✓	**K:** 190,420	**sk:** 2,304
				E: 279,291	**pk:** 992
				D: 306,346	**c:** 1,088
CCA-secure public-key encryption schemes					
NTRUEncrypt [24]	NTRU	159	✗	**K:** 1,194,816[†]	**sk:** 1120
				E: 57,440[†]	**pk:** 1,027
				D: 110,604[†]	**c:** 980
Lizard [21]	LWE, LWR	128	✗	**K:** 97,573,000[†]	**sk:** 466,944[•]
				E: 35,050[†]	**pk:** 2,031,616[•]
				D: 80,840[†]	**c:** 1,072

[†] Compiled using `gcc-4.9.2` and benchmarked on Intel Core i7-4770K (Haswell) computer
[*] Benchmarked on a 2.6 GHz Intel Xeon E5 (Sandy Bridge) with hyperthreading enabled.
[⊗] Benchmarked on an Intel Haswell processor.
[‡] Benchmarked on a Macbook Pro PC with 2.6 GHz Intel Core i5.
[•] Following the explanation provided in [16].
[⊥] Benchmarked on an Intel i7-Haswell, 3.5 GHz processor.

hard problems, offer different levels of post-quantum security, implemented with different levels of optimizations and benchmarked on different platforms. Nevertheless, it is clear from the table that Saber is highly efficient both in terms of bandwidth and computation time.

The implementations of Saber and Kyber use similar building blocks namely polynomial multiplication, generation of random matrix A, sampling of small secret (and error) polynomials and standard symmetric-key primitives for CCA transformations. In Table 2, we compare the performances of these building blocks excluding the symmetric-key primitives. Our Toom-Cook multiplication requires only 3,439 cycles. On the other hand, Kyber uses highly AVX-optimized NTT for polynomial multiplications. Furthermore, Kyber spends much less cycles in polynomial multiplications by generating the matrix A in the NTT domain directly and by keeping the secret polynomials in the NTT domain.

Saber does not require sampling of error polynomials, thus saving in computation time and entropy usage. As already described in Sect. 7 generating the random matrix A is faster in Saber (when same pseudorandom number generator is used) since rejection sampling is not performed, resulting in optimal usage of random numbers. Though in this paper we consider only software implementation on high-end Intel processors, we would like to remark that random number generation is very expensive on resource-constrained platforms. When we compare the high-level C implementations of Saber and Kyber, we see that Saber performs better than Kyber.

Finally note that at the expense of either using larger public keys, or caching the decompressed matrix A, the implementation would run at least 25% faster.

Acknowledgements. This work was supported in part by the Research Council KU Leuven: C16/15/058. In addition, this work was supported by the European Commission through the Horizon 2020 research and innovation programme under grant agreement No H2020-ICT-2014-645622 PQCRYPTO, H2020-ICT-2014-644209 HEAT, Cathedral ERC Advanced Grant 695305 and in part by Flemish Government, by the Hercules Foundation AKUL/11/19.

A   Toom-Cook-4 Polynomial Multiplication

Here we describe the Toom-Cook polynomial multiplication used in our implementation.

Algorithm 6. Toom-Cook Algorithm

Input: Two polynomials $A(x)$ and $B(x)$ of degree $n = 256$
Output: $C(x) = A(x) * b(x)$
// Splitting $A(x)$ into four polynomials of size 64
1 $A(y) = A_3 \cdot y^3 + A_2 \cdot y^2 + A_1 \cdot y + A_0$ where $y = x^{64}$
// Splitting $B(x)$ into four polynomials of size 64
2 $B(y) = B_3 \cdot y^3 + B_2 \cdot y^2 + B_1 \cdot y + B_0$
// Evaluation of the polynomials at $y = \{0, \pm 1, \pm \frac{1}{2}, 2, \infty\}$. These
   multiplications are computed using Karatsuba
3 $w_1 = A(\infty) * B(\infty) = A_3 * B_3$
4 $w_2 = A(2) * B(2) = (A_0 + 2 \cdot A_1 + 4 \cdot A_2 + 8 \cdot A_3) * (B_0 + 2 \cdot B_1 + 4 \cdot B_2 + 8 \cdot B_3)$
5 $w_3 = A(1) * B(1) = (A_0 + A_1 + A_2 + A_3) * (B_0 + B_1 + B_2 + B_3)$
6 $w_4 = A(-1) * B(-1) = (A_0 - A_1 + A_2 - A_3) * (B_0 - B_1 + B_2 - B_3)$
7 $w_5 = A(\frac{1}{2}) * B(\frac{1}{2}) = (8 \cdot A_0 + 4 \cdot A_1 + 2 \cdot A_2 + A_3) * (8 \cdot B_0 + 4 \cdot B_1 + 2 \cdot B_2 + B_3)$
8 $w_6 = A(\frac{-1}{2}) * B(\frac{-1}{2}) = (8 \cdot A_0 - 4 \cdot A_1 + 2 \cdot A_2 - A_3) * (8 \cdot B_0 - 4 \cdot B_1 + 2 \cdot B_2 - B_3)$
9 $w_7 = A(0) * B(0) = A_0 * B_0$
// Interpolation
10 $w_2 = w_2 + w_5$
11 $w_6 = w_6 - w_5$
12 $w_4 = (w_4 - w_3)/2$
13 $w_2 = w_5 - w_1 - 64 \cdot w_7$
14 $w_3 = w_3 + w_4$
15 $w_5 = 2 \cdot w_5 - w_6$
16 $w_2 = w_2 - 65 \cdot w_3$
17 $w_3 = w_3 - w_7 - w_1$
18 $w_2 = w_2 + 45 \cdot w_3$
19 $w_5 = (w_5 - 8 \cdot w_3)/24$
20 $w_6 = w_6 + w_2$
21 $w_2 = (w_2 + 16 \cdot w_4)/18$
22 $w_4 = -(w_4 + w_2)$
23 $w_6 = (30 \cdot w_2 - w_6)/60$
24 $w_2 = w_2 - w_6$
25 **return** $w_1 \cdot y^6 + w_2 \cdot y^5 + w_3 \cdot y^4 + w_4 \cdot y^3 + w_5 \cdot y^2 + w_6 \cdot y + w_7$;

References

1. National Institute of Standards and Technology: SHA-3 Standard: Permutation-Based Hash and Extendable-Output Functions. FIPS PUB 202 (2015)
2. Albrecht, M.R.: On dual lattice attacks against small-secret LWE and parameter choices in HElib and SEAL. In: Coron, J.-S., Nielsen, J.B. (eds.) EUROCRYPT 2017. LNCS, vol. 10211, pp. 103–129. Springer, Cham (2017). https://doi.org/10.1007/978-3-319-56614-6_4
3. Alkim, E., Ducas, L., Pöppelmann, T., Schwabe, P.: NewHope without reconciliation (2016). http://cryptojedi.org/papers/#newhopesimple
4. Alkim, E., Ducas, L., Pöppelmann, T., Schwabe, P.: Post-quantum key exchange - a new hope. In: USENIX Security 2016 (2016)

5. Alperin-Sheriff, J., Apon, D.: Dimension-preserving reductions from LWE to LWR. Cryptology ePrint Archive, Report 2016/589 (2016)
6. Alwen, J., Krenn, S., Pietrzak, K., Wichs, D.: Learning with rounding, revisited. In: Canetti, R., Garay, J.A. (eds.) CRYPTO 2013. LNCS, vol. 8042, pp. 57–74. Springer, Heidelberg (2013). https://doi.org/10.1007/978-3-642-40041-4_4
7. Arora, S., Ge, R.: New algorithms for learning in presence of errors. In: Aceto, L., Henzinger, M., Sgall, J. (eds.) ICALP 2011. LNCS, vol. 6755, pp. 403–415. Springer, Heidelberg (2011). https://doi.org/10.1007/978-3-642-22006-7_34
8. Baan, H., Bhattacharaya, S., Garcia-Morchon, O., Rietman, R., Tolhuizen, L., Torre-Arce, J.L., Zhang, Z.: Round2: KEM and PKE based on GLWR. Cryptology ePrint Archive, Report 2017/1183 (2017). https://eprint.iacr.org/2017/1183
9. Bai, S., Galbraith, S.D.: Lattice decoding attacks on binary LWE. In: Susilo, W., Mu, Y. (eds.) ACISP 2014. LNCS, vol. 8544, pp. 322–337. Springer, Cham (2014). https://doi.org/10.1007/978-3-319-08344-5_21
10. Banerjee, A., Peikert, C., Rosen, A.: Pseudorandom functions and lattices. In: Pointcheval, D., Johansson, T. (eds.) EUROCRYPT 2012. LNCS, vol. 7237, pp. 719–737. Springer, Heidelberg (2012). https://doi.org/10.1007/978-3-642-29011-4_42
11. Bernstein, D.J., Chuengsatiansup, C., Lange, T., van Vredendaal, C.: NTRU prime: reducing attack surface at low cost. Cryptology ePrint Archive, Report 2016/461 (2016). http://eprint.iacr.org/2016/461
12. Bhattacharya, S., Garcia-Morchon, O., Rietman, R., Tolhuizen, L.: spKEX: an optimized lattice-based key exchange. Cryptology ePrint Archive, Report 2017/709 (2017). http://eprint.iacr.org/2017/709
13. Birkett, J., Dent, A.W.: Relations among notions of plaintext awareness. In: Cramer, R. (ed.) PKC 2008. LNCS, vol. 4939, pp. 47–64. Springer, Heidelberg (2008). https://doi.org/10.1007/978-3-540-78440-1_4
14. Bodrato, M., Zanoni, A.: Integer and polynomial multiplication: towards optimal Toom-Cook matrices. In: ISSAC 2007, pp. 17–24. ACM (2007). http://doi.acm.org/10.1145/1277548.1277552
15. Bogdanov, A., Guo, S., Masny, D., Richelson, S., Rosen, A.: On the hardness of learning with rounding over small modulus. In: Kushilevitz, E., Malkin, T. (eds.) TCC 2016. LNCS, vol. 9562, pp. 209–224. Springer, Heidelberg (2016). https://doi.org/10.1007/978-3-662-49096-9_9
16. Bos, J., Ducas, L., Kiltz, E., Lepoint, T., Lyubashevsky, V., Schanck, J.M., Schwabe, P., Stehlé, D.: CRYSTALS - kyber: a CCA-secure module-lattice-based KEM. Cryptology ePrint Archive, Report 2017/634 (2017). http://eprint.iacr.org/2017/634
17. Bos, J.W., Costello, C., Ducas, L., Mironov, I., Naehrig, M., Nikolaenko, V., Raghunathan, A., Stebila, D.: Frodo: take off the ring! practical, quantum-secure key exchange from LWE. In: CCS 2016, pp. 1006–1018. ACM (2016). http://doi.acm.org/10.1145/2976749.2978425
18. Chen, L., Jordan, S.P., Liu, Y.K., Moody, D., Peralta, R.C., Perlner, R.A., Smith-Tone, D.C.: Report on post-quantum cryptography. In: NIST Internal Report (NISTIR) - 8105 (2016). http://dx.doi.org/10.6028/NIST.IR.8105
19. Chen, Y., Nguyen, P.Q.: BKZ 2.0: better lattice security estimates. In: Lee, D.H., Wang, X. (eds.) ASIACRYPT 2011. LNCS, vol. 7073, pp. 1–20. Springer, Heidelberg (2011). https://doi.org/10.1007/978-3-642-25385-0_1

20. Cheon, J.H., Han, K., Kim, J., Lee, C., Son, Y.: A practical post-quantum public-key cryptosystem based on spLWE. In: Hong, S., Park, J.H. (eds.) ICISC 2016. LNCS, vol. 10157, pp. 51–74. Springer, Cham (2017). https://doi.org/10.1007/978-3-319-53177-9_3

21. Cheon, J.H., Kim, D., Lee, J., Song, Y.: Lizard: cut off the tail! practical post-quantum public-key encryption from LWE and LWR. Cryptology ePrint Archive, Report 2016/1126 (2016). http://eprint.iacr.org/2016/1126

22. Diffie, W., Hellman, M.: New directions in cryptography. IEEE Trans. Inf. Theory **22**(6), 644–654 (1976)

23. Ding, J.: New cryptographic constructions using generalized learning with errors problem. Cryptology ePrint Archive, Report 2012/387 (2012). http://eprint.iacr.org/2012/387

24. Hoffstein, J., Pipher, J., Schanck, J.M., Silverman, J.H., Whyte, W., Zhang, Z.: Choosing parameters for NTRUEncrypt. In: Handschuh, H. (ed.) CT-RSA 2017. LNCS, vol. 10159, pp. 3–18. Springer, Cham (2017). https://doi.org/10.1007/978-3-319-52153-4_1

25. Hoffstein, J., Pipher, J., Silverman, J.H.: NTRU: a ring-based public key cryptosystem. In: Buhler, J.P. (ed.) ANTS 1998. LNCS, vol. 1423, pp. 267–288. Springer, Heidelberg (1998). https://doi.org/10.1007/BFb0054868

26. Hofheinz, D., Hövelmanns, K., Kiltz, E.: A modular analysis of the Fujisaki-Okamoto transformation. Cryptology ePrint Archive, Report 2017/604 (2017). http://eprint.iacr.org/2017/604

27. Hulsing, A., Rijneveld, J., Schanck, J.M., Schwabe, P.: High-speed key encapsulation from NTRU. Cryptology ePrint Archive, Report 2017/667 (2017). http://eprint.iacr.org/2017/667

28. Jiang, H., Zhang, Z., Chen, L., Wang, H., Ma, Z.: Post-quantum IND-CCA-secure KEM without additional hash. Cryptology ePrint Archive, Report 2017/1096 (2017). https://eprint.iacr.org/2017/1096

29. Jin, Z., Zhao, Y.: Optimal key consensus in presence of noise. Cryptology ePrint Archive, Report 2017/1058 (2017). https://eprint.iacr.org/2017/1058

30. Kirchner, P., Fouque, P.-A.: An improved BKW algorithm for LWE with applications to cryptography and lattices. In: Gennaro, R., Robshaw, M. (eds.) CRYPTO 2015. LNCS, vol. 9215, pp. 43–62. Springer, Heidelberg (2015). https://doi.org/10.1007/978-3-662-47989-6_3

31. Langlois, A., Stehlé, D.: Worst-case to average-case reductions for module lattices. Des. Codes Crypt. **75**(3), 565–599 (2015). https://doi.org/10.1007/s10623-014-9938-4

32. Lyubashevsky, V., Peikert, C., Regev, O.: On ideal lattices and learning with errors over rings. In: Gilbert, H. (ed.) EUROCRYPT 2010. LNCS, vol. 6110, pp. 1–23. Springer, Heidelberg (2010). https://doi.org/10.1007/978-3-642-13190-5_1

33. Peikert, C.: Lattice cryptography for the internet. In: Mosca, M. (ed.) PQCrypto 2014. LNCS, vol. 8772, pp. 197–219. Springer, Cham (2014). https://doi.org/10.1007/978-3-319-11659-4_12

34. Regev, O.: On lattices, learning with errors, random linear codes, and cryptography. In: STOC 2005, pp. 84–93. ACM (2005). http://doi.acm.org/10.1145/1060590.1060603

35. Saito, T., Xagawa, K., Yamakawa, T.: Tightly-secure key-encapsulation mechanism in the quantum random oracle model. Cryptology ePrint Archive, Report 2017/1005 (2017). https://eprint.iacr.org/2017/1005

36. Schnorr, C.P., Euchner, M.: Lattice basis reduction: improved practical algorithms and solving subset sum problems. Math. Program. **66**(1–3), 181–199 (1994). https://doi.org/10.1007/BF01581144
37. Stehlé, D., Steinfeld, R.: Making NTRU as secure as worst-case problems over ideal lattices. In: Paterson, K.G. (ed.) EUROCRYPT 2011. LNCS, vol. 6632, pp. 27–47. Springer, Heidelberg (2011). https://doi.org/10.1007/978-3-642-20465-4_4
38. Targhi, E.E., Unruh, D.: Post-quantum security of the Fujisaki-Okamoto and OAEP transforms. In: Hirt, M., Smith, A. (eds.) TCC 2016. LNCS, vol. 9986, pp. 192–216. Springer, Heidelberg (2016). https://doi.org/10.1007/978-3-662-53644-5_8

Practical Fault Injection on Deterministic Signatures: The Case of EdDSA

Niels Samwel[✉] and Lejla Batina[✉]

Digital Security Group, Radboud University, Nijmegen, The Netherlands
{n.samwel,lejla}@cs.ru.nl

Abstract. After recent vulnerabilities of implementations of deterministic signatures e.g. EdDSA have been revealed, it became evident that a secure deployment of those will require additional countermeasures. Nevertheless, this is not a simple task, as we show in this work. We demonstrate the easiness of fault attacks on EdDSA as implemented in the lightweight cryptographic library WolfSSL on a 32-bit micro-controller. We achieve a success rates of almost 100% by voltage glitching and electromagnetic fault injection. Even after adding certain checks as a countermeasure, the implementation remains vulnerable to fault injection. As only a single successful fault is needed to recover the key, this kind of implementation is an easy target for the attackers.

Keywords: ECC · EdDSA · Differential fault attack

1 Introduction

In our daily lives the use of small embedded devices have become prevalent due to their numerous deployments in transportation, secure payments and e-health systems, as wearables etc. The accessibility of those devices makes them a perfect target for a side-channel adversary who is able to collect and process leakage signals leading to the secret/private data recovery. On top of this, the protection against this kind of adversary is complicated due to the sparseness of resources such as area, memory, power/energy budgets etc.

Typical services for the IoT and other embedded devices include authentication, which sometimes also needs to be performed off-line. One way to enable strong authentication is to use digital signatures, where Elliptic Curve Cryptography (ECC) is still leading the field for lightweight Public-key cryptosystems (PKC). One of the best known signature algorithms is due to Schnorr [25], which was introduced for discrete logarithm cryptosystems. Other signature schemes have been also proposed such as the Digital Signature Algorithm (DSA) [18]. Later this scheme was extended to a scheme called ECDSA [15] that is using elliptic curves. DSA-like signature schemes require a fresh randomly generated ephemeral key for each signature.

The ephemeral key used in DSA-like schemes has to be truly random. Some recent studies showed how real-world system do not always follow this

© Springer International Publishing AG, part of Springer Nature 2018
A. Joux et al. (Eds.): AFRICACRYPT 2018, LNCS 10831, pp. 306–321, 2018.
https://doi.org/10.1007/978-3-319-89339-6_17

recommendation [13]. The requirement turns out to be a complex issue, especially for resource constrained devices that may not have a true random number generator. Actually, if only a few bits of the ephemeral key are known the private key can be recovered using a specific lattice-based cryptanalysis [14]. To downplay the importance of the true randomness of the ephemeral key an alternative to ECDSA so-called EdDSA was introduced [8]. The selling point of EdDSA is that the ephemeral key is generated deterministically and the requirement for cryptographically secure randomness becomes obsolete. However, a recent side-channel attack on EdDSA has shown that the deterministic feature is not optimal in practice with the adversary that has an access to the device and is able measure side-channel signals [24]. Namely, the promoted feature to make EdDSA deterministic complicates its secure implementation as it makes it a clinical use case for a first order DPA attack using power or EM leakages.

In addition, fault attacks on deterministic signature schemes also appeared recently by Ambrose et al. [2] and Romailler and Pelissier [23]. The former outlines theoretically several scenarios for different fault attacks on deterministic signatures in contrast to the latter which describes a very special practical attack on EdDSA that is feasible on an 8-bit platform only.

The work we present in this paper is a generic fault injection attack that can be applied to a range of platforms and it is using different sources for fault injection. We demonstrate the pervasiveness of it on a 32-bit micro-controller targeting EdDSA implementation within the lightweight cryptographic library WolfSSL. For our attack a single fault during the scalar multiplication algorithm is required for the full key recovery. We give all the details of the setup where this semi-invasive attack is done by applying minor changes to the supply voltage or using electro-magnetic EM signals as the "glitching" sources.

The rest of this paper is organized as follows. First we list related previous work and specify our contributions. In Sect. 2, we provide background information required for the remainder of the paper. Section 3 presents an overview of the attack and more detailed methodology on voltage fault injection and electromagnetic fault injection. Section 4 shows the results of our attack. In Sect. 5, we discuss several countermeasures against this attack and fault attacks in general. Section 6 concludes this paper.

1.1 Related Work

In 1997, the first differential fault attack on public key system RSA-CRT was introduced by Boneh et al. [11]. The authors presented a theoretical concept together with a possible countermeasure. Later Aumüller et al. [3] show the feasibility of the attack by applying it in practice and presenting another countermeasure.

Considering other PKC the first differential fault attack on an elliptic curve cryptosystem was presented by Biehl et al. [10] in 2000. In the scenario they propose the resulting point is not on the original curve anymore. Hence, as a consequence they validate the point as a countermeasure.

Barenghi and Pelosi [5] describe several potential fault attacks on EC-based signature schemes theoretically. In one of the attacks, a fault is introduced during the computation of the hash function. This value is not public and must be recovered by brute forcing over all possible values. The authors implemented the key recovery part and presented their results for this specific scenario.

Recently, a work by Ambrose et al. [2] outlined several differential fault attacks on deterministic signature schemes. However, the authors present no practical results.

The first differential fault attack on Ed25519 was published by Romailler and Pelissier [23]. The authors used the Arduino nano, an 8-bit micro-controller as their target platform where a signing operation takes over 5 s. They introduced a fault in the output of a hash function which is not public so the requirement for the attack is to brute force this value. This issue is complicated with modern platforms using 32- or 64-bit architectures. Therefore, the attack is not so practical for other than 8-bit architectures. In our attack, we introduce a fault during the scalar multiplication which makes it platform-independent.

With the introduction of the Rowhammer attack [17] several papers have been published on injecting faults using software manipulations. Poddebniak et al. [21] used the idea to attack deterministic signature schemes. In their work, they explain how to apply the Rowhammer attack and how to prevent it by presenting several countermeasures. This attack is very different than our attack because the impact of Rowhammer is that an invalid signature is generated, while our attack recovers the relevant part of the key in order to forge a signature.

1.2 Contributions

Here we summarize the main contributions of this paper:

- In this paper we present a conceptually novel and generic differential fault attack on the deterministic signature scheme Ed25519. We inject the fault in the scalar multiplication operation that is unrelated to the hash computation, such that the attacker does not need to brute force the intermediate result.
- The attack is demonstrated on a real-world implementation of Ed25519 from the lightweight cryptographic library WolfSSL on a 32-bit micro-controller. This kind of implementation particularly targets low-cost and/or resource-constrained environments as in the IoT use cases and similar.
- We show that our attack can be effectively executed using voltage glitching and electromagnetic fault injection.
- We also establish the fact on the necessity of suitable countermeasures as we show that even the common point validity check countermeasure cannot counteract the attack.

2   Background

2.1   EdDSA

EdDSA is a known digital signature scheme constructed over so-called Edwards curves [8]. An instance of EdDSA using Edwards Curve25519 in particular (called

Ed25519) is used in Signal protocol, Tor, SSL, etc. There is also an ongoing effort to standardize the scheme, known as RFC 8032. The signature scheme is a variant of the Schnorr signature algorithm [25] that makes use of Twisted Edwards Curves. Compared to ECDSA, EdDSA does not need new randomness for each signature as the ephemeral key is computed deterministically using the message and the auxiliary key that is part of the private key. The security depends on the secrecy of the auxiliary key and the private scalar. This does not create an additional requirement as we need to keep a private key secret anyway. The security of ECDSA depends heavily of a good quality randomness of the ephemeral key, which has to be truly random for each signature. This feature was put forward in promotion of EdDSA as being more side-channel resistant than ECDSA [8].

In Ed25519, a twisted Edwards curve birationally equivalent to Curve25519 [7] is used. Ed25519 sets several domain parameters of EdDSA such as:

- Finite field F_q, where $q = 2^{255} - 19$
- Elliptic curve $E(F_q)$, Curve25519 [7]
- Base point B
- Order of the point B, l
- Hash function H, SHA-512 [22]
- Key length $b = 256$

For more details on other parameters of Curve25519 and the corresponding curve equations we refer to Bernstein [7].

Table 1. Notations EdDSA

Name	Symbol
Private key	k
Private scalar	a (first part of $H(k)$)
Auxiliary key	b (last part of $H(k)$)
Ephemeral scalar of private key	r

To sign a message, the signer has a private key k and message M. Algorithm 1 shows the steps to generate an EdDSA signature.

The first four steps belong to the key setup and are only applied the first time a private key is used. Notation $(x, \ldots, y)$ denotes concatenation of the elements. We call a the private scalar and $b = (h_0, h_1, \ldots, h_{2b-1})$ the auxiliary key (see Table 1). In Step 5 the ephemeral key is deterministically generated.

To verify a signature (R, S) on a message M with public key A a verifier follows the procedure described in Algorithm 2.

Algorithm 1. EdDSA signature generation

Key setup.

1: Hash k such that $H(k) = (h_0, h_1, \ldots, h_{2b-1})$.

2: $a = (h_0, \ldots, h_{b-1})$, interpret as integer in little-endian notation.

3: $b = (h_b, \ldots, h_{2b-1})$.

4: Compute public key: $A = aB$.

Signature generation.

5: Compute ephemeral key: $r = H(b, M)$.

6: Compute ephemeral public key: $R = rB$.

7: Compute $h = H(R, A, M)$ and convert to integer.

8: Compute: $S = (r + ha) \mod l$.

9: Signature pair: (R, S).

Algorithm 2. EdDSA signature verification

1: Compute $h = H(R, A, M)$ and convert to integer.

2: Check if group equation $8SB = 8R + 8hA$ in E holds.

3: If group the equation holds, the signature is correct.

2.2   Fault Attacks

Fault attacks are active attacks and aim at exploiting the leakage of sensitive information due to some irregular conditions i.e. faulty computation. This is distinctive to side-channel attacks that observe signals while the device under attack is working "normally". With fault attacks, an attacker attempts to alter environmental conditions so the device changes it behavior. One way to accomplish this is by "glitching" the device i.e. forcing the changes in the values of relevant physical parameters outside the prescribed intervals. There are several approaches to accomplish this as follows:

- **Clock fault injection** [1]. In this case a glitch is caused by altering the clock signal. This is typically done with devices that allow the use of an external clock.
- **Voltage fault injection** [3]. The attacker can induce this kind of glitch by adding a short positive or negative spike in the power line.
- **Electromagnetic fault injection** [27]. A glitch is caused by emitting a short electromagnetic (EM) pulse towards the device resulting in similar effects as voltage glitching.
- **Optical fault injection** [26]. Optical fault injection is more invasive as the chip typically has to be decapsulated and it often causes permanent damage to a device.

In this paper we focus on glitches caused by voltage and electromagnetic fault injection. If a glitch has an effect that alters the behavior of the device such that it produces a fault, we call this "a successful fault".

Fault Model. A fault model describes the kind and the extent of faults an attacker is able to induce while the device is operating. In this paper our target platform is a micro-controller with a 32-bit architecture so we assume a fault model where a glitch can create an error such that the value of a 32-bit word is modified. This alteration can happen at different stages, for instance when the value is processed by the CPU or when the value is on the memory bus. Typically, a glitch could also alter instructions that affect other sensitive values (e.g. loop counters etc.) or other behavior of the algorithm but our attacks do not rely on this particular assumption.

Differential Fault Analysis. Differential fault analysis (DFA) is a special attack based on faults produced during computation. Typically, the attacker uses the difference between the correct output and one (or more) faulty outputs to recover secret data. This can lead to the total key recovery like in the case of Bellcore attacks on the RSA cryptosystem [11] or merely to forging a signature.

3   Methods

3.1   General Attack Principle

In Ed25519, if an attacker is able to cause a glitch in the computation of the ephemeral public key $R = rB$, or in the computation of the hash $h = H(R, A, M)$ where the same message is signed resulting in R' or h', he can recover the private scalar. Independent of which of the two values is faulty, the hash computation is always faulty as it has R or R' as an input. For a successful attack, we need a correct signature and only a single faulty signature to recover the private scalar a. With private scalar a, a valid signature on any message can be computed as the value of r is arbitrary. From the correct and a faulty signature, the private scalar a can be recovered as follows. The attacker obtains a correct signature (R, S) and a faulty signature (R', S') with the following equations:

$$S = r + ha,$$
$$S' = r + h'a.$$

If we rewrite this, we obtain the following,

$$S - ha = S' - h'a.$$

And we can extract private scalar a

$$a = \frac{S - S'}{h - h'} \tag{1}$$

The output of the hash function h is not public so when a fault is injected in the computation of the hash, an attacker must know or be able to compute hash h'. It can be brute forced as in [23] where the authors use an 8-bit architecture, but their attack does not scale so when a more realistic target is used like a 32-bit or 64-bit architecture, this becomes impractical. Since the ephemeral public key R is part of the signature (hence known), we aim at causing a glitch in the computation of the scalar multiplication $R = rB$. We do not target any particular single bit (or a group of bits), but a fault in any intermediate value of the scalar multiplication is sufficient.

For each execution of the signing algorithm there are three possible outcomes.

– Normal
– Inconclusive
– Successful

A normal outcome denotes the case when no fault occurred and the output is as expected. A successful outcome stands for an induced fault that resulted in the correct key by applying Eq. (1). An inconclusive outcome has several possibilities: (i) a fault was induced and a faulty output was produced but the key could not be recovered, (ii) a fault was induced but no output was produced, and (iii) a fault was induced but no output was produced and the device stopped working. At this point the device had to be power cycled to continue the experiment.

3.2 Voltage Fault Injection

We start with finding the lowest VCC (VCC_L) for which the target still behaves "normally". Next, we under-power the device continuously (VCC_F) so that it still works but faults are introduced, see Table 2 for the settings. Our goal is to maximize the success rate.

Figure 1 shows a schematic overview of the setup. The PC handles communication with the target, collects traces from the oscilloscope and controls the VC Glitcher. The target is powered by the VC Glitcher so it is able to inject glitches in the power line. The glitch amplifier amplifies the current and with the current probe we are able to measure the power consumption and see the effects of the glitch. The oscilloscope and the current probe are only used to collect an overview trace and determine an offset to induce the glitch. Once a suitable offset is located, the current probe and oscilloscope are disconnected and removed from the setup.

Once we identify this offset we try to improve the success rate and we continuously under-power the device by actively inducing faults. To do this we introduce a glitch after a trigger event occurs. We set a trigger at the start of the scalar multiplication in the signature generation. To maximize the success rate there are several parameters to optimize, such as:

– Glitch Voltage (GV),
– Glitch Length (GL),
– Glitch Offset (GO),
– Glitch Repetition (GR).

Table 2. Settings for voltage fault injection setup.

Name	Setting
VCC_L	2.3 V
VCC_F	2.201 V
Glitch Voltage	−0.16 V
Glitch Length	3070 ns
Glitch Offset	1444010 ns
Glitch Repetition	1

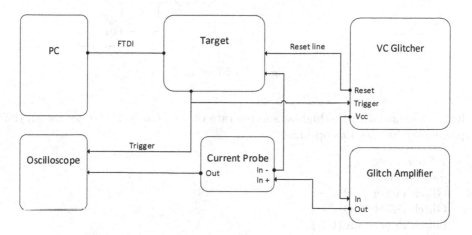

Fig. 1. Voltage fault injection setup

In the experiments we introduce single glitch so we fix the glitch repetition to 1. To optimize those parameters, we did not apply any sophisticated algorithm such as e.g. [12,20], but we applied random search instead. With the first results we manually narrowed down the search ranges to find optimal parameters.

3.3   Electromagnetic Fault Injection

Electromagnetic fault injection (EMFI) is an active attack where the attacker emits a short EM pulse as a glitch from a close distance. If the glitch is strong enough, it can cause a fault. The EM pulse is emitted using a small coil. Different coils could have different effects on the size and the polarity of the EM pulse, but this point is not relevant for our work.

As with voltage fault injection, there exist several parameters to be optimized for EMFI. Those are also different parameters and the most distinctive ones are the x and y coordinates corresponding to a location on the chip where the coil that emits the EM pulse is positioned. Figure 2 shows an overview of the setup. We use the XY-table to precisely position the EMFI probe on the device. With the XY-table we are able to automate a systematic scan of the chip's surface to

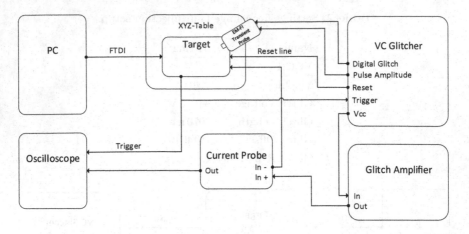

Fig. 2. EMFI setup

find a location with the highest success rate of the attack. Below we list all the parameters we need to optimize.

- x-Coordinate
- y-Coordinate
- Glitch Power (GP)
- Glitch Offset (GO)
- Glitch Repetition (GR)
- Glitch Length (GL)

Again we introduce a single glitch so we fix glitch repetition to 1. The parameter glitch length is fixed to 40 ns due to the EMFI hardware that we used in the attack.

4   Experimental Setup and Results

4.1   Setup

The setups for voltage and EM fault injection are very similar. Our target is a development board containing a Cortex-M4F, more specifically the STM32F407IG. For our experiments we did not have to decapsulate the chip. A signing operation of Ed25519 from WolfSSL takes roughly 30 ms on this platform. Electronic devices have capacitors to keep the power at a stable level so internal or external fluctuations do not influence the behavior of the device. Since we actually want to cause some fluctuations in the power line to alter the behavior with voltage FI, we removed most capacitors on the board. With EMFI we externally cause the fluctuations in the power plane with short EM pulses so the attack also works without removing the capacitors.

Fig. 3. This figure shows the experimental setup. In the top left corner we see the EM-FI transient probe and below that the target board which is fixed to the XY-table. In the center with the blue screen, we see the VC Glitcher under witch is the oscilloscope and the small block on the right is the current probe. (Color figure online)

We use the VC Glitcher[1] to power the board and to cause fluctuations in the voltage. We also need the Glitch Amplifier as the VC Glitcher does not provide enough current to power the board.

To generate the EM pulses we use an EMFI Transient Probe that is connected and controller by the VC Glitcher. An xy-table is used to move the EMFI Transient Probe with high accuracy.

The oscilloscope used to visualize the effect of the voltage fluctuations or the EM pulses is a Picoscope5203. A current probe measuring those changes is connected in series with the power line and it is also a part of the setup. Figure 3 shows a picture of our experimental setup.

We attack the software implementation of Ed25519 in WolfSSL version 3.11.0. Similar implementations can be found in other cryptographic libraries implementing Ed25519. We added a trigger to the code right before the start of the scalar multiplication. We could also have inserted the trigger before the signature generations starts as the code runs in constant time, so it would merely imply the increase in the offset. The attack is also possible without adding a trigger in the code when using hardware that can generate a trigger based on a pattern in the signal [6].

4.2 Voltage Fault Injection Results

The first step of the experiment was to continuously under-power the device. Without introducing glitches we were able to achieve a success rate of 44%. When we actively tried to induce glitches using the described parameters, we

---

[1] https://www.riscure.com/security-tools/hardware/.

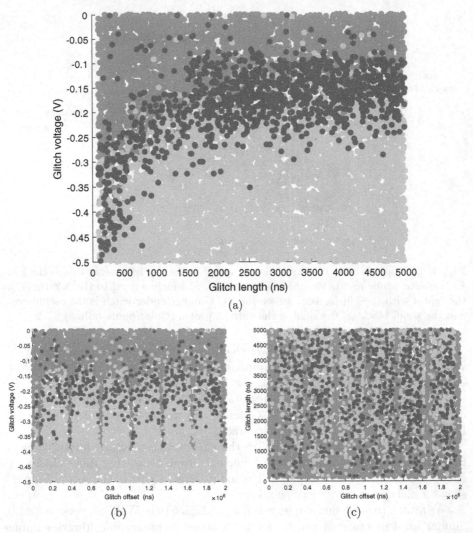

Fig. 4. Voltage fault injection results, Normal (green), Inconclusive (yellow), Successful (red). (Color figure online)

were able to increase the success rate to 69.95% using an optimal set of parameter values we found. We computed the success rates using 10 000 measurements with those optimal parameters.

To visualize the effects of the glitch parameters, we set the parameters to a constant value except for two. For those two parameters we selected random value within a certain range. Figure 4 shows the result of the experiment. In Fig. 4a, we vary the glitch length and the glitch voltage parameters. It shows a typical curve of successful glitches as in [12,20]. A selected set of parameters above the curve means the glitch is not strong enough and the device continues like nothing happened and a selection of parameters below the curve results in a glitch that is too strong and the device stops responding. In Fig. 4b and c we vary offset with the glitch voltage and glitch length and we see a clear pattern that corresponds to an iteration in the scalar multiplication. Each figure contains results of 10 000 measurements.

The results show that inducing exploitable faults is not complicated as even providing a lower voltage results in a reasonably high success rate.

4.3 Electromagnetic Fault Injection Results

In this experiment we start by scanning the surface of the chip to determine good positions for a successful fault injection. Figure 5a shows the surface of the chip.

(a) Target board

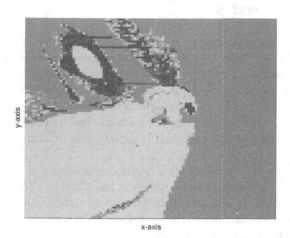

(b) Heat map with EMFI results

Fig. 5. This figure shows a picture of the board and it shows which locations are most effective to inject a glitch.

We divide the x and y-axis up in 100 parts each, resulting in 10 000 positions to scan. We inject a glitch 20 times on each position where the remaining parameters are randomized similar as in the previous section. By manually optimizing the parameters, we were able to achieve a success rate of 99.31%. We did another surface scan with these fixed parameters, the result is shown in Fig. 5b. The figure shows a heatmap, where the color denotes the result of a fault. A color that is a mix between other colors is corresponding to the situations when the resulting faults were mixed.

To scan the surface we performed a total amount of 200 000 measurements. With the best parameters choice of paremetrs, we used 10 000 measurements to compute the success rate.

Since we induce a fault in the scalar multiplication, we expected most resulting points would not be on the curve anymore. In WolfSSL there is no check like this implemented, so we added it ourselves to let the signing operation fail in case of a fault as a countermeasure. We scanned the surface again with optimal parameters and as expected not a single fault was successful.

To have a faulty scalar multiplication where the resulting point still is on the curve, we can modify the scalar itself. However, this is only possible while it is used within the scalar multiplication as the original scalar r must be used to compute S that is leading to the key recovery. In the implementation of WolfSSL (similar in other implementations) the scalar is copied and some computations are done to alter its representation. This takes roughly $36\mu s$ and gives us plenty of time to emit an EM pulse while the original scalar remains unaltered. Optimizing the parameters resulted in a success rate of 70.15%. Although the success rate with the check on the validity of the resulting point is lower, it is still high enough for the attack to remain practical.

5   Countermeasures

There are several approaches to count fault injection attacks, both in hardware [9, 16] and in software [3, 4]. Here we discuss some software countermeasures.

A countermeasure is to add redundancy in the implementation. For instance, in a common countermeasure, the implementation could execute the scalar multiplication again and at the end compare both results. If they are not identical, then the fault occurred and the signature should not be released. The signature could also be verified at the end, if the signature is invalid, do not return the signature.

However, there is a problem with adding redundancy as a countermeasure as this introduces a check in the code that an attacker also could try to skip by injecting a glitch. It also penalizes the performance. Although this adds a significant amount of difficulty to the attack, an attacker only has to be successful once to be able to recover the secret key.

Another solution is to add randomness to the scheme. In [23] the authors propose a countermeasure called "fault infective computations" where 32 random bytes are used together with different implementations of the hash function for each time the hash function is used in the scheme. A second implementation of the hash function adds to the code size and may not be preferred due to resource constraints.

In this attack we exploit that ephemeral scalar r is equal in both signatures. Introducing some randomness in the generation of r counters our attack. New standards where randomness is introduced in the generation of r are proposed like XEdDSA and VXEdDSA [19]. In these schemes 64 random bytes are added, the VXEdDSA scheme also requires several additional scalar multiplications. In [24], the authors propose a cheap countermeasure that requires only 16 random bytes that are used in the generation of r. The randomness does not have to be perfect as with ECDSA as long as the bytes remain unknown to an attacker. On top of that, the countermeasure also protects the key against differential power analysis [24]. Signatures generated using this countermeasure are still verifiable and conformed with the standard.

6   Conclusion

With this paper we improve and generalize previous attacks on Ed25519, using a realistic target platform and a real-world implementation. We show that our attack is possible using voltage FI and EM FI with very high success rates. While we are able to achieve high success rates, close to 100%, we would like to note that an attacker only needs a single successful fault to recover the key. With adding redundancy to the implementation, it would remain in agreement with the standard but still vulnerable to fault injection. To counter fault injection, the standard should be modified to add some randomness in the generation of the ephemeral scalar.

Although we attack the implementation of WolfSSL, the attack is extendable to other implementations of Ed25519 as the issues are with the scheme being implemented straightforwardly and not a particular implementation itself.

Acknowledgments. This work was supported in part by the Technology Foundation STW (Projects 13499 TYPHOON and 12624 SIDES) and The Netherlands Organization for Scientific Research NWO (project ProFIL 628.001.007) and by a project funded by DarkMatter LLC.

References

1. Agoyan, M., Dutertre, J.-M., Naccache, D., Robisson, B., Tria, A.: When clocks fail: on critical paths and clock faults. In: Gollmann, D., Lanet, J.-L., Iguchi-Cartigny, J. (eds.) CARDIS 2010. LNCS, vol. 6035, pp. 182–193. Springer, Heidelberg (2010). https://doi.org/10.1007/978-3-642-12510-2_13
2. Ambrose, C., Bos, J.W., Fay, B., Joye, M., Lochter, M., Murray, B.: Differential attacks on deterministic signatures. Cryptology ePrint Archive, Report 2017/975 (2017). https://eprint.iacr.org/2017/975.pdf

3. Aumüller, C., Bier, P., Fischer, W., Hofreiter, P., Seifert, J.-P.: Fault attacks on RSA with CRT: concrete results and practical countermeasures. In: Kaliski, B.S., Koç, K., Paar, C. (eds.) CHES 2002. LNCS, vol. 2523, pp. 260–275. Springer, Heidelberg (2003). https://doi.org/10.1007/3-540-36400-5_20

4. Barenghi, A., Breveglieri, L., Koren, I., Pelosi, G., Regazzoni, F.: Countermeasures against fault attacks on software implemented AES. In: Proceedings of the 5th Workshop on Embedded Systems Security - WESS 2010. ACM Press (2010)

5. Barenghi, A., Pelosi, G.: A note on fault attacks against deterministic signature schemes (short paper). In: Ogawa, K., Yoshioka, K. (eds.) IWSEC 2016. LNCS, vol. 9836, pp. 182–192. Springer, Cham (2016). https://doi.org/10.1007/978-3-319-44524-3_11

6. Beckers, A., Balasch, J., Gierlichs, B., Verbauwhede, I.: Design and implementation of a waveform-matching based triggering system. In: Standaert, F.-X., Oswald, E. (eds.) COSADE 2016. LNCS, vol. 9689, pp. 184–198. Springer, Cham (2016). https://doi.org/10.1007/978-3-319-43283-0_11

7. Bernstein, D.J.: Curve25519: new Diffie-Hellman speed records. In: Yung, M., Dodis, Y., Kiayias, A., Malkin, T. (eds.) PKC 2006. LNCS, vol. 3958, pp. 207–228. Springer, Heidelberg (2006). https://doi.org/10.1007/11745853_14

8. Bernstein, D.J., Duif, N., Lange, T., Schwabe, P., Yang, B.Y.: High-speed high-security signatures. J. Crypt. Eng. 2(2), 77–89 (2012)

9. Bertoni, G., Breveglieri, L., Koren, I., Maistri, P., Piuri, V.: Error analysis and detection procedures for a hardware implementation of the advanced encryption standard. IEEE Trans. Comput. 52(4), 492–505 (2003)

10. Biehl, I., Meyer, B., Müller, V.: Differential fault attacks on elliptic curve cryptosystems. In: Bellare, M. (ed.) CRYPTO 2000. LNCS, vol. 1880, pp. 131–146. Springer, Heidelberg (2000). https://doi.org/10.1007/3-540-44598-6_8

11. Boneh, D., DeMillo, R.A., Lipton, R.J.: On the importance of checking cryptographic protocols for faults. In: Fumy, W. (ed.) EUROCRYPT 1997. LNCS, vol. 1233, pp. 37–51. Springer, Heidelberg (1997). https://doi.org/10.1007/3-540-69053-0_4

12. Carpi, R.B., Picek, S., Batina, L., Menarini, F., Jakobovic, D., Golub, M.: Glitch it if you can: parameter search strategies for successful fault injection. In: Francillon, A., Rohatgi, P. (eds.) CARDIS 2013. LNCS, vol. 8419, pp. 236–252. Springer, Cham (2014). https://doi.org/10.1007/978-3-319-08302-5_16

13. Checkoway, S., Maskiewicz, J., Garman, C., Fried, J., Cohney, S., Green, M., Heninger, N., Weinmann, R.P., Rescorla, E., Shacham, H.: A systematic analysis of the Juniper Dual EC incident. In: Proceedings of the 2016 ACM SIGSAC Conference on Computer and Communications Security, CCS 2016, pp. 468–479 (2016). http://doi.acm.org/10.1145/2976749.2978395

14. Howgrave-Graham, N.A., Smart, N.P.: Lattice attacks on digital signature schemes. Des. Codes Crypt. 23(3), 283–290 (2001). https://doi.org/10.1023/A:1011214926272

15. Johnson, D., Menezes, A., Vanstone, S.: The elliptic curve digital signature algorithm (ECDSA). Int. J. Inf. Secur. 1(1), 36–63 (2001)

16. Karpovsky, M., Kulikowski, K., Taubin, A.: Robust protection against fault-injection attacks on smart cards implementing the advanced encryption standard. In: 2004 International Conference on Dependable Systems and Networks. IEEE (2004)

17. Kim, Y., Daly, R., Kim, J., Fallin, C., Lee, J.H., Lee, D., Wilkerson, C., Lai, K., Mutlu, O.: Flipping bits in memory without accessing them. ACM SIGARCH Comput. Archit. News 42(3), 361–372 (2014)

18. Kravitz, D.: Digital signature algorithm. US Patent 5,231,668, 27 July 1993. https://www.google.com/patents/US5231668
19. Perrin, T.: The XEdDSA and VXEdDSA Signature Schemes (2017). https://signal.org/docs/specifications/xeddsa/xeddsa.pdf. Accessed 11 Sept 2017
20. Picek, S., Batina, L., Jakobovic, D., Carpi, R.B.: Evolving genetic algorithms for fault injection attacks. In: 2014 37th International Convention on Information and Communication Technology, Electronics and Microelectronics (MIPRO). IEEE, May 2014
21. Poddebniak, D., Somorovsky, J., Schinzel, S., Lochter, M., Rösler, P.: Attacking deterministic signature schemes using fault attacks. Cryptology ePrint Archive, Report 2017/1014 (2017). http://eprint.iacr.org/2017/1014
22. FIPS PUB 180-4: Secure Hash Standard (SHS). Technical report, NIST, July 2015
23. Romailler, Y., Pelissier, S.: Practical fault attack against the Ed25519 and EdDSA signature schemes. In: 2017 Workshop on Fault Diagnosis and Tolerance in Cryptography (FDTC). IEEE, September 2017
24. Samwel, N., Batina, L., Bertoni, G., Daemen, J., Susella, R.: Breaking Ed25519 in WolfSSL. Cryptology ePrint Archive, Report 2017/985 (2017). http://eprint.iacr.org/2017/985
25. Schnorr, C.P.: Efficient signature generation by smart cards. J. Crypt. 4(3), 161–174 (1991). https://doi.org/10.1007/BF00196725
26. Skorobogatov, S.P., Anderson, R.J.: Optical fault induction attacks. In: Kaliski, B.S., Koç, K., Paar, C. (eds.) CHES 2002. LNCS, vol. 2523, pp. 2–12. Springer, Heidelberg (2003). https://doi.org/10.1007/3-540-36400-5_2
27. Velegalati, R., Van Spyk, R., van Woudenberg, J.: Electro magnetic fault injection in practice. In: International Cryptographic Module Conference (ICMC) (2013)

Authentication with Weaker Trust Assumptions for Voting Systems

Elizabeth A. Quaglia[1](✉) and Ben Smyth[2]

[1] Information Security Group, Royal Holloway, University of London, Egham, UK
Elizabeth.Quaglia@rhul.ac.uk
[2] Interdisciplinary Centre for Security, Reliability and Trust,
University of Luxembourg, Luxembourg City, Luxembourg
research@bensmyth.com

Abstract. Some voting systems are reliant on external authentication services. Others use cryptography to implement their own. We combine digital signatures and non-interactive proofs to derive a generic construction for voting systems with their own authentication mechanisms, from systems that rely on external authentication services. We prove that our construction produces systems satisfying ballot secrecy and election verifiability, assuming the underlying voting system does. Moreover, we observe that works based on similar ideas provide neither ballot secrecy nor election verifiability. Finally, we demonstrate applicability of our results by applying our construction to the Helios voting system.

1 Introduction

An election is a decision-making procedure to choose representatives [17,22,30]. Choices should be made freely by voters with equal influence, and this must be ensured by voting systems [24,25,42]. Some voting systems rely on *external* authentication services to ensure choices are made by voters. E.g., Helios [2,26] supports authentication via Facebook, Google and Yahoo using OAuth.[1] Other voting systems use cryptography to implement their own authentication mechanisms. E.g., the voting system by Juels et al. uses a combination of encrypted nonces and plaintext equality tests for authentication [20]. We combine digital signatures and non-interactive proofs to derive a construction for voting systems with their own authentication mechanisms from systems that rely on external service providers. Our construction produces voting systems which require less trust, since systems built upon cryptography are typically preferable to systems trusting external service providers.

Many voting systems rely on art, rather than science, to ensure that choices are made freely by voters with equal influence. Such systems build upon creativity and skill, rather than scientific foundations, and are typically broken in ways that compromise free choice, e.g., [16,39,43,44], or permit adversaries to unduly influence the outcome, e.g., [10,19]. By contrast, we prove that our construction

---

[1] Meyer and Smyth describe the application of OAuth in Helios [23].

© Springer International Publishing AG, part of Springer Nature 2018
A. Joux et al. (Eds.): AFRICACRYPT 2018, LNCS 10831, pp. 322–343, 2018.
https://doi.org/10.1007/978-3-319-89339-6_18

produces voting systems that satisfy rigorous and precise security definitions of *ballot secrecy* and *election verifiability* that capture voters voting freely with equal influence.[2]

We demonstrate applicability of our construction by deriving voting systems with their own authentication mechanisms from Helios. Moreover, we compare those systems to Helios-C [13], a variant of Helios for two-candidate elections in which ballots are digitally signed. Our comparison reveals some subtle distinctions and we show that Helios-C does not satisfy our security definition, whereas our construction produces voting systems that do.

Structure. Section 2 recalls election scheme syntax. Section 3 presents our construction. Section 4 proves that our construction produces systems satisfying ballot secrecy. Section 5 proves that election verifiability is also satisfied. Section 6 demonstrates the application of our construction to the Helios voting system and compares the resulting systems to Helios-C. We conclude in Sect. 7. The appendices recall security definitions for voting systems and present proofs. Definitions of cryptographic primitives and associated security definitions are deferred to an accompanying technical report [28].

2   Election Scheme Syntax

We recall syntax by Smyth et al. [36] for a class of voting systems that consist of the following four steps. First, a tallier[3] generates a key pair and (optionally) a registrar generates credentials for voters. Secondly, each voter constructs and casts a ballot for their vote. These ballots are recorded on a bulletin board. Thirdly, the tallier tallies the recorded ballots and announces an outcome, i.e., a distribution of votes. Finally, voters and other interested parties check that the outcome corresponds to votes expressed in recorded ballots.

Definition 1 (Election scheme [36]). An *election scheme with external authentication* is a tuple of efficient algorithms (Setup, Vote, Tally, Verify) and an *election scheme with internal authentication* is a tuple of efficient algorithms (Setup, Register, Vote, Tally, Verify), such that:[4]

Setup, denoted $(pk, sk, mb, mc) \leftarrow \mathsf{Setup}(\kappa)$, is run by the tallier. Setup takes a security parameter κ as input and outputs a key pair pk, sk, a maximum number of ballots mb, and a maximum number of candidates mc.

---

[2] Quaglia and Smyth [27] provide a tutorial-style introduction to definitions of ballot secrecy and election verifiability, and Smyth [33] provides a technical introduction.

[3] Some voting systems permit the tallier's role to be distributed amongst several talliers. For simplicity, we consider only a single tallier in this paper.

[4] Let $A(x_1, \ldots, x_n; r)$ denote the output of probabilistic algorithm A on inputs $x_1, \ldots, x_n$ and random coins r. Let $A(x_1, \ldots, x_n)$ denote $A(x_1, \ldots, x_n; r)$, where r is chosen uniformly at random. And let $\leftarrow$ denote assignment. Moreover, let $\langle x \rangle$ denote an optional input and $\mathbf{v}[v]$ denote component v of vector $\mathbf{v}$.

Register, denoted $(pd, d) \leftarrow \mathsf{Register}(pk, \kappa)$, is run by the registrar. It takes as input the public key pk of the tallier and a security parameter κ, and it outputs a *credential pair* (pd, d), where pd is a public credential and d is a private credential.

Vote, denoted $b \leftarrow \mathsf{Vote}(\langle d \rangle, pk, nc, v, \kappa)$, is run by voters. Vote takes as input a private credential d (optional), a public key pk, some number of candidates nc, a voter's vote v, and a security parameter κ. The vote should be selected from a sequence $1, \ldots, nc$ of candidates. Vote outputs a ballot b or error symbol $\bot$.

Tally, denoted $(\mathbf{v}, pf) \leftarrow \mathsf{Tally}(sk, nc, \mathfrak{bb}, \langle L \rangle, \kappa)$, is run by the tallier. Tally takes as input a private key sk, some number of candidates nc, a bulletin board $\mathfrak{bb}$, an electoral roll L (optional), and a security parameter κ, where $\mathfrak{bb}$ is a set. It outputs an election outcome $\mathbf{v}$ and a non-interactive proof pf that the outcome is correct. An election outcome is a vector $\mathbf{v}$ of length nc such that $\mathbf{v}[v]$ indicates the number of votes for candidate v.

Verify, denoted $s \leftarrow \mathsf{Verify}(pk, nc, \mathfrak{bb}, \langle L \rangle, \mathbf{v}, pf, \kappa)$, is run to audit an election. It takes as input a public key pk, some number of candidates nc, a bulletin board $\mathfrak{bb}$, an electoral roll L (optional), an election outcome $\mathbf{v}$, a proof pf, and a security parameter κ. It outputs a bit s, which is 1 if the election verifies successfully and 0 otherwise.

Election schemes with internal authentication must always use optional inputs, whereas election schemes with external authentication must not. Both schemes must satisfy *correctness*: there exists a negligible function negl, such that for all security parameters κ, integers nb and nc, and votes $v_1, \ldots, v_{nb} \in \{1, \ldots, nc\}$, it holds that if $\mathbf{v}$ is a vector of length nc whose components are all 0, then

$$\Pr[(pk, sk, mb, mc) \leftarrow \mathsf{Setup}(\kappa);$$

$$\begin{aligned}
&\textbf{for } 1 \leq i \leq nb \textbf{ do} \\
&\quad \left| \begin{array}{l} (pd_i, d_i) \leftarrow \mathsf{Register}(pk, \kappa); \\ b_i \leftarrow \mathsf{Vote}(\langle d_i \rangle, pk, nc, v_i, \kappa); \\ \mathbf{v}[v_i] \leftarrow \mathbf{v}[v_i] + 1; \end{array} \right. \\
&(\mathbf{v}', pf) \leftarrow \mathsf{Tally}(sk, nc, \{b_1, \ldots, b_{nb}\}, \langle \{pd_1, \ldots, pd_{nb}\} \rangle, \kappa) \\
&: nb \leq mb \wedge nc \leq mc \Rightarrow \mathbf{v} = \mathbf{v}'] > 1 - \mathsf{negl}(\kappa),
\end{aligned}$$

where algorithm Register is only applied for election scheme with internal authentication and optional inputs are only used for election scheme with internal authentication.

3   Our Construction

Election schemes with internal authentication can be derived from schemes with external authentication using a digital signature scheme and a non-interactive proof system: Each voter publishes a ballot constructed using the underlying scheme with external authentication, along with a signature on that ballot and a proof that they constructed both the ballot and the signature. Signatures and proofs are used to ensure that each tallied vote was cast by an authorised voter.

Our construction is formal described in Definition 3. It is parameterised by an election scheme with external authentication, a digital signature scheme, and a non-interactive proof system, derived from an underlying sigma protocol and a hash function, using the Fiat-Shamir transformation.[5] Hence, we denote election schemes derived using our construction as $\mathsf{Ext2Int}(\Gamma, \Omega, \Sigma, \mathcal{H})$, where the underlying election scheme, signature scheme, sigma protocol and hash function are Γ, Ω, Σ and $\mathcal{H}$, respectively. To ensure our construction produces election schemes with internal authentication, the non-interactive proof system must be defined for a suitable relation, and we define such a relation as follows.

Definition 2. Given an election scheme with external authentication $\Gamma = (\mathsf{Setup}, \mathsf{Vote}, \mathsf{Tally}, \mathsf{Verify})$ and a digital signature scheme $\Omega = (\mathsf{Gen}_\Omega, \mathsf{Sign}_\Omega, \mathsf{Verify}_\Omega)$, we define binary relation $R(\Gamma, \Omega)$ over vectors of length 6 and vectors of length 4 such that $((pk, b, \sigma, nc, \kappa), (v, r, d, r')) \in R(\Gamma, \Omega) \Leftrightarrow b = \mathsf{Vote}(pk, nc, v, \kappa; r) \wedge \sigma = \mathsf{Sign}_\Omega(d, b; r')$.

Definition 3 (Construction). Suppose $\Gamma = (\mathsf{Setup}_\Gamma, \mathsf{Vote}_\Gamma, \mathsf{Tally}_\Gamma, \mathsf{Verify}_\Gamma)$ is an election scheme with external authentication, $\Omega = (\mathsf{Gen}_\Omega, \mathsf{Sign}_\Omega, \mathsf{Verify}_\Omega)$ is a digital signature scheme, Σ is a sigma protocol for a binary relation $R(\Gamma, \Omega)$, and $\mathcal{H}$ is a hash function. Let $\mathsf{FS}(\Sigma, \mathcal{H}) = (\mathsf{Prove}_\Sigma, \mathsf{Verify}_\Sigma)$. We define $\mathsf{Ext2Int}(\Gamma, \Omega, \Sigma, \mathcal{H}) = (\mathsf{Setup}, \mathsf{Register}, \mathsf{Vote}, \mathsf{Tally}, \mathsf{Verify})$ such that:

- $\mathsf{Setup}(\kappa)$ computes $(pk, sk, mb, mc) \leftarrow \mathsf{Setup}_\Gamma(\kappa)$ and outputs (pk, sk, mb, mc).
- $\mathsf{Register}(pk, \kappa)$ computes $(pd, d) \leftarrow \mathsf{Gen}_\Omega(\kappa)$ and outputs $(pd, (pd, d))$.
- $\mathsf{Vote}(d', pk, nc, v, \kappa)$ parses d' as (pd, d) and outputs $\bot$ if parsing fails, selects coins r and r' uniformly at random, computes

    $b \leftarrow \mathsf{Vote}_\Gamma(pk, nc, v, \kappa; r)$;
    $\sigma \leftarrow \mathsf{Sign}_\Omega(d, b; r')$;
    $\tau \leftarrow \mathsf{Prove}_\Sigma((pk, b, \sigma, nc, \kappa), (v, r, d, r'), \kappa)$,

    and outputs (pd, b, σ, τ).
- $\mathsf{Tally}(sk, nc, \mathfrak{bb}, L, \kappa)$ computes $(\mathbf{v}, pf) \leftarrow \mathsf{Tally}_\Gamma(sk, \mathsf{auth}(\mathfrak{bb}, L), nc, \kappa)$ and outputs $(\mathbf{v}, pf)$.
- $\mathsf{Verify}(pk, nc, \mathfrak{bb}, L, \mathbf{v}, pf, \kappa)$ computes $s \leftarrow \mathsf{Verify}_\Gamma(pk, \mathsf{auth}(\mathfrak{bb}, L), nc, \mathbf{v}, pf, \kappa)$ and outputs s.

Set $\mathsf{auth}(\mathfrak{bb}, L) = \{b \mid (pd, b, \sigma, \tau) \in \mathfrak{bb} \wedge \mathsf{Verify}_\Omega(pd, b, \sigma) = 1 \wedge \mathsf{Verify}_\Sigma ((pk, b, nc, \kappa), \tau, \kappa) = 1 \wedge pd \in L \wedge (pd, b', \sigma', \tau') \notin \mathfrak{bb} \setminus \{(pd, b, \sigma, \tau)\} \wedge \mathsf{Verify}_\Omega(pd, b', \sigma') = 1\}$.

Our construction uses function auth to ensure tallied ballots are authorised and to discard ballots submitted under the same credential (i.e., if there is more

---

[5] Let $\mathsf{FS}(\Sigma, \mathcal{H})$ denote the non-interactive proof system derived by application of the Fiat-Shamir transformation to sigma protocol Σ and hash function $\mathcal{H}$.

than one ballot submitted with a private credential, then all ballots submitted under that credential are discarded). Since election schemes with internal authentication must satisfy correctness, the underlying digital signature scheme must ensure that key pairs are distinct. Hence, correctness of our construction depends on security of the underlying digital signature scheme, albeit in a tedious manner. Since we exploit strong unforgeability of the signature scheme for results in the following sections, we assume the same property here (to ensure key pairs are distinct). Weaker conditions could be used for generality.

Lemma 1. *Let Γ be an election scheme with external authentication, Ω be a digital signature scheme, Σ be a sigma protocol for relation $R(\Gamma, \Omega)$, and $\mathcal{H}$ be a random oracle. Suppose Ω satisfies strong unforgeability. We have* Ext2Int$(\Gamma, \Omega, \Sigma, \mathcal{H})$ *is an election scheme with internal authentication.*

The proof of Lemma 1 appears in our companion technical report [28].

4   Our Construction Ensures Ballot Secrecy

We adopt the definition of ballot secrecy for election schemes with external authentication (Ballot-Secrecy-Ext) by Smyth [32]. That definition appears to be the most suitable in the literature, because it detects the largest class of attacks [32, Sect. 7]. In particular, it detects attacks that arise when the adversary controls the bulletin board or the communications channel, whereas other definitions, e.g., [5–8,11,12,35], fail to detect such attacks. A definition of ballot secrecy for election schemes with internal authentication (Ballot-Secrecy-Int) can be derived from Smyth's definition by a natural, straightforward extension that takes credentials into account. Both definitions are presented in Appendix A. The definition of ballot secrecy we recall challenges an adversary, who has access to the election outcome, to distinguish between ballots.

We can prove that our construction ensures ballot secrecy (a formal proof of Theorem 2 appears in Appendix A), assuming the underlying election scheme satisfies ballot secrecy and the underlying sigma protocol satisfies special soundness and special honest verifier zero-knowledge.

Theorem 2. *Let Γ be an election scheme with external authentication, Ω be a digital signature scheme, Σ be a sigma protocol for relation $R(\Gamma, \Omega)$, and $\mathcal{H}$ be a random oracle. Suppose Γ satisfies* Ballot-Secrecy-Ext, *Σ satisfies special soundness and special honest verifier zero-knowledge, and Ω satisfies strong unforgeability. Election scheme with internal authentication* Ext2Int$(\Gamma, \Omega, \Sigma, \mathcal{H})$ *satisfies* Ballot-Secrecy-Int.

Proof sketch. Ballot secrecy of election scheme Ext2Int$(\Gamma, \Omega, \Sigma, \mathcal{H})$ follows from secrecy of the underlying scheme Γ, because signatures and non-interactive zero-knowledge proofs do not leak information. (Special soundness and special honest verifier zero-knowledge ensure proof system FS$(\Sigma, \mathcal{H})$ is zero-knowledge [7].)   □

We demonstrate applicability of Theorem 2 using a construction for election schemes from asymmetric encryption.[6]

Definition 4 (Enc2Vote [29]). Given a perfectly correct asymmetric encryption scheme $\Pi = (\mathsf{Gen}, \mathsf{Enc}, \mathsf{Dec})$ satisfying IND-CPA, election scheme with external authentication Enc2Vote(Π) is defined as follows:

- Setup(κ) computes $(pk, sk) \leftarrow \mathsf{Gen}(\kappa)$ and outputs $(pk, sk, poly(\kappa), |\mathsf{m}|)$.
- Vote(pk, nc, v, κ) computes $b \leftarrow \mathsf{Enc}(pk, v)$ and outputs b if $1 \leq v \leq nc \leq |\mathsf{m}|$ and $\bot$ otherwise.
- Tally$(sk, nc, \mathfrak{bb}, \kappa)$ initialises vector $\mathbf{v}$ of length nc, computes **for** $b \in \mathfrak{bb}$ **do** $v \leftarrow \mathsf{Dec}(sk, b)$; **if** $1 \leq v \leq nc$ **then** $\mathbf{v}[v] \leftarrow \mathbf{v}[v] + 1$, and outputs $(\mathbf{v}, \epsilon)$.
- Verify$(pk, nc, \mathfrak{bb}, \mathbf{v}, pf, \kappa)$ outputs 1.

Algorithm Setup requires *poly* to be a polynomial function, algorithms Setup and Vote require $\mathsf{m} = \{1, \ldots, |\mathsf{m}|\}$ to be the encryption scheme's plaintext space, and algorithm Tally requires ϵ to be a constant symbol.

Intuitively, given a non-malleable asymmetric encryption scheme Π,[7] Enc2Vote(Π) derives ballot secrecy from Π until tallying and tallying maintains ballot secrecy by returning only the number of votes for each candidate.

Proposition 3 ([29,32]). *Let Π be an encryption scheme with perfect correctness. If Π satisfies IND-PA0, then election scheme with external authentication Enc2Vote(Π) satisfies Ballot-Secrecy-Ext.*

Hence, by Theorem 2, we have the following result.

Corollary 4. *Let Π be an asymmetric encryption scheme with perfect correctness, Ω be a digital signature scheme, Σ be a sigma protocol for relation $R(\text{Enc2Vote}(\Pi), \Omega)$, and $\mathcal{H}$ be a random oracle. Suppose Π satisfies IND-PA0, Σ satisfies special soundness and special honest verifier zero-knowledge, and Ω satisfies strong unforgeability. Election scheme with internal authentication Ext2Int(Enc2Vote$(\Pi), \Omega, \Sigma, \mathcal{H})$ satisfies Ballot-Secrecy-Int.*

Clearly election scheme Enc2Vote does not satisfy universal verifiability, because it will accept any election outcome.

5 Our Construction Ensures Election Verifiability

We adopt definitions of individual (Exp-IV-Ext) and universal (Exp-UV-Ext) verifiability for election schemes with external authentication from Smyth et al. [36]. We also adopt their definitions of individual (Exp-IV-Int), universal (Exp-UV-Int)

---

[6] We omit a formal definition of asymmetric encryption for brevity.

[7] We adopt the formal definition of comparison based non-malleability under chosen plaintext attack, which coincides with indistinguishability under a parallel chosen-ciphertext attack (IND-PA0) [3]. We omit formal security definitions for brevity.

and eligibility (Exp-EV-Int) verifiability for schemes with internal authentication. Those definitions seem to be the most suitable in the literature, because they detect the largest class of attacks. In particular, they detect collusion and biasing attacks [36, Sect. 7], whereas other definitions, e.g., [13,20,21], fail to detect such attacks. The definitions are presented in Appendix B.

The definitions by Smyth, Frink, and Clarkson et al. work as follows: Individual verifiability challenges the adversary to generate a collision from algorithm Vote. Universal verifiability challenges the adversary to concoct a scenario in which either: Verify accepts, but the election outcome is not correct, or Tally produces an election outcome that Verify rejects. Hence, universal verifiability requires algorithm Verify to accept if and only if the election outcome is correct. Finally, eligibility verifiability challenges an adversary, which can corrupt voters, to generate a valid ballot under a non-corrupt voter's private credential.

We can prove that our construction ensures election verifiability. Individual and eligibility verifiability of $\mathsf{Ext2Int}(\Gamma, \Omega, \Sigma, \mathcal{H})$ follow from security of the underlying signature scheme, and universal verifiability follows from universal verifiability of the underlying election scheme Γ.

Theorem 5. *Let Γ be an election scheme with external authentication, Ω be a digital signature scheme, Σ be a sigma protocol for relation $R(\Gamma, \Omega)$, and $\mathcal{H}$ be a random oracle. Suppose Ω satisfies strong unforgeability, Σ satisfies special soundness and special honest verifier zero-knowledge, and Γ satisfies Exp-UV-Ext. Election scheme with internal authentication $\mathsf{Ext2Int}(\Gamma, \Omega, \Sigma, \mathcal{H})$ satisfies Exp-IV-Int, Exp-EV-Int, and Exp-UV-Int.*

Proof sketch. Individual verifiability is satisfied because voters can check that their signatures appear on the bulletin board. Universal verifiability is satisfied because the underlying voting scheme does, and the properties of Ω and Σ ensure only authorised ballots are tallied. And eligibility verifiability is satisfied because anyone can check that signatures belong to registered voters.   □

A formal proof of Theorem 5 follows immediately from our proofs of individual, universal and eligibility verifiability, which we defer to Appendix B (Lemmata 10–12).

We demonstrate applicability of our results for election schemes from nonces.

Definition 5 (Nonce [36])**.** Election scheme with external authentication Nonce is defined as follows:

- Setup(κ) outputs $(\bot, \bot, p_1(\kappa), p_2(\kappa))$, where p_1 and p_2 may be any polynomial functions.
- Vote(pk, nc, v, κ) selects a nonce r uniformly at random from $\mathbb{Z}_{2^\kappa}$ and outputs (r, v).
- Tally($sk, nc, \mathfrak{bb}, \kappa$) computes a vector $\mathbf{v}$ of length nc, such that $\mathbf{v}$ is a tally of the votes on $\mathfrak{bb}$ for which the nonce is in $\mathbb{Z}_{2^\kappa}$, and outputs $(\mathbf{v}, \bot)$.
- Verify($pk, \mathfrak{bb}, nc, \mathbf{v}, pf, \kappa$) outputs 1 if $(\mathbf{v}, pf) = \mathsf{Tally}(\bot, nc, \mathfrak{bb}, \kappa)$, and 0 otherwise.

Intuitively, election scheme Nonce ensures verifiability because voters can use their nonce to check that their ballot is recorded (individual verifiability) and anyone can recompute the election outcome to check that it corresponds to votes expressed in recorded ballots (universal verifiability).

Proposition 6 ([36]). *Election scheme with external authentication* Nonce *satisfies* Exp-IV-Ext *and* Exp-UV-Ext.

Hence, by Theorem 5, we have the following result.

Corollary 7. *Let Ω be a digital signature scheme, Σ be a sigma protocol for relation $R(\mathsf{Nonce}, \Omega)$, and $\mathcal{H}$ be a random oracle. Suppose Ω satisfies strong unforgeability and Σ satisfies special soundness and special honest verifier zero-knowledge. Election scheme with internal authentication* Ext2Int($\mathsf{Nonce}, \Omega, \Sigma, \mathcal{H}$) *satisfies* Exp-IV-Int, Exp-UV-Int, *and* Exp-EV-Int.

Clearly election scheme Nonce does not satisfy ballot secrecy.

6 Case Study: A Secret, Verifiable Election Scheme with Internal Authentication

Helios is an open-source, web-based electronic voting system which has been used in binding elections. The International Association of Cryptologic Research has used Helios annually since 2010 to elect board members [4,18], the ACM used Helios for their 2014 general election [40], the Catholic University of Louvain used Helios to elect the university president in 2009 [2], and Princeton University has used Helios since 2009 to elect student governments. Informally, Helios can be modelled as the following election scheme with external authentication:

Setup generates a key pair for an asymmetric homomorphic encryption scheme, proves correct key generation in zero-knowledge, and outputs the public key coupled with the proof.

Vote encrypts the vote, proves correct ciphertext construction and that the vote is selected from the sequence of candidates (both in zero-knowledge), and outputs the ciphertext coupled with the proof.

Tally proceeds as follows. First, any ballots on the bulletin board for which proofs do not hold are discarded. Secondly, the ciphertexts in the remaining ballots are homomorphically combined, the homomorphic combination is decrypted to reveal the election outcome, and correctness of decryption is proved in zero-knowledge. Finally, the election outcome and proof of correct decryption are output.

Verify recomputes the homomorphic combination, checks the proofs, and outputs 1 if these checks succeed and 0 otherwise.

The original scheme [2] is known to be vulnerable to attacks against ballot secrecy and verifiability,[8] and defences against those attacks have been proposed [7,15,32,35]. We adopt the formal definition of a Helios variant by Smyth

---

[8] Beyond secrecy and verifiability, attacks against eligibility are also known [23,38].

et al. [36], which adopts non-malleable ballots [32,37] and uses the Fiat–Shamir transformation with statements in hashes [7] to defend against those attacks. Henceforth, we write *Helios'16* to refer to that formalisation.

Using our construction we derive an election scheme with internal authentication from Helios'16 and prove privacy and verifiability using our results.

Theorem 8. *Let Ω be a digital signature scheme, Σ be a sigma protocol for relation $R(Helios'16, \Omega)$, and $\mathcal{H}$ be a random oracle. Suppose Ω satisfies strong unforgeability and Σ satisfies special soundness and special honest verifier zero-knowledge. Election scheme with internal authentication* Ext2Int(*Helios'16*, $\Omega, \Sigma, \mathcal{H}$) *satisfies* Ballot-Secrecy-Int, Exp-IV-Int, Exp-UV-Int, *and* Exp-EV-Int.

Proof. Helios'16 satisfies Ballot-Secrecy-Ext, Exp-IV-Ext, and Exp-UV-Ext [32,36], FS($\Sigma, \mathcal{H}$) satisfies zero-knowledge [7], and we conclude by Theorems 2 and 5.   □

Comparison with Helios-C. Schemes derived from Helios using our construction are similar to Helios-C [13,14]. Indeed, they use ballots that include a Helios ballot and a signature on that Helios ballot. The schemes derived by our construction also include proofs of correct construction, unlike Helios-C. We will see that this distinction is crucial to ensure ballot secrecy.

Cortier *et al.* [13, Sect. 5] analysed Helios-C using the definition of ballot secrecy by Bernhard et al. [7]. That definition assumes "ballots are *recorded-as-cast*, i.e., cast ballots are preserved with integrity through the ballot collection process" [32, Sect. 7]. Unfortunately, ballot secrecy is not satisfied without this assumption, because Helios-C uses malleable ballots.

Remark 9. Helios-C does not satisfy Ballot-Secrecy-Int.

Proof sketch. An adversary can observe and block a voter's ballot,[9] extract the underlying Helios ballot, sign that ballot, and post the ballot and signature on the bulletin board. The adversary can then exploit the relation between ballots to recover the voter's vote from the election outcome. (Cf. [15].)   □

Ext2Int(Helios'16, $\Omega, \Sigma, \mathcal{H}$) ballots extend non-malleable Helios'16 ballots with a signature and a proof demonstrating construction of both the embedded Helios'16 ballot and signature, thus, Ext2Int(Helios'16, $\Omega, \Sigma, \mathcal{H}$) uses non-malleable ballots, so it is not similarly effected.

Beyond secrecy, Smyth et al. [36] have shown that Helios-C does not satisfy Exp-UV-Int. Hence, we improve upon Helios-C by satisfying Ballot-Secrecy-Ext and Exp-UV-Int.

Our results can also be applied to the variant of Helios that applies a mixnet to encrypted votes and decrypts the mixed encrypted votes to reveal the outcome [1, 9], rather than homomorphically combining encrypted votes and decrypting the homomorphic combination to reveal the outcome. Tsoukalas *et al.* [41] released

---

[9] Ballot blocking violates the recorded-as-cast assumption used in Cortier *et al.*'s proof.

Zeus as a fork of Helios spliced with mixnet code to derive an implementation of that variant, and Yingtong Li released *helios-server-mixnet* as an extension of Zeus with threshold asymmetric encryption.[10] We could use our construction to derive an election scheme with internal authentication from the mixnet variant of Helios and use our privacy and verifiability results to prove security. Since the ideas remain the same, we do not pursue further details.

7   Conclusion

This work was initiated by a desire to eliminate trust assumptions placed upon the operators of external authentication services. Cortier *et al.* made progress in this direction with Helios-C, which builds upon Helios by signing ballots. We discovered that Helios-C does not satisfy ballot secrecy in the presence of an adversary that controls the bulletin board or the communication channel, and it is known that verifiability is not satisfied either. We realised that proving correct construction of both the Helios ballot and the signature suffices for non-malleability. This prompted the design of our construction and led to the accompanying security proofs that it produces voting systems satisfying ballot secrecy and verifiability. Finally, we demonstrated the applicability of our results by applying our construction to the Helios voting system. The next step would be to select a suitable sigma protocol and signature scheme to instantiate our construction concretely. And an interesting and useful direction for future work will be to consider, in general, the practical challenges of implementing our construction efficiently.

Acknowledgements. In the context of [36], Smyth conceived the fundamental ideas of our construction for election schemes with internal authentication. In addition, Smyth discovered that Helios-C does not satisfy ballot secrecy, whilst analysing election verifiability. Smyth and his co-authors, Frink & Clarkson, decided not to publish these results. This paper builds upon those unpublished results and we are grateful to Frink and Clarkson for their part in inspiring this line of work.

A   Ballot Privacy: Definitions and Proofs

We recall Smyth's definition of ballot secrecy for election schemes with external authentication (Definition 6), and present a natural, straightforward extension of that definition to capture ballot secrecy for election schemes with internal authentication (Definition 7). Our definitions both use predicate *balanced* such that *balanced*$(\mathfrak{bb}, nc, B)$ holds when: for all votes $v \in \{1, \ldots, nc\}$ we have $|\{b \mid b \in \mathfrak{bb} \wedge \exists v_1 \ . \ (b, v, v_1) \in B\}| = |\{b \mid b \in \mathfrak{bb} \wedge \exists v_0 \ . \ (b, v_0, v) \in B\}|$. Intuitively, the definitions challenge an adversary to determine whether the left-right oracle produces ballots for "left" or "right" inputs, by giving the adversary the

---

[10] Smyth [34] shows that vulnerabilities in Helios cause vulnerabilities in implementations of the mixnet variant and proves verifiability is satisfied when a fix is applied.

oracle's outputs, as well as the election outcome and tallying proof. The definitions prevent the adversary from trivially distinguishing ballots by requiring predicate *balanced* to hold.

Definition 6 (Ballot-Secrecy-Ext [32]). Let $\Gamma = (\mathsf{Setup}, \mathsf{Vote}, \mathsf{Tally}, \mathsf{Verify})$ be an election scheme with external authentication, $\mathcal{A}$ be an adversary, κ be a security parameter, and $\mathsf{Ballot\text{-}Secrecy\text{-}Ext}(\Gamma, \mathcal{A}, \kappa)$ be the following game.

$\mathsf{Ballot\text{-}Secrecy\text{-}Ext}(\Gamma, \mathcal{A}, \kappa) =$

> $(pk, sk, mb, mc) \leftarrow \mathsf{Setup}(\kappa);$
> $nc \leftarrow \mathcal{A}(pk, \kappa);$
> $\beta \leftarrow_R \{0, 1\}; B \leftarrow \emptyset;$
> $\mathfrak{bb} \leftarrow \mathcal{A}^{\mathcal{O}}();$
> $(\mathbf{v}, pf) \leftarrow \mathsf{Tally}(sk, nc, \mathfrak{bb}, \kappa);$
> $g \leftarrow \mathcal{A}(\mathbf{v}, pf);$
> **if** $g = \beta \wedge balanced(\mathfrak{bb}, nc, B) \wedge 1 \leq nc \leq mc \wedge |\mathfrak{bb}| \leq mb$ **then**
> | **return** 1
> **else**
> | **return** 0

Oracle $\mathcal{O}$ is defined as follows:[11]

- $\mathcal{O}(v_0, v_1)$ computes **if** $v_0, v_1 \in \{1, \dots, nc\}$ **then** $b \leftarrow \mathsf{Vote}(pk, nc, v_\beta, \kappa); B \leftarrow B \cup \{(b, v_0, v_1)\};$ **return** b.

We say Γ satisfies Ballot-Secrecy-Ext, if for all probabilistic polynomial-time adversaries $\mathcal{A}$, there exists a negligible function negl, such that for all security parameters κ, we have $\mathsf{Succ}(\mathsf{Ballot\text{-}Secrecy\text{-}Ext}(\Gamma, \mathcal{A}, \kappa)) \leq \frac{1}{2} + \mathsf{negl}(\kappa)$.

Definition 7 (Ballot-Secrecy-Int). Let $\Gamma = (\mathsf{Setup}, \mathsf{Register}, \mathsf{Vote}, \mathsf{Tally}, \mathsf{Verify})$ be an election scheme with internal authentication, $\mathcal{A}$ be an adversary, κ be a security parameter, and $\mathsf{Ballot\text{-}Secrecy\text{-}Int}(\Gamma, \mathcal{A}, \kappa)$ be the following game.

$\mathsf{Ballot\text{-}Secrecy\text{-}Int}(\Gamma, \mathcal{A}, \kappa) =$

> $(pk, sk, mb, mc) \leftarrow \mathsf{Setup}(\kappa);$
> $nv \leftarrow \mathcal{A}(pk, \kappa);$
> **for** $1 \leq i \leq nv$ **do**
> | $(pd_i, d_i) \leftarrow \mathsf{Register}(pk, \kappa);$
> $nc \leftarrow \mathcal{A}(pd_1, \dots, pd_{nv});$
> $\beta \leftarrow_R \{0, 1\}; B \leftarrow \emptyset; R \leftarrow \emptyset;$
> $\mathfrak{bb} \leftarrow \mathcal{A}^{\mathcal{O}}();$
> $(\mathbf{v}, pf) \leftarrow \mathsf{Tally}(sk, nc, \mathfrak{bb}, \{pd_1, \dots, pd_{nv}\}, \kappa);$
> $g \leftarrow \mathcal{A}(\mathbf{v}, pf);$
> **if** $g = \beta \wedge balanced(\mathfrak{bb}, nc, B) \wedge 1 \leq nc \leq mc \wedge |\mathfrak{bb}| \leq mb$ **then**
> | **return** 1
> **else**
> | **return** 0

Oracle $\mathcal{O}$ is defined as follows:

---

[11] Oracles may access game parameters, e.g., pk.

- $\mathcal{O}(i, v_0, v_1)$ computes **if** $v_0, v_1 \in \{1, \ldots, nc\} \wedge i \notin R$ **then** $b \leftarrow$ Vote$(d_i, pk, nc, v_\beta, \kappa)$; $B \leftarrow B \cup \{(b, v_0, v_1)\}$; $R \leftarrow R \cup \{i\}$; **return** b; and
- $\mathcal{O}(i)$ computes **if** $i \notin R$ **then** $R \leftarrow R \cup \{i\}$; **return** d_i.

We say Γ satisfies Ballot-Secrecy-Int, if for all probabilistic polynomial-time adversaries $\mathcal{A}$, there exists a negligible function negl, such that for all security parameters κ, we have Succ(Ballot-Secrecy-Int$(\Gamma, \mathcal{A}, \kappa)) \leq \frac{1}{2} + \mathsf{negl}(\kappa)$.

Game Ballot-Secrecy-Int extends Ballot-Secrecy-Ext to take credentials into account. In particular, the challenger constructs nv credentials, where nv is chosen by the adversary. These credentials are used to construct ballots and for tallying. Public and private credentials are available to the adversary. Albeit, the oracle will only reveal a private credential if it has not used it to construct a ballot. Moreover, the oracle may only use a private credential to construct a ballot if it has not revealed it nor constructed a previous ballot with it.

Proof of Theorem 2. Suppose Ballot-Secrecy-Int is not satisfied by Ext2Int$(\Gamma, \Omega, \Sigma, \mathcal{H})$, i.e., there exists a adversary $\mathcal{A}$ such that for all negligible functions negl there exists a security parameter κ and Succ(Ballot-Secrecy-Int(Ext2Int$(\Gamma, \Omega, \Sigma, \mathcal{H}), \mathcal{A}, \kappa)) \leq \frac{1}{2} + \mathsf{negl}(\kappa)$. We construct an adversary $\mathcal{B}$ against Γ from $\mathcal{A}$.

Let $\Gamma = ($Setup$_\Gamma$, Vote$_\Gamma$, Tally$_\Gamma$, Verify$_\Gamma)$, $\Omega = ($Gen$_\Omega$, Sign$_\Omega$, Verify$_\Omega)$, FS$(\Sigma, \mathcal{H}) = ($Prove$_\Sigma$, Verify$_\Sigma)$, and Ext2Int$(\Gamma, \Omega, \Sigma, \mathcal{H}) = ($Setup, Register, Vote, Tally, Verify$)$. By [7, Theorem 1], non-interactive proof system (Prove$_\Sigma$, Verify$_\Sigma)$ satisfies zero-knowledge, i.e., there exists a simulator for (Prove$_\Sigma$, Verify$_\Sigma)$. Let $\mathcal{S}$ be such a simulator. We define $\mathcal{B}$ as follows:

- $\mathcal{B}(pk, \kappa)$ computes $nv \leftarrow \mathcal{A}(pk, \kappa)$; **for** $1 \leq i \leq nv$ **do** $(pd_i, d_i) \leftarrow$ Register(pk, κ); $nc \leftarrow \mathcal{A}(pd_1, \ldots, pd_{nv})$ and outputs nc.
- $\mathcal{B}()$ computes $R \leftarrow \emptyset$; $\mathfrak{bb} \leftarrow \mathcal{A}^{\mathcal{O}}()$; $\mathfrak{bb} \leftarrow$ auth$(\mathfrak{bb}, \{pd_1, \ldots, pd_{nv}\})$ and outputs $\mathfrak{bb}$, handling oracle calls from $\mathcal{A}$ as follows. Given an oracle call $\mathcal{O}(i, v_0, v_1)$ such that $v_0, v_1 \in \{1, \ldots, nc\} \wedge i \notin R$, adversary $\mathcal{B}$ computes $b \leftarrow \mathcal{O}(v_0, v_1)$; $\sigma \leftarrow$ Sign$_\Omega(d_i, b)$; $\tau \leftarrow \mathcal{S}((pk, b, \sigma, nc, \kappa), \kappa)$; $R \leftarrow R \cup \{i\}$ and returns (pd_i, b, σ, τ) to $\mathcal{A}$. Moreover, given an oracle call $\mathcal{O}(i)$ such that $i \notin R$, adversary $\mathcal{B}$ computes $R \leftarrow R \cup \{i\}$ and returns d_i to $\mathcal{A}$.
- $\mathcal{B}(\mathbf{v}, pf)$ computes $g \leftarrow \mathcal{A}(\mathbf{v}, pf)$ and outputs g.

We prove that $\mathcal{B}$ wins Ballot-Secrecy-Ext against Γ.

Suppose (pk, sk, mb, mc) is an output of Setup$_\Gamma(\kappa)$ and nc is an output of $\mathcal{B}(pk, \kappa)$. It is trivial to see that $\mathcal{B}(pk, \kappa)$ simulates $\mathcal{A}$'s challenger to $\mathcal{A}$. Let β be a bit. Suppose $\mathfrak{bb}$ is an output of $\mathcal{B}()$. Since $\mathcal{S}$ is a simulator for (Prove$_\Sigma$, Verify$_\Sigma)$, we have $\mathcal{B}()$ simulates $\mathcal{A}$'s challenger to $\mathcal{A}$. In particular, $\mathcal{B}()$ simulates oracle calls $\mathcal{O}(i, v_0, v_1)$. Indeed, adversary $\mathcal{B}$ computes $b \leftarrow \mathcal{O}(v_0, v_1)$; $\sigma \leftarrow$ Sign$_\Omega(d_i, b)$; $\tau \leftarrow \mathcal{S}((pk, b, \sigma, nc, \kappa), \kappa)$, which, by definition of $\mathcal{B}$'s oracle, is equivalent to $b \leftarrow$ Vote$_\Gamma(pk, nc, v_\beta, \kappa)$; $\sigma \leftarrow$ Sign$_\Omega(d_i, b)$; $\tau \leftarrow \mathcal{S}((pk, b, \sigma, nc, \kappa), \kappa)$. And $\mathcal{A}$'s oracle computes $b \leftarrow$ Vote$(d_i, pk, nc, v_\beta, \kappa)$, i.e., $b \leftarrow$ Vote$_\Gamma(pk, nc, v_\beta, \kappa; r)$; $\sigma \leftarrow$ Sign$_\Omega(d_i, b; r')$; $\tau \leftarrow$ Prove$_\Sigma((pk, b, \sigma, nc, \kappa), (v_\beta, r, d_i, r'), \kappa)$, where r and r' are coins chosen uniformly at random. Hence, computations of b, σ and τ by $\mathcal{B}$ and $\mathcal{A}$'s oracle are equivalent, with overwhelming probability. Suppose $(\mathbf{v}, pf)$ is an output of $\mathsf{Tally}_\Gamma(sk, \mathfrak{bb}, nc, \kappa)$ and g is an output of $\mathcal{B}(\mathbf{v}, pf)$. We have $\mathcal{B}(\mathbf{v}, pf)$ simulates $\mathcal{A}$'s challenger to $\mathcal{A}$, because outputs of $\mathsf{Tally}_\Gamma(sk', \mathsf{auth}(\mathfrak{bb}', L), nc', \kappa')$ and $\mathsf{Tally}(sk', nc', \mathfrak{bb}', L, \kappa')$ are indistinguishable for all sk', $\mathfrak{bb}'$, L, nc', and κ'. Indeed, Tally computes $(\mathbf{v}', pf') \leftarrow \mathsf{Tally}_\Gamma(sk', \mathsf{auth}(\mathfrak{bb}', L), nc', \kappa')$ and outputs $(\mathbf{v}', pf')$. Since adversary $\mathcal{B}$ simulates $\mathcal{A}$'s challenger, with overwhelming probability. It follows that $\mathcal{B}$ determines β correctly with the same success as $\mathcal{A}$ with overwhelming probability. Hence, $\mathcal{B}$ wins $\mathsf{Ballot\text{-}Secrecy\text{-}Ext}(\Gamma, \mathcal{A}, \kappa)$, with overwhelming probability, deriving a contradiction and concluding our proof.   □

B   Election Verifiability: Definitions and Proofs

B.1   Individual Verifiability

Definition 8. (Exp-IV-Ext [36]). *Let* $\Gamma = (\mathsf{Setup}, \mathsf{Vote}, \mathsf{Tally}, \mathsf{Verify})$ *be an election scheme with external authentication,* $\mathcal{A}$ *be an adversary,* κ *be a security parameter, and* $\mathsf{Exp\text{-}IV\text{-}Ext}(\Gamma, \mathcal{A}, \kappa)$ *be the following game.*

$\mathsf{Exp\text{-}IV\text{-}Ext}(\Gamma, \mathcal{A}, \kappa) =$

$\quad (pk, nc, v, v') \leftarrow \mathcal{A}(\kappa);$
$\quad b \leftarrow \mathsf{Vote}(pk, nc, v, \kappa);$
$\quad b' \leftarrow \mathsf{Vote}(pk, nc, v', \kappa);$
$\quad \textbf{if } \ b = b' \wedge b \neq \bot \wedge b' \neq \bot \textbf{ then}$
$\quad | \ \ \textbf{return } 1$
$\quad \textbf{else}$
$\quad \llcorner \ \textbf{return } 0$

We say Γ *satisfies* $\mathsf{Exp\text{-}IV\text{-}Ext}$, *if for all probabilistic polynomial-time adversaries* $\mathcal{A}$, *there exists a negligible function* negl, *such that for all security parameters* κ, *we have* $\mathsf{Succ}(\mathsf{Exp\text{-}IV\text{-}Ext}(\Gamma, \mathcal{A}, \kappa)) \leq \mathsf{negl}(\kappa)$.

Definition 9. (Exp-IV-Int [36]). *Let* $\Gamma = (\mathsf{Setup}, \mathsf{Register}, \mathsf{Vote}, \mathsf{Tally}, \mathsf{Verify})$ *be an election scheme with external authentication,* $\mathcal{A}$ *be an adversary,* κ *be a security parameter, and* $\mathsf{Exp\text{-}IV\text{-}Int}(\Pi, \mathcal{A}, \kappa)$ *be the following game.*

$\mathsf{Exp\text{-}IV\text{-}Int}(\Pi, \mathcal{A}, \kappa) =$

$\quad (pk, nv) \leftarrow \mathcal{A}(\kappa);$
$\quad \textbf{for } 1 \leq i \leq nv \textbf{ do } (pd_i, d_i) \leftarrow \mathsf{Register}(pk, \kappa);$
$\quad L \leftarrow \{pd_1, \ldots, pd_{nv}\};$
$\quad Crpt \leftarrow \emptyset;$
$\quad (nc, v, v', i, j) \leftarrow \mathcal{A}^C(L);$
$\quad b \leftarrow \mathsf{Vote}(d_i, pk, nc, v, \kappa);$
$\quad b' \leftarrow \mathsf{Vote}(d_j, pk, nc, v', \kappa);$
$\quad \textbf{if } \ b = b' \wedge b \neq \bot \wedge b' \neq \bot \wedge i \neq j \wedge d_i \notin Crpt \wedge d_j \notin Crpt \textbf{ then}$
$\quad | \ \ \textbf{return } 1$
$\quad \textbf{else}$
$\quad \llcorner \ \textbf{return } 0$

Oracle C is defined such that $C(i)$ computes $Crpt \leftarrow Crpt \cup \{d_i\}$ and outputs d_i, where $1 \leq i \leq nv$.

We say Γ satisfies Exp-IV-Int, if for all probabilistic polynomial-time adversaries $\mathcal{A}$, there exists a negligible function negl, such that for all security parameters κ, we have $\mathsf{Succ}(\mathsf{Exp}\text{-}\mathsf{IV}\text{-}\mathsf{Int}(\Pi, \mathcal{A}, \kappa)) \leq \mathsf{negl}(\kappa)$.

Lemma 10. *Let $\Gamma = (\mathsf{Setup}, \mathsf{Register}, \mathsf{Vote}, \mathsf{Tally}, \mathsf{Verify})$ be an election scheme with external authentication, $\Omega = (\mathsf{Gen}, \mathsf{Sign}, \mathsf{Verify})$ be a digital signature scheme, Σ be a sigma protocol for relation $R(\Gamma, \Omega)$, and $\mathcal{H}$ be a hash function. Suppose Ω satisfies strong unforgeability. We have $\mathsf{Ext2Int}(\Gamma, \Omega, \Sigma, \mathcal{H})$ satisfies Exp-IV-Int.*

Proof. Suppose $\mathsf{Ext2Int}(\Gamma, \Pi, \Sigma, \mathcal{H})$ does not satisfy Exp-IV-Int. Hence, there exists a PPT adversary $\mathcal{A}$, such that for all negligible functions negl, there exists a security parameter κ and $\mathsf{negl}(\kappa) < \mathsf{Succ}(\mathsf{Exp}\text{-}\mathsf{IV}\text{-}\mathsf{Int}(\mathsf{Ext2Int}(\Gamma, \Pi, \Sigma, \mathcal{H}), \mathcal{A}, \kappa))$. We construct the following adversary $\mathcal{B}$ against strong unforgeability from $\mathcal{A}$:

$\mathcal{B}(pd, \kappa) =$

    $(pk, nv) \leftarrow \mathcal{A}(\kappa);$
    $i^* \leftarrow_R \{1, \ldots, nv\};$
    $\mathbf{for}\ i \in \{1, \ldots, nv\} \setminus \{i^*\}\ \mathbf{do}\ (pd_i, d_i) \leftarrow \mathsf{Register}(pk, \kappa);$
    $(nc, v, v', j, k) \leftarrow \mathcal{A}^C(\{pd_1, \ldots, pd_{i^*-1}, pd, pd_{i^*+1}, \ldots, pd_{nv}\});$
    $\mathbf{if}\ i^* = k\ \mathbf{then}$
        $(pd_j, b, \sigma, \tau) \leftarrow \mathsf{Vote}(d_j, pk, nc, v, \kappa);$
        $\mathbf{return}\ (\sigma, b);$
    $\mathbf{else\ if}\ i^* = j\ \mathbf{then}$
        $(pd_k, b, \sigma, \tau) \leftarrow \mathsf{Vote}(d_k, pk, nc, v', \kappa);$
        $\mathbf{return}\ (\sigma, b);$
    $\mathbf{else}$
        $\mathbf{abort};$

where $C(i)$ outputs d_i if $i \neq i^*$ and aborts otherwise. We prove that $\mathcal{B}$ wins strong unforgeability against Ω.

Since adversary $\mathcal{B}$ chooses i^* uniformly at random and independently of adversary $\mathcal{A}$, and since $\mathcal{A}$ is a winning adversary, hence, does not corrupt at least two distinct credentials, we have that $\mathcal{B}$ aborts with a probability upper-bounded by $\frac{nv-2}{nv}$. Let us consider the probability that $\mathcal{B}$ wins, when there is no abort. Suppose (pd, d) is an output of $\mathsf{Gen}(\kappa)$, (pk, nv) is an output of $\mathcal{A}(\kappa)$, and i^* is chosen uniformly at random from $\{1, \ldots, nv\}$. Further suppose (pd_i, d_i) is an output of $\mathsf{Register}(pk, \kappa)$ for each $i \in \{1, \ldots, nv\} \setminus \{i^*\}$. It is straightforward to see that $\mathcal{B}$ simulates the challenger and oracle in Exp-IV-Int to $\mathcal{A}$. Suppose (nc, v, v', j, k) is an output of $\mathcal{A}^C(\{pd_1, \ldots, pd_{i^*-1}, pd, pd_{i^*+1}, \ldots, pd_{nv}\})$. Since $\mathcal{A}$ is a winning adversary, outputs of $\mathsf{Vote}(d_j, pk, nc, v, \kappa)$ and $\mathsf{Vote}(d_k, pk, nc, v', \kappa)$ collide with non-negligible probability. Hence, if $i^* = k$, then $\mathsf{Vote}(d_j, pk, nc, v, \kappa)$ outputs (pd_j, b, σ, τ) such that σ is a signature on b with respect to private key d_{i^*}, otherwise $(i^* = j)$, $\mathsf{Vote}(d_k, pk, nc, v', \kappa)$ outputs (pd_k, b, σ, τ) such that σ is a signature on b

with respect to private key d_{i^*}. Thus, $\mathsf{Succ}(\mathsf{Exp\text{-}StrongSign}(\Gamma, \mathcal{B}, \kappa))$ is at least $\frac{2}{nv} \cdot \mathsf{Succ}(\mathsf{Exp\text{-}IV\text{-}Int}(\mathsf{Ext2Int}(\Gamma, \Pi, \Sigma, \mathcal{H}), \mathcal{A}, \kappa))$, which is non-negligible.   □

B.2   Universal Verifiability

External authentication. Algorithm Verify is required to accept iff the election outcome is correct. The notion of a correct outcome is captured using function *correct-outcome*, which is defined such that for all pk, nc, $\mathfrak{bb}$, κ, ℓ, and $v \in \{1, \dots, nc\}$, we have *correct-outcome*$(pk, nc, \mathfrak{bb}, \kappa)[v] = \ell$ iff $\exists^{=\ell} b \in \mathfrak{bb}\backslash\{\bot\}$: $\exists r : b = \mathsf{Vote}(pk, nc, v, \kappa; r),$[12] and the produced vector is of length nc. Hence, component v of vector *correct-outcome*$(pk, nc, \mathfrak{bb}, \kappa)$ equals ℓ iff there exist ℓ ballots on the bulletin board that are votes for candidate v. The function requires ballots to be interpreted for only one candidate, which can be ensured by injectivity.

The *if* requirement of universal verifiability is captured by Completeness, which stipulates that election outcomes produced by algorithm Tally will actually be accepted by algorithm Verify. And the *only if* requirement is captured by Soundness, which challenges an adversary to concoct a scenario in which algorithm Verify accepts, but the election outcome is not correct.

Definition 10 ([36]). An election scheme with external authentication (Setup, Vote, Tally, Verify) satisfies *Soundness*, if the scheme satisfies Injectivity [36] and for all probabilistic polynomial-time adversaries $\mathcal{A}$, there exists a negligible function negl, such that for all security parameters κ, we have $\Pr[(pk, nc, \mathfrak{bb}, \mathbf{v}, pf) \leftarrow \mathcal{A}(\kappa); \mathbf{return} \ \mathbf{v} \neq correct\text{-}outcome(pk, nc, \mathfrak{bb}, \kappa) \wedge \mathsf{Verify}(pk, nc, \mathfrak{bb}, \mathbf{v}, pf, \kappa) = 1] \leq \mathsf{negl}(\kappa)$.

An election scheme with external authentication satisfies Exp-UV-Ext, if Injectivity, Completeness and Soundness are satisfied, where formal definitions of Injectivity and Completeness appear in [36].

Internal authentication. Function *correct-outcome* is now modified to tally only authorised ballots: let function *correct-outcome* now be defined such that for all pk, nc, $\mathfrak{bb}$, M, κ, ℓ, and $v \in \{1, \dots, nc\}$, we have *correct-outcome*$(pk, nc, \mathfrak{bb}, M, \kappa)[v] = \ell$ iff $\exists^{=\ell} b \in authorized(pk, nc, (\mathfrak{bb} \setminus \{\bot\}), M, \kappa) : \exists d, r : b = \mathsf{Vote}(d, pk, nc, v, \kappa; r)$. A ballot is *authorised* if it is constructed with a private credential from M, and that private credential was not used to construct any other ballot on $\mathfrak{bb}$. Let *authorized* be defined as follows: *authorized*$(pk, nc, \mathfrak{bb}, M, \kappa) = \{b : b \in \mathfrak{bb} \wedge \exists pd, d, v, r : b = \mathsf{Vote}(d, pk, nc, v, \kappa; r) \wedge (pd, d) \in M \wedge \neg \exists b', v', r' : b' \in (\mathfrak{bb} \setminus \{b\}) \wedge b' = \mathsf{Vote}(d, pk, nc, v', \kappa; r')\}$.

---

[12] Function *correct-outcome* uses a *counting quantifier* [31] denoted $\exists^=$. Predicate $(\exists^{=\ell} x : P(x))$ holds exactly when there are ℓ distinct values for x such that $P(x)$ is satisfied. Variable x is bound by the quantifier, whereas ℓ is free.

Definition 11 ([36]). An election scheme with internal authentication (Setup, Register, Vote, Tally, Verify) satisfies *Soundness*, if the scheme satisfies Injectivity [36] and for all probabilistic polynomial-time adversaries $\mathcal{A}$, there exists a negligible function negl, such that for all security parameters κ, we have $\Pr[(pk, nv) \leftarrow \mathcal{A}(\kappa); \text{ for } 1 \leq i \leq nv \text{ do } (pd_i, d_i) \leftarrow \mathsf{Register}(pk, \kappa);$ $L \leftarrow \{pd_1, \ldots, pd_{nv}\}; M \leftarrow \{(pd_1, d_1), \ldots, (pd_{nv}, d_{nv})\}; (\mathfrak{bb}, nc, \mathbf{v}, pf) \leftarrow \mathcal{A}(M);$ **return** $\mathbf{v} \neq correct\text{-}outcome(pk, nc, \mathfrak{bb}, M, \kappa) \wedge \mathsf{Verify}(pk, nc, \mathfrak{bb}, L, \mathbf{v}, pf, \kappa)$ $= 1] \leq \mathsf{negl}(\kappa)$.

An election scheme with internal authentication satisfies Exp-UV-Int, if Injectivity, Completeness and Soundness are satisfied.

Lemma 11. *Let* $\Gamma = (\mathsf{Setup}_\Gamma, \mathsf{Vote}_\Gamma, \mathsf{Tally}_\Gamma, \mathsf{Verify}_\Gamma)$ *be an election scheme with external authentication,* $\Omega = (\mathsf{Gen}_\Omega, \mathsf{Sign}_\Omega, \mathsf{Verify}_\Omega)$ *be a perfectly correct digital signature scheme,* Σ *be a sigma protocol for relation* $R(\Gamma, \Omega)$*, and* $\mathcal{H}$ *be a random oracle. Moreover, let* $\mathsf{FS}(\Sigma, \mathcal{H}) = (\mathsf{Prove}_\Sigma, \mathsf{Verify}_\Sigma)$*. Suppose* Γ *satisfies* Exp-UV-Ext*,* Ω *satisfies strong unforgeabilityand* Σ *satisfies perfect special soundness and special honest verifier zero-knowledge. Election scheme with internal authentication* $\mathsf{Ext2Int}(\Gamma, \Omega, \Sigma, \mathcal{H}) = (\mathsf{Setup}, \mathsf{Register}, \mathsf{Vote}, \mathsf{Tally}, \mathsf{Verify})$ *satisfies* Exp-UV-Int*.*

Proof. We prove that $\mathsf{Ext2Int}(\Gamma, \Omega, \Sigma, \mathcal{H})$ satisfies Injectivity, Completeness and Soundness: The proofs for Injectivity and Completeness are quite straightforward and can be found in our technical report [28].

Soundness. We prove that $\mathsf{Ext2Int}(\Gamma, \Omega, \Sigma, \mathcal{H})$ satisfies Soundness by contradiction. Suppose $\mathsf{Ext2Int}(\Gamma, \Omega, \Sigma, \mathcal{H})$ does not satisfy Soundness, i.e., there exists an adversary $\mathcal{A}$ such that for all negligible functions negl there exists a security parameter κ and the probability defined in Definition 11 is greater than $\mathsf{negl}(\kappa)$. We use $\mathcal{A}$ to construct an adversary $\mathcal{B}$ that wins the Soundness game against Γ.

$\mathcal{B}(\kappa) =$

    $(pk, nv) \leftarrow \mathcal{A}(\kappa);$
    for $1 < i < nv$ **do**
       $\lfloor \; (pd_i, d_i) \leftarrow \mathsf{Register}(pk, \kappa);$
    $L = \{pd_1, \ldots, pd_{nv}\};$
    $M \leftarrow \{(pd_1, d_1), \ldots, (pd_{nv}, d_{nv})\};$
    $(\mathfrak{bb}, nc, \mathbf{v}, pf) \leftarrow \mathcal{A}(M);$
    return $(pk, nc, \mathsf{auth}(\mathfrak{bb}, L), \mathbf{v}, pf)$

We prove that $\mathcal{B}$ wins the Soundness game against Γ.

Suppose (pk, nv) is an output of $\mathcal{A}(\kappa)$ and $(pd_1, d_1), \ldots, (pd_{nv}, d_{nv})$ are outputs of $\mathsf{Register}(pk, \kappa)$. Let $L = \{pd_1, \ldots, pd_{nv}\}$ and $M = \{(pd_1, d_1), \ldots, (pd_{nv}, d_{nv})\}$. Suppose $(\mathfrak{bb}, nc, \mathbf{v}, pf)$ is an output of $\mathcal{A}(M)$. Further suppose $(pk, nc, \mathsf{auth}(\mathfrak{bb}, L), \mathbf{v}, pf)$ is an output of $\mathcal{B}(\kappa)$. Since $\mathcal{A}$ is a winning adversary, we have $\mathsf{Verify}(pk, nc, \mathfrak{bb}, L, \mathbf{v}, pf, \kappa) = 1$, with non-negligible probability. By inspection of algorithm Verify, we have $\mathsf{Verify}(pk, nc, \mathfrak{bb}, L, \mathbf{v}, pf, \kappa) = 1$

implies $\mathsf{Verify}_\Gamma(pk, \mathsf{auth}(\mathfrak{bb}, L), nc, \mathbf{v}, pf, \kappa) = 1$. Hence, it remains to show $\mathbf{v} \neq$ $correct\text{-}outcome(pk, nc, \mathsf{auth}(\mathfrak{bb}, L), \kappa)$, with probability greater than $\mathsf{negl}(\kappa)$.

By definition of function $correct\text{-}outcome$, we have $\mathbf{v}$ is a vector of length nc such that

$$correct\text{-}outcome(pk, nc, \mathsf{auth}(\mathfrak{bb}, L), \kappa)[v] = \ell$$
$$\Leftrightarrow \exists^{=\ell} b \in \mathsf{auth}(\mathfrak{bb}, L) \setminus \{\bot\} : \exists r : b = \mathsf{Vote}(pk, nc, v, \kappa; r)$$

Since $\mathcal{A}$ is a winning adversary, it suffices to derive

$$\Leftrightarrow \exists^{=\ell} b \in authorized(pk, nc, (\mathfrak{bb} \setminus \{\bot\}), M, \kappa)$$
$$: \exists d, r : b = \mathsf{Vote}(d, pk, nc, v, \kappa; r) \tag{1}$$

Let set $auth^*(pk, nc, \mathfrak{bb}, M, \kappa) = \{b^* | (pd, b^*, \sigma, \tau) \in authorized(pk, nc, \mathfrak{bb}, M, \kappa)\}$. To prove (1), it suffices to show $\mathsf{auth}(\mathfrak{bb}, L) \setminus \{\bot\} = auth^*(pk, nc, \mathfrak{bb}, M, \kappa) \setminus \{\bot\}$, since this would imply that $correct\text{-}outcome$ is computed on sets of corresponding ballots in both the external and internal authentication setting.

- $auth^*(pk, nc, \mathfrak{bb}, M, \kappa) \setminus \{\bot\} \subseteq \mathsf{auth}(\mathfrak{bb}, L) \setminus \{\bot\}$
  If $b^* \in auth^*(pk, nc, \mathfrak{bb}, M, \kappa)$, then $b^* \neq \bot$ and there exists $b \in$ $authorized(pk, nc, \mathfrak{bb}, M, \kappa)$ such that (i) $b \in \mathfrak{bb}$; (ii) $\exists pd, d, v, r, r', r''$: $b = (pd, b^*, \sigma, \tau)$, $b^* = \mathsf{Vote}_\Gamma(pk, nc, v, \kappa; r)$, $\sigma = \mathsf{Sign}_\Omega(d, b^*; r')$, and $\tau = \mathsf{Prove}_\Sigma((pk, b^*, \sigma, nc, \kappa), (v, r, d, r'), \kappa; r'')$, which – by correctness of Ω and completeness of Σ – implies $\mathsf{Verify}_\Omega(pd, b^*, \sigma) = 1$ and $\mathsf{Verify}_\Sigma((pk, b^*, nc, \kappa), \tau, \kappa)) = 1$; (iii) $(pd, d) \in M$, which implies $pd \in$ L by construction; and (iv) $\neg \exists b', v', r, r', r''$: $b' \in (\mathfrak{bb} \setminus \{b\}) \wedge b' = (pd, b^{*'}, \sigma', \tau')$, $b^* = \mathsf{Vote}_\Gamma(pk, nc, v', \kappa; r)$, $\sigma' = \mathsf{Sign}_\Omega(d, b^*; r')$, and $\tau' = \mathsf{Prove}_\Sigma((pk, b^{*'}, \sigma', nc, \kappa), (v', r, d, r'), \kappa; r'')$, which, by correctness of Ω, implies $\mathsf{Verify}_\Omega(pd, b^{*'}, \sigma') = 1$. It follows by (i)–(iv) that $b^* \in$ $auth^*(pk, nc, \mathfrak{bb}, M, \kappa)$ implies $b^* \in \mathsf{auth}(\mathfrak{bb}, L) \setminus \{\bot\}$.
- $\mathsf{auth}(\mathfrak{bb}, L) \setminus \{\bot\} \subseteq auth^*(pk, nc, \mathfrak{bb}, M, \kappa) \setminus \{\bot\}$
  If $b^* \in \mathsf{auth}(\mathfrak{bb}, L) \setminus \{\bot\}$, then $b^* \neq \bot$ such that (i) $(pd, b^*, \sigma, \tau) \in \mathfrak{bb}$; (ii) $\mathsf{Verify}_\Omega(pd, b^*, \sigma) = 1$ and $\mathsf{Verify}_\Sigma((pk, b^*, nc, \kappa), \tau, \kappa)) = 1$, which – by the security of Ω and Σ – implies $\exists pd, d, v, r, r', r''$: $b^* = \mathsf{Vote}_\Gamma(pk, nc, v, \kappa; r)$, $\sigma = \mathsf{Sign}_\Omega(d, b^*; r')$, and $\tau = \mathsf{Prove}_\Sigma((pk, b^*, \sigma, nc, \kappa), (v, r, d, r'), \kappa; r'')$. Indeed, suppose this is not true, i.e., such values do not exist. Then (b^*, σ) and $((pk, b^*, nc, \kappa), \tau)$ could be used by adversaries to break the unforgeability property of Ω and the special soundness and special honest verifier zero-knowledge property of Σ, respectively. Furthermore, we have (iii) $pd \in L$, which implies $(pd, d) \in M$ by construction; and (iv) $b' = (pd, b^{*'}, \sigma', \tau') \notin$ $(\mathfrak{bb} \setminus \{(pd, b^*, \sigma, \tau)\}) \wedge \mathsf{Verify}_\Omega(pd, b^{*'}, \sigma') = 1$, which implies $\neg \exists b', v', r, r', r''$: $b' \in (\mathfrak{bb} \setminus \{b\}) \wedge b' = (pd, b^{*'}, \sigma', \tau')$, $b^{*'} = \mathsf{Vote}_\Gamma(pk, nc, v', \kappa; r)$, $\sigma' = \mathsf{Sign}_\Omega(d, b^{*'}; r')$, and $\tau' = \mathsf{Prove}_\Sigma((pk, b^{*'}, \sigma', nc, \kappa), (v', r, d, r'), \kappa; r'')$, as per definition of $authorized$, concluding our proof. $\qquad \square$

B.3   Eligibility Verifiability

Definition 12 (Eligibility verifiability [36]). Let $\Gamma = (\mathsf{Setup}, \mathsf{Register}, \mathsf{Vote},$ $\mathsf{Tally}, \mathsf{Verify})$ be an election scheme with internal authentication, $\mathcal{A}$ be an adversary, κ be a security parameter, and $\mathsf{Exp\text{-}EV\text{-}Int}(\Pi, \mathcal{A}, \kappa)$ be the following game.

$\mathsf{Exp\text{-}EV\text{-}Int}(\Pi, \mathcal{A}, \kappa) =$
 $(pk, nv) \leftarrow \mathcal{A}(\kappa);$
 for $1 \leq i \leq nv$ **do** $(pd_i, d_i) \leftarrow \mathsf{Register}(pk, \kappa);$
 $L \leftarrow \{pd_1, \dots, pd_{nv}\};$
 $Crpt \leftarrow \emptyset;\ Rvld \leftarrow \emptyset;$
 $(nc, v, i, b) \leftarrow \mathcal{A}^{C,R}(L);$
 if $\exists r : b = \mathsf{Vote}(d_i, pk, nc, v, \kappa; r) \wedge b \neq \bot \wedge b \notin Rvld \wedge d_i \notin Crpt$ **then**
  | **return** 1
 else
  ∟ **return** 0

Oracle C is the same oracle as in $\mathsf{Exp\text{-}IV\text{-}Int}$, and oracle R is defined such that $R(i, v, nc)$ computes $b \leftarrow \mathsf{Vote}(d_i, pk, nc, v, k);\ Rvld \leftarrow Rvld \cup \{b\}$ and outputs b.

We say Γ satisfies $\mathsf{Exp\text{-}EV\text{-}Int}$, if for all probabilistic polynomial-time adversaries $\mathcal{A}$, there exists a negligible function negl, such that for all security parameters κ, we have $\mathsf{Succ}(\mathsf{Exp\text{-}EV\text{-}Int}(\Pi, \mathcal{A}, \kappa)) \leq \mathsf{negl}(\kappa)$.

Lemma 12. *Let* $\Gamma = (\mathsf{Setup}_\Gamma, \mathsf{Vote}_\Gamma, \mathsf{Tally}_\Gamma, \mathsf{Verify}_\Gamma)$ *be an election scheme with external authentication,* $\Omega = (\mathsf{Gen}_\Omega, \mathsf{Sign}_\Omega, \mathsf{Verify}_\Omega)$ *be a digital signature scheme,* Σ *be a sigma protocol for relation* $R(\Gamma, \Omega)$*, and* $\mathcal{H}$ *be a hash function. Suppose* Σ *satisfies special soundness and special honest verifier zeroknowledge, and* Ω *satisfies strong unforgeability. Election scheme with internal authentication* $\mathsf{Ext2Int}(\Gamma, \Omega, \Sigma, \mathcal{H}) = (\mathsf{Setup}, \mathsf{Register}, \mathsf{Vote}, \mathsf{Tally}, \mathsf{Verify})$ *satisfies* $\mathsf{Exp\text{-}EV\text{-}Int}$.

Proof. Suppose $\mathsf{Ext2Int}(\Gamma, \Omega, \Sigma, \mathcal{H})$ does not satisfy $\mathsf{Exp\text{-}EV\text{-}Int}$, i.e., there exists an adversary $\mathcal{A}$ such that for all negligible functions negl there exists a security parameter κ and $\mathsf{Succ}(\mathsf{Exp\text{-}EV\text{-}Int}(\Pi, \mathcal{A}, \kappa)) > \mathsf{negl}(\kappa)$. We construct the following adversary $\mathcal{B}$ against the strong unforgeability of Ω from $\mathcal{A}$.

$\mathcal{B}(pd, \kappa) =$
 $(pk, nv) \leftarrow \mathcal{A}(\kappa);$
 $i^* \leftarrow_R \{1, \dots, nv\};$
 for $i \in \{1, \dots, nv\} \setminus \{i^*\}$ **do** $(pd_i, d_i) \leftarrow \mathsf{Register}(pk, \kappa);$
 $Rvld \leftarrow \emptyset;\ Crpt \leftarrow \emptyset;$
 $(nc, v, i, b) \leftarrow \mathcal{A}^{C,R}(\{pd_1, \dots, pd_{i^*-1}, pd, pd_{i^*+1}, \dots, pd_{nv}\});$
 if $b[1] = pd$ **then**
  | **return** $(b[1], b[3]);$
 else
  ∟ **abort**;

where oracle calls are handled as follows:

- $C(i)$ computes $Crpt \leftarrow Crpt \cup \{d_i\}$ and returns d_i if $i \neq i^*$, and aborts otherwise.
- $R(i, v, nc)$ distinguishes two cases: If $i = i^*$, then $\mathcal{B}$ computes $b \leftarrow \mathsf{Vote}_\Gamma(pk, nc, v, \kappa); \sigma \leftarrow \mathcal{O}(b); \tau \leftarrow \mathcal{S}((pk, b, \sigma, nc, \kappa), \kappa)$, computes $Rvld \leftarrow Rvld \cup \{(pd, b, \sigma, \tau)\}$, and returns (pd, b, σ, τ), where $\mathcal{S}$ is a simulator for $\mathsf{FS}(\Sigma, \mathcal{H})$ that exists by [7, Theorem 1]. Otherwise, $\mathcal{B}$ computes $b \leftarrow \mathsf{Vote}(d_i, pk, nc, v, \kappa)$, $Rvld \leftarrow Rvld \cup \{b\}$ and returns b.

We prove that $\mathcal{B}$ wins the strong unforgeability game against Ω.

Let κ be a security parameter. Suppose (pd, d) is an output of $\mathsf{Gen}(\kappa)$ and (pk, nv) is an output of $\mathcal{A}(\kappa)$. Let i^* be an integer chosen uniformly at random from $\{1, \ldots, nv\}$. Suppose (pd_i, d_i) is an output of $\mathsf{Register}(pk, \kappa)$, for each $i \in \{1, \ldots, nv\} \setminus \{i^*\}$. Let us consider an execution of $\mathcal{A}(\{pd_1, \ldots, pd_{i^*-1}, pd, pd_{i^*+1}, \ldots, pd_{nv}\})$. Let (nc, v, i, b) be the output of $\mathcal{A}$. By definition of algorithm $\mathsf{Register}$, it is trivial to see that $\mathcal{B}$ simulates $\mathcal{A}$'s challenger to $\mathcal{A}$. Moreover, $\mathcal{B}$ simulates oracle C to $\mathcal{A}$, except when $\mathcal{B}$ aborts. Furthermore, $\mathcal{B}$ simulates oracle R to $\mathcal{A}$ as well. In particular, simulator $\mathcal{S}$ produces proofs that are indistinguishable from proofs constructed by non-interactive proof system $\mathsf{FS}(\Sigma, \mathcal{H})$.

We denote by Good the event that $i = i^*$. Now, let us assess $\mathcal{B}$'s probability not to abort, to determine the success probability of $\mathcal{B}$. Since $\mathcal{A}$ is not allowed to corrupt the credential it finally outputs (as $\mathcal{A}$ is a winning adversary, $d_i \notin Crpt$ must hold), a sufficient condition for $\mathcal{B}$ not to be asked for the unknown private credential d_i is to be lucky when drawing $i^* \leftarrow \{1, \ldots, nv\}$ at random and have event Good occurring.

This is the case with probability $\Pr[\mathsf{Good}] = \frac{1}{nv}$ since the choice of i^* is completely independent of $\mathcal{A}$'s view. Therefore we have $\mathsf{Succ}(\mathsf{Exp\text{-}EV\text{-}Int}(\Pi, \mathcal{A}, \kappa)) \leq nv \cdot \mathsf{Succ}(\mathsf{Exp\text{-}StrongSign}(\Omega, \mathcal{B}, k))$. $\qquad\square$

References

1. Adida, B.: Helios: web-based open-audit voting. In: USENIX Security 2008: 17th USENIX Security Symposium, pp. 335–348. USENIX Association (2008)
2. Adida, B., Marneffe, O., Pereira, O., Quisquater, J.: Electing a university president using open-audit voting: analysis of real-world use of Helios. In: EVT/WOTE 2009: Electronic Voting Technology Workshop/Workshop on Trustworthy Elections. USENIX Association (2009)
3. Bellare, M., Sahai, A.: Non-malleable encryption: equivalence between two notions, and an indistinguishability-based characterization. In: Wiener, M. (ed.) CRYPTO 1999. LNCS, vol. 1666, pp. 519–536. Springer, Heidelberg (1999). https://doi.org/10.1007/3-540-48405-1_33
4. Benaloh, J., Vaudenay, S., Quisquater, J.: Final report of IACR electronic voting committee. International Association for Cryptologic Research, September 2010. https://iacr.org/elections/eVoting/finalReportHelios_2010-09-27.html

5. Bernhard, D., Cortier, V., Galindo, D., Pereira, O., Warinschi, B.: SoK: a comprehensive analysis of game-based ballot privacy definitions. In: S&P 2015: 36th Security and Privacy Symposium. IEEE Computer Society (2015)
6. Bernhard, D., Cortier, V., Pereira, O., Smyth, B., Warinschi, B.: Adapting Helios for provable ballot privacy. In: Atluri, V., Diaz, C. (eds.) ESORICS 2011. LNCS, vol. 6879, pp. 335–354. Springer, Heidelberg (2011). https://doi.org/10.1007/978-3-642-23822-2_19
7. Bernhard, D., Pereira, O., Warinschi, B.: How not to prove yourself: pitfalls of the Fiat-Shamir heuristic and applications to Helios. In: Wang, X., Sako, K. (eds.) ASIACRYPT 2012. LNCS, vol. 7658, pp. 626–643. Springer, Heidelberg (2012). https://doi.org/10.1007/978-3-642-34961-4_38
8. Bernhard, D., Pereira, O., Warinschi, B.: On necessary and sufficient conditions for private Ballot submission. Cryptology ePrint Archive, Report 2012/236 (version 20120430:154117b) (2012)
9. Bulens, P., Giry, D., Pereira, O.: Running mixnet-based elections with Helios. In: EVT/WOTE 2011: Electronic Voting Technology Workshop/Workshop on Trustworthy Elections. USENIX Association (2011)
10. Bundesverfassungsgericht (Germany's Federal Constitutional Court): Use of voting computers in 2005 Bundestag election unconstitutional. Press release 19/2009, March 2009
11. Cortier, V., Galindo, D., Glondu, S., Izabachene, M.: A generic construction for voting correctness at minimum cost - application to Helios. Cryptology ePrint Archive, Report 2013/177 (version 20130521:145727) (2013)
12. Cortier, V., Galindo, D., Glondu, S., Izabachene, M.: Distributed elgamal à la pedersen: application to Helios. In: WPES 2013: Workshop on Privacy in the Electronic Society, pp. 131–142. ACM Press (2013)
13. Cortier, V., Galindo, D., Glondu, S., Izabachène, M.: Election verifiability for Helios under weaker trust assumptions. In: Kutyłowski, M., Vaidya, J. (eds.) ESORICS 2014 Part II. LNCS, vol. 8713, pp. 327–344. Springer, Cham (2014). https://doi.org/10.1007/978-3-319-11212-1_19
14. Cortier, V., Galindo, D., Glondu, S., Izabachène, M.: Election verifiability for Helios under weaker trust assumptions. Technical report RR-8555, INRIA (2014)
15. Cortier, V., Smyth, B.: Attacking and fixing Helios: an analysis of ballot secrecy. In: CSF 2011: 24th Computer Security Foundations Symposium, pp. 297–311. IEEE Computer Society (2011)
16. Gonggrijp, R., Hengeveld, W.J.: Studying the Nedap/Groenendaal ES3B voting computer: a computer security perspective. In: EVT 2007: Electronic Voting Technology Workshop. USENIX Association (2007)
17. Gumbel, A.: Steal This Vote: Dirty Elections and the Rotten History of Democracy in America. Nation Books, New York (2005)
18. Haber, S., Benaloh, J., Halevi, S.: The Helios e-voting demo for the IACR. International Association for Cryptologic Research, May 2010. https://iacr.org/elections/eVoting/heliosDemo.pdf
19. Jones, D.W., Simons, B.: Broken ballots: will your vote count? CSLI Lecture Notes, vol. 204. Stanford University, Center for the Study of Language and Information (2012)
20. Juels, A., Catalano, D., Jakobsson, M.: Coercion-resistant electronic elections. In: Chaum, D., Jakobsson, M., Rivest, R.L., Ryan, P.Y.A., Benaloh, J., Kutylowski, M., Adida, B. (eds.) Towards Trustworthy Elections. LNCS, vol. 6000, pp. 37–63. Springer, Heidelberg (2010). https://doi.org/10.1007/978-3-642-12980-3_2

21. Kiayias, A., Zacharias, T., Zhang, B.: End-to-end verifiable elections in the standard model. In: Oswald, E., Fischlin, M. (eds.) EUROCRYPT 2015 Part II. LNCS, vol. 9057, pp. 468–498. Springer, Heidelberg (2015). https://doi.org/10.1007/978-3-662-46803-6_16

22. Lijphart, A., Grofman, B.: Choosing an Electoral System: Issues and Alternatives. Praeger, New York (1984)

23. Meyer, M., Smyth, B.: An attack against the Helios election system that exploits re-voting. arXiv, Report 1612.04099 (2017)

24. Organization for Security and Co-operation in Europe: Document of the Copenhagen Meeting of the Conference on the Human Dimension of the CSCE (1990)

25. Organization of American States: American Convention on Human Rights, "Pact of San Jose, Costa Rica" (1969)

26. Pereira, O.: Internet voting with Helios. In: Real-World Electronic Voting: Design, Analysis and Deployment, Chap. 11. CRC Press (2016)

27. Quaglia, E.A., Smyth, B.: A short introduction to secrecy and verifiability for elections. arXiv, Report 1702.03168 (2017)

28. Quaglia, E.A., Smyth, B.: Authentication with weaker trust assumptions for voting systems (2018). https://bensmyth.com/publications/2018-voting-authentication/

29. Quaglia, E.A., Smyth, B.: Secret, verifiable auctions from elections. Cryptology ePrint Archive, Report 2015/1204 (2018)

30. Saalfeld, T.: On dogs and whips: recorded votes. In: Döring, H. (ed.) Parliaments and Majority Rule in Western Europe, Chap. 16. St. Martin's Press (1995)

31. Schweikardt, N.: Arithmetic, first-order logic, and counting quantifiers. ACM Trans. Comput. Logic **6**(3), 634–671 (2005)

32. Smyth, B.: Ballot secrecy: security definition, sufficient conditions, and analysis of Helios. Cryptology ePrint Archive, Report 2015/942 (2018)

33. Smyth, B.: A foundation for secret, verifiable elections (2018). https://bensmyth.com/publications/2018-secrecy-verifiability-elections-tutorial/

34. Smyth, B.: Verifiability of Helios mixnet. In: Voting 2018: 3rd Workshop on Advances in Secure Electronic Voting. LNCS, Springer (2018)

35. Smyth, B., Bernhard, D.: Ballot secrecy and ballot independence coincide. In: Crampton, J., Jajodia, S., Mayes, K. (eds.) ESORICS 2013. LNCS, vol. 8134, pp. 463–480. Springer, Heidelberg (2013). https://doi.org/10.1007/978-3-642-40203-6_26

36. Smyth, B., Frink, S., Clarkson, M.R.: Election Verifiability: Cryptographic Definitions and an Analysis of Helios, Helios-C, and JCJ. Cryptology ePrint Archive, Report 2015/233 (2017)

37. Smyth, B., Hanatani, Y., Muratani, H.: NM-CPA secure encryption with proofs of plaintext knowledge. In: Tanaka, K., Suga, Y. (eds.) IWSEC 2015. LNCS, vol. 9241, pp. 115–134. Springer, Cham (2015). https://doi.org/10.1007/978-3-319-22425-1_8

38. Smyth, B., Pironti, A.: Truncating TLS Connections to Violate Beliefs in Web Applications. In: WOOT 2013: 7th USENIX Workshop on Offensive Technologies. USENIX Association (2013). First Appeared at Black Hat USA 2013

39. Springall, D., Finkenauer, T., Durumeric, Z., Kitcat, J., Hursti, H., MacAlpine, M., Halderman, J.A.: Security analysis of the estonian internet voting system. In: CCS 2014: 21st ACM Conference on Computer and Communications Security, pp. 703–715. ACM Press (2014)

40. Staff, C.: ACM's 2014 General Election: Please Take This Opportunity to Vote. Commun. ACM **57**(5), 9–17 (2014)

41. Tsoukalas, G., Papadimitriou, K., Louridas, P., Tsanakas, P.: From Helios to Zeus. J. Elect. Technol. Syst. **1**(1), 1–17 (2013)

42. United Nations: Universal Declaration of Human Rights (1948)
43. Wolchok, S., Wustrow, E., Halderman, J.A., Prasad, H.K., Kankipati, A., Sakhamuri, S.K., Yagati, V., Gonggrijp, R.: Security analysis of India's electronic voting machines. In: CCS 2010: 17th ACM Conference on Computer and Communications Security, pp. 1–14. ACM Press (2010)
44. Wolchok, S., Wustrow, E., Isabel, D., Halderman, J.A.: Attacking the Washington, D.C. internet voting system. In: Keromytis, A.D. (ed.) FC 2012. LNCS, vol. 7397, pp. 114–128. Springer, Heidelberg (2012). https://doi.org/10.1007/978-3-642-32946-3_10

Shorter Double-Authentication Preventing Signatures for Small Address Spaces

Bertram Poettering$^{(\boxtimes)}$

Information Security Group, Royal Holloway, University of London, Egham, UK
bertram.poettering@rhul.ac.uk

Abstract. A recent paper by Derler, Ramacher, and Slamanig (IEEE EuroS&P 2018) constructs double-authentication preventing signatures ("DAP signatures", a specific self-enforcement enabled variant of signatures where messages consist of an address and a payload) that have—if the supported address space is not too large—keys and signatures that are considerably more compact than those of prior work. We embark on their approach to restrict attention to small address spaces and construct novel DAP schemes that beat their signature size by a factor of five and reduce the signing key size from linear to constant (the verification key size remains almost the same). We construct our DAP signatures generically from identification protocols, using a transform similar to but crucially different from that of Fiat and Shamir. We use random oracles. We don't use pairings.

Keywords: Signature schemes · Self-enforcement
Identification protocols · Provable security

1 Introduction

Digital Signatures. Digital signature schemes are a ubiquitous cryptographic primitive. They are extensively used for message and entity authentication and find widespread application in real-world protocols. The basic functionality of a signature scheme is as follows: A signer first runs the *key generation* algorithm to create a key pair consisting of a (secret) signing key and a (public) verification key. The signing key can then be used with the *signing algorithm* to create signatures on messages. Such a signature is a short bitstring that serves as an authenticator for a message: Given an authentic copy of the verification key, anybody can invoke the *verification algorithm* together with a message and the signature to check for the latter's validity. The output of this algorithm is binary: either "accept", interpreted as indicating that the message is authentic in the sense that it was fed by the signer into its signing algorithm, or "reject", which means it is not. Signature schemes were first proposed about four decades ago,

---

The full version is available in the IACR eprint archive as article 2018/223 [16].

© Springer International Publishing AG, part of Springer Nature 2018
A. Joux et al. (Eds.): AFRICACRYPT 2018, LNCS 10831, pp. 344–361, 2018.
https://doi.org/10.1007/978-3-319-89339-6_19

and gazillions of constructions are known today. Among the standardized ones, and these are the fewest, are RSA-PSS, RSA-PKCS#1 v1.5, DSA, ECDSA, and EdDSA.

Digital Signatures with Self-enforcement. According to the classic understanding of a signature scheme, signers can, in principle, sign any message they want. Applications, however, might require that specific relations hold between signed messages. For instance, in a public-key infrastructure (PKI), a certificate authority (CA) is expected not to generate certificates on the same identity for different public keys (as this could lead to impersonation attacks), and in cryptographic "currencies" like Bitcoin users shall not double-spend (sign two transactions that transfer the same coins to different recipients). While a regular signature scheme offers no means to enforce specific configurations of signed messages, signature schemes with self-enforcement do. We describe e-cash and double-authentication-preventing signatures as two examples for the latter.

E-CASH. In electronic cash [6], users can transfer virtual coins to each other, and they have a guarantee of anonymity: Nobody, including any central issuing authority, can trace their payments. However, if double-spending happens (this is very explicitly forbidden in e-cash systems) then the spending user's anonymity is automatically revoked in that the user can be identified given the two transactions. This allows for penalizing misbehaving users, for instance by freezing their account.

DOUBLE-AUTHENTICATION PREVENTING SIGNATURES. A signature scheme is double authentication preventing [17], or "has the DAP property", if messages consist of an address and a payload field, and the scheme is such that the signer is penalized if it signs any address twice with different payloads. In this setting the penalty is more drastic than in the e-cash setting: misbehaving signers don't have their anonymity revoked, but instead a verbatim copy of their signing key is leaked to the public. A natural application is in the PKI setting: If domain names are used as addresses, and public keys as payloads, then the DAP property means that the certification authority is penalized if it issues different-key certificates for the same domain. A different application is related to cryptographic currencies: users that double-spend make necessarily also their signing key public, i.e., give everybody access to their funds. Further applications have been proposed in [3, 5,7,17–19], for instance in the context of secure contract signing (and enforcing).

A Brief History of Double-Authentication Preventing Signatures. The first DAP scheme is by Poettering and Stebila [17,18]. Their construction is in the RSA setting. More precisely, it builds on the number-theoretic fact that if one has two square roots of an element modulo a Blum integer, then one also has the factorization of this number.[1] Signatures of the DAP scheme use the factorization as signing key, and signatures consist of a vector of square roots of RSA elements such that the decision about which specific square root is the valid one

---

[1] It is further required that these square roots are not additive inverses of each other.

is a function of the payload. Signing different payloads means releasing different square roots means revealing the signing key. The signatures of this scheme are very large: If a 128 bit security level shall be reached then their size is at least 256 times 2048 bit.

A DAP scheme in the DLP setting was proposed by Ruffing et al. [19, Appendix A], based on Merkle trees based on Chameleon hash functions [13]. The addresses are associated with the leaves of these trees, and signatures consist of vectors of 'openings' of the Chameleon hashes leading to the root. While their signatures are shorter than those of [17,18] (if implemented over elliptic curves), the signature size is linear in the bit-length of the address space, and thus still prohibitively large for many applications.

The work by Bellare et al. [3] improves on the work of [17,18] by compressing DAP signatures, still in the RSA setting and targeting the 128 bit security level, down to the size of 2048 bit. The trick is to evaluate the square root function iteratively, instead of in parallel. While this requires more algebraic properties than [17,18], the Blum integer setting fulfills these. We note that the DAP scheme of [3] is, so far, the only one with tight reductions.

The work of Boneh et al. [5] constructs DAP signatures based on lattice assumptions. The focus is on finding a solution for the post-quantum setting, not to beat the signature size of [3] (which they don't).

The very recent work of Derler et al. [7] reports the smallest DAP signature size so far: 1280 bit at the 128 bit security level, in the DLP-setting. Their scheme, however, can only be used in a restricted setting: As the sizes of signing and verification keys grow linearly in the cardinality of the address space, the scheme is not practical unless the latter is small. Note that all prior works (in particular [3,5,17–19]) support address spaces of exponential size. This drawback is acknowledged in [7], but the authors also report on specific applications where a small address space is just naturally occurring. Technically, the scheme of [7] builds on regular DLP-based signatures like Schnorr and DSA, and achieves the DAP property by including in each signature a payload-dependent share of the signing key, created with a secret-sharing scheme such that from any two shares associated with an address the signing key can be recovered. To show that the shares are well-formed, i.e., indeed allow for key recovery, the DAP signatures also contain a corresponding NIZK proof.

Contribution. In this article we embark on the approach of Derler et al. [7] and study DAP signatures for small address spaces. Also we work in the DLP setting, and build on (EC)DSA or Schnorr signatures. However, we improve drastically on signature and key sizes: Our signatures are five times shorter (namely only 256 bits) and our signing keys are constant size (instead of linear in the cardinality of the address space). While our and their verification keys are roughly the same size, our signing and verification times are better.

In a nutshell, our approach is to draw on the special-soundness property of the identification schemes underlying Schnorr and (EC)DSA signatures, assigning to each address one particular commitment. As these commitments are included in the verification key, the size of the latter is linear in the cardinality of the address space. Note that this linear blow-up is also the case in [7], but in contrast to their scheme we do not build on further primitives (e.g., secret sharing), which overall leads to more robustness, an easier analysis, more compact keys and signatures, and faster algorithms.

2 Notation

We write $\mathbb{Z}$ for the set of integers, and T and F for the Boolean constants true and false, respectively.

Parts of this article involve the specification of program code. In such code we use assignment operator '$\leftarrow$' when the assigned value results from a constant expression (including from the output of a deterministic algorithm), and we write '$\leftarrow_\$$' when the value is either sampled uniformly at random from a finite set or is the output of a randomized algorithm. For a randomized algorithm A we write $y \leftarrow_\$ A(x_1, x_2, \ldots)$ to denote the operation of running A with inputs $x_1, x_2, \ldots$ (and fresh coins) and assigning the output to variable y. Further, we write $[A(x_1, x_2, \ldots)]$ for the set of values that A outputs with positive probability.

Our security definitions are based on games played between a challenger and an adversary. These games are expressed using program code and terminate when the main code block executes a 'Stop with ...' command; the argument of the latter is the output of the game. We write $\Pr[G \Rightarrow \text{T}]$ or just $\Pr[G]$ for the probability that game G terminates by running into a 'Stop with T' instruction. Further, if E is some game-internal event, we similarly write $\Pr[E]$ for the probability that this event occurs. (Note the game is implicit in this notation.)

We use bracket notation to denote associative arrays (a data structure that implements a 'dictionary'). For instance, for an associative array A the instruction $A[7] \leftarrow 3$ assigns value 3 to memory position 7, and the expression $A[2] = 5$ tests whether the value at position 2 is equal to 5. Associative arrays can be indexed with elements from arbitrary sets. We use expressions like $A[\cdot] \leftarrow x$ to indicate that A is initialized with default value x. (That is, for any y, unless $A[y]$ is explicitly overwritten with a different value, $A[y]$ evaluates to x.) When assigning lists to each other, with '_' we mark "don't-care" positions. For instance, $(a, \_) \leftarrow (9, 4)$ is equivalent to $a \leftarrow 9$ (value 4 is discarded).

3 Signature Schemes and Key Extractability

We first reproduce standard definitions associated with signature schemes, and then consider a less common property that signature schemes might have: key extractability.

3.1 Regular Signature Schemes

We recall the definition of digital signatures and their essential security property: unforgeability.

DIGITAL SIGNATURE SCHEMES. A *digital signature* scheme (DS) for a message space $\mathcal{M}$ consists of algorithms gen, sgn, vfy together with a signing key space $\mathcal{SK}$, a verification key space $\mathcal{VK}$, and a signature space $\mathcal{S}$. The key generation algorithm gen outputs a signing key $sk \in \mathcal{SK}$ and a verification key $vk \in \mathcal{VK}$. The signing algorithm sgn takes a signing key $sk \in \mathcal{SK}$ and a message $m \in \mathcal{M}$, and outputs a signature $\sigma \in \mathcal{S}$. The verification algorithm vfy takes a verification key $vk \in \mathcal{VK}$, a message $m \in \mathcal{M}$, and a (candidate) signature $\sigma \in \mathcal{S}$, and outputs either T or F to indicate acceptance or rejection, respectively. A shortcut notation for these syntactical definitions is

$$\text{gen} \to \mathcal{SK} \times \mathcal{VK} \qquad \mathcal{SK} \times \mathcal{M} \to \text{sgn} \to \mathcal{S} \qquad \mathcal{VK} \times \mathcal{M} \times \mathcal{S} \to \text{vfy} \to \{T, F\}.$$

For a verification key $vk \in \mathcal{VK}$ we denote with $\mathcal{V}(vk)$ the set of message-signature pairs that are valid with respect to vk:

$$\mathcal{V}(vk) := \{(m, \sigma) \in \mathcal{M} \times \mathcal{S} : \text{vfy}(vk, m, \sigma) = T\}.$$

A signature scheme is correct if for all $(sk, vk) \in [\text{gen}]$ and $m \in \mathcal{M}$ and $\sigma \in [\text{sgn}(sk, m)]$ we have $(m, \sigma) \in \mathcal{V}(vk)$.

UNFORGEABILITY. For reference we reproduce the definition of the standard security notion for signature schemes: (existential) unforgeability (under chosen-message attacks). For a signature scheme Σ, associate with any adversary $\mathcal{F}$ its forging advantage $\text{Adv}_{\Sigma}^{\text{uf}}(\mathcal{F}) := \Pr[\text{UF}(\mathcal{F})]$, where the game is in Fig. 1. Intuitively, a signature scheme provides unforgeability if all practical adversaries have a negligible forging advantage.

Game UF($\mathcal{F}$)	**Oracle** Sign(m)
00 $L \leftarrow \emptyset$	06 $\sigma \leftarrow_\$ \text{sgn}(sk, m)$
01 $(sk, vk) \leftarrow_\$ \text{gen}$	07 $L \leftarrow L \cup \{m\}$
02 $(m^*, \sigma^*) \leftarrow_\$ \mathcal{F}(vk)$	08 Return σ
03 Require $(m^*, \sigma^*) \in \mathcal{V}(vk)$	
04 Require $m^* \notin L$	
05 Stop with T	

Fig. 1. Security experiment UF modeling the unforgeability of signatures. Adversary $\mathcal{F}$ has access to oracle Sign. We write 'Require C' for a condition C as an abbreviation for 'If not C: Stop with F'.

3.2 Key-Extractable Signature Schemes

We are interested in subclasses of signature schemes where the signing key can be reconstructed from (valid) signatures on specific message configurations. We formalize such extractability properties for *strictly one-time* (SOT) and *double-authentication preventing* (DAP) signatures. In a nutshell, a signature scheme is strictly one-time if the signing key can be recovered from signatures on any two different messages, and it is double-authentication preventing if messages consist of two components, the address and the payload, and the signing key can be recovered if two messages are signed that have the same address but different payloads. While the DAP definition was first developed in [17,18] we are not aware of a prior formalization of the SOT notion.

KEY EXTRACTABILITY. Let $\mathsf{gen}, \mathsf{sgn}, \mathsf{vfy}, \mathcal{SK}, \mathcal{VK}, \mathcal{S}$ be the algorithms and spaces of a digital signature scheme for a message space $\mathcal{M}$. We say that the scheme is *key-extractable* if there exists an auxiliary extraction algorithm ext that takes a verification key $vk \in \mathcal{VK}$ and two message-signature pairs $(m_1, \sigma_1), (m_2, \sigma_2) \in \mathcal{M} \times \mathcal{S}$, and outputs either a signing key $sk \in \mathcal{SK}$ or the failure symbol $\bot \notin \mathcal{SK}$. A shortcut notation for this syntactical definition is

$$\mathcal{VK} \times (\mathcal{M} \times \mathcal{S}) \times (\mathcal{M} \times \mathcal{S}) \to \mathsf{ext} \to \mathcal{SK} / \bot.$$

We formulate two notions of correctness (of extraction):

SOT. The signature scheme is *strictly one-time* if algorithm ext is such that for all $(sk, vk) \in [\mathsf{gen}]$ and $(m_1, \sigma_1), (m_2, \sigma_2) \in \mathcal{M} \times \mathcal{S}$ we have

$$(m_1, \sigma_1), (m_2, \sigma_2) \in \mathcal{V}(vk) \wedge m_1 \neq m_2 \implies \mathsf{ext}(vk, m_1, \sigma_1, m_2, \sigma_2) = sk.$$

DAP. The signature scheme is *double-authentication preventing* if there exist an address space $\mathcal{A}$ and a payload space $\mathcal{P}$ such that $\mathcal{M} = \mathcal{A} \times \mathcal{P}$, and algorithm ext is such that for all $(sk, vk) \in [\mathsf{gen}]$ and $(m_1, \sigma_1), (m_2, \sigma_2) \in \mathcal{M} \times \mathcal{S}$, if we write $m_i = (a_i, p_i)$ and have $(m_1, \sigma_1), (m_2, \sigma_2) \in \mathcal{V}(vk)$ then

$$a_1 = a_2 \wedge p_1 \neq p_2 \implies \mathsf{ext}(vk, m_1, \sigma_1, m_2, \sigma_2) = sk.$$

UNFORGEABILITY OF STRICTLY ONE-TIME SIGNATURES. In SOT signatures, everybody getting hold of two valid message-signature pairs can first recover the signing key and then create signatures on arbitrary messages. For such signature schemes the standard notion of unforgeability, where two message-signature pairs are easily obtained through the signing oracle, is thus not meaningful. We hence formalize a dedicated (weakened) unforgeability notion: For a signature scheme Σ, associate with any adversary $\mathcal{F}$ its (strictly one-time) forging advantage $\mathrm{Adv}_{\Sigma}^{\mathsf{sot}}(\mathcal{F}) := \Pr[\mathrm{SOT}(\mathcal{F})]$, where the game is in Fig. 2.[2] Note that the only difference between the UF and SOT games is the added instruction in line 06 of game SOT which precisely prevents the adversary from posing a second query to the Sign oracle. Intuitively, a SOT signature scheme provides unforgeability if all practical adversaries have a negligible forging advantage.

---

[2] Note that the 'strictness property' of SOT signatures involves only their functionality and is not reflected in the game which formalizes precisely the unforgeability of (regular) one-time signatures. We use the names SOT for the game and sot for the notion merely to allow for a clear association between functionality and targeted security notion.

Game SOT($\mathcal{F}$)	Oracle Sign(m)
00 $L \leftarrow \emptyset$	06 Require $L = \emptyset$
01 $(sk, vk) \leftarrow_\$ \text{gen}$	07 $\sigma \leftarrow_\$ \text{sgn}(sk, m)$
02 $(m^*, \sigma^*) \leftarrow_\$ \mathcal{F}(vk)$	08 $L \leftarrow L \cup \{m\}$
03 Require $(m^*, \sigma^*) \in \mathcal{V}(vk)$	09 Return σ
04 Require $m^* \notin L$	
05 Stop with T	

Fig. 2. Security experiment SOT modeling unforgeability for strictly one-time signature schemes. Adversary $\mathcal{F}$ has access to oracle Sign. We write 'Require C' for a condition C as an abbreviation for 'If not C: Stop with F'.

UNFORGEABILITY OF DOUBLE-AUTHENTICATION PREVENTING SIGNATURES. In DAP signatures, everybody getting hold of two valid message-signature pairs can create signatures on arbitrary messages if the two messages have the same address but different payloads. As we did for SOT signatures, also for DAP signatures we use a dedicated unforgeability notion [17,18]: For a signature scheme Σ, associate with any adversary $\mathcal{F}$ its forging advantage $\text{Adv}_\Sigma^{\text{dap}}(\mathcal{F}) := \Pr[\text{DAP}(\mathcal{F})]$, where the game is in Fig. 3. In the game, note that we replaced the set L (of games UF, SOT) that keeps track of signed messages by an associative array $L[\cdot]$ that manages one such set per address, keeping track of signed payloads. Intuitively, a DAP signature scheme provides unforgeability if all practical adversaries have a negligible forging advantage.

Game DAP($\mathcal{F}$)	Oracle Sign(m)
00 $L[\cdot] \leftarrow \emptyset$	07 $(a, p) \leftarrow m$
01 $(sk, vk) \leftarrow_\$ \text{gen}$	08 Require $L[a] = \emptyset$
02 $(m^*, \sigma^*) \leftarrow_\$ \mathcal{F}(vk)$	09 $\sigma \leftarrow_\$ \text{sgn}(sk, m)$
03 $(a^*, p^*) \leftarrow m^*$	10 $L[a] \leftarrow L[a] \cup \{p\}$
04 Require $(m^*, \sigma^*) \in \mathcal{V}(vk)$	11 Return σ
05 Require $p^* \notin L[a^*]$	
06 Stop with T	

Fig. 3. Security experiment DAP modeling unforgeability for double-authentication preventing signature schemes. Adversary $\mathcal{F}$ has access to oracle Sign. We write 'Require C' for a condition C as an abbreviation for 'If not C: Stop with F'.

4   Constructing DAP Signatures from SOT Signatures

We present a construction of a DAP signature scheme from a SOT signature scheme that offers exceptional performance but requires that the cardinality $n = |\mathcal{A}|$ of the address space is not too large. The basic idea of our scheme is to let the DAP key generation algorithm perform n-many SOT key generations independently of each other, one for each address, and to present the resulting set of SOT signing (resp. verification) keys as a single DAP signing (resp. verification) key. To DAP-sign a message $m = (a, p)$, the SOT signing key $sk[a]$ corresponding to address a is retrieved and payload p authenticated with it. The DAP verification algorithm works analogously. Observe that, without further modification, this design is unforgeable (in the DAP sense) but not key-extractable. Indeed, double-signing, i.e., violating the DAP property, reveals only one of the required n-many SOT signing keys. We apply two tricks to achieve full key extractability: (1) Instead of generating the n-many SOT signing keys independently of each other and with individual random coins, we generate them deterministically as a function of the address they are associated with, using the output of a PRF as the coins required for key generation. More precisely, for each address a we first derive 'random' coins as per $r \leftarrow F(k, a)$, where F is the PRF and k its key (that is stored as part of the DAP signing key), and then compute the SOT key pair corresponding to a as per $(sk[a], vk[a]) \leftarrow \text{gen}\langle r \rangle$, where the $\langle \cdot \rangle$ notation indicates running an (otherwise randomized) algorithm with explicitly given coins. Note that this reduces the size of the DAP signing key from linear (in n) to constant. (2) We include (one-time pad) encryptions of PRF key k in the DAP verification key such that knowledge of any SOT signing key $sk[a]$ suffices to recover it. More concretely, we embed into the DAP verification key the set of values $k + h(a, sk[a])$, for all $a \in \mathcal{A}$, where $+$ denotes (in most cases) the bit-wise XOR operation and h is a random oracle. (This technique is borrowed from [3].) Overall, as we prove, this is sufficient to achieve key-extractability in the DAP sense. We give the formal details of our construction in the following.

SOT-TO-DAP TRANSFORM. Let $\mathcal{A}, \mathcal{P}$ be sets. From a key-extractable signature scheme Σ for message space $\mathcal{P}$ with algorithms gen, sgn, vfy, ext and spaces $\mathcal{SK}, \mathcal{VK}, \mathcal{S}$ we construct a key-extractable signature scheme Σ' for message space $\mathcal{M} = \mathcal{A} \times \mathcal{P}$ with algorithms gen', sgn', vfy', ext' and spaces $\mathcal{SK}', \mathcal{VK}', \mathcal{S}'$ such that if the former is strictly one-time then the latter is double-authentication preventing. As building blocks we employ a pseudorandom function $F : \mathcal{K} \times \mathcal{A} \to \mathcal{R}$ that has a commutative group $(\mathcal{K}, +)$ as its key space[3] and the randomness space $\mathcal{R}$ of algorithm gen as its range, and a hash function $h : \mathcal{A} \times \mathcal{SK} \to \mathcal{K}$. Both F and h will be modeled as random oracles in the security analysis. Let $\mathcal{SK}' = \mathcal{K}$, $\mathcal{VK}' = \mathcal{VK}^{|\mathcal{A}|} \times \mathcal{K}^{|\mathcal{A}|}$, $\mathcal{S}' = \mathcal{S}$, and implement algorithms gen', sgn', vfy' as specified in Fig. 4. (Algorithm ext' is specified in Fig. 5 and discussed below.)

The signature schemes obtained with our transform provide both unforgeability and key extractability.

Theorem 1 (DAP unforgeability). *Let Σ and Σ' be the SOT and DAP signature schemes involved in our construction. If Σ is unforgeable in the SOT sense then Σ' is unforgeable in the DAP sense. More precisely, for any adversary $\mathcal{F}'$ against Σ' there exist adversaries $\mathcal{E}, \mathcal{F}$ against Σ such that in the random oracle model for F and h we have*

$$\text{Adv}_{\Sigma'}^{\text{dap}}(\mathcal{F}') \leq n \cdot \text{Adv}_{\Sigma}^{\text{sot}}(\mathcal{F}) + q_F / |\mathcal{K}| + n \cdot q_h \cdot \text{Adv}_{\Sigma}^{\text{sot}}(\mathcal{E}),$$

---

[3] Consider that same-length bit-strings together with the bit-wise XOR operation form a commutative group to see that this requirement is easily fulfilled in practice.

Proc gen$'$	Proc sgn$'(sk', m)$
00 $k \leftarrow_\$ \mathcal{K}; K[\cdot] \leftarrow \bot$	09 $k \leftarrow sk'; (a, p) \leftarrow m$
01 $sk[\cdot] \leftarrow \bot; vk[\cdot] \leftarrow \bot$	10 $r \leftarrow F(k, a)$
02 For all $a \in \mathcal{A}$:	11 $(sk[a], \_) \leftarrow \text{gen}\langle r \rangle$
03 $\quad r \leftarrow F(k, a)$	12 $\sigma \leftarrow_\$ \text{sgn}(sk[a], p)$
04 $\quad (sk[a], vk[a]) \leftarrow \text{gen}\langle r \rangle$	13 Return σ
05 $\quad K[a] \leftarrow k + h(a, sk[a])$	
06 $sk' \leftarrow k$	Proc vfy$'(vk', m, \sigma)$
07 $vk' \leftarrow (vk[\cdot], K[\cdot])$	14 $(vk[\cdot], \_) \leftarrow vk'$
08 Return (sk', vk')	15 $(a, p) \leftarrow m$
	16 Return vfy$(vk[a], p, \sigma)$

Fig. 4. Our SOT-to-DAP transform (main algorithms). The $\langle \cdot \rangle$ notation in lines 04 and 11 indicates that gen is (deterministically) invoked on random coins r.

where $n = |\mathcal{A}|$ is the cardinality of the address space, q_F and q_h are the numbers of queries to F and h, respectively, and $\mathcal{K}$ is the key space of the PRF. The running times of $\mathcal{E}$ and $\mathcal{F}$ are about that of $\mathcal{F}'$.

Proof sketch. On first sight the security argument for our construction seems to be straight-forward: Any valid DAP signature is in fact a valid SOT signature, so forging the one implies forging the other. Also the DAP signing oracle seems to be easily simulated with the SOT signing oracle. (The latter processes at most one query per key, but this is perfectly matched with the one-query-per-address requirement of DAP unforgeability). The reason why ultimately the proof is not that easy is that the DAP construction uses the SOT scheme in a non-blackbox fashion. More precisely, for a reductionist proof to go through, the random coins of the SOT key generation would need to be freshly drawn right before key generation, and be forgotten immediately afterwards. This is not necessarily the case in our construction, as the coins are generated in a specific and reproducible way, using the PRF. More precisely, as we model the PRF as a random oracle, the coins are uniform and hidden from the adversary as long as the PRF key k is not queried by the latter to its F oracle. However, as h-based encryptions of k are embedded into the verification key, bounding the probability of this event involves arguing about the probability of reconstructing SOT signing keys, and such arguments can only be given if the SOT key generation algorithm receives properly distributed coins, i.e., coins that are drawn uniformly at random. Below we give a more careful analysis that avoids this circularity by cleverly conditioning events on each other.

In the following we refer with E_F to the event that the adversary poses a query with first argument k to its F oracle. We need to bound the probability that E_F occurs to a small value. There are precisely two ways that lead the adversary to posing such a query: (1) Without any knowledge about k but by sheer luck: the adversary guesses $k \in \mathcal{K}$ and hits the right one. As the adversary can try q_F times, the probability for this is bounded by $q_F/|\mathcal{K}|$. (2) By making a more informed guess, i.e., by exploiting obtained knowledge about k. Note that the only information available about k are its random oracle based encryptions, which are information-theoretically hiding up to the point where the adversary poses a corresponding query to the h oracle. Let E_h be the corresponding event that the adversary queries oracle h on one of the n-many SOT signing keys. Instead of deriving individual bounds for $\Pr[E_F]$ and $\Pr[E_h]$, we analyze the probabilities of two closely related events:

Let E_F' be the event that E_F occurs before E_h, including the case that E_h does not occur at all, and let E_h' be the event that E_h occurs before E_F, including the case that E_F does not occur at all. Then, as discussed above, we have $\Pr[E_F'] \leq q_F/|\mathcal{K}|$. Further, as in the E_h' case we can assume perfectly random coins of SOT key generation, we can bound $\Pr[E_h']$ with the probability of SOT key recovery, which is in particular bounded by the SOT forging probability. In particular there exists for each $1 \leq \alpha \leq n$ an adversary $\mathcal{E}_\alpha$ such that $\Pr[E_h' \mid$ the h query happens for address number $\alpha] \leq q_h \mathrm{Adv}_\Sigma^{\mathrm{sot}}(\mathcal{E}_\alpha)$. By defining adversary $\mathcal{E}$ such that it uniformly picks a value $1 \leq \alpha \leq n$ and then behaves like $\mathcal{E}_\alpha$, we obtain $\Pr[E_h'] \leq n q_h \mathrm{Adv}_\Sigma^{\mathrm{sot}}(\mathcal{E})$.

The bounds on E_F' and E_h' can be additively combined as $\Pr[E_F \vee E_h] = \Pr[E_F'] + \Pr[E_h']$. If E_σ denotes the event of a DAP forgery then overall we have $\mathrm{Adv}_{\Sigma'}^{\mathrm{dap}}(\mathcal{F}') = \Pr[E_\sigma] \leq \Pr[E_\sigma \mid \neg E_F \wedge \neg E_h] + \Pr[E_F \vee E_h]$. We already bounded the second term. For the first term note that $\neg E_F \wedge \neg E_h$ means that the adversary does not exploit the random oracle based encryption of the signing key. In this case the initially discussed natural reduction works, showing $\Pr[E_\sigma \mid \neg E_F \wedge \neg E_h] \leq n \mathrm{Adv}_\Sigma^{\mathrm{sot}}(\mathcal{F})$, for a forger $\mathcal{F}$ that results from the reduction.

By combining the above bounds we obtain the one from the theorem statement. $\qquad\square$

Theorem 2 (DAP key extractability). *Let Σ and Σ' be the SOT and DAP signature schemes involved in our construction. If Σ is strictly one-time then Σ' is double-authentication preventing. More precisely, the algorithm* ext' *specified in Fig. 5 is an extraction algorithm for scheme Σ' if its building block* ext *is an extraction algorithm for scheme Σ.*

```
Proc ext'(vk', m₁, σ₁, m₂, σ₂)
00  (vk[·], K[·]) ← vk'
01  (a₁, p₁) ← m₁; (a₂, p₂) ← m₂
02  Require a₁ = a₂ ∧ p₁ ≠ p₂
03  Require (p₁, σ₁), (p₂, σ₂) ∈ 𝒱(vk[a₁])
04  sk[a₁] ← ext(vk[a₁], p₁, σ₁, p₂, σ₂)
05  Require sk[a₁] ≠ ⊥
06  k ← K[a₁] − h(a₁, sk[a₁])
07  Return k
```

Fig. 5. SOT-to-DAP transform (extraction algorithm). We write 'Require C' for a condition C as an abbreviation for 'If not C: Return $\bot$'. Note that the condition in line 05 is always fulfilled.

Proof. The argument is immediate: Having two "colliding" DAP signatures means having two SOT signatures that are valid under the same verification key but are on different messages. The DAP extraction algorithm in Fig. 5 applies the SOT extraction algorithm to this setting to first recover the SOT signing key and then, by decrypting the corresponding h-based ciphertext, the DAP signing key.   □

5   Constructing SOT Signatures

We propose the *Fixed-Commitment transform* that constructs signature schemes from generic identification (ID) protocols, in a way related to that of the classic Fiat–Shamir transform [10]. While the latter turns ID schemes into standard unforgeable signature schemes, the signature schemes obtained with our new transform are strictly one-time. We first recall details of (three-move) identification protocols, then of the Fiat–Shamir transform, and then specify and study our own construction.

5.1   Three-Move ID Protocols

We recall the definition of an important class of identification protocols and of the security properties connected to it: special soundness, (honest-verifier) zero-knowledge, and resilience against key recovery. While we refer to [11,12,14] for general treatments of ID protocols, our notation is in particular close to that of [2].

THREE-MOVE ID PROTOCOLS. A *three-move ID protocol* consists of algorithms G, P_1, P_2, V, an identification secret key space ISK, an identification public key space IPK, a commitment space CMT, a challenge space CH, a response space RSP, and a (prover) state space ST. The key generation algorithm G outputs a secret key $isk \in$ ISK and a public key $ipk \in$ IPK. Algorithms P_1 and P_2 are for the prover: Algorithm P_1 takes a secret key $isk \in$ ISK and a public key $ipk \in$ IPK, and outputs a state $st \in$ ST and a commitment $cmt \in$ CMT. Algorithm P_2 takes a state $st \in$ ST and a challenge $ch \in$ CH, and outputs a response $rsp \in$ RSP. Algorithm V is for the verifier: It takes a public key $ipk \in$ IPK, a commitment $cmt \in$ CMT, a challenge $ch \in$ CH, and a response $rsp \in$ RSP, and outputs T or F to indicate acceptance or rejection, respectively. A shortcut notation for these syntactical definitions is

$$
\begin{array}{rcl}
G & \to & \text{ISK} \times \text{IPK} \\
\text{ISK} \times \text{IPK} \;\to\; P_1 & \to & \text{ST} \times \text{CMT} \\
\text{ST} \times \text{CH} \;\to\; P_2 & \to & \text{RSP} \\
\text{IPK} \times \text{CMT} \times \text{CH} \times \text{RSP} \;\to\; V & \to & \{\text{T}, \text{F}\}
\end{array}
$$

We further write $TR = \text{CMT} \times \text{CH} \times \text{RSP}$ for the transcript space of the ID protocol. A three-move ID protocol is correct if for all $(isk, ipk) \in [G]$ and $(st, cmt) \in [P_1(isk, ipk)]$ and $ch \in$ CH and $rsp \in [P_2(st, ch)]$ we have $V(ipk, cmt, ch, rsp) = \text{T}$.

SPECIAL SOUNDNESS. A three-move ID protocol has *special soundness* if there exists an extraction algorithm that recovers the identification secret key from all (valid) same-commitment-different-challenge transcript pairs. Formally, the notion requires the existence of an algorithm E that takes an identification public key $ipk \in$ IPK and two transcripts $T_1, T_2 \in$ TR and outputs either a secret key $isk \in$ ISK or the failure symbol $\perp \notin$ ISK. For correctness (of extraction) we require that for all $(isk, ipk) \in$ [G] and $T_1, T_2 \in$ TR, if we write $T_i = (cmt_i, ch_i, rsp_i)$ and have that $V(ipk, cmt_1, ch_1, rsp_1)$ and $V(ipk, cmt_2, ch_2, rsp_2)$ evaluate to T, then $cmt_1 = cmt_2 \wedge ch_1 \neq ch_2$ implies $E(ipk, T_1, T_2) = isk$.

HONEST-VERIFIER ZERO-KNOWLEDGE. A three-move ID protocol is (perfectly) *honest-verifier zero-knowledge* if honestly generated transcripts leak nothing about the involved secret key material. Formally, the notion requires the existence of a simulator S that takes a public key $ipk \in$ IPK and outputs a transcript $(cmt, ch, rsp) \in$ TR such that for all $(isk, ipk) \in$ [G] the distributions

$$\{(st, cmt) \leftarrow_\$ P_1(isk, ipk); ch \leftarrow_\$ CH; rsp \leftarrow_\$ P_2(st, ch) : (cmt, ch, rsp)\}$$

and

$$\{(cmt, ch, rsp) \leftarrow_\$ S(ipk) : (cmt, ch, rsp)\}$$

are identical.

RESILIENCE AGAINST KEY RECOVERY. A three-move ID protocol ID is resilient against (blind) key recovery attacks if no adversary can reconstruct the identification secret key from just the identification public key (no sample transcripts are provided). Formally, for all inverters $\mathcal{I}$ we define the advantage $\mathrm{Adv}_{\mathsf{ID}}^{\mathrm{kr}}(\mathcal{I}) := \Pr[(isk, ipk) \leftarrow_\$ G; isk' \leftarrow_\$ \mathcal{I}(ipk) : isk = isk']$. Intuitively, an ID scheme is resilient against key recovery if all practical inverters have a negligible advantage.

5.2 The Fiat–Shamir Transform

A well-known generic construction of a signature scheme from a three-move ID scheme and a random oracle is by Fiat and Shamir [10]. In a nutshell, for creating a signature on a message the signer invokes the P_1 algorithm to obtain a fresh commitment, simulates an (honest) verifier by letting the random oracle, on input the commitment and the message, specify a challenge, and finally invokes the P_2 algorithm to obtain a response that completes the transcript. The signature consists of the commitment and the response. The verification algorithm recovers the challenge by querying the random oracle and checks for transcript validity using the V algorithm. For reference we reproduce the details of this construction in the following.

FIAT–SHAMIR TRANSFORM. Let $\mathcal{M}$ be a message space and let G, P_1, P_2, V be the algorithms and ISK, IPK, CMT, CH, RSP, ST be the spaces of a three-move ID protocol. Let H : IPK $\times$ CMT $\times \mathcal{M} \to$ CH be a hash function. Then the *Fiat–Shamir* transform (FS) converts the ID protocol into a signature scheme Σ: After letting $\mathcal{SK} =$ ISK $\times$ IPK, $\mathcal{VK} =$ IPK, $\mathcal{S} =$ CMT $\times$ RSP, the algorithms gen, sgn, vfy of the scheme are as specified in Fig. 6.

Proc gen	Proc sgn(sk, m)	Proc vfy(vk, m, σ)
00 $(isk, ipk) \leftarrow_\$ G$	04 $(isk, ipk) \leftarrow sk$	10 $ipk \leftarrow vk;\ (cmt, rsp) \leftarrow \sigma$
01 $sk \leftarrow (isk, ipk)$	05 $(st, cmt) \leftarrow_\$ P_1(isk, ipk)$	11 $ch \leftarrow H(ipk, cmt, m)$
02 $vk \leftarrow ipk$	06 $ch \leftarrow H(ipk, cmt, m)$	12 $d \leftarrow V(ipk, cmt, ch, rsp)$
03 Return (sk, vk)	07 $rsp \leftarrow_\$ P_2(st, ch)$	13 Return d
	08 $\sigma \leftarrow (cmt, rsp)$	
	09 Return σ	

Fig. 6. Signature scheme obtained via the Fiat–Shamir transform.

5.3   The Fixed-Commitment Transform

We propose the Fixed-Commitment transform (FC) as an alternative way of constructing a signature scheme from a three-move ID protocol. It differs from the Fiat–Shamir transform in that generating a commitment using the P_1 algorithm happens only once and during key generation, instead of during signing operations. The challenge (of the ID protocol) continues to be a function of commitment and message. Thus, signatures on different messages share the same commitment but use different challenges, allowing for the extraction of the identification secret key via the special soundness property. By using a similar trick as in our SOT-to-DAP transform (see Sect. 4), i.e., by embedding a random oracle based encryption of the remaining signing key components into the verification key, the signature scheme is rendered strictly one-time. We specify the details of the FC transform in the following.

FIXED-COMMITMENT TRANSFORM. Let $\mathcal{M}$ be a message space and let $G, P_1,$ P_2, V be the algorithms and $ISK, IPK, CMT, CH, RSP, ST$ be the spaces of a three-move ID protocol. Assume $(ST, +)$ is a commutative group (see footnote 3). Let $H: IPK \times CMT \times \mathcal{M} \to CH$ and $h: ISK \to ST$ be hash functions, both of which will be modeled as random oracles in the security analysis. Then the *Fixed-Commitment* transform (FC) converts the ID protocol into a signature scheme Σ: After letting $\mathcal{SK} = IPK \times ST \times CMT,$ $\mathcal{VK} = IPK \times CMT \times ST,$ $\mathcal{S} = RSP,$ the algorithms gen, sgn, vfy, ext of the scheme are as specified in Fig. 7.

  The signature schemes obtained with our transform provide both unforgeability and key extractability.

Theorem 3 (SOT unforgeability). *Let* ID *be a three-move ID protocol and let* Σ *be the signature scheme obtained from it via the Fixed-Commitment transform. If* ID *has special soundness, is honest-verifier zero-knowledge, and is resilient against key recovery, then* Σ *is unforgeable in the SOT sense. More precisely, for any adversary* $\mathcal{F}$ *against* Σ *there exists an inverter* $\mathcal{I}$ *such that in the random oracle model for H and h we have*

$$\mathrm{Adv}_\Sigma^{\mathrm{sot}}(\mathcal{F}) \leq Q \cdot \mathrm{Adv}_{\mathrm{ID}}^{\mathrm{kr}}(\mathcal{I}) + (q_H)^2/|CH|,$$

where $Q = q_H + q_h$ *and* q_H, q_h *are the numbers of queries to random oracles H and h, respectively. The running time of* $\mathcal{I}$ *is about that of* $\mathcal{F}$.

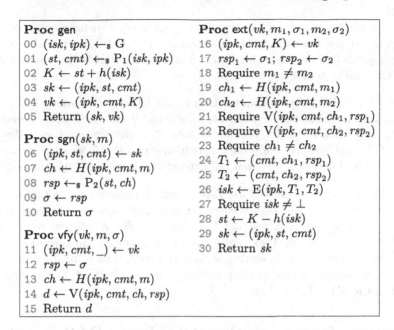

Proc gen
00 $(isk, ipk) \leftarrow_\$ G$
01 $(st, cmt) \leftarrow_\$ P_1(isk, ipk)$
02 $K \leftarrow st + h(isk)$
03 $sk \leftarrow (ipk, st, cmt)$
04 $vk \leftarrow (ipk, cmt, K)$
05 Return (sk, vk)

Proc sgn(sk, m)
06 $(ipk, st, cmt) \leftarrow sk$
07 $ch \leftarrow H(ipk, cmt, m)$
08 $rsp \leftarrow_\$ P_2(st, ch)$
09 $\sigma \leftarrow rsp$
10 Return σ

Proc vfy(vk, m, σ)
11 $(ipk, cmt, \_) \leftarrow vk$
12 $rsp \leftarrow \sigma$
13 $ch \leftarrow H(ipk, cmt, m)$
14 $d \leftarrow V(ipk, cmt, ch, rsp)$
15 Return d

Proc ext$(vk, m_1, \sigma_1, m_2, \sigma_2)$
16 $(ipk, cmt, K) \leftarrow vk$
17 $rsp_1 \leftarrow \sigma_1; rsp_2 \leftarrow \sigma_2$
18 Require $m_1 \neq m_2$
19 $ch_1 \leftarrow H(ipk, cmt, m_1)$
20 $ch_2 \leftarrow H(ipk, cmt, m_2)$
21 Require $V(ipk, cmt, ch_1, rsp_1)$
22 Require $V(ipk, cmt, ch_2, rsp_2)$
23 Require $ch_1 \neq ch_2$
24 $T_1 \leftarrow (cmt, ch_1, rsp_1)$
25 $T_2 \leftarrow (cmt, ch_2, rsp_2)$
26 $isk \leftarrow E(ipk, T_1, T_2)$
27 Require $isk \neq \bot$
28 $st \leftarrow K - h(isk)$
29 $sk \leftarrow (ipk, st, cmt)$
30 Return sk

Fig. 7. SOT signature scheme obtained via the Fixed-Commitment transform. We write 'Require C' for a condition C as an abbreviation for 'If not C: Return $\bot$'. Note that the condition in line 27 is always fulfilled.

Proof sketch. Consider first the variant of the FC transform that does not embed encrypted state information in the verification key. With respect to this scheme, the simulator for game SOT has to provide the adversary with a verification key, a signature oracle that processes at most one query, and access to random oracle H. Insist w.l.o.g. that the adversary poses precisely one signing query, and that before it does so it poses the corresponding query to H. Let m be the message for which the signature is requested, and let $1 \leq i \leq q_H$ be the index of the corresponding H-query. The simulator proceeds as follows: it generates a key pair (isk, ipk) with G; it guesses an index $1 \leq j \leq q_H$ uniformly at random; it aborts, with probability $1 - 1/q_H$, if $j \neq i$; it generates a protocol transcript (cmt, ch, rsp) using the zero-knowledge simulator; it answers the jth H-query with challenge ch (all remaining H-queries are answered with uniformly picked challenges); it invokes the adversary on input the verification key composed of ipk and cmt. Note that the simulator can properly simulate a signature on message m, just by releasing rsp. Note further that with probability $1 - q_H/|CH|$, for the challenge ch^* corresponding to the forgery output by the adversary we have $ch \neq ch^*$. As in this situation the special-soundness extraction algorithm is applicable to recover isk, a natural reduction shows that the forging advantage is bounded by $q_H \text{Adv}_{ID}^{kr}(\mathcal{I}) + (q_H)^2/|CH|$, for an inverter $\mathcal{I}$.

Consider next the full scheme that includes the encryption in the verification key. This additional information is completely useless to the adversary up to the point where it poses a $h(isk)$ query. Each such query can be seen as trying to break a key recovery challenge against scheme ID. That is, to the above bound the term $q_h \mathrm{Adv}_{\mathrm{ID}}^{\mathrm{kr}}(\mathcal{I})$ needs to be added. The overall result is the bound claimed in the theorem statement. □

Theorem 4 (SOT key extractability). *Let* ID *be a three-move ID protocol and let* Σ *be the signature scheme obtained from it via the Fixed-Commitment transform. If* ID *has special soundness then* Σ *is strictly one-time. More precisely, if H is collision resistant then algorithm* ext *in Fig. 7 constructs an extraction algorithm for scheme* Σ *from the extraction algorithm* E *of scheme* ID.

Proof. The argument is immediate: Having two signatures on different messages means having two ID protocol transcripts with the same commitment but different challenges (this requires that hash function H be collision resistant, see line 23 in Fig. 7). Our SOT extraction algorithm applies the special-soundness extraction algorithm to this setting to first recover the identification secret key, and then, by decrypting the corresponding h-based ciphertext, the missing component of the SOT signing key. □

6 Putting Things Together: DLP-Based DAP Signatures

The overall goal of this article is to construct a practical DLP-based DAP signature scheme with short signatures. As in Sect. 4 we constructed DAP signatures generically from SOT signatures, and in Sect. 5 we constructed SOT signatures generically from ID schemes, what is missing is the specification of appropriate DLP-based identification schemes. The classic candidates for this are the schemes by Schnorr [20] and Okamoto [15]. Both of them provide special soundness and honest-verifier zero-knowledge, and thus fit into our ID protocol framework. A less known and less general scheme is the one underlying DSA and ECDSA signatures [1,8] (which can be seen as a variant of Schnorr's scheme, obfuscated to avoid intellectual property issues).

In Figs. 8 and 9 we expose how our overall DAP scheme looks like if the three-move ID protocol is instantiated with the ones underlying Schnorr and (EC)DSA signatures, respectively. In both cases, targeting the 128 bit security level, we propose a PRF key length of $\kappa = 128$ bit and a group order of $2\kappa = 256$ bit. Further, for compactness of verification keys, we suggest using elliptic curve groups. In particular it would be somehow natural to instantiate the Schnorr-based scheme with the parameters of (Schnorr-based) EdDSA signatures [4] (i.e., on Edwards curves) and the (EC)DSA-based scheme with NIST-standardized curves.[4] In both cases the signature size would be 256 bit. No DAP signature

---

[4] That this is "natural" was communicated to us by software engineers. From an academic perspective the choice of curve should be orthogonal to the choice of ID scheme. On the other hand, there seems nothing wrong with the proposal, so we stick to it.

Proc gen	Proc sgn(sk, m)
00 $k \leftarrow_\$ \{0,1\}^\kappa$	10 $k \leftarrow sk;\ (a,p) \leftarrow m$
01 $vk[\cdot] \leftarrow \perp;\ K[\cdot] \leftarrow \perp$	11 $(x,r) \leftarrow F(k,a)$
02 For all $a \in \mathcal{A}$:	12 $X \leftarrow g^x;\ R \leftarrow g^r$
03 $\quad (x,r) \leftarrow F(k,a)$	13 $c \leftarrow H(X,R,m)$
04 $\quad X \leftarrow g^x;\ R \leftarrow g^r$	14 $\sigma \leftarrow r + xc$
05 $\quad vk[a] \leftarrow (X,R)$	15 Return σ
06 $\quad K[a] \leftarrow k + h(a,x,r)$	
07 $sk \leftarrow k$	Proc vfy(vk, m, σ)
08 $vk \leftarrow (vk[\cdot], K[\cdot])$	16 $(vk[\cdot], \_) \leftarrow vk$
09 Return (sk, vk)	17 $(a,p) \leftarrow m$
	18 $(X,R) \leftarrow vk[a]$
	19 $c \leftarrow H(X,R,m)$
	20 Return $[RX^c \overset{?}{=} g^\sigma]$

Fig. 8. DAP signature scheme based on Schnorr signatures, defined in respect to a cyclic group $\mathbb{G} = \langle g \rangle$ of prime-order q. We assume hash functions $F \colon \{0,1\}^\kappa \times \mathcal{A} \to \mathbb{Z}_q \times \mathbb{Z}_q$, $h \colon \mathcal{A} \times \mathbb{Z}_q \times \mathbb{Z}_q \to \{0,1\}^\kappa$, $H \colon \mathbb{G} \times \mathbb{G} \times \mathcal{M} \to \mathbb{Z}_q$.

Proc gen	Proc sgn(sk, m)
00 $k \leftarrow_\$ \{0,1\}^\kappa$	12 $k \leftarrow sk;\ (a,p) \leftarrow m$
01 $vk[\cdot] \leftarrow \perp;\ K[\cdot] \leftarrow \perp$	13 $(x,r) \leftarrow F(k,a)$
02 For all $a \in \mathcal{A}$:	14 $R \leftarrow g^r;\ t \leftarrow f(R)$
03 $\quad (x,r) \leftarrow F(k,a)$	15 $\sigma \leftarrow (H(m) + tx)^{1/r}$
04 $\quad$ Require $x \neq 0 \wedge r \neq 0$	16 Return σ
05 $\quad R \leftarrow g^r;\ t \leftarrow f(R)$	
06 $\quad$ Require $t \neq 0$	Proc vfy(vk, m, σ)
07 $\quad X \leftarrow g^x;\ vk[a] \leftarrow (X,R)$	17 $(vk[\cdot], \_) \leftarrow vk$
08 $\quad K[a] \leftarrow k + h(a,x,r)$	18 $(a,p) \leftarrow m$
09 $sk \leftarrow k$	19 $(X,R) \leftarrow vk[a]$
10 $vk \leftarrow (vk[\cdot], K[\cdot])$	20 $t \leftarrow f(R)$
11 Return (sk, vk)	21 Return $[g^{H(m)} X^t \overset{?}{=} R^\sigma]$

Fig. 9. DAP signature scheme based on (EC)DSA signatures (where we use the notation of the DSA algorithms from [9]). We assume a cyclic group $\mathbb{G}$ as in Fig. 8, and hash functions $F \colon \{0,1\}^\kappa \times \mathcal{A} \to \mathbb{Z}_q \times \mathbb{Z}_q$, $f \colon \mathbb{G} \to \mathbb{Z}_q$, $h \colon \mathcal{A} \times \mathbb{Z}_q \times \mathbb{Z}_q \to \{0,1\}^\kappa$, $H \colon \mathcal{M} \to \mathbb{Z}_q$. We write 'Require C' for a condition C as an abbreviation for 'If not C: Return $\perp$'.

scheme proposed in the past has that short signatures (so far, the shortest DAP schemes have 2048 bit [3] and 1280 bit [7] signatures, which we beat by a factor of 8 and 5, respectively), and likely the length is even optimal (in the DLP setting). The verification keys are considerably less compact, with a size of $640|\mathcal{A}|$ bits. Note this is only slightly larger than those of [7] which are roughly $512|\mathcal{A}|$ bits in size.

References

1. Barker, E.B.: FIPS PUB 186-4 – FEDERAL INFORMATION PROCESSING STANDARDS PUBLICATION Digital Signature Standard (DSS) (2009). https://dx.doi.org/10.6028/NIST.FIPS.186-4
2. Bellare, M., Poettering, B., Stebila, D.: From identification to signatures, tightly: a framework and generic transforms. In: Cheon, J.H., Takagi, T. (eds.) ASIACRYPT 2016. LNCS, vol. 10032, pp. 435–464. Springer, Heidelberg (2016). https://doi.org/10.1007/978-3-662-53890-6_15
3. Bellare, M., Poettering, B., Stebila, D.: Deterring certificate subversion: efficient double-authentication-preventing signatures. In: Fehr, S. (ed.) PKC 2017. LNCS, vol. 10175, pp. 121–151. Springer, Heidelberg (2017). https://doi.org/10.1007/978-3-662-54388-7_5
4. Bernstein, D.J., Duif, N., Lange, T., Schwabe, P., Yang, B.-Y.: High-speed high-security signatures. In: Preneel, B., Takagi, T. (eds.) CHES 2011. LNCS, vol. 6917, pp. 124–142. Springer, Heidelberg (2011). https://doi.org/10.1007/978-3-642-23951-9_9
5. Boneh, D., Kim, S., Nikolaenko, V.: Lattice-based DAPS and generalizations: self-enforcement in signature schemes. In: Gollmann, D., Miyaji, A., Kikuchi, H. (eds.) ACNS 2017. LNCS, vol. 10355, pp. 457–477. Springer, Cham (2017). https://doi.org/10.1007/978-3-319-61204-1_23
6. Chaum, D., Fiat, A., Naor, M.: Untraceable electronic cash. In: Goldwasser, S. (ed.) CRYPTO 1988. LNCS, vol. 403, pp. 319–327. Springer, New York (1990). https://doi.org/10.1007/0-387-34799-2_25
7. Derler, D., Ramacher, S., Slamanig, D.: Short double- and N-times-authentication-preventing signatures from ECDSA and more. Cryptology ePrint Archive, Report 2017/1203 (2017). To appear in the proceedings of EuroS&P 2018. https://eprint.iacr.org/2017/1203
8. Fersch, M., Kiltz, E., Poettering, B.: On the provable security of (EC)DSA signatures. In: Weippl, E.R., Katzenbeisser, S., Kruegel, C., Myers, A.C., Halevi, S. (eds.) ACM CCS 2016, Vienna, Austria, 24–28 October 2016, pp. 1651–1662. ACM Press (2016)
9. Fersch, M., Kiltz, E., Poettering, B.: On the one-per-message unforgeability of (EC)DSA and its variants. In: Kalai, Y., Reyzin, L. (eds.) TCC 2017. LNCS, vol. 10678, pp. 519–534. Springer, Cham (2017). https://doi.org/10.1007/978-3-319-70503-3_17
10. Fiat, A., Shamir, A.: How to prove yourself: practical solutions to identification and signature problems. In: Odlyzko, A.M. (ed.) CRYPTO 1986. LNCS, vol. 263, pp. 186–194. Springer, Heidelberg (1987). https://doi.org/10.1007/3-540-47721-7_12
11. Goldreich, O.: Foundations of Cryptography: Basic Tools, vol. 1. Cambridge University Press, Cambridge (2001)
12. Katz, J., Lindell, Y.: Introduction to Modern Cryptography. Chapman and Hall/CRC Press, Boca Raton (2007)
13. Krawczyk, H., Rabin, T.: Chameleon signatures. In: NDSS 2000, San Diego, CA, USA, 2–4 February 2000. The Internet Society (2000)
14. Menezes, A., van Oorschot, P., Vanstone, S.: Handbook of Applied Cryptography. CRC Press, Boca Raton (2001). http://www.cacr.math.uwaterloo.ca/hac/
15. Okamoto, T.: Provably secure and practical identification schemes and corresponding signature schemes. In: Brickell, E.F. (ed.) CRYPTO 1992. LNCS, vol. 740, pp. 31–53. Springer, Heidelberg (1993). https://doi.org/10.1007/3-540-48071-4_3

16. Poettering, B.: Shorter double-authentication preventing signatures for small address spaces. Cryptology ePrint Archive, Report 2018/223 (2018). https:// eprint.iacr.org/2018/223
17. Poettering, B., Stebila, D.: Double-authentication-preventing signatures. In: Kutyłowski, M., Vaidya, J. (eds.) ESORICS 2014. LNCS, vol. 8712, pp. 436–453. Springer, Cham (2014). https://doi.org/10.1007/978-3-319-11203-9_25
18. Poettering, B., Stebila, D.: Double-authentication-preventing signatures. Int. J. Inf. Sec. **16**(1), 1–22 (2017)
19. Ruffing, T., Kate, A., Schröder, D.: Liar, liar, coins on fire!: Penalizing equivocation by loss of bitcoins. In: Ray, I., Li, N., Kruegel: C. (eds.) ACM CCS 2015, Denver, CO, USA, 12–16 October 2015, pp. 219–230. ACM Press (2015)
20. Schnorr, C.P.: Efficient identification and signatures for smart cards. In: Brassard, G. (ed.) CRYPTO 1989. LNCS, vol. 435, pp. 239–252. Springer, New York (1990). https://doi.org/10.1007/0-387-34805-0_22

Author Index

Printed in the United States
By Bookmasters